FROM PREJUDICE
TO PERSECUTION

FROM PREJUDICE TO PERSECUTION

A HISTORY OF AUSTRIAN ANTI-SEMITISM

BRUCE F. PAULEY

THE UNIVERSITY OF NORTH CAROLINA PRESS   CHAPEL HILL & LONDON

© 1992 The University of North Carolina Press

All rights reserved

Manufactured in the United States of America

The paper in this book meets the guidelines for permanence and durability of the Committee on Production Guidelines for Book Longevity of the Council on Library Resources.

01 00 99 98 97   6 5 4 3 2

Library of Congress Cataloging-in-Publication Data

Pauley, Bruce F.

From prejudice to persecution : a history of Austrian anti-semitism / by Bruce F. Pauley.

p.   cm.

Includes bibliographical references and index.

ISBN 0-8078-1995-6 (cloth: alk. paper)

ISBN 0-8078-4713-5 (pbk.: alk. paper)

1. Antisemitism—Austria—History.   2. Jews—Austria—Politics and government.   3. Austria —Politics and government—1918–1938.   4. Austria—Ethnic relations.   I. Title.

DS146.A9P38   1991

305.892'40436—dc20   91-50249

CIP

Dedicated to the memory of

IRENE HARAND

"I fight anti-Semitism because

it maligns our Christendom"

CONTENTS

ILLUSTRATIONS

PREFACE

The concentration of scholarly and popular attention on the Holocaust has made other forms of modern anti-Semitism seem almost harmless by comparison. Veritable libraries have been written about the destruction of European Jewry during the Second World War, not to mention the production of feature films, documentaries, and made-for-television "docu-dramas." However, relatively little has been written about the immediate forerunner of the Holocaust, the anti-Semitism of interwar Europe. Still less is known about the Jewish responses to this prejudice.

The importance of Austria and especially Vienna for such a study far outweighs the comparatively small size and population of the country. Although the Republic of Austria that was created after World War I could boast little more than 32,000 square miles and scarcely 6.5 million inhabitants, its Jewish population was fairly large. The country's 220,000 Jews were three and a half times more numerous as a proportion of the total population than the 550,000 Jews of Germany. For Vienna alone the numbers were even more significant. In the 1920s over 200,000 self-professed Jews lived in the Austrian capital, making it the sixth largest Jewish city in the world after New York, Warsaw, Chicago, Philadelphia, and Budapest. In Central and Western Europe Vienna had by far the highest concentration of Jewish residents. About 1 in every 9 Viennese (10.8 percent) was Jewish. By contrast, the highest percentage of Jews found in Germany—4.7 percent in Frankfurt am Main—was less than half that of Vienna. Only 3.8 percent of Berlin's population (173,000) was of the Mosaic faith.[1]

Raw statistics alone, of course, do not begin to tell the whole story either of the importance of Austria's Jewish population in the modern history of Western civilization. No other group in Austria between 1848 and 1938 produced so many original thinkers as the Jews,[2] and no other Jews in the world were as culturally creative as those of Vienna during this same period. Such names as Sigmund Freud, Ludwig Wittgenstein, Arnold Schoenberg, Hugo von Hofmannsthal, Arthur Schnitzler, Karl Kraus, and Gustav Mahler, to name only a very few, have immeasurably enriched the culture, not only of Austria, but also of the world. The expulsion of Vienna's Jews has, to some extent, provincialized the Austrian capital and lowered its cultural standards.[3]

Population statistics also tell us little about the nature or intensity of Austrian anti-Semitism and the Jewish response. Neither phenomenon can be understood apart from the country's geographic, economic, and political status. Geographically, Austria was and is at the crossroads of Europe, where North meets South and East meets West. Hence, Austria contained proportionately more Eastern European Jews—who were highly conscious of their Jewish identity—than Germany and Western Europe, which helps to explain why Vienna was also the first city in Europe to have a Zionist-dominated *Kultusgemeinde* (religious community). Nevertheless, the majority of Austria's and Vienna's Jews was thoroughly assimilated or at least acculturated, and very pro-Austrian. Austria's geographic location also exposed it to almost every kind of right-wing extremism from the generally pro-Italian and relatively mildly anti-Semitic *Heimwehr* (Home Guard) to the pro-German and racially anti-Semitic Nazi Party.

The country's economic and social status was similarly transitional. Something like a third of Austria's population lived in industrial centers during the interwar period: Vienna, Wiener Neustadt, the Mur Valley of Upper Styria, Linz, and a few other Austrian towns. Another third of the population made up the modern middle class consisting largely of civil servants and professional people, who were concentrated in Vienna and the provincial capitals. On the other hand, the remaining third of the population was comprised of traditional and usually strongly Roman Catholic peasants. These economic and social divisions were reflected in the country's three political camps: a staunchly anti-clerical Social Democratic Party, which saw both Judaism and anti-Semitism as bourgeois relics; the clerical Christian Social Party, which still espoused traditional Christian anti-Judaism (as well as socioeconomic anti-Semitism); and the pan-Germans, who tended to support the more modern, "racial" form of anti-Semitism.

Consequently, there was little agreement among Austrian anti-Semites about which type of anti-Semitism to pursue, and even less unanimity among the factious Jews on how to oppose it. The "genius" of the National Socialists, in both Austria and Germany, was to unify all forms of anti-Semitism ideology and to implement many of the demands of the separate anti-Semitic groups, instead of merely talking about them, as earlier Austrian anti-Semites had been more inclined to do.

Several disclaimers need to be made at the outset of this book. I have made no attempt in these pages to write a complete history of the Jews of Austria or even of Austrian anti-Semitism. The history of the cultural contributions of Austrian Jews alone would fill many volumes. The internal politics and charitable work of the Viennese Kultusgemeinde likewise lie beyond the scope of this work, except to show how the sharp political divisions within the Jewish community prevented it from presenting the anti-Semites with a common front. On the other hand, the scope of this book is not confined exclusively to Austria. Austrian anti-Semitism was so influenced by anti-Semitism in other countries and was itself so influential abroad that to tell its story is to reveal much about the European-wide phenomenon.

A number of excellent works have already been written about the Austrian Jews and anti-Semitism during the Habsburg Monarchy. The same is true for the period following the "Anschluss," that misnomer commonly used to refer to the annexation of Austria by the Third Reich. However, no comprehensive scholarly studies have been made for the period between the start of the First World War and the German takeover of Austria. The twenty-four years between 1914 and 1938 will, therefore, be the centerpiece of this book. On the other hand, sufficient attention will be paid to the periods before the First World War and after the Anschluss to provide readers with a reasonably complete picture of the whole history of Austrian anti-Semitism from the middle of the nineteenth century to the present.

Any study of anti-Semitism, regardless of the country concerned, runs the risk of being exaggerated and distorted. Condensing several decades of anti-Semitic incidents and publications into a few hundred pages is bound to omit innumerable minute, but collectively significant, expressions of friendly or at least "correct" gentile-Jewish relations. Several interviews with Austrian Jewish refugees now living in the United States—people who certainly have no reason to be biased in favor of Austria—have revealed that at least some Austrian Jews were able to lead fairly normal lives without being seriously affected by Austrian anti-Semitism, prior to the Anschluss.

In order to achieve a balanced view of Austrian anti-Semitism between the world wars it is necessary to place it in an international context. The Austrian variety of Jew hatred was probably the strongest in Central or Western Europe prior to Hitler's takeover of power in Germany in January 1933. On the other hand, it was almost certainly weaker than in such Eastern European countries as Poland, Lithuania, Hungary, and Rumania. The foremost scholar of anti-Semitism in interwar Europe, Richard Coudenhove-Kalergi, went so far as to say in 1935 that "the overwhelming majority of non-Jewish Europeans to-day are more or less anti-Semitically disposed."[4]

This Austrian scholar could have said the same thing of at least a large minority of Americans during the period covered in this book. The reception that Americans gave Jewish refugees of Russian pogroms before and after the turn of the twentieth century was nearly as unfriendly as that given to Galician immigrants in Vienna. During the 1920s the American Congress passed legislation excluding Asians from both immigration and citizenship and sharply limited the number of immigrants from Eastern Europe, an action aimed to a large extent at Jews. Meanwhile, many of the forty-eight states approved laws forbidding racial intermarriage. These measures were closely watched and loudly applauded by Austrian anti-Semites, but similar legislation was never enacted in the Austrian republic. Nor, of course, did anything resembling the relocation of 120,000 Americans of Japanese descent in concentration camps in 1942 ever take place in Austria while it remained an independent country.

Public opinion polls conducted in the United States between 1938 and 1942 revealed that 10 to 15 percent of Americans would have actively supported government-led anti-Semitic legislation and another 20 percent would have been sympathetic to such a policy. Only one-third of the population would have opposed it.[5] Between July 1938 and May 1939, as anti-Semitism in Nazi Germany was entering its violent phase, other polls showed that 66 to 77 percent of the American public opposed raising the immigration quota to help Jewish refugees, even children.[6]

Anti-Semitism in the private sphere and in academic life was also by no means an Austrian monopoly. Whereas Jewish professors in the First Austrian Republic found it nearly impossible to attain promotions, American Jews were not even appointed to the faculties of some of the country's most prestigious universities, and the enrollment of Jewish students at these institutions was often unofficially restricted. Austrian Jews were sometimes excluded from summer resorts and sporting clubs, while American Jews were shut out of country clubs and business organizations. And, of course, independent Austria never experienced anything comparable with the lynchings of scores of blacks that still took place annually in the American South between the world wars, albeit in diminishing numbers.

All contextual considerations aside, the hard fact remains that anti-Semitism was a widespread ideology during the First Austrian Republic. Every major political party, as well as a great many paramilitary formations and private organizations, utilized anti-Semitic propaganda or excluded Jews from membership, or both. Differences of opinion arose mainly over what to do about the "Jewish problem," not about whether Jews were a negative influence on the Austrian state and society. Moreover, much of the discriminatory legislation against the Jews of Germany after 1933 and against those of Austria after the Anschluss had already been discussed, although usually not enacted, in early post–World War I Austria if not before. There is also considerable evidence that Austrian anti-Semitism influenced the German variety, although the reverse was also true. Moreover, it is almost inconceivable that Adolf Hitler would have approved of anti-Semitic legislation in *angeschlossenen* (annexed) Austria, the November 1938 pogrom (popularly known as "Kristallnacht"), and the deportation of Austrian Jews, if he had expected these measures to receive a hostile public reaction. The fact also remains that Austrians played a disproportionately large role in the Holocaust. Simon Wiesenthal, head of the Documentation Center of the Society of Nazi Victims in Vienna, has estimated that half of the crimes associated with the Holocaust were committed by Austrians even though they comprised only 8.5 percent of the population of Hitler's Greater German Reich.[7]

How was the growth of this hateful anti-Semitic ideology possible in Austria? Who were its principal exponents and why? How did it manifest itself? And how did the Jews respond to the insults, allegations, and threats with which they were confronted? These are just some of the questions we must now address.

ACKNOWLEDGMENTS

A scholarly work of any significant scope involves the combined efforts of a great many people. This is especially true of a study of Austrian anti-Semitism, a topic of broad chronological scope that touches on both Austrian and Jewish history. One of the real benefits of doing the research for this book, which was conducted on three continents starting in 1979, was that it enabled me to meet numerous intelligent and extremely kindhearted people.

Several Austrian scholars were instrumental in launching my research into primary and secondary sources in Vienna. Special mention must be made of Professor Gerhard Botz of the University of Salzburg who introduced me to a number of specialists on the subject and who guided me to numerous archives and libraries in addition to finding suitable housing for me and my family while I was working in Vienna. Professor Erika Weinzierl, the director of the Institute for Contemporary History, gave me several useful articles; her own publications on Austrian anti-Semitism are an indispensable starting point for anyone interested in the subject. Her assistants, Gustav Spann and Peter Malinar, were tireless in identifying doctoral dissertations and rare publications. At the Archives of the Austrian Resistance Movement, Director Herbert Steiner was equally helpful in recommending important documentary sources. Dr. Isabella Ackerl of the Austrian Administrative Archives also helped me locate several documentary collections. Equally accommodating were numerous individuals at the Austrian National Library, the library of the University of Vienna, the library of the Vienna municipal government, and the newspaper archive of the Chamber for Workers and Employees in Vienna. Professor Gerald Stourzh, director of the Institute of History at the University of Vienna, also loaned me several important dissertations that had recently been written under his supervision. Professor Anton Pelinka, professor of political science at the University of Innsbruck, graciously volunteered to read portions of the final manuscript.

On this side of the Atlantic, Dr. Wolfgang Petritsch and Dr. Irene Freudenschuss-Reichl, both of the Austrian Press and Information Service in New York, provided me with the results of a recent public opinion poll in Austria and statistics on compensation by the Austrian government to Jewish victims of the Nazi persecution. The fact that this information was by no means all complimentary to the Austrian "image" is a good indication that the Austrian government is attempting to be more forthcoming on the whole question of Austrian anti-Semitism.

Two seminars enabled me to place my topic in a broader historical context. The first, held in the summer of 1985, was "Fascism as a Generic Phenomenon," sponsored by the National Endowment for the Humanities and conducted at Yale University under the masterful guidance of Professor Henry Ashby Turner, Jr. While in New Haven I was able to commute to New York where I could take advantage of the rare book collections on the history of Central European Jewry at the Leo Baeck Institute.

The second seminar—this one on anti-Semitism and the Holocaust—took place the following summer at Yad Vashem, the Holocaust memorial and research center in Jerusalem. The lectures and books of two of the seminar's speakers, Yehuda Bauer and Ezra Mendelsohn, were especially helpful in placing anti-Semitism and the Holocaust in an international perspective. My thanks also go to Eli Dlin for coordinating the many details of the seminar and its accompanying field trips. Herbert Rosenkranz, himself a Jewish refugee from Austria and author of several extremely well-researched studies of the Holocaust period as it involved Austria, was kind enough to read portions of my manuscript and helped me uncover several useful documents in the Yad Vashem archives. While in Jerusalem I was also able to use the archives of the Vienna Kultusgemeinde now housed at the Central Archives for the History of the Jewish People. Its director, Dr. Daniel Cohan, cordially answered my many questions regarding the collections. Dr. Michael Heymann, director of the Central Zionist Archives in Jerusalem, was equally solicitous.

My four research trips to Vienna between 1980 and 1989 as well as my journey to Israel in 1986 would not have been possible without the financial support of several grants. The National Endowment for the Humanities awarded me a research stipend for the summer of 1987. The University of Central Florida provided me with Quality Improvement Program summer research stipends in 1980 and 1982 as well as a sabbatical leave in the spring of 1986. My chairman, Professor Jerrell H. Shofner, was helpful in giving me a teaching schedule that took my research and writing program into account.

UCF presidents Trevor Colbourn and Steven Altman as well as Vice President for Academic Affairs Richard Astro, Vice President for Research Michael Bass, and the dean of the College of Arts and Sciences, Edward Sheridan, were all important to this project in creating an atmosphere conducive to research.

Numerous individuals within the Jewish community of Central Florida have shown a keen interest in this project and have been supportive in many ways. I am especially indebted to Mrs. Tess Wise, executive director of the Holocaust Memorial Resource and Education Center of Central Florida, who has enthusiastically assisted my work almost since its inception and who put me in contact with several Austrian Jewish refugees now living in the Central Florida area. All of those refugees, whose names are mentioned in the bibliography, helped give me a greater appreciation of what it was like to be a Viennese Jew in the First Austrian Republic and immediately after the Anschluss. The Holocaust Center, with the funding of Yumi and Hedy Schleifer, also provided me with a scholarship that made possible my studies in Jerusalem.

More recently, several colleagues at the University of Central Florida and around the country have selflessly devoted countless hours to reading my manuscript and providing me with indispensable suggestions for its improvement. Pride of place clearly belongs to Professor Donald L. Niewyk of Southern Methodist University who meticulously and expeditiously read both the first and second drafts of the manuscript and saved me from numerous errors and contradictions. Professor John Haag of the University of Georgia was particularly helpful on matters regarding his specialty, the history of the University of Vienna. Professor Robert Schwarz, emeritus of Florida Atlantic University, offered me the unique insights of a scholar and Austrian Jewish refugee. My colleague at the University of Central Florida, Moshe Pelli, director of the Judaic Studies Program, was a treasury of information on questions regarding the broader aspects of Jewish history. Professor Elmar B. Fetscher of the UCF history department generously volunteered to proofread portions of the first draft. A former colleague at the University of Wyoming, Professor Emeritus William R. Steckel, provided me with three unique photographs he took in Vienna shortly after the German annexation.

I must also mention three people especially close to me who have always been an inspiration in my labors. From my mother, Blanche M. Pauley, I inherited a love of reading. My father, Carroll R. Pauley, first introduced me to the fascinations of history when I was a child by taking our family to many exciting historical sites in both Europe and the United States. I deeply regret that he did not live to see the final product of this study. My wife, Marianne, who proofread my manuscript, patiently endured the sacrifice of countless excursions and evenings out in order to make a timely conclusion to this project possible.

Finally, I welcome the comments and questions of interested readers, particularly those people who personally experienced events described in this book. Please write me in care of the Department of History, University of Central Florida, Orlando, Florida 32816, or telephone (407) 823-2224.

ABBREVIATIONS

The following abbreviations and acronymns are used in the notes and, where indicated by an asterisk, also in the text. For a list of abbreviations of newspapers, see the Bibliography.

AB   Deutschösterreichischer Schutzverein Antisemitenbund;
            German-Austrian Protective Association League of Anti-Semites
AK   Kammer für Arbeiter und Angestellte in Wien, Abteilung:
            Dokumentation; Chamber for Workers and Employees in
            Vienna, Documentation Department
AVA   Allgemeines Verwaltungsarchiv; General Administrative Archive,
            Vienna
A/W   Austria/Wien (Vienna)
AZ   *Arbeiter-Zeitung* (Vienna)
BJF   Bund jüdischer Frontsoldaten Österreichs; League of Jewish
            Front Soldiers of Austria
BKA   Bundeskanzleramt; Office of the Federal Chancellery
CAHJP   Central Archives for the History of the Jewish People, Jerusalem
CSP*   Christlichsoziale Partei; Christian Social Party of Austria
CZA   Central Zionist Archives, Jerusalem
DB   Deutsche Burschenschaft; German Fraternity Association
DGFP   *Documents on German Foreign Policy, 1918–1945*
doc.   document
DÖTZ   *Deutschösterreichische Tages-Zeitung*
DÖW   Dokumentationsarchiv des Österreichischen Widerstandes;
            Documentation Archive of the Austrian Resistance, Vienna
EB   *Der eiserne Besen* (Salzburg)
FKV   Frontkämpfervereinigung; Front Fighters' Association
FRUS   *Papers Related to the Foreign Relations of the United States*

GDVP*   Grossdeutsche Volkspartei; Greater German People's Party of Austria

IKG*   Israelitische Kultusgemeinde; Jewish Religious Community

K.   Karton; carton

NA   National Archives, Washington, D.C.

n.d.   no date

NS   Nationalsozialistische; National Socialist

NSDAP*   Nationalsozialistische Deutsche Arbeiterpartei; National Socialist German Workers' Party or Nazi Party

NS-P   Nationalsozialistische Parteistellen; National Socialist Party documents of Gau Vienna

R.   reel number

SA   Sturmabteilung; Storm Division or Storm Troopers of the Nazi Party

SD   Sozialdemokratische; Social Democratic

SDAP*   Sozialdemokratische Arbeiterpartei; Social Democratic Workers' Party of Austria

Slg. Sch.   Sammlung Schumacher; Schumacher collection of Austrian Nazi correspondence in the Bundesarchiv of Koblenz, Germany

SS   Schutzstaffeln; Protective Guards of the Nazi Party

T-   microfilm series number; National Archives, Captured German Documents

A NOTE ON TERMINOLOGY

A number of (mostly German) terms used in the text need to be defined at the outset. In many cases these terms have no commonly accepted English equivalent and have therefore been left untranslated. An exception is the name of large cities such as Vienna and Cracow whose English-language names are well known. For lesser-known cities such as Lemberg (Lvov), Brünn (Brno), and Czernowitz (Cernauti), the German names by which they were best known in Austria prior to the Second World War have been retained. To avoid the overuse of italics, names of organizations and frequently used foreign words have not been italicized.

1. *Aryan*. Racists used this term to refer to Europeans who could presumably trace their ancestry back to ancient Persia. In the interwar years, however, it was generally used by both gentiles and Jews simply to refer to non-Jewish Europeans. Between the wars, the term did not have quite the racist and negative connotations it has today.

2. *Assimilationist, assimilationism*. Austrian Jews used these terms to describe Jews who strove for complete cultural and social integration into Austrian society. Those Jews who favored assimilation generally did not intend to abandon all sense of Jewish identity. The terms were used in a positive sense by the Union of Austrian Jews, but in a pejorative way by Zionists.

3. *Burschenschaften*. Nationalistic German-language fraternities that were first founded in the late Napoleonic period. They were hotbeds of German nationalism and anti-Semitism in Germany and even more so in Austria before and after the First World War.

4. *Deutsche Studentenschaft*. An association of Burschenschaften in Germany, Austria, Danzig, and the German-speaking parts of Czechoslovakia. The Nazis took over the leadership of the international association in the summer of 1931. It served each university as a kind of parliament.

5. *Gymnasium, Gymnasien.* Secondary school or schools emphasizing classical subjects like ancient Greek and Latin. In interwar Austria they were favored by Jews over the more practical secondary schools called *Realschulen.*

6. *Heimwehr,* or Home Guard. A paramilitary organization founded in Austria in 1919 to protect the southern states of Carinthia and Styria against the territorial ambitions of the South Slavs. After 1920 it evolved more and more into an anti-Marxist organization and advocated anti-Semitism.

7. *Hochschule, Hochschulen.* The literal translation "high schools" is likely to be confused by the American reader with "secondary schools." Hochschulen were actually institutions of higher learning such as universities and their colleges and institutes. They were centers of anti-Semitism in interwar and pre–World War I Austria, especially in Vienna.

8. *Israelitische Kultusgemeinde* (IKG), or Jewish Community Organization. Every sizable Jewish community in Central Europe after the mid-nineteenth century had its own organization, which regulated religious and social welfare matters pertaining to Jews. Every Jew in the locality was automatically a member unless he formally renounced his Jewish identity. After the founding of modern Zionism by Theodor Herzl in the 1890s, Kultusgemeinden became centers of a power struggle between Zionists and assimilationists.

9. *Juden hinaus!* or Jews get out! The battle cry of anti-Semites, especially at Austrian universities where Jewish students were frequently ordered out of their classrooms and then beaten up by racist students.

10. *Judenrein.* To be free of Jews, or without any Jewish influence.

11. *Judenschutztruppen.* Protective guard of Jews; "Jew lovers."

12. *Middle school.* A secondary school in Central Europe; not to be confused with middle schools in the United States, which serve younger pupils.

13. *Numerus clausus.* A Latin term meaning "closed number." In practice it was a common demand of Austrian anti-Semites that Jews in any particular institution or profession be limited to no more than their numerical percentage. It did not mean, however, that Jews would be guaranteed proportional representation in any given institution.

14. *Ostjuden.* Eastern Jews or Jews from Eastern Europe. In Austria this term usually referred to Jews who had come from the predominantly Polish-speaking province of Galicia in the Austro-Hungarian Monarchy. Such Jews were regarded by both gentiles and assimilated Jews as being relatively coarse, backward, and poorly educated. Anti-Semitic allegations were made most frequently against these Ostjuden.

15. *Parteigenossen,* or party comrades. A term used especially by Nazis to refer to party members.

16. *Westjuden.* Western Jews. In Austria this meant Jews who had come to Vienna and the Alpine provinces from Bohemia, Moravia, and Austrian Silesia. They were much more acculturated into German-Austrian society than the Ostjuden. In practice, Ostjuden frequently became Westjuden after living in the West for one or two generations.

17. *Vereine.* Association, club, or organization.

18. *Verjudet.* Jewified; corrupted by Jewry. Racial anti-Semites frequently used this term to refer to anything in which Jews were involved or in which the "Jewish spirit" played a role. In practice it often meant anything liberal.

19. *Völkisch.* A term that is virtually impossible to translate. Its nearest English equivalent would be "racist-nationalist."

20. *Volksgeist.* A metaphysical word meaning "spirit of the people" coined by the eighteenth-century German philosopher, Johann Gottfried Herder. German and Austrian racists frequently used the term to differentiate the essential "racial" characteristics of Jews and Germans.

1

THE ETERNAL
SCAPEGOAT

Anti-Semitism in Austria, as in other European countries prior to the end of
the Second World War, took so many different forms that, like the term *fascism*, it almost defies definition.[1] The term itself is misleading because almost
all anti-Semites have directed their ire exclusively against Jews, not other
Semites such as Arabs. Moreover, anti-Semites have never even been able to
agree on who is a Jew. Consequently, the definitions of anti-Semitism also
vary widely. One only slightly extreme definition is the following: "a doctrine
which attributes to the Jews an exceptional position among all other civiliza-
tions, defames them as an inferior group, denies their being part of the nation
and categorically refuses them any symbiosis. This definition includes nonviolent social anti-Semitism and 'compulsory Zionism' as possible forms of
anti-Semitism. It transcends the general understanding of Jew-hatred, or combat of Jewry, and emphasizes the latent totality of a phobia, which represents
a secular version of a dichotomous conception of history."[2] A less extreme
and more comprehensive definition that would probably apply to all forms of
anti-Semitism described in this book is "an attitude of hostility towards Jews
as such, i.e. not towards a particular Jew, and not towards a number of people
who, apart from having an attribute that arouses hostility, also happen to be
Jewish. The hostility . . . must be associated definitely with the quality of
being a Jew."[3]

For the more radical anti-Semites in Austria and elsewhere, anti-Semitism
bore some of the characteristics of a religion. Many of its beliefs were beyond
empirical proof and had to be accepted as articles of faith. It seemed to provide answers to mystifying events, assuaged insecurities, and satisfied everyday
psychological demands.[4] Richard Coudenhove-Kalergi perhaps put it most
succinctly when he said that anti-Semitism was "emotional and instinctive,"
and was "older than the theoretical hatred of the Jews. . . . It was [not] based
on a judgment but on a prejudice; not on knowledge, but on instincts."[5] For

the anti-Semite, Jews represented what was disliked and feared. Therefore the term *Jewish* was always a pejorative and only used to describe negative things, never something cultivated or artistic.[6]

ALLEGATIONS TRADITIONAL AND MODERN

Even if anti-Semitism in Austria and elsewhere took an almost infinite number of forms and was justified by an equally infinite number of rationalizations, a large number of allegations were made by nearly all anti-Semites. Austrian anti-Semites contributed little if anything to this stockpile of charges against the Jews, either before or after the First World War.[7] In fact, most of the allegations made against Austrian Jews had been in evidence for centuries, and only the circumstances in which the charges were made had changed.

One Austrian historian has summarized ten frequently made charges against Jews—some very old, others more recent—as follows: (1) Jews everywhere retained their own characteristics, an oriental appearance with a strong bent nose and curly hair; (2) Jews were very rich because of their unscrupulous business practices; (3) they had acquired important offices through the "evil" of emancipation and had formed a clique; (4) the "Jewish press" was a morally corrupting influence because of its unscrupulous nature; (5) Jews wanted to establish a world empire; (6) they had different concepts of right and morality than Germans (including Austrians); (7) the errors of the Jewish religion and theology as well as the corrupting teaching of the Talmud were pernicious, for example, in permitting unchastity and prostitution; (8) Jews were cowards; (9) pogroms were justified because Jews were usurers. Finally, a more recent charge was that (10) Jews were leaders of the Russian Revolution.[8] In reality, this list is far from complete. By 1918 Jews were being held responsible for the defeat of the Central Powers in the world war and the shortages of food, fuel, and housing that accompanied and followed it. What is especially fascinating about this list is that it incorporates every type of anti-Semitism found in Austria in the interwar years and beyond: religious, economic, social, and racial.

So ubiquitous and long-lived were many of these charges that their very universality and longevity became justifications for anti-Semitism. Anti-Semitism must have been valid because so many people, in so many countries had believed it for such a long time. If hundreds of great men from Tacitus to Treitschke subscribed to it, then surely they could not have all been wrong, or so the argument went.[9]

The longevity of Christian anti-Semitism clearly contributed to the idea that Jews had been universally cursed. Christian anti-Semites traced the ideology back to 587 B.C. when the First Temple in Jerusalem was destroyed and the Jews began their captivity in Babylonia. The destruction of the Second Temple in Jerusalem by the Romans in 70 A.D. was seen by Christians both at the time and later as God's wrathful punishment for the Jews' rejection of Jesus.[10] Far more important was the official Roman Catholic view, held throughout the Middle Ages and until recent times, that the Jews were collectively and hereditarily responsible for the crucifixion of Jesus and were therefore the "murderers of God." Some hard-core anti-Semites went so far as to claim that Jesus himself was a "Galilean who considered himself to be a mortal enemy of the Jews and thought they were the children of the devil."[11] Judas Iscariot was held by many of these racists to be a stereotypical Jew.

Another medieval idea that persisted in Austria into the twentieth century was ritual murder—the "blood libel." According to this fantasy, Jews murdered Christian children in order to use their blood for religious rituals. Between 1867 and 1914 there were no fewer than twelve trials for ritual murder in Austria-Hungary and Germany although only one trial ended in a conviction, and that was for ordinary murder, not ritual murder. Anti-Semites were not troubled by these verdicts, however.[12] As late as 1934 a book was published in Austria whose title asked: *Gibt es jüdische Ritualmorde?* (*Is There Jewish Ritual Murder?*), a question that was answered affirmatively after a long list of "cases" had been cataloged.[13] Although the book's publication occasioned a protest from Jews and was ultimately banned, the Styria Verlag in Graz published a pamphlet protesting the confiscation of the book.[14]

Traditional Christian anti-Semitism also appeared in attacks on Jewish business practices. Jewish businessmen were allegedly unethical because they had cut themselves off from the saving grace of Jesus Christ. Christian businessmen, presumably, could not hope to compete with Jews because their religion would not allow them to swindle and cheat. If taken to court, a Jewish lawyer and a sympathetic Jewish judge would be sure to acquit their "blood brother." All the thoughts and aspirations of Jews supposedly revolved around making money and avoiding hard, low-paying jobs. Although some "Aryans" were also concerned with making money, this was not the general rule, or so the anti-Semites argued.[15] Although Christian anti-Semitism was the most important type advocated by Austria's Christian Social Party from the moment of its founding in 1890, it was by no means monopolized by that party.

The alleged exploitation of non-Jews by Jews was one of the most effective weapons used by Austrian anti-Semites of literally every political persuasion.

Thus, Jewish bankers and businessmen were accused of collectively controlling virtually the entire Austrian economy. Most of the millionaires in Austria were allegedly Jews who controlled the banks and stock exchange. Bankers exploited the Christian population in the most "frightful way." The paper factories were all controlled supposedly by Jews as were most of the insurance industry and the wholesale trade of grain, cattle, wine, and other alcoholic beverages. Jewish power even extended over most means of transportation including trains, the Danube Steamship Company, and automobile clubs.[16] (The actual economic influence of the Austrian Jews will be discussed below in Chapter 14, "The Jews in Austrian Society.")

Occasionally anti-Semites, especially those favoring religious and racial explanations, tried to explain the success of Jewish businessmen and the moral and economic failings of their Christian counterparts. The Jews, one writer maintained with at least some plausibility, had had centuries of experience in trading and related professions. Racial anti-Semites thought that Jews had developed a different way of living than Aryans. Living a life of danger and involvement in business affairs had made them more alert, cautious, cunning, and unscrupulous, and they had passed these characteristics on to their children.[17] Another writer was far more explicit in his anti-Semitic feelings by maintaining that when Christian businessmen followed "Jewish economic practices" it was the result of "Jewish infiltration and assimilation."[18] Only rarely did an anti-Semite admit that "the true cause of the downfall of Vienna's German-Aryan population lies in the sons of rich Aryan businessmen who are raised in an undisciplined and effeminate way and waste their inheritance or at least do not exploit it. . . . Only if their business collapses completely do they discover their Aryan heart and find their way to *völkisch* organizations and parties."[19]

Racial anti-Semites loved to use statistics to support their allegations that the Jews were a "criminal people."[20] Figures that disproved their claims were either ignored or explained away, sometimes in a ridiculous fashion. Jewish crimes were not an outgrowth of historical discrimination but an expression of their "racial characteristics." If many statistics on crimes actually favored Jews, it was because they had been "falsified by Jews."[21] Racial anti-Semites also claimed that Jews were more frequently convicted of fraud than either Catholics or Protestants; they were six times as likely to be convicted of not closing their stores on Sundays as Christians and ten times more frequently convicted of employing women and children than the Christian counterparts.[22] Jews were so frequently charged with profiteering—for example, six of twenty-one cases between 1922 and 1924—that the words "Jew" and "profiteer" became almost synonymous.[23]

None of these figures, however, even if taken at its face value, is particularly surprising, much less damning. It is obvious that for Jewish businessmen, for whom Sunday was not the sabbath, remaining open that day would be a far greater temptation than it would be for Christians. Furthermore, most Jewish shops were family-owned and -operated; if women and children were employed, they were likely to be family members.[24] And if a higher percentage of Jews than Christians were convicted of profiteering, there were three times as many Jewish businessmen per capita to begin with.

Anti-Semitic writers conveniently neglected to discuss the low Jewish crime rate in Austria involving theft (209 cases for every 100,000 Jews in 1916 compared with 292 for Protestants and 355 for Catholics). As to their extremely low rate for crimes of violence—4.2 per 100,000 Jewish adults compared with 10.8 for Protestants and 20.3 for Catholics—this only "proved" another favorite anti-Semitic allegation, namely that the Jews were cowards![25]

The theories of nineteenth-century racists such as Count Arthur de Gobineau, Wilhelm Marr (who is "credited" with coining the term "anti-Semitism" in 1879), Houston Stewart Chamberlain, and many others lent an aura of pseudoscientific respectability to age-old prejudices. Racists now claimed that it was a scientifically demonstrable fact that Jews were sensual scoundrels who preyed on German women and girls. They were said to be imitators and exploiters in contrast to Aryans who were supposedly honest, simple, pious, and creative. These "völkisch" anti-Semites thought that Jews had been undermining the original German peasant way of life for two thousand years. In particular, Jews were "materialistic" in contrast to the "idealistic" Germans, among whom völkisch anti-Semites included the German-speaking Austrians.[26]

Racists disagreed about the physical characteristics of Jews. The more radical ones insisted that physical differences were clearly identifiable. The more "moderate" ones, however, conceded that this was not always the case. Even their material culture—their food, shelter, clothing, and so on—admittedly differed little from Aryans. It was not their physical differences, however, that really mattered, but their urban social structure. Without a peasantry they allegedly lacked a spiritual fountain of youth. Racists believed that this spiritual difference was decisive. Therefore, like Negroes and Chinese, albeit not for identical reasons, Jews could never hope to be Germans.[27] Racists turned the American Declaration of Independence upside down: for them it was "self-evident" that all men were created unequal.

Bild 23. Kaftanjude.
Die von liberalen Kreisen und Bekenntnissen gepredigte und gesegnete rassische Vermischung der nordisch-
bestimmten Deutschen mit den vorderasiatisch-orientalisch-negroiden Juden ist die größte Kulturschande
in dieser Welt. (Seite 34.)

Bild 24. Deutsche Bäuerin.

Photographs from Racial Victory in Vienna *by Robert Körber contrasting a Near Eastern caftan Jew and a blonde German peasant woman in traditional dress. The caption reads, "The racial mixing between Nordic-defined Germans and Near Eastern-oriental-negroid Jews, which has been preached and blessed by liberal circles, is the greatest cultural disgrace of the world."*

The lack of a peasantry and the Jews' concentration in big cities—both again the result of their historical discrimination—tended to produce another characteristic that nearly all anti-Semites detested: their social, political, and intellectual modernity. Although anti-Semites generally ignored Orthodox Jews, they occasionally expressed admiration for them because the latter were among the most conservative and traditional people in Europe. However, Orthodox Jews were a small minority in Austria. The vast majority of Jews in Austria, as elsewhere in Central and Western Europe, were acculturated and relatively secular in their outlook. Although by no means all Jews were modernists, and not all modernists were Jews, the freedom from the intellectual dogmas and traditions of the more secularized Jews made them more prone than gentiles to be iconoclastic—even toward Judaism—and exposed them to the charge of attempting to undermine traditional Christian and German-Austrian values. Far from single-handedly initiating intellectual changes, however, they more frequently simply accelerated changes that were already taking place.[28]

Bild 9. Deutsches Mädchen. (Seite 19.)
„Wie es unmöglich ist, aus einem d e u t s c h geborenen Menschen einen J u d e n zu machen, so unmöglich ist es, aus einem J u d e n einen D e u t s c h e n zu machen."

Bild 10. Jüdischer Student. (Seite 20.)
(Staatssekretär Reinhardt.)

Photographs from Racial Victory in Vienna *by Robert Körber contrasting a German girl with long, flowing, blonde hair and a Jewish student with dark, curly hair. The caption, a quotation from a Nazi official (State Secretary Reinhardt), reads, "Just as it is impossible to make a Jew out of a German-born person, it is impossible to make a German out of a Jew."*

Religious, non-Jewish conservatives in Austria, however, saw the gradual secularization of society since the Middle Ages, along with the Renaissance, the Reformation, and the French Revolution, as movements that were increasingly dominated by Jews and were directed against Christianity in general and the Roman Catholic church in particular.[29] Political conservatives held modernistic Jews responsible for all the recent trends that they—both pan-Germans and conservative Catholics—hated, namely capitalism, liberalism, democracy, and socialism.[30]

THE MYTH OF JEWISH WORLD DOMINATION

Probably the most prevalent, notorious, and insidious of all anti-Semitic allegations, as well as one of the most universal, was the idea that the Jews were conspiring to dominate the world. Dating back to the French Revolution, it resembled the belief in Jewish "spiritual," racial characteristics, of which it was a part, insofar as anti-Semites of every type in Austria (and elsewhere) accepted this idea as an article of faith. It lay in the essence of Jewry to strive for power; their drive for world domination was ancient. Hitler was only somewhat more extreme than most racial anti-Semites in frankly telling his friends (but not saying so publicly) that Christianity itself was part of this Jewish plot. St. Paul's extolling of pacifism and egalitarianism had deprived the Roman Empire of its hierarchical and military outlook and had ensured its doom. Hitler maintained that the Jews had continued to propagate their pacifism and egalitarianism in the modern world and thereby brought about the French Revolution, liberalism, democracy, and Bolshevism. Many anti-Semites believed this domination by Jews was already so complete that only the cooperation of völkisch people all over the world could possible break it. This mythical threat, then, became the "warrant for genocide."[31]

The establishment in 1860 of the "Alliance Israelite Universalle," a cultural and educational association for French-speaking Jews, and the first organization to represent world Jewry on a political basis, seemed to lend some credence to the idea of a world Jewish conspiracy.[32] However, much more important for the growing popularity of the myth for countless people was the publication in Russia of *The Protocols of the Elders of Zion* in 1903. Forged in France by agents of the chief of the Russian secret police, General Rachkowski, between about 1894 and 1899, to convince Tsar Nicholas II of the Jewish threat, *Protocols* was based on a pamphlet written by a Frenchman, Maurice Joly, in 1864, which claimed that Napoleon III wanted to dominate the world. The new Russian version merely substituted the Jews for the French emperor. The *Protocols* contained an elaborate plan for the conquest of the world through Jewish-dominated Masonic lodges culminating in the absolute hereditary monarchy of the House of David. The first principle of the "conspiracy" was that the ends justified the means and that most non-Jews were weak, cowardly, and stupid. World domination would be established through the use of merciless violence, cruelty, lies, and demagoguery. Richard Coudenhove-Kalergi wrote that the *Protocols* "constitute an apology of autocracy and of the extremest despotism."[33]

According to the *Protocols* everything had to be done in every state to foster discontent and unrest. This could be accomplished by the Elders through liberalism, which produced confusion through a multiplicity of political parties. The Elders would aggravate the situation by secretly supporting all of the parties. They would pretend to sympathize with the grievances of the workers while secretly maneuvering to increase the cost of living. State authority had to be discredited and all industry had to be concentrated into a few giant monopolies, which would destroy gentile fortunes whenever it pleased the Elders. International relations were also slated to be muddled by emphasizing national differences until international understanding became impossible. Meanwhile, gentile morality would be undermined through the encouragement of atheism and materialism. Drunkenness and prostitution were also to be vigorously encouraged. After years of such intrigue it would be easy for the Elders to organize a war against any nation that resisted them.[34]

From the beginning, the identity of the "Elders" was in doubt. The first Russian translator warned that the Elders of Zion should not be confused with representatives of the Zionist movement and that it was not even known who had copied the minutes of the meetings at which the conspiracy had been hatched.[35] When the book was first published in Central Europe shortly after the world war, this warning did nothing to stop anti-Semites from confidently asserting that the Elders were actually Zionist leaders who met at the first World Zionist Congress in Basel, Switzerland, in 1897.[36]

The publication of the *Protocols* attracted little notice until 1917 when Bolshevik aims and methods—terror, dictatorship, conspiracy, world revolution, and world domination—seemed to validate the forgery and confirm what many people had already believed about the Jews' desire for world domination. The Jewish origins of many of Lenin's close associates—for example, Trotsky, Zinoviev, and Kamenev—lent further credence to the *Protocols*. The *Protocols* helped establish a link between anti-Bolshevism and anti-Semitism. For anti-Semites, every Jew was now suspected of being a Bolshevik.[37] In reality, only 7 percent of the Bolsheviks' membership was Jewish in 1924 even though the urban population of the Soviet Union, which contained most of the party's membership, was 11 percent Jewish. Even at party congresses, only 15 to 20 percent of the delegates were Jewish. Moreover, most of the Bolshevik Jews no longer practiced Judaism or had a Jewish consciousness. For religious Jews the Bolshevik Revolution was a catastrophe; by the end of the 1920s all specifically Jewish activity had been ended or emasculated by Stalin; Jewish religious leaders were either imprisoned or exiled. Nevertheless, anti-Semites preferred to believe that since people of Jewish origins were among the instigators of the revolution, they must have also been its main beneficiaries.[38]

The publication of the *Protocols* in Germany in 1919, in the United States in 1920, and in Great Britain in 1920–21, came just as the hysteria surrounding the "Red Scare" was reaching its height. Even though an investigation by the *London Times* (which for a time had given the *Protocols* the benefit of the doubt) soon revealed them to be a forgery—a conclusion reached again through a libel trial in Switzerland in 1934—they were widely accepted, even to some degree among the general public, as the literal truth and frequently quoted in Austria, especially, but not exclusively, by racist newspapers.[39] By the time Hitler rose to power in 1933 the book had gone through no fewer than thirty-three editions in Germany; one popular edition alone sold nearly 100,000 copies. Even more important, the legal discrediting of the *Protocols* did not completely discredit the myth of a worldwide conspiracy.[40]

None of the anti-Semitic ideas described in this chapter was unique to Austria either before or after the First World War. Still less were any of them inventions of either Austrian or German Nazis. However, the rapidity with which the country entered the modern, secular, industrialized age made the clash between traditionalism, with which anti-Semitism—especially the Catholic variety—was closely associated, and modern secularism, with which the Jews were identified, far more striking than in countries like Britain and France where the process of modernization was much more gradual. Moreover, the Roman Catholic church in Austria was still a powerful and authoritative institution as late as the 1930s and bitterly resented and resisted the trend toward liberalism, democracy, Marxism, capitalism, and especially secularism, all of which it associated with the Jews.

It was not just Roman Catholics, however, who were alarmed about the role of Jews in the development of modernist trends. University students resented the rapidly increasing enrollment of Jewish students, pan-German nationalists detested the cosmopolitan outlook of some Jews, and small shopkeepers hated the large Viennese department stores, which were owned mostly by Jews. Industrial workers often hated the Jewish owners of their factories. Most of these people regarded religious anti-Semitism as antiquated in a world that had become increasingly secular. For them the racial and economic anti-Semitism found in the new bourgeois parties and political movements and in the Marxist Social Democratic Party seemed much more relevant and up to date. For them the ancient Judeophobia and the traditional allegations remained, but the vocabularly had changed. Moreover, unlike premodern times, when Judeophobia was merely a prejudice, albeit a deeply rooted one, there were now well-organized political parties that made anti-Semitism an important part of their programs and propaganda.

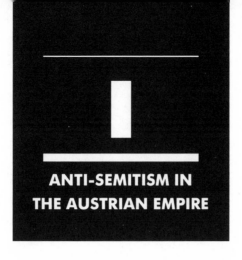

ANTI-SEMITISM IN
THE AUSTRIAN EMPIRE

Anti-Semites were right about one thing: anti-Semitism was scarcely a new phenomenon in the twentieth century, in Austria or elsewhere in Europe. Its roots in Austria can be traced back nearly to the founding of Jewish communities in the tenth century. This is not to suggest, however, that Christian-Jewish relations were always hostile. Nevertheless, three themes predominate for the whole of Austrian history up to the collapse of the monarchy in 1918 and even into the First Republic: (1) Jewish-gentile relations were tolerable during periods of prosperity but rapidly deteriorated during social and economic crises brought on by bad harvests, plagues, wars, or revolutions; (2) Christian theology taught by the Catholic clergy, especially the lower clergy, was a constant cause of popular antipathy toward the Jews; and (3) Jewish survival depended on the protection of the Austrian rulers—whenever it was removed, expulsion or at least harsh social and legal discrimination was the likely result.

In comparison with that of most other ruling dynasties in Europe, the treatment of Austrian Jews by the Habsburgs was usually fairly enlightened, especially after the accession to the throne of Emperor Joseph II in 1780. Habsburg benevolence did not prevent upsurges in popular anti-Semitism, especially in the late nineteenth century, but it did provide Austrian Jews a secure enough setting to leave their ghettos and to enter the modern, secular world and make magnificent cultural contributions to Western civilization.

2

THE HISTORICAL ROOTS

AUSTRIAN JEWS FROM THE MIDDLE AGES TO THE EIGHTEENTH CENTURY

Jews in the late Middle Ages were attracted to Austria by the opportunities to earn a living denied them in many European countries. In other parts of Germany they were subjected to arbitrary rules of lesser clergymen and city councils, as well as to those of the Holy Roman emperor. But in Austria the dukes, like some rulers in other parts of Europe at that time, realized the economic value of Jews and jealously guarded their authority over them much to the displeasure of their gentile subjects. Jews, however, in thirteenth-century Austria were only allowed to engage in money and credit transactions. In 1397 the duke of Austria invited Jews to immigrate to his land from other parts of the Holy Roman Empire. Jews were also lured to Austria by the promise of self-government.[1]

Consequently, Jews settled in several Austrian localities from the tenth to the thirteenth centuries, soon after or in some cases actually before the founding of the cities of which they became a part. Viennese Jews were first mentioned in a document in 966. Jews began settling in Carinthia in the tenth or eleventh century, well before the founding of Klagenfurt, the capital city, sometime between 1161 and 1181. In neighboring Styria, Jews could be found in Judenburg by 1103 at the latest, in Völkermarkt sometime between 1105 and 1126, and in Judendorf bei Graz in 1147. The history of the Jews of the Styrian capital, Graz, began in 1166, only thirty years after the city itself was founded.

Except for Vienna, Jewish communities in Lower Austria were not founded until the thirteenth century. For example, in Wiener Neustadt, which lies only a few miles south of the Austrian capital, Jews first settled in the early thirteenth century, a few years after the founding of the city in 1194. Meanwhile, the Jewish community in Vienna had grown to be the largest in German-speaking Europe; it substantially contributed to the city's improving economy by engaging in business on a grand scale with the nobility and clergy and on a much smaller scale with ordinary townspeople and peasants.[2] On the other hand, the usurious moneylending of some Viennese Jews, even though it was one of the few occupations legally open to Jews, and even though it was indispensable to maintaining the luxurious lifestyle of Austrian dukes, aroused both the envy and distaste of Christians.

The tolerance of the Roman Catholic church toward the collection of interest on loans by Jews served a dual purpose: the church did not have to abandon its condemnation of usury while it could permit its existence in practice; second, usury gave the Jews a new reason for being damned. Christians were already ill-disposed toward Jews because the Catholic church had diabolized them not only for their rejection of Jesus as the Messiah, but also because the church held them collectively and hereditarily responsible for the crucifixion of Jesus or, in other words, the murder of God. The Jews were thus doubly accursed for being exploiters and deicides. The religious and economic arguments reinforced each other and the picture of the Jew as a usurer became permanently fixed in the popular mind.[3]

As early as the First Crusade, at the end of the eleventh century, Jews had also been widely viewed as the children of the Devil and agents employed by Satan to combat Christianity. By the twelfth century they were being accused by the lower clergy of murdering Christian children, desecrating the consecrated wafer (so that they could murder the body of Jesus over and over), and poisoning wells.[4]

Although such allegations were commonplace in the late Middle Ages, they usually resulted in overt persecution of Jews only during times of severe economic or social crisis. Such was the case in 1338 when poor harvests in Lower Austria drove many Austrian peasants to Jewish moneylenders who were then accused of poisoning wells and sacrilege against consecrated wafers. Far worse was in store for the Jews as a result of the black plague, which ravaged Europe in the mid-fourteenth century. Jews were accused of starting the epidemic by poisoning wells in order to stamp out Christianity. Thousands of them were murdered throughout Europe even though Pope Clement VI declared their innocence. In Mühldorf, in the archbishopric of Salzburg, fourteen hundred Jews of all ages and both sexes were burned to death in 1348. The Jews of Upper Austria were far more fortunate. Duke Albrecht II, one of those princes who realized the economic value of the Jews, managed to protect the majority of them in his duchy the following year.[5]

Not all Austrian rulers were so enlightened, or at least so rational, as Duke Albrecht, however. In the early fifteenth century, the Habsburg dynasty, no longer believing that it needed Jews, took away their means of earning a living. In 1420, new charges of desecration and aiding the Bohemian heretic, Jan Hus, and supplying his followers with arms were used as pretexts by Archduke Albrecht V to destroy the Jewish community of Vienna, which numbered between 1,400 and 1,600. In reality, indebtedness to Jewish moneylenders resulting from the Hussite wars, along with increased religious fanaticism, were the chief motivations behind the archduke's actions. Poorer Jews were set adrift in the Danube. Many Jews who were imprisoned in the synagogue committed suicide. The remaining 214 men and women who refused baptism were burned alive outside the city's walls on 12 March 1421. Jewish property was expropriated and Jewish children were forcibly baptized. The events of 1420–21 earned Vienna the title of "the City of Blood" in the memory of Jews.[6]

The Jews were officially banned from Vienna "forever" in 1431. The Renaissance emperor Maximilian, accusing them of sacrilege, ritual murder, and forgery, expelled them from Wiener Neustadt and Neukirchen in 1496. In 1498 the archbishop of Salzburg, responding to popular demand, also drove them out of the city, again "forever." Such expulsions, of course, were scarcely unique to Austria. Jews had been forced out of England in 1291, out of France beginning in 1394, and out of Spain in 1492.

Nevertheless, Jews were never entirely absent from Austria for long. Jewish physicians and merchants could almost always be found in Vienna, at least on a transient basis. During the sixteenth century, individual Jews were once again allowed to settle in Vienna by rulers who needed their services. By the end of the century a new Jewish community had been established. The Jews of this "second ghetto," which was officially founded in 1625, were mostly merchants, in contrast to the moneylenders of the first ghetto. The new Jewish merchants were usually not wealthy; however, they were important because they managed to establish new centers of trade after the old ones had been destroyed by the discovery of America, the Turkish conquest of Hungary in 1526, and the Thirty Years' War. They were also exclusively responsible for providing the Habsburgs and their armies with many of the necessities of warfare. By the mid-seventeenth century about five hundred families were living next to one of the branches of the Danube River in a district later called Leopold-stadt, named after the reigning Austrian emperor Leopold I.[7]

The second Viennese ghetto turned out to be far more short-lived than the first one. Prosperity was elusive in seventeenth-century Vienna, a city that was never out of the shadow of the Turkish armies only a few miles to the east. The end of the wars against the Protestants in 1648 left the Austrian emperor with no more apparent need for Jewish money. The logic of the Catholic Counter-

Reformation also made it likely that it would be turned against all nonbelievers including Jews. Moreover, the Counter-Reformation and the wars of religion left Austria comparatively untouched by destruction, but as a result the disgust for religious bigotry and violence that appeared in some parts of Europe was never created here.[8]

Such bigotry became readily apparent in 1670 when Emperor Leopold I expelled all of the three to four thousand Jews of Vienna who refused baptism. The municipal government of Vienna accused the Jews of being "blasphemers, murderers of God's son, hateful to all Christians, and cursed by God."[9] The chief instigator of the expulsion, however, was Bishop Kollonitsch of Wiener Neustadt. But Leopold's court preacher, Abraham a Sancta Clara, was no less hostile toward Jews calling them "scum of the godless and the faithless" and blaming them for a recent plague. Leopold's Spanish wife, who was well known for her anti-Jewish feelings, interpreted a recent miscarriage and a fire in the imperial palace as omens that she should expel the Jews to avoid further misfortunes. Finally, the Christian merchants of Vienna had long been eager to rid themselves of their Jewish competitors.[10]

Although some of the Jews who had been expelled from Vienna moved as far away as Brandenburg, where they were welcomed by the tolerant and far-sighted Frederick William, the Great Elector, others moved only as far as the Bohemian crownlands of Bohemia, Moravia, and Silesia. By 1673, Emperor Leopold, who was already feeling the financial loss of the absent Jews, allowed a small number of them to return, although they were required to make large initial payments for the privilege of settling in Vienna. The reestablishment of even a small number of Jewish families was enough to provoke Christian burghers once more into petitioning Emperor Karl VI to expel the "accursed and depraved Jews."[11]

A hundred years later, in the middle of the eighteenth century, a small Jewish community once more existed in Vienna. Many of the newcomers were Sephardic Jews, who could trace their ancestry back to Spain and Portugal prior to the expulsion of 1492 and who came to Austria by way of Constantinople, Amsterdam, and various cities in Italy. Although often wealthy, they lacked the political status of the second ghetto; they stood outside the law and were completely dependent on the favor of the monarch. Empress Maria Theresa, who reigned from 1740 to 1780, virtually forced commerce on them by limiting their employment to money changing, general financial operations, and jewel trading; a new law of 1764 also allowed them to trade in domestic (but not foreign) manufactured goods.[12]

Maria Theresa was by no means pleased by even this very limited toleration of Jews. Although enlightened and reforming in many respects, as seen, for example, in her abolition of torture and the founding of schools of higher learning, she was a religious bigot when it came to people of the Mosaic faith. She insisted that Jews keep out of sight when a Catholic procession was passing by as well as on Sunday mornings and holidays. She refused to speak directly with them herself and said that "she knew of no worse plague for the State," a phrase Nazis were fond of quoting two hundred years later.[13] Her outspoken aim was to rid Vienna of them once again; the most she was able to accomplish, however, was the expulsion of the Jews of Prague, on the suspicion they had aided Frederick the Great in his conquest of Silesia. The expulsion lasted for three years (1745–48), but it was enough to earn the empress the distinction of being the last European ruler (before Hitler) to expel Jews.[14]

As late as 1776 the Jews of Vienna remained a tiny community although they were considerably more numerous in other parts of the Habsburg Monarchy. They numbered a scant 317 in Lower Austria, which at that time (and until shortly after the First World War) included Vienna. A mere 37 lived in the Tyrol; in other Alpine crownlands of the monarchy they were not officially allowed to reside at all until 1848. On the other hand, Bohemia and Moravia, from which large numbers of Jews would come to Vienna in the mid-nineteenth century, had a total of about 55,000. The recently annexed crownland of Galicia, which constituted the southern part of Poland before the first partition in 1772, had by far the largest Jewish population in the empire in 1776, amounting to nearly 150,000. In the late nineteenth and early twentieth centuries it became an important source of Jewish immigrants to Vienna.[15]

REFORM AND REACTION: AUSTRIAN JEWS FROM JOSEPH II TO 1848

The accession to the throne of Emperor Joseph II in 1780 marked the beginning of a new era for Austrian Jews. Joseph attributed their real and alleged shortcomings to harsh oppression and economic necessity. As coregent with Maria Theresa after 1765, he had tried unsuccessfully to get his mother to grant religious toleration to Jews in the so-called hereditary lands near Vienna. But it was not until after her death that he was able to issue a decree (in May 1781) that improved the education of Jews in Bohemia in order to make them more useful to the state. In the same year he abolished the wearing of the yellow badge of identification. Then on 2 January 1782 he enacted his famous Patent of Toleration, which applied to the Jews of much of the empire, freeing them from their ghettos. Jewish children were now required to attend German-language schools, could enter all public educational institutions, and could practice any academic profession. They could also found factories, employ Christian workers, and engage in manual labor and any of the arts. Restrictions on their dress were removed, and they were encouraged to wear "Christian" costumes. In 1784 Joseph allowed Jews to practice law and forced them to give up their judicial autonomy. In 1788 he required them to relinquish their use of Yiddish and Hebrew in public and adopt German-sounding family names. In the same year he also required them to perform military service, thus making Austria one of the first countries in Europe to have Jewish soldiers.[16]

Joseph's toleration of Jews was not all inclusive, nor did it make them equal citizens. (They had all the duties of citizens, but not all the rights.) Still less was it based on pure humanitarianism. Jews could not enter the civil service, could not own land, and had to pay ten thousand gulden for the right to settle in Vienna; in some other parts of Austria they were not allowed to reside at all. What it did do was to help fulfill Joseph's goal of increasing their economic and social value to the state by at least partially integrating them into Christian society. Joseph made Austria the first country in Europe to grant Jews naturalized citizenship and to consider them permanent residents; it was also the first to allow complete toleration in religious affairs, thereby preceding even the United States and France. In sum, he was the first modern European ruler to lift the medieval restrictions that had hampered Jewish life.[17]

Joseph's reforms received a mixed response from Jews. The more modern and secularized Jews of Vienna and the Bohemian crownlands were enthusiastic supporters. Elsewhere in the monarchy, however, the reaction was much cooler. Many Jews noted that although Joseph was offering them equal rights as individuals, his reforms did not ensure a bright future for Judaism as a religion. Indeed, their partial integration into Christian society later led to the gradual disintegration of their religious life. These changes eroded even more the Jews' sense of national identity.[18]

Among Catholics the reaction to Joseph's Jewish policies was almost uniformly negative. The government of Lower Austria reacted with barely concealed hostility. Roman Catholic bishops thought the admission of Jewish children to Christian schools would cause conversions to Judaism. Their attempt to get Joseph's brother and successor, Leopold II, to revoke the Patent of Toleration, was refused, however.[19]

The death of Joseph II in 1790 followed by that of Leopold II in 1792 marked the beginning of reaction in the treatment of Jews in Austria that would completely reverse the country's leading role in the emancipation of Jewry. By 1848 the monarchy was the only major European power west of Russia that still imposed medieval restrictions on Jews. Franz II (known as Franz I after Napoleon deprived him of his title as Holy Roman emperor in 1806) was undoubtedly traumatized into becoming a reactionary by the French Revolution, by the Reign of Terror, and especially by the conquering armies of Napoleon, which crisscrossed Austrian territory several times between 1797 and 1813. Like earlier Austrian rulers he still valued the Jews' economic usefulness to the state; but he was unwilling to acknowledge that they had rights. Whereas Leopold had refused a demand by the municipal council of Vienna to revoke Joseph's Patent of Toleration, his son Franz issued no fewer than six hundred decrees that limited Jewish rights guaranteed in the Patent. After 1795 toleration was merely for three years, not for life; and after 1807 it was only for individuals, not for families. Jews who were not tolerated could spend no more than one month at a time in Vienna. Acquiring toleration also required an ability to practice a skilled trade. Whereas foreign Christians could be naturalized after fifteen years, Jews were always considered foreigners.[20]

Despite these renewed restrictions, Jewish integration into Austrian and especially Viennese society continued during the reign of Franz I. In the course of the Napoleonic Wars Jews proved themselves to be especially patriotic and willing to make sacrifices; 35,000 of them fought in the Austrian army in all its branches. Jewish money was needed to help finance the wars. Jews were also beginning to play an important role in supporting the cultural life of the Austrian capital. The salon of Fanny Arnstein was the scene of frequent balls and concerts as well as a place of relaxation for international peacemakers during the Congress of Vienna in 1814–15. Arnstein, who socialized with ladies from the highest Viennese circles, also played a leading role in the establishment of the Gesellschaft der Musikfreunde (the Society of the Friends of Music).[21]

The Jewish community of Vienna had managed to grow numerically and economically during the reign of Franz I, which did not end until 1835. By 1811 the community was large enough to build a prayer house; the following year the first Jewish school was founded. In 1826 a synagogue was built in what is today the Seitenstettengasse near the center of Vienna in the first district. By 1830 there were approximately sixteen hundred Jews living in Vienna who had established various social and charitable institutions for Jewish children, sick people, and widows. Most Jewish men were engaged in small-scale trade as Christian artisans did not want to hire Jewish apprentices. Excluded from the civil service, young Jewish men sought an advanced education in order to pursue careers in law, journalism, literature, and especially medicine, the only professions where Jews faced no restrictions. Some of them had already become successful in these fields even before the Revolutions of 1848. Others were finding jobs in handicraft industries such as textiles and leather.[22]

The reign of Ferdinand I from 1835 to 1848 saw little change in the status of Austrian Jews. Discriminatory laws against Jews were at least administered more leniently than they had been under Franz. Moreover, Prince Clemens von Metternich, Austria's foreign minister between 1809 and 1848 and the most powerful man in the country during the reign of the feeble-minded emperor, Ferdinand, maintained good relations with Jews and generally did not express anti-Jewish sentiments; however, only the social and economic Jewish elite benefited from his policies.[23]

THE REVOLUTIONS OF 1848-1849

The revolutionary year of 1848 proved in some respects a repeat performance of Joseph II's revolutionary Patent of Toleration in 1782. Once again most of the barriers to complete civil equality were removed; but such equality proved to be brief. Ironically a discriminatory law helped Jews to play a prominent role in the revolution. The University of Vienna's Medical College was the only college in the city to which Jews could be admitted; moreover, free speech was more or less allowed during the 1840s. The Jewish students had the right to remain in Vienna indefinitely as long as they paid a fixed fee, thus giving them an incentive to remain students perpetually. Some of these perpetual Jewish students as members of illegal student fraternities helped organize the demonstrations that led to the overthrow of Prince Metternich and later to the enactment of Austria's first constitution.[24]

Jews were prominent in every phase of the revolution, more so than in any other country touched by the revolution. All three men who did the most to initiate the rebellion were Jews as was one of the first victims of the revolution, a student named Spitzer. In May 1848, when a committee of public safety was established, its chairman, Adolf Fischhof, was a thirty-two-year-old Jewish medical student. After the Kaiser's flight from Vienna that summer he became the most powerful political figure in the monarchy.[25] Hermann Jellinek, a radical revolutionary socialist and a Jew, was later executed by the counter-revolutionary military dictatorship for ridiculing religion in a pamphlet.[26] The prominent role played by many Jews in the revolution identified Jews with that episode in the eyes of many conservatives. Those people who opposed the revolution were likely also to oppose Jewish emancipation.[27]

Liberal Jews in Vienna saw the revolution not only as an opportunity to overthrow an unpopular and repressive regime but also to gain emancipation for themselves. They did not ask for much more in 1848 than what Joseph II had granted them in 1782, namely civil and political equality. The constitution of 25 April failed to resolve these issues. However, a newly elected Reichstag removed the special toleration tax on Jews in October. Finally, the new constitution of 4 March 1849 unambiguously declared that the enjoyment of civil and political rights was not dependent on an individual's religion. This meant that Jews could now also own property (except for mines), which in turn meant that they could enter any legal occupation. They were also allowed to marry outside their faith provided they first converted or declared themselves *konfessionslos*.[28]

Jewish academicians who were involved in the Viennese revolution of 1848 were struggling for freedom of press, speech, assembly, and scientific research for all Austrians and not just for their own freedom. Unfortunately, most gentiles were at best indifferent to Jewish emancipation and few non-Jews signed a petition demanding it. Meanwhile, opponents of emancipation were busy circulating a counterpetition and anti-Jewish pamphlets.[29] Jews, in fact, were now confronted with an early example of modern political anti-Semitism, especially on the part of artisans who feared free competition. However, this anti-Semitism was spontaneous and popular and not organized into a political party let alone a mass movement—such developments would have to wait until the late 1870s and the 1880s.[30]

The Jews' new freedoms proved to be even more ephemeral than those granted them by Joseph II. On the last day of 1851, the young emperor Franz Joseph, under the influence of his reactionary mother, annulled the constitution of 1849. Once again Jews were forbidden to own landed estates, although they were allowed to retain those they had already purchased. The medieval law prohibiting the employment of Christian servants was reinstated, and Jews were not allowed to hold public office, including teaching positions. Many Jews were thus driven to baptism, which removed all legal barriers to career advancement.[31]

Not all was lost by the Jews in the reactionary decade following the failed revolution. The Jews of Vienna were allowed in 1849 to establish an autonomous religious communal organization called the Israelitische Kultusgemeinde with its own elected officials. In charge of religious and charitable activities, it functioned continuously until it was dissolved by the Nazis in 1942. *Kultusgemeinden* were subsequently established in other Austrian cities during the next few decades.[32]

FRANZ JOSEPH AND THE JEWS

Despite his renunciation of the March 1849 constitution, Franz Joseph never entirely abolished the gains Jews had made in the revolution. In fact, during the course of his incredibly long reign—nearly sixty-eight years—Jews made enormous progress in almost every aspect of their lives. Even at his most reactionary in 1850, Franz Joseph assured Jews that they would be treated with complete equality in his beloved army. He recognized no confessions in his army, only soldiers, and those who earned it were made officers, regardless of their religion. Moreover, Jews played an active part in the economy during the period of neoabsolutism in the 1850s. They established woolen factories in Bohemia and Moravia; in Hungary they founded the silk-raising industry. Throughout the monarchy they played an important role in the building of steel mills and railroads. Near Vienna they were instrumental in building factories that produced silk, cotton, woolens, laces, and leather, as well as the only factory in Austria that made chocolate. They also founded many of the capital city's more important banks.[33]

Austria's defeat by France in the Italian War of 1859 led to a series of constitutional reforms during the next eight years, many of which directly affected Jews. Franz Joseph's edict of 12 January 1860 again permitted them to own land, enter professions of their own choosing, settle in parts of the monarchy previously forbidden to them, testify against Christians, and employ Christian servants. Jewish manual laborers could now also become masterworkmen.[34]

All remaining laws that discriminated against Jews were removed by the new constitution of 21 December 1867, following Austria's defeat by Prussia and the creation of the Dual Monarchy with Hungary. The constitution confirmed the rights Jews had already obtained in 1860 and stipulated that all public offices including teaching positions were now legally open to all citizens of the state, including Jews. All citizens were now also free to practice or not to practice any religion and to establish cultural and educational institutions.[35]

Thanks in large measure to the new constitution of 1867 and the benevolence of Emperor Franz Joseph, Jews came to regard the last half century of the Habsburg Monarchy as a golden era in their history. Franz Joseph allowed no legislation harmful to Jews to be enacted after 1867. He ennobled twenty Jews and appointed several to the Herrenhaus (the upper chamber of the Austrian Parliament). He appointed one Jew to the highest rank in the army and another to be the chief officer in the army's medical staff. Some men of Jewish origins (although not practicing Jews) even became ministers of state. When anti-Semitic movements first reappeared in Austria in the late 1870s the emperor ordered his prime minister, Count Edward von Taaffe, to stop them immediately. Consequently, when the emperor finally died in 1916 at the age of nearly eighty-six, Jewish newspapers were lavish in their praise of his reign. He had opened the gates of ghettos for Jews, commented one prominent Jewish newspaper. Another writer said that the name of Franz Joseph would always be written in golden letters in Jewish history.[36]

JEWISH DEMOGRAPHY, 1848–1914

The constitutional rights Jews obtained between 1848 and 1867, especially the right to reside wherever they pleased, to own property, and to enter professions of their own choosing, enormously facilitated the growth of the Jewish population in Austrian cities and above all in Vienna. Although Austria as a whole had a Jewish population second only to Russia following the annexation of Galicia and Bukovina in 1772, Vienna's Jewish population still numbered only about 1,600 in 1830. The number grew to approximately 4,000 in 1846, and to 6,217 in 1857. Thereafter, however, attracted by economic opportunities and by the beauty of the city, its exciting cultural opportunities, and its educational institutions, and facilitated by Austria's new railway system, Jews migrated to the Austrian capital in unprecedented numbers.[37]

By 1880, 72,588 Jews lived in Vienna, 118,495 resided there in 1890, 146,926 in 1900, and 175,318 in 1910. The percentage of Jews living in the *Residenzstadt* skyrocketed from 2.16 in 1857 to 10.06 in 1880; thereafter, it declined slowly but steadily to 8.63 in 1910—in part, however, because of the incorporation of the largely non-Jewish suburbs in 1890.[38] For the whole crownland of Lower Austria the growth rate for Jews was five times greater than for non-Jews between 1869 and 1880, and twice as fast in the 1880s.[39] On the other hand, between 1900 and 1910 the overall population of Vienna grew by 21.2 percent compared with only 19.3 percent for the Jews.[40] Nevertheless the growth of Vienna's Jewish population was unmatched anywhere else in Europe except Budapest. In most of the continent's other cities with large Jewish communities, such as Berlin, Frankfurt, Hamburg, Lemberg (Lvov), and Cracow, the percentage of Jews actually dropped, sometimes by nearly half, between the mid-nineteenth century and the outbreak of the First World War.[41]

If the increase of Vienna's Jewish population was dramatic after 1857, the same cannot be said for that of the Austrian half of the Dual Monarchy as a whole. There the Jewish population grew only about 2 percent faster than the non-Jewish population between 1869 and 1900. In Bohemia and Moravia the

Jewish population actually fell sharply in the second half of the nineteenth century, in part because of their migration to Vienna.[42] By 1910 there was a total of 1,313,698 Jews in the Austrian half of the monarchy, or 4.68 percent of the total population. If Jews had still been considered a separate nationality, as they had been before 1860, they would have been the fifth largest in the country, albeit far behind the German-speaking Austrians, the Czechs, the Poles, and the Ruthenes (Ukrainians).[43] These figures should be kept clearly in mind when we later evaluate anti-Semitic charges concerning the size of the Jewish population in Vienna and Austria as a whole.

In the roughly seven decades preceding the outbreak of the First World War, the nature of Jewish immigration to the Austrian capital changed considerably. Until the 1870s Jews came mostly from the Bohemian crownlands of Bohemia, Moravia, and Austrian Silesia. Having already adopted the German language, even before 1848, and being well educated, they had little difficulty adjusting to life in the Austrian metropolis. The same, for the most part, could be said of the second wave of immigrants, which came from Hungary.[44]

After 1867 the geographic origins of Jewish immigrants to Vienna began to change drastically. Immigrants from Galicia, usually non-German-speaking and often Orthodox, now started to outnumber Jewish immigrants from the Bohemian crownlands and Hungary. As early as 1880, 18 percent of Vienna's Jews were from this Polish and Ukrainian province; that figure grew to 23 percent in 1910. The growth in the absolute number of Galician-born Jews was even more impressive: 13,180 in 1880 and 30,325 thirty years later.[45]

Whereas the emigration of Galician Jews until 1880 was motivated primarily by the dire economic backwardness of their homeland, emigration into the empire after 1881 from what had once been Poland was additionally propelled by pogroms organized by the Russian minister of the interior, Nicholas Ignatiev. The Russian Empire thus became the first country in Europe to have officially sponsored pogroms. The tsar's regime was also skillful at playing off Poles, Ukrainians, Lithuanians, and Cossacks against the Jews. The pogroms of Ignatiev spread to over one hundred locations and lasted nearly a year (1881–82); they were followed by a mass of anti-Jewish legislation designed, according to the government, to restrict the antisocial activities of the Jews and to calm popular indignation against them.[46]

Austria was scarcely the only country to be affected by these new Jewish immigrants, nor the only country to react negatively. A massive wave of terrified Jews fled from Russia to urban centers in Western Europe. In England, the Jewish population of 65,000 in 1881 quadrupled during the next thirty years fueling demands by Conservative politicians and trade union leaders alike for immigration controls. Another 20,000 Russian Jews fled to Paris between 1881 and the outbreak of the First World War. The refugees also increased anti-Jewish feelings in Germany just two years after the Hamburg anarchist pamphleteer, Wilhelm Marr, had used the term *anti-Semitism* and had founded an Anti-Semitic League. A year after the onset of increased Russian Jewish immigration to Germany, that is in 1882, the first international anti-Jewish congress met in Dresden.[47]

Thanks in part to these newcomers from Galicia and Russia, Vienna, with 146,926 Jews, had the largest Jewish population in the Dual Monarchy in 1900. However, by 1910, Budapest, with over 203,000 Jews had forged ahead of Vienna, which now had 175,000 Jewish inhabitants. Other Austrian cities with large Jewish populations were Lemberg, the largest city in eastern Galicia, with 44,258; Cracow, in western Galicia, with 25,670; Czernowitz (Cernauti), the capital of the easternmost Austrian crownland of Bukovina, with 21,587 Jews; and Brünn (Brno) in southern Moravia, with 8,238. In the "Inner Austrian" crownlands, those areas that would make up the Austrian republic after 1919, the Jewish population remained tiny. Graz, which had the second largest Jewish population after Vienna, was home to only 1,971 Jews or just 1.3 percent of the Styrian capital's total population in 1910. By contrast, about 100,000 Jews lived in rural parts of Germany after 1900.[48]

Despite the rapid increase in Vienna's Jewish population, it was far from having the highest percentage of Jews in the Dual Monarchy or even in the Austrian half of the monarchy. The 8.77 percent of Vienna's population that was Jewish in 1900 was far below that of Czernowitz, with nearly 32 percent, Cracow, which had 28 percent, and Lemberg, where just under 28 percent of the population was Jewish.[49] The percentage of Jews living in Vienna was even more modest when compared with the 23.1 who lived in Budapest in 1910.[50]

THE OUTLOOK IN 1880

Although there was never a time in nineteenth-century Austria when anti-Semitism was entirely dead, it certainly seemed to be receding during the 1860s and for most of the 1870s, at least as far as the German-speaking population of the country was concerned. Jew-hatred—political, social, and especially religious—appeared to most German-Austrians, particularly educated German-Austrians, to be a mere vestige of the Middle Ages.[51] Until at least 1880, Jews who spoke fluent German were considered to be German-Austrians by the Jews themselves, as well as by non-Jewish German-Austrians and the national minorities of Austria. In fact, German-speaking Jews, out of gratitude for their recent emancipation, identified so closely with German culture and the Austrian state idea that to members of national minority groups who felt oppressed, especially the Czechs, Jews seemed to be accomplices in that oppression, a feeling that could also be found in Hungary.[52] The prominence of German-speaking Jews in the development of Austrian capitalism gave the national minorities, who were far more likely to be peasants, an additional reason for disliking Jews.

However, in Austria, the views of the Czechs and other national minorities hardly counted in the 1860s and 1870s. What mattered was that Jews were accepted, or at least appeared to be accepted, by German-Austrians. True, not all was well even in these two golden decades. Catholics resented the role played by Jews in the Liberal Party in 1870 when the Austrian concordat made with the papacy in 1855 was canceled. Jews were also blamed for the disastrous stock market crash of 1873. That the House of Rothschild, which had not engaged in the speculation preceding the crash, had emerged from the disaster unhurt, only seemed to prove the Jews' craftiness. The crash, however, produced no immediate political repercussions.[53]

In 1867 Austrian Jews had obtained, de jure if not always de facto, complete political and civil equality. Few Jews, or for that matter, probably even non-Jews, would have predicted as late as 1880 that twenty years later anti-Semitism would once again be rampant among both the Austrian elite and the masses. Nor would they have believed that Vienna would have the first municipal government in the world controlled by a political party that officially espoused anti-Semitism.

3

ANTI-SEMITISM
IN FIN-DE-SIÈCLE
AUSTRIA

In retrospect anti-Semitism may have been in one of its periodic dormant phases in the Austria of the 1860s and most of the 1870s. Because many of the very people who would later form the hard-core support for anti-Semitism— small businessmen and artisans—did not yet have the franchise, there was no need for politicians to cater to their prejudices. The situation was chang- ing, however. When anti-Semitism resurfaced in Austria, it was no longer simply an emotion or a religious prejudice as in earlier centuries but was now a political program and a justification for political action.[1]

Austria-Hungary, being almost in the geographic center of Europe, was of course influenced by intellectual trends outside its borders, and anti-Semitism was no exception. The popularity of Darwinism, in both its biological and social manifestations, stressing the "struggle for survival" and the "survival of the fittest," did not leave the Dual Monarchy unaffected. Moreover, at a time when fewer and fewer Christians and Jews alike, especially in the big cities, were still practicing their religion, and at a time when science was reaching its peak of prestige, those people who instinctively disliked Jews, envied their wealth, or rejected their political views felt compelled to justify their feelings on some grounds other than religion or else run the risk of being declared religious bigots. Charges of ritual murder and well poisoning were no longer convincing in a modern, secularized society.

Such views are clearly apparent in Hitler's *Mein Kampf*. If we can believe his own account, the young Hitler, in his Linz years and for a time after his move to Vienna at the age of eighteen, rejected anti-Semitism as being "intol- erant" and "unscientific." "There were few Jews in Linz. In the course of the centuries their outward appearance had become Europeanized and had taken on a human look; in fact, I even took them for Germans. The absurdity of this idea did not dawn on me because I saw no distinguishing feature but the strange religion. The fact that they had, as I believed, been persecuted on this account sometimes almost turned my distaste at unfavorable remarks about them into horror."[2]

Even Hitler's first exposure to anti-Semitic literature in Vienna did not convert him because of its "unscientific" nature. "For a few hellers I bought the first anti-Semitic pamphlets of my life. Unfortunately, they all proceeded from the supposition that in principle the reader knew or even understood the Jewish question to a certain degree. Besides, the tone for the most part was such that doubts again arose in me, due in part to the dull and amazingly unscientific arguments favoring the thesis."[3]

THE ORIGINS OF RACISM AND POLITICAL ANTI-SEMITISM IN GERMANY

The theories about "scientific racism" so cherished by Hitler did not have their origins in Austria or even Germany. Rather it was the Frenchman, Count Arthur Joseph de Gobineau whose three-volume work, *An Essay on the Inequality of the Races* (1853–55), argued that race is the decisive element in history rather than the characteristics or beliefs of individuals. The white races were creative and destined to rule and the other races were bound to follow. The Semites, including the Jews, were merely parasitic. These ideas were to have fateful consequences for the Jews even though de Gobineau himself had no political agenda regarding them.[4]

Although de Gobineau's theories did not attract a particularly large following in his native country, they were popular in Germany and Austria among those urban, educated people who felt alienated from the Christian church and its traditional, religious anti-Judaism. For hard-core racists the racial myth became an all-pervading philosophy of life, which regulated their political and even personal behavior. They could (and did) argue that even baptized Jews should not be accepted as equal citizens in Germany and Austria and should be excluded from the civil service and other influential positions. They interpreted Jewish predominance in trade and moneylending not as historically conditioned but as racially determined. In fact, all negative judgments about Jews were seen by racists as being rooted in nature.[5]

It was for the most part Germans rather than Austrians who elaborated de Gobineau's ideas and applied them to Jews. The man who was probably the most responsible for popularizing the new "scientific" racism in Central Europe was Wilhelm Marr, who is also "credited" with coining the pretentious term anti-Semitism in 1879, which soon gained wide acceptance in part because of its lack of clarity. In his book entitled *Der Sieg des Judentums über das Germanentum* (*The Victory of Judaism over Germandom*), which went through twelve editions in six years, Marr contrasted Jews not with Christians but with Germans along lines that were immutable and eternal. Marr deliberately rejected many of the Christian accusations against Jews as unworthy of an enlightened thinker, but replaced them with the idea of a cunning, rootless, and conspiratorial race. The Germans had lost the battle to the Jews, according to Marr, through their own stupidity without ever realizing that a war was taking place. The only solution to the "Jewish problem" was the strict segregation of the races, an idea perhaps inspired by his unhappy marriages to three Jewish women. Although Marr would eventually become a critic of the anti-Semitic movement, he is still remembered as the "patriarch of anti-Semitism" and the person who changed the image of the Jews from being a small, weak group to that of a world power; now Jews could be depicted as being much stronger than the Germans.[6]

One reason why the term anti-Semitism gained such rapid momentum, especially in German universities, was its incidental use by the immensely popular German historian, Heinrich von Treitschke, in an essay he wrote in November 1879 in which he identified the Jews with every negative aspect of German life. The Jewish question was not one problem among many, but the very essence of evil. Nevertheless, Treitschke differed sharply from most German racists in not opposing Jewish conversions to Christianity and in actually favoring their assimilation into German society.[7]

Neither Marr nor Treitschke were political activists. The first German to create an anti-Semitic ideology based on biology, philosophy, and history was a professor of philosophy and national economy at the University of Berlin, Eugen Dühring. Dühring carried anti-Semitism to new extremes in his book, *Die Judenfrage als Racen-, Sitten- und Culturfrage* (*The Jewish Question as a Race, Morals and Cultural Question*) published in 1881. Dühring contradicted Treitschke in denying that Jews could ever become Germans; he also rejected Treitschke's advocacy of Jewish conversion, which he believed would only make it easier for Jews to infiltrate and corrupt German society. Jews were irredeemably depraved because of their racial characteristics, which had even shaped their religion. The Jewish problem could only be solved by the revocation of their emancipation. They had to be governed by special laws and their influence removed from all public affairs including education and the press as well as from business and finance.[8] Although Dühring, through his students, influenced the Austrian pan-German and racial anti-Semite Georg von Schönerer (to be discussed later), his influence was limited even within racism's lunatic fringe, not to mention the larger German society, in part because of his outspoken atheism and his desire to go beyond a mere "cleansing" of Christianity of its Jewish elements.[9]

Much less extreme than Dühring but more influential was Adolf Stöcker. The imperial court chaplain in Berlin, Stöcker thought that the emancipation of the Jews had been a serious mistake but was irreversible. However, he favored the German government's de facto policy of excluding unconverted Jews from civil service positions and especially from teaching Christian children. He deplored anti-Semitic violence and like Treitschke demanded the complete assimilation of Jews. Although Stöcker failed in his attempt to win over the German working class to anti-Semitism, his Christian Social Party was the first organized political expression of anti-Semitism during its brief existence between 1878 and 1885. His effort to merge "German socialism" with anti-Semitism made it one of the early forerunner's of Hitler's National Socialism.[10]

Thanks to Stöcker, Dühring, Marr, Treitschke, and other anti-Semites, Germany became the first country in the world to develop a modern political anti-Semitic movement. This is not to say that anti-Semitism did not exist in other countries. But anti-Semitism as a well-organized political movement aimed against liberalism, socialism, and clericalism flourished first and most vehemently in Germany and very soon thereafter in the German-speaking parts of Austria. Even after its spread to France, England, Eastern Europe, and the United States, German-speaking Europe remained the center of the movement.[11]

ACADEMIC ANTI-SEMITISM IN AUSTRIA BEFORE THE FIRST WORLD WAR

Although the racial component in Austrian anti-Semitism was largely imported from Germany, nonreligious and "racial" anti-Semitism first appeared in Austria even before the publication of Marr's book. Universities and other so-called Hochschulen or schools of higher learning were already espousing the new creed in the late 1870s at about the same time that Jewish enrollments were exploding. Unfortunately, the rapid increase in Jewish enrollments coincided with a downturn in the economy, which was not completely reversed until 1896. Nowhere was this first "Great Depression" more obvious than in the academically trained professions, especially between 1880 and 1900. Non-

Jewish students in both Austria and Germany saw their careers threatened by the shortage of jobs and blamed their new Jewish classmates.[12]

Jewish enrollments in Austrian institutions of higher learning had been modest until the middle of the nineteenth century. In the years 1851 to 1855 there had been an average of only 484 Jews or 7.9 percent at all the Austrian universities and technical Hochschulen. Between 1876 and 1880 these figures rose sharply to 1,685 or 14.2 percent and reached a relative peak between 1886 and 1890 with 3,301 or 21.5 percent before the percentage of Jewish students began to decline, at least for the monarchy as a whole.[13] At the University of Vienna the number of Jews increased especially rapidly during the early 1880s from 1,298 in the winter semester of 1881 to 2,095 four years later. During the same period the Christian enrollment rose only slightly from 3,525 to 3,831. Thereafter, however, it continued to rise to 5,422 in 1903–4 while the number of Jewish students declined to only 1,693.[14]

Anti-Semites, however, either ignored this decline by citing only those years in which Jewish enrollment had been high,[15] or else simply invented inflated statistics.[16] They were also oblivious to the fact that many of the Jewish students were foreigners (well over a third in 1918–19)[17] who were likely to return to their homelands at the completion of their studies and not compete for positions in Austria.

Although academic anti-Semitism in Austria was by no means confined to Vienna—it was also strong at the University of Innsbruck, for example, even though the Jewish student population never exceeded 1.5 percent before (or after) the First World War[18] — it was most intense in the Austrian capital probably because more than half of all the Jewish students in the Austrian half of the monarchy were located in the *Kaiserstadt*.[19] Likewise, the *percentage* of Jewish students was substantially higher in Vienna, both at the university and at the Technical College, than elsewhere in the monarchy with the exception of the much smaller German University of Prague and the tiny University of Czernowitz in far away Bukovina.[20] Moreover, ethnic German students and professors in Prague were inclined to see German-speaking Jews as allies against the Czechs; in Graz and Innsbruck the primary enemies were the large minority of South Slav and Italian-speaking students rather than Jews.[21]

The origins of racial anti-Semitism among students at the University of Vienna can be traced to Dr. Theodor Billroth, a world-famous German-born surgeon and professor at the Medical College of the University of Vienna. Jewish enrollment at the Medical College had been high since before the Revolution of 1848 and about half the teaching staff was also Jewish after 1890.

Billroth objected to the large number of new Jewish medical students coming from Eastern Europe; their poverty and poor command of German, he assumed, would lower the academic standards of his college. In his book, *Über das Lehren und Lernen der medizinischen Wissenschaften* (*About the Teaching and Learning of Medical Science*), published in 1875, he warned against the dangers of Jewish predominance in medicine. He argued that the Jewish students did not simply belong to a different religion but also to a different race. Although Billroth later reversed this view and actually became a member of the Verein zur Abwehr des Antisemitismus (League to Combat Anti-Semitism), substantial damage was already done.[22]

Another member of the faculty at the University of Vienna who contributed to the idea of Jewish racial characteristics was Adolf Wahrmund. In his book *Das Gesetz des Nomadenthums und die heutige Judenherrschaft* (*Law of Nomads and Contemporary Jewish Domination*), which he published in 1887, Wahrmund argued that the central Jewish racial characteristic was their need to wander, which had been created by their origins as nomads in the Sinai desert. This fact explained their shiftlessness in commerce and their rootless, cosmopolitan way of thinking, and their inability to build a state of their own in contrast to Aryans whose racial characteristics had been formed by their peasant ancestors. Wahrmund thus used secular and pseudoscientific environmental arguments to describe Jewishness instead of the traditional religious explanations.[23]

Of the two Viennese academicians, Billroth appears to have had the greater influence on Austrian students. His assertion that Jews belonged to a separate race was enthusiastically received by gentile students at the University of Vienna even though the university had been a bastion of liberalism during the 1850s and 1860s. Most university students rejected religious anti-Judaism as reactionary and unenlightened. Racial anti-Semitism, on the other hand, seemed modern and scientific. Moreover, the treatment of Jews as a separate race and not merely as a different religion would eliminate the opportunities for social and economic advancement Jews enjoyed in Central Europe when they converted to Christianity.[24]

In the same year that Billroth published his book, a nationalistic student organization in Vienna called the Leseverein der deutschen Studenten (Reading Club of German Students) supported his racial thesis. Two years later a student fraternity (or *Burschenschaft*) in Vienna called Teutonia was the first to make itself *judenrein*, followed the next year by another fraternity called Libertas. In both instances the exclusion was based on "race," not religion.

Not even a pseudoscientific test was used, however, to determine race. Most Burschenschaften were satisfied with a simple declaration by the candidate that he knew of no Jewish ancestors.[25]

Once established in the Burschenschaften, anti-Semitism developed a dynamics of its own. Actually, Jews had been underrepresented in the fraternities in relation to their proportion of the student population, and those who did belong tended to be well-assimilated German nationalists. These facts did not prevent them from being excluded from one fraternity after another during the 1880s; even the fraternities' Jewish alumni (*alte Herren*) were expelled. By 1890 all of the Burschenschaften of Vienna had become anti-Semitic. Even in the United States Greek letter societies began excluding Jews, beginning at the City College of New York in 1878.[26]

The anti-Semites of the Austrian Burschenschaften were well ahead of their fraternity brothers in Germany who, though nationalistic, were not specifically anti-Semitic in the 1870s, accepting new members without regard to their ancestry, political affiliation, or faith. Germany even had a national organization of students that was categorically opposed to anti-Semitism, the Deutscher Allgemeiner Burschenbund (German General League of Fraternities). However, German university students were the largest single supporters of a nationwide petition in 1881 calling for the end of Jewish immigration. By 1890 German Burschenschaften no longer accepted practicing Jews; in contrast to Austria, however, they did admit baptized Jews. Even in the heyday of student anti-Semitism in the 1880s and 1890s, therefore, German academic anti-Semitism was somewhat less extreme than in Austria, much to the frustration of Austrian university students.[27]

These differences became readily apparent in the matter of dueling between Jews and "Aryans." As early as 1881 Libertas had forbidden its members to duel with Jews. Then in 1896 the "Waidhofner Principle" was adopted by the Waidhofner Verband, an umbrella organization of pan-German dueling fraternities that had been established in 1890. This doctrine, named for a town in central Austria, stated that there were deep moral and psychic differences between Jews and Aryans; Jews had no honor or character in the sense that Germans (including German-Austrians) defined these terms. Therefore, students accepting this principle swore to refuse to give Jews the "satisfaction" of fighting duels with them. The practical effect of this policy was to enable anti-Semitic and nationalistic students to insult and assault Jews without the unpleasant prospect of having to fight a duel with them as a consequence. (The prohibition may have been induced in part by the rapid improvement of fencing skills by Jewish students, which thus deprived nationalistic students of activity in which they had previously demonstrated a clear superiority over their Jewish classmates.)[28]

The Austrian Burschenschaften wanted the Deutsche Burschenschaften, which included chapters in Germany as well as in German-speaking parts of Austria, to forbid all members from giving satisfaction to any Jew or person of Jewish origins. However, these attempts to persuade German universities to adopt the Waidhofner Principle enjoyed only limited success prior to the First World War. Although the more nationalistic fraternities refused to give satisfaction to Jews, they did not officially adopt the Waidhofner Principle.[29]

Even in Vienna the implementation of the Waidhofner Principle was not without its difficulties. The government of Vienna tried to dissolve every corporation that adopted the principle even though dueling itself was actually illegal in Austria! Government opposition was overcome, however, by the organizations simply changing their names so that eventually the government gave up its opposition. More serious, however, was the refusal of the Austro-Hungarian army to accept the idea. Students who were also reserve officers were therefore faced with the choice of either dropping out of their fraternity or losing their commission.[30]

The Waidhofner Principle also enjoyed little success in Prague where, as noted previously, student anti-Semitism never achieved the same intensity as in Vienna. Pro-Jewish students continued to dominate the "Lesehalle" so that German nationalist students seceded to form their own anti-Semitic "Germania" organization in 1892. A turnaround in favor of anti-Semitic students in Prague, which also intensified student anti-Semitism in Vienna, came in the latter part of the decade during the political fire storm caused by the ill-fated language laws of Prime Minister Count Casimir Badeni; these proposed laws would have put the Czech language on an equal footing with German in the Bohemian crownlands.[31]

Despite their setbacks, student anti-Semites at Austrian universities had, by the turn of the century, succeeded in making anti-Semitism intellectually "respectable" among the very people who were most likely to reject it as archaic a quarter century earlier.[32] Nevertheless, it is possible to exaggerate this prewar academic Jew-hatred. The world-renowned Jewish-Austrian author, Stefan Zweig, who was born in 1881 and was a student at the University of Vienna at the beginning of the new century, wrote in his memoirs that "neither in school nor at the University, nor in the world of literature, have I ever experienced the slightest suppression or indignity as a Jew."[33]

GEORG VON SCHÖNERER AND RACIAL ANTI-SEMITISM

Although academic anti-Semitism in Austria had its own origins and developed for the most part independently, it was encouraged and certainly supported by some politicians, above all by Georg von Schönerer, a man who Hitler later both praised and criticized in *Mein Kampf*. Described by his most recent biographer as the "most prominent propagandist and symbol" of anti-Semitism in his day, Schönerer believed that race ought to be the criterion for all civic rights.[34] Ironically, Schönerer's father had been ennobled in 1860 for his work as one of the monarchy's leading civil engineers and for being the chief executive of the giant railroad lines that had been founded by the Rothschilds. The younger Schönerer, who was born in 1842, would one day assail the same Jewish capital that had made possible his father's fortune.[35] It was perhaps not a mere coincidence that he was elected to the lower house of the Austrian Reichsrat (Parliament) from the very district, Waidhofen-Zwettl, from which the movement to ban dueling between Aryans and Jews had originated.

Although Schönerer made contact with fraternities in Vienna as early as 1876, for several years their common interest was primarily pan-Germanism rather than anti-Semitism. As a left-wing Liberal deputy he helped to draft the famous Linz Program of 1882, which demanded an extension of the franchise and the protection of the German-speaking people of Austria by making German the official language in predominantly German areas.[36] Anti-Semitism was not originally even part of this program, as was demonstrated by the fact that Schönerer's chief collaborators on the document, the historian Heinrich Friedjung and the later Socialist leader, Viktor Adler, were both of Jewish origin. Schönerer was simply against a "preponderance" of Jewish political influence in 1882 and wanted Jews to be no more than the foot soldiers of pan-Germanism rather than the officers. Three years later, however, he added a twelfth point to the Linz declaration, stating that "the removal of Jewish influence from all sections of public life is indispensable for carrying out the reforms aimed at."[37]

Why did Schönerer suddenly develop so strong an aversion to Jews between 1882 and 1885? The answer may lie in the broadening of the franchise in 1882 that Schönerer himself promoted. Until then voting laws had favored the aristocracy and the liberal bourgeoisie, which together made up only about 3 percent of the population. Neither of these classes had been particularly anti-Semitic. Indeed, the latter included a good many Jews. The electoral reform gave the vote to all men over twenty-four who paid at least five florins a year in direct taxes. Overnight the electorate in Vienna tripled from 15,385 to 45,695. (A few years later it nearly doubled again to 78,387 when the city's boundaries extended to include several lower-middle-class suburbs.) The primary beneficiaries were anticapitalistic artisans who saw in big business and mass production a threat to their economic well-being. On the other hand, the industrial working class, which depended on industrialization and which later proved to be relatively immune to anti-Semitism, was still denied the right to vote.[38]

It is a sobering fact that the sudden rise of political anti-Semitism after 1882 was a result of the partial democratization of Austrian politics. Schönerer was not alone among the politicians who now tried to appeal to the new voters through antielitist, anti-individualistic, and anti-intellectual demagoguery, but he did play an increasingly dominant role.[39]

In June 1882 Schönerer founded the Deutschnationaler Verein (League of German Nationalists), whose membership was made up of a few hundred journalists, primary and secondary school teachers, and some successful small businessmen as well as members of student fraternities and ruined artisans. Schönerer hoped these groups would be the nucleus of a national following. He unashamedly declared that he and his Deutschnationalen regarded anti-Semitism not as a regrettable symptom or a disgrace, but as the very pillar of German nationalist thought; it was nothing less than "the most important expression of genuine popular consciousness and the greatest national achievement of the century." In contrast to most Austrian anti-Semites of his day, Schönerer stressed that their fight ought not to be against the Jewish religion but against the racial characteristics of the Jews. Contradicting the spirit of the Linz Program of 1882, he welcomed the help of Slavic and Romance people. He claimed that his party alone, of all the parties in the Reichsrat, was not *verjudet* (jewified) which led one journalist to ask him if there was anything he did not consider jewified.[40]

Throughout the 1880s, as Jewish immigrants continued to settle in Vienna, and at that time when the Austrian economy was in a prolonged depression, "the knight of Rosenau" (as Schönerer was popularly called) introduced one piece of anti-Semitic legislation after another in the Reichsrat. In 1882 he brought petitions signed by 37,068 people living in 2,206 communities demanding that Parliament prevent the settlement of victims of the recent Russian pogrom, which, the petitions alleged, had been provoked by the Jews themselves. The next year Schönerer demanded the dismissal of all Jewish teachers. In 1884 he led a campaign for the nationalization of Austrian railroads to take them out of Jewish hands.[41]

The Reichsrat elections of 1885 as well as the Viennese city council elections of 1886 demonstrated the popularity of anti-Semitism and encouraged von Schönerer and five of his parliamentary colleagues to revive his bill restricting Jewish immigration into Austria. This time he made his proposed law a verbatim copy of the Chinese exclusion law that had been approved by the U.S. Congress between 1882 and 1884. The one difference was that the word "Jew" was substituted for the word "Chinese." Jewish immigrants, however, were evidently viewed with less alarm in Austria than Chinese newcomers were in the United States because, once again, Schönerer was defeated when his bill received only 19 votes out of 572.[42]

Schönerer's political activities were not confined to proposing new legislation to the Austrian Parliament. In 1880 he founded the Deutscher Schulverein (German School League), which four years later had ninety thousand members. However, he turned into its enemy when it refused his demand to stop supporting Jewish schools and hiring Jewish teachers. Not until 1898 did it go so far as to establish purely Jewish local organizations. Its willingness to accept Jewish members induced Schönerer and his followers to quit the organization in 1885, but not before he made an angry speech in which he said he could no longer belong to an organization that was verjudet; the next year he and his supporters founded the Schulverein für Deutsche (School League for Germans).[43]

Although the liberal press in Vienna praised Schönerer for a time in the early 1880s because of his courageous defense of the civil liberties of workers, his demands for far-reaching advances in political and economic democracy, and his denunciations of police censorship and press confiscations, it turned against him when he began to advocate racial anti-Semitism. Although this same racism drew fanatical support from Burschenschaften, gymnastic clubs, and some small quasi-political organizations, it never proved attractive to the Austrian masses, most of whom were anything but "racially pure." Many other issues also cost Schönerer potential supporters, especially his anti-Catholic "Los von Rom" (Away from Rome) movement which put him on the side of the Liberals and the Marxists in the eyes of religious conservatives. Most unpopular of all was his anti-Habsburg stand and his call for the breakup of the monarchy with the predominantly German-speaking areas going to the German Reich. Schönerer's anti-Austrianism, was in fact, closely connected with his anti-Semitism because he correctly identified the Jews as the monarchy's preeminent state people, that is, the only people (at least in the 1880s) wholly committed to the empire, with no irredentist desires.[44]

Schönerer's career suffered a gigantic setback because of two incidents toward the end of the 1880s. In 1887 a Viennese newspaper published documentary proof that his wife had a Jewish ancestor. Then in March of the following year Schönerer and a band of his followers broke into the editorial offices of the *Neues Wiener Tagblatt* and attacked the staff with sticks because of an article prematurely announcing the death of Kaiser Wilhelm I. For this assault the knight of Rosenau was sentenced to four months in prison and the loss of his political rights for five years. His patent of nobility was also revoked.[45]

Georg von Schönerer returned to political life in the 1890s and even led the agitation against the Badeni language laws. But his Pan-German Party was able to win only forty thousand votes in the parliamentary elections of January 1901. Even if we include those people who admired Schönerer but did not belong to his party, his total support probably never exceeded 3 or 4 percent of the German-speaking population of Austria and even this was to decline in the parliamentary elections of 1907, which put a definite end to his career.[46] Schönerer's own lack of personal popularity, however, should not be confused with the overall popularity of anti-Semitism within fin-de-siècle Austria.

THE ORIGINS OF CATHOLIC POLITICAL ANTI-SEMITISM

Georg von Schönerer and his racist-nationalist followers, who resented the internationalism and pro-Habsburg outlook of most Austrian Jews, represented just one reaction to the mid-nineteenth-century emancipation of Austro-Hungarian Jewry. Another response came from conservative Roman Catholics, both from the clergy and the laity. Belonging to an international institution par excellence, they could hardly fault the Jews for their cosmopolitanism per se. Nor could they object to their Austrianism, which they shared. Rather it was the secularization and modernization of society—democracy, Marxism, and capitalism, all of which were entering Austrian life at a breathtaking pace, especially after 1867—that Catholics identified with Jews. These new ideologies proved to be the major source of conflict, surpassing even religion, which had previously been the traditional cause of antagonism.

The secularizing and modernizing role of Jews in Austrian society had been especially apparent during the Revolutions of 1848–49 when the laicization of the state had been one of the primary goals of the revolutionaries (though by no means only Jewish revolutionaries). Far worse, however, in the eyes of Roman Catholic clergymen and the more conservative Catholic laity, was the anticlerical legislation introduced and supported by the German Liberal Party and passed by the Austrian Parliament between 1867 and 1870. The largest parliamentary faction between 1867 and 1879, the German Liberals, were an upper-middle-class party that drew inspiration from the French Enlightenment of the previous century and the Viennese Revolution of 1848. The party was definitely supported by Austrian Jews but was by no means dominated by them. On the contrary, the party was careful not to allow any Jew to hold a high government office.[47]

The Liberal government of Prime Minister Count Karl Auersperg restricted clerical influence wherever it could. Impetus to do so had been given by papal criticism of the constitution of 1867 with its articles on religious toleration and freedom of the press. One by one, clerical prerogatives were eliminated: civil marriage was legalized and divorce proceedings were transferred from church to secular courts. The new legislation prompted Catholic prelates to walk out of the "infidel" upper chamber of the Parliament but created general rejoicing among the Viennese population and high praise from the city's press, much of which was owned and edited by Jews. Another law passed by the Reichsrat in 1869 nationalized all Austrian schools. From then on religious institutions were only responsible for religious education. Pope Pius denounced the new laws as "truly unholy," "destructive, abominable, and damnable," and "absolutely null and void." Some clerical leaders even defied the laws and encouraged the faithful to do likewise.[48]

The civil influence of the Roman Catholic church was diminished still further in 1870 when the concordat made in 1855 between Austria and the Vatican was canceled at the urging of the Liberal Party. Among other things the concordat had given the Catholic church the right to approve all instruction given to Catholic children both in public and private schools; the church had also been given the right to designate a book as objectionable on religious or moral grounds and the state was then obligated to prevent its circulation. The concordat had, furthermore, restored the jurisdiction of the church on all questions relating to marriage laws.[49]

Rather than attacking modern trends directly, Catholic spokesmen often found it more politically expedient to identify them first with Jews and then hold the Jews responsible for them. This is not to suggest that anti-Semites were always insincere, but their technique of disguising their true aims by hiding them behind an anti-Semitic smoke screen became a favorite ploy of anti-Semites of all types and descriptions in the late nineteenth century and during the years between the world wars of the twentieth century.

An early clerical anti-Semite in Austria was Prelate Sebastian Brunner who published the *Wiener Kirchenzeitung*. Catholics in Paris knew him as the "Father of Austrian anti-Semitism." He was succeeded as editor by another

Catholic theologian, Albert Wiesinger, who has been described as a "devoted fanatic of hate." These men were actually only two of the many priest-journalists who spoke at anti-Semitic public rallies, authored numerous anti-Jewish tracts, and tried to compete with the anti-Semitism of Georg von Schönerer and his German nationalist followers.[50]

Brunner and Wiesinger and their *Kirchenzeitung* were the immediate forerunners of the far more influential Catholic politician, Baron Karl von Vogelsang and his newspaper, *Vaterland*, which he edited from 1875 to his death in 1890. Vogelsang, a Catholic convert who moved to Vienna from Mecklenburg in 1859, was the first to synthesize the disparate elements of early Austrian political anti-Semitism into a coherent critique of the liberal-capitalist order. He identified the Jews with all the evils of modern society, especially liberalism, materialism, and atheism. He also regarded capitalism as a Jewish invention and advocated the restoration of a medieval Christian economic order. Without this reform, artisans, peasants, and industrial workers would be ruined by Jewish capitalism just as the moral fabric of society would disintegrate because of the "Jewish press." Only in a completely re-Christianized society in which Jewish emancipation was rescinded would people be safe from "Jewish domination." On the other hand, Vogelsang, like most Catholics, was not a racial anti-Semite and did not attack the Hebrew religion; instead he called on Jews to convert to Roman Catholicism. His wrath was directed only against secularized Jews.[51]

The man who inherited these ideas and was the first to exploit them to their full political potential was Karl Lueger. Born in 1844, two years after Schönerer, Lueger entered politics in 1875 as a Liberal member of Vienna's city council; a decade later he was elected to the Reichsrat, although municipal politics continued to interest him more than national politics. Even though he espoused no anti-Semitic views during his early political career, in 1887 he was one of the nineteen parliamentary deputies to vote in favor of Georg von Schönerer's bill to restrict the immigration of Russian and Rumanian Jews. Like Schönerer he used anti-Semitism to appeal to the same unstable elements of the population: artisans and university students. And like Schönerer, Lueger favored political platforms that denounced the emancipation of Jews. However, that is where the similarities ended. Lueger, in sharp contrast to Schönerer, was pro-Catholic and pro-Habsburg. He hoped to unite all Christians and all the nationalities of the monarchy against a common Jewish enemy. Moreover, Lueger's anti-Semitism lacked the bitterness, consistency, and above all the conviction of the knight of Rosenau. Whereas Schönerer was a racial anti-Semite and, at least after about 1885, uncompromising in his intolerance of Jews, Lueger's anti-Semitism was opportunistic, economic, religious, and cultural. When opponents criticized Lueger for associating with converted Jews, he retorted half jokingly and half cynically that he "determined who a Jew was." It was this very lack of principle that made him much more adept at building coalitions than the doctrinaire Schönerer.[52]

By far the most important way in which Lueger differed from Schönerer was in the former's enormous personal and political popularity. Lueger's old-fashioned brand of religious, cultural, and economic anti-Semitism remained for half a century the integrating force of political Catholicism because it was far more in accord with Viennese traditions than Schönerer's more modern racial anti-Semitism. (As noted already, racism was a rarity in the ethnically mixed capital of the multinational empire and was anathema to the international Roman Catholic church.) The Viennese also loved Lueger's vulgar jokes, Viennese dialect, elegant appearance, humble bourgeois origins, and general *Gemütlichkeit*.[53]

Lueger, like other Catholic politicians of his day, realized that Vienna's economic tribulations could not be ascribed to the Jews alone but rather to capitalistic modes of production. However, he cared far less about the validity of anti-Semitic allegations than he did about their effectiveness in taking the wind out of the sails of the Schönerer movement and destroying the Liberal Party. Viennese artisans and tradesmen were struggling to survive in the late nineteenth century against competition from above in the form of far more efficient factories and large retail distributors — the latter frequently being the new Jewish-owned department stores on Mariahilferstrasse — which were mass producing and selling textiles, machines, and furniture. They also feared competition from below by peddlers. Since many of these factories and stores were owned by Jews, and many of the peddlers were recent Jewish immigrants from Galicia, it was tempting to assume that their problems would be solved through anti-Semitic legislation, all the more so because the lower middle class had little understanding of economics. As the historian John Boyer has noted, "nowhere else did artisan antisemitism become the basis for a major successful upheaval in municipal politics."[54]

The common enemy of the anti-Semites in the 1880s and 1890s, especially in Vienna, was the Liberal Party. The master of both the government of Austria and the municipal government of Vienna in 1879, twenty years later it had been driven from power at both levels and was on the verge of extinction. In large measure its downfall was its own fault. The main beneficiaries of the highly restricted voting system, the Liberals had remained isolated from the common people and had made no effort to resolve the many legitimate grievances of artisans and industrial workers. Nor did they even make use of a new generation of talent.[55]

The first organization to exploit the grievances of artisans through anti-Semitism was the so-called Verein zum Schutze des Gewerbestandes (Association for the Protection of Tradesmen), which was constituted in 1881. Even more explicitly anti-Semitic was the Reformverein zur Betreibung der gewerblichen Interessen (Reform Association for the Prosecution of Trade Interests), which was organized the next year and demanded the expulsion of Jews from their political, economic, and social positions. Jewish businesses were to be boycotted and all social contact between Jews and Christians was to be eliminated. Most important of all for the anti-Semitic movement was the Christlichsozialer Verein (Christian Social Association), established in 1887. According to Lueger's contemporary, Richard Charmatz, "in its fifth plenary assembly Dr. Karl Lueger declared himself to be an anti-Semite. The new movement found in him a leader with incomparable energy, unscrupulousness and astonishing cleverness."[56]

In 1888 the Christian Social Association briefly joined with Georg von Schönerer's German Nationalists to form an alliance called the United Christians. The only common denominator of this motley collection of lower-level clerical conservatives, pan-German nationalists, and social reformers was anti-Semitism. Their manifesto combined earlier demands by Vogelsang and Schönerer for the exclusion of Jews from such professions as teaching (except for the teaching of Jewish children), medicine, law, retail trade, and the civil and military service. They also wanted restrictions placed on Jewish immigration. Their slogan was "all Jews are capitalists." The solidarity of the United Christians proved to be short-lived. Hardly had the alliance been concluded when Schönerer fell into political disgrace because of his storming of the offices of the *Neues Wiener Tagblatt*. Schönerer's racial anti-Semitism also proved to be unacceptable to conservative Catholics in the coalition. Lueger and Schönerer soon went their separate ways, joining forces only occasionally on an ad hoc basis. Schönerer's newspaper, *Unverfälschte deutsche Worte*, did not hesitate to launch periodic attacks against Lueger and the United Christians.[57]

As early as 1885 Lueger had become sympathetic to Karl Vogelsang's clerical, aristocratic, conservative program that rejected capitalism, rationalism, and materialism, all of which allegedly threatened the Christian *Weltanschauung*; he then combined these views with the populist anticapitalism of the small artisans to form the Christian Social Party in 1891. The new party stressed the importance of the Jewish question, but declared it to be a social one, rejecting both racial and religious anti-Semitism. Although it was adept at coining anti-Semitic slogans, it refrained from proposing specific anti-Semitic legislation because it could not even agree on a definition of what constituted a Jew. Its followers did not demand that the party do more than insult Jews. As John Boyer has succinctly put it: "Austrian Christian Socialism was a movement of nineteenth-century social protest, not a protofascist crusade or a total break with nineteenth-century Viennese political values and institutions."[58]

Only four years after its creation, the Christian Social Party, with the help of its official daily newspaper, the *Reichspost* (founded in 1894), and its pan-German allies, had won an absolute majority in the Vienna municipal elections of April 1895; wealthy Jews threatened to move to Hungary while other Jews in Vienna lived in a constant state of panic until Franz Joseph assured them that he would protect all his subjects, regardless of their faith or traditions. Four times in the space of two years Lueger won smashing electoral victories and four times the emperor refused to appoint him mayor, vetoes that earned him the title of *der Judenkaiser* among fanatical anti-Semites and served only to increase Lueger's popularity. Finally, after a fifth electoral victory, this one in the Reichsrat elections of April 1897, the emperor relented and Lueger became the first mayor in the western half of Europe elected to office on an anti-Semitic platform. He was now the leader of the most successful anti-Semitic movement in nineteenth-century Europe.[59]

In that fifth election the Liberal Party gained a scant 10,000 votes in Vienna compared to over 117,000 for the Christian Social Party and other anti-Semitic parties.[60] The Liberals, who had lost control of the Austrian Parliament in 1879, were now finished as an effective party even though they continued to exist as a very minor party during the First Republic. Although the Liberals had been crushed in large measure because they had failed to adjust to the democratic (and demagogic) politics of the last two decades of the nineteenth century, their defeat was also a punishment for being pro-Jewish, or at least for being perceived as pro-Jewish, even though in reality they were by no means free of anti-Semitism themselves.[61]

Although the Liberals never gave their unqualified support to the political, economic, and legal tenets of classical liberalism, they had been consistent in their endorsement of equality for all citizens during the sixties, seventies, and early eighties.[62] To be sure, they did become somewhat ambivalent toward anti-Semites in the mid-eighties; nevertheless, their demise was a major setback from which the more assimilated Viennese Jews perhaps never fully recovered. Gentile and Jewish Liberals had all fought for constitutionalism, administrative centralism, religious tolerance, and private enterprise. As the British historian Peter G. J. Pulzer has so ably put it: "Because Jews had staked more on [the Liberal Party's] success than any other group in the monarchy, they felt its failure most keenly."[63] The disappearance of Liberalism left the Austrian Jews—or at least those who belonged to the bourgeoisie—politically homeless; never again would they find a political party with which they were so completely compatible.

4

AUSTRIA'S JEWS
ON THE EVE OF THE
GREAT WAR

THE APPARENT DECLINE IN AUSTRIAN ANTI-SEMITISM, 1897–1914

The appointment of Karl Lueger as mayor of Vienna in 1897 had an astonishing short-term outcome. Far from marking the beginning of the end for the city's Jews, it marked the beginning of a new if all-too-brief golden age, not only economically but also in their contributions to the arts and sciences as well as to sociology, psychology, law, architecture, and philosophy.

Austrian Jews—or at any rate those in the middle and upper classes—prospered as never before or since. Between 1900 and 1910 they made up 71 percent of Vienna's financiers, 63 percent of its industrialists, 65 percent of its lawyers, 59 percent of its physicians, and over half of its journalists.[1] A well-known German-Jewish writer, Jakob Wassermann, who visited the city in 1898 remarked that "all public life was dominated by the Jews. The banks, the press, the theatre, literature, social organizations, all lay in the hands of Jews. The explanation was easy to find. The aristocracy would have nothing to do with such things."[2] What Wassermann and above all anti-Semites failed to note, however, was that Jews were also very underrepresented in certain other aspects of Austrian society. For example, there were only 10 Jews among the 512 representatives in the lower house of the Parliament.[3]

Unfortunately, the combination of Lueger's unfulfilled anti-Semitic threats together with the Jews' prewar economic and cultural successes led Vienna's Jews to reach unwarranted conclusions about the true nature of anti-Semitism, which would have catastrophic consequences forty years later: the threats and ravings of anti-Semitic demagogues could be safely ignored because they would never be carried out.

The character of Lueger's thirteen-year administration was revealed in his inaugural speech when he ignored the "Jewish question" completely and instead discussed what proved to be the hallmarks of his rule, the improvement of the city's public services, especially mass transit, parks, and schools. These achievements were so impressive that his bitter rival, the Social Democratic Party, tolerated the erection of a statue in his honor in 1926 in a square that still bears the mayor's name.[4]

As the years passed, it became more and more apparent that, to quote Lueger himself, anti-Semitism was simply "an excellent means of getting ahead in politics, but after one [had] arrived, one [could not] use it any longer; it [was] the sport of the rabble."[5] It may also be that with Franz Joseph looking over his shoulder, the mayor felt constrained to keep his anti-Semitic proclivities in check. That explanation alone, however, would not account for the many favors Lueger was willing to do for his Jewish friends. More revealing is the connection between Austria's improving economy and the decline in anti-Semitism. By 1897 the "Great Depression" had definitely ended and by 1903 the economy of western Austria was booming. It was keeping pace with Germany's and partially catching up with those of Britain, France, and Belgium.[6]

During the Lueger years Jews were faced with no mass violence and little physical abuse. The mayor even paid them the left-handed compliment of saying that they were not as bad as the Hungarian Jews and that Vienna could not get along without them because they were the only people who were always active. Lueger also avoided antagonizing influential Jews by not insisting on the segregation of Jewish school children. On the other hand, Jews had difficulty getting contracts from the municipal government and few Jews were hired or promoted in the municipal service, although the practices of the preceding Liberal government had not been much better in this regard. Worst of all, Lueger's legacy made anti-Semitism seem normal and respectable.[7]

The improving Austrian economy also helps explain why the Jewish population of Vienna grew more slowly between 1900 and 1910. As noted earlier, the city's overall population grew by 21.2 percent in this decade, whereas the Jewish population slowed to 19.3 percent.[8] In particular it was the decline in the immigration of Galician Jews to Vienna, and their emigration instead to America, that help account for this diminution.

In the Alpine provinces of Austria the growth rate of the small Jewish population was similar to that of Vienna. In Graz, Linz, Salzburg, and Innsbruck the number of Jews reached an all-time high in the last decade before the Great War, but the Jewish communities were not growing rapidly, and their absolute numbers were still very small. Graz, for example, had the second-largest Jewish population of Inner Austria, with only about two thousand souls. Linz was second in size with just one thousand members in its community. Salzburg

compensating for the declining number of readers of pan-German newspapers. Although anti-Semitism was an important feature of the paper from the very beginning, it was not an obsession. Moreover, even though the *Reichspost* enjoyed considerable success already before the world war, it could not begin to compete in popularity and still less in the prestige with some of Vienna's great Jewish-owned newspapers, especially the *Neue Freie Presse*, whose reputation extended far beyond the boundaries of the Austro-Hungarian Monarchy.[22]

THE BEGINNINGS OF JEWISH SELF-DEFENSE

Austrian Jews were not entirely passive in the face of the growing number of insults they encountered after about 1880. Their response was muted, however, by the firm belief on the part of assimilated Jews—who made up the overwhelming majority of German-speaking Jews in the monarchy—that anti-Semitism was not a serious problem; it was at most a relic of an earlier and benighted age, which was bound to disappear in the near and more enlightened future. Such Jews also tried to ignore the problem. For example, in the 1880s the twelve Jewish members of Vienna's city council took an oath to each other to ignore all but the worst expressions of anti-Semitism. Other Jews immersed themselves in scientific or literary studies.[23]

On several occasions in the late nineteenth century anti-Semitic attacks on Judaism became so outrageous that rabbis and other Jewish scholars, as well as some political leaders of Jewish origins could no longer remain silent. Such was the case already in 1860 when Ignaz Kuranda successfully defended himself against a libel suit by Sebastian Brunner after accusing Brunner's *Kirchenzeitung* of spreading long disproven lies about the Jewish religion. The *Kirchenzeitung* claimed that Judaism permitted Jews to disregard their oaths and required them to use Christian blood for religious purposes. Brunner's defeat forced him to resign as editor of his Jew-baiting newspaper and helped launch Kuranda's political career in the German Liberal Party, which for twenty years he led. Kuranda also became the president of the Jewish Community of Vienna in 1871. Another example of Jewish self-defense occurred in 1869 when the chief rabbi (Oberrabbiner) of Vienna, Adolf Jellinek, wrote a book entitled *Der jüdische Stamm*, in which he paid an enthusiastic tribute to the Talmud at a time when recent anti-Semitic attacks had made even some Jews ashamed of it. In so doing he also raised Jewish national consciousness.[24]

The most celebrated case of Jewish self-defense took place in 1882. A few years before, in 1871, a priest named August Rohling, who considered the Jews a nation of deicides, published a book entitled *Der Talmud Jude* (*The Talmud Jew*), a plagiarism of a book written by Johann Eisenmenger in 1700 called *Entdecktes Judentum* (*Essence of Jewishness*) which was a compilation of anti-Semitic allegations that previously only marginally respectable individuals had made. Within six years *The Talmud Jew* went through six editions; by the time the seventeenth and final edition was printed, the book had been sold (or perhaps in some cases given) to hundreds of thousands of readers. Following this "achievement" Rohling was appointed professor of Bible Studies and the Old Testament at the German University of Prague in 1876. After securing this prestigious position, Rohling offered to serve as an expert in trials involving accusations of ritual murder and to substantiate other charges against Jews. The Jewish community tried to ignore Rohling's book until 1882 when he published a series of articles in a Viennese newspaper in which he accused Rabbi Jellinek and his assistant, Moritz Gudemann, of "arrant knavery" for having denied that the Talmud teaches Jews to hate the Christians. The articles were reprinted in book form and 200,000 copies of it were circulated.[25]

A partly self-educated, Galician-born rabbi named Josef Samuel Bloch suddenly appeared on the scene to defend the Talmud, the collection of Jewish legal codes and interpretations of Biblical laws. Within a twenty-four-hour period, Bloch wrote a detailed refutation of Rohling's accusations. Bloch's newspaper article was literally an overnight sensation; published as a supplement, three editions of 100,000 were sold in a single day, and subsequently it was translated into several foreign languages. When Rohling tried to make a rebuttal, Bloch offered to pay him three thousand gulden if he could correctly translate a single page from the Talmud, a challenge Rohling declined to accept.[26]

Some months later Rohling published the allegation that "the Jew was required by his religion to exploit non-Jews in every possible way, and to destroy them physically and morally, to corrupt their lives, honor, and property openly and with force, secretly and treacherously . . . in order to bring about the world domination of his people."[27] Later, at a ritual murder trial, Rohling maintained that the shedding of the blood of a non-Jewish virgin was an "extraordinarily holy affair."[28] Bloch counterattacked by publicly calling Rohling an "ignorant plagiarist," a charge that Rohling could not ignore without admitting guilt. Rohling filed a lawsuit against Bloch; preparations for the trial took a year, but at the last moment Rohling withdrew his charge. His action was considered an admission of guilt and he was dismissed from his professorship. But if this incident terminated Rohling's career, it did not mark the end of the popularity of *The Talmud Jew*, or the end of charges of Jewish ritual murder within Austrian and German Catholicism. However, the allegation was at least made less frequently than before Bloch's time.[29]

On the other hand, the Rohling–Bloch confrontation marked only the beginning of Bloch's career as a highly respected and influential Jewish leader, a career that was to last until his death in 1923. In 1883 Bloch was elected to the Reichsrat and for a time was the only one of twelve Jewish deputies to defend specifically Jewish issues.[30] In January 1884 he founded *Dr. Bloch's Oesterreichische Wochenschrift*. The newspaper's subtitle, *Zentralorgan für die gesamten Interessen des Judentums* (*Central Organ for the Collective Interests of Jewry*) revealed Bloch's aversion to dissension within the Jewish community and his desire to serve as a mediator of conflict and as a creator of consensus. For thirty-seven years, until just two years before his death, Bloch remained the paper's editor. It became an indispensable source for the history of Viennese Jewry during its golden age. Far from evading the "Jewish question" as the liberal press usually did, the *Wochenschrift* was a world forum for its discussion and an organ for the refutation of hostile criticism of Jewry.[31]

Josef Bloch favored a stronger expression of Jewish identity and tried to educate his readers about the history and ethics of Judaism. On the other hand, he was not a Jewish nationalist or Zionist. His *Wochenschrift* encouraged Jews to develop their own spiritual and political sphere in Austria and was opposed to complete assimilation. He wanted the Jews to have their own political party and not simply help other nationalistic parties. Rare among German-speaking Austrians of his day, he actually called himself as well as his newspaper "Austrian" (rather than German) and sought to make the Jews the pillars of the state. He therefore could not support Zionism, regarding it as divisive. Moderate as Bloch's Jewish self-consciousness was, it still aroused resentment among Vienna's numerous politically liberal and pro-German Jews. The Jewish upper classes in Vienna regarded Judaism almost exclusively as a religion.[32]

Bloch was not simply an inspiring writer, but also a practical man of action. He was the first Austrian Jew to advance a coherent defensive strategy based on a Jewish political organization. Disgusted with the passivity of the Viennese Kultusgemeinde in the face of the virulent anti-Semitism of the 1880s, Bloch founded the Österreichisch-Israelitische Union (Austrian-Israelite Union) in 1886. Its first task was to raise Jewish pride and self-consciousness. Second, it was committed to expose anti-Semitic errors and prejudices and to fight the passage of any discriminatory religious or racial laws. As the first Jewish self-defense organization in Central Europe, it preceded by seven years the similar Centralverein deutscher Staatsbürger jüdischen Glaubens (Central Union of German Citizens of the Jewish Faith) in Germany.[33]

Although Bloch himself was not an assimilationist, the Austrian-Israelite Union appealed mainly to young middle-class Jews who were so inclined; members therefore included mostly liberal professors, businessmen, politicians, and lawyers, all people who were particularly concerned about the de facto deterioration of Jewish rights and the rapid growth of anti-Semitism. By sponsoring lectures on Jewish history and scholarship and keeping the Jewish community informed about the activities of the Austrian Parliament that might affect them, the union followed a middle road between assimilation and Jewish nationalism.[34]

In March 1895 the union decided to establish a Rechtsschutz Comité (Legal Defense Committee) to cope with the increasing number of appeals for assistance. In December 1897 the committee was transformed into the Rechtsschutz und Abwehr-Büro (Legal Aid and Defense Bureau), which was staffed by a small but efficient office force. Unfortunately, the bureau proved to be less than a spectacular success. Although it was effective on minor issues, like having anti-Semitic government clerks reprimanded, in more serious cases, such as economic boycotts, satisfactory results were obtained only about 15 percent of the time.[35]

Already in 1889 the leaders of the union had also become the leaders of the Kultusgemeinde. By 1900 the union, including Bloch himself, had lost some of its original militancy, but by then the Jewish establishment was much less timid about expressing Jewish pride than it had been earlier.[36]

The union was not the only Austrian organization to fight in the defense of Jewish rights. In 1891 a predominantly Christian Verein zur Abwehr des Antisemitismus (Society to Combat Anti-Semitism) was founded by Baron Arthur Gundacher von Suttner, his wife Berta, and Count Hoyos. Other famous Viennese Christians such as the composer Johann Strauss and the surgeon Theodor Billroth (who by now had completely reversed his earlier view of Jews) were also founding members. Modeled after a German society of the same name established four months before in Berlin, it sought to fight anti-Semitism by stressing the common ideals of Christianity and Judaism and by exposing the falsehoods of anti-Semitic publications, rather than taking direct political action. Despite its promising beginnings, however, the organization met with little success—its membership rose to only 4,520 in 1895—in large part because the Suttners were far more involved in the pacifist movement (for which Berta was to win a Nobel Prize for Peace) than fighting anti-Semitism.

Although liberal professors as well as members of the nobility were well represented, prominent clergymen were conspicuous only by their absence. Equally damaging was the reluctance of many well-known Jews to join because of their continuing desire not to give anti-Semitism any publicity by confronting it.[37]

Another prominent Christian defender of Jews from the 1890s until his death in 1934 was the writer, Hermann Bahr. His early book, *Der Antisemitismus: Ein internationales Interview* (*Anti-Semitism: An International Interview*), published in 1894, contained the answers of thirty-eight of Europe's leading intellectuals to Bahr's questionnaire asking them to explain their views about anti-Semitism. Bahr drew the doubtful conclusion from their responses that anti-Semitism was an end in itself. But he was on much firmer ground in also pointing out that rational arguments made little impact on people whose views rested on illogical feelings. Anti-Semitism, Bahr maintained, was the "morphine of little people"; critics of Jews were usually people who had the same faults as the Jews they condemned. Bahr never became an uncritical philo-Semite despite his marriage to a Jew, Rosalie Jokl. He did not hesitate to criticize individual Jews himself and insisted only that Jews not be judged as a group.[38]

Bahr's attitude toward Jews was not always so enlightened. He had been something of an anti-Semite himself in his early years as a student at the University of Vienna. In 1881 he had joined an anti-Semitic fraternity called Albia and at the same time was a member of Georg von Schönerer's German National Party. But in 1882 his view started to change when his fraternity expelled several of his Jewish friends including Theodor Herzl, the future leader of political Zionism. Another friend, Viktor Adler, was ejected from Schönerer's party at about the same time. Bahr also noticed that his Jewish uncle in no way fit Schönerer's stereotype of Jews. In 1884 Bahr broke with Schönerer. Then, a sojourn in Berlin between 1889 and 1891 convinced him that the best of Berlin's traditional culture was being preserved almost exclusively by Jews.[39]

THE RISE OF JEWISH NATIONALISM AND ZIONISM IN AUSTRIA

Probably the best known reaction to late nineteenth-century anti-Semitism was the birth of modern secular Zionism. Often mistakenly attributed to the Viennese journalist and friend of Hermann Bahr, Theodor Herzl, the movement actually began among Galician Jews already in the 1880s as a result of the impoverishment of Jewish small-time traders and merchants. It was not simply a reaction to anti-Semitism but was also an integral part of the rise of nationalism in general that was occurring all over Europe, especially in the second half of the nineteenth century. Herzl was not even the first Jew in modern times from the German-speaking part of Austria to conceive of the idea of a Jewish state in the Holy Land.[40]

That distinction belongs instead to a little-known Galician-born journalist and long-time resident of Vienna, Nathan Birnbaum. In 1882 he was one of the founders of the first prominent Jewish nationalist fraternity in the world called the Akademischer Verein Kadimah at the University of Vienna. Although Jewish nationalism at this early date was confined almost exclusively to Eastern European Jews, it was mostly assimilated Westjuden who joined Kadimah. Even though it attacked assimilationism, Kadimah soon adopted many of the customs of the German-nationalist Burschenschaften including ritualized beer drinking and, in 1890, dueling. Previously Jews had considered dueling "un-Jewish," but newer members refused to tolerate taunts that they were inherent cowards. By 1910, 35 percent of the Jewish students at the University of Vienna including half of the Jewish medical students considered themselves Jewish nationalists and by 1914 there were close to twenty-five Jewish nationalist or Zionist organizations at the University of Vienna. By this time some of the early Kadimah members had already become leaders in the world Zionist movement and Kadimah-inspired Jewish fraternities had been founded in Germany and elsewhere in Europe and America.[41]

In 1885 Birnbaum established a journal called *Selbst-Emancipation* (*Self-Emancipation*) in which he introduced the word *Zionism*. In 1892 he first used the term Zionism publicly at a discussion meeting in Vienna. The following year he expounded his Zionist views in a pamphlet with the explicit title, *Die nationale Wiedergeburt des jüdischen Volkes in seinem Lande als Mittel zur Lösung der Judenfrage* (*The National Rebirth of the Jewish People in Their Land as a Means to the Solution to the Jewish Question*). In the same year Birnbaum formed an organization in Vienna called Zion: Verband der österreichischen Vereine für die Kolonisation Palastinas und Syriens (Zion: Union of Austrian Societies for the Colonization of Palestine and Syria). Birnbaum, however, did not see a mass Jewish migration to Palestine as the sole answer to the "Jewish question." Rather it would be complemented with cultural autonomy for Jews in countries where they already resided. Birnbaum and his ideas found little favor among Viennese Jews, so in 1907 he moved to Galicia where his ideas had always enjoyed a more receptive audience.[42]

Although Nathan Birnbaum can be considered the "father of Austrian Zionism," his impulsiveness, inconsistency, and self-criticism prevented him from enjoying major success. Consequently, it was Theodor Herzl who made Zionism a household word and established a movement which eventually created a Jewish state in Palestine. In many respects Herzl was an unlikely hero of Jewish nationalism. Born in Budapest, he attended German-language schools and entered adulthood as an ardent partisan of assimilation into German-Austrian culture. Although he was trained to be an attorney, his real ambition was to be a famous playwright and in fact he wrote several moderately successful plays. However, he ultimately found much greater success as a journalist for the *Neue Freie Presse*. His degree of assimilation was manifested in his never having his son circumcised and in marrying a Jewish woman with very Nordic features. During the Christmas season he and his family gathered around a Christmas tree to sing carols. Herzl even loved to tell self-effacing jokes, once writing his parents a postcard from Ostend, Belgium, saying: "Many Viennese and Budapest Jews on the beach. The rest of the holidaymakers very pleasant."[43]

Although Herzl's expulsion from his fraternity in 1882 must have dampened his enthusiasm for assimilation, it was not until 1895, a year after attending the treason trial of Alfred Dreyfus as a newspaper reporter that he abandoned the idea altogether. He had become accustomed to Viennese anti-Semitism, but it came as a depressing shock that in Paris, the classic land of freedom and a birthplace of Jewish emancipation, politicians in the French Parliament could call for the prevention of Jewish "infiltration" in much the same way as Schönerer had done a few years before in the Reichsrat. Two days after witnessing these anti-Semitic speeches, Herzl learned that Karl Lueger had just won a majority in Vienna's city council for the first time. Herzl was now convinced that Jews neither could nor should assimilate and that anti-Semitism, far from being a mere vestige of the Middle Ages, was a product of emancipation.[44]

Soon after his return to Vienna, Herzl published his epoch-making book *Der Judenstaat (The Jewish State)* in which he in effect repeated Nathan Birnbaum's call for a state exclusively for Jews. Coming as it did from the literary editor of the *Neue Freie Presse*, however, the book created far more of a stir than Birnbaum had ever managed to make. Although Herzl was more specific than Birnbaum about the logistics of creating such a state—the need for a congress of Jewish representatives, for money, for engineers and technicians— nowhere in his book did he insist on Palestine as the location of this state; he even mentioned Argentina as a possibility. Herzl also differed from Birnbaum in trying to avoid arguments over the nature of Jewish culture and the role of Jewish tradition and religion. In fact, there was to be nothing especially Jewish about the Jewish state he hoped to create; there would be no common language, not even Hebrew. The state was to be an open, pluralist society, but not a particularly Jewish one.[45]

Given the type and location of the Jewish state Herzl advocated, it is a supreme irony that, with the exception of university students and some middle-class young people in Bohemia and Moravia, his ideas found favor almost exclusively among religious Jews from Eastern Europe (but not the *most* religious Jews); even among these people, however, the reception was at first lukewarm because Herzl had said nothing about a Jewish cultural renaissance and claimed no special virtues for the Jewish race. From the politically and religiously liberal assimilated Jews in Western Europe (Westjuden) the reaction was one of scorn and ridicule. They believed that assimilation had made great strides in the last century and felt more in common with their non-Jewish compatriots than they did with Jews from Eastern Europe, North Africa, or Yemen. Herzl represented a threat to their complete acceptance into gentile society. In Vienna assimilated Jews regarded Herzl's ideas as "the fantasies of a madman who mistook himself for the Messiah." Not even Herzl's friends took his plan seriously, and he soon came to regard assimilated Jews as his worst enemies. He also resented Josef Bloch's willingness to have his (Herzl's) ideas discussed in the *Oesterreichische Wochenschrift* by non-Zionists. Herzl, therefore, founded his own Zionist organ, *Die Welt*.[46]

Although Herzl's plans were far from universally popular outside Austria, they did at least receive the backing of some influential supporters. In Vienna, on the other hand, aside from Jewish university students, they were almost completely rejected, at least prior to Herzl's death in 1904. In 1902, for example, there were only 862 dues-paying Zionists in the Austrian capital despite the presence of the headquarters of the international organization. In elections held by the Viennese Kultusgemeinde the Zionists appeared to do fairly well, winning 27 percent of the vote in 1902, 32 percent in 1906, 22 percent in 1908, and 34 percent in 1912. However, these figures are misleading. Between 1900 and 1912 as few as 10.5 percent of the Gemeinde's 13,000 to 18,000 dues-paying members actually voted in communal elections. The nonvoters were almost certainly assimilated Jews who had no interest in the politics of the Jewish community; if they had voted it would not have been for the Zionists. On the other hand, the restrictive franchise no doubt did exclude many potential Zionist voters. However, by the same token, even among the active supporters of Zionism in Austria and elsewhere in Europe prior to 1914 (or even up to 1933), the vast majority had no intention of actually emigrating to Palestine.[47]

CONVERSIONS, INTERMARRIAGE, AND THE DECLINING SENSE OF JEWISH IDENTITY

The modest progress of the Zionists in Vienna and the apathetic attitude most Viennese Jews took toward communal elections illustrates the weak sense of Jewish identity felt by most Jews in Vienna and in other parts of Central and Western Europe in the early twentieth century. Although even the more acculturated Austrian Jews tended to socialize mainly with other Jews, thousands belonged to no Jewish organizations and did not take part in the activities of their Kultusgemeinde. Younger Jews in the West were by the early twentieth century much more attracted to the messianic appeal of socialism than they were to Jewish community politics. Whereas most Jews, even in Western Europe, would have agreed as late as the mid-nineteenth century that they were a separate nation, by 1914 assimilated Western Jews considered themselves to be members of the surrounding gentile nationality. On the other hand, the passionate rejection of this notion by anti-Semites forced most Jews to retain at least some sense of Jewish identity, however ambiguous or weak.[48]

Although the evidence is not clear-cut, the rapid integration of Jews into German-Austrian culture after their partial emancipation in 1848, the relatively high rate of Jewish conversions to Christianity or at least to a "confessionless" status, and the large number of Jewish-Christian marriages probably all resulted from this declining sense of Jewish identity. It was also the most likely road to total assimilation and a complete loss of Jewish identity. Even the mundane desire to avoid paying taxes to the Jewish Kultusgemeinde should not be overlooked as a motivation for renouncing their ancestral faith for some Jews.[49]

Until the 1880s the number of Jews who left the Jewish community was small and was compensated by a nearly equal number of Christians who converted to Judaism, mostly through marriage. This situation changed drastically, however, in the last decades of the century, and nowhere in Austria more so than in the capital. Between 1868, when records began to be kept, and 1900, the number of Jewish conversions to Christianity in Vienna increased eighty times with the largest number of conversions taking place in 1883, 1893, and 1900. Between 1891 and 1914, 12,000 Jews left the religion of their forefathers, or slightly less than 0.5 percent per annum. By the eve of the world war something like 20,000 Viennese had formally left the Jewish fold either by conversion or by a declaration of no religious affiliation.[50]

The most likely candidates for conversion were young, single males between the ages of twenty and thirty; their most likely motivation was either to marry a Christian or to increase their chances of gaining a government job; baptism was still a de facto though not a de jure requirement for the highest civil (but not military) positions. For example, there were few professors at the University of Vienna who were Jews by religion before the world war but many who were baptized Jews. Converts were frequently university students, members of the free professions, or high-level business employees. For example, marriages between wealthy Jewish men and beautiful Christian women were particularly common as were marriages between Jewish women and Christian army officers. Until 1903 slightly more than half of the converts (53.6 percent) chose Roman Catholicism, just under a quarter (23.1 percent) became Protestants, whereas the remainder (19.9 percent) were affiliated with no religion. Of all the Viennese who declared themselves confessionless between 1886 and 1903, just over one-third (33.9 percent) were of Jewish origins. By 1900 four to five times as many Jews converted to Christianity as the other way around.[51]

The conversion rate in Vienna was by far the highest in the monarchy, or for that matter anywhere in Europe. The conversion rate for the 28,000 Jews of Prague was only one-fifth as great as in Vienna and only half as many Jews married gentiles, no doubt in large measure because there was less social interaction among Jews and gentiles in the Bohemian capital than in the Kaiserstadt.[52] However, none of the statistics for Jewish conversions in Austria can be taken entirely at their face value. Around 1900, 38 Viennese Jews per 10,000 converted annually compared to only 13 in Berlin, but the discrepancy may have been in part a product of differing marriage laws. In prewar Austria, in contrast to Prussia, marriage between Jews and Christians was illegal. This law could be evaded only if one or the other of the potential marriage partners either converted to his or her future spouse's religion or ceased any religious affiliation whatsoever. Before the war the Jewish partner was more likely to convert to Christianity; after the war it was more common for the prospective Jewish bridegroom or bride to renounce any religious affiliation. Further encouraging conversions in Austria was a law requiring children under fourteen to have the same religion as their parents. In Prussia, on the other hand, parents could have their children baptized while remaining Jews themselves. It is therefore doubtful whether the desire for assimilation was any greater in Vienna than it was in Berlin.[53] Whatever the motivation, however, the conversions certainly accelerated assimilation and blurred distinctions between Jews and Christians.

Jews who hoped that converting to Christianity or renouncing their faith would remove the last social and psychological barriers to full integration into Austrian society were likely to be disappointed. The long-time Austrian diplomat, Hans J. J. Thalberg, who converted to Protestantism as a child, wrote in his memoirs that "nothing had changed as a result of my baptism. On the contrary, baptism was a social obstacle because I belonged neither to the one group nor to the other."[54] On the other hand, the relations of converted Jews with their former coreligionists were certainly not as bad as they had been prior to the nineteenth century when apostate Jews were considered as good as dead.[55] Jewish newspapers did publish the names of Jews who had renounced their religion, but this act appears not to have discouraged further renunciations, and may even had encouraged them by demonstrating how common such decisions were and showing that many worthy people were doing it.[56]

Although most Austrian Jews by 1914 no longer considered themselves to be members of a separate Jewish nationality but instead German-Austrians (or occasionally, Czech-, Polish-, or Italian-Austrians), it should not be assumed that they had no sense of Jewish identity at all. Anti-Semitism, particularly the racial variety, constantly reminded them of their religious roots. Moreover, on the positive side, there were literally hundreds of Jewish social, educational, political, cultural, and economic organizations, especially in Vienna (more than in any other city in the world), which made it possible for even the most westernized Jew to associate on a daily basis with other Jews. These organizations also, no doubt, substantially reduced the number of mixed marriages, at least in Vienna where less than 10 percent of the Jews married non-Jews. By sharp contrast, in Graz, with its relatively small Jewish population, two-thirds of the Jewish marriages were with non-Jews, although half of the Christian partners—usually women—then converted to Judaism.[57]

THE OUTLOOK IN 1914

After two decades of virulent anti-Semitism at the end of the nineteenth century, the prospects of Austrian Jews on the eve of the First World War looked almost as bright as they had shortly before 1880. Overt acts and statements of anti-Semitism were becoming increasingly rare, at least among German-speaking Austrians. The Christian Social Party, which had so frightened Austrian Jews seventeen years before, had lost its leader and much of its electoral support, especially in Vienna. Georg von Schönerer was a political has-been. Jews were prospering both economically and intellectually as never before. Intermarriage between Jews and Christians had become fairly commonplace, and many Jews had ceased practicing their religion, had renounced it, or had even converted to Christianity.

On the other hand, however alarming conversions were to the Jewish community, they were not numerous enough to threaten its existence. Austrian Jews were still not well integrated into Christian society; they tended both to work and socialize with each other. These circumstances helped sustain their sense of Jewish identity even if that consciousness was undoubtedly weaker than seven decades earlier. Anti-Semites who claimed that Jews did not cease being Jews merely because they were baptized or attempted to assimilate were not entirely wrong, even though this assertion was to a large extent a self-fulfilling prophecy.

Even at the University of Vienna, where anti-Semitism had flourished from the late 1870s to the 1890s, a new spirit of tolerance prevailed after the turn of the century. Whatever the private feelings of gentile faculty members toward Jews may have been, they did not prevent Jews from being promoted, especially in the Medical College. The influence of the Burschenschaften was waning and even the infamous Waidhofner Principle was revoked a few days before the outbreak of the world war.[58]

Knowing what we know today about the catastrophe that was about to engulf the Jews of Austria, it is easy to say that they were living in a fool's paradise in 1914. Yet our knowledge should not blind us to the very real progress toward civil equality Austrian Jews had achieved since 1848 and especially since 1867. One Jewish historian has recently noted that, "the history of the Jews in Germany from 1870 to 1930 represents the most spectacular advance any branch of Jewry has ever achieved."[59] Much the same could be said of the Jews in Vienna. As for the Jews of the Habsburg Monarchy as a whole, another American historian has recently concluded that "nowhere else in the world has the large-scale transformation of eastern Jewry taken place so relatively peacefully, indeed so relatively without major violence."[60]

The shots that killed the heir apparent to the Austro-Hungarian throne, Franz Ferdinand, on 28 June 1914, brought an almost instant end to the golden age of Viennese Jewry. They proved to be as catastrophic for Austrian Jews as they were for the monarchy as a whole and far surpassed the consequence of the demise of Liberalism. The more than four grueling years of war and famine revived Austrian anti-Semitism to its greatest intensity since at least the seventeenth century. Although the war helped awaken Jewish self-consciousness as well, the combination of increased anti-Semitism and growing Jewish awareness resulted in less, not more, unity within the Jewish community.

5

A WORLD COLLAPSES

JEWISH SUPPORT FOR THE WAR

Although it is easy today for the historian to see in the First World War the catastrophe that ended the golden age of Viennese Jewry, there was no sense of forboding in the Jewish press (as distinguished from Jewish-owned or edited newspapers having both gentile and Jewish readers) when the war broke out. Nor, for that matter, did Jewish journalists have much anti-Semitic news to report before about the last year and a half of the war. On the contrary, with the exception of the iconoclastic writer, Karl Kraus, and Friedrich Adler, the son of the Socialist leader, Viktor Adler, nearly all Austrian Jews, including the Zionists, like the Jews of other belligerent countries, supported the war enthusiastically as an opportunity to prove their loyalty to the Habsburg dynasty and to the Austro-Hungarian state. For assimilationist Jews in Austria (and Germany) it was also a chance to complete their integration into society. A victory would be "the start of a new centuries-long era of peace and work."[1]

Moreover, the war was widely regarded as a chance to disprove one of the oldest anti-Semitic allegations, namely that Jews were cowards. *Die Wahrheit*, the organ of the liberal and more assimilated Viennese Jews, thought that "the worst enemies of the Jews . . . would be shamed into silence by the long lines of Jews" volunteering for service in the Austro-Hungarian army.[2] The monthly newsletter of the Austrian-Israelite Union expressed these views succinctly in its July–August issue of 1914: "In this hour of danger we consider ourselves to be fully entitled citizens of the state. . . . We want to thank the Kaiser with the blood of our children and with our possessions for making us free; we want to prove to the state that we are its true citizens, as good as anyone. . . . After this war, with all its horrors, there cannot be any more anti-Semitic agitation in Austria. . . . We will be able to claim full equality."[3]

Although nearly all the Austro-Hungarian nationalities supported the world war, especially at the outset, it was particularly easy for Jews to do so. For them Russia, home to more than half the world's Jewish population and by far the worst and most powerful oppressor of their coreligionists, was the instigator of the war and the monarchy's principal enemy. Jewish newspapers even held the Russian government responsible for the murder of Franz Ferdinand in Sarajevo. Princip, the assassin, and the Serbian government were no more than tools of the Russians.[4] When the Russian "steamroller" swept through most of Galicia in the fall of 1914, it was interpreted not so much as a defeat for Austria-Hungary as it was proof of Russia's preparedness for an invasion.[5] Rumania's entry into the war in August 1916 merely reinforced the war's legitimacy and gave Austrian Jews another opportunity for revenge against a country that had always denied Jews equal rights.[6]

Support for the war effort remained unwavering among most Jews until the end. In January 1917 *Dr. Bloch's Oesterreichische Wochenschrift* declared that "we have the knowledge that Austria-Hungary's cause is just; the cause that our army and the armies of our allies have served has brought our fatherland glorious successes. To be sure, there have also been setbacks, which in a great war are unavoidable and which must be endured with strong hearts. The result, however, is more than favorable for our weapons. . . . Except for the diplomatic cabinets of the Entente governments, there is probably no one who does not want peace."[7]

The same newspaper was puzzled, however, by the outbreak of war between Germany and the United States in April, stating that there had been no political or economic conflicts between the two countries or even any tradition of enmity. The paper rejected the contention of pan-Germans and anti-Semitic newspapers that American Jews were anti-German and offered as proof a recent meeting of Jews in Philadelphia that protested the U.S. entry into the war. Anti-Germanism in America had been provoked by the aggressiveness of pan-German propaganda, not Jewish agitation.[8]

JEWISH SOLDIERS IN THE FIRST WORLD WAR

Austrian Jews supported the Austro-Hungarian war effort not only verbally and financially—through their heavy subscription to war loans—but militarily as well. Even before the war Jews had been overrepresented in the army among its officers, especially its reserve officers because of the need for educated young men with linguistic skills. Whereas Jews made up only about 4.5 percent of the Dual Monarchy's population, they comprised 8 percent of the army's officers in 1900 and nearly 19 percent of its reserve officers, making Austria-Hungary the only country in the world with such an overrepresentation. In fact, prior to the establishment of the Israeli Defense Force no army even came close to having as many Jewish officers in its army as Austria-Hungary.[9]

The total number of Jews who served in the Austro-Hungarian army during the First World War cannot be determined because no census was ever taken during the war. Erwin Schmidl, an Austrian military historian, has estimated the figure to be 300,000 Jewish soldiers.[10] Furthermore, we know that 25,000 Jewish officers served in the war compared with only 2,000 for Prussia. All of the Austrian Jewish refugees interviewed for this book reported that many of their relatives had fought in the war. Nevertheless, it is entirely possible that Jews were underrepresented at least among soldiers who served and were killed on the fighting fronts. The simple fact is that most infantry soldiers were peasants in all the belligerent armies of the First World War, and peasants, for historical reasons described previously, were overwhelmingly gentiles. The urban population of Austria-Hungary, whether Jewish or gentile, was far more likely to be used in safer military jobs requiring training and education like transportation corps, construction units, or military administration. Jews were especially numerous among medical officers who played an indispensable role ministering to the wounded on the front. Nevertheless, 30,000 to 40,000 Austro-Hungarian Jews were killed in the war.[11]

Although little information is available, anti-Semitism does not appear to have been a serious problem within the Austro-Hungarian army during the war, in sharp contrast to the army of imperial Germany.[12] Fights between Christian and Jewish officers did break out in prisoner-of-war camps, however. Moreover, military authorities showed their mistrust of Jewish (as well as Czech and Italian-speaking) soldiers by not allowing them to guard prisoners of war after March 1917.[13]

For the first few months of the fighting, Jewish hopes that the war would inaugurate a new and far more amicable era of Christian-Jewish relations seemed realistic. In October *Die Wahrheit* observed that "the earlier antipathy for Jews has quickly quieted down both within the government and within the Aryan masses of Middle Europe. Even the Viennese and Lower Austrian press . . . has since the start of the war maintained an honorable and objective tone vis-à-vis the Jewish population."[14]

Moreover, the Jews' hope of refuting anti-Semitic charges about their alleged cowardice seemed to be realized during the war. Members of the imperial family as well as senior officers were lavish, both during and after the war, in their praise of Jewish bravery. Archduke Ferdinand declared that the Jews in his division had fought like heroes and that he was "very satisfied" with their performance.[15] Franz Joseph and his successor, Karl, who came to the throne in November 1916, repeatedly recognized Jewish patriotism and steadfastness both on and off the field of battle. Major General G. Glasser Edler von Jarten and Colonel-General Count Viktor Denkl stated after the war that they did not notice any difference in the fighting ability of Jewish and non-Jewish officers and soldiers. A member of the general staff, Colonel-General R. E. Allexin said he had witnessed numerous heroic and self-sacrificing achievements of both Jewish officers and soldiers. Field Marshal Edler von Kaltenborn praised both the bravery and reliability of the Jewish soldiers under his command.[16]

Jewish optimism about the war causing a remission of anti-Semitism, however, turned out to be pathetically naive and short lived. The trust that the military in general gave to Jews seems to have aroused the distrust of non-Jews outside the army. Gentiles accused Jews of acting as spies for the Russians. Occasionally wartime psychoses led people to take these stories seriously. As early as February 1915, the Austrian-Israelite Union's *Monatschrift* reported that Jews were accused by various types of people of being cowards and traitors.[17] In 1916 Galician Jews were charged with trying to avoid military service by pretending to be rabbinical students. An investigation at the time revealed that only a few Jews had taken advantage of the unclear qualifications that existed in the eastern part of the monarchy for becoming rabbinical students. The matter was quickly settled when the government and a committee of rabbis established new rules. These actions did not prevent anti-Semites from repeating the allegations after the war, however.[18]

As the war progressed and turned increasingly against the Central Powers in 1917, the government's censorship of anti-Semitic hate articles grew lax and verbal attacks against Jews became more frequent. At first they were done mostly by innuendo. But by 1917 and especially throughout 1918 they became increasingly frequent and vociferous. Anti-Semites accused the Jews of cowardice, saying that only a few had been cited for bravery; the trenches, they claimed, were virtually "judenrein." Instead, Jews filled the comparatively safe Red Cross centers far from the front lines, worked in warehouses where they stole goods, or evaded military service altogether and became profiteers. Jewish physicians were accused of coddling Jewish soldiers while sending Aryans back to the battlefields prematurely. (After the war Zionists made inverse accusations against gentile officers.) By war's end Jews were being charged, as in Germany, with undermining the homefront and causing the defeat of the Central Powers.[19]

THE FLIGHT OF THE GALICIAN JEWS

Anti-Semitic charges against Jewish soldiers were mild and infrequent compared with those made against Jewish refugees from Galicia and Bukovina. These refugees represented a second wave of Ostjuden who had migrated to the Austrian capital. As noted in Chapter 2, between 1867 and 1910 some 30,000 Galician Jews had moved to Vienna. This first "wave" of Jewish immigrants had aroused a great deal of anti-Semitic resentment even though their numbers were insignificant compared with the 467,000 immigrants who came from Bohemia and Moravia. And whereas the generally Yiddish-speaking Galician immigrants quickly learned the closely related German language, Slavic immigrants from the Bohemian crownlands often preferred to establish their own private Czech-language schools.[20]

Even in the most prosperous prewar years, Galician immigrants to Vienna had been overwhelmingly poor. Although Galician Jews were legally equal to the Jews of western Austria, economically they were far more like the Jews of Russia. In Galicia, as elsewhere in Eastern Europe, Jews handled the money economy between landowners and peasants; the latter were usually gentiles and saw the Jews as economic exploiters. This entire traditional social order, however, began to change with the coming of capitalism and the Industrial Revolution in the late nineteenth century. The emergence of Polish and Ukrainian nationalism also helped lead to economic competition between Jews and gentiles. All of these factors caused the decline of Galician villages and the rise of unemployment among Galician Jews, sometimes to levels above 50 percent. Therefore, young people, both gentiles and Jews, had to seek employment in the cities. Galician Jews were attracted to Vienna not only by economic opportunities but also by the prospects of greater social equality and frequently by the presence of friends and relatives who had emigrated earlier.[21]

Although second generation Ostjuden often transformed themselves into Westjuden by entering the professions, the older generation and the new immigrants remained for a long time a culturally and religiously distinct entity. While they resided in Galicia, Jews had lived in well-established communities, geographically and culturally isolated from the West and so culturally and economically superior to the surrounding Polish and Ukrainian population that they had no temptation to assimilate, at least in rural areas. When they moved to Vienna, they often retained the Orthodox faith and occasionally the dress, manners, and life-style that were typical of Ostjuden all over Eastern Europe. Many of these Eastern Jews considered themselves to be a distinct nationality with their own rich and unique literature and *Volksgeist* and were

Galician Orthodox Jews on the Karmeliterplatz in the Leopoldstadt about 1915.
Franz Hubmann, The Habsburg Empire. *In* Mein Kampf *Hitler said of this*
section of Vienna, "Particularly the Inner City and the districts north of the
Danube Canal swarmed with a people which even outwardly had lost all
resemblance to Germans."

therefore often attracted to Zionism. They were frequently startled, when first arriving in Vienna, to discover that it was practically impossible to tell the difference between most of the Jews and gentiles whom they encountered on the street.[22]

There were then, on the eve of the First World War, two Jewish communities in Vienna. The majority consisted of westernized, very pro-Austrian, politically liberal Jews who adhered to "reform" Judaism or who were frequently even nonobservant; most had been born in Vienna itself or else in Bohemia or Moravia. The minority, about 25 percent, consisted of recent immigrants from Galicia, many of whom retained their Orthodox faith. The westernized Jews usually regarded their eastern coreligionists with suspicion if not outright contempt and rarely intermarried with them. They saw the Ostjuden as loud, coarse, dirty, immoral, and culturally backward. As in Germany they were seen as apparitions from an earlier period of Jewish history the assimilated Jews wanted to forget. Well-established Viennese Jews even held them responsible for arousing anti-Semitism. The hostile reception Galician Jews encountered in Vienna was not unlike that which Russian Jews received in the eastern cities of the United States after 1905 or that which Japanese immigrants experienced in California at about the same time.[23]

The world war vastly accelerated the migration of Jews from Galicia and Bukovina to Vienna, increasing in a matter of months the city's Jewish population by as much as 125,000,[24] or almost 75 percent. This veritable population explosion, consisting mainly of penniless peddlers, artisans, or cattle dealers, was produced mostly by the Russian invasion of northeastern Austria at the outset of the war; a few thousand Galician Jews were also expelled from France and Belgium as enemy aliens and made their way to Vienna.[25] Facilitated by the deployment of much of the Austro-Hungarian army on the Serbian front when the war broke out, the Russian conquest momentarily reached to within twelve miles of Cracow, in extreme western Galicia, by 29 November 1914. By January nearly all of Bukovina was also under tsarist control. The Central Powers managed to drive the Russians out of most of the occupied territories between May and September of 1915, only to see the majority of the same area fall again to the Russians during the "Brusilov" offensive of June 1916. Not until 1917 were Galicia and Bukovina liberated once and for all.[26]

When the Russians approached, Austro-Hungarian military authorities ordered the evacuation of civilians from the battle zones; Jewish inhabitants, well aware of the anti-Semitic policies of the Russian government in recent decades, needed little prodding to leave. By the fall of 1915 the army reported that 340,000 refugees had fled to the West, including some who had been expelled by the Russian army command for having allegedly caused the Russian defeat. Although the Austro-Hungarian military authorities attempted to direct the refugees to several different unoccupied territories, the Jews were free to go where they wished; some went to Bohemia and to Linz in Upper Austria, but the majority chose Vienna with its large and well-organized Jewish community.[27]

The first refugees who reached Vienna before the end of August 1914 were met with considerable sympathy, especially by their coreligionists, or with nothing worse than indifference. Even so rabid an anti-Semitic newspaper as the *Ostdeutsche Rundschau* at first ignored the refugees. It contradicted the initial enthusiasm for the war to mention refugees at a time when there were supposed to be victories in the East. Even police reports did not indicate the presence of strong anti-Semitic feelings during the first months of the war. In any case, the refugees were not expected to remain in the capital for long, and until at least 1915, food shortages were not too serious in the Austrian capital.[28]

The reaction of the "native" Jewish population of Vienna to the arrival of the Jewish refugees from the East was complicated. The upper class was shocked by the poverty and backwardness of these Ostjuden. The Austrian-Israelite Union's *Monatschrift* for November–December 1914 described the unfortunate living conditions in the barracks where most of the refugees were housed. They were at least equipped with electricity, kitchens, and washrooms, all of which would have been suitable for soldiers, but which were very inadequate for whole families. The *Monatschrift* appealed to its readers to supply the refugees with jobs, clothes, and shoes, which were desperately needed with winter approaching.[29] Jewish officials praised the work done by the government to establish children's homes, schools, kitchens, and libraries for the refugees. *Dr. Bloch's Oesterreichische Wochenschrift* stated in March 1915 that the friendliness of the Christian Social mayor and administration of Vienna toward Jews would not be forgotten by them.[30]

As time went on and tens of thousands of the refugees remained in Vienna far longer than anyone, including the refugees themselves, had anticipated, resentment against them began to grow for consuming the already short supplies of housing, food, and fuel. Upper-class Jews now began to see them as a threat to their goal of complete social acceptance by the Christian Viennese. Meanwhile, poorer Viennese Jews, fearing economic competition from the refugees, saw them as a danger to their existence.[31]

In fairness to the Jews and gentiles of Vienna, it should be pointed out that their hostility to Jewish refugees was not unique. Many Berlin Jews reacted in the same way to the 70,000 Ostjuden who immigrated to the German capital between 1917 and 1920.[32] Hungarians and Czechs were even less friendly toward the refugees. As late as April 1918 there were still 41,365 Jewish refugees in Bohemia out of a total of slightly fewer than 65,000, and in neighboring Moravia there were 18,487 Jewish refugees among the 35,413 people who had fled their war-ravished homelands.[33]

When Galicia was temporarily cleared of Russian troops in the summer of 1915, the Viennese municipal government considered interning Jewish refugees who refused to return to their homes, an idea that was repeatedly discussed after the war. In 1915, however, the minister of interior, Baron Haynold, was sympathetic to the refugees, calling them "victims of war," so no such drastic action was taken. But the city council still put pressure on remaining refugees to leave by removing their public assistance and offering free transportation back to Galicia. The number of Jewish refugees consequently declined from 125,000 to 77,000 by October 1915. For many of the remainder, however, a return to their native villages (*shtetl*) was a virtual impossibility because they had been rendered uninhabitable by the fighting. A new Russian offensive in 1916 sent another 200,000 refugees (both Jews and gentiles) fleeing to the West, 40,000 to 50,000 of whom reached Vienna and other parts of Lower Austria. The loss of most of Galicia, one of the prime breadbaskets of the Austrian half of the monarchy, also meant that grain and meat shortages became ever more acute in the Austrian metropolis. An offensive launched by the Central Powers in 1917 finally enabled most of the refugees to return to their homes. By April 1918 only 38,772 refugees without means remained in Vienna, of whom 34,233 were Jews. By the following March there were no more than 20,000 to 25,000 Jewish refugees left in Vienna.[34]

JEWISH REFUGEES, WARTIME SHORTAGES, AND PROFITEERING, REAL AND IMAGINED

Although the number of Jewish refugees in Vienna was never as large as anti-Semites believed, especially by 1918, the refugees and other Jews were blamed for every conceivable problem afflicting Austria at the end of the war and in the early postwar period. In reality, the refugees (both Jews and gentiles) at no time occupied more than 7,700 Viennese apartments. Although it is impossible to describe the living conditions within these apartments with any precision, we can get some idea from the districts of Leopoldstadt and neighboring Brigittenau, where nearly half of all of Vienna's Jews lived, and far more than half of the Galician Jews lived. An average of four to six people inhabited single rooms as late as 1919.[35]

The real problem, however, was that even before the war there had been a severe housing shortage in the Austrian capital. In 1910, 1.24 Viennese lived in every room in the city, including kitchens, bathrooms, and front halls. During the war, the housing question was aggravated not only by the influx of refugees but also by the absence of residential construction. All this made the temptation to blame the Ostjuden for the hardships more and more irresistible. Anti-Semites charged that the refugees were living in comfortable quarters or even in palaces while 19,000 honest Aryans had no place at all to live. The whole issue could be resolved overnight if only the unwanted guests were compelled to return to their homelands.[36]

Worse than the charges of creating shortages of housing and food were the allegations that the Jewish refugees were war profiteers. Indeed, so numerous were the accusations that by the end of the war the words, "Ostjude," "Galician," "profiteer," "hoarder," "speculator," and "usurer" had become practically synonymous. Anti-Semitic articles in newspapers such as the *Reichspost* were usually not pure inventions, but they gave the very false impression that only Jews were involved in illegal activities.[37] Anti-Semites typically used the wrongdoings of individual Jews to generalize about the whole Jewish community. Even Jewish authors admitted that some Jews "speculated in money and indulged in other reprehensible practices to ward off starvation."[38] The great Austrian defender of Jews, Count Richard Coudenhove-Kalergi, acknowledged that some Jewish refugees had managed to become rich during the war and had acted in a tasteless way. Jewish businessmen were also charged with making enormous profits in procuring goods for the army. During the war they had supposedly taken over whole branches of industry as well as the grocery business. Central government offices that were set up by the government in order to regulate war industries were allegedly run by Jews who employed their Jewish friends and favored their own private industries.[39]

In reality, however, the number of Jews in Vienna who were enriched by the war was tiny in comparison to those impoverished by it. The biggest profits were made in the armaments industries and in agriculture, two areas from which Jews were almost completely excluded. Peasants not only enjoyed a huge demand for their harvests but were also able to pay off their debts with inflated money. And even if by some chance a higher percentage of Jews in Vienna did profit from the war, this could easily be explained by the fact that a far higher percentage of Jews than Christians was engaged in business.[40]

Despite press censorship, anti-Semitic articles began appearing in Viennese newspapers as early as 1915, especially in the *Reichspost*. An article in an October issue of this official organ of the Christian Social Party blamed Jews for opposing papal efforts for a peace of understanding without annexations. Four days earlier the *Ostdeutsche Rundschau* complained that Jews were standing in the way of an annexationist peace. Another article in the *Reichspost* in November described allegedly treasonous activities of German-American and German-English Jews against their former homeland without mentioning the activities of Christian immigrants that were directed against the Central Powers. In October 1917 the *Reichspost* claimed that Alexander Kerensky and Vladimir Lenin in Russia, and Lord Northcliffe, the propagandist in Britain, were all Jews. It also maintained that President Woodrow Wilson had fallen completely under Jewish influence. After March 1918 anti-Semitic articles became increasingly common in several Viennese newspapers, with the *Reichspost* still setting the pace.[41]

Newspapers were not the only medium for anti-Semitic statements during the last year and a half of the Habsburg Monarchy. In the summer of 1917 a

Christian Social politician named Heinrich Mataja, who represented Lower Leopoldstadt, the most heavily Jewish populated district in Vienna, wrote a memorandum to his party's leader, Prince Alois Liechtenstein, curtly reminding him about the party's anti-Semitic principles and demanding the lifting of the *Burgfrieden* (civil peace) that the mayor of Vienna had proclaimed at the beginning of the war. But whoever had heard Mataja's own public speeches as well as those of two other Christian Social politicians, Anton Jerzabek and Leopold Kunschak, not to mention Georg von Schönerer's old follower, K. H. Wolf, could have no doubt that the Burgfrieden was already a thing of the past. The reopening of the Austrian Parliament at the end of May 1917 provided a new forum for anti-Semitic delegates of the Christian Social Party and various German nationalist parties. In July, Jerzabek told the Reichsrat that Jewish refugees were stealing instead of working. Indeed, in the summer of 1917 the German-Austrian parties in the Reichsrat were making anti-Semitism their main program.[42]

The failure of Austria-Hungary's last offensive on the Italian front in June 1918 along with the approach of defeat and increasingly desperate food, housing, and fuel conditions in the summer and fall combined to produce a need to find a scapegoat; the Jews, especially the Ostjuden, were the most convenient target. The new wave of anti-Semitism expressed itself in public demonstrations, which began in the summer of 1918 and which became ever more massive and sometimes violent until 1923, when improving economic conditions and the settlement of the Galician refugee issue finally dampened, but by no means extinguished, the passions of anti-Semites.

This wave of anti-Semitism, which was tolerated by both imperial and municipal authorities, reached an early high point in mid-June 1918 with mass demonstrations; they were part of a so-called German People's Assembly (Deutscher Volkstag), which met in the Austrian capital ostensibly to proclaim the unswerving loyalty of the Christian Social and pan-German participants to Kaiser Karl. In fact the demonstrators denounced the Jews as war profiteers and held them responsible for the food shortages. One speaker even called for a pogrom as a way to heal the state.[43]

The Jewish response to the renewed agitation was at first tepid. The Austrian-Israelite Union quietly, and for a while successfully, protested anti-Semitic activities to the Ministry of the Interior. However, Vienna's Israelitische Kultusgemeinde for a long time tolerated anti-Semitic pronouncements, hoping that in so doing it was providing a service to the fatherland by observing its part of the Burgfrieden. Not all Jews were satisfied with such passivity, however. One private individual by the name of Sigmund Schönau wrote an open letter to the president of the organization, Alfred Stern, complaining that a proposal he (Schönau) had made in January 1916 for the formation of a committee to fight anti-Semitism had been ignored. Schönau claimed that he had succeeded in getting the pope to forbid priests in Vienna and elsewhere in Austria-Hungary from delivering anti-Semitic sermons. Despite Schönau's efforts, most Viennese Jews started to become alarmed only in the second half of 1918 and even then deluded themselves into thinking that the renewed anti-Semitism was only temporary.[44]

In retrospect it is clear that well before the final collapse of the Austro-Hungarian Monarchy, the establishment of the First Republic, and the emergence of the Social Democratic Party as the leading political force in Vienna, anti-Semitism had reappeared in the Austrian capital and elsewhere in the Dual Monarchy, especially in its German-speaking regions. The First World War had proved to be a major turning point in the relations between Jews and German-speaking people in both Austria and Germany.[45] Bad as things were in the summer and fall of 1918, however, they were but a foretaste of things to come.

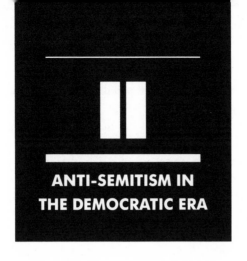

ANTI-SEMITISM IN
THE DEMOCRATIC ERA

The end of the Habsburg Monarchy also brought a temporary end to authoritarian government in Austria. Tragically, from the accession of Joseph II in 1780 to the end of Austrian independence in 1938, Austrian Jews were far better protected by authoritarian regimes than they were when executive powers were weak and democratic institutions were strong. Thus, anti-Semitism flared briefly during the democratic Revolutions of 1848 and again after the extension of the franchise in 1882. It was largely suppressed during the first three years of the First World War when the Austrian Parliament never met and the press was censored. It was at least partially quelled once again with the establishment of the authoritarian regime of Chancellor Engelbert Dollfuss in 1933 who dissolved all the political parties, including his own Christian Social Party, and partially censored the press.

It was during the intervening years, between the fall of the Habsburg Monarchy and the establishment of the "corporative state" by Dollfuss that anti-Semitism enjoyed its most luxuriant expressions. Freedom of speech and freedom of assembly also meant freedom to shout anti-Semitic slogans and to hold anti-Semitic demonstrations. Anti-Semitism, in fact, flourished in all the new democracies of East Central Europe after 1918, with the exception of Czechoslovakia and Yugoslavia. And it is no mere coincidence that the rebirth of freedom in Eastern Europe in the early 1990s is also being accompanied by a rebirth of anti-Jewish hatred.

At the very moment when Austrians enjoyed almost unlimited freedom of expression, they had an incredible number of newspapers to voice their newfound freedom as well as a large number of ideologically doctrinaire political parties. The bibliography of this book lists no fewer than thirty-two newspapers for Vienna alone. Nearly all of them represented the views of a different political party or faction. The almost completely nonideological pragmatism, which has generally characterized the politics of the Second Austrian Republic since 1945, was unknown in the First Republic. Extremists in interwar Austria, of which there were many, saw their rivals not as honest, if mistaken men, but as heretics to be eliminated one way or another. Anti-Semitism was just one of many deeply entrenched passions of interwar Austria. Anti-Marxism and hatred of the newly autonomous "Red Vienna," anticlericalism, and fascism all had their fanatical devotees. Nor were such passions limited exclusively to non-Jews.

If it is sobering to acknowledge the connection between democracy and anti-Semitism, it is downright depressing to note that there was also a parallel between anti-Semitism, education, and religiosity. Thus Socialists, with their eighth-grade educations and atheistic philosophy, were far less likely to be anti-Semitic than regular churchgoers and holders of academic degrees.

Still another relationship with anti-Semitism, albeit a much less surprising one, was the connection between economic crises and Judeophobia. The new Austrian state was never economically sound in the interwar period. Landlocked and with few natural resources including arable land, it was now cut off from former markets. At no time (in contrast to Germany) did Austria fully recover its prewar prosperity. But it was precisely in the worst of economic times, from 1918 to the end of 1923 and again after 1930 that anti-Semitism was at its height. Nevertheless, the connection between unemployment and anti-Semitism was never exact. Even during periods of high unemployment a laid-off industrial worker was less likely to be anti-Semitic than a still-employed member of the bourgeoisie.

One final connection should be noted. However much democracy may have made the expression of anti-Semitic sentiments easier, it was not the *cause* of anti-Semitism. On the contrary, anti-Semites were the enemies of democracy. It is at least encouraging to note that in general Austrians who were the strongest supporters of democracy were the least likely to be anti-Semitic and in some cases were actually philo-Semitic. Those people who were the most fanatically anti-Semitic were also the most likely to be archenemies of democracy. By 1933 the anti-Semites had helped bring about the premature death of the fledgling Austrian democracy.

REVOLUTION AND RETRIBUTION

The end of the First World War and the establishment of the First Austrian Republic came as mixed blessings for Austria's Jews. They generally regretted the passing of the monarchy in which they had gained complete constitutional equality and considerable prosperity. Its demise represented the triumph of narrow national self-interest, something that most Austrian Jews had rejected.[1] On the other hand, the end of the war at least meant the cessation of the slaughter on the front lines and the promise that the dreadful shortages of food, fuel, and housing would soon be alleviated. However, the war's end and the collapse of the monarchy also left the Jews, along with other Austrians, bitterly divided about their own future.

THE JEWISH IDENTITY CRISIS AND LEFT-WING POLITICS

The collapse of the Habsburg Monarchy created a severe identity crisis for all Austrians, both Jews and gentiles. Most Austrians, including many Jews, were confronted with the question of whether they were Germans, just like those of the new Weimar Republic, or whether as Austrians they formed a distinct nationality that ought to remain in a separate state. Most Austrians, for the moment at least, preferred the first alternative.

Austrian Jews who were still self-consciously Jewish faced a second problem: were they primarily Austrians and only secondarily Jews, or did they, as Jews, belong to a distinct nationality? Unlike Austrian gentiles, most Jews, especially in the 1920s and early 1930s, continued to think of themselves as German-Austrians by birth, customs, education, culture, and feeling, and had no wish to be anything else. They asked only for equal treatment in the new republic. In view of the growing anti-Semitism late in the war, however, they were apprehensive about this goal being achieved.[2]

Complicating the sense of identity for Austrian Jews were the Bolshevik revolutions in Russia and Hungary and the prospect of a new Jewish homeland in Palestine. The questions of identity and their future role in the Austrian state were to cause hostile feelings among the Jews themselves, which lasted to the very day of the German annexation of Austria in 1938 and made it impossible for them to present the anti-Semites with a common front. The wartime renaissance of anti-Semitism and the arrival of so many unassimilated Galician Jewish refugees in the Austrian capital were strong stimuli to the growth of Zionism.[3] As early as April 1918 a Zionist delegation demanded that the Austrian government recognize Jews as a separate nationality with proportional representation for themselves in the Reichsrat.[4] By October the Zionists were insisting on national self-determination in accordance with the principles laid down during the war by the Entente. They asked for a homeland in Palestine and a separate national assembly for those Jews remaining in Austria.

The Zionists failed to gain recognition for themselves as a separate nation in Austria; nor did the new Austrian constitution grant them their own national assembly. However, the Treaty of St. Germain concluded by the Allies with Austria in September 1919 did contain minority clauses that promised Jews equal treatment. The Paris Peace Conference also recognized the right of Jews to establish a homeland in Palestine. If a minority of Austrian Jews, especially Galician immigrants and university students, enthusiastically supported the rapidly growing Zionist movement, the others—assimilated and Orthodox Jews, who until 1932 constituted the majority—ardently opposed it, not just during and immediately after the First World War, but also during the entire First Republic. Assimilationists feared that Theodor Herzl's idea that Jews were a separate nation would simply confirm the prejudices of anti-Semites who had long argued that Jews were foreigners deserving no civil rights.

For some Austrian Jews, especially those who had recently arrived from Galicia or Bukovina, the search for a new identity produced an interest in left-wing or even revolutionary politics, much to the alarm of Austrian conservatives. During the war a Jewish youth group called Shomer (Guardian), whose members were mostly Galician students and workers, evolved from a scouting organization into a revolutionary youth movement. Influenced by the Russian revolutions, it tried in 1917 to get workers to sabotage war production.[5] Far more important as a radical left-wing organization, however, was the Viennese section of the international Zionist workers' organization known as Poale Zion (Workers of Zion).

The membership of Poale Zion also included many Galician and even Russian Jews, who were strengthened during the war by the flight of much of their leadership from Galicia to Vienna. These leaders, however, were mostly intellectuals with no real following. Like the Shomer they were influenced by the Russian revolutions and opposed both nationalism and the war. In a more general way they were often rebellious young people who sought to compensate for the petite bourgeois values of their parents by attempting to be proletarian in their outlook. After the war some of them joined Socialist groups or even the Communist Party as a means of rejecting their Jewish heritage.[6]

The Shomer and the Poale Zion were strongest in the Leopoldstadt with its large Jewish and working-class population. Their resistance to the war and to the prowar policy of the Social Democratic Party existed from the start of the fighting. By January 1918 the seemingly endless war, hunger, and overcrowded housing drove nearly one million Austrian workers to go on a general strike, a strike in which a disproportionately large number of those arrested (for distributing leaflets) were Jews and members of the Poale Zion. So important, in fact, was Jewish participation in the January strike that imperial officials jumped to the conclusion that the whole revolutionary movement was part of an international Jewish conspiracy; thereafter, they no longer tried to hinder counterrevolutionary anti-Semitic propaganda.[7] However, even if Jewish participation in the January strike was comparatively high, most Jews were not industrial workers and therefore did not support the strike. For that matter even the official organ of the Socialist Party, the *Arbeiter-Zeitung*, worked to contain it. And the overwhelming majority of the Jewish population of Austria remained devoted to the Habsburg Monarchy to the very end. These facts, however, did not prevent anti-Semites from holding Jews responsible for the monarchy's downfall.[8]

The same could be said for the Communist revolutions in Russia and Austria's neighbors, Bavaria and Hungary; in all three places a high percentage of the revolutionaries were of Jewish origins. In Russia this was not surprising. Although the Communists persecuted Judaism as a religion, they granted secularized Jews equal rights, were officially opposed to anti-Semitism, created an autonomous district for Jews in Siberia, and allowed Jews to hold high offices in the party.[9] Nevertheless, as noted in Chapter 1, only 7 percent of the Communists' membership was Jewish in 1924, even though Jews made up 11 percent of the population of Soviet cities where most of the party's membership was located.

In Hungary Jewish involvement was even more modest in absolute numbers. All 5,000 revolutionaries—Jews and gentiles combined—represented only 1 percent of Hungary's 500,000 Jews.[10] Nevertheless, Austrian anti-Semites were fond of quoting Hungarian clergymen, such as a bishop named

Dr. Ottokar Prochaska, who said that Hungarian Jews had "walked over the mass graves of Christian soldiers in order to make a revolution and trampled Christendom with Social Democracy." [11]

In addition to Jewish involvement in the Russian, Bavarian, and Hungarian revolutions, Jews were overrepresented in the Austrian Social Democratic Party. Indeed, the Jewish drift toward Socialism before the war accelerated after 1918, resulting in about 75 percent of the Viennese Jews voting for the Socialists after the world war (although this figure is less startling than it may appear when compared with the 54 to 60 percent of the general Viennese population that voted for the Socialists). [12] About 80 percent of the Socialist intellectuals were Jewish: most members of the Socialist university students' organization, nearly all the Socialist lawyers and physicians, and about 90 percent of the editors of the Arbeiter-Zeitung. [13]

The explanation for this phenomenon is not hard to find. As has already been observed, the Liberal Party began disintegrating in the mid-1890s and by 1918 had disappeared almost completely, thus leaving the Austrian Jews in search of a new home. Although the Social Democrats frequently resorted to anti-Semitic rhetoric by attacking "Jewish" capitalism, they at least ignored smaller Jewish businesses and never espoused or practiced racial anti-Semitism; nor was anti-Semitism ever part of the party's official program. They favored welfare and housing programs beneficial to impoverished Jews and, like the Liberal Party, they ardently believed in progress and education, staunchly opposed tyranny, and supported the separation of church and state. Finally, any Jew who had not converted to Christianity and hoped to hold an office in a major political party had no alternative but to join the Social Democratic Workers' Party. Thus Jewish involvement in the party was both a result and a cause of anti-Semitism. [14]

Many Austrian Jews were disturbed by the large number of people of Jewish origins among the Bolshevik leadership in Russia, Hungary, and Bavaria and were aware of the implications for themselves. [15] But the Zionist daily newspaper, Wiener Morgenzeitung, pointed out that there were also large numbers of Russian, German, and Czech Bolsheviks. The Jews had been more seriously affected by the war than any other people. The Morgenzeitung also noted that the Jewish revolutionaries were fighting for other nationalities, not for a specifically Jewish cause. [16] Bourgeois Jews in Austria obviously objected to the Marxism in the Austrian Social Democratic Party, although their objections did not necessarily prevent them from voting for the party's candidates. Bourgeois Jews were also embarrassed by the prominent role which some Jews played in the party. Most of all they resented being held collectively responsible for the actions of those Socialist leaders who had Jewish backgrounds.[17] None of these protestations, however, prevented anti-Semites in Austria, as well as Germany and elsewhere, from habitually equating Jews with Marxism and revolution.[18]

POSTWAR POLITICAL AND ECONOMIC CRISES

This Jewish involvement in revolutionary movements and left-wing politics coincided with Austria's defeat in the world war and the punitive Peace Treaty of St. Germain. At the same time, the food, housing, and fuel shortages as well as a staggering inflation reached their zenith in the first few postwar years. These circumstances combined to produce a need to find a scapegoat. The Jews, above all the Ostjuden, were for many Austrians the most obvious targets, especially now that Austria had lost nearly all of its other minorities. Even Viennese-born Jews sometimes joined in the chorus of complaints.[19]

The Treaty of St. Germain was similar to the Treaty of Versailles, except harsher. In contrast to Germany, which lost only about 10 percent of its territory and population, Austria was forced to cede all but 23 percent of the territory of just the Austrian half of the Austro-Hungarian Monarchy, and all but 26 percent of its former population. Not only did Austria lose all of its outlying and predominantly non-German-speaking provinces, but also territories inhabited by about 3.5 million German-Austrians. The majority of these lost Austrians lived in northern parts of Bohemia and Moravia as well as in Austrian Silesia. But another 650,000 were left in compact areas just beyond the new Austrian borders in southern Czechoslovakia, northern Yugoslavia, and the South Tyrol in Italy. Moreover, Austria was denied the right of self-determination by agreeing "not to alienate its independence" by joining the new German republic. Worst of all, nearly all the 6.5 million inhabitants of the new Austria were left with the firm conviction that what remained of their country could not possibly survive economically, a feeling that to some extent became a self-fulfilling prophecy.[20]

Not only pan-German nationalists, who until the end of the war had hoped for an annexationist *Siegfrieden,* but virtually all Austrians, including Austrian Jews, were outraged by the treaty's terms. The treaty's sharpest critics held the Socialist Party responsible, especially the Jewish leader of the party's left wing, Otto Bauer, who as the country's foreign minister was the most important component of the Austrian delegation at the peace conference. Bauer, however, resigned his post on 26 July 1919 because of the refusal of the Allies to permit the Anschluss with Germany. So it was actually Chancellor Karl Renner, a gentile, who ultimately signed the Treaty of St. Germain.[21]

Although all segments of Austrian society were hurt by the loss of Austria's former markets and natural resources, it was middle-class industrialists and civil servants who were the hardest hit. The same was true of the inflation. The bourgeoisie was traditionally the most thrifty of all the segments of Central European society and was therefore the group whose savings for all practical purposes were wiped out. A savings account that before the war would have been enough to buy a small house was worth only a postage stamp by 1922. Rent control, which began during the war and has lasted with some modifications to the present day in Vienna, also hurt middle-class landlords by making rent receipts practically worthless. Probably no other group in Austria was more affected by these economic developments than the Jews, who made up a disproportionately large percentage of the bankers, landlords, and merchants. Inflation hurts lenders and savers the most and was a major cause for the bankruptcy of twelve banks in the early 1920s, ten of which were largely Jewish owned. Yet once again, anti-Semites held Jews responsible for the inflation.[22]

The favorite whipping boys for all of the problems of early postwar Austria were the Jews, especially the continued presence in Vienna of Jewish refugees from Galicia. The *Wiener Morgenzeitung* described the status of the Ostjuden in Vienna by observing that "since the collapse the good people of Austria have condensed everything into the little word 'Ostjude.' . . . It is a wonderous expression which alleviates every pain and takes away every shame. Complaints over the rising costs of bread, and the falling morals of women, over bad railroad transportation, the lack of coal, the unruliness of school children, and the watering down of milk find their solution: Out with the Ostjuden! Their persecution and banishment have become a popular sport. . . . Not only the honorable German Christians express this hatred, but also Jews."[23]

The size of the Jewish refugee community itself became the subject of demagogic speculation. In October 1919 the *Reichspost* estimated that there were a fantastic 600,000 Jews in Austria, or more than double the prewar figure. Not to be outdone, a committee of the Greater German People's Party calculated that the total number of Jews of all types living in Vienna—refugees, "natives," Christian converts, and "part Jews" was 583,000 or nearly one-third of the city's population; another 137,000 Jews allegedly lived in the federal states.[24] In December of the same year the *Reichspost* estimated that there were still 100,000 Jewish refugees in the capital city who were living off the charity of the city and state.[25] In August 1920 the paper claimed that the 20,000 families with their 100,000 members who were without living quarters could be housed if only the Eastern Jews were deported.[26]

The actual number of Jews living in the whole of Austria was revealed by the census of 1923 to be only about 220,000, of whom 201,513 lived in Vienna. This represented an increase in absolute numbers of just over 26,000 since the census of 1910, and a rise in the percentage from 8.6 to 10.8. However, the increase was actually smaller than the 28,500 Jews who were added to Vienna's population between 1900 and 1910; the increase in the *percentage* of Jews simply resulted from the decline in Vienna's overall population following the departure of thousands of Czechs and other national minorities.[27] As to the number of people of Jewish origins in the country, the figure of 300,000 has frequently been cited; however, when the Nuremberg Laws were enforced after the Anschluss, only 34,500 people were reclassified as Jews who had not been so identified in the census of 1934 when there were officially 200,000 Jews in the whole of Austria.[28]

ANTI-SEMITIC DEMONSTRATIONS AND
COUNTERDEMONSTRATIONS, 1918–1923

The political and economic crises of the early postwar years induced many politicians to hold the Jews responsible and fostered a series of noisy and sometimes violent demonstrations, which did not end until the Austrian economy slowly began to recover in the spring of 1923. An anti-Semitic rally in the plaza in front of Vienna's huge neo-Gothic city hall on 25 September 1919 drew 5,000 participants who heard eight speakers complain that Aryan women and children were going without food and shelter because of Galician Jews. A second rally on 5 October, which was aimed primarily at the "plague of Eastern Jews," attracted 15,000 onlookers and prompted the *Ostdeutsche Rundschau* to remark that the Viennese population was far more anti-Semitic than it had been in the 1880s and 1890s. Now the whole "German" intelligentsia was involved in the movement along with large numbers of workers.[29]

In 1920 such demonstrations sometimes turned violent. After a joint meeting in June called by the Antisemitenbund (League of Anti-Semites) and a monarchist paramilitary formation known as the Frontkämpfervereinigung (Front Fighters' Association), a number of passersby with long noses were assaulted because they looked Jewish.[30]

In September the Austrian Nazi Party held a rally in the Prater amusement park near Leopoldstadt attended (according to its own estimate) by 3,000 people. The party's leader, Walter Riehl, demanded that Vienna's "200,000 Ostjuden" be deported to Poland to make room for the city's 150,000 homeless people. (Prophetically, twenty years later all of Vienna's Jews—and not just the Ostjuden—were forced to emigrate or were deported to death camps, in part to solve Vienna's housing shortage.) A street march after the rally by 1,000 of the participants led to clashes with outnumbered Socialists and Jews. The latter were chased down side streets until police finally intervened. Jewish shopkeepers in the neighborhood were hastily forced to close up and flee to their homes while the Nazis hurled stones and insults at the police.[31]

One of the biggest rallies in early postwar Vienna was an international congress held between 11 and 13 March 1921. The product of over eighteen months of preparation by the Antisemitenbund and especially its leader, Dr. Anton Jerzabek, it was attended by about 40,000 people. Participants came not only from Austria, but also from Germany, Czechoslovakia, and Hungary. Austria alone was represented by sixty-two anti-Semitic corporations and clubs having a total of 400,000 members. Many of the organizations brought all of their members, including their marching bands, which performed on the final day.[32]

The speakers at the congress covered all the usual anti-Semitic allegations and demands. Colonel Hermann von Hiltl, the leader of the Front Veterans, demanded that Austrian Jews be stripped of their citizenship rights, including the right to serve in the army and to own land; land already owned by Jews should be expropriated. The Catholic writer, Anton Orel, called Jews the "incarnation of the anti-Christ" whose strength was used to destroy Christian-German culture. Either German Romanticism would triumph or there would be world domination by the Jews. The congress concluded by approving a resolution calling on the Austrian government to limit the number of Jewish middle-school and university-aged students to their percentage of the country's population. Another resolution, advanced by Jerzabek demanded the expulsion by 1 April 1921 of all Jews who had immigrated to Vienna after the start of the world war. Some young people celebrated the end of the rally by breaking the windows of Jewish stores and attacking Jewish streetcar passengers.[33]

Anti-Semitic rallies diminished in 1922 only to reach new heights in the first three months of 1923. In January a newly founded Racial Anti-Semitic Fighting Committee (Völkische-antisemitische Kampfausschuss) organized a huge rally between the City Hall and the Burgtheater attended by anywhere from 20,000 (the estimate of the *Wiener Morgenzeitung*) to 100,000 people (the *Reichspost* calculation). Several paramilitary formations, including the Austrian Nazis and the Front Veterans' Association marched to the rally, "looking not unlike real storm troopers," and listened to speeches demanding that the Austrian government recognize the Jews as a separate nation and count them as such in the next census. The director of the Burgtheater, Hofrat Milenkovich, demanded that a *numerus clausus* (cap on representation) for Jews be applied not just to Vienna's Hochschulen, but to all public positions.[34]

Anti-Semitic outbursts in the early 1920s were not limited to street rallies and demonstrations. For example, in early February 1923 a group of young Nazis broke up a public lecture on "The Aberrations of Erotic Passion," which was given at the Konzerthaus (a large concert hall) by a Jewish sexual therapist from Berlin named Magnus Hirschfeld. At a prearranged signal the storm troops fired pistols blindly, threw stink bombs and rotten eggs, and threatened members of the audience with rubber knuckles and knives while shouting "Saujud [pig Jew] shut up" and "out with the Schweinhund [swine]," all of which created a panic and caused some people to be trampled. The tactics prompted the *Wiener Morgenzeitung* to comment that the medieval spirit of Jew burning had been reawakened.[35]

The *Morgenzeitung* did not content itself with editorializing. A month after the Nazi outrage in the Konzerthaus the Zionist paper helped sponsor a mass rally protesting anti-Semitic rallies that had taken place in front of the city hall. The rally, attended by Jews of all political orientations, took place in the people's hall of the Rathaus, the site of many earlier anti-Semitic demonstrations, and was intended to give Jews a chance to express their feelings about the recent anti-Semitic agitation. Six thousand people crowded into the hall and perhaps another ten thousand listened to the speeches outside on loudspeakers. The vice president of the Israelitische Kultusgemeinde, Dr. Desider Friedmann, criticized the Austrian government for doing nothing to stop the anti-Semitic excesses. Members of the audience had to leave the building by rear exits under police protection. But not everyone was able to escape the armed Nazi youths who attacked Jews with rubber clubs and heavy sticks along with various other weapons, in actions that the *Reichspost* said were provoked by Zionist guards. Ninety-nine armed anti-Semites were arrested.[36]

DEMANDS FOR EXPULSION OR INTERNMENT OF GALICIAN REFUGEES

The hate campaign against the Ostjuden also included the universities (to be described in the next chapter), parliamentary bodies, and above all the newspapers. The common denominators in all of this anti-Semitic agitation were calls for the expulsion or even the internment of Jewish refugees. These became almost routine in Vienna and in other parts of Austria after the summer of 1915 when the municipal government first made such a proposal. In December 1917 the Christian Social mayor of Vienna urged the city council to compel the repatriation of the city's remaining refugees now that there was an armistice on the eastern front. In July 1919 the Christian Social deputies in the city council, no doubt angry over their party's defeat in a recent municipal election, demanded that the Ostjuden (whom they blamed for their defeat) either be forced to emigrate or be placed in internment camps. The Social Democratic governor of Lower Austria (which still included Vienna at the time), Albert Sever, ordered all foreigners, except those with special temporary permission, to leave the federal state. Similar demands were made during the next several years by members of both the Christian Social Party and the Greater German People's Party.[37]

Brutal as these demands were, it should at least be pointed out that once again Austria's anti-Semitism at this time was not unique in Central Europe or elsewhere. The governments of Czechoslovakia and Hungary also tried to send Galician refugees back to their Polish homes after the First World War (even though the Czech government later became a bulwark of tolerance toward Jews). In August 1923 the police of Amsterdam gave Ostjuden who had arrived in the city after the start of the war just eight days in which to leave. Even in the United States, the Bolshevik scare was associated with radical Jews and helped produce immigration restrictions in the early 1920s that were aimed in large measure against Eastern European Jews.[38]

The response in Germany to the continued presence of Eastern European Jewish refugees was equally sharp. In December 1919 Prussian Minister of the Interior Wolfgang Heine announced his intention to establish internment camps for the refugees; in April 1920 the Bavarian government tried to expel 5,000 Ostjuden who had entered the state after August 1914. In August 1923 internment was limited only to criminals, people under serious suspicion of having committed crimes, and enemies of the state. These camps were hardly comparable with the Nazi concentration camps established a decade later and even German Jews did not object to their stated intention. But they did set something of a precedent.[39]

To force, or at least encourage, the departure of the Ostjuden, politicians made all sorts of proposals, none of which was ever implemented by the Austrian government, but all of which were eventually enacted by the Nazi government in Germany after 1933 and in Austria after the Anschluss. In February 1919 Anton Jerzabek along with nineteen of his Christian Social colleagues in the Austrian Parliament proposed a bill that would have expelled Jewish refugees if they had infectious diseases, had committed economic crimes, or had carried out political subversion. The sponsors of the bill warned that if it were not enacted the outraged masses would resort to "self-help." The Jews were not singled out in the language of the bill, but the motivation was clear and the alleged habits and customs of the Jewish refugees were openly discussed by the parliamentary deputies. In March 1919 a so-called German People's Council (Deutsche Volksrat) for Vienna and Lower Austria, an anti-Semitic group of German nationalist clubs, demanded that all refugees have their ration cards and freedom to conduct business withdrawn. The following month the two largest parties in the Parliament, the Social Democrats and the Christian Socials, agreed to control more strictly the dispersement of ration cards to refugees.[40]

Actually, the attitude of the Social Democratic Party toward Jews on this as well as many other issues was ambivalent. During these early postwar years the party sometimes favored the expulsion of the Ostjuden in principle but opposed it in practice. For example, as mentioned previously, on 10 September the Social Democratic governor of Lower Austria, Albert Sever, ordered the expulsion by 20 September of all foreigners who had not been residents at the start of the world war on the grounds that there was not enough housing and work available for them. Already on 23 September, however, he had to acknowledge that the shortage of trains and the coal to fuel them made this order impractical. He also called the idea of concentration camps for refugees a "cultural disgrace." The reversal of the governor's decision sparked a major protest demonstration by the Nazis and the League of Anti-Semites a few days later.[41]

It is possible that Governor Sever was never serious about expelling the foreigners and had only made a gesture to appease the anti-Semites. It is also likely, however, that he was reacting to a warning by the American consul general in Vienna, Albert Halstead. The consul told Chancellor Karl Renner on 25 September that American opinion would be prejudiced against Austria if the expulsions should actually occur. The warning came at a time when Austria was desperately dependent on the United States for famine relief. A few weeks later (in November) Halstead repeated his warning, this time to the Austrian Foreign Ministry, saying that reports coming out of Vienna about anti-Jewish agitation had created a very unfavorable impression in the United States, which could make it difficult in the future for Austria to obtain American credit.[42]

Verbally at least, the Catholic Christian Social Party was much less equivocal about the Ostjuden, especially the party's leader in the early 1920s and simultaneously the head of its "Workers' Union" (Arbeiterverein), Leopold Kunschak. Although he was more extreme in his anti-Semitism than most other members of his party, the other party leaders gladly tolerated the expression of his views. On countless occasions in 1919 and 1920 Kunschak demanded that the Jewish refugees either be deported or, if that proved impossible, placed in concentration camps. To the objection that such imprisonment would be impossibly expensive, Kunschak replied that the taxpayers would willingly pay the cost. In a debate in the Vienna provincial assembly (Landtag) in January 1921 Kunschak demanded that the Jewish refugees be expelled because they were profiteers and because they were a threat to law and order. The Socialist mayor, Jakob Reumann, responded that he was opposed to all profiteers, not just those who were Jewish. The Zionist councilman, Dr. Leopold Plaschkes, added that in the name of culture, humanity, and the honor of the city of Vienna the expulsion of Jewish refugees could not be carried out.[43]

Even Kunschak moderated his tone after his Christian Social Party assumed the leading role in the federal government in 1920. He now argued that the expulsion of the Ostjuden was not the responsibility of the federal government but of the Socialist mayor of Vienna. The federal chancellor and the minister of interior, both also members of the Christian Social Party, maintained that an energetic deportation of the Ostjuden would cause great international difficulties, especially with the Poles, and have the worst possible consequences for Austria.[44]

THE OPTION QUESTION

To many Austrian anti-Semites the most promising way to expel the unwanted Eastern Jews appeared to lie in article 80 of the Treaty of St. Germain, which stipulated that "persons who live in a former territory of the Austro-Hungarian Monarchy and are differentiated there from the majority of the local population by race and language may within six months of the enforcement of the state treaty of St. Germain-en-Laye, that is, including 15 January 1921, opt for Austrian citizenship if they according to their race and speech, belong to the German majority of the people of Austria."[45]

When the Treaty of St. Germain began to be enforced in August 1920, the Austrian government at first considered German-speaking Jews who sought Austrian citizenship to be "Germans" because Jews had not been regarded as a distinct race or nationality in the Dual Monarchy. To prove one's nationality it was only necessary to show one's conscription or demobilization papers, workbook, or marriage certificate. Some lower-level officials, however, would accept only proof of having had a German-language education. Anti-Semites like Kunschak claimed that Ostjuden forged documents to make false claims about having attended a German school.[46]

Anti-Semites appeared to have won a great victory when an Austrian administrative court ruled on 9 June 1921 that the word *race* could be interpreted in a völkisch or biological sense rather than as nationality in a cultural sense. Thereafter the minister of the interior and member of the Greater German People's Party, Dr. Leopold Waber, began to reject citizenship petitions even from Jews who had been born in Vienna or some other German-speaking city. This new policy meant that sometimes members of the same family were treated as belonging to different "races."[47]

Domestic and foreign pressure eventually forced Waber and the Austrian government as a whole to retreat from their anti-Jewish position on the option question. As early as March 1921 the Council of the League of Nations, with British Foreign Secretary Lord Arthur Balfour leading the discussions with the Austrian government, decided it was permissible for Austria to expel foreigners. However, this concession was hedged with so many exceptions—old and sick people, those whose towns were destroyed in the war and were not yet rebuilt, people who had been working for a long time on projects for the common good, and certain categories of students—that the *Deutschösterreichische Tages-Zeitung*, at the time an organ of the Greater German People's Party, complained that the league's decision would make the expulsion of Ostjuden a legal impossibility.[48]

In August 1921 the Union of German-Austrian Jews made an urgent appeal to the Viennese representatives of the signatory powers of the Treaty of St. Germain to request their governments to give an authoritative interpretation of article 80. At the same time the union urged its friends in London, Paris, and Rome to support this step through direct representations at their foreign ministries.[49] Pressure on the Austrian government to change its policy on the option question also came from international Jewish organizations. Armed with information provided him by the Union of German-Austrian Jews, Lucien Wolf, the general secretary of the Joint Foreign Committee of the Jewish Board of Deputies in London, together with the Alliance Israelite Universelle in Paris, remonstrated in September 1921 to the league about the Austrian government's interpretation of article 80. When the league secretariat asked the Austrian government for its response, Minister of Interior Waber replied disingenuously that the condition of "the Jews in Austria was, as is well known, favorable both economically and socially and that the treatment of the 190,000 people seeking citizenship was being handled in a liberal spirit." [50]

The option question was finally laid to rest in April 1922 when an Austrian administrative court repealed an earlier decision by saying that the usual legal definition of race in Austria was merely "nationality" and not a biological or cultural community as interpreted by the Ministry of the Interior. Thereafter, Austrian anti-Semites were deprived of any legal grounds for protesting the naturalization of Ostjuden and the issue finally faded away as it did in Germany about the same time. [51] The demagogic nature of the whole debate over the option question is revealed in the fact that, even with the favorable interpretation (from the Jewish point of view) of article 80, only 20,360 Jews opted to become Austrian citizens between 1920 and 1925, or less than one-ninth the number claimed by Leopold Waber in his reply to the League of Nations.

7

ACADEMIC
ANTI-SEMITISM IN
THE EARLY POSTWAR
YEARS

JEWISH ENROLLMENT AT AUSTRIAN UNIVERSITIES
AND MIDDLE SCHOOLS

One important area in which Ostjuden caused real and not just imaginary overcrowding, albeit only temporarily, was in Vienna's institutions of higher learning or Hochschulen, especially at the University of Vienna and at the College for International Trade (Hochschule für Welthandel). A high percentage of Eastern European Jews had attended Austrian universities even before the outbreak of the First World War. For example, during the summer semester of 1913, 24 percent of the medical students at the University of Vienna were from Galicia and Bukovina, of whom the majority was Jewish. The same was true of 16 percent of the law students and 12 percent of the arts and sciences students.[1] Jews from all geographic locations made up over 27 percent of the total enrollment at the University of Vienna during the last five semesters preceding the assassination at Sarajevo.[2]

The high proportion of Jewish students, even though it had been declining since the 1880s, produced a keen competition for jobs and helped create an academic anti-Semitism that was even worse than in Germany. But like Germany no other group in Austria was so racially, passionately, and violently anti-Semitic as students of university age. Jewish students were frequently attacked and anti-Semitism was so common that it was almost taken for granted.[3] This anti-Semitism was tolerated both by sympathetic administrators and, until the 1930s, by the tradition of academic freedom or autonomy, dating back to the Middle Ages, which allowed Central European universities to police themselves.[4]

During the early part of the First World War both the percentage and the absolute number of Ostjuden in Viennese Hochschulen rose rapidly, reaching a peak in 1917–18 when 46 percent of all the students were Jewish—exactly half of the 92 percent claimed by one postwar anti-Semitic pamphlet. It was still slightly over 42 percent in 1920–21, but thereafter the percentage rapidly declined so that by 1925–26 it was below 25 percent.[5]

Anti-Semites claimed that the high percentage of Ostjuden in Vienna's colleges and institutes during the war was the result of the Jews' desire to evade military service. The reality was considerably more mundane. The overall enrollment at the University of Vienna dropped precipitously from a prewar high of 10,424 students just before the outbreak of the war to 3,942 during the summer semester of 1916 and to just 2,500 a year later. With most of the male students now in the Austro-Hungarian armed forces the percentage of the female students rose dramatically, from 7 percent in early 1914 to 36 percent in 1917–18. Nearly all of these coeds were Jewish: most westernized Jews encouraged higher education for women whereas pan-Germans regarded such education as undesirable at best. The upsurge of Jewish enrollment also resulted from the Russian invasion of the monarchy's northeastern provinces in the fall of 1914, which forced the closing of several universities that had large numbers of Jewish students. Many of these students, especially young women, then transferred to schools in militarily secure Vienna.[6]

An attempt was made already during the war to place a limit on the number of Galician students. The student fraternities, in fact, wanted to have a numerus clausus for all Jewish students, not just Ostjuden.[7] The issue of the Galician students became more critical again just after the war when the virtual exclusion of Jews from numerous Eastern European universities, particularly in Poland, caused many Jewish students to seek entry into the somewhat less anti-Semitic universities of Central Europe. Unfortunately, this new wave of students coincided with the return of Austrian war veterans to create a shortage of space and an increase in anti-Jewish sentiments.[8]

The students, often the offspring of government officials, military officers, and small businessmen, were the people who were most likely to feel declassed by the military defeat and the breakup of the Austro-Hungarian empire. Their prospects were bleak at best in the shrunken territory of the Austrian republic with its huge surplus of civil servants and soldiers. This situation was greatly aggravated by Austria having by far the highest percentage of students in all of Europe. As late as 1933 there were still 38.3 students per 10,000 population in Austria or almost twice as many as that of the next country, France, which had only 20.9.[9]

The oversupply of students and the undersupply of jobs only worsened in 1922 when in the so-called Geneva Protocols the British, French, Italian, and Czechoslovakian governments insisted that the Austrian government enact an austerity program that resulted in the dismissal of thousands of civil servants as the quid pro quo for a guaranteed twenty-year loan equal to $126 million.[10] The hopes students harbored of moving into the free professions—medicine, law, journalism, and the arts—also appeared slim to nonexistent because they were already dominated in Vienna by Jews.

The shortage of space at Vienna's colleges and institutes in the early post-war years was very real although far from being exclusively the result of the enrollment of foreign Jews. In March 1919 the *Arbeiter-Zeitung* described the facilities at the University of Vienna as being "obviously overcrowded." In one of the anatomy institutes there were 1,308 students in an area designed to accommodate 360 to 400 students. At the Institute for Medical Chemistry 1,286 students were trying to make do with space intended for 464 students. The Surgical Clinic had 557 students working where there should have been only 120 to 150 trainees. At the Ear Clinic there were 232 students instead of 50, and so on.[11]

The lack of space combined with the student and professorial anti-Semitism persuaded authorities at the University of Vienna and the Agricultural College to cap enrollment in 1919. Preference was given to native applicants, thus in effect discriminating against Jews who constituted the majority of the foreign students. Even so, two years later there were still 4,000 foreign students among the 10,851 students at the University of Vienna. These foreign students, however, paid a higher tuition than natives, were not eligible for any public welfare, and through their purchases contributed in a minor way to improving the economy of Vienna.[12]

The high percentage of Jews at Austrian and especially Viennese institutions of higher learning was not caused solely by a large number of foreign Jews. A basic cause, of course, was the venerable and well-known Jewish love of and respect for education and scholarship, especially in medicine and the law. These two professions were also attractive to Jews because they could be self-employed and not dependent on employment by Christians. The medical and teaching professions were especially advantageous because they could be practiced anywhere in the world if anti-Semitism became too extreme. Jewish parents evidently also realized more than most Christians the importance of an education. Certainly, poor Jewish immigrants were far more likely to send their children to Vienna's elite *Gymnasien*—the prerequisite for entry into universities—than was true of gentiles from comparable social positions.

Even more important, however, was the relatively high percentage of Jews who belonged to the Austrian middle class, the class that was by far the most academically inclined in Europe.[13]

Jews, especially Jewish girls, were also found in disproportionately large numbers in Austria's middle schools. Between 1851 and 1903 the number of Christian pupils in these schools in the whole Austrian half of the Dual Monarchy increased from 21,213 to just under 100,000. Jewish attendance, however, increased from 1,251 to nearly 16,000 in the same period or three times as quickly as the Christian rate. After 1896, however, the percentage of Jewish pupils began to decline although their absolute numbers continued to increase slowly.[14] As for Vienna, the percentage of Jews in middle schools of all types stabilized at 28.8 percent already in 1885 and thereafter declined slightly to 27.6 percent in 1912. The same was true at the more prestigious classics-oriented Gymnasien where Jewish enrollment was 30.9 percent in 1885, reached 35 percent in 1913, and attained an all-time high of just under 37 percent in 1923, making Jews three times more likely to attend these schools than Christians. Thereafter the absolute number of Jewish pupils steadily decreased while the total number of pupils gradually increased.[15] Such figures, however, did not prevent anti-Semites from claiming that a fantastic 65 to 70 percent of all middle school students were Jewish in the mid-1920s.[16]

Although anti-Semites loved to cite enrollment statistics for middle schools as proof that the Jews were "taking over" the city's elite positions, Jewish and gentile students themselves in primary and middle schools appear, for the most part, to have socialized well with each other, in sharp contrast to Vienna's Hochschulen. Numerous memoirs by former Viennese Jews, as well as interviews conducted by the present author, have confirmed this fact. George Clare remembers some mutual exchanges of insults, but on the whole the children "played and worked happily enough together, Jews and Christians, and whenever there was, thanks to Lehrer Schneider's temporary absence, an opportunity of creating havoc in class, the little Jewish and Catholic devils formed a firmly united front."[17]

THE DEUTSCHE STUDENTENSCHAFT AND DEMANDS
FOR A NUMERUS CLAUSUS

Anti-Semitism itself, of course, was nothing new in Austrian universities after the war. What was new, however, was the cooperation between two former foes, völkisch and Catholic students. In February 1919 traditional völkisch organizations founded the Deutsche Burschenbund (German Fraternity League), which, in its initial assembly, saw as its "first duty the execution of the fight of the German people in Austria and chiefly against Jewry." The Burschenbund formed an alliance with Catholic students, with whom pan-German students had fought before the war—an alliance that lasted until 1933 and was based largely on anti-Semitism and partly on a common dislike of Marxism and democracy.[18]

The same was true of the Deutsche Studentenschaft (German Student Organization), which was also founded in 1919. The Studentenschaft, which included students from Germany, Czechoslovakia, and Danzig as well as Austria, declared in a leaflet published in 1927 that "belonging to one people will no longer be given mere lip service. . . . The intellectual liberation from racially alien assaults" would be the greatest cultural accomplishment since the world war.[19] Consisting at first largely of recently returned veterans from the front, it eventually grew to include the vast majority of students. Professors at colleges and universities in Vienna, Graz, and Leoben (in Upper Styria) were also allied with it.[20]

Academic authorities granted the Deutsche Studentenschaft official recognition and financial support, and provided it with space for its meetings. It did the same for numerous other racist and nationalistic organizations that sprang up in Austria in the 1920s, such as the Institute for the Cultivation of German Consciousness, founded in 1924. Ardently promoted by Robert Körber, the leader of the Deutsche Studentenschaft at the College for International Trade, it sponsored sixty-seven lectures during its three-year existence, twenty-four of them by university professors. The most common theme of the lectures was the "scientific" treatment of the "Jewish question"; other topics included attacks on liberalism, democracy, the Weimar constitution, and modernity.[21]

One of the Deutsche Studentenschaft's principal demands was the enactment of a numerus clausus in all of Austria's Hochschulen. For example, if the Jews of Vienna made up only 10.8 percent of the city's total population they should comprise no more than 10.8 percent of the students and professors in the city's institutions of higher education. Interestingly enough, when the Studentenschaft and other racist organizations wanted to limit Jewish "influence" to their proportion of the total population of Vienna or Austria, they used statistics based on religion, not their own inflated statistics based on "race," which, if utilized, hardly would have reduced the number of Jewish students and professors at all.

The Deutsche Studentenschaft was far from being the only organization that called for limited enrollment of Jewish students. Similar policies, which flouted the minority treaties, had been adopted in Hungary, Poland, and the Baltic states during the 1920s. Austrians were also well aware that private American universities on the East Coast including Harvard, Yale, and Princeton informally restricted Jewish enrollment starting between 1919 and 1923 and lasting into the mid-1940s. For example, Harvard's freshman class which was 27.6 percent Jewish in 1925 was only 15 percent (or less) Jewish a few years later.[22]

Within Austria a numerus clausus for students and professors at Austrian Hochschulen as well as for public and professional jobs was probably the most common demand made by anti-Semites of all types both before and after the First World War. During the war an attempt was made by the völkisch fraternities to limit the number of Jews and other minorities in Vienna's colleges and institutes to their percentage in the census of 1910 for the whole of Austria. The demand, which was directed primarily against Jews from Galicia and Bukovina, was expanded after the war by the Burschenbund as well as the Deutsche Studentenschaft and various Catholic student organizations to include Jews of all kinds.[23]

These demands became more strident in 1922, the same year in which tuition at Austria's universities rose sharply. Hostility between German nationalist and Jewish students increased rapidly in the fall over a dispute at the College of International Trade. In the summer the European Student Relief, an American charity that for three years had provided needy European students with clothing, shoes, and books, announced the cessation of its activities, but encouraged Austrian students to form a committee to continue the work on their own. Attempts by German nationalist students to control the distribution of the funds led to an exchange of insults between them and Jewish students and ultimately to a demand by the Deutsche Studentenschaft to the rector of the University of Vienna, Karl Diener, that he implement a numerus clausus.[24]

Angered by the recent election of a Jew, Professor Samuel Steinherz, as rector of the German University of Prague, the Deutsche Studentenschaft further demanded that no Jew ever be elected rector, dean, or any other academic officer. The memorandum furthermore demanded that the number of Jewish students and professors in Vienna be limited to 10 percent. Diener, who blamed the recent controversy at the College of International Trade on Jewish students, agreed that only Germans should occupy posts of honor at the University of Vienna, but doubted whether a Jew could be elected in any case at that time. As for students, those with Austrian citizenship could not be denied entry on religious or racial grounds, but students from Poland, Rumania, and

Russia (who were likely to be Jews) could be restricted. He went on to declare that "the large number of Eastern European students at the University represents a downright shocking invasion of racially and organically alien elements, whose culture, upbringing, and morals are far below every native German student; therein lies the true cancerous damage to our academic conditions. The reduction of the Eastern Jews must today take a leading place in the program of every rector and senate of a German Hochschule. The progressive orientalization of Vienna must at least be stopped at the Hochschulen."[25]

No restrictions were ever placed on Jewish enrollments at the University of Vienna, perhaps because of promises made by Chancellor Ignaz Seipel in response to protests made by the Israelitische Kultusgemeinde that the demands made by the Deutsche Studentenschaft would violate the Austrian constitution.[26] But the idea of a numerus clausus never disappeared from the Austrian academic scene, at least for foreign Jews. Such an idea was raised in January 1923 at a meeting of university students attended not only by nationalist students but by many professors as well and was under the honorary chairmanship of Rector Diener.[27]

Finally, in March 1923, the "College of Professors" at the Technical College (Technische Hochschule) in Vienna, where the Jewish enrollment was over 41 percent, unanimously approved of a numerus clausus regulation stipulating that Jewish students from foreign countries could enroll in a particular discipline only if the number of Jewish students already enrolled, both foreign and native, was no more than 10 percent of the total. Although this policy did not violate the Austrian constitution, it marked the first time since the final emancipation of Austrian Jews in the nineteenth century that a distinction was drawn at an Austrian Hochschule between Jews and non-Jews, a distinction that had nothing to do with scholarship or ability.[28]

Somewhat surprisingly, the College of Professors at the Agricultural College in Vienna moved in the opposite direction as their colleagues at the Technical College. In October 1924 and March 1925 they removed the restrictions on the enrollment of foreign Jews that had existed since 1919 by declaring "that a rejection in principle of the acceptance of foreign Jews as students at the College of Agriculture is uncalled for." Jewish enrollment, however, was hardly a pressing issue at the college where there was a grand total of only thirteen Jewish students, or 1.61 percent of all those enrolled![29]

ANTI-SEMITIC VIOLENCE AT AUSTRIAN UNIVERSITIES

Student anti-Semites did not content themselves with mere verbal abuse in interwar Austria. Organized beatings of Jewish students, which had been rare before the First World War, became commonplace during the First Republic. This was especially true during the early postwar years when war veterans, accustomed to violence, confronted the large Jewish minority. Ironically, some of the brawling may have been a product of the Waidhofner Principle forbidding members of the Burschenschaften from dueling with Jews. Unwilling meekly to tolerate insults, members of Kadimah and other Jewish fraternities would slap the face of any non-Jewish student who tried to invoke the Waidhofner Principle, thereby often setting off fights and melees between Jews and anti-Semitic students. Such fights were particularly common at beer and wine gardens and at sporting events.[30]

In April 1920 between five hundred and one thousand German nationalist students from the Technical College assaulted twenty Zionist students at the dining hall for poor Jewish students and drove the other students out. Some Jews were even forced to show that they had been circumcised, a favorite tactic of Nazis a few years later.

Later in the same day some nationalist students marched on the Anatomy Institute of Dr. Julius Tandler, one of many such episodes directed against the world famous scholar. Tandler's institute became something of a focal point for student anti-Semitic demonstrations during the 1920s even though Tandler had converted to Roman Catholicism in 1899 and even though the professor himself did not scruple to bait Eastern European Jewish students during examinations. Nevertheless, Tandler's institute attracted mostly Jewish and Socialist students because in addition to his Jewish origins he was a major reformer of Vienna's welfare institutions for children, young people, the aged, and the poor in Vienna's Socialist administration. Meanwhile, a second anatomy institute headed by Professor Ferdinand Hochstetter became a magnate for völkisch-nationalist students.[31]

On the day following the invasion of Tandler's institute, anti-Semitic students demolished a dining room that had been established a short time before by the American Joint Distribution Committee, a New York consortium of Jewish welfare organizations. Finally, the next day they occupied the main entrance to the University of Vienna in order to prevent Jewish students from entering the building.[32]

The attacks provoked a raucous debate in the National Assembly (Nationalversammlung as the Parliament in the Republic of Austria was called). Leopold

Kunschak, while conceding that nothing was possible without law and order, was loudly applauded when he said that the "demonstrations" by Christian students were an expression of legitimate grievances and long-held resentments. The students believed that they had been abandoned by the government. Christian students were especially upset by civil service offices allegedly hiring Jews when they were not supposed to hire anyone. Kunschak went on to say that since the beginning of the republic many people thought they had to curtsy to Jews three times so they wouldn't be accused of snubbing them. Kunschak begged the students not to repeat the violence, but added that it was up to the government to remove the causes of the students' grievances. A member of the Greater German People's Party, Dr. Josef Ursin, told the Parliament that the demonstrations at the university were simply intended to protest the predominance of Jews at Austrian Hochschulen. Jews could count on Christian support if they wished to emigrate to Palestine.[33]

Anti-Semitic violence at Vienna's colleges quieted down in 1921 and 1922, but revived again in 1923. However, the introduction of enrollment restrictions at the Technical College in early March 1923 inspired members of the Deutsche Studentenschaft to demonstrate the "German character" of the University of Vienna, the Technical College, and the College of Veterinary Medicine by using sticks and hard rubber clubs to prevent Jews from entering the main buildings of these institutions and by spreading false rumors about Jews forcibly driving Aryan students out of the University of Vienna.[34]

These events were but a prelude, however, to a pitched battle which took place at the University of Vienna in the fall of 1923. On 19 November, Nazi students from the Technical College, reacting to an order by academic authorities forbidding the wearing of student colors and other insignia and requiring them to carry student identification, invaded the lecture hall of Professor Tandler's Anatomy Institute, and shouting "Juden hinaus," gave Jews just three minutes to vacate the room. The next day, fifty Nazis from the College of Agriculture carried out a similar action at the College for International Trade. After storming into the lecture hall of Professor Siegmund Grünberg, they demanded, "in the name of the Deutsche Studentenschaft," the removal of all Jewish students from the classroom and the implementation of a numerus clausus. Those who did not leave within three minutes and who, in the words of the *Reichspost* "acted provocatively toward the Aryans," were beaten with rubber clubs and sticks, dragged to the top of the ramp in front of the main building of the University of Vienna, and thrown off. The police, standing only a few feet away, did nothing because of "academic freedom." The rector's response was to close the university.[35]

After the violence subsided, the University of Vienna chapter of the Deutsche Studentenschaft issued a statement rejecting all responsibility for the recent events and blaming them on the academic authorities who had allegedly failed to keep their promise to maintain the German character of the university. For example, a Jew, Professor Fischl, had been appointed dean of the Medical College. The demand of the Deutsche Studentenschaft for the reduction of students from Eastern Europe had also not been fulfilled. Moreover, no chair of racial-oriented "Germanic Studies" had been created and Aryan students were forced to hear lectures about German economics from an alien (Jewish) professor. These circumstances led to the enormous agitation of the German students and made it possible to understand the reasons behind the recent events. Therefore, the Deutsche Studentenschaft could not guarantee the restoration of peace and order.[36]

The violence at the several Viennese Hochschulen was so extreme that for once it drew criticism from people who normally would have excused or at least ignored it. One professor by the name of Othenio Abel, who was well known for his German nationalist views, told Professor Grünberg, in the presence of a group of students, that the disruption of his lecture by Nazi students was "loutishness."[37] Even the *Reichspost* had to admit that every thinking person had to condemn the acts of violence. The student riot "was not only a great wrong, but also a great stupidity" because it gave the enemies of Christian German culture a strong argument for ending the autonomy of the university and weakened the forces of those people who wanted to support Christian and German culture. The University of Vienna was supposed to be a place of intellectual competition, not violence. Students who defied academic authorities courted disaster when they made demands that could not possibly be fulfilled. Jewry would cease to be dangerous only through the spread of German education. Positive work was more powerful and lasting than destruction.[38]

The *Arbeiter-Zeitung* was even less equivocal in its condemnation of the riot calling it a "scandal." The Nazi terror had to be stopped at any cost. The violence had gone beyond anything that had taken place in any other country, including Germany, because it had disrupted research and teaching. If workers had committed the same acts, the police would have attacked them with sabers.[39] *Die Wahrheit*, speaking for assimilated Jews, called the violence "purely criminal in the legal sense." Nazi students who acted like criminals ought to be treated like criminals.[40]

Vienna was not the only site of student academic anti-Semitism. The violence at Vienna's colleges and institutes in November 1923 was repeated at the same time at the University of Graz. Anti-Semitism was also very strong in the Tyrol even though only a few hundred Jews lived there. A particularly notorious event at the University of Innsbruck occurred in February 1920 when Karl Kraus was supposed to give two recitals from his recent play, *The Last Days of Mankind*. The second recital never took place, however, because of a student-led protest when Kraus read passages ridiculing Kaiser Wilhelm and the German generals. Students at the University of Innsbruck went so far as to condemn one Professor Alfred Kastil merely for applauding Kraus's readings. Shortly after the aborted recital, students at the University of Innsbruck demanded that the school's Academic Senate restrict the appointment of administrators to people of German descent and mother tongue and that a numerus clausus of 5 percent be applied to professorial appointments and the admission of Jewish students—demands that the Senate of course could not implement because of their unconstitutionality. It did, however, recommend to the rector that foreign Jewish students, especially Ostjuden, not be allowed to matriculate.[41]

THE INFLUENCE OF AUSTRIAN ACADEMIC ANTI-SEMITISM ON GERMANY

The impact of increased academic anti-Semitism in Austria during the early postwar years was not confined to Austrian Jews. Student anti-Semites worked hard and enjoyed considerable success at persuading their fellow students in Germany to accept their more radical and racial views.

As noted in Chapter 3, the development had already begun in the late 1870s when fraternities in Austrian universities began excluding Jews, including those who had been baptized, at a time when even nationalistic German fraternities accepted new members without regard to their ancestry, political affiliation, or faith.[42] The situation began to change after the First World War as German universities became increasingly infected with radical forms of anti-Semitism. Nevertheless, at a general assembly in 1919 Austrian representatives found it almost unbelievable that fraternity chapters in northern Germany, for example at Frankonia-Bonn, still insisted that new members ought to be accepted on the basis of their ability and character traits and not on the basis of the beliefs of their ancestors. The assembly finally decided merely to *recommend* to its individual chapters that Jewish members not be accepted.

Not satisfied, the Burschenschaft Frankonia-Graz persuaded a working committee of the all-German Deutsche Burschenschaft to approve a change in the organization's principles to state that it "supports the racial standpoint; only

German students of Aryan descent who openly acknowledge Germandom, will be accepted into the German Burschenschaft."[43] However, it was still left to individual chapters to determine who had Jewish blood. Moreover, the organization rejected an Austrian motion that the fraternities expel all past and current members who were Jewish or of Jewish origins.[44]

Austrian students were also only partially successful at spreading the Waidhofner Principle to Germany after the war. In 1920 the Austrian Burschenschaften tried to persuade the international organization to forbid all members from giving satisfaction to any Jew or person of Jewish origins. Instead, the Deutsche Burschenschaft merely agreed to the almost meaningless statement that local chapters could forbid such duels if their members unanimously approved.[45]

This pattern of Austrian anti-Semitism playing an influential role within private all-German organizations can also be seen in the Deutsche Studentenschaft. Its members from the former Habsburg territories in Austria and Czechoslovakia soon pushed for the exclusion of Jews from the entire international organization. However, because the German constitution forbade such blatant discrimination, only in Austria and the Sudetenland was membership in the Studentenschaft limited to members of "German descent and mother tongue."[46]

THE DECLINE OF ANTI-SEMITISM IN 1924

The student Krawalle (brawls) in November 1923 could be considered the climax of the early postwar period in Austria so far as anti-Semitism was concerned. Although there were Christian-Jewish confrontations in 1924–25, only occasionally were they accompanied by acts of violence. A major cause of the diminution was almost certainly the declining overall enrollment at Austrian Hochschulen, and particularly the decline in Jewish enrollment. For example, total enrollment at the University of Vienna declined from roughly 10,800 in 1920–21, of which over 42 percent was Jewish, to 8,088 in 1925–26, less than 25 percent of which was Jewish. At the Technical College, always a hotbed of anti-Semitism, enrollment declined even more sharply, from 3,460 in 1920–21 to just 2,279 only three years later, although the percentage of Jewish enrollment remained high at around 41 percent in 1923–24. Perhaps even more important than these raw numbers was the graduation of most of the militant veterans of the world war by 1924.[47]

At the very time when far fewer graduates were coming out of Austrian universities, there were considerably more jobs waiting for them, thus substantially reducing economic competition between Jews and gentiles. The year 1924 saw a marked improvement in the economy of Austria as well as of Germany thanks in part to the United States. As noted previously, the United States had already played a role in lessening anti-Semitism in the early postwar years through its diplomatic protests. On the more positive side, its food shipments and medicine supplied by the American Relief Administration headed by the future president, Herbert Hoover, went a long way to reducing the physical suffering that to a large extent was the root cause of anti-Semitism between about 1918 and 1923. Domestically, the chancellorship of the relatively moderate Ignaz Seipel from 1922 to 1924 and 1926 to 1929 along with the $126 million loan from the League of Nations, and the introduction in 1924 of a new and far more stable currency, the Austrian schilling, were all important in reviving the Austrian economy. And just as anti-Semitism in Germany tended to decline with an improving economy so too did it in Austria. The main office of the World Zionist movement may also have had something to do with the lessening of anti-Semitism at Austrian universities. We know that in December 1922 the Zionist State Committee for Austria appealed to the executive office of the organization in London to use its political connections to put pressure on the Austrian government to stop the anti-Semitic excesses at Austrian universities by threatening to stop efforts to restore the Austrian economy. However, we do not know what concrete measures, if any, resulted from this appeal.[48]

With brief interruptions Austrian anti-Semitism in general remained dormant, but certainly not dead, until a new economic crisis struck the Alpine republic in 1929. By the end of 1926, *Der eiserne Besen*, undoubtedly Austria's most viciously anti-Semitic newspaper at the time, admitted that it had not been easy to be an anti-Semite that year. Many had dropped out of the struggle and the German people of Austria were divided into several antagonistic camps.[49]

ASSASSINATION AND INTIMIDATION

Although the higher educational institutions of Austria and particularly Vienna remained the focal point of anti-Semitic violence through the entire period of interwar Austria, they did not have a monopoly on the phenomenon. Never was this more true than in 1925 when two major but unrelated anti-Semitic events occurred: the murder in March of Hugo Bettauer, a popular novelist of Jewish origins; and massive demonstrations organized against the XIVth World Zionist Congress, which was held in Vienna in August.

THE ASSASSINATION OF HUGO BETTAUER

Although Hugo Bettauer is almost entirely forgotten today, except by scholars of modern Austrian literature, he was enormously popular during the first half of the 1920s; his many novels sold by the hundreds of thousands. Born in 1872, he converted to the Protestant faith in 1890, an act that later made not the slightest impression on his anti-Semitic enemies. In the 1890s he lived in the United States just long enough to lose his entire inheritance through a bad investment. After returning to Europe in 1899 he became the editor of the *Berliner Morgenpost*, but was expelled from Prussia in 1901 as an undesirable alien after attacking purported police corruption. In 1904 Bettauer returned to the United States, working for several German-language newspapers in New York and writing installment novels about German and Austrian immigrants. In 1908 he returned to Vienna and began to publish novels on topical themes, many of which became motion pictures. Bettauer scandalized conservative Austrians and provided ammunition for anti-Semites by coediting in 1921 a journal called *Er und Sie*, which was devoted to sexual questions along with the rights of women and homosexuals.[1]

Bettauer is best known for his satiric and prophetic novel, *Die Stadt ohne*

Juden: Ein Roman von Übermorgen (*The City without Jews: A Novel about the Day after Tomorrow*), one of five books he wrote in 1922. Bettauer was far from being the only Austrian novelist to write about anti-Semitism in the 1920s— it was perhaps the theme of the decade in Austrian literature—nor was he even the first writer to fantasize about a judenrein Vienna. *The City without Jews*, which sold over 250,000 copies including many in translation, tells how a Christian Social politician, named Dr. Karl Schwertfeger—modeled after mayor Karl Lueger—is brought to power after an election in which he promises to expel all Jews from Austria because of their "domination." Although Jews are permitted to sell their homes and businesses and take cash out of the country with them, the financial provisions of the law are designed to take advantage of them. Those who remain underground in Austria are to be punished with death. When the last of the Viennese Jews are hauled away on thirty huge trains using all available rolling stock and locomotives borrowed from neighboring countries, the remaining million Viennese celebrate. Food is cheaper and housing is plentiful. However, it is not long before disillusionment sets in. The city's remaining newspapers are colorless, and the unemployment rate rises. Without Jewish patronage, the opera house closes and the theaters stagnate as do the art salons, the publishing houses, and the libraries. Without Jewish physicians and lawyers the hospitals and law courts become hopelessly congested. Vienna degenerates into a provincial city culturally and economically.[2]

Although *The City without Jews* was probably the most powerful attack made on anti-Semitism during the First Austrian Republic, it was far from being uncritically philosemitic; nor was it uniformly well received by Austrian Jews. Bettauer used the same stereotypes of Jews as did anti-Semites, although his purpose was to encourage mutual tolerance. He mentioned tensions between old Viennese Jewish families and recent immigrants from Eastern Europe. The sole Zionist member of Parliament in the novel votes in favor of the expulsion because it furthers Zionist goals. And although the book was remarkably prophetic in many respects, in one area it was anything but accurate. In the novel the "Aryan" Viennese realize that they cannot do without Jewish business expertise, money, style, taste, and cosmopolitanism. Chancellor Schwertfeger, seeing his mistake, invites back all those Jews who had settled in the city before 1914. No such invitation was made after 1945 following the real-life deportation of Austrian Jews.[3]

By 1925 Bettauer had become a highly controversial figure, even within the Jewish community being both extremely popular and hated. Whereas his supporters considered him to be an apostle of a new morality and a servant of enlightenment, his detractors in the Christian Social Party, the Greater German People's Party, and the Nazi Party considered him to be a "Red poet," a "shameless corrupter of youth," and the embodiment of pornography and all that was evil. The Nazis later referred to him as "the father of the erotic revolution." During his lifetime his writings were denounced by dozens of women's organizations for their alleged "filth." Even the *Wiener Morgenzeitung* described his work as "pornographic." Attacks made on Bettauer by Anton Orel, a Christian Social member of the Vienna City Council and the editor of a weekly newspaper called *Volkssturm*, were so extreme that the *Reichspost*, certainly no fan of Bettauer, felt compelled to censor them. Even the normally liberal *Neue Freie Presse* said that the public needed to be protected against Bettauer, who appealed to the instincts of the half educated and half grown.[4]

Bettauer's notoriety reached a climax in September 1924 when he was charged with sixteen counts of harming "public morality." After three hours of deliberation the jury acquitted the accused of all sixteen counts, usually by a vote of nine to three. Even Bettauer's friends had not expected such a favorable outcome. Instead of ending the controversy surrounding the author, however, the verdict merely added to it, while at the same time it encouraged radicalism and sharpened the political atmosphere.[5]

Meanwhile, since the middle of 1924, Kaspar Hellering, a Sudeten-born gymnastics and mathematics middle-school teacher in Vienna and member of the Austrian Nazi Party, began writing a series of articles, pamphlets, and poems in various völkisch newspapers and magazines in which he openly called for "radical self-help" and "lynch justice against all polluters of our people."[6]

Hellering's plea was heard by an unemployed twenty-year-old man with a Sudeten German father and a Czech mother named Otto Rothstock. On the morning of 10 March 1925 Rothstock walked into Bettauer's office and shot him several times; Bettauer died of his wounds two weeks later. Newspaper reaction to the shooting was just as mixed as the reviews of his writings had been. The *Neue Freie Presse*, *Neues Wiener Tagblatt*, *Volkszeitung*, and *Deutsch-österreichische Tages-Zeitung* all ascribed it to popular moral indignation. The *Tag*, *Neues Wiener Journal*, and the Communist *Rote Fahne* all condemned the act. The *Arbeiter-Zeitung* held leaders of the Christian Social Party indirectly responsible for the shooting because they had polemicized so much against Bettauer. The *Wiener Morgenzeitung*, certainly no friend of Bettauer's, said the murder was not directed against Bettauer alone, but against every intellectual who wrote on behalf of a cause.[7]

Neither the investigation of the crime nor the trial of the killer showed the

Austrian republic at its best. In fewer than forty-eight hours the police declared that there were no grounds for believing that there was a conspiracy, even though they had not yet collected all the evidence. The public prosecutor actually suppressed important documents, including one that proved that Rothstock had been a member of the Nazi Party since 1920. Nor did the police check out Rothstock's connections with the Nazi Party, despite a report that the murderer had been seen wearing a Hitler shirt and carrying a Nazi flag at a Nazi demonstration just two days before the assassination. The uncertain origin of the murder weapon was never investigated, and Hellering's possible connections to the murder were ignored.[8]

The Bettauer murder trial turned out to be one of the most politicized events in interwar Austria. Anti-Semites and other right-wing extremists saw it as an opportunity for reversing the results of Bettauer's pornography trial of the previous year by putting Bettauer rather than the murderer on trial. They were enormously aided in this endeavor by the judge and the prosecuting attorney, who were both völkisch.[9] Rothstock, who was defended by the former leader of the Austrian Nazi Party, Dr. Walter Riehl, admitted that he had belonged to the Nazi Party until December 1924 but had resigned his membership in order to avoid implicating the party in his planned assassination. He testified that he knew what he was doing when he shot Bettauer, and had done it because he wanted to "drive Bettauer out of this world and into another one in order to protect his people and cohorts." Christ, he said, had come to earth to lead the fight against Jewish writers and scholars; he, Rothstock, was merely continuing that work and fulfilling a prophecy. He had a right to shoot Bettauer because he was a good Christian and had the blessing of God. Riehl therefore described Rothstock's deed as "gallant" and claimed that he had acted out of religious, not political motives.[10]

The sensational trial resulted in the jury voting twelve to nothing that Rothstock had murdered Bettauer, but the vote was evenly divided as to whether Rothstock was insane at the time of the murder. Rothstock's only punishment, therefore, was to spend two and a half years in mental hospitals from which he was released at the end of 1927. Even such a ridiculously light sentence was enough to make Rothstock a "martyr for the German people" in the opinion of the Nazi *Deutsche Arbeiter-Presse*. Rothstock rejoined the Austrian Nazi Party in 1932, but was expelled in January 1933 after criticizing the Gauleiter of Vienna, Alfred Frauenfeld. However he joined the SS Standarte 11 in time to take part in the Nazi *Putsch* of July 1934, which resulted in the death of Chancellor Engelbert Dollfuss. After the war he moved to Germany where he was still living in 1976.[11]

Sandwiched between the assassination of Hugo Bettauer and the violence attending the meeting of the XIVth World Zionist Congress was the murder of an entirely unknown twenty-one-year-old man named Josef Mohapl on 1 August 1925. The killing itself by another obscure youth by the name of Josef Seidl was entirely nonpolitical as neither Mohapl nor Seidl was active in politics. Nor did the killing have anything directly to do with anti-Semitism as neither the victim nor the murderer was Jewish or particularly anti-Semitic. Nevertheless, as with so much else in the First Austrian Republic, the murder had political consequences and heightened the already tense political atmosphere.

Although Seidl was completely nonpolitical, preferring the company of prostitutes to politicians and enjoying violence for its own sake, his murder of Mohapl ignited a war of words between Vienna's political press organs, a battle of headlines that was a novelty at the time but was to become commonplace in the early 1930s. Right-wing papers claimed that Mohapl had been murdered by Socialists, and his burial became a big show for the entire "Christian population." On the other hand, the *Arbeiter-Zeitung* charged that Mohapl had been chased by five or six Nazis after their party comrades had deliberately provoked a Socialist crowd. The only common goal of the papers was their desire to gain political advantage from the senseless tragedy. And the only satisfactory outcome of the murder was that Seidl received a twelve-year sentence, the only time in the First Republic that a murder that afterward became politicized resulted in a severe sentence.[12]

ZIONISM AND THE AUSTRIAN ANTI-SEMITES

As it turned out, the political reactions to the murders of Hugo Bettauer and Josef Mohapl were mere preludes to agitation surrounding the holding of the XIVth World Zionist Congress in Vienna in August 1925. The events were completely unrelated, but once more anti-Semites were far less concerned about the actual events involved than they were in gaining as much publicity for themselves as possible. The political reactions to the Zionist Congress were especially hypocritical because prior to the meeting anti-Semitic attitudes toward Zionism were by no means entirely negative, and those people who did oppose Zionism were not always anti-Semitic.

The Christian Social Party usually adopted a favorable stance toward Zionism because, like Kaiser Wilhelm II, it saw the movement as an excellent way of ridding the country of Jews. The *Wiener Stimmen*, which was in most respects even more anti-Semitic than its sister paper, the *Reichspost*, editorialized in 1919 that it had always favored an alliance between anti-Semites and Zionists against things Jewish. The *Reichspost* supported Zionism not to protect the rights of a minority, but to limit Jewish influence in the state. It backed Zionist demands for the separation of people "who don't belong together for the benefit of both." The *Reichspost* was opposed to Jews controlling Christian holy places in Palestine and doubted whether Palestine could ever accommodate more than 500,000 Jews. Nevertheless, on the eve of the Zionist Congress it remarked that Zionists were forthright in their goals and ought to be treated like any other political opponent. They were at least preferable to assimilated Jews. The Catholic and usually very anti-Semitic journal *Schönere Zukunft* was also favorably disposed toward Zionism, admitting that Jewish settlers in Palestine had proved that Jews could be successful farmers, miners, and construction workers.[13]

The Roman Catholic church was far less favorably disposed toward Zionism than the Christian Social Party. For example, the *Katholische Kirchenzeitung* in Salzburg called a possible Jewish state in Palestine at best a headquarters for Jewish world domination, an idea frequently repeated in völkisch newspapers. And while the Zionist Congress was meeting in Vienna, the bishop of Innsbruck, Sigismund Waitz, organized a counter congress in the Tyrolean capital consisting of Roman Catholic academics from Austria and Germany who were warned by the bishop about the "world Jewish danger."[14]

The *Arbeiter-Zeitung* was not openly hostile to the Zionist goal of establishing a homeland for Jews in Palestine, but regarded it as at best a bourgeois utopia that detracted efforts away from the class struggle. Moreover, like many Catholic periodicals it doubted whether such a state would solve the Jewish problem. No more than a small percentage of the world's Jews could live in Palestine and therefore the relationship between Jews and non-Jews in other countries would remain essentially unchanged. Just prior to the gathering of the Zionist Congress, the *Arbeiter-Zeitung* claimed that the meeting was being funded by a few Jewish magnates who had enough influence in the League of Nations, the United States, and Great Britain to prevent Austria from receiving loans.[15]

The nationalist camp usually took a much less sanguine approach to Zionism and its goals. Ironically, nationalistic anti-Semites in Germany and probably Austria as well gave serious consideration to the idea of a Jewish state long before a significant number of Jews did. Pro-Zionist statements were fairly common in Germany even before the First World War, being made by those people who wanted to expel the Jews.[16] In Austria the völkisch *Ostdeutsche Rundschau* remarked shortly before the end of the war that nothing would please Germans more than if all Jews would move to Palestine. It was a utopian idea, however, because Central European Jews were too used to making money. Only a few Jews from Russia would actually be willing to emigrate. Both *Der eiserne Besen* and the *Deutsche Arbeiter-Presse* agreed that the migration of Jews to Palestine was an excellent idea in and of itself. However, they thought that Palestine would then become merely the first stage on the road to Jewish domination of the world. The *Deutsche Arbeiter-Presse* expressed a common view among anti-Semites that a Jewish state would never be realized because Jews could not create anything on their own and did not know the meaning of work. However, the paper loved to quote Zionists who said that assimilationist Jews were foolish to deny that the Jews were a race with specific characteristics. As the Zionist Congress approached, the attitude of the *Deutsche Arbeiter-Presse* became increasingly belligerent. Zionism, it said, was only an advanced form of Judaism that did not differ in its essentials from Judaism in general. The building of a Jewish state in Palestine was a farce. Most Zionists wanted someone else to emigrate there.[17]

THE XIVTH WORLD ZIONIST CONGRESS

In the last few weeks before the opening of the Zionist Congress, anti-Semitic newspapers in Vienna returned to their favorite pastime of estimating Jewish numbers. As in the case of the Eastern European Jewish refugees, there was a kind of bidding war to see who could make the highest estimate. The *Deutsche Arbeiter-Presse*, after remarking that Leopoldstadt should be made a ghetto again until all Jews were expelled from Vienna, stated that there would be 25,000 Jewish observers at the congress in addition to the 500 delegates. The Christian women and girls of Vienna would be in great danger with this horde of foreign Jews around. Three weeks later the newspaper raised that estimate to 50,000, a figure that also appeared on Nazi posters. *Der eiserne Besen* put the number of Jewish visitors at 50,000 to 80,000. The *Deutschösterreichische Tages-Zeitung* was more modest in estimating that only 30,000 Jews would attend the international meeting, but claimed that 25,000 of these would be from Eastern Europe. As many as 20,000 would use the meeting as a pretext to remain in Austria permanently in order to take control of the country. When in reality only 10,000 Jews came to the congress, the Nazis interpreted that figure as proof not that their predictions were grossly exaggerated but that they had discouraged the others from attending through their work of "enlightening" the Christian population of Austria about the dangers of the congress.[18]

Nazis were not the only Austrians "alarmed" about the forthcoming "invasion" of congress participants. Three members of the Bundesrat, the upper house of the Austrian Parliament—Leopold Stocker, Theodor Berger, and Martin Drescher—warned the Christian Social chancellor, Rudolf Ramek, that allowing so many Jewish delegates to enter the country would create a "sanitation problem," would cause Austrian trains to get dirty, and would overcrowd Vienna's hotels, thus discouraging other tourists from visiting the country.[19]

The attitude of the Austrian government and the police of Vienna toward the Zionist Congress both before and during the meeting itself can be described as "correct." After the *Deutsche Arbeiter-Presse* had published a series of articles insulting the congress and threatening its participants with violence, Chancellor Ramek warned the Nazis against using terror and threatened to use vigorous countermeasures if his warnings were ignored.[20] At the same time Ramek also assured two worried Austrian Zionist leaders that his government would do everything possible to protect the congress. He would certainly find the means to keep "the few undesirable screamers away from the Congress." He was convinced that there would be no surprise attacks against the Jewish visitors because the government would find a way to render them harmless long before the congress began. At the end of the conference Ramek declared that he would write a letter to the Zionist state organization of Austria in which he would put these promises in writing. It would then be free to publish this letter abroad in order to dissipate any fears.[21]

The same two Zionist leaders also visited Police President Johannes Schober, a member of the Greater German People's Party, who told them that he would defend the congress "at all costs."[22] True to his word, Schober met on 15 July with a group of representatives of völkisch groups calling itself the Verband deutschvölkischer Vereine (League of German Völkisch Clubs) and also including the chairman of the Austrian Nazi Party, Karl Schulz, and advised them of the importance of the congress to the Austrian economy. They in turn promised not to hold any demonstrations against the congress. On the contrary, they would influence their followers to allow the meeting to take place undisturbed, a promise they soon utterly ignored.[23]

Ramek and Schober publicly repeated their support for the congress shortly before it met. On 8 August Ramek said that his government had no reason to limit those people attending the congress to elected delegates as many anti-Semites had demanded. He did not fear any sanitation problems. The next day Vienna's police headquarters explained to the public the importance of the congress for Vienna's economy and international reputation. The congress would establish worthwhile contacts for the future.[24]

The Austrian chancellor and Viennese police president fulfilled their promises to protect the congress even though in doing so they had to turn Vienna into a veritable armed camp. The most important public buildings were surrounded by cordons of police. During the congress Ramek held a press conference in which he made an appeal for reason. A particularly inflammatory edition of the *Deutsche Arbeiter-Presse* was also confiscated during the congress. Much to the disgust of the anti-Semitic press, a member of Ramek's cabinet attended the opening of the congress and greeted the delegates on behalf of the Austrian government. The whole attitude of the Austrian government caused the *Deutsche Arbeiter-Presse* to claim that it was completely under the influence of Jewish world capital.[25]

ANTI-ZIONIST DEMONSTRATIONS

Nazis and other anti-Semites broke their promise to Schober not to demonstrate against the congress even before the congress officially began on 18 August. Already on 13 August, 10,000 demonstrators gathered in three halls to protest the congress, a rally that inspired some Nazis to break the windows of Jewish-owned coffee shops. A second demonstration and march planned by several völkisch and Christian Social organizations for 17 August was forbidden by police because no single organization could guarantee the peaceful behavior of members of the other organizations. The police also objected to the meeting starting at 7:00 in the evening, which meant it would not have ended until after nightfall and therefore would have attracted hooligans.[26]

In order to make sure that the forbidden gathering did not take place, the police occupied the Freiheitsplatz (now called Rooseveltplatz) in front of the Votiv Church early in the afternoon of Monday, 17 August. People who approached the square were repeatedly warned that the demonstration was illegal, warnings that were ignored. At 6:15 a whistle sounded in the vicinity of the nearby University of Vienna, signaling the mobilization of the crowd that had already gathered. Ten thousand people listened to three speakers, two of whom were Nazis. One of the speakers, Walter Gattermayer, the leader of a Nazi trade union, used the occasion to appeal to the paramilitary Frontkämpfervereinigung, nationalistic gymnasts, and members of the Greater German People's Party to join the Nazis in opposing the Zionist Congress.[27]

Antisemiten Wiens!

An Stelle der für den 10. d. M. einberufenen und von der Polizei verbotenen Versammlung findet

Donnerstag, den 13. August 1925, in Weigls Katharinenhalle (bei Bedarf in den anschließenden Sälen)
12. Bez., Schönbrunnerstraße 307, eine

⊞ Riesen- ⊞
Massenkundgebung

des deutsch-christlichen Wien statt, in welcher Parteiobmann **Karl Schulz** und die Pg. Jugendobmann **Bauer** und **Walter Gattermayer** als Hauptredner über

„Die Stellungnahme des arisch-christlichen Wien zum Zionistenkongreß"

sprechen werden. Außerdem werden Vertreter verschiedener völkischer Verbände Erklärungen abgeben.

Jeder antisemitische Wiener ohne Unterschied der Parteirichtung muß zu dieser Massenkundgebung des deutsch-christlichen Wien erscheinen.

Hie christliche Bodenständige!   Hie jüdische Gäste!

Kostenbeitrag 30 Groschen. Arbeitslose ab ¹/₂8 Uhr gegen Ausweis frei.

Saaleröffnung 7 Uhr abends.   Beginn 8 Uhr abends.
Juden ist der Eintritt verboten!

Nazi poster announcing a demonstration on 13 August 1925 to protest the Zionist Congress in Vienna. The chairman of the Austrian Nazi Party, Karl Schulz, and Walter Gattermayer, among others, were scheduled to speak on the topic "The Attitude of Aryan-Christian Vienna toward the Zionist Congress." Every anti-Semite, regardless of political affiliation, was urged to attend. Jews were forbidden to enter. DÖW.

At 8:00 the police, estimated by anti-Semites to number 6,000, belatedly began to break up the rally. In groups of 100 to 150 the demonstrators, shouting anti-Semitic slogans, showered the police with stones and attacked them with sticks and even guns. Not until 8:30 did the crowd begin to disperse. About 1,000 of the demonstrators tried to march into the Leopoldstadt and the inner city, but were stopped by the police. However, the demonstrators remained masters of the Ringstrasse until about 11:00 and attacked Jews or suspected Jews in automobiles, streetcars, and coffee shops. Other demonstrators yelled anti-Semitic insults in front of hotels catering to foreign guests. Not until 12:30 did the city return to normal after 132 people had been arrested and later sentenced to eight to fourteen days in jail. However, 53 of these people were released after just two days as the result of the intervention of the Christian Social Party. All but 34 were released by 22 August. Altogether, 40 people were injured in the melee, 21 of them policemen; fifteen horses were also injured. In addition, $4 million in damage was caused by the rioters not counting the lost patronage of hotels and restaurants from delegates who had been too frightened to come to Vienna.[28]

Tuesday, 18 August, proved to be considerably quieter than the preceding day, perhaps because the police took even greater precautions, especially around the Konzerthaus where the congress was taking place. The police allowed crowds to gather no closer than the Schwarzenbergplatz, one block away from the Konzerthaus; there anti-Semites shouted "Juden hinaus" and sang the pan-German "Wacht am Rhein." This time only 73 demonstrators—most of them young and many of them girls—were arrested and all of them were set free within three days.[29]

Of the 202 demonstrators arrested on 17 and 18 August for anti-Semitic disturbances, 62 were Nazis, 41 came from various other völkisch organizations, 29 were members of the Social Democratic Party, 6 were Christian Socials (probably because the party's leadership had forbidden its members to take part in illegal demonstrations), just 2 were members of the Greater German People's Party, and 41 had no political affiliation, probably because they were too young to have any real interest in politics but were old enough to enjoy a brawl and an opportunity to plunder.[30]

A final and this time entirely peaceful demonstration took place on 22 August. Among the approximately 8,000 people taking part in the rally were 2,000 members of the Vaterländische Schutzbund (Patriotic Protection League), the predecessor of the Austrian Nazis' Sturmabteilung; 800 uniformed members of the Frontkämpfervereinigung; 1,200 members of various gymnastic organizations; and 800 students wearing nationalistic colors. They all marched from the Votiv Church next to the University of Vienna to the Karlskirche (Charles Church) where they heard Walter Gattermayer boast that the anti-Semitic movement had cut expected attendance at the Zionist Congress from 30,000 to 4,000. Anti-Semitism, he continued, must be spread to the proletariat so that it would understand that its greatest enemy was the bestial international capitalist Jew. After the crowd approved of a resolution stating that the public life of Vienna was becoming more and more "jewified," the demonstration ended with the participants singing Germany's national anthem.[31]

Although no Christian Social organization was involved in the violent anti-Semitic demonstrations of 17 August, and few of the party's members were arrested, the party's leadership and official organ, the *Reichspost*, as ever fearful of losing one of its most effective political weapons to its rivals, felt compelled not to condemn the violence but to defend the demonstrators and use the Zionist Congress as an excuse for venting its anti-Semitic feelings. In an official communiqué the party's leadership in Vienna said that the recent demonstrations were

> caused by the deep excitement of the Viennese population which did not start with the Zionist Congress. The anti-Semitism of the native population [was] not directed against the strivings of Zionist Jews, but instead against that part of Jewry which, through its insidious agitation in cultural affairs and its arrogance in economic and political areas, and the excesses in the press which it leads, undermines the morals and economy of our people. The leadership in this righteous defensive struggle, which the Christian Social Party has resolved to continue with every legal means, cannot be turned over to irresponsible groups.[32]

Christian Social newspapers were unanimous in blaming everyone except the anti-Semitic rioters for the violence. The *Wiener Stimmen*, far from denouncing the demonstrations, said the violence was the work of "Jewish and Communist provocateurs" who had tried to provoke the crowds against their own "blood brothers." According to the paper, the population of Vienna was outraged not by the violence of the anti-Semites but by the actions of the police who were to blame for discouraging some of the expected 60,000 to 70,000 participants of the congress from coming to Vienna.[33] The *Reichspost* traced the violence to the deep bitterness that had been growing within the Christian population as a result of month after month of Jewish arrogance and provocations in the press, and by the terroristic acts of the Jewish leaders of the Social Democratic Party. These leaders had been treated too leniently by the authorities. The honor of upright men who had given valuable service to the state was ridiculed every day by the depraved Jewish press. The morals and beliefs of the Christian population were being attacked by impudent posters and publications. All this had strained the patience of the Viennese population and had caused the biggest demonstrations in six years. The Zionist Congress and the exaggerated concern about it by the authorities was simply the last straw. People from all walks of life had taken part in the demonstrations, not just Nazis. There would have been no violence if the authorities had permitted a legal demonstration on 17 August, the *Reichspost* concluded. When the final anti-Semitic demonstration accompanying the Zionist Congress took place peacefully on 22 August, the *Reichspost* used that fact as proof that had the demonstration planned for 17 August been authorized by the police there would have been no violence.[34]

Whereas the *Reichspost* did its best to excuse and explain away the violence of the anti-Semitic demonstrations, the independent and liberal *Neue Freie Presse*, probably Austria's only newspaper with an international circulation and reputation, unequivocally condemned the violence. It noted that the same kinds of people took part in the violence of 17 August as were involved in the murder of Josef Mohapl near the Praterstern three weeks earlier. It was

intolerable that a few hundred people [*sic*, actually several thousand] led by a few dozen agitators could put their stamp on the city's reputation, disturb the peace . . . and hurt completely innocent bystanders and cause losses to businessmen. [It was also intolerable] that it was necessary to pay millions . . . for security forces which, according to the police president, had the strength of a brigade. During the last years we have experienced enough unrest and several times Vienna has been the site of excesses; but at those times there was at least a certain excuse because the demonstrators were people who were suffering from material need of the first postwar years and had nerves that had been strained by hunger and cold. There is no longer any question of such circumstances today. And the excitement surrounding the meeting of a great international congress in Vienna has been artificially created by men who wanted to satisfy their personal ambitions. . . . In the long run it will not help to mobilize the police. . . . It is not their duty to eradicate the evil. . . . It is the task of the political parties.[35]

The *Arbeiter-Zeitung* had surprisingly little to say about the Zionist Congress apart from its strictly factual reports concerning the riots. One article, however, did say that the Christian Social government of Chancellor Ramek had welcomed the congress as an opportunity to cultivate relations with international high-finance capital. The day after the worst rioting the *Arbeiter-Zeitung* published an editorial that was even more revealing about the general attitude of the paper and the Socialist Party in general toward the congress and anti-Semitism as a whole. The headline read: "Lies and Again Lies!" The column indignantly denied an allegation recently published in the *Wiener Allgemeiner Zeitung* claiming that the Social Democrats had held a secret meeting of their parliamentary deputies to plan strategies for the defense of the Zionist Congress. Moreover, all leaders of the party's paramilitary Schutzbund had been put on highest alert in case of trouble. Not one word of the report was true, according to the *Arbeiter-Zeitung*. The congress and the Nazi actions against it were solely the concern of the federal government, which was controlled by the Christian Social Party. That party had welcomed the congress as an opportunity to cultivate relations with international finance capital.[36]

Austrian newspapers were far from being the only ones to report on the anti-Zionist violence. In England the *Times*, the *Morning Post*, and the *Manchester Guardian* all gave the story extensive coverage. In the United States the congress was front-page news in the *New York Times*, which reported that in one parade ten thousand men, women, and children marched down the Ringstrasse shouting "Clear out the Jews" and "Kill the Jews."[37] The New York paper also printed a telegram from an American member of the executive committee of the congress, Louis N. Jaffe, to President Calvin Coolidge complaining about the riots and asking the American government to issue a formal protest. An even more prominent American Zionist, Stephen S. Wise, one of the vice-presidents of the congress as well as the president of the American Jewish Congress, was also reported by the *Times* as having denounced the rioting, saying: "May Austria be spared the shame and curse of the reaction which would follow in the wake of anti-Semitism triumphant."[38] The Austrian consul in New York, however, responded to these reports by saying that they were "grossly exaggerated" in the U.S. press.[39]

Most of the blame for Austria's declining international reputation in 1925 must be laid at the doorstep of the country's political parties. Far from eradicating the evil of anti-Semitism and political extremism in general, the political parties of Austria had either aggressively contributed to it in 1925 or had done nothing to stop it. Every violent incident during the year from the murders of Hugo Bettauer and Josef Mohapl to the anti-Semitic demonstrations accompanying the Zionist Congress was used by the parties and their presses (although not to the same degree) as an opportunity for holding their rivals responsible for the "underlying causes" that had led to the incidents. Gaining some momentary advantage over one's political opponents, or at least preventing that opponent from gaining an advantage, was seen as far more important than denouncing the violence and hatred in unambiguous terms.

Although the murder of Hugo Bettauer and the trial of his assassin, along with the demonstrations accompanying the World Zionist Congress, attracted a great deal of national and even international attention, these incidents did not permanently reverse the general decline in Austrian anti-Semitism, which had set in at the end of 1923. The years 1926 through 1929 proved to be by far the quietest four-year period in the entire history of the First Austrian Republic not only with regard to anti-Semitism but in other aspects of political life as well (with the notable exception of the burning of the Palace of Justice by a mob of enraged workers in July 1927). In part the political calm was due to a split in the Austrian Nazi Party, which occurred in 1926 between a faction loyal to Karl Schulz and another fanatically devoted to Adolf Hitler, a schism that was not overcome until the followers of Hitler gained the upper hand in 1930. Even more important, however, was the improving Austrian economy, which reached its apogee in the late 1920s, and the absence of any spectacular incident that could restore anti-Semitic passions.

9

SEGREGATION AND RENEWED VIOLENCE

During the democratic years of the First Austrian Republic it was the large and well-organized anti-Semitic demonstrations against Ostjuden in the early postwar years, the XIVth Zionist Congress in 1925, and anti-Semitic brawls at Austrian universities that attracted national and even international attention. These public and noisy displays of anti-Jewish hostility became less frequent in the second half of the 1920s only to return again after the onslaught of the Great Depression. Even during those times when Austrian anti-Semitism was the least overt and public, however, it continued to flourish in a wide variety of private and professional organizations, especially those catering to the academically trained middle class. Not surprisingly therefore, these organizations—with the exception of those that were avowedly Roman Catholic—excluded Jews from membership primarily for "racial" reasons.

PRIVATE CLUBS

Private organizations, unlike, for example, tourist and health resorts, were legally free to discriminate as far as their membership was concerned. Even though these organizations were technically nonpolitical, they were very much influenced by contemporary political ideologies when it came to anti-Semitism. And like the anti-Semitism of bourgeois parties, that of the various *Vereine* of Austria became increasingly racist and radical after the First World War until many of them were disbanded by the Austrian government after 1933 for their close connections to Nazism.

One of the largest and most anti-Semitic of these organizations was the Deutsch-österreichischer Alpenverein (German-Austrian Alpine Club), a mountaineering organization that provided members with hundreds of protective shelters during their hikes. Founded in 1874, the 250,000-member Alpenverein resembled student organizations such as the Deutsche Studentenschaft in being "all-German," having 84 chapters in Austria and 220 in Germany. In May 1921 the "Austria" chapter of the Alpenverein, the oldest, and with 7,000 members, the largest of the organization's chapters, introduced a bill to the Alpenverein's general assembly that would have excluded Jews from the entire organization. Although two-thirds of the chapters approved the motion, it fell short of the three-fourths majority needed for acceptance.[1]

Nevertheless, many individual chapters of the Alpenverein did expel their Jewish members. The "Austria" chapter itself did so in October 1921 by a vote of 2,420 to 46 after its leader, Otto Wagner, gave a speech advancing the extreme racist argument that a large number of Jews had criminal, not human instincts, and he blamed the Jews for dividing the German people into classes. Some of the Jews who had been expelled from various chapters of the Alpenverein subsequently formed their own "Donauland" chapter in Vienna in late 1921, which was admitted into the Alpenverein by a 14-to-12 vote of the executive committee. Even this apartheid solution was unacceptable to the Klagenfurt section of the Alpenverein, which in 1924 demanded the expulsion of Donauland. Ninety-nine chapters, nearly all of them Austrian, sponsored the bill, which was accompanied by a threat from the Klagenfurters that they and the other Austrians would withdraw from the organization altogether if their demand was not met. The motion was approved by the main assembly by a vote of 1,660 to 70. This expulsion did not entirely end the matter, however, because the "Austria" section of the Alpenverein continued its enmity toward Donauland. It blamed Jews for the Treaty of St. Germain and for the growing influx of tourists into Austria, many of whom, according to the chapter, were obtrusive Jews who wore offensive clothing and destroyed the landscape.[2]

Another organization having pronounced anti-Semitic proclivities was the Österreichischer Touristenklub or Austrian Tourist Club. In theory the club was merely supposed to protect the Austrian Alps from "undesirable elements." The club began excluding Jews informally in 1920 and then made it official a year later.[3]

Gymnastic organizations in Austria were even more nationalistic and anti-Semitic, tracing their ideological heritage back to the early nineteenth-century teachings of "Turnvater" Friedrich Jahn. Like the Alpenverein, they were often more anti-Semitic than their counterparts in Germany. The Turnerbund ridiculed the parent Deutsche Turnerschaft in Germany for accepting Jews as members and considering them Germans if they had German citizenship and had converted to Christianity. Already in 1897 the Erster Wiener Turnverein (First Viennese Gymnasts' Club) introduced the so-called Aryan paragraph, which excluded Jews from membership. Its successor was the Deutscher Turnerbund 1919 (German Gymnasts' League 1919). Founded in September 1919, it fought against the "enemies of the German people": Marxism, Bolshevism, and Judaism and all other "un-German" influences. No Jews or foreigners could join the organization, and members could not be married to Jews. Any contact with a Jew was thought to make one dirty. By 1932 the Turnerbund had 70,000 adult members and another 45,000 who were children.[4]

A Catholic gymnastic association called the Christlich-deutschen Turnerschaft incorporated the German-völkisch ideology of the Deutscher Turnerbund in opposing Jewish influence in social life and in the press. It wanted to restore the privileged position that Christians enjoyed before the emancipation of Jews. It differed from the nationalistic groups in rejecting rowdiness in favor of boycotting Jews in order to ruin their businesses. The association also differed from other gymnastic organizations in adding elements of Roman Catholic beliefs in, for example, regarding the Jews as the murderers of Jesus. Typical of Catholic anti-Semitism was also the injunction that members should fight the "disintegrating" influence of Jews through not buying Jewish newspapers or magazines and by not showing any enthusiasm for works created by the "Jewish spirit." Unfortunately, however, "idealistic" Christians were at a disadvantage when fighting "materialistic" Jews. None of this contradicted Nazi ideology, and indeed the Christlich-deutschen Turnerschaft admired the Nazis' outspoken German nationalism. However, like most other Catholics, the gymnasts considered the Nazi stand on racial questions too extreme.[5]

The Österreichischer Schiverband (Austrian Skiing Association) was still another, though much smaller, private anti-Semitic organization, which in 1927 had 2,435 members in forty-six chapters. It had introduced the Aryan paragraph in 1922 causing several of its chapters to withdraw and leading to the founding of a second organization known as the Allgemeiner österreichischer Schivervand (General Austrian Skiing Association), which did not insist on racial purity. The statutes of the Österreichischer Schiverband during the 1920s and early 1930s moved in an ever more racial direction. In 1932 the statutes mentioned "cultivating and encouraging German racial consciousness." By this time and later there was some Nazi activity going on within the association, although it cannot simply be called a cover for the Nazi Party.[6]

Professional organizations for physicians and lawyers were also far from being above anti-Semitism in the First Austrian Republic. In their practices, physicians and apothecaries were obliged by law to serve anyone who sought their services. Lawyers, however, were under no such obligation. The only

Jewish clients that the early Nazi leader, Dr. Walter Riehl—himself a lawyer—would accept were those who wished to prosecute other Jews. Professional organizations, being private, were also not legally bound to accept Jews. For example, the Vereinigung christlichdeutscher Ärzte Österreichs (Union of Christian-German Physicians of Austria) stipulated in its "Cultural and Political Principles" of September 1935 that it would accept Jews only if they unquestionably belonged to the German cultural community. The union did not, however, adopt an extreme racial philosophy because it was willing to accept Jews who had "honorably" converted to Christianity. However, such Jews would be entrusted with active collaboration only after special precautions had been taken. The principles also stated that race was part of the natural order and was to be respected and cultivated. Indiscriminate mixing between very different races was to be taken more seriously than in the past. The disintegrating influence of Jews was to be decisively fought.[7]

Viennese lawyers were, if anything, generally even more anti-Semitic than physicians, at least by the early 1930s. However, in the 1920s they all belonged to a Chamber of Lawyers, which in 1922 departed from tradition by electing a Jew as its president. He was succeeded by a gentile, but then in 1932 another Jew, Dr. Siegfried Kantor, was elected. At a time when Nazism was rapidly growing in Austria and Germany, Kantor's election proved to be intolerable for many of the non-Jewish members of the chamber, who formed their own League of German-Aryan Lawyers of Austria. In 1934 the German-Aryan Lawyers complained that Austria was "overrun" with foreigners, especially Jews, and noted that there were only 320 Aryan lawyers in Vienna, compared to 1,834 Jewish lawyers. The league also refused, as a matter of principle, to collaborate with Jewish colleagues or Jewish judges in professional matters. Its newsletter, the *Mitteilungen des Verbandes deutsch-arischer Rechtsanwälte*, supported radical racial anti-Semitism and demanded a strict numerus clausus; it was also responsible for publishing a "Guide to Aryan Businesses" for its readers.[8]

However much professional organization in Austria may have practiced anti-Semitism in admitting members and in regulating their conduct with Jews, their journals usually avoided the "Jewish question" and confined themselves to issues pertinent to their profession.[9]

THE CONTINUATION OF ACADEMIC ANTI-SEMITISM, 1925–1932

Meanwhile, Austrian university students, who often did or who soon would belong to these private interest groups and professional organizations, were keeping anti-Semitism alive and well in the academy. For Austria as a whole there was a substantial diminution of overt anti-Semitism beginning in 1924 and continuing with some interruptions until the end of the decade. However, this decline was only barely noticeable in Austria's Hochschulen. There, anti-Semitic demonstrations continued with almost monotonous regularity, especially at the University of Vienna and the Technical College, despite the steady and rapid decline of Jewish enrollment at these and other institutions of higher learning. One should point out, however, that although Austria's economy in general had nearly reached prewar levels by the late 1920s, the prospects for young university graduates continued to be poor if not as bleak as the early postwar years, thus encouraging gentile students to cling to the belief that their career opportunities could be improved only through eliminating Jewish predominance in the professions.

Although the number of Jewish students at Vienna's colleges and institutes had undoubtedly been high before and especially during and immediately after the First World War, their enrollment was far lower by the late 1920s and even lower during the 1930s. Jewish enrollment in all of Vienna's Hochschulen still stood at 42 percent in 1920–21; by 1925–26, however, it was already below 25 percent. By 1927 only 17.5 percent of the students at the University of Vienna were Jewish, and only 9.1 percent were Jews at the Technical College. The 2,204 Jewish students who attended the university in 1928 dropped to only 1,553 in 1936 out of a total of 9,675. In 1933 the 1,213 Jewish students in the Medical College made up about a third of the 3,774 total students; however in the arts and sciences division there were only 554 Jews among the 4,450 students, or just 12 percent.[10]

Statistics alone do not begin to describe the declining status of Jews in Austrian universities during the First Republic. Even the most outstanding Jews among the faculty were unable to obtain appointments as full professors. Some (but not all) Jews were convinced that their gentile professors used any excuse to fail them. By the same token, outside university halls Jews were never appointed to be directors of primary or secondary schools.[11]

Anti-Semitism in Vienna's Hochschulen was expressed by far more than complaints about Jewish overrepresentation and demands for the implementation of a numerus clausus. The *Neue Freie Presse* reported in March 1925 that a walk around the main building of the University of Vienna would reveal little except anti-Semitic posters and literature of the lowest kind, including the *Protocols of the Elders of Zion*, which was on sale everywhere with the rector's approval. To the reporter of Austria's most venerable liberal newspaper it seemed as though the students were interested in nothing but the "Jewish question." This was especially true for members of the Deutsche Studentenschaft, whose numbers and influence were constantly growing. The hate propaganda was finally forbidden by the academic authorities in October 1925, much to the indignation of Nazi students, but only the rector of the College of International Trade was strict about enforcing the new rule.[12]

The anti-Semitic violence in Vienna's institutions of higher learning of the early postwar years abated only slightly in the middle and late twenties. The Anatomy Institute of Professor Julius Tandler continued to be a favorite target of völkisch students, being spared attacks only in 1928 and the first ten months of 1929.[13] In May 1925 Nazi students broke into the institute and demanded that Jewish students get out. One of the Nazi students then made a speech in the entry hall of the building in which he called for the murder of leading Socialists such as Karl Renner, Otto Bauer, and Julius Deutsch. This incident caused the Austrian government, which had the ultimate authority over Vienna's higher academic institutions, to close them all. The federal chancellor, Rudolf Ramek, very possibly responding to a complaint contained in a long letter from the Israelitische Kultusgemeinde, and mindful of the World Zionist Congress that was to meet that summer in Vienna, also issued a stern warning to the leaders of the Deutsche Studentenschaft.[14]

Another anti-Semitic brawl took place at the College of International Trade in March 1927 when two hundred to three hundred students from other Hochschulen—led by Robert Körber, who by this time had graduated and become a businessman but had lost none of his interest in radical student politics—invaded the building and attacked anyone who looked Jewish with rubber clubs and sticks. The director of the college, Dr. Grunzel, was called a "Jewish pig," a "dirty pig-Jew," and a "stinking Hebrew," whereas the police who arrived on the scene to restore order were called "Jew lovers." Körber delivered a short speech in which he denounced Grunzel for not allowing any anti-Semitic posters.[15]

During observances in November 1927 celebrating the founding of the republic, Nazi students with the help of thirty men from the Sturmabteilung attacked the predominantly Jewish Socialist Student Association at the University of Vienna. After ten minutes eight Jewish students had to be carried away to receive first aid while the Nazi students triumphantly sang a party song.

*Theodor Innitzer as rector of the University of Vienna. He aided poor Jewish
students at the university and later as cardinal helped baptized Jews (but not Jews
who had not been converted) escape from Austria.
Library of the City of Vienna Picture Archive.*

This episode was merely the first of a series of eight pitched battles at the university in which Nazi students destroyed kiosks that displayed announcements and posters of Jewish organizations, disrupted lectures of Jewish professors, captured and held campus security officials for hours at a time, issued ultimatums, and besieged the office of the university's chancellor and later Roman Catholic cardinal, Theodor Innitzer.[16]

Meanwhile, over a two-year period the National Socialist League of Students distributed 100,000 propaganda leaflets, held a dozen mass meetings, and organized countless "lecture evenings." By such self-styled "heroic" tactics, the Nazi students attracted two to three thousand followers by the beginning of 1930 and claimed to be the "masters" of one of the world's most distinguished universities.[17]

Nazi students did not, however, have a monopoly on anti-Semitic activities at Austria universities in the late 1920s. A protest by Socialist workers in Vienna against the results of a politicized trial culminated in the burning of the Palace of Justice in Vienna in July 1927 and sparked a sudden upsurge in the popularity of the anti-Marxist and paramilitary Austrian *Heimwehr* or Home Guard. By the fall of 1929 it was Heimwehr, not Nazi students, who attracted the attention of even the *New York Times* because of its frequent attacks on Jewish students at the University of Vienna and other Hochschulen. In October Heimwehr students at the Technical College barred the entrance to Jews and then marched to the main building of the University of Vienna where they drove Jews out of lecture halls into the streets and then assaulted them. A few days later rioting Heimwehr students invaded Professor Tandler's Anatomy Institute and attacked Jewish students with such viciousness that onlookers summoned five fire brigades to help the victims escape and ambulances were called for the injured. Seven people were seriously hurt, one having a badly fractured skull. Mounted police were present but did not set foot on academic soil. Following similar incidents a year later rectors at the Institute for International Trade scolded Jewish students for provoking nationalist students while politely reminding the latter that they ought to resist responding to "provocations."[18]

By 1931 Nazi students in Vienna had regained the upper hand following the great Nazi electoral victory in Germany the preceding September. Early February witnessed a renewal of Nazi violence, this time at the Chemistry Institute on Währingerstrasse, at the Technical College, and on the ramp in front of the main building of the University of Vienna on the Ringstrasse. The "provocation" for the three days of demonstrations was a poster by Socialist students (who, it will be recalled, were mostly of Jewish origins) protesting the conditions of a forthcoming student election and calling for a boycott. Nazis at the Technical College hauled away a kiosk with the offending poster, set it on fire, and then tried to prevent firefighters from putting it out. At the Chemistry Institute they invaded the building, shouted their usual anti-Semitic slogans, and sang the German national anthem; anyone who refused to stand up for the anthem was assaulted. The *New York Times* said the scene outside the university "at times resembled a battlefield with hundreds of foot police massed in double cordons against the khaki-uniformed Hitlerite detachments." On the third day of the rioting the rector of the University of Vienna, the historian Hans Uebersberger, met some of the völkisch students and told them that the Socialist poster had indeed been a provocation and would be banned.[19]

THE CREATION OF STUDENT "NATIONS"

The climax of student anti-Semitic violence probably came in 1931 after the constitutional court of Austria disallowed a regulation at the University of Vienna that had divided the student body into "nations," including one for Jews. Under pressure from the increasingly Nazified Deutsche Studentenschaft, the Viennese rectors' conference, chaired by the rector of the University of Vienna and legal scholar, Count Wenzel Gleispach, decided on 1 February 1930 that Hochschule students should be divided into four nations— in the manner of medieval universities—if they formed at least 1 percent of the total enrollment. According to the new rule, which was approved by the Academic Senate of the University of Vienna on 8 April 1930, students themselves could not decide to which nation they belonged: German, non-German (Jewish), mixed, or "other." Declaring oneself an Austrian or an American was not an option! A student would be regarded as a non-German, even if he was an Austrian citizen and his native language was German, unless he could prove that his parents and all four of his grandparents had been baptized. The latter stipulation was far more stringent than the infamous Nuremberg Laws implemented in Nazi Germany in September 1935.[20]

The regulation, which was similar to one that had been enforced at the Technical College since 1924, was a thinly disguised plan to disenfranchise Jewish students in campus politics and in a broader sense to segregate them from the rest of Austrian society and turn them into second-class citizens. It would have been the basic principle around which Austrian society as a whole would have been reorganized if its proponents had had their way. One Austrian anti-Semite called it the first time in the history of the anti-Semitic movement that a segregation of Germans and Jews had been carried out. Only a few months after the approval of the new rule Nazi students were able to take control of the Deutsche Studentenschaft following elections in February 1931 from which Jews had been excluded. It also assured that students belonging to the "German Student Nation" would enjoy a privileged status in helping to administer the university. The Catholic periodical, *Schönere Zukunft*, thought that Jews disliked the new ruling only because they did not want others to see how predominant they were at the university.[21]

The enforcement of the new student ruling turned out to be short-lived even though the Ministry of Education shied away from getting involved in the controversy and the federal cabinet as a whole wanted to treat the whole question as an internal academic matter. On 23 June 1931 the constitutional court of Austria announced that the academic rule violated an Austrian law dating back to 1867 regulating the formation of associations. The creation of separate student nations per se was legal; however, because students could be assigned to a nation against their will by a student court, they were deemed involuntary and hence unconstitutional. The regulation also violated the constitutional principle of the equality of all citizens because under the plan students would not enjoy the same privileges. The court's decision amounted to a slap in the face for the academic authorities and the minister of education, the historian Heinrich Srbik, who had supported the rule; both he and the academic authorities had said it was an internal matter of the university.[22]

The decision by the constitutional court, which appeared to threaten the ascendancy of the Deutsche Studentenschaft, unleashed three days of the worst academic violence in the history of the First Austrian Republic. After a hundred Nazi students, most of them wearing party insignia, heard the court's ruling, they marched in closed formation from the courtroom in the Parliament building to the University of Vienna, just two blocks away. There they met hundreds of other well-armed Nazi students in the entrance of the main University building and began attacking Jewish and Socialist students with rubber truncheons and steel clubs, seriously injuring fifteen of them. Rear exits from the building were blocked by other Nazi students, who would let no one pass without identification proving that he belonged to the Deutsche Studentenschaft. Campus guards made no effort to break up the brawl; Rector Uebersberger refused to allow municipal police to enter the building and protested their charging the ramp in front of the building to drive off the assailants. (Out of gratitude for his sympathies, Nazi students serenaded the rector a few days later.) Nazi students who had previously attacked Jews had always claimed to have been "provoked." This time no such claim was advanced.[23]

The demonstrations led to the closing of the university, the Technical College, the College of Veterinary Medicine, and the Agricultural College for the remainder of the academic year for all students except those taking final examinations. After the fighting died down, the rectors of the Viennese Hochschulen expressed their "disapproval" of the fighting but also assured the Deutsche Studentenschaft of their support for its continued existence. Likewise the Academic Senate of the University of Vienna in November 1931 expressed its approval of the goals and methods of the Deutsche Studentenschaft.[24]

Even though the *Reichspost*, which was usually sympathetic to the demands of völkisch students, said that the decision of the constitutional court was final and had to be respected, Nazi demonstrations against the announcement continued.[25] In fact, even the issue of the student nations was not quite over. In April 1931 the minister of education and member of the Christian Social Party, Emmerich Czermak, tried unsuccessfully to get the Austrian Parliament to approve a new student order similar to the one that had been disallowed by the constitutional court in the previous year.[26]

AN END TO ACADEMIC VIOLENCE?: JEWISH AND AMERICAN PROTESTS

The attempt partially to segregate Jewish students at the University of Vienna thus ended in failure. Jews, however, had little reason to be optimistic about the future. Official Jewish complaints to the Ministry of Education about the abuse of students received polite assurances that the government would make every effort to treat all citizens, including Jewish students, equally. However, no concrete measures were ever taken prior to 1932 to implement the reassuring words. Numerous interventions with the governor and mayor of Vienna and with the police president about Nazi outrages at the colleges and institutes in Vienna also proved to be equally ineffective. In October 1930 the former police president and then chancellor of Austria and member of the Greater German People's Party, Johannes Schober, told the director of the international Jewish Telegraph Agency, Jakob Landau, that Austrian anti-Semitism did not have any manifestations that required government intervention. There had been some noisy incidents, but they had not affected the equal rights of Jews. The occasional Nazi student demonstrations did not deserve the attention they had received abroad. They were not as bad as those that took place when he (Schober) was a student thirty-six years earlier.[27]

The violent Nazi demonstration that accompanied the decision of the constitutional court of Austria to disallow the regulation regarding student nations induced the board of directors of the Kultusgemeinde to send a sharp protest to the federal chancellor in which it denounced the highest academic authorities even more strongly than the "misguided" students. By not denouncing the outrages and not providing protection for the Jewish students, the authorities had encouraged the illegal and violent attacks of the German nationalist students. The same demonstrations caused Jewish students to hold a massive but peaceful demonstration of their own on 27 June 1931; "Radical Zionists" held another demonstration in late November to protest Nazi activities at the University of Vienna.[28]

The protest of the Jewish students received reinforcement from a surprising quarter. The violence that accompanied the decision of the constitutional court of Austria to disallow the "student nations" prompted the executive committee of the American League for the Protection of Foreign Students in Vienna, which consisted of prominent members of the American Medical Association, to issue a sharp note of protest; copies were sent to the Austrian government, the rector and College of Professors of the University of Vienna, the American minister to Austria (American envoys did not yet have the title of ambassador), President Herbert Hoover, and all newspapers in the United States having large circulations. The letter denounced the "cowardly, inhuman and unsportsmanlike" conduct of the bands of Nazi students. The note also objected to the absence of protection provided the victims by the rector of the university. The American minister, Gilchrist Baker Stockton, also made an informal complaint to Foreign Minister Johannes Schober at this time, which apparently was instrumental in preventing serious disturbances for the next year.[29]

The American government had monitored Austrian anti-Semitism during the First Republic because of the relatively large numbers of Americans who were studying in Vienna at the time, the great majority of whom were Jewish medical students. Vienna had long been a mecca for such scholars. Between 1870 and 1914 two-thirds of the two to three hundred Americans who annually came to Central Europe to study medicine in the decade before the outbreak of the World War came to Vienna, a number that if anything increased in the interwar period. No doubt some of the students were simply following in the footsteps of their fathers. Others, however, were there because of increasingly restrictive quotas against Jews at American medical colleges where Jewish enrollment fell from 16.4 percent in 1918 to 12.7 percent in 1946.[30]

By the time the next major round of anti-Semitic violence at the University of Vienna occurred in October 1932, the American legation in Vienna was prepared to take an even firmer stance to protect American students. A Nazi attack with steel rods, whips, brass knuckles, and knives on Jewish students at Professor Tandler's Anatomy Institute resulted in fifteen being injured, three of them Americans. Following the attack, twenty American students called on Minister Stockton to demand the protection of the American government.[31]

Consequently, Stockton had a series of three meetings with the Austrian chancellor, Dr. Engelbert Dollfuss, to protest the Nazi violence. During the first meeting the chancellor was visibly irritated by the "gross stupidity of the National Socialist students" and promised to do everything he could to prevent a recurrence. Nevertheless, the disturbances continued, causing Stockton to seek a second audience in which he "expressed the opinion that if the university authorities were unable to extend protection the state should intervene." Stockton sought still another meeting with the chancellor after four more American students were injured in a new incident. This time Dollfuss was defensive, blaming the unruly spirit of the students on their lack of discipline which in turn, he claimed, was the result of Austria not having compulsory military service. Stockton was not impressed with this argument and replied that university officials in the United States managed to maintain law and order despite a similar absence of compulsory military service. The meeting ended with Stockton again saying that it was the duty of the Austrian state to intervene if the authorities at the University of Vienna could not extend adequate protection to students.[32]

The formal demarche of the American minister along with similar protests from the envoys of Poland, Bulgaria, Yugoslavia, and Romania to the federal chancellery was widely publicized both in Austria and abroad. The recently elected völkisch rector of the University of Vienna, Professor Othenio Abel, was forced to make a formal and public apology to the American envoy. Abel also issued a proclamation at the University of Vienna urging students not to precipitate further disorders, threatening to expel students who disturbed the academic peace and even having them prosecuted criminally. No one would be allowed on academic premises without an identity card. The recent excesses had been injurious to the prestige of the university and had placed in jeopardy its special centuries-old privileges, Abel concluded.[33]

The pro-Nazi *Deutschösterreichische Tages-Zeitung* called Abel's apology a "humiliation" and warned ominously that "the time in which such things are impossible is just around the corner." It went on to allege that, based on their surnames, at least 74 percent of the American students were Jewish and therefore not really Americans. "The Jew belongs to a nation with special characteristics like no other people. It is therefore irrelevant where he happens to live, he still remains a Jew."[34]

Shortly after the American protest, the Austrian minister of education, Anton Rintelen, assured the president and vice-presidents of the Israelitische Kultusgemeinde of Vienna that the government disapproved the recent regrettable incident. He had discussed necessary security measures with the rector of the university, who had assured him that the guilty would be punished to the fullest extent of the university's rules and receive whatever civil punishment might be appropriate. Further discussions regarding security measures would take place during the next few days between the rector's office and the Ministry of Education.[35]

By the end of 1932 violence at the University of Vienna had subsided. However, Austrian Jews could hardly have been encouraged by other events that had occurred during the year. In April Nazis won nearly 17 percent of the vote in local elections throughout Austria, including over 200,000 votes in Vienna alone, up from 27,500 in November 1930. Then in July the National Socialists won over 37 percent of the vote in the Reichstag elections in Germany. Austrian Jews, who were being subjected to increasing social segregation and violence in the early 1930s, now faced the imminent prospect of a Nazi takeover in neighboring Germany. Would Austria be next?

THE VARIETIES OF
AUSTRIAN ANTI-SEMITISM

It is far easier to describe the many anti-Semitic incidents that occurred during the democratic years of the First Austrian Republic than it is to analyze
the political forces that produced them. Obviously, many different groups disliked Jews for one reason or another: university students, practicing Roman
Catholics, small shopkeepers, industrial workers, pan-German nationalists,
and others. All of them feared that their political goals and ways of life were
threatened by political and economic developments, especially in the early
postwar years and again after the start of the Great Depression.

Anti-Semitism in Austria (and most other European countries, for that matter) can best be understood if it is divided into categories and if those categories
are associated with various political parties and movements. The categories in
interwar Austria remained the same as they had been in the late nineteenth
century: religious, economic, social, and racial. Any reader expecting to find
airtight divisions between these types will be both disappointed and confused,
however. Economic and social motivations could be found in every form of
Austrian anti-Semitism. Religious anti-Semitism was naturally most closely
associated with the Catholics in their Christian Social Party, but was by no
means eschewed by the country's other bourgeois parties. Even the Social
Democrats might be accused of religious anti-Semitism, except in their case
they distrusted all religion, not just Judaism. Racial anti-Semitism was most
frequently found in the pan-German parties; but some of the more extreme
Catholics came close to accepting it by refusing to accept baptized Jews as
full-fledged Christians for up to three generations.

To make the incredibly complex task of categorizing Austrian anti-Semitism
as simple as possible this survey will begin at the political "left" with Marxist
anti-Semitism, the most moderate and the most "verbal" of the various types;
the Social Democrats and Communists were also the only people who had

no specifically anti-Semitic program and who directed their wrath exclusively against capitalists, especially Jewish capitalists; the latter could be salvaged by abandoning their exploiting ways. To their credit, the Marxists also occasionally opposed anti-Semitism as an antileftist snare.

Traditional Catholic anti-Semitism will be considered the "middle-of-the-road" variety although it encompassed both moderate and extreme forms of anti-Semitism. Catholics usually "limited" their demands to the reduction of Jewish "influence" though some favored the expulsion of Jewish newcomers. Catholics also considered Jews redeemable if only they converted to Catholicism.

The analysis will conclude with the most violent and modern form of anti-Semitism, that which was espoused by the Austrian Nazis and other ultra-right-wing groups. For them, Jewish salvation was impossible because their evil characteristics were racially inherited. Even the racists disagreed, however, as to how many Jewish ancestors made one hopelessly corrupt and how the "Jewish problem" was to be solved. In practice, most joined the traditionalists in favoring the limitation of Jewish influence or at most the expulsion of the Ostjuden.

This organization has the added advantage of conforming roughly with chronological developments. The Marxists were strongest in the early postwar years when they gained control of the Vienna municipal government in May 1919 (holding it until February 1934) and shared control of the federal government from November 1918 until October 1920. The Christian Socials took sole command of the federal government and were usually in control until the end of the democratic era in 1933 as well as during the authoritarian regime that followed. It was also during the democratic era, especially between 1927 and 1932 that the paramilitary Austrian Heimwehr enjoyed its heyday. Thereafter the Austrian Nazi Party figured ever larger in the politics of the country until, with the help of the German invasion of March 1938, it gained control, or at least partial control, of the annexed state.

THE MARXISTS

The anti-Semitism that manifested itself in Austria's universities and in the violent street demonstrations that accompanied the Zionist Congress in 1925 was merely a reflection, albeit in a more violent form, of the anti-Semitism of Austria's political parties. In the First Austrian Republic *all* of the major political parties, and most of the minor ones as well, were anti-Semitic to one degree or another; and for all of them anti-Semitism was a weapon to be used to embarrass their enemies. To be sure, there were differences on the issue of race and how the "Jewish problem" was to be solved. But there were also many common denominators, especially in terminology and in the use of political caricatures.

Of all the major political parties of Austria, the Marxists in the Social Democratic Workers' Party (SDAP) and the tiny Communist Party were the least anti-Semitic. Neither party included anti-Semitism in their official programs. Likewise, neither party can be accused of racial anti-Semitism. When they did give in to anti-Semitic demagoguery, they at least "limited" their attacks to Jewish capitalists and did not specifically include Jews in general. Socialist anti-Semitism was less severe than that of other major political parties of Austria, probably in part because the industrial workers, who made up the rank-and-file membership of the party, could identify with Jews as another oppressed minority. There was also next to no economic competition for industrial jobs between Jews and non-Jews because few Jews sought employment in this sector. What anti-Semitism there was within the party tended to be defensive, being a response to anti-Semitic attacks directed against the SDAP from other parties.

MARX, ENGELS, AND THE "JEWISH QUESTION"

To a large extent the philosophy the Austrian Socialists and Communists adopted toward Jews was inherited from the founding fathers of Marxism: Karl

Marx and Friedrich Engels. By the same token, some of the Marxist philosophy may have been a subtle inheritance from Judaism. It is, of course, a well-known fact that Marx had a Jewish background, his father having converted to Protestantism from Judaism. Although Marx never practiced Judaism, his idea of a Communist millennium in which the state disappears along with the class struggle resembled Jewish apocalyptic thought and messianism; it might be called a kind of messianic heresy. His methodology also may have been partly rabbinical: his own research was based solely on books and not on personal observation (although he did benefit from the firsthand experiences of Engels).[1]

Despite the possible influence of his Jewish background on his economic theories, some historians have suggested that Marx was an anti-Semite.[2] Superficially there is ample justification for this charge. Marx did, in fact, make far more negative comments than positive ones about Jews, comments that a half century after his death Nazis were fond of quoting. Most of these statements can be traced to an essay he wrote in 1844 called "On the Jewish Question." Among the more provocative things he said were:

> Let us look for the secret of the Jew not in his religion, but let us look for the secret of religion in the actual Jew.
>
> What is the secular cult of the Jew? Haggling. What is the secular god? Money. . . .
>
> Thus we recognize in Judaism a general contemporary anti-social element which has been brought to its present height by a historical development which the Jews zealously abetted in its harmful aspects which now must necessarily disintegrate.
>
> In the last analysis the emancipation of the Jews is the emancipation of humanity from Judaism. . . . The Jews have emancipated themselves in so far as the Christians have become Jews.
>
> What was the implicit and explicit basis of the Jewish religion? Practical need, egoism. . . . Money is the jealous god of Israel before whom no other god may stand. . . . The god of the Jews has been secularized and has become the god of the world.[3]

The Jews also determined the whole fate of the Austrian empire through their money. Their religion showed a contempt for theory, art, and history. They had made economic man an end in himself.[4]

Taken out of context, Marx's comments on Jews would indeed tend to confirm the view that he was an anti-Semite. However, "On the Jewish Question" was written early in his career and represents just the first of four distinct phases of his philosophy vis-à-vis Jews. If his career began with aggressive hostility toward Jews, it ended with indifference. He did not want to rid the world of Jews, but the spirit behind Judaism which he equated with capitalism. Merely disestablishing the religion would not eliminate the religious beliefs or the social ills that gave rise to those beliefs. The Jews and their capitalistic spirit would only disappear in a future classless society, he argued. Marx could not have been an anti-Semite because for him anti-Semites were only people who opposed the struggle against capitalism. He had only one enemy: the capitalists, not the Jews. Nevertheless, the terminology Marx used to describe Jews resembled that used by anti-Semites and made Jews appear to non-Marxists as pure money-makers who were parasitic, clannish, and antisocial.[5]

It was Marx's linkage of capitalism and Judaism that provided much of the material used by both later-day socialists and the bourgeoisie against Jews. Some of Marx's followers thought that if the proletariat would hate Jewish capitalists, they would eventually hate even those capitalists who were not Jews. An early Austrian Socialist bank employee of Jewish origins, Isidor Ehrenfreund, was one of those who believed that anti-Semitism could be used to increase the hatred of capitalists by the proletariat. It was, he wrote to Friedrich Engels in 1890, a necessary road to socialism in a country like Austria where so many prominent capitalists were Jews. According to Ehrenfreund, many Viennese thought that socialism was a movement that wanted to deprive property owners of all of their possessions in order to give them to the proletariat. Engels was already well informed about Austrian anti-Semitism and its oppositionist and democratic associations through the early Austrian Socialist leader Karl Kautsky. Kautsky had written Engels a few years before that it was difficult to prevent socialist workers from fraternizing with anti-Semites.[6]

Engels was not impressed by Ehrenfreund's arguments and told him in a letter that was published in May 1890 in the Austrian party's official organ, the *Arbeiter-Zeitung*, that anti-Semitism was a product of backward societies and therefore was strong in Russia, Prussia, and Austria. In the more modern countries of England and the United States it was considered ridiculous. Anti-Semitism existed, Engels wrote, in places where the lower bourgeoisie and artisans could not compete with big capitalists. Only after the destruction of the lower middle class in Austria would Austria become a modern country. Engels concluded his letter by denouncing anti-Semitism as being only the reaction of dying medieval social classes against modern society and able to serve only reactionary purposes.[7]

Although Ehrenfreund had no desire either to defy Engels or to appear to be a follower of Georg von Schönerer, the attitude of other Socialists toward

Jews and anti-Semitism both before and after the First World War in Austria, as well as in other countries, wavered ambiguously between Marx's equating of Jews and capitalism, Ehrenfreund's desire to exploit anti-Semitism, and Engels's outright rejection of anti-Semitism. Their most consistent belief was that anti-Semitism, the Jewish question, and Jews themselves would vanish with the establishment of socialism and the disappearance of capitalism. "History" alone would eliminate anti-Semitism. At that time the Jews would simply be assimilated into the general population. In other words, cultural, economic, and social progress would eventually overcome national exclusivity, including that of the Jews. In the meantime, Social Democratic leaders expected Jewish workers to get rid of any distinctive traits that might repel their gentile comrades. This was not an attitude likely to win them fast friends among Jews who were conscious of their heritage, especially Zionists. Zionism was regarded by international socialism and Austrian Socialists in particular, both before and after the First World War, as a reactionary, bourgeois, nationalistic movement. Not surprisingly, the Zionists responded by accusing the Socialists of being anti-Zionist or even anti-Semitic. The *Arbeiter-Zeitung* counterattacked by saying that Zionism served the cause of English imperialism.[8]

All of these attitudes were readily apparent almost as soon as the Socialist Party of Austria was founded in 1889. Viktor Adler, one of the founding fathers and himself an apostate Jew, spoke against a condemnation of anti-Semitism at an international party congress in Brussels in 1891 because he said that it would work to the advantage of the party by driving persecuted Jews into the party's ranks. He thought that anti-Semitism was only a form of anticapitalism. However, he did not believe that Jews had invented capitalism; at most they had accelerated its development and worsened its manifestations. Taunted by hecklers about his Jewish background he tried to avoid any appearance of defending Jews. Therefore he did not appoint Jews to leadership positions and admitted that his own Jewish background was a handicap. He was forced to change his policy toward utilizing talented Jews as the party grew into a mass movement. However, the new Jewish intellectuals in the party hierarchy tended to view their Jewish background with the same disdain as Adler.[9]

During the 1890s the Social Democratic Party of Austria maintained a kind of benevolent neutrality toward anti-Semitism. Adler stressed that the Austrian workers should not allow themselves to be exploited by either Jews or Christians. He did believe, as did later Austrian Socialists, that anti-Semitism obscured social questions. However, the party only sporadically attacked anti-Semitism and occasionally indulged in it itself. For example, in 1892 the

Die Sozialdemokratie und die Juden.

Die oben- und untenstehenden Zeichnungen sind originaltreue Wiedergaben **sozialdemokratischer Wahlplakate,** die an allen Ecken und Enden Wiens kleben. Hohn und Verhetzung, wie sie giftiger und bösartiger von Radauantisemiten nicht erdacht werden könnten. Um **christliche Stimmen zu fangen,** appellieren die Sozialdemokraten **an die niedrigsten antisemitischen Instinkte.** Sie prägen in die Seelen der Wähler und der Jugend blutrünstigen Hass und wilde Verachtung für lange Zeit, weit über die Wahlen hinaus.

Anderseits fordern die Sozialdemokraten die Stimmen der Juden!

Jüdische Wähler und Wählerinnen!

**Weist diese schamlose Zumutung zurück! Wahret die Selbstachtung!
Wahret jüdische Ehre und jüdisches Recht!
Wählet am 21. Oktober in allen Wiener Bezirken die Liste der**

„Jüdischen Wahlgemeinschaft!"

Aguda Jisroël   Aguda Jisroël

A Jewish nationalist election poster of 1923 reprinted in Racial Victory in Vienna by Robert Körber depicting the use of anti-Semitic stereotypes by the Social Democrats. The cartoons, which originally appeared in Social Democratic publications, show Jewish capitalists and rabbis cavorting with Roman Catholic and Christian Social officials in an attempt to win over Christian Social voters to the Social Democratic Party.

Arbeiter-Zeitung said that many Galician Jewish immigrants were crooks and swindlers.[10]

THE APPEAL OF SOCIALISM FOR AUSTRIAN JEWS

Until the catastrophic electoral defeats of the Liberal Party in 1895, the Social Democrats were militantly anti-Liberal because of sharp ideological disagreements regarding capitalism, free trade, and the Liberals' opposition to extending the vote to industrial workers. (The working class was not fully enfranchised at the local level in Vienna until after the First World War when they also gained control of the municipal government for the first time.) After 1896, however, Socialist hostility began to shift toward Lueger's Christian Social Party. In that year Socialist representatives in Vienna's city council, reacting to anti-Semitic charges of the Christian Socials, sardonically began using the term "Jewish banks" and referred to the Christian Socials as *Judenschutztruppen* because their party contained a number of (mostly converted) Jews. In language that resembled the anti-Semitism of pan-German nationalists, the *Arbeiter-Zeitung* claimed that Jews controlled the liberal press of Vienna, big industry, the universities, and the arts and sciences, in addition to the major banks. The newspaper's editor, Friedrich Austerlitz, of Jewish origins himself, even wrote that the anti-Semitism of the Lueger period had been "a justified reaction against the indubitable preponderance of the Jews . . . in all spheres of influence of Viennese public life." However, after 1900 Socialists began to take a less neutral attitude toward anti-Semitism and started to see its attacks on free thought, education, and progress as attacks on civilization itself. But this change of heart never induced Socialists to give up their own occasional indulgence in anti-Semitic rhetoric.[11]

With the virtual collapse of the Liberal Party after 1895 a growing number of its Jewish members switched their allegiance to the Socialists. By 1918, when the Liberal Party had become minuscule, the drift had become a flood. Although the Liberals and Socialists had been rivals, the changeover was by no means irrational for Jews. Both parties were heirs of the eighteenth-century Enlightenment. They had secular philosophies and favored reducing the privileges of the Roman Catholic church and the importance of religion in general. Both believed in progress and saw education as the most important instrument of that progress. And both believed in the full range of civil liberties, including freedom of religion and freedom of the press.

For Jews, who in general supported all of these ideas, the Socialist Party had a number of additional advantages. It favored a social welfare program very much in keeping with the three-thousand-year-old Jewish tradition of social justice, which was particularly important for recent Jewish immigrants. Party members were relatively free of anti-Semitic prejudices themselves, and middle-class Jews could identify with their exclusion from society. Finally, Socialism, with its cradle-to-grave-involvement in all aspects of life, became a substitute religion that would bring about a heaven on earth for those Jews who no longer practiced the religion of their ancestors. It was a secular form of messianism.[12]

Only Jews who had completely renounced their religion and who did not regard themselves as big businessmen or capitalists could accept Socialism without any reservations. Many Jewish businessmen, especially small businessmen, voted for the SDAP despite their repugnance for the Marxist critique of capitalism. And practicing Jews could not be pleased with the party's attack on religion. But for most Austrian Jews, there were simply no realistic alternatives aside from political abstention. All the other parties of Austria were overtly anti-Semitic and in some cases even flatly refused to accept Jews as members. Consequently, about 75 percent of the Jews of Austria voted for the Socialists. Unfortunately, this combination of factors also meant that the SDAP did not have to make any special effort to win the Jewish vote. By the same token, its mild anti-Semitism seemed relatively harmless in comparison to the much more vicious anti-Jewish hostility of the other political parties.[13]

A few Jews voted for the Greater German People's Party in 1930 and 1932 perhaps because they favored an Austrian Anschluss with Germany or because the leader of the Greater Germans, Johannes Schober, had been helpful toward Jews during his tenure as police president at the time of the Zionist Congress in 1925. Wealthy Jews were sometimes able to ignore the anti-Semitism and clericalism of the Christian Socials and vote for the party's candidates because of its procapitalist philosophy. And a few thousand other Jews voted for tiny Jewish parties, which, however, never had any representation in the Austrian Parliament after 1920.[14]

Not only did the Socialist Party accept Jews as members, but it also allowed them to play leading roles. By the beginning of the First Republic an estimated 80 percent of the Socialist intellectuals were of Jewish origins. Karl Renner was the only one of the top Socialist leaders who did not have a Jewish background. Sixteen of the twenty-three Socialist literary writers who contributed to *Jung Wien* were Jewish, as were the great majority of the editors of Socialist newspapers. Socialist lawyers, physicians, and secondary-school students and teachers were also predominantly Jewish, as were the overwhelming percentage of the members of the Socialist organization for university students. Socialists, however, did not like to mention statistics such as these for fear of giving ammunition to their enemies.[15]

The leader of the left wing of the Socialist Party and without doubt the party's best-known theoretician, Otto Bauer, was Jewish. Unlike other prominent Socialists who bent over backward to dissociate themselves from their coreligionists, Bauer never left the Jewish community of Vienna even though he was not a practicing Jew. Bauer considered the Jewish people to be a nation, but thought that their extraterritoriality, along with the development of capitalism, condemned them to assimilation. Although he opposed forced assimilation, he urged Jewish workers to resemble native workers culturally. He once assured an English Zionist that he was not antagonistic toward Zionism. Bauer himself was also the object of a good deal of anti-Semitic abuse. On one occasion a stone was hurled at him by a Heimwehr deputy in a meeting of the Parliament's Finance and Budget Committee. Nevertheless, like other Austrian Socialists, Bauer was not willing to renounce the attempt to take the anti-Semitic wind out of bourgeois sails by claiming that the SDAP was the better opponent of Jewish big capitalism and high finance. Ironically, Bauer, like Marx and other Socialist leaders, espoused an ideology resembling the nineteenth-century Catholic philosophy of Karl Vogelsang by equating the "Jewish spirit" with capitalism. They were also careful to point out Christian Social leaders who had Jewish backgrounds in order to demonstrate the hypocrisy of that party's anti-Semitism.[16]

MARXIST ATTACKS ON "JEWISH CAPITALISM"

Although as Marxists the Austrian Social Democrats were theoretically opposed to all capitalists without distinction, in practice they frequently gave the impression of being opposed only to Jewish capitalists. They called on the "real anti-Semites" to join them to fight Jewish capitalism. In order to avoid offending their own Jewish constituency, however, Socialists confined their attacks only to big Jewish businessmen and ignored the small Jewish shopowners.[17]

Examples of such attacks on the big Jewish bourgeoisie in the Socialist press are legion. On 5 October 1919 the *Arbeiter-Zeitung* said that big Jewish capitalists were in agreement with the anti-Semites about Social Democracy. The Jewish factory owners, together with the anti-Semites in the Greater German People's Party and the Christian Social Party, were all opposed to the nationalization of factories. On the other hand, Jewish capital had long since recognized the Social Democratic Party to be its mortal enemy. The 16 March 1921 issue of the *Arbeiter-Zeitung* claimed that the Jewish bourgeoisie did not even mind students, officers, and members of the petite bourgeoisie carrying out violent, anti-Semitic demonstrations because the supposedly anti-Semitic parties never passed any anti-Semitic legislation. The Aryans and the big bourgeoisie knew how to stick together on important issues. In September 1922 the *Arbeiter-Zeitung* called Chancellor Seipel a "puppet of the Jews" who wanted to turn Austria over to the enslavement of Jewish international finance capital by signing the Geneva Protocol, which gave Austria a loan of $126 million.[18] Bold headlines of the 12 September 1923 issue of the same newspaper announced that "the Christian Social anti-Semites were begging Jewish capitalists" for money for the parliamentary elections scheduled for November. The League of Front Fighters was also accused of accepting money from Jews in the Industriellenverband (Union of Industrialists); a few years later similar charges were leveled against the Nazis.[19]

The founding of "Aryan" and "Christian" banks in the provinces during the early 1920s gave the Socialists still more opportunities to attack Jewish capitalists. The banks had presumably been founded to free gentiles from "Jewish" capital. After these banks had gone bankrupt by 1926, a prominent Jewish Socialist in the Austrian Parliament, Robert Danneberg, pointed out how these anti-Semitic banks had lost their money by making poor investments with funds given them by Jewish speculators.[20]

Many if not all of these charges were probably true and were not necessarily inspired by anti-Semitism. There was indeed considerable capitalist class solidarity in Austria; and one could legitimately argue that it was hypocritical of groups to espouse anti-Semitism—often in blatant forms—yet at the same time accept handouts from Jewish capitalists. Nevertheless, the attacks also reinforced the stereotype of Jews being moneygrubbers and manipulators and caused confusion in readers' minds as to whether their real sin was being capitalists or being Jewish.

Socialist publications were also fond of using terms like *Bankjuden, jüdische Borsenpresse* (Jewish stock-market press), and *Borsenjuden* (stock-market Jews) to describe Jewish capitalists. Opponents of the Socialists were often caricatured in cartoons as looking like Jews. In some Socialist publications and posters even Orthodox Jews were ridiculed. Chancellor Seipel was lampooned in 1923 in a Socialist cartoon for making a welcoming speech to the first international congress of the Orthodox Jewish organization called Agudas Jisroel (Association of Israel). Political cartoons in the *Arbeiter-Zeitung* and *Das Kleine Blatt*, like Socialist publications in Germany, often showed capitalists with the same "Jewish" features depicted in strictly anti-Semitic publications.[21]

Sometimes the Socialists' satire was part of an attempt to ridicule racial theories in order to show their absurdity. At times, however, the satire was too subtle and not in good taste. For example, in 1923 the *Arbeiter-Zeitung* said, with tongue in cheek, that Seipel's long nose was the product of a secret and presumably Jewish great grandmother or a legitimate or illegitimate great grandfather.[22]

The *Arbeiter-Zeitung* was by no means the only Socialist publication to identify rich Jews with capitalism. In 1923, a time when anti-Semitism was at its postwar high, a Socialist by the name of Christian Hinteregger published a booklet, with the party's approval, called *Der Judenschwindel*, a pun whose secondary meaning was "the swindle about the Jews." In ninety-six pages the author reiterated all the recent charges that Socialists had made regarding wealthy Jews while at the same time he defended poor Jews. The latter had just as much stake in the November 1918 revolution as poor Christians, but rich Jews and Nazis supported the Seipel government. In a chapter called "The Jewified Anti-Semites," Hinteregger said that anti-Semitism was a tool for diverting people's attention away from the true cause of their troubles, namely capitalism, and from the class struggle. While making war on Jewish peddlers and trying to close the doors of universities to Jewish students, the anti-Semites accepted money from Jewish banks; they built a unity front with Jewish capitalists against workers and employees. Despite its many anti-Semitic tirades, the Christian Social Party named a Jew, Grunberger, to be the minister of food and agriculture in the government it formed in November 1920. A few weeks later they nominated Dr. Kienbock, a half Jew, to be their presidential candidate. After claiming that there were many Eastern European Jews who were unscrupulous money changers and stock-exchange speculators, he charged that the Christian Social government of Chancellor Michael Mayr was doing nothing to stop their activities. And the government of Ignaz Seipel had been dependent on rich Jews from the very beginning, according to Hinteregger.[23]

Der Judenschwindel also defended Jews by pointing out how during the world war Christian Social newspapers supported the war as a great cause willed by God; only after the conflict was over did they blame it on Jews. Likewise, German nationalists tried to hold Jews responsible for the dictated peace treaties when it was really Clemenceau who was to blame. Hinteregger also said that the Social Democratic Party did not object to the idea per se of having a Jew as a state minister, but thought it was a swindle for the anti-Semitic Christian Social Party to have one. Although Hinteregger's goal was to deflate the impact of anti-Semitism, which was being directed against the SDAP, by noting the sharp contrasts between the theories and practices of the anti-Semites, like many other Socialists he attacked Jewish capitalists as much for being in collusion with bourgeois anti-Marxists who were also anti-Semites as for being capitalists. In the end, the reader is confused as to whether the author objected to anti-Semitism itself, or merely to the way that anti-Semitism was being used by the enemies of the Socialist Party.[24]

Although Socialist anti-Semitism was directed primarily against wealthy Jews, other forms of Socialist anti-Semitism, or at least ill will toward Jews, did exist. The newly formed Jewish National Council established by Zionists in October 1918, perhaps hoping to win over Jews in the SDAP, complained to the board of directors of the Social Democratic Party in November of the same year about recent articles and advertisements in the *Arbeiter-Zeitung* that the council considered anti-Semitic (but which may have been actually merely anti-Zionist). If continued, they could arouse the general population against the Jews in a dangerous way. The *Arbeiter-Zeitung* did not take kindly to this criticism and replied that now that there was no longer any censorship it would say anything it wanted. If the Jews were a nationality, they could be criticized like Czechs, Hungarians, or any other nationality.[25]

We have already noted how Albert Sever, the Social Democratic governor of Lower Austria, which at the time still included Vienna, favored the expulsion of all foreigners who had been harming the economy, including (but not limited to) Ostjuden. The attempt to expel the "army of profiteers," which had the support of the whole Social Democratic Party, failed, ostensibly because of an insufficient number of available trains, but more likely, as we saw in Chapter 6, because of diplomatic protests.[26]

Although the Socialists usually opposed anti-Semitism in summer resorts, some exceptions did occur, especially in the federal states during the desperately hard early postwar years. For example, a workers' council in Frohnleiten in Styria warned Jews in August 1919 to leave the health resort within twenty-four hours because they were allegedly eating too much food and driving up the prices. During the same summer many people, but especially Jews, were having difficulty receiving permission from a Socialist workers' council even to enter the province of Tyrol to take a summer vacation.[27]

The anti-Semitic feelings of individual members of the Social Democratic Party may have also reappeared in August 1925 during the Zionist Congress in Vienna. Although the SDAP did not adopt any official policy toward the congress (apart from its already negative attitude toward Zionism in general), as we noted in Chapter 8, 29 of the 202 people arrested during the violent anti-Zionist demonstrations were members of the Social Democratic Party.

Occasionally Socialist leaders denounced anti-Semitism unequivocally as, for example, when Mayor Seitz assailed anti-Semitic rowdyism at the University of Vienna in August 1924. Such comments were not part of any unified Socialist program, however, and only rarely did Socialists denounce anti-Semitism as such instead of simply violence in general.[28]

Equivocation toward anti-Semitism was also the order of the day for Socialists in Germany. At the heart of their reluctance to take a strong stand against anti-Semitism was their inability to take the threat seriously. Racial anti-Semitism seemed like nothing more than a pretext for exploitation. It was also difficult for them to feel much sympathy for a group that prior to 1933 and even more so prior to 1914 was less victimized by discrimination than industrial workers. Consequently, there appeared to be no good reason why they should be singled out for special consideration. To the extent that anti-Semitism needed to be fought at all, the best way to do so seemed to be by simply fighting Nazism. The German Socialists also resembled their Austrian (and Polish) brethren (as well as all other political parties in Germany) by reducing the number of Jews in their party who were parliamentary deputies.[29]

Nevertheless, the Jewish policies of the Austrian and German Socialists were far from identical. There were few instances of anti-Semitism among the German Socialists either before or after the First World War. Even though they made no concerted campaign against anti-Semitism, they frequently ridiculed it, especially during the years that it was strong, and did not ignore its corrupting influences on German society as a whole. They did not even accept anti-Semitic allegations that Jews used unfair economic practices or were unpatriotic.[30]

How does one account for the apparent differences the German and Austrian Socialists had toward the "Jewish question?" Any answer to such a question must, to some extent of course, remain speculative. In all likelihood, however, Austrian Socialists were sensitive of the strength of anti-Semitism particularly in Vienna, which was their own stronghold. It required real political courage for any Austrian politician to fly in the face of such a strong popular current. Another likely explanation lies in the leadership of the two parties. Whereas around 80 percent of the leadership of the Austrian SDAP was of Jewish origins, the comparable figure in Germany was only 10 percent. These facts made the Austrian party extremely vulnerable to the charge of being "jewified" and made their leaders all the more anxious to take no action that would seem to confirm the allegation. Many of them also viewed their Jewish heritage with disdain and did their best to dissociate themselves from their origins.[31]

ANTI-SEMITES AND THE SOCIAL DEMOCRATIC PARTY

Socialist anti-Semitism found in a book like Hinteregger's or in many articles published by the *Arbeiter-Zeitung* and other Socialist newspapers cannot be fully understood apart from anti-Semitic attacks made against the Social Democratic Party. This question will be examined in more detail in subsequent chapters dealing with the other political parties of Austria; a few remarks need to be made here, however, as well.

There was in fact a flood of anti-Socialist pamphlets published during the 1920s, most of which had the goal of convincing the readers that the Socialist Party was thoroughly *verjudet* and that working-class *Volksgenossen* (blood brothers) were being led astray by racial enemies, namely the Jews. These pamphlets, along with countless articles in newspapers making essentially the same arguments, were challenges that the Social Democrats simply could not ignore. Because they could not deny that there were Jews within their party, the simplest counterattack was to point out Jews who were members of other parties or suggest that those anti-Semitic parties were dependent on Jewish capital.

One of the best known and most vicious of the anti-Socialist and anti-Semitic pamphlets was one written by Karl Paumgarten called *Judentum und Sozialdemokratie (Jewry and Social Democracy)*, published in 1920. Paumgarten began his book with an attack on other anti-Semites who did not understand the "essential characteristics" of Jews. Violently anti-Semitic pamphlets that could not explain why Jews were exploiters, arrogant, and greedy for power only made Jewish refutations easy and gave anti-Semitism a bad name. Paumgarten's answer to the mystery of Jewish behavior lay in race. The Jews were racially different from "Aryans" and therefore could no more become Aryans than Mongolians could become Negroes or Germans could become American Indians. Races were basically different from each other and not just physically but also spiritually, intellectually, ethically, and aesthetically. Moreover, these psychic characteristics of races remained unchanged from generation to generation. Poor Jews were just as materialistic as wealthy ones. All of them were born to lie, cheat, and swindle; they did not even regard these things as bad. Jews therefore could no more change their racial instincts than they could

Title page from Jewry and Social Democracy *by Karl Paumgarten.*

change the shape of their skulls. Jews simply could not understand the material and spiritual way of life of the German people. Whereas the Germans were essentially idealistic and creative, the Jews were materialistic and were good only for accumulating goods.[32]

It was these racially alien Jews who had taken over the Social Democratic Party, according to Paumgarten. Jews like Karl Marx and Kurt Eisner (the leader of the Communist revolution in Bavaria in 1918–19) had dropped their Jewish names and adopted German ones in order to make themselves more acceptable to German workers. Socialism, like liberalism, was merely a means for attaining Jewish world domination. The power of Jewry was greater now than ever before. The German workers had not been working for themselves but for Jews. Workers ought to be red with shame that they had been siding with the mortal enemy of the German people against their blood brothers.[33]

Other anti-Semitic pamphlets charged that Jewish Socialists held the most important positions in the federal government after the war. The Jewish domination of the Social Democratic Party was even greater after the war than before. During the war the Jews had allegedly occupied all the free professions so these positions were not available to returning veterans, thus forcing thousands of German Austrians to emigrate to other countries. Otto Bauer had presumably aggravated the problem by preventing the Jewish refugees from being expelled. The SDAP was delighted with the immigration of the Ostjuden because it gave the party new voters.[34]

The idea that the Social Democratic Party was led, or misled, by "alien" Jews was not confined entirely to nonparty members. Such allegations were also leveled from within the party itself. This was especially true after the collapse of the brief uprising in February 1934 when Socialist workers in Linz, reacting to the tightening dictatorship of Chancellor Engelbert Dollfuss, initiated a desperate revolt which quickly spread to Vienna. After just three days, however, it was suppressed by the government with excessive brutality and the party was outlawed. Some of the party's rank-and-file members could not resist the temptation to accuse the party's "Jewish" leadership, including Otto Bauer and Julius Deutsch, the leader of the party's paramilitary Schutzbund, of first preaching revolution and then deserting the party and fleeing to Czechoslovakia once that revolution took place.[35]

Any latent anti-Semitism that existed within the SDAP was exploited by both the Austrian government and the, by now, illegal Austrian Nazi Party. Both groups, but especially the Nazis, tried to foster the idea that the workers had been seduced, misled, and then abandoned by Jewish "word slingers" and "cafe revolutionaries." The Nazis' hopes of winning over at least half of the

Cartoon from Jewry and Social Democracy *by Karl Paumgarten showing an
"Aryan" worker attacking an "Aryan" capitalist.
The supratitle reads, "Kill him! He is your brother!"*

Socialists' membership were never fully realized, however.[36] By June 1934 a German observer in Austria noted that Socialist conversions had lasted for "only a short time" after the February revolt. A more important long-term effect, however, was a reluctance by the party's membership to invite its former Jewish leadership to return to the country after 1945.[37]

Thrown on the defensive by anti-Semitic charges about the close connection between Judaism and Socialism, the Socialists felt obliged to strike back. Instead of simply denouncing anti-Semitism, however, they often preferred to respond with what bordered on anti-Semitic charges of their own and implied that their opposition to "Jewish capitalism" made them superior to their anti-Semitic opponents.[38] Although they did not formally espouse anti-Semitism in a party platform, they were no more willing than the other political parties of Austria to be Judenschutztruppen. As in Germany, the espousal of the Jewish cause could hurt the party attempting it more than it would help the Jews. And Jewish support in both Austria and Germany was regarded as more of a liability than an asset.[39] At most the Austrian Socialists were willing to provide spiritual and material support for poor and lower-class Jews while attacking Jewish capitalists with the same rhetoric used later by the Nazis. But such attacks were not motivated by racial or religious antagonism. For them the world was not divided between Jews and Christians but between capitalists and the proletariat.[40]

11

THE ROMAN CATHOLICS

For Austrian Marxists the Jewish bourgeoisie represented a conservative social force that blocked the Socialists' goals of nationalizing industries by upholding the social and economic status quo. Ironically, Austrian Catholics saw them in exactly the opposite light. For them, Jews were revolutionaries or at least extreme modernists who were determined to secularize society by undermining the Catholic faith and traditional Christian values.

Roman Catholic anti-Semitism was also far more diffuse than the Marxist variety. Marxists limited their attacks to Jewish capitalists and, to a much smaller extent, the Zionists. Catholics sometimes also attacked "Jewish capitalism" as well as "Jewish materialism" and, in theory at least, agreed with Socialists in rejecting racial anti-Semitism. But by far their greatest wrath was reserved for the Jewish intellectuals, especially those in the Social Democratic Party. The secularism and modernity of these Jewish savants were in direct conflict with the religious traditionalism of Catholics. In premodern times practicing Jews had been the chief objects of Christian anti-Semitism; however, after the mid-nineteenth century, the Catholic church, not only in Austria but also in Poland and other European countries, saw "freethinkers"— whether or not they still belonged to the Jewish community, had nominally converted to Christianity, or had renounced religion altogether—as by far its greatest threat. Such Jews were held responsible for all the trends of modern society that Catholics abhorred: atheism, Bolshevism, revolution, liberalism, capitalism, and pornography. On the other hand, as we already saw with the Zionist Congress of 1925, Austrian Catholics assumed a fairly benevolent attitude toward Zionism. Likewise, Catholics did not object to Orthodox Judaism, no doubt because Orthodox Jews, even more than Zionists, tended to live in a world of their own and posed no threat to the Catholic religion or to traditional Christian values.[1]

After the First World War "the Jew" remained for both the Roman Catholic church and its political arm, the Christian Social Party (CSP), almost entirely negative in contrast to their own absolutely positive characteristics. The church and the party were Christian, Social, and patriotic. The Jews, on the other hand, were in Catholic eyes the advocates of anticlericalism, anarchical democracy, egalitarianism, irresponsible freedom, rationalism, and doctrinaire individualism.[2]

TRADITIONAL CATHOLIC ANTI-JUDAISM

Although political, diplomatic, and military history can be divided into separate eras with relative ease, the same cannot be said for social, economic, or intellectual history. In these fields historical epochs do not end all at once. Rather there is a very large amount of untidy overlapping. These generalizations are especially true of the history of anti-Semitism in both Austria and Germany. Although Marxist anti-Semitism was of far more recent vintage than the Catholic variety, it by no means replaced it. Even though some newly emerging social groups such as the industrial working class and the academically trained bourgeoisie—both of them militantly anticlerical—abandoned religious anti-Semitism in favor of "progressive" economic or racial anti-Semitism, the more traditional form remained surprisingly tenacious, especially among such traditional social groups as the clergy, the peasantry, and the lower middle class.[3] Crucifixes in classrooms and along country paths were reminders of the Catholic belief that Jews were the murderers of God.[4] So widespread was anti-Semitism among Austrian Catholics that organizations that carried the name "Christian" in their title could almost be assumed to be hostile toward Jews.

Catholic journals and newspapers in the First Republic were filled with articles denouncing Jews in very traditional terms. Such denunciations could be found in almost every issue of the prestigious new weekly magazine, *Schönere Zukunft*. Founded in 1925, it was far from being considered an extremist publication featuring as it did commentaries on current events by Catholic bishops, professors of theology, and leading Catholic politicians, not only from Austria but from Hungary and Germany as well. The editor of *Schönere Zukunft*, the German-born Josef Eberle, considered the Jewish question to be the most important of all questions and was himself a frequent contributor of anti-Jewish articles, introductions, and editorials.[5] Eberle proved to be one of the primary moving forces of Catholic anti-Semitism, and not just because of his work for *Schönere Zukunft*. Already in 1920 he had demanded the restriction of Jewish involvement in all aspects of Austria's cultural and economic life to the Jewish percentage of the country's population. Jews, he wrote, ought to be placed under special laws, and the assets of wealthy Jews above a certain point ought to be confiscated for the good of society. In 1926 Eberle was apparently instrumental in making sure that the new program of the Christian Social Party contained an anti-Semitic section. In 1929 he complained in the pages of *Schönere Zukunft* that anti-Semitic efforts of the CSP had been pushed into the background during the previous ten years compared with such efforts in the early history of the party. The Jews, with only 5 percent (*sic*) of the population, played a leading role in the country and formed a kind of state within a state. This was the fault of Christians themselves, however, because they continued to shop at Jewish stores and read Jewish newspapers.[6]

Eberle's primary function was advocating the cause of traditional Catholicism, including traditional Catholic anti-Semitism. In one of the early issues of *Schönere Zukunft*, Eberle claimed that the Talmud predicted future wealth for Jews. This creed had created a type of person who was dangerous to those tolerating him. The one-sided approval of wealth, property, and power by the Jewish religion gave Jews an advantage over Christians, who sanctioned these things only to a very limited extent. The fight against Jews was not a matter of hatred or of racism, but a fight against the contradiction of the Christian idea. The triumph of Jews in the modern world was God's way of punishing Christians for the Renaissance and Reformation, and for rejecting the ideas and organizations of Christianity. Elsewhere Eberle maintained that the fundamental answer to the threat posed by Jewry was the re-Christianization of society. On other occasions, however, Eberle advanced more secular proposals, such as special laws for Jews. He also published articles calling for boycotts of Jewish department stores.[7]

Another contributor to *Schönere Zukunft* was a Catholic theology professor from Salzburg, Dr. Alois Mager, who wrote in 1928 that the radical rejection of Christ and his manifestations had given Jews their special character and attitudes. Jews throughout the centuries had always reacted against anything Christian, and Judaism was still present in all anti-Christian movements. Nothing was so anti-Christian as capitalism, which expressed the essence of Judaism.[8] Another theology professor, Dr. Karl von Balas of Budapest, added that the great goal of the Jews was ruling the world, although they were clever enough to disguise their methods of achieving this aim.[9]

Of course, *Schönere Zukunft* was far from being the only outlet for Catholic anti-Semitism. An anonymous pamphlet called *Die Juden im Staate Deutsch-Österreich* (*The Jews in the State of German-Austria*) was published in 1920. Modern Jewry, the author claimed, poisoned both economic life and Christian morality. The Jewish spirit was one of naked profit and heartless egotism. Jews believed that their natural enemy was the Roman Catholic church, which they wanted to undermine through spreading disbelief, by organizing strife between different Christian denominations, and through the use of slander and ridicule. Jews had invented anticlericalism and were responsible for the hatred of Christianity within the Social Democratic Party. Jews and revolution were inseparable; in Russia Kerensky, Lenin, and Trotsky were all Jews, as were Karl Liebknecht, Rosa Luxemburg, and Kurt Eisner in Germany. In defending themselves against this menace, Christians did not want to fight the Jewish religion or use force against Jews, some of whom were upright. Rather, Jews ought to be treated as a separate nation, just as the Zionists demanded. The Jewish press, which was the main source of Jewish influence, also had to be fought. The latter was the task of the recently organized "Piusverein." The best method of immunization against Jewish influence, however, was through a religious revival.[10]

Catholic anti-Semitism was also very much in evidence at a conference of Catholic academicians in Innsbruck in 1925. Bishop Sigismund Waitz called the Jews an "alien people" who had corrupted England, France, Italy, and especially America. Americanism, he said, was nothing more than the Jewish "spirit." Thanks to Jewish control over banks and newspapers, their power in the last few years had grown in an uncanny way. If people did not cultivate Christianity, Jews would become even more powerful. On the other hand, the more Christian life flourished, the more protected the Christian people would be against the corrupting influence of unbelieving Jewry.[11]

Other similar publications included *Kikiriki*, a satirical magazine that specialized in attacks on "stock-market Jews" and carried inflammatory caricatures of Orthodox Ostjuden with the sidelocks. It has even been described as a forerunner of Julius Streicher's infamous *Stürmer* in Nuremberg.[12] Anti-Semitic articles and editorials were also commonplace in such newspapers as the *Grazer Volksblatt*, the *Salzburger Volksblatt*, *Der Bauernbündler*, the *Klerus Zeitschrift für soziale Arbeit*, the *Kleines Kirchenblatt* (a newspaper written for Roman Catholic youth), and countless other Catholic or Christian Social newspapers and journals.[13]

By far the most important of these periodicals was the *Reichspost*. However, its circulation of 50,000 made it only the fourth largest newspaper in Austria after 1925; the *Arbeiter-Zeitung*, with 112,000 readers, the *Neue Freie Presse* with 75,000, and the *Neues Wiener Tagblatt* with 55,000, were all larger. In fact, the *Reichspost's* inferior circulation, which caused financial difficulties, and the absence of journalists comparable with those of the great

Jewish-dominated newspapers, were doubtless behind some of the *Reichspost's* anti-Semitism.[14]

Although it was the official organ of the entire Christian Social Party, its readers came mostly from the conservative right wing of the party, which supported Ignaz Seipel. Since the first year of its publication in 1894, the paper dealt with all aspects of the Jewish question in a way designed to evoke an emotional response. The attacks were always aimed against Jews in general, rather than particular Jews. The paper's editor, Friedrich Funder, like Karl Lueger, determined who was a Jew and did not hesitate to socialize with individual Jews as long as they were baptized.[15]

Anti-Jewish articles were endemic in the *Reichspost*, especially in the early postwar years. Shortly after the armistice, the *Reichspost* complained that Jewish soldiers were stealing valuable items from the Habsburg palaces of Schönbrunn and the Hofburg. In 1919 it claimed that six million Germans in Austria were being ruled by a tiny percentage of Jews who belonged not only to a different nation but also to a different race. Other articles dealt with the overrepresentation of Jews in Austrian schools and universities, the supposed prominence of Jews in the Austrian government, and the need for expelling the Ostjuden. The *Reichspost* was also fond of attacking its rival, the *Neue Freie Presse,* and its predominantly Jewish editorial staff. Almost all of the anti-Semitic articles were linked to the Social Democratic Party, which was blamed for allowing Jewish refugees to remain in the country.[16]

A favorite topic for the *Reichspost* was the alleged effort by "the Jews" to take over the world, a thesis that the paper tried to prove with contradictory evidence and illogical arguments. Jewish mastery of the world was portrayed not as a question, a possibility, or even an eventuality, but as an established fact. Not surprisingly, therefore, the *Reichspost* ended an article about the *Protocols of Zion* by speaking of their "shocking nature" even though the beginning of the same article expressed doubt about the very authenticity of the *Protocols.*[17]

Not all of the articles in the *Reichspost* that dealt with Jews were negative. The paper consistently supported Zionism; it praised the founding of the Jewish National Council in the fall of 1918. We have already noted its generally positive stand toward Zionism at the time of the Zionist Congress.[18] The *Reichspost* favored the same policy of dissimilation advocated by the Zionists, but went even further by wanting to revoke the Jews' equal rights. It favored special laws for Jews that would have limited their freedom of choice in business and the professions as well as where they lived; it also wanted to prevent Jews from holding public office or even from voting.[19]

The anti-Semitism of Friedrich Funder and the *Reichspost* paralleled almost

Friedrich Funder, anti-Semitic editor of the Reichspost.
Austrian National Library Picture Archive.

exactly Austrian anti-Semitism in general. It was very strong between the founding of the newspaper in 1894 and Lueger's appointment as mayor in 1897, declined during Lueger's administration only to rise again after the Christian Social Party was defeated in the national elections of 1911. Its anti-Semitism subsided once again during the First World War, no doubt in part due to press censorship, but rose again after Austria's defeat, which the paper blamed on the influence of international Jewry. It remained strong in the early postwar years, but almost disappeared between 1926 and 1930, possibly due in some measure to Seipel's influence, only to reappear once more with the economic crisis and the meteoric rise of the Nazis.[20]

Most criticisms of Jews in *Schönere Zukunft*, the *Reichspost*, and other Catholic and Christian Social publications were extremely general. There were, however, also some specific points of conflict with Jews. Catholics strenuously objected to attempts made by Socialist politicians of Jewish origins, Lucian Brunner and Julius Ofner, to eliminate the use of public revenues for building Catholic churches in Vienna and efforts to make divorces easier to obtain. In the latter case, Ofner's effort to abolish the old marriage law, which differed according to the religious beliefs of the marriage partners, created an enormous reaction not only from Catholics but also from Zionists. The latter saw Ofner's proposed reform as an unwarranted intervention in internal Catholic affairs, which would inevitably provoke Christian hostility. The church and the Christian Social Party also differed sharply with secularized Jews in the Social Democratic Party about the role of religion in public schools. Socialists continued the Liberal tradition of treating religion as just one subject in the schools. The Socialist school reformer, Otto Glöckel, even wanted the teaching of religion in public schools replaced by instruction in morality. Roman Catholics, on the other hand, led by the *Reichspost*, wanted religion to permeate all subjects.[21]

THE POSTWAR CHRISTIAN SOCIAL PARTY

The Roman Catholic church and its defenders such as *Schönere Zukunft* could only denounce Jews; they could not legislate against them. The organization that had that power was the Christian Social Party. We have already observed in Chapter 3 how anti-Semitism was central to the propaganda of the first great leader of the CSP, Karl Lueger. Lueger and his supporters, however, did not enact any anti-Semitic legislation in Vienna or elsewhere in Austria—nor, for that matter, did Christian Social politicians in the First Republic. But anti-

Semitism remained an important part of Christian Social propaganda and was a major integrating factor in holding the socially heterogeneous party together. The anti-Semitism of the Christian Socials also remained opportunistic and like Lueger, they could never even agree on how to define a Jew. The CSP used anti-Semitism when it saw some political advantage to be gained, or at least to prevent some other political party from gaining an undue advantage. The party was consistent only in almost never allowing Jews, even baptized Jews, to serve in the cabinets of Christian Social chancellors. On the other hand, the party was not above accepting money from Jewish capitalists to fight Social Democrats, just as the *Arbeiter-Zeitung* charged.[22]

An enormous new impetus to Christian Social anti-Semitism was the party's massive defeat in the Vienna municipal elections of May 1919. Having controlled the city's government without interruption since Karl Lueger's appointment as mayor in 1897 the CSP now found itself outnumbered by the Social Democrats—with their many Jewish leaders—one hundred deputies to fifty in the city council. The *Wiener Stimmen* blamed the electoral annihilation on the Ostjuden, a ridiculous charge since few of them were citizens with the right to vote. This fact did not prevent the Christian Socials from continuing to charge that the Socialist majority in the municipal government was produced by the votes of Eastern European Jews, even though between 1920 and 1925 only a little over 20,000 Jews were ever granted the *Heimatrecht* (right of residency) needed to vote and only about half of them were Ostjuden.[23]

Although the Christian Socials never actually enacted any anti-Semitic legislation, unlike the Social Democrats they did include anti-Semitism in the official programs of individual federal states in 1918 and 1919. The program of the CSP in Vienna in December 1918 promised to fight a defensive struggle against Jewish "corruption and thirst for power." The Jews ought to be "recognized as a nation with self-determination, but they ought not be allowed to become the masters of the German people." The CSP's Vienna program in November 1919 was a little more specific. In order "to protect the German character of Vienna," it demanded that the naturalization of *Volksfremde* (foreigners) be made difficult and that a numerus clausus for Jewish university students and instructors be enacted. Jewish pupils were also to be segregated into their own schools or else into their own classes. It declared that Jews were a separate nation and ought to be recognized and counted as such.[24]

Individual Christian Social politicians also made other anti-Semitic proposals in 1919. In July several party members sent a bill to the Parliament, aimed primarily against Jews, that would have prevented name changes. In October a group of ten Christian Social parliamentary deputies proposed that Jews not be allowed to serve in the Austrian army, a right they had enjoyed since the time of Joseph II. On the same day an equal number of Christian Social deputies asked Parliament to count Jews as a separate race in the next census.[25]

Provincial branches of the Christian Social Party were also busy formulating anti-Semitic programs in the early postwar years. The Salzburg branch demanded the expulsion of Jews from all public offices. The Salzburgers as well as the party in Carinthia insisted that Jewish participation in public life (apparently meaning the free professions) be limited to their percentage of the population. The party as a whole, however, never demanded a general numerus clausus for Jews in all aspects of Austrian life.[26]

A more unified approach for the Christian Social Party was taken in 1926 when the party drew up its first national program at a congress in Linz. Reflecting the overall decline in Austrian anti-Semitism during the previous three years, the new document no longer talked about the Christian Social Party fighting Jews or their influence in intellectual and economic affairs, but instead condemned "the predominance of the disintegrating Jewish influence." This vague wording could be interpreted in two quite different ways: it could mean that all the Jewish influence was a disintegrating element or it could mean that the party would fight Jewish influence only when it was a disintegrating element. The second interpretation was preferred both by Chancellor Ignaz Seipel and by Jews, who saw the program as a major revision of the party's anti-Semitic policy. The program also observed that Jews had been prominent among the leaders and propagandists of the Russian Bolsheviks, the Communists of Central Europe, and the Socialists of Austria. But Seipel also softened the impact of this statement by commenting that these facts did not result from the national character of Jews or from the essence of their religion, but from their being oppressed for hundreds of years.[27]

LEOPOLD KUNSCHAK AND THE EXTREME CATHOLIC ANTI-SEMITES

Without any doubt, a major driving force in the anti-Semitism in the Christian Social Party of the early postwar years, and to a lesser extent in later years as well, was a former saddlemaker's apprentice named Leopold Kunschak. Possibly the most versatile and talented organizer in the party after Lueger, Kunschak's power base was his leadership of the party's Arbeiterverein (Workers' Association), which he founded in 1892, when he was twenty-one. Kunschak had at first strongly sympathized with both the anti-Semitism and the antiliberalism found in the *Deutsches Volksblatt*. Ultimately, however, he split with the paper and with Georg von Schönerer over the question of German nationalism. Like his close friend Lueger, Kunschak remained loyal to the Habsburgs and to the monarchy. Kunschak's anti-Semitism was also even more irrational and mythical than Schönerer's; Kunschak glorified the Middle Ages and wanted to return Jews to their medieval ghettos.[28]

Kunschak's workers' movement almost inevitably had to be as anticapitalist as it was antimodern. Not surprisingly it was especially opposed to "Jewish capitalism," another similarity it had with Karl Lueger's anti-Semitism. For Kunschak, capitalism and Marxism were both the creations of Jews. By merely attacking "Jewish" capitalism, Kunschak could avoid any direct confrontations with the capitalist system in Austria and the capitalist supporters of the Christian Social Party; likewise, latent class conflicts could be covered up.[29]

To distinguish themselves from the attacks made on Jewish capitalism by Marxists, Kunschak and his followers gave to their anti-Semitism a religious and racial element. Kunschak was far from being the first Catholic to introduce a biological element into Judeophobia. In the late Middle Ages it had been common to identify proselytes as former Jews. During the Spanish Inquisition certificates of "purity" were given to people with purely Christian ancestry. In the early twentieth century Karl Lueger had publicly warned that Christians ought to beware of Jewish converts.[30]

Kunschak's racism could be seen in his use of such terms as *Abstammung* (descent), *bodenständig* (native), and *Kulturgemeinschaft des deutschen Volkes* (cultural community of the German people) as well as in his criticisms of Negroes and Slavs. Jews were immoral, dishonest middlemen, profiteers, and smugglers. They were not capable of creating anything positive. Even the reputations of Freud and Einstein rested on Jewish propaganda. Jews could not eradicate their characteristics merely by not practicing Judaism. Consequently, even baptized Jews could not be assimilated for at least two generations.[31]

With the easing of wartime censorship in 1918, Kunschak began to make public speeches denouncing the Jews. He accused them of stabbing the country in the back by corrupting civil and military authorities and making huge profits in the process. The military defeat therefore was also the fault of the Jews, as was the postwar economic misery, for which the Ostjuden in particular were responsible. Kunschak was one of the primary agitators for the expulsion of all Jewish refugees; if that proved to be impossible, he wanted them interned in concentration camps.[32]

In 1919 Kunschak drew up a detailed proposal for the solution to the "Jewish problem," which he submitted to the Christian Social parliamentary club (delegation) in November. It was designed to limit Jewish influence in public

Ignaz Seipel (fourth from left), chancellor of Austria, 1922–24 and 1926–29, being greeted in Hütteldorf by Leopold Kunschak (holding hat), leader of the Christian Social Workers' Association. Austrian National Library Picture Archive. "Either one solves [the Jewish question] in a timely way, inspired by reason and humaneness," Kunschak declared in a 1936 speech, "or it will be solved in the way an unreasoning animal attacks his prey, with enraged, wild instincts" (Deutsches Volksblatt, 21 March 1936).

life by declaring them a separate nationality with limited rights and segregating them from the "German" majority. Resignations from the Israelitische Kultusgemeinde would not be recognized even for people who converted to Christianity. Jews would have been required to attend separate primary and secondary schools, and a numerus clausus would have been implemented for Jews in Austrian universities. Likewise, Jews would not have been able to serve in the army, police, judiciary or parliamentary body at any level. They would have been able to practice various professions only if they did not exceed their percentage of the total population in each Austrian state.[33]

Ignaz Seipel made moderating comments on each one of Kunschak's proposals. But Seipel also remarked that the proposed law, if implemented, would have required a similar one for the Czech minority. He concluded that although the plan might ultimately be realistic, for the moment it could not be enacted because of foreign and domestic political considerations. In all likelihood Seipel feared that Kunschak's bill would violate the Treaty of St. Germain and result in sanctions being imposed on Austria. He also realized that such a plan had no chance of being approved by the Social Democrats or even by some Christian Social deputies.[34]

Even though Kunschak's legislative proposal for Jewish dissimilation was never approved, he continued to advocate his brand of racial anti-Semitism within his own Christian Social workers' movement. A congress of the Arbeiterverein in Linz in 1923 demanded that "the leaders of [Austrian] workers belong to the native Christian population both in their descent and in their way of thinking and that the disintegrating influence of Jewry must be driven out of the intellectual and economic life of the German people." An official commentary on the program stated that the Austrian people had the right to protect themselves against Jews in the same way that Americans defended themselves against the Chinese.[35]

Leopold Kunschak's brand of extreme and racist-tinged anti-Semitism remained a minority element within the Christian Social Party, particularly after his resignation as chairman in 1922. Nevertheless, he continued to be an important factor within the party. As chairman of the Christian Social Club in Vienna's city council until 1932, he was able to strengthen the anti-Semitism of other Christian Social politicians and prelates. The rise of the Nazis seems only to have increased his fanaticism. After proudly describing himself as a "lifelong anti-Semite" in a public speech to a group called the Freiheitsbund in March 1936, he declared that there were only two possible solutions to the Jewish problem: "Either one solves [it] in a timely way, inspired by reason, and humaneness, or it will be solved in the way an unreasoning animal attacks his prey, with enraged, wild instincts." The Nazis, who quoted this speech at length, could hardly have described the alleged alternatives more forcefully.[36]

Leopold Kunschak was by no means the only de facto racist within the Catholic camp. Father Georg Bichlmair, the Jesuit leader of a missionary group for the conversion of Jews called the "Paulus-Missionswerke," declared in a public speech in March 1936 that Jews belonged to a different race than the German people. Sympathy for the Jews should not blind Christians to the dangerous, contagious effects of the Jewish national character and to the spiritual homelessness of the Jews. Because of their race, Bichlmair believed, Jews remained different from Christians even if they were baptized. He therefore opposed baptized Jews holding any high office in the church hierarchy or the civil service up to the third generation. In this respect, Bichlmair's policy was

P. Georg Bichlmair, leader of the Paulus-Missionswerk to convert Jews. Austrian National Library Picture Archive. "The Christian culture and tradition of the German-[Austrian] people has fallen too much under the influence of the Jewish people in the last decades," he claimed in a speech entitled "The Christian and the Jew" delivered in March 1936 (Reichspost, 19 March 1936).

in accord with that of the Jesuits, who would not accept as novices anyone whose grandfather had not already converted to Catholicism. Bichlmair also believed that the "Aryan paragraph" was necessary for certain organizations in order to defend Christian ethics.[37]

THE MODERATE ANTI-SEMITE: IGNAZ SEIPEL

Much more influential within the Christian Social Party than either Leopold Kunschak or Georg Bichlmair was Dr. Ignaz Seipel, professor of theology at the University of Vienna and chancellor of Austria from 1922 to 1924 and again from 1926 to 1929. As chancellor he protected the rights of all citizens regardless of their religion and refused to allow a numerus clausus in Austrian universities even though in 1922 he had declared that "German" students needed to be protected from the competition of Jewish students by such a cap on Jewish enrollment. He denounced racial anti-Semitism in his book *Staat und Nation*, published in 1916, and on numerous other occasions, including a statement he made to the leadership of the Union of German-Austrian Jews in 1923. He spoke out against the forced expulsion of Jews in 1919 and never indulged in vulgar, public anti-Semitic outbursts. In 1927, in order to win over liberals and democrats for a "Unity List" for the parliamentary election of that year, he declared that for him there was no Jewish question. Seipel also toned down the already fairly moderate official party program of the previous year. These opinions caused the radically anti-Semitic *Deutsches Volksblatt* to call Seipel's Jewish policy "treason toward Christian-German culture." *Der eiserne Besen* doubted in 1927 whether Seipel's party could still be called anti-Semitic.[38]

If Seipel's views toward Jews can be characterized by restraint, they were also at times ambiguous and even tinged with racial overtones. He thought Jews had their own characteristics and had not become Europeans even after having lived in Europe for many centuries. He considered the Jews to be a national minority of a special kind, partly because they had no compact territory of their own and partly because they also were a class representing mobile capital. Consequently the struggle of non-Jews against Jews was to some extent a class struggle. Christians felt economically threatened by Jewish big capital and because they could not compete with Jewish business practices. They also felt a special need to defend themselves when the allegedly unscrupulous Jewish business spirit was carried over into politics, the press, scholarship, literature, and art. The danger to Christians of being dominated by Jews was especially strong because of their leading role in the Social Democratic Party. The best solution to these problems was to recognize the Jews as a separate nation with national autonomy, including their own schools, something the Zionists were already demanding. If this proved unacceptable to the majority of Jews, they could be granted proportional representation in Austria's political, cultural, and educational institutions. In this he agreed in principle with many points made by Kunschak in his unsuccessful legislative proposal of 1919. He also agreed with Kunschak that Jews did not cease to be Jews simply by leaving the Jewish Community. On the other hand, he differed from both Kunschak and Bichlmair in believing that Jews ceased to be Jews once they converted to Christianity.[39]

Although Seipel gave some indication of becoming more alarmed about Jews in three death-bed interviews he gave in 1932, on the whole Austrian Jews appear to have held him in high esteem if only because his anti-Semitism was so much more moderate than that of many other Austrian politicians. The Zionist *Wiener Morgenzeitung*, which naturally would have approved of Seipel's call for separate Jewish schools, remarked editorially in June 1924, shortly after an unsuccessful attempt on his life had failed, that the chancellor had never acted as a blind zealot of the church and had given no inflammatory speeches against Jews. He had also rejected "active" anti-Semitism. Likewise, the assimilationist *Wahrheit*, in an obituary written in August 1932, said that the former chancellor had treated Jews fairly, particularly on religious questions. The paper criticized him only for having tolerated the anti-Semitic programs of the Christian Social Party and for having sympathized with the "student nations" academic reform of 1930. In general, however, the paper said that Austrian Jews would remember him as an honorable man, a point also made by Seipel's long-time political foe, Otto Bauer, in a famous parliamentary tribute made immediately after the former chancellor's death.[40]

EMMERICH CZERMAK AND THE PRO-ZIONISTS

Leopold Kunschak and Ignaz Seipel were not the only Catholics to favor the dissimilation of Jews from Austrian society. The idea was revived by a former minister of education, leader of the Sudeten Germans in Austria, and prominent Christian Social politician, Emmerich Czermak. Together with a well-known Zionist author, Oskar Karbach, Czermak published in 1933 a lengthy proposal for the segregation of Jews entitled *Ordnung in der Judenfrage: Verständigung mit dem Judentum?* (*Order in the Jewish Question: An Under-*

Emmerich Czermak, chairman of the Christian Social Party in 1934 and author of
Order in the Jewish Question (Ordnung in der Judenfrage). *Austrian National
Library Picture Archive. "Assimilation has failed; in the middle of the host people
the Jews, with their equal rights, remain an alien body," Czermak asserted.
"A special minority law must be created."*

standing with Jewry?). Although little in the book was really new, it needs to be examined here in some detail if only because Czermak was in charge of "solving the Jewish problem" for the Christian Social Party,[41] and because he became chairman of the party only a few weeks after the book's publication. The book itself also evoked an enormous public response.

The Czermak–Karbach proposal was a radical solution to the "Jewish problem"—at least as measured by contemporary Austrian standards though not by the standards of Nazi Germany—expressed in disarmingly moderate language. "Any solution based on the principle that one race [was] more valuable than another [was] rejected," as was the Old Testament law of revenge. Both Jews and gentiles had to have an opportunity to earn a living and mutual hatred had to be eliminated. However, the proposal was also based on the principle that the mixing of Jews and Germans had been bad for both people. The authors declared that the liberal, socialist, Bolshevik Jewry of their day was degenerate. This was also clear to Jews who regarded themselves as Jewish nationalists.[42]

In his section of the book Czermak argued that when Christians fell away from their ancient laws of an ordered *Volksgemeinschaft* (people's community), Jews increasingly began to influence the social life of different peoples. From liberalism, which had been influenced by Jews, came all the other ideologies, such as humanism and pacifism. But they all remained rigid and soulless because they were all far removed from the concept of brotherly love. Moreover, only a few people had benefited from the growth of material things that liberalism helped bring about. Liberalism had ended with a complete moral collapse. Liberalism as a political party was destroyed; the only remains of it could be found in assimilated Jewry. The majority of the assimilated Jews, according to Czermak, had moved with "flying colors" into the Marxist camp. Even more decisively than liberalism, Marxism tried to build an international world. It made religion not just a private matter but tried to exterminate it altogether. Bolshevism was also the most radical advocate of assimilation and for this reason was fought, among others, by Jewish nationalists.[43]

Despite the political and material influence of the Jewish spirit in all aspects of modern life, the Jewish people, Czermak maintained, were threatened with complete national disintegration. They could only be saved by reversing assimilation and undergoing a religious revival. Assimilation had failed; even most Jews recognized this. A Jew could not become a member of another nationality simply by leaving Judaism if the host people rejected him. Czermak thought that the current hatred of Jews was regrettable, but equally untenable was the senseless excitement that Jews expressed over not being able to hang on to all the economic and intellectual positions they had won almost without a fight.[44]

Czermark thought that Palestine offered a partial solution to the Jewish question, but it was not large enough to hold even the 560,000 Jews of Germany. The best solution was to place Jews under a special minority law that would regulate their economic and social activities within the host nationality in such a way that all causes of hatred would be removed. In economic affairs there was to be a thoughtfully conceived boundary between Jews and gentiles. In cultural matters Jews would have been able to speak only as guests. If this solution were followed, Jews would return to the original conservative character that they had abandoned. Christians demanded only that Jews be loyal to the state; the leadership of the state would remain exclusively in Christian hands.[45]

In his second and shorter section of the book, Oskar Karbach pointed out that Nazi Germany regarded Jews as an enemy power that had to be conquered, not reformed. Positive norms for Jews to follow were not even being discussed. Karbach thought that if there were such guidelines there would be no occasion for continued enmity. Arguments over Jewish refugees could be avoided by authoritarian states if such positive reforms were implemented. No solution to the Jewish question could be found if one tried to solve it in a piecemeal way. Dissimilation alone would be a catastrophe for the Jews. The German people of Austria would have to convince the Jews that a reform would lead to a lasting and equitable involvement in the state.[46]

The reaction to *Ordnung in der Judenfrage* was swift, intense, and predictable. Not surprisingly, most Jewish and philo-Semitic newspapers reacted scornfully to the book's publication. The assimilationist newspaper, *Die Wahrheit*, pointed out the obvious parallels between the Czermak–Karbach proposal and laws that had already been enacted in Nazi Germany. The newspaper said that Jews were willing to negotiate a change in the status quo but would never voluntarily surrender their equal rights.[47]

Speaking for mainstream Zionists, *Die Stimme* noted that Czermak wanted to implement a numerus clausus in areas where Jews were overrepresented, but did not support any changes where Jews were underrepresented, as, for example, in the civil service. *Jüdische Front*, representing Jewish war veterans, said that Czermak mentioned only Jews who had had a harmful effect on society and not those who had played a positive role. *Der jüdische Arbeiter*, the organ of working-class Zionist Jews in the Poale Zion, thought that Czermak's proposal would deny Jews equal rights.[48]

Irene Harand, the editor of the philo-Semitic newspaper *Gerechtigkeit*, was also not fooled by Czermak's polite language. She saw nothing new in the book; what Czermak was proposing amounted to exceptional laws for Jews. Forcing Jews to say that they belonged to a separate *Volk* and then segregating them from German-Austrians would not win Austria the sympathy of foreigners. She would not reject Czermak and doubt his loyalty to Austria simply because he had a Czech name.[49]

Anti-Semitic publications, both Catholic and nationalist, were enthusiastic about the new book by Czermak and Karbach. Josef Eberle in *Schönere Zukunft* warmly recommended the book to his readers after summarizing its contents. The violently anti-Semitic and thinly disguised Nazi newspaper, *Der Stürmer,* thought the book "could be taken seriously," especially because Czermak was a leading member of the Christian Social Party.[50]

ROMAN CATHOLICS AND NAZI ANTI-SEMITISM

The publication of *Ordnung in der Judenfrage* was part of a larger effort by Roman Catholics in Austria to respond to the challenge confronting them by the revived Austrian Nazi Party, which had won nearly 17 percent of the vote in local and provincial elections held in several parts of Austria in April 1932. In July of the same year the German Nazis had garnered a spectacular 37.4 percent of the vote in national parliamentary elections. After Adolf Hitler was appointed chancellor of Germany in January 1933 Austrian Nazis were supremely confident that they, too, would soon be in power.[51]

A major part of the appeal of the Austrian Nazis was their unscrupulous anti-Semitic propaganda, which threatened to attract many young Catholics and Christian Socials. Anti-Semitism was a major part of the Christian Social Weltanschauung from the very beginning. Even though it became less important after 1922, it remained a significant integrating factor in the heterogeneous party. Indeed, there had to be serious doubts in the minds of the party's leaders whether the party could survive if denied this political weapon. Members of the Roman Catholic hierarchy were anxious to convince young people that the church had been anti-Semitic centuries before anyone had heard of National Socialism.

Thus, the bitter competition to determine who was best qualified to deal with the Jewish question revived with renewed intensity in the 1930s. First it had been between Lueger and the pan-German nationalists, then it was Kunschak and other Christian Social anti-Semites and the Social Democrats. Now it was primarily between the Catholics and the Nazis. This time, however, the

Catholics found themselves at a distinct disadvantage because of their unwillingness to embrace racial anti-Semitism wholeheartedly; the financial support the Christian Socials received from capitalists, some of whom were Jews, was another major embarrassment.

The approach many Catholics took in this competition was reminiscent of arguments made by private Austrian organizations—namely, that the Germans were too weak or too insincere in their anti-Semitism. Josef Eberle made this point in one of the early issues of *Schönere Zukunft* in 1926, long before the Nazis had become a serious factor in German politics. German Catholics were allegedly not really aware of the Jewish question because their own Catholic press ignored the issue and even accepted advertisements from Jews. Shallow humanism and dangerous tolerance would only benefit Jews at the expense of Christians. Hatred and pogroms were not necessary, but Jewish influence had to be limited to their numbers.[52]

Eberle and *Schönere Zukunft* were only mildly critical of the Nazis' persecution of Jews after Hitler's takeover of power in 1933, even though Eberle had written in 1931 that the Nazis' handling of the Jewish question was both un-Christian and barbaric. *Schönere Zukunft* could agree with the Nazis that the Jewish "race" was inferior, but ultimately could not accept the Nazis' idea about the total depravity of Jews or the even broader notion that race is of decisive importance for whole peoples as well as individuals.[53]

Christian Socials could not help but admire the Nazis' anti-Marxism as well as their passionate opposition to the Paris Peace treaties. The *Reichspost* was therefore generally sympathetic to the new Nazi regime in Berlin but faulted its policy toward Jews. The newspaper maintained in March 1933 that the Nazis had betrayed their own anti-Semitic program. Jewish citizens in Germany were being treated just like everyone else. Then, after the brief boycott of Jewish stores on 1 April 1933, the *Reichspost* complained that Nazi anti-Semitism in Germany was not legal and was disturbing the economic order. Other articles about anti-Semitism in Germany were simply printed without comment by the *Reichspost* and other Catholic periodicals. On the other hand, *Christliche Ständestaat*—a Catholic weekly that employed a number of recent Jewish converts—published an article in 1936, warning against trying to take the wind out of Nazi sails through the use of anti-Semitism instead of simply rejecting both Nazism and anti-Semitism.[54]

Schönere Zukunft likewise remained critical of the methods, but not the goals, the German Nazis used in "defending themselves" against the "culturally and morally destructive work of the Jews." In May 1933 the weekly magazine claimed that National Socialism had its positive points. Hitler was serious in wanting the German people to preserve their Christian faith. Likewise the magazine declared its "solidarity" with the German regime after the book burning ceremonies of 10 May.[55] In November 1933 *Schönere Zukunft* rejected contentions by what it called the "Jewish boulevard press" that anti-Semitism was unpatriotic and a threat to the state. On the contrary, it was patriotic to say when the Jews held too many positions. The "Jewish press," furthermore behaved as if "a few anti-Semitic excesses in the Third Reich were the most disgraceful and terrible crimes in world history."[56]

Catholic newspapers were not alone in fearing the increased popularity of Nazi anti-Semitism. The anti-Semitism of the Christian Social workers' movement responded to the new competition by intensifying its long-standing anti-Semitic policy. The Jews provided a convenient scapegoat for the disastrous Austrian economy so that neither the non-Jewish capitalist supporters of the Christian Social Party nor the party's leadership would be blamed. Leopold Kunschak also hoped that by renewing his attack on Jews he could prevent the younger members of his Arbeiterverein from deserting to the Nazis.[57]

Kunschak thought that the Nazi takeover in Germany was a natural reaction to "formal democracy" and party domination. However, he criticized the new regime for its "moderation" toward Jews. The regime and the German Jews had allegedly reached a modus vivendi so the anti-Semitic slogans of the Austrian Nazis did not need to be taken seriously. The true anti-Semites were in the Arbeiterverein, not in the Nazi Party. When a few hundred Jews from Nazi Germany sought refuge in Austria, Kunschak's Arbeiterverein attacked them as sharply as it had the Ostjuden during the First World War. In 1936 Kunschak republished his legislative proposal of 1919 in order to prove that he had favored the segregation of Jews sixteen years before the Nazis in Germany enacted the Nuremberg Laws. At no time prior to 1938 did any of the publications of the Arbeiterverein complain about the Nazi persecution of Jews.[58]

The Catholic church did not remain entirely silent regarding the excesses of Nazism and anti-Semitism. Unfortunately, however, its efforts to denounce these phenomena were often so equivocal that it is uncertain whether they did the Nazis more harm than good. The most celebrated case of such an ambiguous denunciation was a pastoral letter of the bishop of Linz, Johannes Maria Gföllner, on 23 January 1933, exactly one week before Hitler became the German chancellor.

Much of the long letter, when read today, is a praiseworthy defense of Christian values. Gföllner wrote that humanity was one family that had descended from Adam and Eve. Race hatred like class hatred was not compatible with true Christianity, which is a religion of love, not revenge. Revenge was a matter left to God. As for nationalism, it was willed by God and approved by the church. But it became unnatural and un-Christian when it degenerated, as it had done in Gföllner's time, to racism and the blood myth. The racial standpoint of nationalists, including the radical anti-Semitism preached by Nazism, was completely incompatible with Christianity and had to be rejected. It was inhuman to hate, despise, and persecute Jews simply because of their descent. All things considered, National Socialism suffered internally from racial madness, from un-Christian nationalism, and from a nationalistic concept of religion. It was impossible, the bishop concluded, to be both a good Catholic and a real Nazi.[59]

If Bishop Gföllner had limited himself to these remarks, his letter might still be remembered today as a courageous, timely, and insightful denunciation of the Nazi ideology, which in part it was. Unfortunately, however, the letter also included a long list of anti-Semitic clichés that had been repeated for decades by anti-Semites of various political persuasions. He charged that undoubtedly many godless Jews exercised a harmful influence in all areas of modern cultural life, trade and business, the legal profession, and medicine. Recent social and political revolutions had been carried out on the basis of materialist and liberal principles that originated from the Jews. The press, advertisements, theater, and cinema were often filled with frivolous and cynical tendencies that poisoned the Christian soul and were also nourished and spread by Jews. Degenerate Jews, in league with Freemasons, were also primarily responsible for capitalism and were the principal founders of socialism, communism, and Bolshevism. To fight and to break these harmful influences of Jewry were both the right and the duty of a convinced Christian. If Nazism limited itself to these tasks there could be no objection to it as long as the National Socialists remembered that the Roman Catholic church was the strongest bulwark against Jewish atheism.[60]

Not surprisingly, anti-Semites were far more receptive to Gföllner's pastoral letter than were Jews or philo-Semites. After two thousand members of the paramilitary League of Jewish Front Fighters held a demonstration in Vienna on 30 January to protest the letter, Leopold Kunschak's Arbeiterverein held a counterdemonstration in support of the bishop's statement. Georg Glockemeier, the anti-Semitic author of a book called *Zur wiener Judenfrage*, applauded Gföllner for denouncing Jewish business morality and the Jewish international *Weltgeist* (world spirit). Even Nazis loved to quote from the letter, without, of course, mentioning its anti-Nazi contents. Nor did the Nazis mention that the Austrian episcopate condemned the letter in December 1933 for causing racial hatred and conflict.[61]

In 1937 another Austrian bishop, Alois Hudal, the rector of the German charity in Rome called "Anima," published in Leipzig *Die Grundlagen des Nationalsozialismus (The Foundations of National Socialism)*, which was even more pleasing to the Nazis than Bishop Gföllner's pastoral letter because it attempted to establish an understanding between Catholicism and National Socialism. Hudal (who dedicated the first copy of his book to Adolf Hitler himself whom he called "the Siegfried of German hope and greatness"),[62] praised the idea of a Volksgemeinschaft, the German ideal of racial unity, and the Nazis' attempt to find a solution to the Jewish question. In contrast to Gföllner, Hudal said that the nationalism and racism of the Nazis were compatible with Christianity as long as fundamental Christian dogmas were not violated. Although all races were equal in the eyes of God, this did not make them equal in the eyes of man as far as their intelligence, customs, and physiology were concerned. The avoidance of race mixing for the sake of producing healthy children was therefore justified. There could also not be any serious objection to special laws preventing a flood of Jewish immigrants. Bishop Hudal went on to criticize the "Jewish" press in Austria for playing off Austrians against Germans and said that the Nazis should be supported as long as they were carrying on their fight against left-wing radicalism. Hudal's book was criticized by *Christliche Ständestaat* for using Nazi polemics and terminology. However, the prelate received support from Archbishop Theodor Innitzer of Vienna, Friedrich Funder's *Reichspost*, and Chancellor Kurt von Schuschnigg.[63]

This brief survey of Catholic attitudes toward anti-Semitism clearly reveals that there was no single unambiguous policy. Most Catholics, including even people like Leopold Kunschak, rejected racial anti-Semitism in theory as being contrary to the teachings of the church. In practice, however, most Catholics made sharp distinctions between Catholics who had converted from Judaism and people whose families had belonged to the church for many generations. No member of the church's hierarchy or leader of the Christian Social Party approved of anti-Semitic pogroms, but nearly all of them appear to have supported some kind of legislation limiting the "influence" of Jews in Austria's cultural life and many also favored restricting their numbers in Austrian universities. A nostalgic longing to reverse the emancipation of Jews and return them to their medieval spiritual or even physical isolation was unmistakable. Catholics saw Marxism as the greatest threat to their religion and conservative way of life and held Jews responsible for this modern phenomenon. Without Jews there would presumably be no Marxism, atheism, or secularism. Therefore anti-Semitic Catholic propaganda was directed primarily against these "Jewish Marxists."

The rise of the Nazis and their expropriation of the Catholics' anti-Semitic slogans put most (but not all) Catholics in the awkward position of being able to do little more than quibble about Nazi racial theories and occasional use of violence if they did not wish to contradict centuries of their own beliefs. Moreover, the official anti-Semitic program of the Third Reich prior to the Anschluss in 1938 rarely went beyond that which had been proposed by Leopold Kunschak and others long before 1933. In short, neither the Catholic clergy nor the Catholic laity managed to denounce either Nazism in general or Nazi anti-Semitism in unequivocal terms. Guenter Lewy's judgment of the Catholic church in Germany is also applicable to Austria: "A Church that justified moderate anti-Semitism and merely objected to extreme and immoral acts was ill-prepared to provide an effective antidote to the Nazis' gospel of hate."[64] The compromising attitude toward Nazism, which characterized the Catholic church after the Anschluss, had its origins long before 1938.

12

THE MINOR POLITICAL PARTIES AND MOVEMENTS

The Social Democratic Workers' Party and the Christian Social Party were by far the two largest parties in Austria during the democratic era, usually winning a combined total of over 80 percent of the seats in the lower house of the Austrian Parliament.[1] The remainder of the seats were divided between several minor bourgeois parties nearly all of which espoused anti-Semitism at least some of the time as well as a measure of pan-German nationalism. In addition there were a number of usually nonparliamentary political organizations with anti-Semitic agendas. The intensity and type of anti-Semitism varied from one group to another and from one time to another.

None of these minor parties and organizations displayed anything remotely resembling originality when it came to the "Jewish question." Rather, they all belonged to one of the dominant types of bourgeois anti-Semitism: religious, economic, or racist, or very often a combination of these types. Although these organizations all existed from the early postwar years until at least 1934, those with stronger religious proclivities tended to predominate in the early or middle years of the republic whereas those that were more racially inclined either increased in strength after the meteoric rise of Nazism in Germany and Austria after 1930 or else were absorbed by them.

THE LANDBUND

Possibly the least anti-Semitic of all of Austria's political parties, other than a few tiny ones of no consequence, was the Landbund or Agricultural League. In 1920 various nationalistic peasant leagues of Austria organized themselves into the German Peasant Party which in 1922 changed its name to the Landbund. Its political principles, written in 1923 during the height of the postwar anti-Semitic hysteria in Austria, closely resembled the traditional and religious anti-Semitism of the Christian Social Party in declaring that it fought the Jewish race as a "disintegrating" element in society. The overwhelming influence of the Jews on the political, economic, and cultural life of Austria had to be fought at all times. The attempt of the Jews, through their leadership of the internationally organized proletariat to eliminate state power and to dominate the world was opposed by the Landbund, which considered itself a bulwark of European civilization.[2]

After 1923 the Landbund was only intermittently anti-Semitic. In the more prosperous year of 1925 its new party program said nothing about anti-Semitism. On the other hand, after the revival of anti-Semitism in the early 1930s still another official declaration in 1932 included an anti-Semitic statement. Most Austrian peasants probably resembled other Central European farmers in being anti-Semitic only when their specific economic interests were involved.[3]

PARAMILITARY FORMATIONS: THE HEIMWEHR AND
THE FRONTKÄMPFERVEREINIGUNG

A larger and certainly more strident organization than the Landbund was the Heimwehr. Whereas the Landbund was one of the more democratic parties of Austria, the Austrian Heimwehr or Home Guard, especially its pan-German wing in Styria known as the Styrian Heimatschutz, has often been described as "fascist," because of its advocacy of the "leadership principle"; its open admiration for its financial patron, Benito Mussolini; and its anti-Semitism.[4]

In the spectrum between the demagogic, religious, but usually nonracial anti-Semitism of the Christian Socials, on the one hand, and the racial and sometimes violent anti-Semitism of the Nazis on the other, the Heimwehr stood squarely in the middle, with one foot in both camps. The Heimwehr was a paramilitary formation founded shortly after the collapse of the monarchy in order to defend Austria's southern borders against Yugoslav incursions. It soon evolved, however, into a primarily anti-Socialist movement.

At the height of its popularity in the late 1920s, 70 percent of the Heimwehr's 300,000 to 400,000 active members and sympathizers were peasants, many from traditionally völkisch and anti-Semitic areas like Styria and Carinthia. Their religious suspicion of Jews now combined with their hatred of Socialists and their distrust of the great metropolis, Vienna, with its new Socialist government. On the other hand, most Heimwehr members in other provinces, while sharing the anti-Socialism of their comrades in the south, were too

Catholic to indulge in overt racial anti-Semitism. Moreover, the two wings of the movement were badly split over the issue of Anschluss with Germany; the pan-German Styrian Heimatschutz was in favor of the union, but the Catholic wing, which was closely associated with the Christian Social Party, was opposed, especially after Hitler's takeover in 1933.

Complicating the issue of anti-Semitism still further was the much needed financial support of some Jewish bankers such as Rudolf Sieghart, Jewish industrialists like Fritz Mandl, and the predominantly Jewish Phönix Insurance Company, which sympathized with the Heimwehr's staunch anti-Marxism. Richard Steidle, who came from the ultra-Catholic province of Tyrol and was the Heimwehr's coleader from 1928 to 1930, said the movement was not anti-Semitic, but merely opposed to Jewish Marxists and destructive Ostjuden. Patriotic Jews, Steidle said, were welcome comrades against Marxism.[5]

If the attitude toward Jews was somewhat ambiguous, the attitude of at least the more politically conservative Jews toward the Heimwehr was also equivocal. *Die Wahrheit*, the mouthpiece for upper-middle-class assimilated Jews, wrote in October 1929 that "Austrian Jews" approved of the Heimwehr's opposition to the high taxes imposed by Vienna's Socialist government. Jews also favored the Heimwehr's demand for strict proportional representation in Parliament, according to the paper. It is also true that some Jewish businessmen gave in to Heimwehr demands to dismiss their Social Democratic employees, thus doubtless increasing anti-Semitism in the working class. Moreover, according to the Heimwehr's most recent historian, not a few Jews actually joined the Heimwehr, although none of them ever became leaders.[6]

The tolerant attitude that some Jews held toward the Heimwehr began to change in 1930 as the Heimwehr became more outspokenly anti-Semitic. In October, Dr. Franz Hueber, a minister of justice in the federal government and brother-in-law of Hermann Göring, announced that Austria "ought to be freed from this alien [Jewish] body." As a minister he "could not recommend that the Jews be hanged, that their windows be smashed, or that their shop display windows be looted. . . . But we demand that racially impure elements be removed from the public life of Austria." Not surprisingly, Jewish members of the Heimwehr began resigning about this time and by 1934 the organization was no longer accepting Jews as members.[7]

In the ideological middle of the Austrian Heimwehr, trying to balance its pan-German and racist wing with its Catholic-conservative branch, was its leader for most of the period between 1930 and 1936, Prince Ernst Rüdiger Starhemberg. Like the organization as a whole, he was caught between the need to appease the Heimwehr's Jewish financiers and his desire to maintain and attract the support of anti-Semites. He was also indebted to the House of Rothschild for helping him out of some personal financial difficulties.[8]

Consequently, Starhemberg could be either moderate or radical on the Jewish question, depending on the audience and the situation. In a speech delivered to a Heimwehr crowd in 1930 he proclaimed that "the object of our movement is to create a people's state in which every *Volksgenosse* [blood brother] will have the right to a job and to bread. [The Nazis' slogan was *Arbeit und Brot*.] By a *Volksgenosse* I mean only one inspired by the race instinct of the Germans in whose veins German blood flows. In 'the people' I do not include those foreign, flat-footed parasites from the East who exploit us. [This was an apparent attempt to distinguish between the Ostjuden and the West-juden.] We want the German people's state to be on Christian foundations."[9] In February 1933 Starhemberg told a Heimwehr audience in Vienna that he was pleased that a national government had just come to power in Germany. Later in the same speech he said that Austria had lost the world war because of a foreign race sitting in coffeehouses.[10]

Starhemberg became much more temperate in his public pronouncements while a member of the federal cabinet from 1932 until 1936, particularly when he was speaking to foreign journalists. To a French newspaper reporter he said in March 1934 that he merely wanted to break Jewish "predominance." At about the same time he told a Hungarian newspaper that all Jews who rejected internationalism and who were not a burden to the state were not part of the Jewish problem. A few weeks later Starhemberg told English and American reporters that it would be crazy to solve the Jewish problem by force or through a numerus clausus. The government wanted to retain "valuable" Jews who would take part in rebuilding the state. Who these valuable Jews were, Starhemberg did not say. The only solution to the Jewish problem, he added ambiguously, was through laws that took into account the sensitivities of the Christian majority.[11]

The Styrian branch of the Heimwehr, which also had followers in neighboring Lower Austria and Carinthia, was much less equivocal about anti-Semitism than Prince Starhemberg. Its leader, Dr. Walter Pfrimer, a lawyer from the Upper Styrian town of Judenburg, said on numerous occasions that Jews ought to be treated as a foreign race and complained that his coleader, Steidle, was too moderate on the Jewish question. Pfrimer's racism increased in the early 1930s when his Styrian Heimatschutz began to compete with the Austrian Nazi Party. The statutes of his organization, which went into effect on 1 March 1933, specifically excluded Jews from membership. A few weeks later, Pfrimer's newspaper, *Der Panther*, proudly stated that the Styrian

Prince Ernst Rüdiger Starhemberg, leader of the Austrian Heimwehr. Austrian National Library Picture Archive. "In 'the people,' I do not include those foreign, flat-footed parasites from the East who exploit us," he told a Heimwehr audience in 1930 (Franz Winkler, Die Diktatur in Österreich*).*

Heimatschutz followed the same völkisch ideology that had been preached by Georg von Schönerer.[12]

The Heimwehr's attempt to bridge the gap between the relatively moderate, traditional, Catholic anti-Judaism of the Christian Social Party and the modern, racial anti-Semitism of pan-German groups ultimately proved to be impossible. The Nazis' brand of violent racial anti-Semitism together with their promise to bring about an Anschluss between Germany and Austria, proved too appealing for pan-Germans within the Heimwehr to resist. Consequently, in 1933 Walter Pfrimer and his Styrian Heimatschutz allied themselves with the Austrian Nazis and were later absorbed by them.[13]

A paramilitary formation that was far more unified on the Jewish question than the Heimwehr was the Frontkämpfervereinigung or League of Front Fighters. Organized in 1920, it claimed to be a mutual aid society that merely wanted to cultivate comradeship among veterans of the world war and work for the reconstruction of the German fatherland, leading to the eventual union of the entire German people. Its secret program, however, was to unite all bourgeois elements against "Jewish Marxism." In other words, its objectives were similar to those of the Heimwehr except as a whole it was not armed and it was distinctly more anti-Semitic, probably because the majority of its 50,000 members (in late 1920) came from Vienna.[14]

From the beginning the league was staunchly anti-Semitic. Its leader, Colonel Hermann von Hiltl, blamed the Jews for the breakup of the Austro-Hungarian Monarchy. He opposed the immigration of Jews and wanted to make their emigration easy, although he did not favor their expulsion. He was also against the persecution of individual Jews if they had not been provocative. But he did want to limit their representation in the press, medicine, and law, as well as their ownership of property to no more than their percentage of the population. Hiltl vociferously advanced these views in numerous anti-Semitic rallies in which the Front Fighters participated, especially in the early 1920s.[15]

The heyday of the Frontkämpfervereinigung was definitely in the early postwar years. When the Heimwehr underwent an explosive growth in the late 1920s the Front Fighters were left in the shadows. However, when the Austrian Nazi Party was outlawed in 1933, the league experienced a rebirth with many Nazis switching their allegiance. To accommodate these new members the paramilitary formation once again stressed its anti-Semitism and refused to join the government-sponsored umbrella organization called the Fatherland Front. Eventually, however, it acquired the well-deserved reputation of being a Nazi front and was outlawed in June 1935.[16]

THE GREATER GERMAN PEOPLE'S PARTY

The further one went up the social scale in late nineteenth- and early twentieth-century Central Europe, the more secular, cultural, and racial anti-Semitism tended to become; by the same token it became less and less religiously motivated. This helps to explain why the peasant-dominated Heimwehr was not particularly racist. On the other hand, the middle-class Greater German People's Party or Grossdeutsche Volkspartei (GDVP) was extremely racist.[17]

Anti-Semitism was apparently a necessary ingredient of the German nationalist ideology. Since the days of Georg von Schönerer its exponents had rejected liberalism, rationalism, Marxism, and democracy as "un-German." Jews were blamed for alienating Germans from their presumably unspoiled characteristics. Because there was traditional anti-Jewish resentment in broad sections of the public in Central Europe, it was easy to depict the Jews as foreign even if they were culturally integrated. Rather than blaming concrete, individual Jews, however, the German nationalists spoke about Verjudung (jewification) and the hidden and all-pervasive Jewish Geist (spirit). If Jews were not openly influential, it only showed how cunning and dangerous they really were. Racial theories were a pseudoscientific reinforcement for people who rejected emancipation, self-determination, and equality.[18]

The German nationalists did not regard the Jews as inferior in every way. On the contrary, Jews had an excellent "business spirit" and were clever, shrewd, intelligent, and energetic. These qualities made German nationalists think they were defending themselves against a superior foe. After 1918 they were also convinced that they were being ruled by foreigners.[19]

All of these ideas were present in the Greater German People's Party. A middle-class coalition of seventeen nationalistic splinter parties and organizations left over from the monarchy, it was founded in 1920 by groups that came together more out of necessity than conviction. To some extent it was a collecting point for all those people who could not find an ideological home in one of the two major parties. Of the nationalistic parties of Austria, only the German Workers' Party (which soon evolved into the Austrian Nazi Party) and the Landbund remained outside this loose coalition. Because it was created from "above," it had no strong organization. People who voted for the GDVP were nationalistic, but otherwise uninterested in politics and did not want to engage in routine political work. Consequently, the party was often like a general staff without an army.[20]

In addition to its racial anti-Semitism, the party favored free trade and an Anschluss with Germany. It also supported the concept of a Volksgemeinschaft, or people's community. This idea had the dual advantage of ending the Marxist class struggle while excluding the "parasitic" Jews, who were allegedly responsible for Marxism, liberalism, individualism, and capitalism. Because Jews were not ethnically Germans, they could never be part of the Volksgemeinschaft.[21]

The concept of a Volksgemeinschaft was very much present in the party's first declaration of principles drawn up in Salzburg in 1920. The Jews' ability to dominate depended on their destroying the people's community by dividing the Volk into mutually quarreling groups. In other respects the document was filled with most of the usual anti-Semitic clichés. Jews were stylized into everything negative. They were guilty of moral depravity and for all economic misery. The idea of an absolute moral code was alien to them. The Christian attitude toward morality was just the opposite, so it was inevitable that Jews would fight it. The Jews were parasitic because they could not maintain a state of their own. Their racial characteristics made them try to dominate productive people. They could only sell things, not make them. Their highest goal was to become rich in order to avoid work. Even art for them was not a matter of creativity but a means of making money. They had recently enjoyed a great increase in political power, in part because of democracy, which made it easy for them to dominate the state.[22]

The only means of combating these evil Jewish racial characteristics and their threat to the Volksgemeinschaft was to treat them as a separate nation, a demand that some of the Jews (the Zionists) favored. In this the GDVP openly subscribed to racial anti-Semitism with all that that implied. "Verbal anti-Semitism" was simply not enough to restore the people's community. Propaganda about the essence of the Jewish intellectual characteristics and their danger to the German people would lead to their influence over the culture, economy, and public life of the country being reduced and to the disappearance of the Jewish way of thinking within the German people.[23]

When read today the party program of the GDVP as well as that of other anti-Semitic parties of interwar Austria seems so extreme and so utterly irrational that one is inclined to doubt seriously whether the framers of such documents took them seriously themselves. Surely the authors were doing nothing more than appealing to the worst prejudices of their audiences in order to gain votes. However, there is hard evidence available that proves that at least some prominent members of the Greater German People's Party did indeed believe their own propaganda.

The Administrative Archives in Vienna contain minutes of numerous private meetings of a special committee of the GDVP that was formed in order to study the Jewish question and to make recommendations to the party as a whole. The committee's meetings were private, and it is unlikely that any member thought that the minutes would ever be made public. The committee, whose meetings began in April 1921 and lasted until at least February 1924, estimated that there were an incredible 730,000 Jews living in Austria, of whom 220,000 were foreign and 260,000 were baptized. The committee, which consisted of "experts" on the Jewish question from both inside and outside the Parliament, was charged with exploring the following points: Ostjuden, the option question (in which, it will be recalled, subjects of the former Austro-Hungarian Monarchy had the option to choose which successor state they wished to live in), rent control, the race question, banking matters, Hochschulen, the press, and changes in the party's principles with regard to membership and marriage to Jews. The committee also wanted to establish an anti-Semitic archive and library. Already in its second meeting the committee approved a motion to exclude all racial Jews from membership in the Greater German People's Party.[24]

The chairman of the committee, parliamentary deputy Dr. Josef Ursin, who accepted the authenticity of the *Protocols of Zion*, was convinced that the Jews, not the Entente, were the real winners of the world war. Another member of the committee believed that the Jews also represented a greater danger to the preservation of the German people and their economy than the Entente. The latter at least was obvious in its desire for destruction, whereas the Jews were secretive. Another member cautioned that the Treaty of St. Germain protected the rights of minorities, including Jews. During a meeting in May 1921, the committee discussed the possibility of a complete separation of Jews and "Aryans" in all their social organizations, including sporting, academic, and professional associations. It was agreed that Aryans should not even allow Jews in their homes. In this regard, cooperation with other anti-Semitic organizations such as the Schutz- und Trutzbund (Offensive and Defensive League) was thought to be helpful as long as it was not done publicly.[25]

Despite their efforts to combat Jewish influence through the publication and distribution of leaflets and pamphlets, members of the committee themselves admitted that they had not been very successful up to 1924, except in promoting social segregation. The power of the Jews, far from being curbed, was actually still growing. The committee was not even sure whether the Jews were a divided people, united only by instinct, or whether they were, as one member suggested, a united and international great power led from New York.[26]

Chairman Ursin did not confine his anti-Semitic activities to the committee on Jews. Early in 1923 he and Anton Jerzabek, a Christian Social parliamentary deputy and chairman of the League of Anti-Semites (Antisemitenbund), sponsored a bill in Parliament that would have required Jews to state their *Volkszugehörigkeit* (roughly "nationality") and race when the Austrian census was taken that March. *Die Wahrheit* was adamantly opposed to such a question being included in the census, arguing that there was no such thing as a "Jewish race" because of intermarriage between Christians and Jews, which had been taking place in Austria since 1914 (actually much earlier than that). The Union of German-Austrian Jews denounced the proposed bill as anti-Semitic. On the other hand, Zionists such as Leopold Plaschkes favored the bill, as did Robert Stricker when a similar bill was first proposed in 1919. The bill enjoyed the support of both the Greater German People's Party and the Christian Social Party, but was ultimately defeated in Parliament by the Social Democrats.[27]

Although the official program of the Greater Germans was the most anti-Semitic and racist of Austria's political parties apart from the Nazis, in practice the party was more moderate than its program suggested.[28] Its best-known leader, Johannes Schober, had taken every precaution as Vienna's police president to protect the Zionist Congress in 1925. His chancellorships in 1921–22 and 1929–30 were marked by equal restraint. The unwillingness or inability of the party to back up its extreme rhetoric vis-à-vis the Jews with concrete actions no doubt accounts at least in part for its losing 90 percent of its followers to the National Socialists in 1932–33.

THE ANTISEMITENBUND

The close agreement and cooperation between the Christian Social Party and the Greater German People's Party can be seen not only in their joint sponsorship of the parliamentary bill on racial identity, but also in the involvement of both parties in the German-Austrian Defensive League of Anti-Semites, the full title of the organization which was better known as the Antisemitenbund. In fact, members of all the bourgeois parties and paramilitary formations of Austria including the Landbund, the Heimwehr, the Frontkämpfervereinigung, and the Austrian Nazi Party (until 1924 and after 1933) participated in the activities of the Antisemitenbund. For example, the CSP member and parliamentary deputy, Anton Jerzabek, and Robert Körber, a member of the GDVP and later the Nazi Party, were the organization's first cochairmen in 1919; Anton Orel, leader of the Christian Social Party's League of Working Youth of Austria and editor of its newspaper called *Volkssturm*, was on the Executive Committee of the Antisemitenbund until it was officially dissolved

Dr. Anton Jerzabek, Christian Social member of Parliament and leader of the Antisemitenbund. Austrian National Library Picture Archive. Addressing an international congress of anti-Semites in Vienna in March 1921, he proclaimed, "Only the debilitating disintegration of the German people by the Jewish poison is responsible for the Entente victory over us" (Der eiserne Besen, 20 March 1921).

shortly after the Anschluss. Richard Steidle, the one-time coleader of the Heimwehr, was a prominent member of the Antisemitenbund in the Tyrol in 1919 at a time when it was the leading exponent of anti-Semitic propaganda in the province. Even Engelbert Dollfuss, chancellor of Austria from 1932 to 1934, repeatedly spoke at league meetings in 1920 while he was a leader of the Catholic Students. Leopold Kunschak of the CSP, Josef Ursin of the GDVP, and the Nazi leaders Walter Riehl and Walter Gattermayer were also frequent speakers at meetings and rallies of the Antisemitenbund.[29]

The Antisemitenbund was founded during the height of the anti-Semitic hysteria in 1919, and thereafter its success mirrored the rise and fall of anti-Semitic feeling in Austria. It began in Salzburg, but by the middle 1920s it had established chapters all over the country. The first mass meeting of the league took place in September of 1919 with five thousand people attending. By March 1921 it was able to attract forty thousand people to an international congress of anti-Semites in Vienna. The organization continued to prosper until about 1924 or 1925, but thereafter its popularity declined, as did the popularity of anti-Semitism in general in Austria; then a revival of both occurred with the coming of the Great Depression.[30]

The first task of the Antisemitenbund, and the element that made it unique among anti-Semitic organizations in Austria, was its desire to assemble all anti-Semites into a single umbrella organization in order to protect them from the economic, social, and political influence of the Jews. The Antisemitenbund stood squarely in favor of the racial principle; it defined as a Jew anyone having one Jewish great-grandparent, a definition far more rigorous than that found in the legal commentaries on the Nuremberg Laws of 1935. The latter considered a person Jewish who had two Jewish grandparents and practiced Judaism or, for nonobservant Jews, three Jewish grandparents. On the other hand, the league's definition was no more exacting than legal definitions used to identify racial minorities at that time in the United States. Therefore, one of its most important responsibilities was informing the Austrian people that the Jews were a separate nation. However, like nearly all other anti-Semitic organizations in Austria, the Antisemitenbund also fought the "Jewish spirit" among Aryans. Unlike many anti-Semites, league members did not waste much time on scholarly analysis of the Jewish question. Instead, they preferred taking such action as encouraging boycotts of Jewish businesses.[31]

In general the League of Anti-Semites wanted a legal separation of Jews and non-Jews in education, administration of justice, and social welfare. More specifically it wanted to expel all Jews who had immigrated since 1914; forbid all future Jewish immigration; identify as "Jewish" all newspapers and businesses where Jews worked; establish a numerus clausus for Jews in the arts; exclude Jews from the professions of law, medicine, and teaching; take away their right to vote; and deny them the right to hold public office and to own land.[32]

Members of local chapters of the Antisemitenbund, consisting of at least twenty members, were supposed to report the names of all Jews living in their building together with their professions, the size of their apartments, when they were born, their arrest record, their service in the army, and where they spent their summer vacations so that a complete registry of all Jews could be compiled by the national organization. These records would make it possible someday for Jews to be required to carry special identification. The *Reichspost* asked its readers to assist in this survey, much to the alarm of the Viennese Jews who feared a pogrom. Local chapters were also supposed to help establish judenrein schools and to monitor the influence of Jews on the press, education, scholarship, and art in their locality. They also encouraged summer resort communities to exclude Jewish guests, an effort at which they were only partially successful, however.[33]

Although the *Deutschösterreichische Tages-Zeitung* in Vienna maintained close ties with the Antisemitenbund, as did the *Reichspost* (which advertised its meetings), the *Deutsches Volksblatt*, and the *Neuigkeits-Weltblatt*, the official newspaper of the organization until 1932 was *Der eiserne Besen*. Founded in Vienna in 1921, it was forced to move its editorial offices to Salzburg in 1923. Its circulation remained quite small, never exceeding six thousand. Even by the low standards of predominantly anti-Semitic newspapers, the contents of *Der eiserne Besen* were primitive; its specialties were detailed descriptions of private sex scandals involving Jews and stories about alleged Jewish ritual murders. It also liked to list the names of Jewish shops together with the names of their "Aryan" customers. The scandal mongering evidently proved to be too much for three newspapers in Salzburg, which won a libel suit against *Der eiserne Besen* in March 1932, a victory its editors ascribed to "Jewish-Roman concepts of right and wrong."[34]

The Antisemitenbund virtually disappeared from public view during the relatively prosperous late 1920s, in part because the leadership of the Austrian Nazi Party required its *Parteigenossen* (party comrades) to give up their membership in the Antisemitenbund in 1924, a decision that came about the same time that overall interest in anti-Semitism in Austria substantially declined. For the next nine years or so the activities of the Antisemitenbund remained infrequent and were far overshadowed by those of the Nazis. However, it experienced a major renaissance after the prohibition of all the political parties of Austria, beginning with the Communists and Nazis in 1933. From then until early 1937 the Antisemitenbund led a precarious existence because Austrian security forces were convinced, with good reason, that it was a mere cover for the illegal Austrian Nazi Party. From mid-1935 until early 1937 it was not even allowed to hold public meetings after the police discovered that as many as 60 percent of the people in its audiences were Nazis. Thereafter, however, it resumed its public activities with the permission of the government, which evidently thought that such limited tolerance would allow it to monitor the illegal Nazis and distract them from more dangerous activities. In arguing its own case, the leadership of the league maintained that their anti-Semitism was strictly defensive. Their model, it said, was not Julius Streicher, the rabble-rousing Gauleiter of Nuremberg, but Karl Lueger.[35]

By March 1937 the Antisemitenbund had chapters once again in nearly all the federal states of Austria and by November of the same year it was holding two meetings a week in Vienna alone in addition to others in the provinces, especially in Graz. The frequency of these meetings increased in the last few months before the Anschluss in March 1938. In Vienna the meetings were attended by an average of two hundred to six hundred enthusiastic people, mostly young Nazis. Speakers who praised the anti-Semitic policies of the German government—for example, a proposal to put 6.5 million unemployed Germans back to work by supposedly removing the Jews from the German economy—and denounced the high percentage of Jews in the professions in Austria were loudly applauded. Meanwhile, the league was also busy distributing anti-Semitic propaganda in an attempt to penetrate every segment of society, but especially young people, students, the military, gentile businessmen, and women. The Antisemitenbund had to exercise extreme caution, however, in order to avoid difficulties with the authorities. It had to notify the government ten days in advance of all planned activities, and the government had the right to change the topics of the speakers.[36]

During the last three years or so of its existence the Antisemitenbund was anxious to prove that it was a patriotic organization with no ties to the Nazi Party. A new statement of twenty principles drawn up by the league in the spring of 1936 began with the declaration that the organization "recognized without reservation the Christian-German, independent fatherland of Austria." The principles also carefully avoided calling the Jews a "race," preferring instead the more politically neutral word "Volk." The declaration furthermore claimed that the organization, since its founding, had been strictly nonpolitical and consisted of native Austrians.[37]

The Antisemitenbund's managing director and deputy chairman, Karl Peter, a former *Truppführer* (section leader) in the Nazis' Sturmabteilung, also wrote a twenty-four-page pamphlet in 1936 called *Der Antisemitismus* which reaffirmed the league's loyalty to the state. League members, Peter claimed disingenuously, were not Nazis because anti-Semitism was only one part of the Nazi program. Anti-Semitism was no imported idea but had long played an important role in Austrian history. The notion that the Jews were a people (Volk) was also not an exclusively Nazi idea, but one admitted by most Jews themselves. The Antisemitenbund did not preach hatred of the Jews but merely love of its own people. Zionism was the only solution to the Jewish problem, and the league did not care whether the Jews moved to Palestine, Madagascar, or somewhere else.[38]

Despite these denials, relations between the Antisemitenbund and the illegal Nazi Party were very close, especially in the last two years before the Anschluss. *Der eiserne Besen* had continued to urge its readers to vote for the Nazi Party as the only genuinely radical anti-Semitic party even after Nazis had withdrawn from the organization in 1924. After a major Nazi victory in local and state elections in April 1932, *Der eiserne Besen* described Hitler as the "only politician . . . of the German people who is willing to oppose Jews openly and ruthlessly."[39]

For its part, the leadership of the outlawed Austrian Nazi Party, especially Leopold Tavs, the Gauleiter of Vienna, had good relations with the leaders of the Antisemitenbund and allowed their members to join the latter organization and to attend its meetings. But the relationship remained a loose one, probably in order to prevent the league from being outlawed.[40]

The fate of the Antisemitenbund was similar to that of other racist and pan-German organizations of Austria. It was founded and flourished at a time of extreme anti-Semitism when few people had heard of National Socialism. The popularity of the Antisemitenbund, the Front Fighters' Association, the Greater German People's Party, and the Heimwehr all declined in the middle 1920s as anti-Semitism began to recede with the return of at least a modicum of prosperity. Only the Heimwehr enjoyed an early revival between July 1927 and 1930 because of the anti-Socialist hysteria surrounding the burning of the Palace of Justice by a crowd of workers. In the meantime, the Landbund temporarily dropped its anti-Semitic philosophy, and the Greater German People's Party chose the pragmatic Johannes Schober as its leader for the elections of November 1930.

The deepening of the Great Depression and the rising popularity of Nazism in Germany ultimately revived Austrian anti-Semitism, and no group benefited more than the Austrian Nazi Party. For a time, the Heimwehr, the

GDVP, the Landbund, and also the Christian Social Party all tried to compete with Nazi anti-Semitism. In this they all failed, however. The Nazis, with their more uncompromising stand on anti-Semitism and monopoly (after 1933) of the Anschluss issue, absorbed 90 percent of the Greater Germans, at least a third of the Heimwehr, and perhaps a quarter of the CSP. Of the non-Nazi organizations of Austria, only the Antisemitenbund continued to flourish after the mid-1930s, and that was only because it had become largely a cover—its protestations to the contrary notwithstanding—for the now-outlawed Austrian Nazi Party.

13

THE AUSTRIAN NAZI PARTY

The most infamous of the anti-Semitic organizations of Austria was without doubt the Nationalsozialistische Deutsche Arbeiterpartei (NSDAP). But once we look beyond the Nazi Party's popular reputation, we discover that its ideas and methods of propaganda were in no respect completely novel. It is even doubtful whether its Jewish policy prior to the Anschluss was much more extreme than that of the Antisemitenbund, the Christian Social Workers' Association, or some elements of the Greater German People's Party. Only in their greater willingness to use violence against Jews did the Nazis differentiate themselves to some extent from other political parties.[1]

If Nazi anti-Semitism was unusual in any way it was in how it combined different aspects of anti-Semitism from all other political parties in order to bind together the very heterogeneous party membership as well as to attract new followers. One could find an anticapitalism resembling that of the SDAP, the same attacks on the Jewish leadership of the SDAP made by the CSP and the Heimwehr, the same charge of "Jewish materialism" made by the GVDP and the Antisemitenbund, the same violent criticism of Jews for their supposed domination of the Viennese press and cultural life found in all the non-Jewish political groups of Austria, and the same racism as in Schönerer's Pan-Germans, the GVDP, the Antisemitenbund, and part of the Heimwehr.[2] However adept the Nazis may have been at combining various forms of anti-Semitism, their eclecticism itself cannot be considered unique. As we have already seen, there were no pure forms of anti-Semitism in Austria. Many political groups, especially the Christian Social Party, attempted to combine religious, economic, cultural, and, to a certain degree, even racial varieties of anti-Semitism.

The Nazis were more consistent in their anti-Semitism than their rivals. Their "scientific" racism and aggressive opposition to Jews avoided the semireligious, semiracist, and basically "defensive" anti-Semitism of most Christian Socials. (On the other hand, it is ironic and instructive that the Nazis were able to define who belonged to the Jewish "race" only by using the religious affiliation of grandparents.) Unlike the Socialists they denounced all Jews, not just those who were capitalists; and unlike the Heimwehr and the CSP, the Nazis did not accept money from Jewish financiers. In contrast to all their anti-Semitic rivals, except Greater Germans and the Antisemitenbund, Nazis were not supposed to associate with even baptized Jews. Thus, the Nazis, unlike most other anti-Semites, could claim to be fully *kompromisslos* (uncompromising) on the Jewish question, although this did not mean that their rivals did not accuse some of their leaders of having Jewish blood or business associates.

It may also be that anti-Semitism played a more important (but not all-important) role in Nazi ideology than it did in the ideology of the other political parties of Austria. The centrality of the Nazis' anti-Semitism can best be seen in six of the party's official twenty-five points, announced (but not drafted) by Hitler in February 1920, being devoted to the Jewish question.[3] The Christian Socials, on the other hand, were primarily concerned about the defense of Christianity; the Socialists were interested above all in defending the interests of the working class against those of the capitalists and in establishing economic equality. But the Nazi ideology was so antirational and pseudoreligious that perhaps only something equally antirational and pseudoreligious like anti-Semitism could hold it together. Neither Nazi dogma nor anti-Semitism could be exposed to critical thinking.

It is obvious by now that the Austrian Nazi Party was far from having a monopoly on anti-Semitism in the First Republic, especially prior to about 1934. It was, however, ultimately the most successful party in exploiting traditional Austrian anti-Semitism as well as current events and problems in which Jews were associated or at least alleged to be associated. In doing so the Austrian Nazis employed mostly the traditional techniques of anti-Semites, ranging from attacks on the alleged cultural influence of Jews to boycotts. Their solutions for the Jewish "problem" were equally shopworn and included such things as reducing Jewish representation in the professions and academic life to their proportion of Austria's (or Vienna's) population to expelling the Jews or at least the Jewish newcomers from Eastern Europe.

THE GERMAN WORKERS' PARTY

The prewar Austrian Nazi Party, or German Workers' Party (*Deutsche Arbeiterpartei*), as it was known until 1918, was not particularly vociferous in its opposition to Jews. Although founded in Bohemia in 1903, it was not until

1913, when its Iglau Program was drafted, that anti-Semitism was even mentioned. Even then the program merely made the rather unexceptional assertion (for anti-Semites) that the party would "combat . . . the ever-increasing Jewish spirit in public life."[4]

During and immediately after the war the Austrian Nazis, who started calling themselves the German National Socialist Workers' Party in May 1918, began to intensify their anti-Semitic message, as indeed did all of Austria's parties. Rudolf Jung, a Bohemian and the party's principal theorist, wrote an article during the war calling for the nationalization of monopolies, department stores, and large landed estates that were not the product of "honest work," a disguised form of anti-Semitism. Jung was also most responsible for drawing up a new program for the party in August 1918 which opposed "all alien influences, but above all . . . the parasitic power of the Jewish trading spirit in all spheres of public life." In particular the predominance of Jewish banks in Austria's economy had to be eliminated. Shortly after the war the party's leading newspaper, the *Deutsche Arbeiter-Presse*, put *Judenherrschaft* (Jewish domination) at the top of a list of evils the party opposed.[5]

A major driving force behind the party's anti-Semitism, almost from its founding, was one of its early leaders, Dr. Walter Riehl, who, like Jung, came from the party's original heartland in northern Bohemia. To be sure, anti-Semitism was not quite the all-consuming obsession it was for such bourgeois radical nationalists as Georg von Schönerer, although Riehl did resemble the knight of Rosenau in being a racial rather than a religious anti-Semite. Nor did Riehl emulate the adult Hitler in refusing even to associate with Jews socially. Still, as his early biographer, Alexander Schilling, noted, Riehl related almost all of Austria's problems, foreign and domestic, to Jews.[6]

Riehl's primary demand with regard to the Jews was one that could be found in all of Austria's interwar parties: the political, cultural, and economic "predominance" of the Jews had to be reduced to their proportion of the country's total population, roughly 3 percent.[7] Even though Riehl's anti-Semitism was less extreme than that of either Hitler or Schönerer, he was far from being regarded as innocuous by Viennese Jews who were the brunt of his fiery oratory. For *Die Wahrheit*, Riehl was the "embodiment of wild street terror and violent racial anti-Semitism. . . . He was the personification of unredeemed hatred and bitter enmity toward Jews."[8]

Walter Riehl, chairman of the Austrian Nazi Party. Austrian National Library Picture Archive. "Our housing shortage could be completely solved if the approximately 200,000 Eastern Jews were expelled because there are about 150,000 Viennese without homes," he declared in a speech to a Nazi Party rally on 31 August 1920 (Deutsche Arbeiter-Presse, 4 September 1920).

NAZI DEMONSTRATIONS AND VIOLENCE IN THE EARLY REPUBLIC

The minuscule size of the Austrian Nazi Party in the early 1920s—its membership reached only 34,000 in August 1923—condemned it to relative obscurity in the anti-Semitic developments of early postwar Austria. Between
the summer of 1918 and the spring of 1923, Vienna witnessed numerous anti-
Semitic outbursts. These included mass demonstrations similar to those that
occurred in Berlin and Munich at the same time. In these demonstrations the
Austrian Nazis played a leading role, or at least claimed to do so. In none
of these events were Nazis acting alone, however. As we saw in Chapter 6,
many of the participants came from the Greater German People's Party, the
League of Anti-Semites, the Front Fighters' Association, or the right wing of
the Christian Social Party, particularly Leopold's Kunschak's Workers' Association. Not until 1923, when the Nazis first appeared at the Technical College
in Vienna and began their brutal assaults on Jewish students, did they attract
much attention.[9]

One early instance of Nazi violence directed against Jews occurred in August
1923. Julius Streicher, the infamous Jew baiter from Nuremberg, spoke at a
Nazi meeting in Vienna. In one two-hour speech he claimed that Jews alone
profited from the world war whereas all non-Jews had to be considered conquered peoples. Streicher furthermore repeated the medieval legend of Jewish
ritual murder and warned the women and girls in the audience about the Jewish "white slave trade." Any German woman or girl who had any sexual contact
with a Jew would be lost to the German people. The effect of one of Streicher's speeches was illustrated when one of his listeners hit a Jewish-looking
pedestrian in the face following the meeting.[10]

The Nazis first succeeded in pushing their way to the forefront of the Jewish
question in 1925. That was the year in which Walter Riehl regained some
of the prestige he had lost—following his resignation from the chairmanship
of the Austrian Nazi Party in August 1923—by defending Otto Rothstock,
the murderer of Hugo Bettauer.[11] In July the party gained additional notoriety when eighty Nazis, youths between fifteen and twenty years old, attacked
several hundred people in a fashionable restaurant in Vienna while shouting
"Juden hinaus."[12]

The highlight of 1925 for the Nazis, however, was the Zionist Congress in
August, another occasion when the Nazis made their presence known through
their stormy protests and organized "riots." The impact of the Nazis' demonstrations, however, was undoubtedly blunted by the inclusion of countless

other anti-Semitic groups. Moreover, the Nazis could not prevent the congress from taking place, a number of their members were arrested by the police, and they found themselves financially exhausted by their propaganda expenditures. Karl Schulz, the leader of the Austrian Nazis, had also alienated many of his followers; he had secretly promised the Vienna chief of police, Johannes Schober, that he would persuade his party comrades not to disturb the congress in order to prevent damage to Vienna's economy and to the good name of the city. Even though Schulz did not (or perhaps could not) live up to his promise, the whole episode cost him the respect of many of the younger Nazis.[13]

An epilogue to the Zionist Congress not previously mentioned was a trial in March 1926 of the Nazi union leader, Walter Gattermayer, and a former editor of the *Deutsche Arbeiter-Presse*, Josef Müller. The charges, which were raised by the *Arbeiter-Zeitung, Der Abend*, and the *Wiener Morgenzeitung*, accused Gattermayer of trying to provoke a pogrom. In the *Deutsche Arbeiter-Presse*, he reprinted a speech entitled "Wien, wach auf!" ("Vienna, Wake Up!") and wrote two other articles called "Christian Pogrom" and "The Plague in Vienna." He also authored a pamphlet entitled "A Collective Call against Jews and the Servants of Jews." In the first of these articles Gattermayer wrote that the God of the Jews was a "hardened swindler": "The beast Jehovah teaches the pleasure of making strangers work and the brutal rape of everything which is not Jewish." Gattermayer defended himself against the charge of blasphemy by quoting from the works of several scholars, including the discredited theology professor, August Rohling. Gattermayer was acquitted of blasphemy and provocation against the government, but was sentenced to three weeks of jail and three years of probation for writing and distributing his pamphlet. Müller also received three years of probation, and six weeks of jail.[14]

The late 1920s and early 1930s, as we observed in Chapter 9, saw Nazi students start to dominate Austria's universities. By 1931 they had gained control over the Deutsche Studentenschaft and had created a veritable academic Third Reich a year and a half before Hitler came to power in Germany. In addition to their violent attacks on their Jewish classmates, Nazi students busied themselves compiling and publishing lists of Jewish professors, which were practically honor rolls of internationally renowned scholars, and then boycotting the classes of these professors.[15]

THE GREAT DEPRESSION AND THE RESURGENCE OF
THE AUSTRIAN NAZIS

Outside of Austria's academic institutions, however, Nazi anti-Semitism did not appear to be very threatening, at least not before the beginning of the 1930s. For example, as late as 1929 *Die Wahrheit* was so confident about the declining significance of Nazi anti-Semitism that its 4 October issue said that "we Austrian Jews have outlasted many anti-Semitic movements including the now-finished Nazis." [16]

This relatively happy state of affairs proved to be all-too-short-lived. The Great Depression raised the already high number of unemployed to over 600,000 Austrians and caused the collapse of Vienna's two great Jewish-owned banks, the *Bodencredit-* and the *Creditanstalt* (as well as a great many non-Jewish banks in other countries). One Austrian émigré reflected years later that "these failures did more than hurt the Jewish community financially; they undermined the belief that Jews were particularly gifted, and indeed vitally needed, for the conduct of financial transactions and enterprises. Added to the substantial losses suffered by hundreds of thousands of gentile bank depositors . . . the end of the myth of Jewish competence in money matters gave a renewed impetus not only to anti-Semitic feelings, but even more so to the idea that anti-Semitic actions could be taken without harm to the economy." [17] The Nazis, in fact, made a point of this very issue in their propaganda. [18]

The economic catastrophe, combined with the impact of the impressive Nazi electoral victories in Germany starting in September 1930, helped the Austrian Nazis to garner over 201,000 votes in the municipal elections in Vienna in April 1932 compared with just 27,500 votes seventeen months earlier. With the increase in the Nazi vote came a far more aggressive attitude toward Viennese Jews. By June 1932 Nazi youths sometimes attacked people in the streets of Vienna who simply looked Jewish. The next month a group of young Nazis attacked a country club in Lainz near Vienna which had an international membership including many Jews; tables were overturned and furniture and windows were damaged. [19]

One particularly ugly incident occurred in October 1932 when forty Nazis, claiming they had been attacked by Jews while they were peacefully walking down a street, stormed a coffee shop that Jews used for prayers. Shouting "Juda verrecke" (roughly "Jews go to hell!") they destroyed windows and furniture. Further damage was prevented when members of the recently organized League of Jewish Front Soldiers (Bund jüdischer Frontsoldaten) came to the rescue. In February 1933 a Viennese court sentenced a Nazi to four-teen days in jail for threatening a Jewish store owner across the street from the Nazis' "Brown House" (headquarters) on the Hirschengasse in the sixth district called Mariahilf. Jewish shopkeepers and their families in that neigh-borhood were often beaten up and told to move to Palestine as soon as possible before they suffered the same fate as Jews in Germany, where Hitler had just come to power. Attacks by Nazis on Jewish individuals and businesses con-tinued throughout the winter of 1932–33. By May, so many Jewish stores had been wrecked that non-Jewish businessmen began to display swastikas in order to gain immunity. A climax was reached in June when the Jewish jeweler, Norbert Futterweit, was killed, one of the Nazi acts of terror that led to the outlawing of the party on 19 June.[20]

The degree of violence, including homicide, which the Austrian Nazis were willing to employ, and not simply discuss, surpassed the physical intimidation used by their bourgeois rivals and predecessors. Likewise, their anti-Semitic propaganda *as a whole* was more extreme in its content and rambunctious in its techniques than anything Austrians had seen before or since the First World War, with the probable exception of the propaganda of the League of Anti-Semites and the Greater Germans.

On the other hand, there was little if anything new in the specific charges the Nazis leveled against the Jews or even in their "solutions" to the Jew-ish "problem." As a matter of fact, the Nazis went out of their way to prove that their anti-Semitism was *not* something new or unique. The *Deutschöster-reichische Tages-Zeitung*, which had previously been an organ of the Greater Germans but was now moving into the Nazi camp, announced at least as early as 1926 that the greatest thinkers of all nationalities had been anti-Semites.[21] The Nazis' Office for the Handling of the Jewish Question sent out a long list of anti-Semitic quotations by great German intellectuals and Catholic clergy-men, including Bishop Gföllner's pastoral letter of January 1933, as well as statements by Jewish leaders that could be used by Nazi speakers and news-papers.[22] The pro-Nazi weekly newspaper, *Der Stürmer*, asserted that hatred of Jews dated back to ancient times and existed wherever Jews had lived. Even the famous American automobile manufacturer, Henry Ford, subscribed to the principle, as did the Ku Klux Klan, according to the paper.[23] *Die Wahrheit* pointed out that many of the Nazis' favorite quotations from Goethe, Herder, Luther, Moltke, Bismarck, Voltaire, and others had been taken out of context, and did not take into account temporary moods, historical circumstances, or even later changes of mind.[24] But few Nazis had such critical insight and even fewer read *Die Wahrheit*! Austrian Nazi newspapers also liked to publish false quotations from the Talmud and other Jewish works but would have to retract them a few months later.[25]

SCANDALMONGERING: THE THEATER, THE CINEMA, AND THE PRESS

The Nazis were particularly incensed about three aspects of Vienna's cultural life where Jewish influence was especially strong: the theater, the cinema, and the press. The Nazis charged that Jews completely controlled the legitimate theater in Austria and Germany. Most of the playwrights were allegedly Jewish as were the theater directors and actors. Classical and purely German plays were rarely performed anymore. Furthermore, the purpose of the Jewish plays was not to idealize life but to show it in all its fluctuations between good and evil. They made people look wretched and hopeless, and their jokes were mere obscenities without any deeper meaning.[26]

The Nazis believed that films were one of the most effective ways Jews had of spreading their influence because of their appeal to the masses. Films produced by Jews were allegedly filled with "kitsch" and stupid jokes and melodies. Only one film company in Central Europe was even partly non-Jewish. Jewish control over American films, which were frequently shown in Germany, was equally great according to the Nazis.[27] As a matter of fact, the percentage of Jews involved in the film industry was high and thus gave a certain plausibility to the complaints of Nazis and other anti-Semites, which was also true in Germany. For example, an estimated 63 percent of Vienna's cinemas were owned by Jews.[28]

Nazi anger with American "Jewish" films and the Viennese Jewish cinemas that showed them reached its peak in the winter of 1930–31. Several weeks of demonstrations by perhaps as many as 10,000 Nazis and other anti-Semites against the movie *All Quiet on the Western Front*, which allegedly "ridiculed the memory of two million dead German soldiers," resulted in several people being injured, considerable property being destroyed, and the picture finally being banned.[29]

As for the press in Vienna, the Nazis claimed that twenty-two of the city's newspapers were in Jewish hands and that "Jewish" newspapers had a daily circulation of 1.3 million compared to only 400,000 for the nine "purely German" papers. One Nazi author complained that "at no time in history has so small a group of foreigners been able to exercise the unlimited domination the way the Jewish press has and does today in Austria."[30] While publicly railing against the "Jewish press," the Nazis privately fumed about the willingness of the Viennese to read the hated Jewish newspapers and were concerned about their own financial woes, which in the 1920s made the purchase of a single typewriter a major expense and the payment of phone bills a constant headache. Even in the (for them) more affluent 1930s, their newspapers were poorly written and confined largely to party affairs. The rapid growth of dues-paying members meant better times for the party's press in the early 1930s. The NSDAP's social heterogeneity, which was far greater than that of any other party in either Austria or Germany, continued to be a serious problem, however, making it difficult for any paper to satisfy the literary and intellectual tastes of peasants, industrial workers, and professional people at the same time.[31]

The Nazis attempted to solve this dilemma by borrowing the Antisemitenbund's tactic of reporting crimes and scandals, especially those involving Jews.[32] For example, in Graz *Der Kampf*, the official organ of the NSDAP in Styria, accused a Jewish-owned clothing firm by the name of Rendi of failing to pay income taxes and investing money in Switzerland. Stories about the scandal dominated the paper's headlines for several weeks.[33] Such articles could sometimes boomerang, however. When *Der Kampfruf*, the party's official mouthpiece in Vienna, warned its readers against patronizing the Phönix Insurance Company because it had Jewish directors, the newspaper was flooded with angry letters from the company's non-Jewish employees who complained that a boycott would threaten their jobs. The Austrian Nazi press chief soon advised the editors of the *Kampfruf* to publish an apology. The Phönix Insurance Company was the focus of a genuine scandal a few years later, however. In 1936 the business collapsed because of faulty speculations, in part by Jewish managers; anti-Semites were thereby presented with a propaganda bonanza.[34]

The *Deutschösterreichische Tages-Zeitung* in Vienna was still another Nazi newspaper that enjoyed relating horror stories about Jews. One article claimed that an "Aryan" country girl had been lured into the house of a Jew and threatened with bodily harm. She was seriously injured after trying to escape by jumping from a second-story window. A whole Jewish band of abductors was at work, but the authorities were silent about it, the headlines screamed. Another piece told about the conviction of a Jewish child-molester. "Jewry is conducting a systematic, tenacious fight against the morally upright German people. Everywhere sexual revolutionaries preach Jewish morality and succeed, at least among a portion of the subhumans who have been benumbed by Marxism."[35]

The ultimate Jewish scandal and proof of Jewish destructiveness, so far as the Nazis were concerned, were revealed in the *Protocols of the Elders of Zion*.

Despite the growing evidence that the *Protocols* was a crude forgery, Nazi newspapers, including the *Deutsche Arbeiter-Presse, Der Kampf*, and especially *Der Stürmer*, continued to maintain its authenticity, claiming that its prophecies had come true.[36]

Ironically the Nazis themselves were not free of "Jewish scandals." The Gauleiter of Vienna between 1930 and 1933, Alfred E. Frauenfeld, was frequently charged with having Jewish ancestors and associating with Jews. In early 1931 *Die Volksstimme*, edited by Frauenfeld's rival in Upper Austria, Alfred Proksch, called Frauenfeld a "Jewish shyster" and said that the Gauleiter had written for a pornographic magazine and dedicated a book to a Jewish bank president. Frauenfeld was also accused of having patronized a Jewish dentist. However, the controversy was at least temporarily stilled when Frauenfeld was acquitted of the charges by a special party court.[37]

A somewhat similar scandal occurred in 1937 when the leader of the Austrian Nazi Party, Josef Leopold, appointed Franz Schattenfroh to be his deputy. A great controversy ensued when it was discovered that Schattenfroh had been married to a Jew for two years. After trying unsuccessfully to gain permission from Hitler to keep his Jewish wife Schattenfroh was forced to give up his position. The whole episode was used by Leopold's rivals to undermine his authority.[38]

NAZI SOLUTIONS TO THE "JEWISH PROBLEM"

When it came to actual solutions to the alleged Jewish problem, the Nazis had nothing new to offer. Indeed, neither the Austrian nor the German Nazis themselves had any preconceived and officially approved party plans about how to deal with the Jews once they came to power. The Nazis' anti-Semitic policy in Germany after Hitler's *Machtergreifung* (takeover of power) "developed largely through internal ideological and political processes [and] continually caught the German Jews by surprise because it was not developed with any relevance to them save that they were hurt by it and ultimately killed by it."[39]

Austrian Nazi leaders, like those in Germany, issued statements at different times and in different places that ranged from bloodcurdling to fairly moderate. As early as June 1925 the *Deutsche Arbeiter-Presse* demanded that Vienna's second district, Leopoldstadt, be made a ghetto for all Viennese Jews as a prelude to their being expelled from the country.[40] In 1931 Walter Riehl demanded the legal emasculation of any Jew who had sex with an "Aryan" girl.[41] When he entered Vienna's city council in 1932, Riehl demanded the expulsion of the Jews from the municipality.[42] On the other hand, the normally fire-breathing *Stürmer*, perhaps with an eye to the government's censors, stated in October 1933 that it rejected a violent solution to the Jewish problem.[43] One Nazi author, Dr. Erich Führer, writing in 1935, insisted that "no seriously thinking anti-Semite who is familiar with the latest research wants the return of the ghettos or the yellow star. A new time demands new viewpoints. From this [assumption] the Jewish problem of Austria can and will be solved in a satisfactory way."[44] The Nazis also loved to cite—without necessarily endorsing—Zionists who advocated proportional representation for Jews in various fields of endeavor. At other times they recommended "modest jobs" for Jews in accordance with their numbers.[45]

Until a permanent solution was found, the Nazis liked to organize boycotts of Jewish businesses. Here again, there was nothing new in this tactic. Anti-Semites had been trying to boycott Jewish establishments since at least the time of Mayor Karl Lueger. Such attempts were particularly common during the Christmas season, when Jewish-owned shops enjoyed brisk sales. But boycotts had little success, at least before the end of 1932.[46] Already in the early 1920s *Der eiserne Besen* began publishing the names of Jewish shops together with the names of "Aryans" who patronized them. In 1930 Nazis put up posters all over Vienna calling for a boycott of Jewish stores and saying that Jews were sorry that the Virgin Mary did not have a second son during the summer so that there could be two Christmas shopping seasons.[47] In 1931 they posted placards listing Aryan shops and pasted stickers on Jewish shop windows saying "Don't buy from Jews."[48] The legally published *Deutsches Volksblatt* also printed a list of Aryan shops in 1935,[49] a practice that was resumed by the illegal *Österreichischer Beobachter* in 1937. In December 1932 the Nazis even tried posting party members in front of Jewish shops, four months before the famous Nazi boycott of Jewish stores in Germany on 1 April 1933.[50] None of these actions, however, made much of an impression on Christian shoppers, who still preferred Jewish stores because of their generally lower prices or because they were unwilling to break long-established shopping habits.[51] Moreover, even partially successful boycotts damaged the Austrian economy and cost Christian sales clerks their jobs. Not until Nazis began throwing small bombs into Jews' shops in late 1932 and early 1933 did non-Jewish shoppers become frightened.[52]

ANTI-SEMITISM AS A UNIFYING ELEMENT

Anti-Semitism was undoubtedly an important cause of the success enjoyed by the Austrian Nazi Party after 1930. Walter Riehl, in commenting on the Nazi breakthrough in the local elections of April 1932 said that most bourgeois voters "did not understand the true nature of our movement. They valued only our anti-Semitic and above all our anti-Marxist positions. . . . The whole Aryan intelligentsia and a large part of the academic and higher civil servants have voted for us as well as many businessmen and architects." [53] These social groups all faced direct economic competition from Jews and were highly anti-Semitic.

Politically, the Nazis also enjoyed their greatest success with winning votes from precisely those parties that were the most ardently anti-Semitic although this fact does not prove that anti-Semitism was the Nazis' only attractive feature. In the same local elections of April 1932 to which Walter Riehl referred, the Greater German People's Party, which at the very least equaled the Nazis in the intensity of its anti-Semitism, saw its vote in Vienna decline from 124,400 in 1930 to 8,800. In Lower Austria the combined vote of the GDVP and the Agricultural League (Landbund) dropped from 70,100 in 1930 to 28,000 in 1932. [54] The other Nazi votes came mostly at the expense of the Heimwehr and the right wing of the CSP. Consequently, between 1930 and 1934 the Nazis absorbed virtually all of the pan-German and ultra-anti-Semitic right in Austria just as they did in Germany. [55]

The conservative bourgeois camp had many differences with the Nazis, especially the CSP on church-state relations. Anti-Semitism, on the other hand, was one of the few things that brought the very heterogeneous elements of the bourgeoisie together, even though there were some differences in how they approached the "Jewish question." It was the main ingredient fostering cooperation between Catholic and nationalistic students in Austrian universities and was important in helping the Nazis to win over huge segments of the bourgeois political parties and movements. Anti-Semitism served a similarly unifying function in Poland between the wars. With the very important exception of the Anschluss question, it is doubtful whether any other single issue in Austria, even the hated Treaty of St. Germain, appealed to so large a cross-section of the Austrian population as anti-Semitism. [56]

In competing with other anti-Semitic organizations, the most important advantage the Nazis enjoyed after January 1933 was that their comrades in Germany were actually doing something about the "Jewish problem," whereas Austrian anti-Semites had seldom done anything except talk. In the Reich,

Jewish influence was being eliminated from the civil service and cultural life of the country; German Jews had been deprived of their full citizenship rights and were being stripped of their wealth.

Of course, anti-Semitism should not be used as an all-encompassing explanation for Nazi electoral successes. Anti-Semitism had been part of Austrian Nazi ideology since 1913 and a very important part since 1918; yet it was not until the Great Depression hit Austria, and the NSDAP began to enjoy an astonishing series of electoral successes in Germany, that the Austrian NSDAP began its rapid growth. Moreover, as Walter Riehl suggested, the party's anti-Marxism was also an important key to its success in a country with the largest (per capita) and most powerful Marxist party outside the Soviet Union.[57]

Equally important for Nazi successes was the impact of Hitler's Machtergreifung in Germany on the Anschluss movement in Austria. The dissolution of the Catholic Center Party and the German Social Democrats along with their subsidiary organizations caused their brother parties in Austria to drop the Anschluss from their political platforms. By default then, the Austrian Nazi Party became the only political force in the Alpine republic with a realistic chance of implementing the union with Germany. All those political elements in Austria, which still regarded the Anschluss as being crucial to Austria's economic survival at a time when the Great Depression was reviving the whole question of the country's viability, were now drawn to the Nazi camp. For some of these people anti-Semitism was a kind of bonus for joining the party. Others undoubtedly joined the party *despite* its anti-Semitism. For only a minority, however, was it the most important reason for siding with the Nazi cause. Nevertheless, the Nazis' anti-Semitism found widespread support in interwar Austria simply because it was very much in accord with a long-standing tradition dating back to the Middle Ages.[58]

IV

AUSTRIA'S JEWS AND THE ANTI-SEMITIC THREAT

Oddly enough, scholars have devoted far more attention to anti-Semitism than they have to the victims of that prejudice. This is particularly true of the Jews of Austria and most especially for the interwar years. Judging from their propaganda, even Austrian anti-Semites knew little about the people they were so quick to condemn.

A single, monolithic Jewish community of Austria existed only in the fervid imagination of anti-Semites. In reality, there was not one Jewish community but several. There were, to begin with, well-assimilated or at least well-acculturated Jews whose ancestors, as we have seen, generally came from the Bohemian crownlands or from Hungary. They almost always adhered to the "Reform" type of Judaism if they were still observant at all. They tended to be upper-middle-class businessmen or professional people and were deeply devoted Austrian patriots. In contrast to these "Westjuden" were the more recent immigrants to Vienna and the smaller Jewish communities of Austria who had usually come from Galicia or Bukovina. Consisting largely of peddlers, very small businessmen, or industrial workers, they too soon spoke fluent German. Vienna, in fact, had no Yiddish or Hebrew newspapers in the interwar period. Nevertheless, these "Ostjuden" were much less well assimilated than the Westjuden, at least for a generation or two. Younger immigrants from the East tended to be either Zionists or Socialists whereas the older generation often still clung to the Orthodox faith and, even more than the Zionists, shunned assimilation.

Only when these basic divisions are understood can the reader appreciate how bitterly divided was the Jewish community of Austria and why it was utterly incapable of presenting anti-Semites with a united front. Their religious, political, and economic differences colored how they interpreted events not only in Austria but in neighboring Germany as well. Only after Adolf Hitler came to power in Germany in January 1933 could Austrian Jews finally agree on something: the need to support the federal government of chancellors Engelbert Dollfuss and Kurt von Schuschnigg.

14

THE JEWS IN
AUSTRIAN SOCIETY

A study of Austrian anti-Semitism would hardly be complete without a discussion of the objects of so much passionate hatred and propaganda by so many people and organizations. Anti-Semitic propaganda was often effective precisely because it seemed to correspond with known facts. As two American specialists on the subject have put it: "No propagandist worth his mettle will prefer an untruth to a truth, if the truth will do the job."[1] It is highly unlikely that anti-Semites would have won any converts if their claims had borne no relationship to reality. No intelligent person in interwar Austria could deny that there were some very wealthy Jews and many Jewish bankers in the country, that Jews were overrepresented in certain professions, and that they played an important role in Vienna's newspaper press and various fields of entertainment. What was important about anti-Semitic propaganda, however, was not only what it said, but what it did *not* say.

ANTI-SEMITIC ESTIMATES OF "ETHNIC" JEWS IN AUSTRIA

Anti-Semitic propaganda was perhaps weakest on the fundamental issue of determining how many "ethnic" Jews there were in Vienna and the whole of Austria between the world wars. As Mark Twain once said, there are "lies, damned lies, and statistics." Anti-Semites were fond of citing statistics, some of them real, some of them out of date, and almost all of them highly tendentious. We have already noted this penchant with regard to estimates made of Eastern European Jewish refugees and the number of people expected to attend the Zionist Congress in 1925.

Although the census of 1923 revealed that there were just over 201,000 registered Jews in Vienna and about another 19,000 in the federal states, no one knew how many people there were of Jewish origins in Austria (or for that matter in Germany). As noted earlier, the Nazis themselves discovered after the Anschluss that there were only 34,500 Viennese who met the Nuremberg definition of a full-blooded Jew who had not already been counted as such in the most recent Austrian census.[2] (The Nuremberg Laws, it will be recalled, defined a full-blooded Jew as someone with at least three Jewish grandparents or someone who practiced Judaism and had two Jewish grandparents.) Members of the Greater German People's Party—who, incidentally, could not be party members if there was the slightest doubt about their racial background or if they were married to Jews—made the most extravagant estimates. Probably using a much broader definition than that used later by the Nazis, they claimed in 1921 that there were 730,000 "racial" Jews in the whole country and 583,000 in Vienna alone, or nearly one-third of the city's entire population![3] The Nazis' *Deutsche Arbeiter-Presse* was actually considerably more modest in its estimate of 300,000 which it made in 1925.[4] The *Deutschösterreichische Tages-Zeitung*, by 1932 an unofficial organ of the Austrian Nazi Party, spoke of an "incredible increase of Jews in Vienna." By counting the "Jewish-sounding names" in the phone book, it estimated that there were 375,000 "racial" Jews in the Austrian capital.[5]

Walter Pötsch, in an anti-Semitic tract published in 1932, estimated that there were at least 750,000 Jews in Vienna, counting converts to Christianity, Jews without any religion, and "part Jews." At the rate Jews were multiplying they would make up half the city's population by 1935! He estimated that there must have been at least 165,000 racial Jews who had not been counted in the census of 1923.[6]

When not frightening Austrian gentiles about the supposed rapid increase of Jews in their country, anti-Semites were making dire predictions about Jewish population growth in other countries. In the early 1930s several Nazi newspapers and public speakers were fond of quoting from a book by E. van Winghene and A. Tjorn entitled *Arische Rasse, christliche Kultur und das Judenproblem* (*Aryan Race, Christian Culture and the Jewish Problem*) published in Erfurt in 1931 by the notoriously racist U. Bodung Verlag. These authors quoted a so-called *Illustrierter jüdischer Kalendar* (*Illustrated Jewish Calendar*) for the year 1924, which claimed that there were 18 million Jews in the world, a figure that the publication said would increase to 30 million by 1950, making the Jews the most rapidly growing people in the world. This "terrifying" increase was caused, Winghene and Tjorn claimed, by a life expectancy for Jews that was 40 percent higher than for Aryans, the result of greater Jewish wealth and therefore better health care. According to the same obscure *Jewish Calendar* there were really 280,000 religious Jews in Vienna instead of the official figure of 201,000. Winghene and Tjorn, however, said they had "secret" information that there were actually 420,000 religious Jews in Vienna and 450,000 "racial" Jews. Extrapolating from these discrepancies with official census figures, they estimated that there must really be 27 million observant Jews in the world and 38 million racial Jews altogether.[7] By contrast, the Nazis in an internal memorandum written in January 1933 admitted that at least as far as the Jews of Germany was concerned their future was doubtful without constant immigration from the East because their birthrate was far lower than for Catholics or Protestants.[8]

THE DECLINING JEWISH POPULATION IN AUSTRIA

Far from increasing at a "frightening" pace, the Jewish population of Vienna and the rest of Austria steadily and rapidly declined during the entire First Republic. The population of Vienna, where over 90 percent of Austria's Jewish population lived after the fall of the monarchy, probably reached its peak in 1915 or 1917 when during the First World War the city was filled with Jewish refugees. The highest number ever recorded in an official census, however, occurred in 1923 when 201,513 Jews were counted, or 10.8 percent of Vienna's shrunken population of 1,868,000. Another 18,695 Jews lived in the other eight federal states, thus giving Jews 3.37 percent of the country's total population, compared with a Nazi claim of 4.6 percent.[9] After that the Jewish population in the Austrian capital declined to 176,034 in 1934 and to just under 170,000 on the eve of the German annexation. Except for Lower Austria, where there was a slight increase in the Jewish population, the number of Jews declined in the Austrian provinces even more rapidly than in the capital. By 1938 there was a total of only 185,000 practicing Jews in the entire country, a remarkable decline of 17 percent in just fifteen years.[10]

Several reasons account for this diminution. Even during the period 1870 to 1910, when Vienna's Jewish population was increasing at its most rapid rate, the growth came almost exclusively from immigration, not births. After 1918 Vienna and the rest of Austria was cut off from its previous reservoir of potential immigrants in the Bohemian crownlands and especially Galicia, where the vast majority of the Jewish population of the Austrian empire had lived.

Vienna's Jewish birthrate was always low. In 1896 there had been 999 more births than deaths; after that the ratio steadily changed until after 1908 there were always more deaths than births. By 1918 2,424 more Viennese Jews died than were born, although this was a situation caused in part by deaths resulting from the world influenza epidemic of 1918–19. After the war the situation momentarily improved; in 1921 there were only 406 more deaths than births. However, between 1920 and 1930 the number of births declined by well over 50 percent, from 2,744 to 1,214. By 1937 only 720 Jews were born compared with 2,824 who died, a shortfall of 2,102. According to the census of 1934 only 1.1 percent of all babies born in Austria were Jewish even though Jews made up 2.8 percent of the country's total population.[11]

The birthrate for Jews in Vienna was probably the lowest for Jews anywhere in the world. Already in 1925 there were only 8.5 live Jewish births in Vienna per one thousand people, about half of what was needed to maintain a stable population. By comparison, the Jewish birthrate in Berlin was 11.9; in New York it was 18.0; in Warsaw, 14.4. The Jewish birthrate in Rumania was 19.3 and 23.4 in Czechoslovakia.[12] Nowhere were there the 32 births per 1,000 Jews mentioned by Winghene and Tjorn, and least of all in Vienna where over half of all Jewish families had only one child and less than a quarter had two or more. The only favorable statistics for Viennese Jews were the decline in the number of people leaving their ancestral faith from 1,236 in 1923 to just 472 in 1935 and the rise in the number of people converting to Judaism or returning to it from 290 in 1932 to 369 just three years later. Altogether, about 17,000 Jews left the fold between 1919 and 1937 whereas 7,000 people (three-fourths of them women) converted to Judaism. Meanwhile, although the gentile population was not exactly booming in the First Republic, a surplus of births over deaths was recorded nearly every year.[13]

Considering the declining Jewish birthrate in Vienna it is not surprising that the number of marriages also nosedived from 2,955 in 1920 to 1,244 in 1930.[14] Jews tended to marry much later than gentiles—usually between the ages of 30 and 40 compared with ages between 20 and 30 for Christians—which obviously also contributed to the low Jewish birthrate; moreover, far more Jews than gentiles remained single. Even more alarming for Jews was the fact that by 1929, 28 percent of all Jewish marriages were with Christians. As before the war, the Jewish partner converted to Christianity in the great majority of these marriages. The number of mixed marriages increased by perhaps as much as 100 percent between 1914 and 1930.[15]

Finally, a minor factor in the declining Jewish population of Vienna was the relatively high suicide rate after the First World War, probably reflecting deteriorating economic and psychological circumstances. Whereas only 9.06 percent of all suicides in Vienna during the years 1907–13 were committed by Jews, or just slightly over their percentage of the population, this percentile rose to over 12 in 1926–27, or somewhat above their 10.8 percent of the total population during that period.[16]

Although the Jewish population of Austria steadily declined between the wars, it was still highly visible because it was concentrated in the capital city. Whereas Jews made up only 3.8 percent of Berlin's population, their percentage in Vienna was nearly three times as high. By contrast, Jews made up only 0.64 percent of the population of the other federal states in 1923; with the exception of the Burgenland, most of these provincial Jews lived in the state capitals or larger towns. By 1938 the provincial population of Austria had declined by about 20 percent, from around 19,000 to little more than 15,000. Only 8,000 Jews lived in Lower Austria, 3,200 in Burgenland, just over 2,000 in Styria, fewer than 1,000 in Upper Austria, and only a few hundred in each of the other states, except for Vorarlberg, where a mere 18 Jews lived at the beginning of 1938.[17]

In Vienna itself Jews were also unevenly distributed. Nearly 60,000 of them lived in the former ghetto and still largely impoverished district of Leopoldstadt, or 38.5 percent of that district's total population in 1923. The even poorer twentieth district, called Brigittenau, had another 17,600 Jews in 1923, or 18 percent of that neighborhood's population. At the opposite end of the social scale, the wealthy first district had 10,460 Jews, or 24.3 percent of the total. Nearly 24,000 residents, just over a quarter, of the middle-class ninth district of Alsergrund were Jewish, and the middle-class sixth district of Mariahilf contained nearly 9,000 Jews, or 16.4 percent of the entire population. On the other hand, the percentage of Jews in the other districts of Vienna was well below the average for the city.[18]

The concentration of 60 percent of Vienna's Jewish population in just four of the city's twenty-one districts and 75 percent of the Jews in eight districts made it easy for Jews to socialize with each other, but it also made a complete assimilation into the general population much less likely, a phenomenon also found in cities like Warsaw and even Paris.[19] Sigmund Freud's son Martin wrote that even though his family was completely alienated from the Jewish religion and Jewish rites and was thoroughly assimilated into German-Austrian culture, it moved in exclusively Jewish circles. Their friends, physicians, lawyers, and business partners all tended to be Jewish. Even when they went on vacations, it was to places where Jews were in the majority.[20]

The experience of the Freud family was typical of all but the most culturally assimilated Viennese Jewish families. The pattern of housing and social segregation, according to Marsha Rozenblit, created the impression among both Jews and non-Jews that they were a distinct group and prevented intimate relations between them.[21] *Die Wahrheit* was disturbed by this situation and editorialized in 1931 that "contact between Jews and non-Jews [was] declining at a frightening rate." Equality, the paper continued, could "never be based on laws alone, but instead on the sympathy or at least respect of the non-Jewish population."[22] This lack of personal contact and friendship between Jews and non-Jews, which was partly voluntary on the Jewish side but also to a large extent the result of anti-Semitism, was to have dire consequences for Vienna's Jews after the Nazi takeover in 1938 when Jews often found themselves with tragically few gentile friends to protect them.

JEWISH WEALTH, POVERTY, AND EMPLOYMENT

It is easier to enumerate the size and location of Austria's Jewish population than it is to describe its wealth or poverty. Such is not the case for German Jews because we know that their average income was more than three times that of the general population during the Weimar Republic. In Austria, no statistics were ever kept about the wealth of different religious groups so that one is forced to speculate by way of very indirect evidence and the personal observations of contemporaries. There were certainly some wealthy Jews living in the First Austrian Republic, but it does not follow that all Viennese Jews were rich. The only completely safe generalization that can be made about the economic status of Jews is that it varied enormously from one individual to another. The idea that Jews made up just one economic group was one of the more absurd myths perpetrated by anti-Semites.[23]

What evidence is available suggests that more Jews were poor than rich. In the four districts of Vienna where 60 percent of the Jewish population lived nearly 19 percent more people were housed in large apartment buildings than in the other seventeen districts of the city. The percentage of employed Jews (54) was almost identical to that of non-Jews (53) according to the census of 1923. Many Jews were businessmen who had generally prospered in the last decade and a half before the First World War. However, businessmen were especially hard hit by the breakup of the Habsburg Monarchy and the subsequent loss of markets. Then, little more than a decade later, the Great Depression and the drying up of international trade proved to be a second blow to Austrian commerce. The declining Jewish population was almost certainly a symptom of these disastrous economic circumstances. The depression was the main reason why the number of Jews who could afford to pay taxes to the

Israelitische Kultusgemeinde declined from 60,000 in 1927 to little more than 48,000 six years later. In 1934 no fewer than 55,000 Viennese Jews were receiving assistance from the Kultusgemeinde, and fully 65 percent of all Jewish burials were made at the expense of the communal organization.[24]

Two areas in which the anti-Semitic stereotype of the rich Jew bore some relation to the truth were credit institutions and big industries. Jewish bankers had been powerful in Vienna as early as the eighteenth century and had actually begun to dominate Vienna's financial structure as early as the first quarter of the nineteenth century. Ever since the time of Joseph II Jews had administered Austria's tobacco monopoly, probably because of their trade relations with the Near East, from where the raw tobacco was imported.[25] Fully 60 percent of the people engaged in finance and industry were Jewish, or about six times as many per capita as gentiles, at least in 1900.[26] Although most of these people were undoubtedly wealthy, they were also among those who suffered the most catastrophic losses during the depression, when ten of the twelve Austrian banks that failed were Jewish-owned.

Another area in which Austrian Jews were definitely overrepresented was in the so-called free professions such as law, medicine, and higher education. Anti-Semites charged that this was because of a specifically Jewish characteristic of seeking lucrative jobs and avoiding manual labor. These same anti-Semites never explained which people preferred low-paying jobs to high-paying ones. Nor did they attempt to prove that Christians preferred manual labor to white-collar work.

There were, however, some concrete reasons why Jews were particularly anxious to enter the professions. In many cases Jews hoped to avoid problems created by centuries of legal and social discrimination. Before 1848 it had been impossible for them to own land and become farmers; and even after 1867 it was virtually impossible for them to become civil servants without first becoming Christians. Jews were seldom hired by Christian employers, and observant Jews could not work on Saturdays. Many of these problems could be avoided in the free professions. The traditional Jewish emphasis on scholarship, and the observance of daily rituals prescribed by 613 Jewish laws, also made a move into the professions a natural one. The law profession had the additional advantage of not requiring too much money to get started.[27]

Anti-Semites were especially exercised about the number of Jews in the free professions. The *Deutschösterreichische Tages-Presse* claimed that only 300 of 1,940 Viennese lawyers were Aryans and 75 to 85 percent of physicians in the Austrian capital were Jews. Georg Glockemeier, a somewhat more restrained anti-Semitic author frequently cited by other anti-Semites, alleged in 1936 that 85.5 percent of all lawyers and 1,541 of 3,268 physicians in Vienna were Jewish. The pamphleteer Walter Pötsch thought that 90 percent of all Viennese lawyers and 45 percent of all university instructors were Jewish. Only rarely did anti-Semites admit that these Jewish professionals could not have continued their practices without the heavy patronage of Christians.[28]

Although these figures may have been somewhat exaggerated, there is no doubt that in interwar Vienna the free professions were dominated by Jews. According to one Jewish calculation made in 1936, 62 percent of all Viennese lawyers were Jewish, as were 47 percent of all physicians, and almost 29 percent of the city's university instructors. Vienna, in fact, had a higher percentage of Jewish lawyers and physicians than any other city in Europe.[29]

Before the First World War the Jewish domination of certain professions was not a terribly pressing issue because Christians preferred the security of civil service or military jobs, over which they had a near monopoly.[30] After the war, however, in the shrunken territory of the First Republic, the civil service, which had been overstaffed even before the war, now had a huge surplus. The Austro-Hungarian army, whose officers had come primarily from the German-speaking population, was now only a memory, and the new army of the First Republic was far smaller than the 30,000-man limit allowed it in the Treaty of St. Germain. Not unnaturally, Christians now turned to the traditionally "Jewish" professions, only to find that they too had no room for novices. Only a reduction of the number of Jews in the professions to their percentage of the overall population—a numerus clausus—or an even more drastic deportation of Jews seemed to offer hope to anti-Semites of creating new jobs for themselves.

Jewish professional people (as well as other Jews), facing an uphill struggle against discrimination, were convinced that they had to work 120 percent as hard as Christians to get even 90 percent as much recognition. They had to do everything better and more thoroughly than others and could not allow themselves the luxury of making any mistakes. This perfectionist attitude resulted in many magnificent Jewish contributions to Austrian culture and society, but it did not necessarily make the Jews more popular with their Christian competitors.[31]

Below the socioeconomic level of the Jewish financiers, big industrialists, and professionals came the businessmen. The Nazis estimated just after their takeover of power in 1938 that 36,000 of the 146,000 business enterprises in Vienna, or 25 percent, were owned by Jews, or about three times their percentage of the city's population. The great majority of these businesses, however, were small, old-fashioned family affairs. This large number of Jewish businesses helps explain why some 45 percent of all Viennese Jews were self-employed compared with just over 28 percent for non-Jews. The Jewish desire for self-employment was not a great deal different from that of Viennese Christians, however, and was part of a common reluctance to modernize, which only the Nazis would be able partially to overcome after 1938.[32]

The percentage of Jews engaged in various businesses differed substantially, but in nearly all of them they were overrepresented. Over 76 percent of the book salesmen in Vienna were Jewish in the 1930s, 74 percent of the retailers of wine, 73 percent of the textile handlers, 63 percent of the owners of motion picture theaters, 53 percent of the shoe merchants, 40 percent of the jewelers, 34 percent of the photographers, and 26 percent of the druggists, to cite only a few examples.[33]

The high proportion of these Jewish merchants created a great deal of anti-Semitism among Christian small-time merchants and shopkeepers. It was not numbers alone, however, that aroused their resentment. Christian merchants were used to long, leisurely lunch hours, coffee breaks in a nearby cafe, and early closings. Jewish merchants, by contrast (not unlike recent immigrants to the United States from southeast Asia), anxious to become established in what for them was often a new city, frequently disregarded these Viennese traditions, forcing their Christian competitors either to keep pace or lose customers. Many Jewish merchants, especially owners of department stores, were able to offer their customers lower prices, which also did not endear them to their Christian competitors. One particularly innovative and successful Jewish grocery store owner in Vienna's ninth district by the name of Jakob Lehrer attracted a loyal clientele by being the first to offer "specials." His store, the largest of its kind in Vienna with no fewer than twenty-one employees, was also the first to have a machine that roasted imported coffee beans, the aroma of which filled the store. Even his cash register, imported from the United States, was a novelty that amazed his customers.[34]

Jewish writers in interwar Austria were able to point out that Jews benefited the Austrian economy by being responsible for 60 percent of the country's exports; they employed 212,000 Christians, which meant that including dependents, 600,000 to 800,000 Viennese derived their livelihood from Jewish employers. By contrast, Christian firms rarely employed Jews. Jews also paid a disproportionately high percentage of the taxes in Austria, which helped pay the salaries of civil servants, virtually all of whom were Christians. None of these facts impressed anti-Semites, however, who complained that almost half of the workers and employees of Vienna worked for "Jewish gold." They also complained bitterly when the depression forced some Jewish businesses to reduce the wages of their employees; even more anger was created when a Jewish business had to close altogether, thus throwing gentiles out of work.[35]

Further down the social and income scale were Jewish tailors, money changers, and peddlers, most of whom were recent immigrants from Eastern Europe. The latter would usually sell easily transportable items like soap, suspenders, buttons, pencils, and the like. With some luck a son would establish a more substantial business and a grandson would become a professional person. A grandson might even convert to Christianity and become an anti-Semitic Christian Social politician.[36] At the very bottom of the social ladder one could find some Jewish shoe shiners, newspaper salesmen, and even beggars. However, just 2.9 percent of Vienna's industrial workers were Jewish on the eve of the First World War.[37]

Almost too small to be counted were the Jewish peasants of Austria, all 760 of them, who in 1934 made up just 0.7 percent of Jewish employment. Anti-Semites regarded the virtual absence of a Jewish peasantry as particularly damning, thus completely ignoring the laws that prevented Jews from owning property in Central Europe before 1848. After that date Jews could, in theory, become farmers; but by that time Europe was moving inexorably toward urbanization and industrialization. Few Christians moved from the city to the countryside after the mid-nineteenth century, not even when encouraged to do so by Adolf Hitler in the 1930s. In any event, Jews would have found it next to impossible to accommodate themselves to the peasant customs of Alpine Austria, which revolved in large part around the Catholic church.[38]

A common characteristic of all the occupations where Jews were highly represented—be they finance, commerce, or the liberal professions—was that they were all "unproductive" in the eyes of Christian traditionalists. Unlike premodern artisans and peasants, the "Jewish professions" literally produced no tangible products. Instead, Jewish bankers made money by charging interest on loans; Jewish businessmen lived from the profits charged on goods produced by Christians, and Jewish lawyers and physicians profited from the hardships of their Christian clients: hence the myth of the "unproductive" and "exploiting" Jew.[39]

When anti-Semites cataloged the economic fields in which Jews were overrepresented, they carefully avoided mention of the civil service. If a numerus clausus had meant guaranteed proportional representation for Jews instead of capping Jewish representation it would have been an enormous boon to Austrian Jews. There had been a tradition of excluding Jews from public service in Austria, and most of the rest of Europe, since the Middle Ages when imperial charters forbade their employment. This tradition was supposedly ended by the Austrian constitution of 1867; in practice, however, it remained extremely difficult for a Jew to obtain a government position—either local, state, or federal—unless he was baptized. This policy continued into the First Republic. In 1935 the Austrian government employed 160,692 civil servants, but only a pathetic 682, or 0.28 percent, were Jews. In Vienna there were only 152 Jews, most of them physicians, who were employed by the municipality, out of 42,113 positions. Since the establishment of the republic, no Jew was ever made a judge anywhere in Austria, whereas before the war there had been thirteen Jewish judges in Vienna alone. The Zionist Robert Stricker was the only politician representing Jewish interests exclusively in the Austrian Parliament during the entire First Republic, and he served only from 1919 to 1920; in the early 1930s there were no Jews from the bourgeois parties in the National Assembly. Almost certainly the large number of Jewish lawyers and professors in Vienna would have been reduced if some of them could have found government employment.[40]

THE "JEWISH PRESS"

Two professional activities in which Jews were heavily involved in interwar Austria and before, which have been intentionally omitted until now, were writing and publishing. Probably nothing else the Austrian Jews did so incensed anti-Semites, particularly the editors of anti-Semitic newspapers.

All manner of evils were ascribed by anti-Semites to this "Jewish press," which was above all responsible for the "decay" of German intellectual and spiritual life. It was supposedly leading Christian Germans like a "herd of sheep." Whenever the Germans were about to defend themselves, the Jewish press managed to incite them against each other. The sale of pornographic books was allegedly solely in the hands of Jews and was causing Christians to lose their morality. Jews were also said to control the most important literary magazines and through them "created" great men who "of course" were always either Jews or friends of Jews. They also controlled literary criticism and had good things to say only about Jewish authors and playwrights. Hitler echoed this idea when he wrote in Mein Kampf that the "glorification of the theater critics [of the Jewish press] was always reserved for Jewish authors, and their rejection never affected anyone but German[-Austrians]." However, on rare occasions even a Nazi newspaper would admit that Jewish families did a great deal to encourage the development of their children's talents whereas "Aryan" families often discouraged their children.[41]

Some Jewish writers or writers of Jewish origins did play into anti-Semitic hands. Most were nonpracticing Jews and often felt alienated from society. Therefore Jewish publications were sometimes critical of Austrian culture. An extreme example was the baptized Jew, Karl Kraus, and his journal *Die Fackel* (*The Torch*), which he edited from 1899 until his death in 1936. *Die Fackel* set new standards for aggressive satire, much of it aimed against Jews such as Herzl and Freud. Anti-Semites condemned Kraus for defending homosexuals and prostitutes. Kraus was a half century ahead of his time in arguing that a person's sexual activities were his business alone as long as they did no one any harm. Prostitutes, he said, were more heroic than soldiers. Like the latter, they served the existing social order by facing injury, disease, and death, but unlike soldiers, prostitutes were subject to social and legal penalties.[42]

Jewish newspaper editors in interwar Austria also sometimes provided anti-Semites with ammunition. Even Jewish historians have admitted that not all were respectable. *Pressefreiheit* (freedom of the press) could sometimes lead to *Pressefrechheit* (insolence). A tasteless, sensationalistic boulevard press, edited largely by Jews, grew up between the wars. And there was also some corruption in the press of the First Republic. None of these phenomena was unique to Austria, however. They were also common in New York and in London where there were very few Jewish editors. More important, in comparison to anti-Semitic newspapers like *Der eiserne Besen*, *Der Stürmer*, the *Deutsch-österreichische Tages-Zeitung*, *Kikeriki*, *Wiener Stimmen*, and *Der Kampfruf*, Jewish-owned papers like *Der Tag*, *Der Abend*, and *Die Stunde* were absolute models of decorum and restraint.[43]

It is a fact that the creation of the liberal Viennese press, like much of the metropolitan press in Germany, was to a large extent a Jewish achievement. Jews wrote the leading articles, advertisements, essays, and business news; they were also highly influential in the publication of books and magazines. One British writer claimed shortly before the First World War that 75 percent of the editors of Vienna's daily newspapers were Jewish.[44] However, when anti-Semites referred to the "Jewish press," they rarely meant those newspapers which were written by and exclusively for a Jewish audience, such as the assimilationist weekly, *Die Wahrheit*, the daily Zionist paper, *Die Wiener Morgenzeitung*, and its successor, the weekly *Die Stimme*. Because these newspapers exercised no influence over the non-Jewish population, anti-Semites mentioned them only when they might contain a statement that they, the anti-Semites, found damaging to Jewish interests.

Rather it was the secular and liberal press, owned and edited predominantly by Jews, that drew the wrath of anti-Semites. Though they never said so directly, it was actually the liberalism of the Jewish press to which nationalistic anti-Semites objected; Catholic newspapers like the *Reichspost* and *Wiener Stimmen* detested both their liberalism and secularism and not just their association with Jews. This is why anti-Semites referred to Austrians who expressed liberal ideas as being infected by the "Jewish spirit." Pan-German nationalists used "the Jews" and "Jewish influence" to explain why some Austrians did not think as they did. As in so many other aspects of Austrian culture and society, it was easier for anti-Semites to condemn something because of its association with Jews than it was to criticize an idea or practice on its own merits. Although liberal newspapers like the *Neue Freie Presse* certainly depended on well-educated upper-middle-class Jews for much of their readership, they also could not have survived without a large gentile audience, another fact that infuriated hard-core anti-Semitic editors and politicians.[45]

Far from supporting specifically Jewish causes, the liberal Jewish-owned and edited newspapers of Vienna actually bent over backward to avoid even mentioning Jewish issues such as Zionism or Palestine. Even in the liberal causes that Jewish-owned newspapers did support, it may be doubted just how much influence they really had. Liberalism itself was a dying ideology after the mid-1890s and never more so than during the entire First Republic. Liberal, Jewish-owned newspapers fought the Christian Social Party, as did the Socialist press, which was also edited primarily by people of Jewish origins; yet they did not prevent the Christian Social Party from controlling the government continuously after the breakup of the early postwar coalition government in 1920. Such papers were occasionally critical of anti-Semitism, but certainly did not eliminate it. They were staunchly pro-Austrian and anti-Nazi yet failed to prevent the Nazi takeover in 1938.[46]

About the only safe generalization that one can make about the Jews in Austrian society during the First Republic is that it is impossible to make grand generalizations that would apply to all of them. All of the anti-Semitic clichés about the Jews did have some basis in fact, but only some. There were wealthy Jews, but there were also a large number of impoverished ones. And if anything, Jews were hurt by the breakup of the Habsburg Monarchy and the Great Depression even more than gentiles. Some Jews did live in palatial quarters in the inner city of Vienna and elsewhere, but far more were crowded into the slums of the Leopoldstadt and Brigittenau. They were overrepresented in certain fields such as banking, law, and medicine, but grossly underrepresented in the civil service. There were a large number of Jewish-owned and -edited newspapers, magazines, and publishing houses, but they did not defend specifically Jewish causes and had only a limited ability to influence public opinion; and they were often critical of Jews themselves.

These fine distinctions were almost always lost on the anti-Semites. They talked only about "die Juden" or "das Judentum." Crimes or perversions of individual Jews became "typical" of all Jews. Achievements of individual Jews, if mentioned at all, were called exceptions or manufactured creations of other Jewish writers. For the true believing anti-Semite, anti-Semitism was an article of faith. Facts that contradicted that faith either had to be ignored or explained away as exceptions. Jews and the friends of Jews discovered to their dismay that rational arguments made almost no impact on these people.

15

A HOUSE DIVIDED
Internal Jewish Politics

Austrian Jews were by no means passive during the First Republic when they were being regularly assaulted, first verbally and then increasingly physically. However, their reaction was far from united. In fact, their responses were just as varied as the many types of anti-Semitism they encountered. Not only did they differ according to particular incidents but also according to the religious, political, social, and economic background of the Jews themselves. We have seen how the non-Jewish Austrians were bitterly divided into pan-German nationalists, conservative Roman Catholics, and relatively radical Social Democrats. The Jews of Austria were also split into at least as many acrimonious political factions as the gentiles, who outnumbered them by a thirty-to-one ratio. One Viennese Jewish magazine went so far as to describe Jews as "the most divided people in the world."[1] In no respect was the mythical Nazi view of Jews more absurd than in its depiction of them as monolithic world conspirators. Indeed, Jews could not even agree on the most fundamental questions of survival.

THE ZIONIST CHALLENGE

The most important reason for the acrimony within the Jewish community after 1918 not only in Austria but throughout the rest of Europe and America as well was the rise of Zionism. Before the war the Zionists had been little more than a vocal minority. As late as 1913 there had been only fifteen hundred dues-paying Zionists, over a third of whom were university students who encountered anti-Semitism and even physical assaults almost on a daily basis. However, their use of Herzl's inflammatory language along with their aggressive tactics and philosophy, which would so outrage wealthy and well-assimilated Jews, were already well established before the First World War.

Assimilationists accused the Zionists of rejecting liberal and tolerant politics aimed at harmony and compromise, and refusing to make a clear distinction between the common anti-Semitic enemy and the leadership of the Jewish community. Stefan Zweig, who knew Theodor Herzl personally, openly admitted that he disliked the Zionists' "quarreling and dogmatic spirit, the constant opposition." Another famous Jewish author, Joseph Roth, rejected Zionism because he thought its nationalism was the scourge of the twentieth century. In many respects the rejection of liberal and assimilationist values by young Zionists was part of a rebellion against parental authority, including in some cases their parents' religious orthodoxy.[2] Zionists themselves were convinced that it resulted from their clearer perception of the dangers facing the Jewish community.

Zionists did not share the optimism of the liberal assimilationists, whose philosophy was rooted in the eighteenth-century Enlightenment. The assimilationists in the Union of German-Austrian Jews (renamed the Union of Austrian Jews in 1931) stubbornly held to their belief in the powers of persuasion and in the ultimate reasonableness of mankind, even when contemporary events seemed to be proving the exact opposite. They were determined to defend themselves by uniting with progressive and liberal elements in other political parties and were not about to sacrifice what they saw as a bright future because of a gloomy present. They regarded the revolutionary disturbances of the early postwar years and the disintegration of traditional moral concepts as merely passing phenomena.[3]

Most Zionists, on the other hand, were much less sanguine about being able to solve the Jewish problem in Europe and the likelihood of the anti-Semites ever changing their views as a result of education and reasonable persuasion. Consequently, Herzl thought that combating anti-Semitism was futile. On the contrary, the intensification of anti-Semitism would actually benefit Zionism by exposing the assimilationist philosophy as an illusion. However, Zionists tended to be optimistic about their own prospects of creating a separate, prosperous, and culturally creative Jewish society either in their present homeland, on a temporary basis, or in Palestine. They reversed the logic of the anti-Semitic stigma by rejoicing in the distinctiveness of their Jewishness rather than by denying or minimizing the differences between Jews and gentiles, as assimilationists were prone to do.[4]

Indeed, most Zionists were so convinced of the uniqueness of the Jewish people that they considered themselves to be a separate nationality. It was this fundamental belief, even more than their extreme propaganda tactics, that alienated assimilated Viennese Jews. Only baptized and nonpracticing

Jews fell outside the fold as far as the mainstream Austrian Zionist organ, *Die Stimme,* was concerned. However, many Zionists went even further, refusing to regard religion as essential to membership in the Jewish community. Assimilated Jews, on the other hand, regarded themselves as first and foremost Austrians and only secondarily as Jews. Indeed they were probably the most patriotic Austrians of both the monarchy and the First Republic. To assimilated Jews, the Austrian loyalties of the Zionists were very much in doubt. (In reality, Zionists were loyal to Austria both before and after 1918, but unlike the assimilationists they were not devoted to it.)[5]

The second fundamental point of conflict between the Zionists and the assimilationists, and one that was related to the first point, was the Zionist desire to establish and preserve a modern Jewish culture that was separate and distinct from the German-Austrian culture, not only in Palestine, but also in Austria and elsewhere. Among other things, this entailed the establishment of Hebrew-language schools, clubs, choirs, literary societies, youth groups, and sporting associations. The demand for separate Jewish schools was especially dear to Zionists because they believed, with good reason, that the public schools of Austria were heavily infused with Catholicism in the textbooks and other teaching materials. Such schools were a harmonious extension of Catholic family life, but not of Jewish values. Austrian Zionists hoped that such "dissimilation" would reduce conflicts with gentiles and would even win their respect. (Such hopes might have actually been realized if Catholic rather than Nazi anti-Semitism had prevailed.) Assimilation, on the other hand, they regarded not only as a major cause of anti-Semitism, but also as moral bankruptcy and treason toward the Jewish people.[6]

Actually the Zionist program was not as radical as it was often portrayed by the assimilationists. Zionists did not propose a complete separation of Jews and gentiles. Jewish schools would at first only be at the elementary level and would be voluntary. Eventually, it was hoped (and finally realized) that Jewish secondary schools (*Gymnasien*) could be created. However, Jews would continue to attend public universities and technical schools in Austria. Zionists, like assimilationists, rejected a numerus clausus in any form. They demanded to be treated as citizens with completely equal rights, including unrestricted access to public jobs. Austrian Zionists were also nearly as acculturated into German-Austrian society as were the assimilated Jews and expected to teach the local language, culture, and history in their Jewish schools. Their adaptation to the Austrian way of life was evident in their unwillingness to leave the country, at least before the depression and the rise of Nazism in the 1930s. In 1926, a year in which some prosperity was beginning to return to Austria, only thirty-nine Jews left Vienna for Palestine. The next year the number dropped to a mere nine. And because Vienna was something of a jumping off point for the Holy Land, it is quite likely that a majority of these forty-eight Jews were from Eastern Europe rather than from Vienna.[7]

THE ASSIMILATIONIST RESPONSE TO ZIONISM

Both assimilationist Jews and Zionists in Vienna tended to emphasize differences rather than commonalities. Opponents of Zionism thought that labeling Jews as anything other than Austrian citizens, and particularly calling Jews a national minority, would be but the first step in curtailing the rights of Jews as equal citizens. Identifying Jews as a separate nationality would only confirm what racial anti-Semites had been saying all along—that Jews were an alien people who ought to be segregated from the rest of society—and would lend justification to whatever discriminatory measures they chose to take against Jews, as indeed turned out to be the case. *Die Wahrheit* called Zionism the counterpart of racial National Socialism and thought that the Nazis had borrowed many of their slogans from the Jewish nationalists.[8]

The one area where there was at least some agreement between assimilationists and Zionists was Palestine. *Die Wahrheit* sometimes published articles about Arab terrorism in Palestine and warned that there could never be any peace in the Holy Land until there were equal rights for both Arabs and Jews. Nevertheless, the newspaper supported Jewish efforts to establish a homeland there for Jews who could not or were not allowed to assimilate elsewhere. Left unspoken was the desire to rid Vienna of troublesome Ostjuden who might create an anti-Semitic backlash. Prior to a Jewish communal election in 1936 the Union of Austrian Jews raised the constructive work in Palestine to second place in their list of priorities. Of course Palestine could never be the first concern of assimilationists because they never expected to move there themselves.[9]

Although the Zionists' policy toward Palestine differed substantially from that of the assimilationists, their practices did not. Palestine was the focus of their attention; it received more space in their newspapers than did events in Austria or Germany. Whereas the assimilationists pointed out the difficulties of life in Palestine, the Zionists tended to minimize them. Nevertheless, most Zionists, in both Austria and Germany, did not expect to emigrate to Palestine at any time in the near future, if ever. And just as Palestine grew more important in the program of the assimilationists, so too did expressions of loyalty to Austria by Zionists as the Nazi threat loomed ever larger.[10]

ZIONIST FACTIONALISM

The rise of Zionism did not merely divide Austrian Jews between those whose first loyalty was Austria, both politically and culturally, and those who wanted to develop a distinct Jewish culture. Austrian Zionists themselves were also badly split into a large number of factions that were prone to quarrel even during good times. This is probably best explained by the greater social heterogeneity of the Zionists when compared with the Union of Austrian Jews as well as by the ideological nature of the movement. No doubt Zionist factionalism also simply reflected the divisions within the Jewish community in general. In any event, there were at least four or five different Zionist groups in interwar Austria and, indeed, throughout Europe, since the Zionist organizations were all international. The only thing these factions had in common was their belief that the Jews were a distinct nationality and their desire to help Jews to emigrate to Palestine who wanted to do so. However, they had almost irreconcilable differences about the form and size of the new Palestinian state, about its social organization, and about the role of religion.[11]

Membership in all Zionist political organizations ranged from about 10,000 in the mid-1920s to around 16,000 a decade later. In Austria, most of these Zionists belonged to bourgeois or conservative factions. The middle-of-the-road General Zionist organization included Jews of all religious practices and social backgrounds. Its newspaper had been the *Wiener Morgenzeitung*, the only daily Jewish newspaper in German-speaking Europe from its founding in 1919 until its demise in 1927; after 1928 the weekly *Stimme* became the organ of mainstream Zionism represented in the Landeskomitee für Österreich (State Committee for Austria). The Misrachi (literally: "Of the East") was a group of religious Zionists that was founded in 1901 as a special section within the General Zionist organization. The Poale Zion (Workers of Zion), which had been founded in 1907 and whose newspaper was *Der jüdische Arbeiter*, was a bridge between Zionism and Marxian socialism. It was itself divided as to whether Palestine or a proletarian revolution was the answer to the Jewish question; the organization was dissolved by the Austrian government in 1934 because of its connections to the recently outlawed Social Democratic Party. The non-Marxist People's Socialist Zionists, to which the Hitachduth

(Association) and the Zeire Zion (Youth of Zion) belonged, rejected the class struggle advocated by the Poale Zion and emphasized the importance of agricultural work in Palestine. Minor revisionist organizations included the Zionist Revisionists, whose newspaper was *Die Neue Welt* edited by Robert Stricker; the New Zionist Organization, founded in 1935 by Vladimir Jabotinsky in Vienna, which stressed militancy, strict discipline, ceremonies, and symbols; and the Radical Zionists, with *Der jüdische Weg* as its press organ.[12]

ORTHODOX JUDAISM IN AUSTRIA

The third and smallest group of Jews in Vienna comprising approximately 20 percent of the community's total population was the Orthodox. Not much space needs to be devoted to them because they had little to do with either Jewish politics or general Austrian politics. Indeed they did not even participate in politics of the Kultusgemeinde until 1920, being convinced that the communal leadership neglected religious education, Hebrew education, and the needs of poor Jews. Orthodox Jews dropped out of the organization altogether in 1932. Instead they had an unofficial communal organization of their own. They tended to be older than the assimilated Jews and much older than the Zionists. They most frequently immigrated to Vienna from either Hungary or Galicia. They rejected on religious grounds both the idea of a modern secular Jewish state, which only the Messiah could restore, and assimilation into gentile society. Consequently, they tended to be relatively oblivious of what was going on around them, and their newspaper, *Jüdische Presse*, only barely noticed the rise of National Socialism.[13]

JEWISH INTERNAL POLITICS AND
THE ISRAELITISCHE KULTUSGEMEINDE

Much of the intra-Jewish feuding took place within the Jewish communal organization of Vienna, the Israelitische Kultusgemeinde Wien (IKG). From 1888 until 1932 the IKG was controlled by assimilationist Jews organized in the Union of German-Austrian Jews, which had 5,500 members in 1923 but only 3,000 in 1938. Having lived in Austria, or at least some other German-speaking area, for at least two generations, they spoke German fluently and considered themselves to be Austrians in every respect. They were by far the wealthiest Jews as well as being older and more "established" than most other

Austrian Jews. Therefore, they had the most to fear from a Nazi takeover and the least to expect from a move to Palestine, or anywhere else. Their list of thirty-six candidates for the 1936 elections of the IKG reveals, for example, that six were lawyers, two were physicians, three were factory owners, and most of the others were businessmen, head clerks, or people with substantial training and education.[14]

The Viennese IKG, like other Jewish communal organizations in Central Europe in the late nineteenth and early twentieth centuries, consisted of three parts: a president, an elected Community Council, which in 1932 had thirty-six men, and affiliated organizations (in Vienna there were an incredible 450 such organizations in the 1930s). All Viennese Jews who had not explicitly renounced their faith automatically belonged to the organization.[15]

From at least as early as the turn of the century, a philosophical conflict existed within the IKG between politically conservative Unionists and Orthodox Jews, on the one hand, who wanted to restrict the organization to its original religious and social functions as laid down in the bylaws of 1890, and Zionists, who saw it as a potential means of bringing about major changes in the community. Already at the first Zionist congress in Basel, in 1897, Herzl had made the conquest of Jewish communal organizations a major Zionist goal. Almost certainly, most Viennese Jews were content with the limited role of the IKG because only a small percentage of them even bothered to vote in the communal elections, although prior to 1912 this was in part due to the restriction of the franchise to just the twelve thousand wealthy, dues-paying members. Their apathy ultimately redounded to the benefit of the Zionists, who were anything but apathetic.[16]

The influx of Jewish refugees into Vienna not only affected Austrian politics in general, but internal Jewish politics as well. Most of the refugees were poor and came from areas of the monarchy where there was still a strong sense of Jewish national identity. The younger refugees supported Zionism; the older ones often remained Orthodox. The added support for the Viennese Zionists alarmed the assimilated Jews.[17]

With their ranks swollen by these newcomers, and with revolutionary enthusiasm spreading all over Central Europe, Zionists in both Austria and Germany thought the time was propitious to rally their fellow Jews to the cause of Jewish nationalism. Assimilationist ideas appeared to be especially vulnerable at a time when everything old was being questioned and when anti-Semitism was on the rise.[18] Consequently, in November 1918 the Austrian Zionists (like Zionists in other countries) formed a fifty-member National Council (Nationalrat) and demanded that the government recognize the Jews as a separate nationality with self-determination in cultural and religious affairs, including all those matters controlled until then by the IKG. It also demanded proportional representation for Jews in the Austrian Parliament and all other legislative bodies. Jewish nationalists hoped that the National Council would gain publicity for their cause. In reality, however, only pan-German and Christian Social anti-Semites even paid much attention to the demands of the Nationalrat, and the assimilated Viennese Jews were horrified.[19] The Community Council formally declared in December 1918 that the Jewish National Council had no right to speak for all the Jewish people; Jews had a right to identify with whatever nationality they chose.[20]

However, assimilated Jews were disturbed about the growing rift in the Viennese community and, fearing bloodshed, agreed in the same month to the formation of an "Action Committee" to study the reform of the antiquated and undemocratic franchise of the IKG with a view toward giving Zionists more representation. The minimum tax making one eligible to vote was greatly reduced at the end of 1918, thus nearly doubling the franchise. Another rule reserving one-third of the deputies elected to the parliamentary body of the IKG to those people who paid the highest taxes was also eliminated. The next few years saw further electoral reforms, all of them beneficial to Zionists. In 1924 the citizenship requirement for voting was rescinded, thus raising the IKG electorate, which had been only about 12,000 as late as 1910, to 35,000 in 1924 and 49,000 in 1932. An agreement between the Zionists and Unionists concluded in 1920 stipulated that seats on the Community Council, the legislative body of the IKG, would be distributed on the basis of proportional representation.[21]

These rule changes helped the Zionists steadily to increase their representation within the Community Council. In the elections of July 1920, the first since the electoral reform of 1918, the number of their mandates rose from eight to thirteen, and they won 39 percent of the vote. The Zionists gained only modestly in the elections of December 1928 at a time of maximum Austrian prosperity; the Unionists won over 9,000 votes whereas the Zionists received just under 6,000.[22]

The big breakthrough for the Zionists came in the elections of December 1932, the same year in which the Nazis had won major electoral victories in both Austria and Germany and when Austria was wallowing in the depths of the Great Depression. For the first time anywhere in Europe the Zionists gained an absolute majority of the vote in a communal election. Nevertheless, it is doubtful whether a majority of the Viennese Jews were actually Zionists or pro-Zionists. Almost half of the eligible voters did not cast ballots, and it can reasonably be assumed that nearly all of them were non-Zionists.[23] However, in the elections of November 1936 the Zionist majority in the IKG grew when 70 percent of the eligible voters cast their ballots, doubtless reflecting increased Jewish self-consciousness and fear of anti-Semitism since Hitler's takeover of power in Germany. By comparison, only 51 percent had voted in 1932 and 42.3 percent in 1924. The Zionists' vote of 17,466 represented a 5,000-vote increase since 1932. The Unionist vote also increased, but only by 1,412 to a total of just 11,633.[24]

All of the IKG elections, especially those of the 1930s, were bitterly fought affairs accompanied by a great deal of mudslinging and name-calling and even physical violence—mostly attempts by young Zionists to disrupt Unionist electoral meetings. At first *Die Wahrheit* only gently rebuked the Zionists saying in 1920 that the majority of Viennese Jews were accustomed to mildness and tolerance in their politics. The Zionist Jews, the paper continued, needed to learn that Viennese Jews behaved differently from those in Eastern Europe. They should not adopt the political practices of the Socialists and Karl Lueger. Later, however, *Die Wahrheit* used stronger language. In 1936 it accused the Zionists of using lies, slander, terror, swindles, boycotts, and physical obstruction in the campaign. The politics of the Jewish nationalists had allegedly copied those of the anti-Semites. The Unionist organ quoted the *Deutsches Volksblatt* as strongly approving of the Zionists' victory. *Die Wahrheit* also charged that the Zionists had won the election of 1936 because they had received the votes of 12,000 non-Austrian Jews.[25] In reality, the union had won only 45 percent of the vote of Austrian citizens and just 36.5 percent of the total vote.

The Zionist press was equally intemperate in its attacks on the Unionists. *Die Neue Welt* said that the Jewish men and women of Vienna had had to put up with the drumroll of lies, slander, denunciation, and terror slogans. The paper also claimed that no more than 5,330 non-Austrian Jews had voted in the election of 1936. After the election of December 1932, the principal Zionist paper, *Die Stimme*, complained that the Unionists' campaigning had been marked by lies, distortions, hatred, the calling into question of the Zionists' loyalty to the state, and the breakdown of all political decency. A flood of dirt and stupidity had swept over the electoral arena.[26]

The more activist policy of the Zionists within the IKG once they had gained a majority embittered the Union of Austrian Jews and caused it temporarily to withdraw its deputies from the IKG parliament in 1936. It complained to the mayor of Vienna that the Zionists made illegal use of the communal organization for their own political purposes by establishing a Zionist elementary school and by allegedly filling the administration of the IKG exclusively with Zionists. The protest was in vain, however.[27]

Apart from the Jewish communal elections, only a single avowed Jew representing Jewish interests, Robert Stricker, was ever elected to the Austrian Parliament. He was elected in 1919 with 7,706 votes. However, a change in the voting rules caused his defeat the following year, even though his vote nearly doubled to 13,358. A Zionist coalition gained nearly 25,000 votes in 1923, but still won no parliamentary seat. After that the Zionist vote in parliamentary elections declined to 10,717 in 1927 and to just 2,135 in 1930, after which no more Zionists ran for office. Jewish nationalists were only slightly more successful in Vienna's city council, gaining three representatives in 1919 but only one in the municipal elections of 1923 under more unfavorable election regulations.[28]

In many ways the split in Jewish ranks was a microcosm of divisions in Austrian society as a whole. Just as Jews could not agree on whether they comprised a distinct Volk, gentile Austrians were divided on whether they were Germans or Austrians. Just as the nationalistic Zionists were themselves split into many different factions, so too were pan-German Austrians, at least until the Nazis absorbed most of them after 1932. Religious-secular and capitalist-socialist rivalries could also be found in both gentile and Jewish circles.

If anything, however, fundamental disagreements among Jews were even more profound than among gentiles. Very few Christian Austrians considered leaving their homeland (except, perhaps, to move to neighboring Germany), much less establishing a new language and culture within Austria. Moreover, a far higher percentage of Jews consisted of recent and unassimilated immigrants than was true among gentiles. Even religious differences among Jews were probably more serious than among Christians. It is hardly surprising, therefore, that Austrian Jews found it almost impossible to unite against the common anti-Semitic danger.

16

THE VIEW FROM
THE SOUTH

The factionalism of the Jewish community in Austria can be easily seen in the way the press organs of the particular Jewish parties viewed current events in both Austria and in the neighboring Third Reich. Every Jewish newspaper of Austria—and here we are speaking only of those newspapers that were written exclusively by and for practicing Jews—interpreted events through the prism of its own passionately held ideology. And every paper looked for events that would prove that its group's program was the only one that held hope for the salvation of all Jews in the future.

The Jewish newspapers of Austria present a unique perspective on Jewish reactions to anti-Semitic events in the Third Reich. As German-speaking Jews living just beyond the boundaries of Nazi Germany, the Jews of Austria were probably better informed about events on the other side of the Inn River than Jews anywhere else in the world. At the same time, because Hitler had made his intentions toward Austria clear on the first page of *Mein Kampf*, it was obvious that Austrian Jews would share the fate of their German brethren if the country were annexed or *gleichgeschaltet* (coordinated). Therefore events in Germany affecting the Jews dominated the pages of Austria's Jewish newspapers, above all the *Die Wahrheit*, at least in 1932 and 1933. Moreover, even though Austrian papers began to be censored in 1933, the censorship was largely confined to reports involving the Austrian government. There is no evidence that it colored reporting on Nazi Germany.[1]

Die Wahrheit, with its optimistic, liberal philosophy, was inclined to put the most hopeful interpretation on the events of the day. For *Die Wahrheit* and the Union of Austrian Jews, the Hitler movement was no more than a temporary phenomenon, a view that allowed the union to retain its liberal, assimilationist Weltanschauung.[2] In surveying articles from *Die Wahrheit*, and a few from other Jewish newspapers, it is easy to conclude that the writers were naive, grossly optimistic, or simply grasping at straws. Before arriving at so harsh a conclusion, however, it should be remembered that Jewish writers, and, for that matter, other Austrians and Germans, did not have the benefit of our hindsight. Almost no one, Jew or gentile, in his wildest nightmare foresaw the coming Holocaust.

Moreover, the Nazis themselves had not outlined any clear-cut policy toward the Jews prior to their takeover of power. Although some regional Nazi leaders like Julius Streicher had made frightening statements about the future of German Jewry, top Nazis often made relatively mild comments. For example, in the early months of 1930 an American journalist asked Hitler to describe his anti-Semitism. The Führer answered that his party had no plans to deny Jews their rights; it used anti-Semitic slogans only because the voters expected to hear them. And despite the sharp increase in verbal anti-Semitism after the First World War, direct physical assaults on Jews were comparatively rare in Germany, especially after the early postwar years. Except for the Viennese Hochschulen, the same was also generally true in Austria.[3]

THE JEWISH PRESS AND THE RISE OF THE NAZIS

References to Nazis, Austrian or German, were infrequent in the Jewish newspapers of Vienna prior to 1930. Die Wahrheit did mention Nazi participation in the public demonstrations of the early 1920s as well as Nazi activities in Viennese colleges and institutes throughout the decade. In December 1925 it commented that "the mentality of these boys, some of whom have hardly outgrown their childhood, is truly frightening. Shooting, shouting, marching, and destroying appear to be their real purpose in life." However, as late as October 1929 it referred to the Austrian Nazis as being "finished."[4]

Already in July 1930, several weeks before the German Nazis won their stunning electoral victory in the Reichstag elections of September, Die Wahrheit expressed concern over Nazi victories in local German elections. Jews had to recognize that hatred of Jews was the most important part of the Nazis' program. However, the paper took some comfort in noting that the Nazis' gains had come mostly at the expense of other anti-Semitic parties, especially the German National People's Party. Moreover, Hitler's domestic program, especially as it concerned Jews, was simply utopian and would be catastrophic and doomed to failure if actually implemented. Nazism was one of those phenomena that grew stronger as long as it was fought, but which would fall apart as soon as someone tried to put its program into practice.[5]

Die Wahrheit was slightly less optimistic in late August. It noted an increase in anti-Semitism among state officials in Germany, in the right-wing bourgeois parties, in the Ministry of Justice, and in the economy and society of Germany. The Center Party and the new State Party were acting responsibly, but not the German National People's Party and the German People's Party. The German government was also not doing anything to counteract the Nazis' pogrom-fostering propaganda. Austrian Jews could eventually be affected by developments in Germany.[6]

The German elections in September 1930, when the Nazis suddenly became the second largest party in the Reichstag and won 6.4 million votes after having received only 810,000 two years before, shocked the Jewish newspapers of Austria. *Die Wahrheit* thought the elections showed that Germany was suffering from a sickness caused by the continuing humiliation of its national consciousness by the Versailles peace treaty and reparations. The younger generation was filled with despair and hopelessness. The elections had sent a message to the Western democracies to abandon their spirit of revenge and to think in pan-European terms regarding economic matters. The German Jews were also guilty of displaying a regrettable spirit of confusion and division.[7]

The prognosis of the Zionist-Revisionist *Neue Welt* regarding the Reichstag elections was much gloomier than that of *Die Wahrheit*. Half of the German population had voted for anti-Semitic parties. The children of the intelligentsia had voted for the Nazis, which meant that the next generation would be anti-Semitic. The idea that 60 million Germans had to fight 500,000 Jews had triumphed. The German Jews had tried to fight anti-Semitism with lofty words, as though it were a temporary phenomenon. Instead of considering themselves Jews, the Jewish leaders in Germany wanted to be considered Germans.[8]

The year 1931 was a relatively quiet one politically in both Germany and Austria because no major elections were held in either country. Nevertheless, *Die Wahrheit* was aware that the Austrian Nazis had gained in popularity recently even though they were still well behind their German comrades in that regard. The paper did not think that the Austrian Nazis were as fanatical as their counterparts in the Third Reich, but correctly noted that their methods were the same, especially their propaganda techniques.[9]

By 1932 the Nazis in both Germany and Austria had grown enormously and had to be taken seriously. Commenting on the Prussian Landtag elections of 24 April, when the Nazis won 36 percent of the vote, *Die Wahrheit* noted that the Nazis now represented a real danger to Jews in the Reich. However, the Nazis could not form a government because the Catholic Center Party would not agree to forming a coalition with them. There also remained the hope that, if the Nazis should eventually come to power, their bite would not be as bad as their bark. If the Nazis wanted to be considered capable of governing they would have to become more moderate. *Die Neue Welt* thought that the election results in Prussia and those from regional elections in Austria on the same day proved that Jews could rely only on themselves for help and not on any predominantly Christian party.[10]

The fall of the federal government of Heinrich Brüning in June 1932 caused alarm in Jewish circles. But *Die Wahrheit* soon commented that the government of Franz von Papen did not appear to be paving the way for Hitler, as earlier feared. To the contrary, the Junkers were using Hitler for their own purposes. The conservative and democratic elements of Germany had not given in to Hitler, and the organized workers and the Center Party also strongly opposed him. Moreover, President Hindenburg had promised to uphold the constitution. Although these were dangerous days, they were no more so than those of the anti-Semites Adolf Stoecker and Heinrich von Treitschke in the nineteenth century.[11]

Even though the Nazis won a smashing victory in the Reichstag elections in July 1932, more than doubling their vote of September 1930, *Die Wahrheit* thought that Hitler had not won the victory that he had expected. The political fronts could not be changed any further because the Center Party had declared its absolute opposition to joining a Nazi-dominated coalition government. Jews could also take comfort in the Nazis' very slow growth since April. The Nazis, in fact, had probably already passed their peak strength. Parties that could no longer grow as a rule declined.[12]

By September *Die Wahrheit*'s optimism was getting stronger. Although all the signs were not yet positive, it appeared that the Nazis were on the verge of a decline. Hitler had been foolish to turn down the recent offer of Chancellor Franz von Papen to be the vice-chancellor of Germany and the prime minister of Prussia. Papen had proved himself a better strategist than Hitler. Hitler's popularity with his own followers had been based on the belief that he would soon gain power. That no longer appeared to be the case, and his prestige had been hurt. The Nazis were now in an irreversible decline.[13]

Die Wahrheit's super optimism seemed amply justified when the Nazis lost over two million votes in the November 1932 Reichstag elections. The Nazis' final collapse was now imminent. The day was perhaps not far off when Hitler's career would resemble that of some of his famous anti-Semitic predecessors such as Adolf Stoecker and Georg von Schönerer. Moreover, the Austrian Nazis, who had always been able to bask in the glory of the "great" Adolf

Hitler, would lose their popularity as well now that Hitler's reputation had been so badly tarnished.[14]

On the other hand, *Die Neue Welt* was much less cheerful following the November elections. Although the Nazis had indeed lost many votes, the outcome was not advantageous for Jews. The lost Nazi voters had simply gone to other anti-Semitic parties, such as the German National People's Party. The success of the Communists would also likely attract impoverished Jews away from the Zionist idea.[15]

The largest of Austria's Zionist newspapers, *Die Stimme*, devoted relatively little space to anti-Semitic developments in neighboring Germany. It and other Zionist newspapers did, however, use the Nazi threat in 1932 as a rallying cry for Jews to join the Zionist movement. "Divided into parties we are nothing, united we are a mass which can influence our future in Austria. . . . We are up against a great danger. But nothing would be more dangerous than to give in to a fear psychosis. . . . We will outlive these difficult times despite Hitler."[16] In December, the paper added that "we will . . . outlive Hitler . . . if we can convince Jews that only the blue and white flag of the Zionists can lead to a better future."[17]

THE AUSTRO-JEWISH PRESS AND THE THIRD REICH

Hitler's relatively sudden reversal of fortune and appointment as chancellor at the end of January 1933 came as a terrible shock to Jewish newspapers in Austria. *Die Wahrheit* believed Hitler's chancellorship would be a real testing time for Jews. But it would also be a "testing time for the Nazis to see if they could actually put their theories into practice. . . . No radical party has ever been spared a contradiction between theory and practice when it took over power. . . . For us Viennese Jews the developments in Germany are nothing new. We went through the same thing during the rise of the Christian Social Party."[18]

When the Nazis won nearly 44 percent of the vote in the parliamentary elections of March 1933, *Die Wahrheit* remained unruffled. Hitler's victory had been expected because of the Nazi use of terror against opponents, which had prevented the latter from employing their propaganda and had intimidated weaklings. The Unionist organ expressed hope that the anti-Semitic measures of the new German government would be only temporary. Two weeks later, however, *Die Wahrheit* said that there was so much brutality taking place in

Germany that it was hard to believe that such things could transpire in the land of poets and thinkers. Why did the German government want to attack Jews when they had rejected the Communist Party so vehemently? Nevertheless, Jews were being equated with Communists.[19]

Just when things appeared bleakest for German Jews in the late winter of 1933, *Die Wahrheit* was greatly encouraged by statements regarding Jews by leading Nazi officials. The paper's hope that current anti-Semitic measures in Germany would soon moderate seemed confirmed by an interview Hermann Göring had with a Swedish newspaper. The Prussian prime minister said that if Jews remained loyal and went about their business as usual they would have no cause to worry. The Nazi government would merely not allow them to lead the Reich. Perhaps even more reassuring was an angry denial by the party's official mouthpiece, *Der Völkischer Beobachter*, that a pogrom was being planned.[20]

A few weeks later *Die Wahrheit* was able to report even more encouraging news from Germany when Adolf Hitler himself was quoted as saying that he would treat all religions with justice provided only that all religious groups and races fulfilled their legal responsibilities. Göring also told a reporter that no one would be persecuted simply because he was a Jew. The remarks about tolerating the Jewish religion, however, were actually much less significant than they sounded. For years most racial anti-Semites, including Hitler himself in *Mein Kampf*, had boasted that they were free of religious prejudice and only rejected Jews for their race, not their religion. However, *Die Wahrheit* chose to attribute this apparent change in attitude toward German Jews to the current international boycott of German exports. In reality, however, the boycott was not particularly effective because even many Jews around the world could not agree on its usefulness; they feared it would only lend credence to the idea that there was an international Jewish conspiracy and might harden Nazi policies toward Jews. They also doubted whether a boycott would be extensive enough to make any real difference.[21]

Die Wahrheit was much more cautious in interpreting the significance of Hitler calling off the boycott of Jewish shops in Germany just one day after it had been implemented on 1 April 1933. It disagreed with those optimists who thought that conditions would now improve for German Jews. The German government was trying to eliminate the Jews from the country's economic and cultural life, and this had already been largely accomplished. The early end to the boycott did nothing for those Jews who had already lost their jobs in national and local governments, medicine, journalism, teaching, and the arts.[22]

The pessimistic mood of *Die Wahrheit* continued into the fall of 1933, when the paper compared the fate of the German Jews with the fate of Jews in Spain during the Inquisition. The one big difference noted by the paper, however, was that in the sixteenth century a Jew could, as a last resort, escape persecution by converting to Christianity (actually this was not entirely true), an option not available in the Third Reich. Even families whose Jewish ancestors had converted to Christianity two generations earlier were being affected by the Nazis' anti-Semitic legislation.[23]

Die Wahrheit's pessimism was nothing, however, compared with that of Zionist newspapers in Austria. Just three days after Hitler's appointment as chancellor on 30 January 1933, *Die Stimme* again used events in Germany as a dire warning about the need to join the Zionist cause before it was too late. "The situation of Jews in Germany is deplorable hopelessness, fear, lack of organization, and helplessness. These are the people who did not recognize, or who did not want to recognize, that liberalism had been passed by. They ridiculed the Zionist idea. They did not realize that their desire for assimilation and their cringing made them look silly."[24]

Die Stimme used the burning of 45,000 "Jewish" books on 10 May as the occasion to renew its criticism of assimilated German Jews. Their superpatriotism was now coming back to haunt them. They ought to get rid of their past illusions. But if the future of Jews in Germany looked dismal, the future of Zionism was bright. "We are just as certain of final victory as we are sure that culture will always win over barbarism, morality over naked power, justice over the power-politics of despots." The Zionists would never desert the Jews of Germany, but they demanded the same loyalty from the German Jews.[25]

Der jüdische Arbeiter was a little less moralistic in its assessment of Hitler's takeover, and was more direct and descriptive. The paper remarked that for the first time a government was in power in Germany whose political path was marked by murder and bloodshed and whose party program was characterized by hatred of other races. But *Der jüdische Arbeiter* also could not resist the temptation to seek political gain. Hitler, it said, could only appear in a capitalist society. The extreme champions of the capitalist order had helped put him in power. After the Reichstag elections in March, the paper noted (for the most part correctly) that it was the middle classes that had voted for Hitler, not the proletariat.[26]

Die Neue Welt considered Hitler's assumption of power proof that Herzl was right in saying that only the gathering of all Jewish strength on a national basis could resist anti-Semitism. The disaster that was befalling the Jews of Germany was the result of their being politically leaderless, which left them defenseless. Anti-Semitism could be avoided only if German (and by implication, Austrian) Jews did not interfere in the cultural affairs of Christians. Great harm had come when Jewish writers had criticized German artistic taste and morality. The German Jews had been suffering from the illusions of the emancipationist and socialist ideologies that viewed Zionism as unpatriotic and suspect. A few months after dispensing these opinions, *Die Neue Welt*, alone among Austrian Jewish newspapers, made the remarkable statement that "Hitler-Germany was preparing to murder hundreds of thousands of Jews," [27] although the comment was probably intended more as a scare tactic than as a sober prediction.

Jüdische Presse, the organ of Austrian Orthodox Jews, also found it impossible to pass up the opportunity to moralize about the sins of liberal, assimilated German Jews. Their problems were all caused by their not having been given a religious education, the paper editorialized just after Hitler's takeover. "Orthodox Jews in Germany will certainly be negatively affected by Hitler's takeover of power. But it is undeniable that those assimilated Jews who have turned their backs on Judaism will be hurt the most." Other religions were no less endangered than the Jews. The greater part of the first page of this issue, however, was devoted not to events in Germany, but to denouncing the full enfranchisement of women for Viennese Jewish communal elections! [28]

AUSTRIAN JEWS AND NAZI GERMANY IN THE MIDDLE 1930S

Both the deep pessimism of *Die Wahrheit* and the attention paid to Jewish affairs in Nazi Germany by Zionist papers proved to be short-lived. From 1934 until the Anschluss, reports in the liberal paper about the Jewish persecution in Germany became less frequent, and those that were published were considerably more hopeful. The main reason for this relative lack of interest was that after the initial outburst of persecution in early 1933, life for German Jews settled down into somewhat more tolerable, if uncertain, circumstances. Many Jews who had emigrated in 1933 actually returned after failing to find employment abroad or after encountering more anti-Semitism in their host country than they had left behind in Germany. Aside from the 5,433 high-level Jewish civil servants who had lost their jobs in the first six months of the Nazi era, many Jewish businessmen actually prospered. At the beginning of 1937 there were still 40,000 Jewish-owned businesses in Germany, and some even received government contracts. German Jews also experienced little intervention by the Nazi government in the operation of their school system. Jews were not hindered in the practice of their religion or in the functions of their institutions. Therefore it appeared to many Jews in Germany and Austria that German Jews might be granted a special autonomous position within the Nazi state.[29]

Already by July 1934 *Die Wahrheit* was beginning to regain some of its lost confidence. In that month it expressed pleasant surprise that the recent campaign of the Nazi government to stamp out criticism had ended not with a pogrom, as feared, but with a purge of the Sturmabteilung. It expected this "Röhm Purge" to undermine the Nazi regime.[30] *Die Wahrheit* was not alone in this assessment. The American Jewish scholar Jacob R. Marcus expressed the opinion that "any day may witness the collapse of Hitler and his cohorts. The implacable logic of internal, economic decline and foreign encirclement would seem at the date of this writing (August, 1934) to presage the speedy and almost inevitable fall of Hitler."[31]

The biggest news to come out of Nazi Germany in the middle 1930s regarding Jews was the publication of the infamous Nuremberg Laws. Approved by the Nazified German Reichstag on 15 September 1935, they classified Jews as subjects rather than citizens of the Third Reich. Since the Holocaust the Nuremberg Laws have been seen as a major step in the Nazis' anti-Jewish program. Far from reacting in horror, however, as one might presume, the reaction of *Die Wahrheit* and many other Jewish newspapers was relatively restrained. Both Jews and non-Jews actually welcomed the new laws as a return of order. The German Jews now at least appeared to have a permanent albeit lowly status. A decree implementing the citizenship law in November narrowed the definition of a Jew to include only those people who had at least two Jewish grandparents and who practiced Judaism or who had three or more Jewish grandparents if they were nonpracticing Jews. This definition was the least comprehensive of the four presented to Hitler and was designed to make the Führer look moderate at a time when a worldwide boycott of the 1936 Olympic Games still seemed likely. Jews were partially excluded from public life and were increasingly isolated from German society; but this merely codified what had long since been implemented.[32]

The Nuremberg Laws were designed first of all to fulfill the Nazi Party's original Twenty-five Point Program of 1920 concerning Jews, and secondly to comply, at least superficially, with the demands of German Zionists for cultural autonomy. The German government, in fact, went out of its way to claim that the laws conformed to demands made by a recent Zionist congress in Switzerland. It did not object to Jews as long as they wanted to be members of a separate Jewish Volk. *Die Wahrheit* said that the laws only proved that the opposition of the Union of Austrian Jews to declaring Jews a national minority had been justified. The desire of Zionists for such minority status had led to the loss of basic rights for German Jews.[33]

After two months of reflection, *Die Wahrheit* admitted in November that the Nuremberg Laws did not actually involve a worsening of the long-declining status of German Jews. They were mild in comparison to what German Jews had had to endure in practice up to then. The few Jews remaining in lower-level civil service positions had to give up their jobs by the end of 1935 unless they were veterans of the First World War. Jews also lost their right to vote, but that right had been a farce even for gentiles since March 1933. Surprisingly, the laws had already been revised since September so that the minimum age for Aryan women working in Jewish households had been lowered from forty-five to thirty-five in order to preserve some jobs. In sharp contrast to *Die Wahrheit*, however, was the reaction of the bimonthly Zionist newspaper, *Der Jude*, which denounced the Nuremberg Laws for condemning the German Jews to a death by hunger. The slaves of Abyssinia enjoyed an enviable status compared with the Jews of Germany.[34]

As the Winter and Summer Olympic Games of 1936 approached, the status of German Jews once again faded from Jewish newspapers in Austria. *Die Wahrheit* was not entirely fooled by this diminution of anti-Semitic activity, however. In April 1936 the paper observed that there had been fewer anti-Semitic measures and demonstrations taking place in the Third Reich than at any time since 1933. This happy turn of events, however, could be attributed to the Olympics. The future still looked ominous for Germany's Jews. By November *Die Wahrheit* already noticed a worsening of the status of the Jews since the end of the Olympics and noted that the Nazi government's policy toward the German Jews was determined by both domestic and international politics.[35]

In 1937 almost nothing was reported in Austrian Jewish newspapers about the status of Germany's Jews. *Die Neue Welt* did comment in May, however, that the anti-Semitic measures in Germany had the purpose of destroying the Jews not just economically but spiritually as well. Anti-Semitism had nothing more to do with so-called cultural Bolshevism and had become a kind of sport.[36]

The changing moods of Austrian Jewish newspapers, particularly *Die Wahrheit*, toward events in Nazi Germany closely reflected the moods of Jews inside Germany. A few months of stability could produce a spirit of optimism, which then quickly dissipated with the next wave of persecution.[37] However, in general it would appear that there was far less apprehension about Nazi Germany in the Austro-Jewish press at the beginning of 1938 than there had been in the first half of 1933. It is entirely possible, of course, that after five years Nazi persecution had lost some of its shock value or newsworthiness. It is even more likely, however, that Austrian Jews, like so many Jews and non-Jews outside Nazi Germany, were overly impressed by the comparatively secure and still reasonably prosperous status of the Jews of Berlin and did not realize the extent to which provincial German Jews were subjected to forced "Aryanization" and emigration.

What is more certain is that a large percentage of those articles that had been published during the first five years of Hitler's rule had been designed more to achieve some partisan advantage by proving that the ideology of one's own political faction offered better protection against the Nazi threat than that of one's rivals. The persecution of the German Jews had done nothing to bring the Austrian Jews together in a common front. If anything, they were more divided than ever as they were about to face their ultimate challenge.

17

THE DEFENSE AGAINST
ANTI-SEMITISM

It is easy to imagine that Austrian Jews and gentiles were silent and passive in the face of the anti-Semitic campaign. Indeed, there were far more anti-Semites than there were Jews, and many Jews did remain silent either because they did not experience anti-Semitism personally or because they hoped that it would not get worse and would eventually disappear by itself.

JEWISH FACTIONALISM AS A HINDRANCE TO SELF-DEFENSE

The factionalism in the Jewish community in Vienna that produced such bitter rivalries within the Israelitische Kultusgemeinde and such widely differing interpretations concerning the rise and triumph of National Socialism also meant that there would almost never be a common front against the anti-Semitic enemy during the entire history of the First Austrian Republic. Nor was there a great deal of cooperation between Austrian Jews and the few Christians who were willing to help them. Of course, even a solid alliance between all Austrian Jews and their Christian allies could not have prevented the Holocaust and the death of most of the 65,000 Austrian Jews who perished in it, but it might have preserved more Jewish rights while Austria remained an independent state.

To a large extent the various Jewish factions regarded their ideologies as providing their best protection against anti-Semitism, at least in the long run. The Unionists with their liberal, assimilationist philosophy were convinced that anti-Semitism would disappear as soon as Jews were fully integrated socially and economically into Austrian society and Christians had become convinced that the Jews were unequivocally patriotic Austrians. Jews could also defend themselves by uniting with progressive and liberal elements of other political parties. This policy would require decades if not centuries to be fully imple-

mented, however. Unfortunately, the Unionists' philosophy was also something of a handicap in combating anti-Semitism. Their desire to blend into
Austrian society made them reluctant to do anything that might emphasize
their Jewishness.[1]

Jews who belonged to the Social Democratic Party and who fully accepted its Marxist philosophy were likely to hold views on the question of
self-defense somewhat similar to those of the assimilationists. Marxism taught
that the Jews would eventually disappear in the classless society of the future.
A self-conscious expression of Judaism was therefore simply not compatible
with Socialism. For example, one of the most prominent members of the
Social Democratic Party, Julius Deutsch, the leader of the party's paramilitary
Schutzbund, never once mentioned his Jewish wife in his memoirs, *Ein weiter
Weg* (*A Long Road*).[2] At best, therefore, anti-Semitism could be resisted only
on the grounds that it was a disguised form of anti-Socialism, which to some
extent it was.

The Zionists thought that anti-Semitism would end only after the Jews had
established their own autonomist society, thus removing all sources of conflict with Christians. "The organizing of all Jews into a Volk [would] change
the situation with a single blow. . . . It [was] unthinkable that a government
could for long ignore the wishes and complaints of a united nation. . . .
Anti-Semitism would not disappear entirely, but it would no longer be born
exclusively on the weak backs of individual people."[3]

Like the Zionists, Orthodox Jews also believed that a partial withdrawal from
Austrian politics and culture represented the best means of combating anti-
Semitism. They did not, however, believe that the formation of a single Jewish
society could prevent the kind of tragedy that was then afflicting the Jews of
Germany. Their belief that they were "the most worthwhile element repre-
senting the real Judaism"[4] virtually precluded cooperation with other Jewish
factions. With them religion was the primary means to combat anti-Semitism.
The inner strengthening of religious belief and following the laws of Orthodox
Judaism would win the respect of non-Jews, including anti-Semites. Besides,
the Messiah would come only after conditions for Jews had become dire. Their
intense religiosity, however, contributed to passivity vis-à-vis anti-Semitism.
The past and present suffering of the Jewish people was beneficial, they believed, because it helped to "purify their souls" and "to understand God's word
and way."[5]

THE LEGALISTIC APPROACH TO SELF-DEFENSE

The defensive strategy favored by the Union of Austrian Jews and the IKG, especially during the years up to 1932 when the latter was controlled by the Unionists, was *shtadlanut* or lobbying behind the scenes with government officials for the enforcement of Austrian laws and issuing formal protests. The Unionist leaders of the IKG, many of whom were lawyers themselves, hoped that their grievances could be resolved through normal legal channels: police authorities, law courts, and district attorneys. Formal declarations and personal remonstrances to government officials were also employed. For example, the Kultusgemeinde frequently adopted resolutions demanding that the government stop the violence at Austria's universities. It also protested anti-Semitic posters, pamphlets, newspapers, and books as well as certain laws such as those described in the next chapter. The results, however, were mixed, especially with regard to academic anti-Semitism. Usually government officials replied that existing laws made it impossible for them to do anything; this was especially true with regard to academic autonomy.[6]

The Union of Austrian Jews also took legal actions of its own, quite independent of those of the Kultusgemeinde. Among the most successful of these actions was the union's campaign against discrimination in summer resorts. At a time when country clubs and hotels in the United States and other countries often excluded Jews, many health spas in Austria, and even entire communities catering to summer holiday visitors, sought to do likewise, though generally with much less success than their American counterparts. Anti-Semitic newspapers such as *Der eiserne Besen* and the revived *Deutsches Volksblatt* published lists of summer resorts that catered exclusively to "Aryans" or else republished lists from Jewish or Jewish-edited newspapers such as the *Wiener Morgenzeitung* and *Die Stunde*, which enumerated hotels and pensions where Jews were not welcome. Those establishments involved in providing food and lodging were obliged by law to serve Jews if they demanded it; however, they were free to post signs saying they preferred Aryan customers. Not surprisingly, that was usually enough to keep Jews away. Private individuals who merely rented out rooms were completely free to serve whomever they pleased.[7] Numerous city councils, particularly in the Alpine areas of Upper and Lower Austria, Salzburg, and the Tyrol, passed resolutions saying they did not want to have Jews as summer guests or even to have them stop there.[8]

The union, sometimes supported by the *Neue Freie Presse*, made numerous complaints to the federal chancellery about the prohibitions. For once the union was effective in protesting this kind of discrimination, probably because the Austrian constitution was clearly on its side. For example, the Propaganda Bureau of the Austrian federal railways agreed not to distribute brochures, such as one published in Schladming in Upper Styria, because of anti-Semitic statements such as "Jews are not welcome." Upon hearing this news, *Der eiserne Besen* said the Alpine communities would now have to resort to "self help" to keep the Jewish tourists out.[9] The union also claimed to have succeeded in keeping the Austrian army accessible to Jews. By its own admission, however, the protests of the union were not always effective. For example, a protest against the holding of a meeting by the Antisemitenbund in March 1937 did not prevent the meeting from actually taking place.[10]

A major obstacle in the way of greater legal successes by the union was the Austrian press law both before and after the First World War. It allowed newspapers and individuals to attack groups such as Jews, but not individuals, without fear of being sued for slander. And no Jewish individual or association, not even the IKG, had a right to sue in cases where Jewry as a whole had been slandered. Moreover, parliamentary immunity protected legislators who, in their own newspapers, attacked individual Jews, at least prior to the First World War. Consequently, the union, which tried but failed to change the press laws, was unable to prevent newspapers from publishing stories about Jewish ritual murder. It was probably also in part because of the wording of this law that Austrian anti-Semitism tended to have a very abstract character, usually being directed against Jews in general rather than specific Jews.[11]

The union's official organ, *Die Wahrheit*, frequently published editorials and articles that were obviously intended to counter anti-Semitic arguments and to reassure its readers that their assimilationist philosophy was viable. The paper asserted that the Austrian Jews were not a people without a country. "Our homeland—and that cannot be said too often or too clearly—is Austria. We love this beautiful land; we love it just as much as our non-Jewish fellow citizens. We don't recognize any other homeland." *Die Wahrheit* denied that Jews belonged to a separate race or nationality; Jews undoubtedly belonged to the white or Caucasian race. The paper also emphasized that Jews were strongly traditional and conservative, otherwise they would not have survived so long. Only a small number of Jews, the renegades, were radical.[12]

ZIONIST SELF-DEFENSE

The Unionists' conviction that anti-Semitism was an aberration that could be fought through public enlightenment and legal measures encouraged a comparatively strong if not always effective response to anti-Semitic actions and allegations. Zionists, on the other hand, viewed anti-Semitism as being permanent, at least as long as Jews were culturally, economically, and socially integrated with Christians. Moreover, their belief in an ultimate emigration to Palestine, even if that day might be in the indefinite future, fostered a more ambiguous commitment toward Austria although Zionists were far from being disloyal citizens. However, their philosophy produced a somewhat fatalistic attitude toward anti-Semitism and a tendency to ignore all but the most outrageous manifestations of the prejudice.[13]

Zionists believed that if anti-Semitic attacks became severe they could appeal to the League of Nations to enforce the provisions of the Treaty of St. Germain guaranteeing minority rights. American Jews of Eastern European origins had fought hard to have such rights included in the treaties not only for Austrian Jews, but also for other Jews throughout Eastern Europe where persecutions had been common. The only problem was that the minority treaties contained no provisions for enforcement, an omission that was already pointed out in *Dr. Bloch's Wochenschrift* in January 1920 and repeatedly by *Die Wahrheit* thereafter. Such impotence had by the early 1930s already been demonstrated many times through the ineffectiveness of German and Jewish complaints to the league over the treatment of minorities in Poland. Another, and much more secret Zionist tactic, was to appeal to the headquarters of the World Zionist Organization in London to apply pressure on the Austrian government to prevent anti-Semitic excesses.[14]

CALLS FOR JEWISH UNITY

Austria's Jews were very much aware of their own disunity; most of them believed that they could better defend themselves against anti-Semitism if they were united. Consequently, appeals were made for Jewish unity time and again by nearly every Jewish faction in the First Austrian Republic. The problem, however, was that nearly every group wanted unity only on its own terms; other Jews were supposed to give up their ideology and identity and join the group making the latest call for unity.

In this the Austrian Jews were no different from other Jews throughout both Eastern and Western Europe between the two world wars. At a time when Jews faced their most mortal threat since ancient times, they were everywhere badly divided. Nowhere in Europe did Jews effectively unite in the face of the growing anti-Semitic and fascist danger. Without a unified concept of what constituted Jewry, such unity was probably impossible. Moreover, at a time when class consciousness was particularly strong in Europe, the class divisions between Jews simply added to strongly differing opinions about religion and nationalism.[15]

If anything, divisions between Austrian Jews may have been deeper than between Jews in other European countries. In Western Europe, especially England and Germany, assimilationist Jews were in the majority, although even there bitter rivalries existed. In Eastern and East Central Europe, on the other hand, Zionist and Orthodox Jews were prominent. In Austria assimilationists and Zionists met on fairly equal terms, at least in the IKG, rendering their rivalry all the more intense. Zionists were already an important minority in the 1920s, and by the beginning of 1933 they had taken control of the Israelitische Kultusgemeinde in Vienna, the first such Zionist takeover in Europe. In Germany, by contrast, nearly all Jews regarded themselves as highly patriotic and thoroughly assimilated, or were, at least, eager to become so. They also enjoyed the distinct advantage of having a leader in Leo Baeck, the leading rabbi of Berlin, whom nearly all Jews — liberal, Orthodox, and Zionist — respected. No leader with Baeck's universal prestige ever emerged in Austria, at least not in the interwar years.[16]

At times when Austrian anti-Semitism became particularly extreme there were some Jewish efforts to create a unified response, but they were never long-lived or very effective. For example, in February 1923, when postwar anti-Semitism was reaching a climax, an "Executive Committee of Austrian Jews" was created consisting of representatives of several different Jewish parties. The committee organized a rally to show that Jews were loyal to the republic. A few months later Unionists and Zionists managed to agree on an electoral coalition for the forthcoming municipal elections in order to help defend Jewish rights against the anti-Semitic wave sweeping over the country. However, this *Wahlgemeinschaft* managed to gain only 2.4 percent of the vote, even though Jews made up 10.8 percent of Vienna's population.[17]

Probably the most impressive Jewish means of self-defense in interwar Austria, and also the most nonpartisan, was the Bund jüdischer Frontsoldaten or League of Jewish Front Soldiers. Far more militant and aggressive than the Unionists, Zionists, or Orthodox Jews, this organization was in some respects the successor to several early postwar self-defense organizations, the Stadtschutzwache (City Guard), the Selbstwehr (Self-Defense Force), and the Schutzkorps (Protection Corps).[18]

None of these organizations apparently outlasted the anti-Semitic wave of the early postwar years. However, when anti-Semitism revived a decade later, more militant and dangerous than before, three new defensive organizations were founded: the Zionist Jüdischer Wehrsport- und Schützenverein Haganah (Jewish Armed Sporting and Defense Association Haganah); the Jüdischer Schutzverband (Jewish Protection League), an umbrella organization to protect the Jewish population of Austria and to support Jewish sport and hiking clubs; and the Bund jüdischer Frontsoldaten, by far the largest and most important.[19]

Founded in Vienna in the summer of 1932, shortly after the Austrian Nazis' great electoral victory in April, the organization's statutes declared that its purpose was "to protect the honor and respect of the Jews living in Austria."[20] Its program was likely inspired both by the older and larger Reichsbund jüdischer Frontsoldaten (National League of Jewish Front Soldiers) in Germany (though it was less political) and the Heimwehr in Austria.[21] Like the Heimwehr, at least in its heyday prior to 1930, the Bund was supposed to be *überparteilich* or nonpartisan. By deliberately avoiding partisan politics and emphasizing military virtues like discipline, obedience, and physical fitness, it hoped to overcome the chronic divisiveness of the Jewish community in Austria. Although only men who had actually served at the front could be regular members of the organization, other Jews who agreed with its goals could be extraordinary members. Starting in January 1933 it had its own newspaper, *Jüdische Front*, and by February 1934 it could boast having some eight thousand members in Vienna, Graz, Linz, and Baden bei Wien—including both Zionists and assimilationists—making it the largest single Jewish organization in Austria apart from the Kultusgemeinde in Vienna.[22]

The League of Jewish Front Soldiers was typical of many political organizations of interwar Austria—the Zionists, the Heimwehr, the Social Democrats, the Communists, and the National Socialists—in claiming to be a "movement of renewal." Hence, there were a myriad of subsidiary organizations like a Frauengruppe for women, a sports organization for youth, and a symphony orchestra for older adults. Young people would not only acquire military discipline but would also learn not to tolerate the insults of anti-Semites.[23]

Most of all, the Bund was a highly patriotic veterans' organization and partly a paramilitary formation dedicated to the preservation of Austrian independence. Its members proudly wore their military decorations well before Chancellor Dollfuss attempted to create a sense of Austrian identity. It shared the Heimwehr's love of uniforms, marching, roll calls, and admiration for military virtues. The Nazis were outraged that Bund members were allowed by the government to wear brown uniforms at a time when the NSDAP was prohibited.[24]

The Jewish Front Soldiers had a number of ways of defending Jews against anti-Semitism. First, and perhaps foremost, it sought to provide physical protection against sometimes brutal Nazi attacks (although it was handicapped by having no special self-defense units within its ranks). Like the Union of Austrian Jews, it would respond to false accusations against Jews. Also resembling Unionist activities were direct complaints and open letters to high government officials about anti-Jewish violence at state institutions of higher learning or anti-Semitic speeches and publications. The Bund sometimes organized protest rallies as, for example, in January 1933 when two thousand members protested the pastoral letter of Bishop Johannes Gföllner of Linz.[25]

The Bund jüdischer Frontsoldaten sought strength and encouragement from Christian veterans as well as from Jewish veterans in other countries. Letters from Christian officers testifying to the bravery and loyalty of Jewish soldiers during the war were published in *Jüdische Front*.[26] The Bund was also buttressed through its membership in the world organization of Jewish Front Fighters. The latter held its second annual meeting in Vienna in 1936—without any of the violent protests that accompanied the Zionist Congress of 1925—and elected Captain Edler von Friedmann, the leader of the Austrian chapter, as the president of the congress.[27]

Although all the political and religious factions of Austria were painfully aware of their divisions and made frequent appeals for unity, *Jüdische Front* did so more insistently than any other Jewish group. Nevertheless, its many attempts to form a "unity front" with the Jewish parties all failed. Even its pleas for Jewish newspapers to stop attacking each other, for an indefinite postponement of the IKG election of 1936, and for Jews to stop complaining to non-Jews about internal Jewish problems were made in vain.[28] Still worse, the Bund was not even able to prevent divisiveness within its own ranks. In April 1934 its founder, Emil Sommer, together with his monarchist followers, broke away to form their own organization.[29]

An entirely different approach to Jewish unity also achieved only limited success. As early as 1918 attempts were made by the various Jewish communities of Austria to form a *Gemeindebund* (federation) that would have enabled Jews to present a united front vis-à-vis the Austrian government when complaining about anti-Semitic acts. Proponents of such a federation thought that it would be more useful than parallel actions taken by different Jewish organizations. However, the most that was ever achieved was a voluntary *Arbeitsgemeinschaft* or working committee, which was formed in 1935. Even this modest organization was not all-inclusive, however, because the predominantly Orthodox Jewish communities in the Burgenland in eastern Austria pre-

Emil Sommer, founder of the League of Jewish Front Soldiers.
Austrian National Library Picture Archive.

ferred to remain in their own *Landessekretäriat* (state secretariat). The working committee had no political authority to do anything beyond making nonbinding resolutions. The president of the study group, Desider Friedmann, who was also the president of the IKG in Vienna, lamented, in a speech he gave to the Arbeitsgemeinschaft in November 1937, only four months before the Anschluss, that Austrian Jews were fighting each other and all claiming to be better Jews than the others because they were more religious, native, or patriotic.[30]

Many Jews, especially those who were not Zionists, realized that, to defend themselves against anti-Semitism, more was needed than a united front of Jews alone. As early as January 1920 *Dr. Bloch's Wochenschrift* called on Jews to form a unity front with Christians against anti-Semitism similar to one that had just been formed in Berlin. When anti-Semitism revived again in the early 1930s, *Die Wahrheit* warned prophetically that "one day the Christian Socials will realize that the ghosts which they have conjured up cannot so easily be abolished. They will [learn] . . . that the Hitlerites will not be satisfied with taking over the Hochschulen, but will also want to take over the state, something that a good Catholic cannot really want. But then it will be too late." A few years later *Die Wahrheit*, commenting on recent articles in the *Reichspost*, said that if Catholics did not have the sense to realize that anti-Semitism represented a common enemy to both Jews and Catholics they should at least stop complaining about Nazi attacks on the Catholic church while applauding attacks on Jews.[31]

CHRISTIAN ALLIES

Jewish appeals for Catholic cooperation did not go entirely unheeded. The *Wiener jüdisches Familienblatt* reported in February 1934 that the discussion about the Jewish question in Austria had made good progress during the previous year. In March 1935, the editor of the *Familienblatt* was invited to speak to a Catholic academic association about the Jewish question. At about the same time a Catholic biweekly magazine called *Die Erfüllung (The Fulfillment)* was founded, which was dedicated to bringing down the walls of misunderstanding between Jews and Christians, according to Cardinal Innitzer of Vienna. The publication was designed to acquaint Jews with the spirit of Jesus and Christians with the mission of Israel. It also spoke of the Godly clarity and human sublimity of the Bible and the wisdom and piety of the Talmud. It ridiculed the myth that the Jews formed a monolithic bloc bent on dominating the world. It acknowledged that the Christian Occident was in mortal danger, but that danger arose from the Nazis, not the Jews.[32] However, the fact that its editor was a converted Jew, Johann Oesterreicher, almost certainly decreased the credibility of the periodical among mainstream Catholics.

These contacts and gestures of goodwill between Catholics and Jews represented a promising beginning for increasing mutual understanding and can perhaps be seen as forerunners of much more active cooperation between the two faiths in post–World War II Austria. At the time, however, only a small number of Austrian Catholics were willing to collaborate with Jews against anti-Semitism.[33] Such contacts as there were, were much too few and too late.

Fortunately, there were some Christians who were willing to go beyond opening a mere dialogue with Jews and who attempted both to analyze the causes of anti-Semitism and to fight it. Probably the most famous of these people were the two Austrian noblemen Count Heinrich Coudenhove-Kalergi and his son Count Richard, who is best known as the founder and leader of the pacifistic Pan-Europe movement.[34] Their two-part book, translated into English as *Anti-Semitism throughout the Ages*, was first published by the elder Coudenhove-Kalergi in Berlin in 1901 and was then edited and brought up to date by the son and republished in Vienna and Zurich in 1935. It was the only major work published in Austria during the interwar period that dealt objectively with anti-Semitism. The authors identified several critical features of the phenomenon: its link with anti-Marxism; the impact of the bad economic situation in Europe following the First World War; the irrational nature of anti-Semitism, which made it almost impossible to combat with rational arguments; and the special fear and hatred anti-Semites felt toward secular, assimilated Jews, whose ideas seemed to threaten their traditional ideas and economic status. The Jews, *Anti-Semitism throughout the Ages* concluded, were "for the most part what the nations in whose midst they have lived have made them."[35]

The Coudenhove-Kalergis were not the first Christian defenders of Jews in Austrian history. The novelist Hermann Bahr, for example, remained a friend of the Jews until his death in 1934. His prediction, however, that Hitler was nothing more than a passing grievance who would soon destroy himself, though shared by many Jews, turned out to be wildly overoptimistic.[36]

One of the most outspoken critics of anti-Semitism in interwar Austria was Wilhelm Boerner. Some of the arguments that Boerner used in a booklet called *Antisemitismus, Rassenfrage, Menschlichkeit* (*Anti-Semitism, Racial Question, Humanity*) resembled those of the Coudenhove-Kalergis. Many negative characteristics of Jews were actually the fault of non-Jews. Anti-

Semites looked for justifications of their hatred, emotional disturbances, and instincts in religious, economic, or racial explanations. Therefore it was naive to think that anti-Semites could be dissuaded by facts. If Jews had a low homicide rate, anti-Semites thought it was because they were cowards. When Jewish children did well in school, it was because they were pushy. If they had a quick wit, they were arrogant.[37]

Boerner regarded the religious, economic, and racial arguments used against Jews as no better than crude generalizations. He denied that there were any constant Jewish racial characteristics and therefore rejected the idea that there was a real "Jewish race." Certainly there was no scientific proof that Jews were inferior. He praised the Jewish success in the modern world of cultivating internationalism, but was critical of Zionists for encouraging nationalism, of which, he said, there was too much already. On the other hand, he acknowledged that Zionism was a defensive reaction to anti-Semitism. Anti-Semitism of any kind or degree was unethical because it was based on generalizations. He could not see how one could be both a good Christian and an anti-Semite when one considered that Jesus was a Jew.[38]

Incisive as Boerner's ideas were, he was far from being the most prominent critic of anti-Semitism in interwar Austria. The most courageous opponent of both anti-Semitism and Nazism that Austria, or very likely the whole of Central Europe, produced in the 1930s was a previously unknown and politically inexperienced young woman by the name of Irene Harand. A less likely heroine is difficult to imagine. Born in 1900, for a decade after the world war she lived the life of a conventional middle-class housewife, far removed from the turmoil of Austrian politics. She was, however, profoundly distressed to witness local examples of church-sanctioned intolerance. Slowly, painfully, she began to question two of the most fundamental principles of her upbringing: first, that those in the highest positions of church and state were absolutely clear and correct in their moral judgments; and second, that a woman who had never even attended a university could presume to get involved in politics. And yet, almost by accident, she became very much involved.[39]

Irene Harand's ethical awakening resulted from a chance meeting with an attorney in Vienna in the late 1920s. The lawyer was a Jew named Dr. Moritz Zalman, who agreed to assist her in fighting for the estate of a destitute and elderly nobleman. When the question of fees was raised, Zalman told Frau Harand that if she could devote her time to helping a poor old man with no hope of personal compensation, so too could he volunteer his legal services. Years later Harand explained the significance of this minor episode. Unconsciously she had accepted the almost universally held notion in Vienna that

Irene Harand, leader of the World Organization against Racial Hatred and Human Need. DÖW. "I fight anti-Semitism because it maligns our Christendom," she declared in the masthead of Gerechtigkeit.

Jewish lawyers were greedy and unscrupulous. Before meeting Zalman she had not known about his Jewish origins; this fact, combined with clear evidence that he displayed none of the supposed "Jewish traits," shocked her into the realization that she had been looking at the world through anti-Semitic eyes.[40]

This collaboration with Moritz Zalman marked the beginning of Harand's career as an outspoken opponent of anti-Semitism. In the next few years both she and Zalman became increasingly alarmed by the growth of anti-Semitism and its most aggressive manifestation, National Socialism. Soon after the Nazi electoral victory in Germany in September 1930, Harand appeared at a Catholic political meeting and warned about the growing menace of Nazism. She was rudely rejected by the conservative audience, which dismissed her as having no political experience; they taunted her as a foolish, hysterical woman—the Nazis referred to her as "arme Irre," poor, crazy Irre—and booed her off the stage before she could finish her talk. Later she would receive a large number of insulting letters and phone calls. Far from being intimidated, however, she wrote a brochure in March 1933, shortly after Hitler came to power, entitled *So oder So? Die Wahrheit über den Antisemitismus (Either This or That? The Truth about Anti-Semitism)*, 50,000 copies of which she had printed and distributed at her own expense. In August of the same year she established her own weekly newspaper, *Gerechtigkeit (Justice)*, which by December 1936 had twenty thousand readers in thirty-six countries. A year later it was being published in French, Czech, and Hungarian, in addition to German. In 1935 Harand also wrote *Sein Kampf: Antwort an Hitler (His Struggle: An Answer to Hitler)*, a 347-page rebuttal to the ideas that Hitler had laid out in *Mein Kampf*.[41]

In October 1933 Harand and Zalman founded a movement with the ambitious title of the World Organization against Racial Hatred and Human Need, popularly known as the Harand Movement. It eventually grew to nearly forty thousand members, including six thousand outside Austria. Branches of the organization were established in no fewer than twenty-seven countries. To encourage the growth of her movement, Harand traveled all over Austria, other parts of Europe, and even to the United States, giving public speeches, often several a week, against anti-Semitism and Nazism.[42]

The essence of Harand's commitment to fight anti-Semitism was her conviction—repeated at the top of every issue of *Gerechtigkeit* and in all of her other publications—that anti-Semitism was harmful to Christianity. She was "fighting not so much in behalf of the Jews as to save Christians from becoming beasts." Anti-Semitism was an attack on the soul of humanity and a sin against the Savior. Nazism wanted to rob humanity of its reason and every noble feeling. She also tried to help the Jews because otherwise she would have been ashamed of her own passivity and because she was filled with sympathy for the victims of persecution. She knew that most Christians were not anti-Semites, but it was not enough simply to reject it. "One [did] one's duty only when one *actively* took part in defense against it."[43]

What was most unusual about Harand's writing and public speeches was that she attacked not only the manifestations of anti-Semitism but also their causes, which she saw in the desperate economic conditions of the 1930s. It was no accident that her organization was against *both* racial hatred and human need. It was not hard, she wrote in *Gerechtigkeit*, to implant hatred into people who were suffering. Therefore one of her movement's goals was to raise Austrian exports and increase the number of foreign tourists. Unemployment was the government's biggest problem. But the hundreds of thousands of jobless workers would not be helped one bit if they had only Christian physicians, lawyers, and merchants to serve them, she wrote. Harand's movement did more than lament Austria's dire economic circumstances. From its inception it distributed food and clothing to needy people, paid for by the extremely modest membership fee of twenty groschen a month, and even took poor children from Vienna into the countryside for vacations.[44]

Much of Harand's writing was devoted to exposing anti-Semitic myths. In *So oder So?* she asked if it was reasonable to blame all Christians because some of them had become rich capitalists. The Great Depression was the indirect result of the world war, which the Jews had not started. There were no Jews in the German diplomatic corps in 1914 or in the German general staff. Nor were any of the other world leaders Jewish in 1914. Jews, she concluded, were neither better nor worse than other people.[45] In *Gerechtigkeit*, Harand pointed out the absurdity of the statement, frequently made by anti-Semites, that they had nothing against "honorable" Jews. No one, including Jews, she said, was going to defend a dishonorable Jew. It was the responsibility of the state to deal with such people. The anti-Semites, Harand continued in the same article, saw around them only Jewish bankers and factory owners, not the sixty thousand Jews who were dependent on the charity of the Kultusgemeinde.[46]

Harand also praised the virtues of famous Jewish men at a time when Hitler was busy barring Jewish professors from German universities and Jewish physicians and lawyers from practicing their professions. In addition to publicizing outstanding Jewish men in her publications, Harand came up with the novel idea of doing the same thing through a series of propaganda labels in postage stamp format. The well-designed postage seals depicted famous Jewish scientists, artists, writers, and scholars and carried texts in all the major European languages; they were distributed monthly to subscribers of *Gerechtigkeit* for use on their correspondence.[47]

Current events, as they involved anti-Semitism and Nazism, consumed most of the space in *Gerechtigkeit*. Harand was critical of anti-Semitic acts carried out by government officials in Austria, although she believed that they were committed by subordinates without the approval of their highest superiors. When Chancellor Dollfuss was murdered, she unambiguously declared that the true murderers, who wanted to put the world back a thousand years, were in Berlin and Munich. No government should have further diplomatic relations with Germany. She denounced what she called "cold anti-Semitism" that resulted in the dismissal of Jewish physicians from municipal hospitals. She was apprehensive about the German-Austrian agreement of 11 July 1936, which reestablished normal diplomatic relations between the two countries because it would allow Nazi culture to reenter the country. However, she overoptimistically thought the government was aware of the problem so that the fears of Jews and Christians were groundless. Likewise, she tried to be reassuring about the Berchtesgaden agreement between Schuschnigg and Hitler in February 1938, calling it a positive step toward world peace.[48]

Harand also responded to anti-Semitic charges made in recently published books and public speeches. She denounced *Zur Wiener Judenfrage* by Georg Glockemeier, which used statistics in a tendentious way, and *Ordnung in der Judenfrage* by Emmerich Czermak and Oskar Karbach. There was no "Jewish question," but instead a "human question." The real issue in Austria was poverty; anti-Semitism was no better than a distraction from this crucial issue. All Austrians, including Jews, were needed to rebuild the country. If there were a Jewish question that needed clarification, then the same was needed for the Czech and Protestant minorities. When a book called *Gibt es jüdische Ritualmorde? (Is There Jewish Ritual Murder?)*—a rhetorical question answered in the affirmative—was published by a Catholic publishing house in Graz, Harand did more than criticize. Her denunciation of the book persuaded the federal chancellery—which feared it might cause foreign policy problems—to have the book confiscated. And when the leader of the Antisemitenbund, Anton Jerzabek, declared that Austrian Jews were a guest people who had never been invited to the country, Harand asked who had invited his Czech ancestors to come to Austria. She did not deny his right to be an Austrian citizen just because his ancestors could not speak German.[49]

Although Jewish newspapers like *Die Wahrheit*, *Die Stimme*, and the American Jewish journal, *B'nai Brith Magazine*, sometimes wrote flattering articles about the Harand Movement, in general Irene Harand did not receive a great deal of support from Jews. The Nazis charged that the Harand Movement was created and financed by Jewish gold from Amsterdam and New York and was led by Moritz Zalman. In reality, however, it had only about 3,500 Jewish members and only one Jew in its twelve-member executive committee. Indeed Harand sometimes complained about her lack of Jewish support. Many Jews, she said, were indifferent to Nazism, including many she had met in Germany in 1932. They were divided into too many organizations and committees. They frequently did not even answer their critics, either out of false shame or false pride. Much of their money was going to Palestine instead of to the resistance against Nazism. It was depressing, she said, to see how they behaved in the face of danger. Their indolence was downright criminal.[50] The philo-Semitic Abwehr-Verein in Germany had expressed similar disappointment around the turn of the century about Jewish silence in the face of anti-Semitic charges.[51]

THE DEFENSE AGAINST ANTI-SEMITISM: HOW EFFECTIVE?

It is difficult to assess the effectiveness of the Harand Movement or any of the other organizations in Austria that attempted to combat anti-Semitism. It is tempting to discount them since they obviously did not prevent the Holocaust or even greatly reduce anti-Semitism. Clearly, they relied too heavily on rational arguments to fight what were largely irrational beliefs, although there were few if any alternatives to this strategy. Already in the 1890s the liberal German historian, Theodor Mommsen, told Hermann Bahr that anti-Semites would "listen only to their own hatred and envy, to the meanest instincts."[52] It is also obvious that Jews and philo-Semites were hurt by their own disunity and even, in some cases, by their underestimation of the Nazi threat. Almost certainly, however, the most important reason for failure was the relatively small size of the Jewish population in Austria as well as the small number of Christians willing to help them. These same fundamental problems existed all over Europe, especially in Poland, where the Jewish population was much larger than in Austria.[53]

Perhaps the most effective type of defense against anti-Semitism was the satire found in Hugo Bettauer's book, *The City without Jews*. Bettauer's novel enjoyed a huge readership and was later even made into a motion picture. By contrast, the propaganda of the Jewish self-defense organizations, and even the Harand Movement, was almost certainly read and heard mostly by those already converted to the cause.

Even so, the defense against anti-Semitism did make a real difference. The complaints of the Kultusgemeinde, the Union of Austrian Jews, the League of Jewish Front Fighters, and the Harand Movement all achieved at least some short-term legal successes. And it is certainly possible that without pressure from these groups, the Austrian government might have felt free to follow a much harsher anti-Semitic policy.

Dr. Bloch's Wochenschrift pointed out another easily forgotten advantage of self-defense: it helped counteract Jewish indifference. Through it Jews learned more about their own religion and heritage. Josef Bloch believed that Jews simply had to defend themselves against false accusations; it was a social duty and was demanded by self-respect.[54] As for the Harand Movement, its followers must have surely gained a sense of self-worth at a time when some of the fundamental principles of civilization were being ruthlessly attacked.

18

FRIEND OR FOE?
The Dollfuss–Schuschnigg Regime

By themselves Austrian Jews were too splintered and their Christian allies were too few to be effective against the anti-Semitic onslaught in the early 1930s. However, just when the Nazis in both Austria and Germany were marching from one electoral victory to another, and just when anti-Semitic violence at the University of Vienna was reaching unprecedented proportions, the Jews of Austria gained an unexpected ally: the Christian Social chancellor of Austria, Engelbert Dollfuss. Although Austrian Jews found it difficult to agree on much of anything, they could at least agree on their almost unqualified support of the young chancellor.[1]

Neither Dollfuss, who had become the youngest head of government in Europe at age thirty-nine in May 1932, nor his successor, Kurt von Schuschnigg, resorted to the use of anti-Semitism in their public or private statements even though as late as 1932 the official program of the Christian Social Party still said that anti-Semitism was an essential part of the party's ideology and was no mere piece of agitation material. The program spoke of the "corruptive, revolutionary" influence of Jewry, although it still rejected racial anti-Semitism. By contrast, when the Christian Social Party celebrated the birthday of its founder, Karl Lueger, in October 1933, neither Dollfuss nor any other Christian Social speaker, nor even the *Reichspost* mentioned Lueger's anti-Semitism, even though anti-Semitism had been the cornerstone of the mayor's ideology and campaign tactics.[2]

THE JEWISH PRESS AND THE DOLLFUSS REGIME

Jewish support for Dollfuss seldom wavered, even when in March 1933 the Austrian Parliament dissolved after all three of its presidents resigned in protest over a minor voting procedure. Dollfuss was under pressure from his mentor,

Mussolini, to abolish democracy. The four-foot-eleven-inch chancellor took advantage of the situation by declaring that Parliament had dissolved itself, and he forcibly prevented it from reconvening. He used this unforeseen turn of events as a pretext for establishing an authoritarian regime which was to last until the annexation of the country by Germany almost five years later.

Although Dollfuss's commitment to democracy has long been a matter of some dispute—he was a member of that "front generation" that was accustomed to giving and taking orders—there can be little question that his immediate motivation was to block the Anschluss following Hitler's consolidation of power in Germany and the rapid rise of the Nazi Party in Austria. The chancellor wished to prevent the Nazis from using Parliament to increase their popularity through demagogic agitation the way they had done in Germany.[3]

Whatever the Socialists, democrats, and some historians may have thought about the chancellor's antidemocratic moves, there can be no debate that they had the strong and nearly unanimous support of Austria's Jews, even many who in normal times supported the Socialist Party. Although press censorship also began about this time, it did not require active support of the government, in sharp contrast to that of the Third Reich. Even the liberal *Wahrheit* thought the dissolution of Parliament was "the lesser of two evils."[4]

Moreover, the termination of parliamentary democracy in Austria did not mean the end of democratic Jewish politics. As discussed in Chapter 15, the politics of the Israelitische Kultusgemeinde continued unchanged until the Anschluss. Oddly enough, Jews were the only Austrians to retain their political parties after 1934 (albeit only for their Kultusgemeinde) as well as to have the right to elect representatives through democratic elections; all other political offices in Austria were appointed from above. Even stranger is the existence of the same situation in Nazi Germany until 1938.[5]

Both Zionists and assimilationists were unstinting in their support of Dollfuss. *Die Stimme* praised the chancellor for trying to maintain peace and order. Although forbidding assemblies (a policy also initiated by Dollfuss) was regrettable, the Nazis had misused freedom of assembly and would do so even more after Hitler's victory in Germany. Peace and order were also essential for Austria's ailing economy. Leading Austrian Zionists such as Oskar Grünbaum, the president of the Zionist Federation of Austria, were convinced that the Dollfuss government would be succeeded by a Nazi one if it were to fall. And an Austrian Nazi government would be more disastrous for Jews than the Hitler dictatorship because of the large number of despised Ostjuden in Vienna. Zionist support for Dollfuss, which included attempting to influence the English press through their connections in London, had to be kept secret, however, so as not to embarrass the chancellor.[6] When in late April Doll-fuss took the further step of forbidding future elections, Die Wahrheit thought that these measures had been taken to preserve Austria's independence. At a time when Nazi membership in Austria was growing rapidly, "even the most convinced democrats realize[d] that the Austrian government, in the present chaotic circumstances, need[ed] to take unusual measures to bring Austria out of dangerous times and into a better future."[7]

In June Die Wahrheit was even stronger in its support of the Dollfuss government, saying that the chancellor, "with prudence and decisiveness, [had done] everything possible to fend off the brown [Nazi] threat to Austria." The paper also accepted at face value the chancellor's statement to a foreign reporter that all races and religions were being treated equally by the Austrian government. It likewise approved the use of police in Vienna's Hochschulen to prevent Nazi violence, even though this move violated Austria's ancient tradition of academic autonomy. The paper had long been calling for such action to protect Jewish students. Later in the summer of 1933 the Austrian government announced that it would organize a new security force for Austrian universities. It also prohibited the Deutsche Studentenschaft in Austria because it was just one part of an organization that had been coordinated by the German government. The government even censored public notices of other student organizations, many of which had anti-Semitic contents.[8]

Die Wahrheit was so impressed by the government's anti-Nazi actions that it thought that "the spread of the brown plague [had been] banished. The measures of the political doctors of Austria [had been] so radical that they had localized the contagion." This interpretation appeared to be well justified when on 19 June the government outlawed the Austrian Nazi Party and shut down its press after the Nazis had perpetrated a series of terrorist actions.[9]

Such high praise from Jewish circles was not appreciated by all members of the government, however, At a cabinet meeting held on 14 June Minister of the Army Carl Vaugoin remarked that the government's anti-Nazi policies were being pursued for the benefit of the country's "Aryan" population, not for the Jews. He did not like the enthusiastic support given the government by Jewish newspapers, preferring the times when Jews had insulted him.[10]

Austrian Jews were also well disposed toward the new authoritarian constitution that went into force on 1 May 1934. Die Wahrheit said that although Jews would regret the passing of the old constitution of 1867, which had first brought about their emancipation, they would not regret the downfall of the misused parliamentary democracy, which had created an anti-Semitic plague. The paper welcomed the equality of all citizens and the free exercise and autonomy of all religions guaranteed in the new constitution. The patriotism, intelligence, endurance, and above all the courage of the chancellor was the reason why the future again looked bright. The *Jüdische Presse* likewise did not mourn the passing of the "party state" into which Orthodox Jews had had so much trouble fitting.[11]

Government support for Jews was not confined to legal theories or statements to foreign reporters. When summer resort communities tried to exclude Jews and when landlords refused to rent to them, the authorities stepped in, as before, to enforce the law. The government also created a new Unity Trade Union in March 1934 that encompassed all workers and employees, including Jews. Finally, professional and sporting organizations that were even suspected of harboring Nazi ideas were dissolved. All things considered, Austrian Jews felt that for the first time since the halcyon days of Liberalism in the 1870s the head of the government was an ally.[12]

The popularity of Chancellor Dollfuss among Austrian Jews was so great that when he survived an assassination attempt in the fall of 1933, Jewish newspapers expressed profound relief. *Die Stimme* wrote that "one can easily affirm that Jews of all classes and parties are sympathetic with the manly and self-sacrificing struggle of the head of the government to defend Austria's independence. . . . Dollfuss's popularity rests in part on the support of the world's Jews. It is an immortal achievement that he has kept the murdering brown beast away from Austria."[13]

Such praise was modest, however, in comparison to the eulogies written about the chancellor after his assassination by Austrian Nazis on 25 July 1934. *Die Wahrheit* wrote that Dollfuss had been loyal to the Jews and that they had returned that loyalty with true attachment. "His enthusiastic patriotism and the energy with which he defended Austria's independence assure[d] him a lasting and honorable memory in the hearts of patriotic Austrian Jewry."[14] *Die Stimme* lauded Dollfuss as "the only statesman in the world who defended humanity and morality against the Nazis."[15]

RESTRAINING INFLUENCES ON
GOVERNMENT-SPONSORED ANTI-SEMITISM

The administrations of Engelbert Dollfuss and Kurt von Schuschnigg were undoubtedly marked by improvements in some of the ways in which Jews were treated by the Austrian government. Although the documentary evidence reveals no hostility toward Jews by either of the two chancellors—despite the speeches made by Dollfuss for the Antisemitenbund in 1920—the chancellors' attitude toward the Jewish community cannot be attributed to personal feelings alone. Both men were subjected to numerous domestic and foreign influences on questions regarding Jews that made it politically opportune to avoid at least obvious signs of anti-Semitism.

This is not to imply that either Dollfuss or Schuschnigg was simply a cynical opportunist. Neither man was megalomaniacal nor naturally inclined to giving demagogic speeches. Dollfuss exuded personal warmth and great courage. The American minister to Austria, Gilchrist Baker Stockton, was "much impressed with [the chancellor's] sincerity" when he denounced the "gross stupidity" of Nazi students who had attacked their Jewish classmates.[16] Kurt von Schuschnigg, who was thirty-four when he succeeded the murdered Dollfuss in 1934, came from an officer's family—not the kind of background likely to produce a rabid anti-Semite. It is also reasonable to assume that both men were following the long-established tradition of the Austrian government, dating back to the monarchy, of protecting the legal rights of all minorities.

At the same time there is no denying that there were real political advantages to be gained from eschewing open anti-Semitism. As practicing Catholics and convinced Austrian patriots, the chancellors ardently sought to preserve the independence of both Austria and the Catholic church. But to do so they desperately needed political, economic, and military assistance from both domestic and foreign sources. After Dollfuss abolished parliamentary democracy in March 1933, the renunciation of anti-Semitism was one important way in which both Dollfuss and Schuschnigg could put ideological distance between themselves and Hitler. Aid was unlikely from the Anglo-Saxon powers—Britain and the United States—if Austria were perceived as an anti-Semitic country at a time when anti-Semitism and Nazism were more and more being equated in the popular mind. Anti-Semitic policies would also not have been helpful in maintaining good relations with France, Czechoslovakia, or even Italy. For a country already suffering from high unemployment and a trade boycott imposed by Nazi Germany between 1933 and 1936, foreign tourists were essential. The consequences of a world Jewish boycott, such as Germany experienced after 1933, were painfully obvious. Moreover, neither chancellor had any desire to alienate the wealthy Jews who gave large sums of money to the government at critical times.[17]

Dollfuss did not have to speculate on the attitude of the American government regarding anti-Semitism. As early as 1919 American threats to withhold food shipments to Austria if anti-Semitic demonstrations continued may very well have cooled anti-Semitic passions at that time and possibly even prevented the deportation of Jewish war refugees from Eastern Europe.[18] Likewise, in 1931 and again in 1932 (after Dollfuss had become chancellor in May), repeated American diplomatic protests to the Austrian government concerning the treatment of American students at the University of Vienna led to Dollfuss taking a much harder line toward anti-Semitic violence.[19]

The protests of the American minister appear to have quieted anti-Semitism at the University of Vienna for a few months. However, Hitler's appointment as chancellor in January 1933 inspired Austrian Nazis to imagine that they too would soon be able to take over Austrian political and educational institutions. Consequently, Nazi violence increased rapidly in the spring of 1932 not only at the University of Vienna, but also throughout the whole country. Following two waves of attacks by Nazi students on Professor Tandler's Anatomy Institute in March and May and a new protest from Minister Stockton over the injuring of American students, Dollfuss revoked the institute's academic autonomy, thus allowing police to enter the premises in order to protect students. Nazi students were also forbidden to wear their insignia, although they did so anyway.[20]

In November 1933, the new American minister to Austria, George H. Earle, stated publicly that Austria could count on the sympathy of and better trade relations with the United States if it rejected anti-Semitism. (The minister received eighty-two threatening letters in response to this warning.) A second and more direct semiofficial warning was published in the Austrian press in January stating that the American government could not cooperate with a country that persecuted people because of their birth. The warning may have been partially responsible for Dollfuss making a radio broadcast to the American people the next month.[21]

Not everyone in Austria appreciated the Americans' remarks, however. To some Austrians such warnings understandably sounded hypocritical. *Schönere Zukunft* observed that the minister's comments were strange coming from a country that practiced strict racial segregation in the southern states against people having only a trace of Negro blood. Only dirty railroad cars were available for such people; and they were forced to drink from separate fountains. Even in some of the northern states marriage between whites and Negroes was forbidden.[22] A later article in the *Deutsches Volksblatt* reported a speech by Rabbi J. X. Cohen to the American Jewish Congress in which the rabbi noted the number of large businesses, utility companies, and banks in New York City that discriminated against Jews in their hiring practices.[23]

THE JEWISH PRESS, THE SOCIALIST UPRISING, AND
THE SCHUSCHNIGG CHANCELLORSHIP

Domestically, the Austrian government and the Jews became more dependent on each other as a result of Dollfuss crushing a Socialist uprising and outlawing the Social Democratic Party in February 1934. The three-day uprising against the federal government was initiated by radical elements of the Social Democratic Party and took place four and a half months before the assassination of Dollfuss. Although it involved few if any observant Jews, the brief civil war aroused genuine fears among Austrian Jews.

As early as 1927 *Die Wahrheit* had expressed concern and embarrassment about the large number of people of Jewish origins—but people who no longer practiced Judaism or even considered themselves Jews—in the Socialist Party. "The more Jews there are among the leaders of Social Democracy, the stronger the desire will become to square accounts through a show of anti-Semitism. We have in Austria not only religious but also racial and economic anti-Semitism which is a result of Jewish circles which direct the Social Democratic financial policies. . . . The anti-Semites will not make just the Jewish leadership alone, but all Jews responsible for the unreasonable financial policies of city hall which threaten the existence of many Viennese even though they fall most heavily on the Jews." Nearly three years later, *Die Wahrheit* warned ominously that Jewish history taught that if a civil war came to Austria, the Jews would be the first victims.[24]

Consequently, assimilated and Zionist Jews alike were worried that the Jewish community in general would be blamed for an uprising in which some people of Jewish origins had played minor roles. *Die Wahrheit* reiterated that "most Jews reject radicalism, the class struggle, and anticlericalism pursued by part of the SDAP."[25]

After defending the Austrian government against foreign criticism for the way in which it put down the uprising, *Die Stimme* wrote that it was ridiculous to blame "the Jews" for all aspects of the February revolt. The Jewish leaders of the SDAP had long ago turned against religious Judaism and could, therefore, no longer even be considered Jews.[26]

Jewish newspapers not only feared that the Socialist uprising would revive Austrian anti-Semitism, but they were also apprehensive that one or more of their rivals would inherit the remnants of the Social Democratic Party. *Die Wahrheit* worried that allegations by Christian Social politicians that the "Jewish" leaders of the party had led the workers astray (charges that were in fact also made by the leaders of the illegal Nazi Party) would only drive them into the arms of the underground Austrian Nazi Party. *Die Stimme* thought the moment was ripe to appeal to working-class Jews to forget Socialism and join the Zionist movement. Because the Socialist Jews had been "unfaithful to their own house, ancestry, and Jewish pride, a catastrophe was bound to happen." The Jews in the Austrian Social Democratic Party had suffered the same fate as the assimilationist Jews in Germany, and like them they had no choice but to turn to the Zionist cause as soon as possible. The *Jüdische Presse* also got into the act by calling on the Jewish members of the SDAP to return to their religious home.[27]

Relations between Jews and the Austrian government under the chancellorship of Kurt von Schuschnigg followed essentially the same pattern as those established during the Dollfuss years. Jewish newspapers responded gratefully to occasional comments by the chancellor to foreign reporters and directly to Jewish representatives that he would continue to uphold the May Constitution of 1934 guaranteeing equal rights for all Austrian citizens. For example, in September 1934 Schuschnigg told leaders from the World Jewish Congress, the Board of Deputies of British Jews, and the Comité des Délégations Juives that there were no second-class citizens in Austria and no restrictions on the personal freedom of Jews. In March 1935 he told the Jewish Telegraphic Agency in London that there was no Jewish question in Austria in the usual sense of the term. The government would never consider expelling Eastern European Jews. In October 1937 the chancellor qualified his support a bit when he told reporters from a Belgian newspaper that he drew a distinction between Jews who had lived in Austria for generations and those who had immigrated since 1914, mostly from Poland. However, these Jews represented a national, not a social or religious problem.[28]

Chancellor Schuschnigg, like his predecessor, at times also went beyond these reassuring words to provide Austrian Jews with real protection. The disgustingly anti-Semitic newspaper, *Der Stürmer*, was banned shortly after the July Putsch that had resulted in the death of Dollfuss. In September 1937 he prevented the Salzburg provincial parliament from enacting a law prohibiting the kosher slaughter of animals.[29] A few Jews, most of them Zionists, were even appointed to high positions in the federal government and the municipal government of Vienna.

QUIET ANTI-SEMITISM

Superficially, then, the contrast between Hitler's Germany and the Austria of Dollfuss and Schuschnigg could hardly have been greater. In the Third Reich the government itself ostentatiously dismissed Jewish civil servants, journalists, and people in the fine arts; it sponsored the boycott of Jewish shops of 1 April 1933 and the burning of Jewish books six weeks later. In 1935 it codified a "racial" definition of Jews and increased their social segregation. In Austria, Jews were guaranteed equality of legal rights by the constitution, the government actively suppressed physical assaults on Jews, and the chancellors never indulged in Jew baiting. These differences were significant, but they do not tell the whole story.

The fact is that whereas the Austrian government was under pressure from a number of sources to protect the country's Jews, it was also under a great deal of popular pressure from Austrian anti-Semites, and economic pressure from Nazi Germany after 1936, to do just the opposite. The government therefore chose a middle position, tolerating political and economic anti-Semitism of middle- and lower-level officials while not promoting it at the highest levels. For example, the vice-mayor of Vienna, Josef Kresse, made several anti-Semitic speeches advocating that Jews be banned from trade unions and that their businesses be boycotted by Christians.[30] And while Dollfuss and Schuschnigg were assuring foreigners and Jews that they opposed anti-Semitism and were in favor of equal rights for Jews, they often tolerated newspapers and organizations that specialized in hate mongering as long as they had no known connections with the illegal Austrian Nazi Party.

We have already noted in Chapter 11 how Christian Social and Catholic publications and organizations like the *Reichspost*, *Schönere Zukunft*, and the Christian Social Arbeiterverein actually stepped up their anti-Semitic tirades in 1933 in an effort to compete with the Nazis. Even *Sturm über Österreich*, the organ of Chancellor Schuschnigg's own paramilitary organization called the Ostmärkische Sturmscharen, talked about the need for a "better anti-Semitism." However, it also said that the "Jewish danger" had to be met with justice, and it rejected the racial anti-Semitism of the Nazi variety. It even went so far as to say that religious and national Jews should not be regarded as enemies. But it added that Austria had to "escape from the evil spirit of Jewish economics."[31]

In addition to the anti-Semitism of the Christian Social periodicals, there were several thinly disguised Nazi newspapers after the official party press had been banned along with the party itself in June 1933. Nazis purchased the inexpensive Viennese newspaper called *Depeschen* through "straw men" and for a time were able to operate the paper as an "independent daily" despite the close scrutiny of the police. Two other Viennese newspapers, the *Neue Zeitung* and the *Zwölf-Uhr Blatt*, were secretly financed by a pro-Nazi German, Prince Philipp Josias von Coburg. Far better known and more successful, at least for a time, was the *Wiener Neueste Nachrichten*. Having fifty thousand readers, it too was subsidized from Germany. It praised economic developments in the Third Reich and printed numerous anti-Semitic articles while carefully avoiding direct attacks on the Austrian government, in order to escape censorship. Beginning in December 1934, the government allowed Walter Riehl, who, it will be recalled, was one of the first leaders of the Austrian Nazi Party, to resume publication of the *Deutsche Arbeiter-Presse*.[32]

By far the most notorious of the pro-Nazi, anti-Semitic newspapers between the outlawing of the Austrian Nazi Party in 1933 and the Nazi Putsch of July 1934 was *Der Stürmer*. In its contents, at least, it was the successor of *Der eiserne Besen*. Scarcely an article in *Der Stürmer* did not encourage hatred and contempt for Austrian Jews. It frequently published falsehoods about Jews— for example, that the Talmud contained instructions that allowed Jews to cheat Christians and that Jews drank the blood of Christians at Easter—that had long since been disproved by scholars and judicial courts. Every week *Der Stürmer* carried an article about a Jewish criminal, but never about Christian criminals. And, of course, there were the usual articles about all the great thinkers of world history who had been anti-Semites.[33]

Anti-Semitic publications were not limited to newspapers in the Dollfuss–Schuschnigg era. Oswald Menghin, a specialist in prehistory and archaeology at the University of Vienna, published a book in 1934 called *Geist und Blut* (*Spirit and Blood*) in which he argued that every race tried to avoid mixing with foreigners who threatened to change their character. Anton Orel, the Catholic youth leader, also published a book in 1934 entitled *Wahre Ständeordnung* (*True Corporative Order*), which by January 1935 had already gone through three editions. In explaining the collapse of capitalism, Orel described how Jews had destroyed the corporative order in the Christian Middle Ages in the process of building a new liberal-capitalist social and economic system.[34]

When Jews complained about these anti-Semitic publications, Chancellor Schuschnigg disingenuously replied that Jews had their own press with which to answer these allegations. It is unclear whether the chancellor was referring to the strictly Jewish press that was read only by Jews, not by the general public, or to those newspapers that had Jewish editors, or both. The former, of course, had a very limited readership which certainly did not include anti-Semites. The latter usually ignored Jewish questions. In any event, most of the anti-Semitic accusations—for example, about the existence of a world Jewish conspiracy and a "Jewish spirit" influencing Austrian culture—were essentially outside the bounds of rational argument, being neither provable nor disprovable. Schuschnigg's response also ignored the government's own unwillingness to tolerate attacks against itself.[35]

Apart from anti-Semitic propaganda, Jews suffered some concrete disabilities during the Dollfuss–Schuschnigg regime. Soon after the Socialist uprising in February 1934, large numbers of Jewish physicians who had worked in municipal hospitals did not have their contracts renewed. Officially, these Jews lost their jobs because they belonged to the now illegal Social Democratic Party, not because they were Jews. However, fifty-six of fifty-eight physicians who were released were of Jewish origins, even though four-fifths of them had in no way been active in Social Democratic politics but had merely joined the party as a prerequisite for obtaining their jobs. Moreover, many non-Jewish physicians who had been members of the party were allowed to keep their jobs. No Jewish physicians—defined racially—were hired at federal hospitals after the dissolution of Parliament or at any public health-care center in Vienna after February 1934. The government's plan was to have a freeze on Jewish appointments until the number of Jewish physicians at such institutions fell below 20 percent. It need hardly be added that Jews continued to be almost completely excluded from other federal, provincial, and municipal positions. The city of Vienna employed only 154 Jews out of their 22,600 municipal employees in 1937.[36]

Jews were also gradually eased out of various aspects of Austria's cultural life after 1934. They had no influence in the Ministry of Education, and the various art associations had long been "Aryan." By 1935 few publishing houses were open to Jewish authors. At the state theaters only Jewish actors with international reputations were able to perform, although at private theaters there remained both Jewish actors and directors. There were still many Jewish journalists in Vienna after 1934, but they dealt mainly with nonpolitical subjects like sports and art critiques. Even the great *Neue Freie Presse*, which had been founded by a Jew in 1864, had become judenrein by 1937. Austrian films were produced without Jews so that they could be shown in Nazi Germany. Austrian sports teams that competed with German teams could have no Jewish athletes.[37]

Jewish lawyers were somewhat more successful than other professionals in maintaining their positions because, unlike physicians, they were not affiliated with any government institutions or insurance programs. However, when the government dissolved the bar association at the end of 1935, all but two of the twelve Jewish members of the executive committee of the bar, including the president, were not reappointed to a new association created by the Justice Ministry. The long-range plan of the Schuschnigg government, according to the American ambassador in Germany, was to reduce the number of Jews in the legal profession, medicine, and banking to their percentage of the total Austrian population.[38]

The role of Jews in the commercial life of Austria was left mostly unimpeded. Even here, however, there were instances of large export houses discharging their Jewish employees, especially those doing business with Nazi Germany. After 1 December 1934, syndicates that previously had only an advisory capacity could now decide whether a new business could be started. Not a single Jew was appointed to the section of the Economic Council dealing with trade, credit, and insurance.[39] If it is admitted that, despite these measures, Jewish commercial life was not too seriously disturbed during the Dollfuss–Schuschnigg years, it should be remembered that at least larger Jewish enterprises were also able to operate in Nazi Germany prior to 1938.

The same kind of quiet, creeping anti-Semitism existed in the government's own Fatherland Front (Vaterländische Front), an all-encompassing political organization created by Dollfuss shortly before his death to replace the defunct political parties. Although anti-Semitism was not in the statutes of the Fatherland Front, and although it resembled the Roman Catholic church and the now dissolved Christian Social Party in rejecting racial anti-Semitism, it in fact practiced religious and cultural anti-Semitism, albeit to a lesser degree than the Nazis. As in the government and the Heimwehr, it was usually lower-level officials rather than the leaders who openly espoused anti-Semitism. They still associated Jews with liberalism, individualism, and Socialism.[40]

The anti-Semitism of the Fatherland Front manifested itself in a variety of ways. Although Jews were allowed to join the organization, they could not rise within its hierarchy. Along with the illegal Nazis, it encouraged the idea after the Socialist uprising in February 1934 that the workers had been misled by their Jewish leaders. In December 1934 Prince Starhemberg, the leader of the Fatherland Front at the time, disbanded its motor corps because it was 80 percent Jewish. The general secretary, Guido Zernatto, thought that Jews ought to be gradually excluded from public positions and the cultural life of

Austria. Perhaps for this reason no Jews were appointed to a special commit-tee of physicians within the Fatherland Front. The Trade Association and the 400,000-member Trade Union, both associated with the Fatherland Front, barred Jews from membership and openly agitated in favor of a boycott of Jew-ish businesses in 1937. Finally, a separate organization for Jewish children was created in January 1938 within the Jungvolk (Young People), which was part of the Fatherland Front. Orthodox and Zionist Jews, however, applauded this move as a step toward Jewish autonomy.[41]

Barriers to the teaching profession, always difficult to overcome even in the monarchy and during the democratic era before 1933, became virtually impossible to penetrate during the years of the corporative state. There were about 180 Jews among Vienna's 5,000 school teachers. Of the Jewish teachers who were dismissed after 1934, only one-fifth had belonged to the outlawed Social Democratic Party.[42]

An educational issue that aroused a much stronger reaction from Jews was a regulation issued by the Ministry of Education in September 1934 establish-ing "parallel" (that is to say, segregated) classes for all non-Catholic students—Jews and children without religious affiliation. To be sure, *Jüdische Presse* wel-comed the policy as a partial fulfillment of its goal of having religious schools, although it preferred religious Jews being separated from nonreligious ones. *Die Wahrheit*, however, vehemently objected that the new classes would en-large the already deep gulf between Christians and Jews. Even *Die Stimme* was not pleased with the new ruling because it did not provide for Jewish teach-ers or a Jewish curriculum. On 26 September the Kultusgemeinde adopted a resolution formally protesting against the action of the Austrian government. The Schuschnigg government responded to these objections by saying that it was simply trying to make religious instruction easier, in accord with Jewish desires. Actually, the ruling was implemented only where there were too many pupils for a single classroom (in just eleven middle-school classes by the end of 1937), in part because of the opposition of most Viennese Jews, but more likely because of potential opposition from abroad.[43]

Austrian anti-Semitism also manifested itself in relatively trivial and yet sig-nificant ways. In January 1937 an Austrian court adopted the Third Reich's racial principles by granting a divorce because of the "racial incompatibility" of the partners, one a Protestant and the other a Jew. In March of the same year two Jewish musicians from the Manhattan String Quartet Anglicized their names on the program of a concert at the insistence of the management of the Konzerthaus; the concert itself was an artistic success. Then in April, after considerable agitation by anti-Semites, the bust and memorial tablet of the

German Jewish poet, Heinrich Heine, was removed from an apartment house in Vienna on the orders of Mayor Richard Schmitz.[44]

By the beginning of 1938 the status of the Jews of Austria was in some respects similar to that of the Jews in Nazi Germany. To be sure, there were no headline-catching denunciations of Jews from the highest government offices, no Jewish books were burned, and no physical assaults on Jews were permitted, let alone encouraged by the government. However, the government did tolerate verbal abuse of Jews by newspapers and private organizations such as the Antisemitenbund, which, as we saw in Chapter 12, experienced a real renaissance in the last year or two of the First Republic. Many Jews, especially physicians, lost their jobs, and most others found themselves more socially isolated than ever. The Fatherland Front segregated Jewish children in the Jungfront, some schools were at least partially segregated, and even the Boy Scouts had separate sections for Jews.[45]

An important difference in the treatment of German and Austrian Jews after 1934 is that discrimination in Austria was quieter and did not attract much worldwide attention. The Austrian Jews themselves referred to it as "rubber-soled anti-Semitism."[46] The Austrian government and economy, unlike the Nazi regime in Berlin, was not nearly strong enough to defy world public opinion or a boycott. However, an even greater distinction with Nazi Germany was that in Austria there was no systematic attempt by the government to pauperize the country's entire Jewish population or to force its emigration.

The governments of Engelbert Dollfuss and Kurt von Schuschnigg inherited the inconsistent Jewish policies of both the Christian Social Party and the Roman Catholic church. Racial anti-Semitism was officially *verboten*, but not economic and social anti-Semitism. The two chancellors apparently hoped to appease both domestic and foreign Jews, who would consider their policy enlightened in comparison with Germany, while at the same time satisfying the prejudices of Austrian anti-Semites and the German government. As it turned out, this middle-of-the-road anti-Semitism was moderate enough to retain the fervent loyalty of Austria's Jews to the very last day of the First Austrian Republic. However, it was not nearly radical enough to pacify the extremists among Austrian or German anti-Semites.

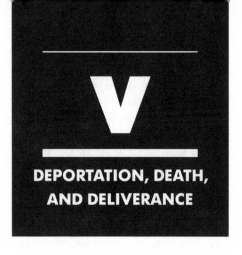

V

DEPORTATION, DEATH, AND DELIVERANCE

The night of 11–12 March 1938 marked the dramatic end of a thousand years of Austro-Jewish history. On Friday, 11 March, all the Jewish newspapers of Vienna published their usual weekly editions. By the next day their offices and those of other Jewish organizations had been seized by Nazis. Within a matter of days, or at most a few months, nearly all Austrian Jews had lost their means of livelihood and in many cases their homes as well. By 1942 almost all of the country's 220,000 Jews (using the Nazis' own definition) had either been forced to emigrate or had been deported to work and extermination camps in Poland. By the end of the war, 65,000 of them had lost their lives.

Anti-Semites, especially the hard-core, racial variety, regarded Jews as having a completely corruptive and injurious influence on Austria's politics, culture, and economy. In fact Austria's well-being and that of its Jewish population have nearly always coincided. The golden age of Viennese Jewry between 1867 and 1914 occurred at a time when Viennese growth, prosperity, and cultural creativity as a whole reached a peak. Jews and Austrians in general shared in the calamity of the late war years and the early years of the First Republic. When a modicum of prosperity returned in the mid- and late 1920s Jews and gentiles alike benefited, and both suffered again from the Great Depression.

This pattern seemed to change immediately after the annexation of Austria by Nazi Germany. The year and a half between the Anschluss and the outbreak of the Second World War saw unemployment in Austria rapidly disappear at the very time when Austria's Jews were suffering an almost unimaginable disaster. The apparent difference in fate, however, was only momentary and illusory. By 1941, hundreds of thousands of Austrians were freezing and dying on the Russian front. By 1944 American and British bombs were being dropped on Vienna, Linz, and Wiener Neustadt. By April 1945 the once-mighty Third

Reich was in ruins and the eastern third of Austria was overrun by Russian troops.

The common fate of Austria and its Jewish population to a limited extent resumed after 1945. Austrian independence (though not yet sovereignty) and the Jewish community of Austria were both reborn. This time, however, Austria's Jewish community was too small to make a significant contribution to what, by the 1960s, was a prosperity unprecedented in the country's entire history. But if the Second Republic has proved that the welfare of its economy is not dependent on Jewish businessmen, the same cannot be said of Austria's academic, cultural, and scientific creativity, which to date has shown little of the brilliance of the First Republic (although Austria continues to be a world leader in the performing arts).

Austrian anti-Semitism has not vanished with the virtual disappearance of the country's Jewish community. Ancient stereotypes have survived to the present, but one can no longer speak of an anti-Semitic "movement" and few if any Austrians would suggest that any important problem could be solved if only the "Jewish problem" were solved.

19

FROM THE ANSCHLUSS
TO EXTERMINATION

JEWISH OPTIMISM IN THE LAST DAYS OF AUSTRIAN INDEPENDENCE

In the last six weeks of the First Austrian Republic two Jewish attitudes remained constant: support for Chancellor Kurt von Schuschnigg, and confidence that Austria would remain independent. Even the most ominous news never shook these beliefs for long. Stefan Zweig was shocked to discover, on his last trip to Austria in November 1937, that his friends were not worried about a Nazi takeover. The family of Hans Thalberg, a post–World War II Austrian diplomat, never considered emigration, not even in the last days before the Anschluss.[1]

Although Adolf Hitler had made it absolutely clear on the first page of *Mein Kampf* that his ultimate goal was to annex Austria, the practical realities of German military weakness and the strong opposition to any such move by Britain, France, Italy, and Czechoslovakia induced Hitler to scale back his ambition vis-à-vis Austria to an interim policy of *Gleichschaltung*, or coordination. Austria was to have a Nazi government that would fully cooperate with the Reich in political, military, social, and economic affairs until a full-fledged annexation could be safely consummated. Hitler apparently saw that time rapidly approaching when he called his famous "Hossbach Conference" in November 1937 and discussed possible foreign policy options with the top military and political leaders of the Third Reich. One option the Führer specifically mentioned was the takeover of Austria.

The first indication of an impending aggressive foreign policy came in late January and early February 1938. On 26 January Hitler dismissed his war minister, General Werner von Blomberg, on the pretext that he had recently married a prostitute. Then on 4 February the Führer announced the resignation of the commander in chief of the German army, Werner von Fritsch, and Foreign Minister Konstantin von Neurath, both of whom, like von Blomberg, had been outspoken opponents of Hitler's expansionist plans discussed at the Hossbach Conference. Hitler now became the supreme commander of all the German armed forces, and the ardent Nazi Joachim von Ribbentrop became the new foreign minister.

Although the Hossbach Conference was ultrasecret, the dismissal of the conservative nationalists, who had helped the Führer come to power, was completely public. Because Jews had long been counting on these conservative politicians and military leaders to restrain Hitler, if not overthrow him, one might assume that they would have been alarmed by these changes. Not necessarily. George Clare's Uncle Paul, the family's highly respected political pundit, probably typified the almost inexhaustible optimism of Austrian Jews in being convinced that the conservative nationalists, now freed from political responsibility, would get rid of Hitler within months if not weeks.[2]

The Clare family was not alone in clinging to these illusions. The *Jüdische Presse*, while admitting that the ministerial changes represented a turning point, thought it was possible that these events would have a favorable result by causing world public opinion to realize the increased danger to peace. In any event, Austrian Jews needed to rally around Schuschnigg. The *Jüdische Presse* was even less alarmed by the meeting at Berchtesgaden between Hitler and Schuschnigg at which the Austrian chancellor was forced to make a number of concessions to the Austrian Nazi Party. Fears of a "Trojan Horse" arising from the meeting were highly exaggerated, according to the mouthpiece of Austrian Orthodox Jewry. The same fears had existed after the July Agreement in 1936, but the aftermath proved that these fears were unjustified. The new pro-Nazis in the cabinet were friends of Schuschnigg; patriots had no reason to distrust the Austrian chancellor. A week later the *Jüdische Presse* commented that Austria had overcome greater crises in the past than the present one. Any anti-Jewish measures the government might take would only hurt the Austrian economy. As long as Schuschnigg was in charge, the Jews were in no danger. *Die Wahrheit* thought that the only purpose of the Berchtesgaden meeting was to restore peace between Germany and Austria. The Germans had assured Schuschnigg that they would not intervene in Austrian affairs and would not support the Austrian Nazis.[3] Schuschnigg himself sought to quiet Jewish fears — a move he would later regret — by telling a group of Jewish industrialists that there would be no further changes in the Austrian government.[4]

More alarming to Austrian Jews was the increase in Austrian Nazi activity following the Berchtesgaden meeting, and especially after Hitler's speech to the Reichstag in which he mentioned the sufferings of ten million "Germans" in Austria and Czechoslovakia, but failed to make any assurances regarding Austrian independence. *Die Neue Welt* was concerned by the increased aggressiveness of the Austrian Nazis, but thought that Austrian independence could best be served by the Jews remaining quiet and unprovocative. The Clare family believed Austrian newspapers, which said that Hitler had not mentioned Austrian independence in his Reichstag speech because the Berchtesgaden agreement had reaffirmed the July Agreement of 1936, which had guaranteed the independence of Austria. The seventeen-year-old George Clare even thought that the demonstrations by Austrian Nazis in late February and early March 1938 were more exciting than threatening.[5]

Never were the Austrian Jews more solidly behind the Austrian government and never were they more united than after Schuschnigg announced on 9 March that a plebiscite on the question of Austrian independence would be held four days later. Following the meeting at Berchtesgaden, Schuschnigg was far more forthright with Dr. Desider Friedmann, the president of the Israelitische Kultusgemeinde, than he was with the press or with foreign diplomats. The chancellor described in detail Hitler's ravings and threats. Schuschnigg asked Friedmann to travel abroad and do what he could to bolster the sagging Austrian schilling. Then on 10 and 11 March, Dr. Friedmann presented Schuschnigg with two checks worth a total of 800,000 schillings, or about $120,000 in the currency of that time. After the Anschluss the Nazis ransacked the headquarters of the IKG and discovered a list of contributors to this fund. The Jewish community was fined a sum equal to this amount and Friedmann and other IKG officials were arrested.[6]

ARRESTS AND "ARYANIZATION"

The fate of the officials of the Kultusgemeinde was representative of the plight of thousands of Austrian Jews immediately after the German invasion and annexation of Austria, beginning on 12 March 1938. The optimism that most Jews clung to in the last years and months of Austria's independence nearly vanished, although wishful thinking never entirely disappeared. The Clare family knew at once that their life in Austria was over as soon as the Anschluss occurred. On the other hand, Hans Thalberg's father thought that things might not be too bad for Jews. Perhaps they would merely have to work harder and their economic status would be lowered. Many other Jews tried to console each other with rumors that Hitler had throat cancer and was expected to die any day.[7]

The change in the political atmosphere from the Schuschnigg regime to the Nazi dictatorship was incredibly swift and dramatic. One Austrian émigré recalled fifty years later that when she entered a cinema at five o'clock on the afternoon of 11 March Vienna was festooned in red-white-red Austrian flags. When she emerged from the theater two hours later the city was bedecked with red, white, and black swastika flags. Another émigré remembered feeling as though she were suddenly surrounded by enemies who wanted her dead. On the other hand, still other refugees recounted years later how their fathers had advised their anti-Nazi employees to wear swastikas on their lapels as a security measure. Still other refugees had fathers who were confident that their war record would protect their families.[8]

The first few days following the German annexation witnessed a veritable orgy of plundering and brutality perpetrated against the Jews. Only rarely were these acts committed by German Nazis, and still less by German soldiers; rather it was Austrian Nazis and even non-Nazis who now released the hatred they had pent up against the Jews, especially since the outlawing of the Nazi Party in 1933. With the blessings of the new Nazi government, anti-Semitism now became a patriotic virtue and crypto-anti-Semites could freely exhibit their long-suppressed prejudices. Nazis ordered Jewish women to dress in their best clothes and scrub pro-Schuschnigg slogans off sidewalks with their bare hands or with toothbrushes; Jewish children were forced to write the insulting word "Jud" on the windows of their fathers' shops. Supposedly these actions were in retaliation for earlier incidents when Austrian authorities had forced Nazis to clean off illegal swastikas from sidewalks and walls. The two actions were hardly parallel, however. The Nazis who had been punished had been the same people who had painted the swastikas, and their punishment was carried out in the middle of the night. The Jews who were degraded had committed no crimes, and their punishment was inflicted during the day in order to make it as humiliating as possible.[9] Other petty tortures inflicted immediately after the Anschluss included actresses from the Theater in der Josefstadt being forced to clean toilets of the Sturmabteilung (SA); other, more fortunate Jews, cleaned cars. Hitler Youths pulled Orthodox Jews around by their beards; Jews in the Leopoldstadt were forced to call each other insulting names; and Jews at the Praterstern were compelled to lie down and eat grass.[10]

During the 1930s Nazi sympathizers had not purchased Jewish property because they thought they would some day get it for free. Now gangs of Nazis invaded Jewish department stores, humble Jewish shops in the Leopoldstadt, the homes of Jewish bankers, as well as the apartments of middle-class Jews, and stole money, art treasures, furs, jewelry, and even furniture. Some Jews were robbed of their money on the street. All automobiles owned by Jews were

A Jewish store in Vienna with the insulting word "Jud" written on its display
windows, late April 1938. Photograph by William R. Steckel.

confiscated immediately. Jews who complained to the police about the thefts
were lucky if they escaped arrest or physical violence. Even after this initial
looting rampage subsided, about a week after the Anschluss, bargain hunters
could buy Jewish possessions at nominal prices when word got around that a
particular Jewish family was desperate for money.[11]

Many Jews, especially prominent ones who were in great danger, attempted
to flee to Czechoslovakia. However, a train carrying a large group of refugees,
both Jewish and gentile, was halted at the Czechoslovak border, and all the
passengers were ordered to return to Austria by the Czech minister of the interior. Other Viennese Jews were more shrewd and took trains to Berlin where
they resided for several days or weeks in comfortable and secure hotels. These
Jews were amazed at how much better they were treated in Berlin than in
Vienna. Later, other Viennese Jews were even more surprised when they discovered that they could shop in almost any store or attend the cinema long
after they had been banned from these activities in Vienna.[12]

When Hermann Neubacher, the new Nazi mayor of Vienna, was asked by
foreign reporters about the anti-Jewish outrages, he replied that they were only

A shoe store in Vienna displaying a picture of Adolf Hitler and a swastika flag to distinguish it from boycotted Jewish stores, late April 1938. The sign reads, "Aryan German business." Photograph by William R. Steckel.

temporary and the result of the previous persecution of the Nazis.[13] In a very limited sense Neubacher was right. Outright violence against Austrian Jews ended a week or so after the Anschluss and did not resume until October. The persecution of Jews, however, was actually just beginning. For example, on 1 April 1938, 60 of the 154 political prisoners sent from Austria to the Dachau concentration camp in Bavaria were Jewish; they were released early only if they promised to emigrate from Austria immediately. From 23 to 25 April, a boycott of Jewish stores in Vienna took place. SA men stood in the entrances of Jewish shops; Christians who entered the stores were arrested and forced to wear signs saying they were "Christian pigs." A new wave of arrests began in May, this time of members of the Schuschnigg government along with many Jews who had held some kind of political or cultural position; the result was another 5,000 people (2,000 of them Jews) being sent to Dachau. Those arrested had long been on black lists of the Austrian Nazis.[14]

Within a few hours or at most a few days all Jewish actors, musicians, and journalists lost their jobs. By mid-June 1938, just three months after the An-

A store in Vienna with a sign saying "only Aryan guests desired," late April 1938. Photograph by William R. Steckel.

schluss, Jews had already been more thoroughly purged from public life in Austria than in the five years following Hitler's takeover of power in Germany. Tens of thousands of Jewish employees had lost their jobs. Only rarely were they given any warning or severance pay. Among those dismissed were all state and municipal employees (what few there were), including 183 public schools teachers, and employees of banks, insurance companies, theaters, and concert halls. Meanwhile, private Jewish businesses large and small were either confiscated outright or their owners were paid only a small fraction of the property's true value.[15]

Jews were also excluded from most areas of public entertainment and to some extent even public transportation by the early summer of 1938; similar rules were not imposed on German Jews until November. Austrian Jews were also subjected to all kinds of personal insults and indignities that were not the result of official Nazi legislation. If a gentile streetcar passenger did not like the looks of a Jewish fellow passenger in the summer of 1938, he could have the trolley stopped and the Jew thrown off. The number of coffeehouses and restaurants that would not serve Jews grew from day to day. All of the public baths and swimming pools were closed to Jews. Park benches all over the city had the words "Juden verboten" stenciled on them. Jews were not admitted to theater performances, concerts, or the opera. Numerous cinemas had notices saying that Jewish patronage was not wanted. Sometimes Jews were ejected from a motion picture theater in the middle of a performance if gentiles complained about them. SA men at times even stood at the last tramway stop in the suburb of Neuwaldegg in order to prevent Jews from strolling in the nearby Vienna Woods.[16]

The initial weeks of the persecution of Austrian Jews were accompanied by a huge increase in Jewish suicides, especially among the wealthier and better-educated Jews. For example, 213 Jews committed suicide in March 1938, three times as many as in the previous March; during the next four months there were over 140 suicides per month, about twice as many as for the same period in 1936–37. If Jewish converts to Christianity are included, about 55 to 60 percent of all the suicides in Vienna were by Jews, or ten times the rate among gentiles. By the end of the Nazi occupation, some 1,200 Jews had died in despair by their own hands, not counting suicides by Austrian Jews who had already been forced out of the country.[17]

A MODEL FOR THE THIRD REICH?

Much of the persecution of Austrian Jewry that occurred after April 1938 was simply part of the larger persecution of Jews that took place all over the Third Reich and therefore cannot strictly speaking be considered "Austrian" anti-Semitism. Nevertheless there are numerous examples of Austrians initiating anti-Semitic policies that were later adopted in the Third Reich as a whole.

For example, the "Aryanization" of Jewish property and jobs in Austria after the Anschluss transpired so precipitously—being delayed only by administrative and legal technicalities—that on 4 April Josef Bürckel, the Reich commissioner for the reunification of the Ostmark with the Reich and former Gauleiter of the Saar, halted further arbitrary confiscations of Jewish property in order to prevent any more damage to the Austrian economy and to help restore Austria's trade, which had been hurt by an international boycott of its products. Bürckel even went so far as to institute criminal proceedings against some of the 25,000 Austrian Nazi "commissars" who had seized Jewish property without instructions from their superiors. In an attempt to modernize the Austrian economy, Bürckel allowed only the largest and most productive enterprises—about 20 percent of the 26,000 Jewish businesses that existed in March 1938—to remain operational, and even these were usually managed by Reich Germans. None, of course, was ever returned to its original Jewish owner. The Nazi state rather than individual Austrian Nazis proved to be the biggest profiteer from the Aryanization of Jewish businesses.[18]

The Austrian historian Gerhard Botz has noted that as a consequence of the anti-Jewish activities of the Austrian Nazis in March, "'Aryanization Instructions' were speeded up, dictated by events in Vienna for the whole Reich at the end of April 1938. Administrative methods developed in Austria soon became models for the 'old Reich' as well as for the 'newly acquired territories of the Reich.'"[19] Another Austrian historian, Erika Weinzierl, has described Austria as a "training ground for the German policy toward Jews."[20] For example, a Jewish enterprise could only be Aryanized if such an act did not harm the general interest of the German economy. The principles Bürckel developed for taxing Aryanized property were also used later in the Reich.[21]

Austrian Nazis not only raced ahead of their German Parteigenossen as far as Aryanization was concerned—by May 1939 only 6 percent of the Viennese Jews were still employed compared to 30 percent in Berlin—but also in segregating Jewish pupils and teachers and prohibiting Jewish professionals from having gentile clients. The same was true of their plans, never actually implemented, for interning Jews in concentration camps near Vienna.[22]

The "achievements" of the Austrian Nazis vis-à-vis the Jewish population did not go unnoticed by leading German Nazi Party institutions and members. Only six weeks after the Anschluss the official SS journal, *Das Schwarze Korps*, noted with some envy that the Viennese had managed to do almost overnight what the Germans had failed to do after several years. The Austrians could even organize anti-Jewish boycotts without any supervision. None other than Hermann Göring complained in the fall of 1938 that the "dejewification" of the economy in Germany was not progressing as rapidly as in Austria. Austrian methods were therefore introduced into the Altreich in 1939. The *Völkischer Beobachter* also noted that whereas in northern Germany it was the duty of the party to educate the people about the Jewish danger, in Austria the duty of the party was to preserve the purity of the movement by restraining overly exuberant radicalism.[23]

To some extent Austria indeed served as a model to the rest of the Third Reich for the persecution of the Jews. Certainly Nazi officials from Germany found the enthusiasm of their Parteigenossen in Austria a useful tool with which to shame their German comrades into a more energetic implementation of Nazi goals. However, Austria's role in the persecution of Central European Jewry cannot be understood apart from developments that occurred within the Nazi Party shortly before the Anschluss.

Aryanization and persecution of Jews in general had been slowed by several factors prior to 1938, the most important of which was Hitler's reluctance to do anything that might disrupt the German economy at a time when unemployment was still high. It is no accident therefore that Aryanization began to speed up rapidly in Germany in 1937 at the very moment when unemployment disappeared. Hermann Göring's appointment at the end of 1936 as head of the Four-Year Plan also represented a shift in the balance of power within the Nazi Party toward the more radical elements. More important, however, was the dismissal of Economics Minister Hjalmar Schacht in November 1937, which removed another obstacle to Göring's economic ascendancy and to more drastic forms of Aryanization, even though Schacht had not been opposed to "legal" confiscations. Consequently, by January 1938, 60 to 70 percent of the enterprises that had been in German-Jewish hands in 1933 had been Aryanized and half of all Jewish workers and employees were unemployed. After 1 March 1938 no more government contracts were given to Jewish firms except for a few vital to the rearmament program; nearly all the Jewish banks in Germany were also Aryanized by early 1938, well before the Anschluss.[24] Therefore it is safe to say that Aryanization (and also emigration) measures carried out by Austrian Nazis at most only slightly accelerated trends already well underway in the Altreich.

THE NOVEMBER POGROM

Essentially the same thing can be said about Kristallnacht. The November Pogrom in Vienna, far from being a turning point, merely completed the economic destruction of the Jewish community in Vienna as well as in other cities of the Third Reich. Nazi outrages against Austrian Jews, which had abated during the summer of 1938, began increasing again in early October when numerous Jews were hauled out of their beds by Nazi functionaries. In the middle of the month some Jewish religious places and stores were damaged.[25] As it turned out, however, all of this was merely a prelude to the November Pogrom, more popularly known by the euphemistic name "Kristallnacht" or "Crystal Night" given it by its chief promoter, Propaganda Minister Josef Goebbels.

Although the Nazi instigators of the pogrom wanted it to appear like a spontaneous popular outburst of indignation aroused by the assassination of a German diplomat in Paris by a Polish-German Jewish refugee, the pogrom was actually carefully planned. Two days before the "action" the Vienna edition of the *Völkischer Beobachter* carried an article describing the location and appearance of the temples. The members of the SS and Hitler Youth (including the League of German Girls), who were the principal perpetrators of the pogrom in Vienna, especially those between the ages of fourteen and thirty, were ordered to leave their uniforms at home and told not to plunder. The police were instructed to protect the property of non-Jews and foreign Jews.[26]

Probably no one in Vienna was fooled into thinking the pogrom was really spontaneous in its origins. Nevertheless, there were elements of spontaneity that the instigators themselves had probably not envisioned. Not only were all but one (or by some reports two) of the twenty-four temples and synagogues and seventy prayer houses in Vienna destroyed by fires started by hand grenades, in addition to the few Jewish religious houses that existed in the provinces, but they were also plundered and sacrilege committed against their sacred contents. Over four thousand Jewish shops were looted and their inventory was partially or sometimes even completely destroyed; afterward they were closed and sealed by the police. On some streets so many shops were shut down that it looked like Sunday on weekdays. Nearly two thousand Jewish apartments in the first district alone were Aryanized by the SA, in the process of which a great deal of furniture and mattresses was destroyed while the looters searched for silver, jewelry, and other valuables. Men who tried to defend their homes against the looters were sometimes beaten to death. Six hundred eighty Viennese Jews committed suicide during the night of burning and looting and in the following few days; another twenty-seven were murdered and eighty-eight seriously injured. Over sixty-five hundred Jews were arrested in Vienna and about twelve hundred in the rest of Austria, of whom thirty-seven hundred were sent to Dachau.[27]

Many of the actions carried out by the SA against Jews were nothing more than pure sadism. Jewish men who were arrested were placed in schools, prisons, and even the Spanish Riding School next to the Habsburg Hofburg Palace and forced to do calisthenics, go without food, and sleep while standing up. Some Jewish women were forced to strip and perform lesbian acts with prostitutes for the entertainment of the storm troopers. Other Jewish women were forced to dance naked. One Gestapo agent in Vienna later reported that he and his colleagues had difficulty in preventing crowds from manhandling still more Jews.[28]

Outside of Vienna the situation was similar though perhaps not quite as bad; in Graz and Linz this may have been because all Jewish shops had already been Aryanized and therefore could not be plundered. There was looting, however, in Salzburg and Klagenfurt. The main difference between Vienna and the provinces is that the SA was in charge of burning synagogues in the federal states, not the SS. There also appears to have been less violence perpetrated against Jews except in Innsbruck, perhaps indicating a closer sense of small-town solidarity between Jews and gentiles than existed in a more impersonal metropolis like Vienna. In Graz, most of the young SS men were actually on friendly terms with their former Jewish classmates.[29]

Many historians believe that the November Pogrom was even more severe in Austria than in the Altreich. The only evidence to support this contention, however, is anecdotal. There are no statistics to compare property damage in Austria with that in the Altreich. The number of Jews arrested in Vienna—6,547 out of somewhere between 20,000 and 40,000 for the entire Reich—was no more than proportionate to Vienna's share of the Third Reich's Jewish population in November 1938. Equally proportionate was the twenty-seven murders in Vienna compared with ninety-one for the whole Reich. Individual acts of cruelty toward Jews may have been more common in Vienna than elsewhere, but this has not been proved statistically. There were many private individuals who condemned the senseless destruction of property in Germany, but such expressions were not unknown in Austria either, even among party members. Two things are reasonably certain, however. Kristallnacht was at least as brutal in Austria as elsewhere in the Third Reich; and 10 and 11 November proved that the robbery and murder of defenseless Jews would not cause a collective protest. The Nazi government therefore had little to fear from the Austrians when it decided to accelerate the process of destroying what remained of the Jewish community.[30]

THE SOLUTION TO VIENNA'S HOUSING PROBLEM

The confiscation of Jewish homes and other kinds of wealth by Austrian Nazis both before and after Kristallnacht probably had less to do with Nazi ideology than it did with economic self-aggrandizement—that is, pure old-fashioned greed. In addition, Hitler, Bürckel, and the Austrian Nazis intended to solve the housing shortage in Vienna by driving out the Jews, as well as Czechs and other foreigners. It was a solution to a problem that had been chronic in

Vienna since the beginning of heavy industrialization and urbanization in the late nineteenth century and that had become far more acute during the First World War with the rapid influx of refugees, many of whom had been Jewish. Of course it was also a way of rewarding *alte Kämpfer* (old Nazi fighters) for their services during the illegal period and tying them more closely to the regime. Likewise, the confiscation of Jewish jobs was also an answer to Viennese unemployment, which had been endemic during the entire interwar period, and especially in the 1930s. The confiscation of Jewish homes was also a critical step on the road to their emigration and deportation. Without homes, Jews could hardly hope to remain in Austria for long.[31]

Confiscation of Jewish homes began immediately after the Anschluss. Then a few days after Kristallnacht the Vienna edition of the *Völkischer Beobachter* openly called for robbing Jews of their apartments. Already by December 1938, 44,000 Jewish apartments had been Aryanized out of a total of about 70,000. In early May 1939 various officials in the city housing office complained that a new law against Jews was not stringent enough.[32]

The housing situation for Jews after the November Pogrom can only be described as appalling, although far worse conditions awaited those Jews who were eventually deported to concentration camps in Poland. Jews were sometimes notified by a piece of paper on their front door that they had only a few days or even hours to move out of their apartments. And leaving their own apartments was the first of as many as six moves they had to make between 1940 and 1942. By 1940, up to five or six families were living in a single apartment; the married and unmarried, young and old, and people of both sexes were all living in one room without plumbing or cooking facilities. Telephone calls could be made only from a central office.[33]

One of the cruelest ironies of this horrible housing situation was that Nazi officials blamed the sanitary conditions that resulted from the overcrowding on Jewish "character traits." In reality, of course, it was Nazi discriminatory policies in employment, housing, and even shopping that created in some cases the stereotype of the filthy Jew that the Nazis and other anti-Semites had long depicted in their propaganda and political cartoons. Making the Jews disgusting alienated them all the more from their gentile neighbors (if they still had any) and made it easier for the Nazis to depict them as subhuman and worthy only of deportation.[34]

LEGAL DISCRIMINATION

With the loss of their homes came special laws intended to segregate Jews completely from the rest of society and to make them want to leave Austria as soon as possible. Although the laws became really severe only after the beginning of the Second World War in September 1939, some were first introduced immediately after the Anschluss. By the end of Nazi rule in 1945, some 250 anti-Jewish laws had been enacted in the former Austrian territories.[35]

One of the first such discriminatory laws to be enacted was a numerus clausus for Jewish university students, which was introduced on 24 April 1938, thus fulfilling one of the oldest and most cherished demands of Austrian anti-Semites. Only 2 percent of the students at Austrian universities could be Jews, a figure which was actually considerably below the 2.8 percent of religious Jews in the country in 1934 and far less than the percentage of "racial Jews" that pan-Germans had always cited when speaking of Jewish "domination." After 8 December even the few remaining Jewish students were excluded from the universities. In some cases unqualified gentile professors replaced world-famous Jewish scholars who had been dismissed. In the meantime, in April 1938 the 16,000 Jewish primary and secondary pupils of Vienna were placed in segregated classes and were later forced to transfer to eight purely Jewish schools, often far from their homes; at the end of the school year in 1939, they were no longer allowed to attend even these public schools.[36]

On 20 May 1938 the Nuremberg Laws were introduced into Austria. One of the surprises resulting from this action was the discovery that there were only 34,500 people who qualified as full-blooded "racial Jews" according to the Nuremberg definition who were not already registered as Jews. This figure was only a fraction of that which had been claimed by Austrian racists, particularly in the Greater German People's Party. After 2 July Jews were not allowed to enter certain public gardens and parks, and none at all after September 1939. At the end of September 1938 both Jewish physicians and Jewish lawyers lost their right to serve gentile clients. Only about fifty Jewish lawyers were able to make a living even briefly under these circumstances. After 5 October Jews were not permitted to enter sports stadiums as spectators. Shortly after the November Pogrom the Jews were not even allowed to appear in public during certain times of day. After January 1939 they could not use sleeping or dining cars on railroad trains.[37]

By far the harshest anti-Semitic laws were introduced just before and during the Second World War when they developed a kind of dynamic of their own that went far beyond the previous "moderate" steps. On the eve of the war, in August 1939, the Nazis requisitioned all rare metals and jewelry except for wedding rings, watches, and table service for two people. On 25 September, shortly after the outbreak of the war, Jews were forbidden to go out after eight o'clock in the evening and were not allowed to listen to the radio or to visit any public places (although there were few they could still visit anyway). The curfew was to facilitate mass arrests, which always occurred at night. By May 1941, Jews could not leave Greater Vienna without special permission. After 1 September of the same year, all Jews over the age of six had to wear the Star of David, thus removing their last measure of anonymity. The penalty for noncompliance was six to eight weeks imprisonment followed by deportation to Poland. In 1942, the few Jews who still remained in Vienna could not use public means of transportation without police permission; they could not go to "Aryan" barbershops or buy newspapers or magazines. In April non-Jews who were married to Jews had to move to Jewish housing. In November Jews had to surrender all their electrical appliances.[38]

In 1939, just as the persecution of Austrian Jews was entering its harshest phase, a book was published in Vienna with the obvious intent of soothing any troubled consciences. The book, *Rassesieg in Wien: Der Grenzfeste des Reiches* (*Racial Victory in Vienna: The Border Fortress of the Reich*), was written by Robert Körber, one of Vienna's most rabid anti-Semites since his days as a student at the University of Vienna just after the First World War. Körber's book, which was lavishly illustrated with unflattering photographs of Jews and reprints of political cartoons, was one of the longest and viciously anti-Semitic works of interwar Austria.

Rassesieg in Wien purported to be a historical survey of all the crimes and cultural degradations committed by Austrian Jews since the Middle Ages, and especially since the First World War. The Galician Jews who had immigrated to Vienna during the war were no more than "human mire" and "pirates of war." It was not a legend but a historical fact that the Jews had stabbed Germany in the back in November 1918. The revolution in that month was a Jewish, not a German one. The Christian Social Party had abandoned Lueger's anti-Semitic program and had become a party of converted Jewish bank presidents and stock-market capitalists. The anti-Semitism of the Landbund and the Greater German People's Party was only for show. The Dollfuss regime was unconstitutional and had fought Austro-Marxism in February 1934 not because of its Weltanschauung and culture, but only because the SDAP had risen up against the government. The Nazi Putsch in 1934 was a desperate uprising against Jewish executive organs. And Jews dominated Vienna's cultural life during the Schuschnigg regime.[39]

Bild 235 a und 235 b. Das häßlichste Volk auf dieser Welt wurde der sicherste Bundesgenosse einer „christlich-deutschen" Regierung. (Seite 241.)

Photographs from Racial Victory in Vienna *by Robert Körber showing deformed Jews. The caption reads, "The ugliest people of the world were the most certain allies of the 'Christian-German' government [of Dollfuss and Schuschnigg]."*

Körber's view of Jews followed the uncompromising Nazi line. It was "dangerous" to draw any distinctions between Westjuden and Ostjuden or between Jews who practiced their religion and those who did not. The enemies of Germany and the friends of the Jews wanted the Viennese to feel sorry for them. But the Aryans of Vienna were not dealing with normal people but with a criminal group that had been waging clandestine war against the Germans for centuries. One could not have any sympathy for criminals; they had to be punished through restitution and expulsion. What was happening to the Jews might seem hard, but it was mild in comparison with what would have happened to Vienna if the Jewish Bolsheviks had taken over. The Austrian Jews had lost their thousand-year war with Germandom and now had to vacate their occupied territory. But they could emigrate wherever in the world they wished.[40]

EMIGRATION AND DEPORTATION

Whereas German Jews had, until the November Pogrom, often hoped that they might remain in Nazi Germany indefinitely, albeit with an inferior legal and social status, most Austrian Jews were disabused of any such illusion soon after the Anschluss. Hermann Göring announced already in March 1938 that Vienna had to be a German city once again, by eliminating Jews from the city's economy. A month later, the *Völkischer Beobachter* said that this task had to be completed within four years, a goal that was reached. Most Viennese Jews wasted no time in helping Göring to realize his dream, standing outside the consulate of every possible host country in lines that sometimes stretched for miles, and which were subject to constant attack by anti-Semites. Some Jews, however, waited too long to apply for visas, and others—estimated by Jewish leaders as comprising one-third of all Austrian Jews—were simply too old, sick, or settled in their ways to contemplate emigration.[41]

The Kultusgemeinde of Vienna lost its autonomy on 18 March 1938. Thereafter its only functions were to provide welfare and to facilitate emigration (and later deportation). Over 42,000 Jews enrolled in its courses, which trained people in the skills they would need in their new homelands. Young Jewish women had comparatively little trouble finding work as domestic servants, particularly in Britain, in 1938 and 1939. They hoped to bring the rest of their families to them later, but often their loved ones perished in extermination camps instead.[42]

Obtaining an immigration visa was probably the most difficult obstacle for an Austrian Jew trying to escape from the Third Reich. Neighboring countries like Czechoslovakia, Hungary, and Switzerland required Jews to have a visa merely to cross their borders. Switzerland also insisted that German-Jewish passports be clearly identified with the letter J. The worldwide depression only made potential host countries all the more reluctant to accept penniless Jewish refugees. The German ambassador to the United States, Dieckhoff, when reporting to Berlin on the American reaction to the Anschluss, noted with apparent glee that "the realization that large numbers of Austrian refugees, especially of the Jewish race, would constitute no blessing for America, might also have contributed to this sobering up [of hostile public opinion]; and it was interesting to note the letters to the papers, especially from the middle strata of the population, criticizing the American Government's readiness to admit such refugees and thus further depress the labor market."[43]

Once an immigrant's visa had been obtained, there were still other roadblocks to overcome before a Jew could leave Austria. The Nazis hoped to export anti-Semitism and enrich the Third Reich by allowing only penniless Jews to go. Therefore Jews were allowed to take only thirty marks (later reduced to only ten) in German and foreign currency when they left Austria. This problem could be surmounted only with the aid of Jewish organizations abroad. The American Jewish Joint Distribution Committee, the Jewish Agency for Palestine, and the Central British Fund for Refugees all set up soup kitchens for Jews while they remained in Vienna and paid all the costs of Jewish emigration. Unfortunately, such aid ended with the American entry into the war in 1941. In the meantime, however, the Third Reich was able to make a profit of $1.6 million by the end of November 1939 from the emigration of Austrian Jews alone. Still more difficulties were caused by fake travel agencies, which swindled desperate Jews.[44]

With so many obstacles to overcome, emigration from Austria after the Anschluss was at first slow; only 18,000 Jews left in the first three months following the German annexation compared with 32,000 for the next three months. By the end of November 1939 over 126,000 had escaped, including 80 to 90 percent of the Jewish intelligentsia. Having been the first to lose their jobs, they had the most time to emigrate and the least difficulty in obtaining immigrant visas.[45] Only 66,000 Jews remained in Vienna along with another 30,000 "racial" Jews. During the next two years only 2,000 more managed to get out of the country before legal emigration was completely ended in November 1941. A plurality of the departing Austrian Jews, 30,850, moved to Great Britain. The 28,615 who went to the United States (along with the Jewish refugees of the Altreich) were probably the largest single influx of talent in American history even before the arrival of another 17,000 Austrian Jewish refugees between 1945 and 1954. However, the United States virtually closed its doors to further immigration in July 1940. China was the recipient of 18,124 refugees most of whom settled in Shanghai. Palestine received 9,195. Smaller numbers emigrated to eighty-five other countries all over the world.[46]

The deportation of Austrian Jews to work camps began in October 1939, shortly before legal emigration came to a virtual standstill. The exiled Austrian Socialist newspaper, *Der Sozialistische Kampf*, published in Paris, preserved a survivor's vivid description of the very first transport to leave Vienna for Poland.[47] Early on the morning of 20 October, 912 Viennese Jewish men between the ages of eighteen and fifty were notified by a registered letter from the Kultusgemeinde that they were to appear that same afternoon at five o'clock at the Aspang railroad station and would leave an hour later for a work camp in Nisko, a swamply area in southeastern Poland. Failure to appear at the appointed time and place would have the most serious consequences. Each member of the transport was allowed to take along 110 pounds of baggage and three hundred German marks. However, at the station they were immediately forced to exchange their marks for Polish zlotys at only one-fourth of the official rate. They were robbed not just of money, however; during the trip all of their personal documents were taken from them, including passports and birth certificates. The train trip lasted four days; anyone asking for water during the many hours the train stood at depots along the way was beaten by a Viennese policeman who was assigned to each passenger car.

The real brutality, however, began only after the train reached Poland. Perhaps because the work camp at Nisko did not have the necessary facilities to accommodate these men, all but 150 of them were driven by SS guards to the vicinity of San River. There the commandant announced that he was giving the "pig Jews" two hours to get away. Anyone found within three miles after that time would be shot. To emphasize the point he fired three bullets into the crowd. In a panic the Jews dropped their baggage and began running in every direction. After five days of hiking through forests and making many detours to avoid field gendarmes, small groups of Jews reached the Bug River, which divided the German and Russian occupation zones. There German border guards robbed them of their last possessions and forced them to swim across the icy waters to the Russian side of the river where they were cordially received by the Russians; they were then sent to labor camps in Siberia. Remarkably, all but about a hundred men survived the death march. In comparison with the fate of the later transports, these men were fortunate indeed. After this experience, Heinrich Himmler ordered that further transports be suspended for "technical reasons."[48]

Many of the deportation policies originated in Berlin and, like many other aspects of the post-Anschluss persecution of Austrian Jews, cannot properly be considered "Austrian" anti-Semitism. Certainly the idea of the Jews' wearing some identification on their clothing, driving them into ghettos and work camps, and ultimately deporting them was not conceived exclusively in Vienna. The Franconian Gauleiter Julius Streicher was apparently the first to propose, already in November 1938, the idea of interning Jews as a means of solving a housing problem. Nevertheless the Austrians frequently did take the initiative and did not simply wait for instructions from the Altreich. In the Third Reich, personal advancement was more likely for innovators than followers; some Austrians therefore may have felt compelled to catch up with their colleagues through aggressive new policies.[49]

The most important of the Austrian initiators, aside from the inspiration of Adolf Hitler himself, was Adolf Eichmann, a man whose name would one day become almost synonymous with crimes against humanity. A member of the Austrian Nazi Party and the SS since 1932, he soon became the departmental head for Zionist affairs at the Reich Security Head Office (Reichssicherheitshauptamt). After the Anschluss he told Jewish dignitaries that he had been ordered to solve the Jewish problem in Austria in the quickest and most effective way and demanded their complete obedience. His aggressive leadership resulted in the establishment of the Central Office for Jewish Emigration in Vienna with himself as head. No project having to do with the emigration of Austrian Jews could take place without his approval.[50]

Eichmann's appointment came at a critical time in the emigration of Jews from the Third Reich. By the end of 1937 only 129,000 Jews had been coerced into leaving Nazi Germany, not counting thousands of Jews who returned to the Reich thinking that the worst of the persecutions was over. The sudden addition of nearly 220,000 "racial" Jews to Germany's population made the solution to the "problem" more "urgent" than ever. The efficiency of Eichmann's office soon caught the attention of his German superiors. In January 1939 a group of officials in charge of Jewish emigration from Berlin visited Vienna to study Eichmann's organization. They were astounded to see that in one day Eichmann could accomplish what had been taking weeks in the Altreich. A Jew would enter Eichmann's "fully automated emigration factory" still possessing some wealth and within a matter of hours would emerge from the building with nothing more than a passport stating that he was required to leave the country within a fortnight.[51] Göring was so impressed with Eichmann's example that he established a Committee of the Central Reich Office for Jewish Emigration on 24 January. Later even Eichmann's well-trained "Jewish Police" was ordered to Berlin to show officials there how to conduct a nighttime deportation raid. On 11 February, Reinhard Heydrich, the head of the Nazis' security police, cited the Austrian experience as a model for how to obtain foreign exchange from international relief organizations so that the deportations could be made without any expense being incurred by the Reich. Eichmann's conveyor-belt system of emigration in Vienna proved to be so successful that he was finally rewarded by being put in charge of Jewish deportation for the entire Reich beginning in October 1939.[52]

Austrians were involved not only in planning and administering the deportations, but also in operating the death camps themselves where they constituted 40 percent of the staff and three-fourths of the commandants. Odilo Globocnik, who had joined the Austrian Nazi Party in 1920 and who became the Gauleiter of Vienna for a time shortly after the Anschluss, exercised overall supervision over Treblinka, Sobibor, and Belzec, three concentration camps whose only purpose was to kill Jews as expeditiously as possible. The commandant at Treblinka, the largest of these three camps, was likewise an Austrian. The Austrian concentration camp of Mauthausen, near Linz, was by far the harshest of all the camps within the territory of the Third Reich. The prisoners were worked to death in quarries within a few months. However, relatively few Austrian Jews were sent there. Simon Wiesenthal, the internationally renowned hunter of Nazi war criminals, has estimated that Austrians were directly or indirectly responsible for the death of 3 million Jews during the Holocaust. Austrians also comprised 13 to 14 percent of the SS even though they comprised only about 8 percent of the population of the Greater German Reich.[53]

When the deportations were resumed in 1941, it was again an Austrian, Eichmann's deputy, SS Captain Alois Brunner, who issued the order in late September, three weeks before a similar decision was made for Jews in the Altreich. Would-be deportees were seized in the middle of the night and given only three or four hours to pack their bags. Only people with permission to emigrate, war invalids, people working in essential industries or for the IKG, "part Jews" (Mischlinge), and baptized Jews were temporarily exempted. In the end, only the last two categories escaped deportation, although in all special cases much depended on the mood of local SS men.[54]

The actual transporting of the 48,000 Jews who remained in Austria began on 15 October 1941 and ended (with a few exceptions) on 9 October 1942 when the last two transports—there had been seventy-one altogether—took prominent Viennese Jews to the "model" concentration camp of Theresienstadt in northern Bohemia. From there 70 percent of the Viennese prisoners were sent to the gas chambers of Auschwitz-Birkenau. Many of those who remained at Theresienstadt died of starvation or disease. Another 15,000 Austrian Jews were killed after falling into Nazi hands in occupied countries. By October 1942 only 8,100 Jews remained in Vienna. Other Austrian cities were "cleansed" of Jews even earlier than Vienna; the last Jews left Graz in May 1940 and Linz in the summer of 1942.[55]

By the time the Second World War ended in May 1945, a total of 65,459 Austrian Jews had been killed in one way or another, or slightly more than half of the 128,500 who successfully escaped by emigration. Some 2,142 had been in concentration camps and around 6,200 survived because they were married to Christians or had been baptized before 1938 (or both). Only 1,747 deportees ever returned to Vienna. Of those who survived as "U-boats," 700 were hidden by friends in Vienna. This should be compared to the 5,000 Jewish "submarines" in Berlin, which had had a considerably smaller prewar Jewish population, no doubt a testimony to the greater integration of Berlin Jews into gentile society.[56]

CARDINAL INNITZER AND CATHOLIC ASSISTANCE TO BAPTIZED JEWS

That so many baptized Jews survived the war in Austria was largely due to the efforts of the Sudeten-born pan-German, Theodor Cardinal Innitzer of Vienna. Innitzer had had good relations with Jews, particularly impoverished Jewish students, since his days as a professor at the University of Vienna. When he was rector, he threatened to close the university for a year after Jewish students were assaulted. He was also the honored guest of the Zionist fraternity, Kadimah. In 1934 the cardinal made critical comments about the Nazi treatment of Catholics in Germany.[57]

However, the day after the Anschluss Cardinal Innitzer committed a major blunder by pledging the loyalty of the Catholic church to the new regime in exchange for a promise from Hitler that he would respect the independence of the church formally promised it by Nazi Germany in the Concordat of July 1933 (and subsequently violated). He even ordered church bells rung in Vienna when Hitler entered the city on 14 March and in a pastoral letter instructed Catholics to vote for the Anschluss. Whatever illusions he may have had about the efficacy of these gestures must have soon disappeared. In 1940 he started a new welfare agency that fully supported three hundred Jewish Catholics and partially assisted another one hundred. In 1941 he personally opposed Jews having to wear special identification and to their being required to attend separate church services for Jewish converts; this he felt would have been an unwarranted concession to Nazi racial theories. He obtained money from the Vatican to help about 150 Jewish Christians escape to North and South America by way of Portugal and Spain. Perhaps most important of all, he informed Pope Pius XII in April 1943 that the Nazis were planning to dissolve "legally" all mixed marriages between Christians and Jews; the Jewish partners would then be deported to the East, Innitzer said, where they would face an uncertain future. But Innitzer, like the rest of the Catholic hierarchy of Austria and Germany, did not extend his assistance to religious Jews or those who were not married to Christians.[58] Of course, he may have simply believed that Jewish converts were the only ones he had any hope of saving.

The German annexation of Austria in March 1938 clearly represented a sharper turning point for Austrian Jews than it did for the country's anti-Semites. For Jews it marked an immediate end to all of the country's Jewish newspapers. In Vienna, only 3 of 450 Jewish organizations survived the take-over: the Kultusgemeinde; the "Pal-Amt" (Palestine Office), a Zionist umbrella organization; and the Bund jüdischer Frontsoldaten.[59] Within a matter of months if not weeks nearly all Jews lost their livelihoods and soon thereafter their homes. Within an equally short time, all but the most naive realized that they must emigrate from Austria as soon as possible.

For anti-Semites, the change was much less drastic, at least prior to the Kristallnacht. Restraints on violence against Jews imposed by Dollfuss and Schuschnigg were removed. But this simply meant a return to the type of activity that had been commonplace in Viennese Hochschulen before 1933 and even to some extent on the streets of Vienna until 1925, with the important distinction that now Austrian Jews could no longer turn to the authorities for protection. The imposition of a numerus clausus in Austrian universities, the segregation of Jewish school children, and the elimination of Jewish cultural influence fulfilled old demands that had been made by nearly all bourgeois Austrian anti-Semites, even some of the more "moderate ones."

The economic spoliation of the Jews was especially popular with broad sections of the Viennese public. *Der Sozialistische Kampf,* while reporting with considerable horror the violence and humiliations perpetrated against Jews in the spring of 1938, acknowledged that although the workers had not taken part in these actions they did approve of measures taken against "unloved Jewish department stores and individual capitalists." The petite bourgeoisie had approved of the economic campaign against all the Jewish classes but had rejected the violence.[60] Even the expulsion of Austrian Jews was hardly a new idea, although the less rabid anti-Semites would have confined such a move to Ostjuden.

Whether Austrians knew about or approved of the Holocaust is an entirely different question, although it is certain that more Austrians knew about the slaughter than admitted to knowing. Recent research into what Americans and even Jews themselves knew at the time about the Holocaust, however, has shown that "knowing" and "believing" are two quite different things.[61] (One refugee recalled years later that Americans refused to believe what she told them about anti-Semitism in Austria; finally she simply gave up talking about it.)[62] It would probably be reasonable to say that there was nothing in the ideology of even the more radical forms of Austrian anti-Semitism that made the Holocaust "inevitable." Certainly no Austrians openly called for such a thing, and even the more radical anti-Semites often said that they opposed pogroms, that is to say, random violence, preferring instead an orderly elimination of Jewish economic competition. Yet the idea that Jews were a "criminal group" so emphatically expressed by Robert Körber in his book, *Rassesieg in Wien*, was by no means new. There are many ways of punishing criminals: fines, incarcerations, and exile, all of which were exacted against Austrian Jewry. Still another alternative is capital punishment.

20

RESTITUTION AND RECOVERY

ANTI-SEMITISM AFTER THE HOLOCAUST

Whereas 185,000 Jews lived in Austria on the eve of the Anschluss, the country's Jewish population was little more than 11,000 shortly after the war. Today just 6,500 are registered with the Israelitische Kultusgemeinde in Vienna and perhaps another 6,000 Jews (mostly recent immigrants from the Soviet Union) live in Vienna but do not belong to the IKG. Of this remnant, only about 1,600 lived in Austria before the war. Only 4,500 Jewish émigrés ever returned to their former homeland; the remainder had no desire to return to the scene of so many painful memories. The exceptions were mostly baptized, were married to gentiles, or had (naive) hopes of recovering their businesses. The Austrian government, for its part, issued no blanket invitation for the refugees to return until after Kurt Waldheim became president in 1986. The Jewish newcomers were mainly Hungarian, Polish, Romanian, or more recently Russian immigrants. As before the war, over 90 percent of the Austrian Jews today live in Vienna. Graz has the second largest community with just 80 Jews.[1]

One might suppose that the virtual disappearance of Austria's Jewish population along with its cultural influence and economic power would have been accompanied by the disappearance of anti-Semitism. However, neither the minuscule number of Jews nor knowledge about the Holocaust—which was at first viewed by Austrians as crude Allied propaganda—eliminated anti-Jewish attitudes, especially in the early years following the Second World War. A public opinion survey conducted in 1946 by Americans in their zone of occupation revealed that 44 percent of the Viennese, 50 percent of the Salzburgers, and 51 percent of the Linzers believed that although "the Nazis had gone too far in the way they dealt with the Jews, something had to be done to place limits on them."[2] Another survey conducted in the same year showed that 46 percent of the respondents opposed a return of those Jews who had survived the slaughter, compared with just 28 percent who favored their return. In 1973,

21 percent still opposed their repatriation, the same percentage that favored it. Even Social Democratic politicians, who had been among the least anti-Semitic people in the First Republic, were not anxious to see too many Jews come back to the country, including their own former leaders. It is not certain, however, whether this feeling resulted from resentment against émigré Jewish leaders for sitting out the war in safe havens (even though that was hardly the result of their own free will), or whether it was a product of the exiled leaders' Jewish backgrounds.[3]

For a time there was an eerie resemblance between the anti-Semitism of post–World War II Austria and that which occurred after the Great War of 1914–18. A major cause of anti-Semitism at the beginning of the First Republic had been the refugees who had flooded the country after 1914. Between 1945 and about 1953, 170,000 Jewish refugees from Eastern Europe spent some time in Austria and again became a cause of anti-Semitic agitation. The parallels between the two postwar periods were far from exact, however. After 1945 the refugees were not Austrian citizens; nor did they have any intention of remaining in the country any longer than was absolutely necessary. Rather they were Jewish displaced persons (DPs) who were in transit from their old homes in Poland, Russia, or Hungary to Palestine or the United States. Contrary to a widely held belief among Austrian gentiles, the refugees were not being fed or housed from scarce Austrian sources. Instead, they were being cared for exclusively by the American army and by the American Jewish Joint Distribution Committee. Nor were there huge numbers of them in Austria at any one time. In March 1947, for example, when the tide of refugees was probably at its height, there were only about 32,000 in Austria, not counting the 10,000 who had made Austria their home.[4]

As so often happens in history, however, the reality was less important than the perception. Many Austrians, desperately poor, cold, and underfed in the early postwar years, were convinced that the Jewish refugees were taking food out of their mouths. Others disliked them for exactly the opposite reason, envying them for receiving four hundred to five hundred more calories per day than Austrians did because of the Jews' outside assistance. A few Austrians smeared swastikas on the newly opened synagogue in Graz and sent threatening letters to the IKG in Vienna. The British occupiers did not help matters by openly sympathizing with the Austrians. At the same time, however, the DPs, who had barely survived the Holocaust and who were hypersensitive to anti-Semitic affronts, did not always behave in an irreproachable manner, accusing everyone who did not agree to their demands of being anti-Semitic.[5]

Another, almost bizarre similarity between the two postwar periods is that

Leopold Kunschak was still around after 1945 to make anti-Semitic speeches. Seven years in a Nazi concentration camp had done nothing to change his attitude toward Jews. One of the founding fathers of the Second Republic and the first president of the postwar National Assembly, Kunschak protested the entry of Polish Jews into Austria and continued to boast at a big rally in December 1945 that he had always been an anti-Semite.[6]

Kunschak's speech was a rarity, however, even in early postwar Austria because government officials were eager to avoid offending the occupying powers by doing anything that might jeopardize an early state treaty and the return of Austria's sovereignty. Consequently, Kunschak's speech was never published. Mayor Theodor Körner of Vienna even went so far as to say in February 1947 that Viennese anti-Semitism was nothing more than a "fairy tale." On the other hand, there were instances of former prominent anti-Semites apparently undergoing a genuine change of heart. For example, Friedrich Funder, who had been editor of the *Reichspost*, was transformed by his experience in Nazi concentration camps. No trace of his former anti-Semitism could be found in his newspaper, *Die Furche*, which he edited after the war.[7]

Even after Austria finally regained its independence in 1955, naked anti-Semitism expressed in speeches or demonstrations remained uncommon, especially when compared to the First Republic. Unlike many other European countries, no tombs have been desecrated and the number of swastikas painted as graffiti has probably not been any greater than on Long Island, at least prior to the Waldheim affair.[8] The worst offenders could again be found in the country's institutions of higher learning during the first two postwar decades. This was true even though between 50 and 60 percent of all university teachers were dismissed after 1945 as part of de-Nazification. However, by 1950, many of these professors had returned to their posts. Worst of all, however, was a right-wing organization called the Ring Freiheitlicher Studenten or Circle of Freedom-loving Students. In 1961 members of this organization beat up an American and told him to get out of the country. Four years later a professor of history at the College of World Trade, Dr. Taras Borodajkewycz, a self-described Nazi long before Hitler took over Austria, became the center of a controversy because of his outspoken anti-Semitic and pan-German opinions. His remarks produced demonstrations both for and against him, which resulted in an elderly Communist being beaten to death by a neo-Nazi student. After these incidents, however, there was a marked decrease in right-wing extremism in Austria's universities. By the late 1980s neo-Nazi student politics were not nearly as significant as they were during the first twenty years of the Second Republic, not to mention the interwar years.[9]

Street sign in Vienna with anti-Semitic grafitto reading "short-term parking zone in Vienna, fee required for Jews." *Photograph by the author, 1987.*

In 1966, Franz Olah, the leader of the tiny Democratic Progressive Party, created a minor uproar by saying that Jews in the Socialist Party were trying to grab power.[10] Otherwise, avowed political anti-Semitism has been a virtual taboo ever since 1945. No Austrian politician of the 1980s or 1990s would dare to brag about being a life-long anti-Semite. Moreover, in contrast to the First Republic, no public servant would suggest today that if only the "Jewish problem" could be solved, all other problems would automatically disappear. No longer do any of Austria's political parties or private associations use anti-Semitism as an integrating device.

One obvious proof of the very substantial decline in Austrian anti-Semitism during the Second Republic was the chancellorship of the Jewish Socialist,

Bruno Kreisky, from 1970 to 1983. A cynic could, of course, retort that Kreisky's popularity was based in part on his coolness toward Zionism and sympathetic treatment of the Palestine Liberation Organization. The fact remains, however, that no Jew of any political persuasion (with the possible exception of Otto Bauer) could have become a chancellor during the First Republic let alone remained the popular leader of the country for thirteen years.

None of this is intended to suggest that anti-Semitism has disappeared in Austria, but it has been restricted largely to code words and private prejudicial feelings. Indeed, it has been called "anti-Semitism without anti-Semites" and "anti-Semitism without Jews." Few Austrians openly admit to being anti-Semites. As in the First Republic, prejudice is directed only against Jews in general, especially those living abroad, and not specific Jews, particularly not those living in Austria. Austrian anti-Semitism is also strongest in the provinces where almost no Jews live today and very few have lived in the past, and weaker in Vienna, the home of nearly all of Austria's contemporary Jewish population and the traditional heartland of Austrian anti-Semitism.[11]

ANTI-SEMITISM AND PUBLIC OPINION POLLS

That prejudices still exist has been demonstrated in numerous public opinion surveys conducted since the early postwar years. All of them have shown that anti-Semitism remains stronger in Austria than in Germany, France, or the United States. For example, polls conducted in 1986 showed that 60 percent of the Austrians surveyed thought that all Jews ought to move to Israel. Only 44 percent of the Germans agreed with that statement, 35 percent of the French, and just 13 percent of the Americans. Sixty-three percent of the Austrians said they would not want to live next to a Jew, compared with 48 percent in Germany, 15 percent in France, and 9 percent in the United States.[12] In general the surveys have shown that about 75 percent of all Austrians privately articulate at least some anti-Semitic views, about 20 to 25 percent have fairly strong anti-Semitic opinions, and about 7 to 10 percent can be described as extreme anti-Semites.[13] A poll conducted in 1970 revealed that 35 percent of the respondents would not marry a Jew; 45 percent thought that Jews acted only out of self-interest; and 21 percent thought it would be better if there were no Jews in Austria.[14]

Ancient stereotypes have remained especially tenacious in Austria. A survey in 1973 showed that 44 people in 100 thought that most Jews did not want to work with their hands. In 1976, 34 percent thought one could not have an honest competition with Jews, and 15 percent thought that wherever there was some shameless exploitation at least one Jew was sure to be involved. (The latter question was an almost verbatim quotation from Hitler's *Mein Kampf* in which he asked: "Was there any form of filth or profligacy, particularly in cultural life, without at least one Jew involved in it?") Sixty-four percent thought that Jews had too much influence in international finance and business. In the same year (1976) 18 percent agreed that restrictions should be placed on Jews entering influential professions in Austria; 33 percent answered the same question affirmatively in 1986.[15]

A survey completed early in 1987 drew criticism from intellectuals because it claimed that an average of only 7 percent of the respondents agreed that Austrian Jews were unpleasant, that they would find it difficult to shake hands with a Jew, that they found nothing wrong with discrimination against Jews, and that they would break off a friendship if they discovered the person was a Jew. However, 15 percent said that Austria would be better off with no Jews; 59 percent did not object to Jews being run down in Austrian newspapers; 25 percent did not care if politicians tried to seek political advantages by making anti-Semitic remarks; and 23 percent thought that efforts ought to be made to keep Jews out of influential positions. One of the more depressing aspects about the survey is that there was a positive correlation between church attendance and anti-Semitic views, something that was also true of German and no doubt also Austrian anti-Semites in the 1930s. An incredible 50 percent of the respondents to surveys in 1976 and 1980 thought that Jews still comprised 10 percent of the country's total population or over 700,000 people, one hundred times the actual Jewish population![16]

The most recent public opinion poll conducted in early 1989 revealed a reversal in the decline of anti-Semitism that had been apparent in earlier polls since at least 1973. For example, in 1973, 21 percent of the Austrians polled replied that their country would be better off with no Jews whatsoever. This figure declined to just 8 percent in 1988, but rose to 13 percent a year later. In response to other questions, 18.5 percent thought that Jews are responsible for the disintegration of ancient religious values, 29.4 percent thought that Jews have proved themselves to be calamitous throughout history, and 21.9 percent said that Jews cannot become good Catholics and therefore assimilation is impossible. Altogether the poll revealed that 10.2 percent of the respondents could be categorized at "vehemently" anti-Semitic, 27 percent as mildly anti-Semitic, and 62.8 percent as neutral or philo-Semitic. It also showed that more men (14.8 percent) than women (7 percent) were hard-core anti-Semites. One encouraging statistic shown by the poll was that only 7.5

percent of young people were ardent anti-Semites compared with 11.5 percent for those over forty years of age. On the other hand, it is disconcerting to learn that anti-Semitism did not decline with educational attainment although that generalization apparently does not apply to people with advanced degrees.[17]

Another interesting revelation of the public opinion polls is the striking similarity between the political anti-Semitism of the First and Second Republics. The poll of 1989 showed that the Socialist Party still had the fewest hard-core anti-Semites with 6.5 percent, followed by the conservative Austrian People's Party (the successor to the Christian Social Party) with 8 percent. On the other hand, 35.5 percent of the members of the Freedom Party (which might be considered the successor to the Greater German People's Party) were hard-core anti-Semites or (according to an earlier poll conducted in 1970) about half of all those who were so designated.[18]

RESTITUTION AND DE-NAZIFICATION

Probably in response to these popular feelings, the Austrian government, until recently at least, has not been anxious to compensate those former Austrian Jews who lost their homes, jobs, and property after the Anschluss. The Austrian press was almost unanimously opposed to the negotiations over reparations that took place between representatives of the Austrian government and the Jewish Claims Committee during the 1950s and early 1960s and even today *Wiedergutmachung* (reparations) is a dirty word as far as the Austrian public is concerned. Therefore, the history of the attempts by Jews to gain compensation is a long and torturous one, which is not entirely resolved even today.[19]

Apart from the political unpopularity of compensating Jewish victims of Nazism, the other fundamental difficulty has been the unwillingness of the Austrian government to consider itself a successor to the Third Reich. To a certain extent this policy was at the outset part of a perfectly understandable effort to legitimize the Second Republic by putting as much distance between Austria and Germany as possible. Consequently, the Austrian government, which from 1945 to 1966 was a coalition of both major parties, at first rejected any responsibility for reparations, saying that Austria had been an occupied country between 1938 and 1945; therefore it was the Germans rather than the Austrians who were accountable for the suffering of the Austrian Jews. The Federal Republic of (West) Germany had the opposite motivation. By accepting the role of successor to the Third Reich it hoped to strengthen its claim to speak for all Germans on both sides of the Iron Curtain and therefore fully cooperated with the Jewish Claims Committee. Chancellor Konrad Adenauer also realized as early as 1950 that reparations would be an important factor in the international rehabilitation of West Germany, help achieve an early end to the occupation, and lead to better relations with the United States. On the other hand, having no desire for a new Anschluss with Austria, the Federal Republic refused to accept responsibility for illegal or violent acts against Austrian Jews committed by Austrian citizens.[20]

It is extremely unlikely, however, that political legitimacy was the only factor causing the Austrian government to reject responsibility for Jewish property losses, which amounted to $1.2 billion. The new owners of the "Aryanized" property, like the owners of confiscated Jewish property in Poland and other Eastern European countries, had no desire to return it to its original owners (if they were still alive) and were able to exercise enormous pressure on the Austrian government to limit any possible restitution. At first the Austrian government argued that 50 percent of the Austrian Jews in 1938 were baptized and therefore could not be represented by a Jewish organization. Only in 1953, after some diplomatic pressure had been put on the Austrian government by the State Department of the United States, the British Foreign Office, and world public opinion did the Austrian government consent to negotiate with the Committee for Jewish Claims on Austria, a coalition of the Jewish communities of Austria and twenty-three international Jewish organizations. Even then the Austrians agreed only to a moral, not a legal responsibility for making compensations, a position it still subscribes to today. After nine years of negotiations the government eventually settled on a sum of $6 million plus 10 percent to cover administrative costs compared with $822 million agreed to by the West Germans, not counting the $33 billion Bonn gave to Israel up to 1990. Jews who lost land in 1938 (a relatively small number since Jews were not large landowners) received only two-thirds of its actual value; those who had lost property were awarded only one-fourth of its real value. Left completely uncompensated was the almost complete loss of income the Jewish refugees had suffered during the first two or three years following their departure from Austria, interrupted educations, lost promotions, illnesses induced by the persecutions, and, of course, the lives of 65,000 murdered Jews.[21]

The Austrian government has been especially opposed to making lump sum payments to any international group of victims. On the other hand, in recent years it has been more forthcoming with regard to pensions for individual Jews now living abroad and especially in assisting the tiny Jewish communities remaining in Austria. In addition to the modest one-time payment of between $250 and $500 granted in 1988 by the Austrian government to Jewish victims of the Anschluss on its fiftieth anniversary, the government in 1990 approved a "48th Social Insurance Amendment," which will eventually amount to $165 million in social insurance benefits to Jews who were between six and fourteen in 1938. Another $30 million will be paid to assist homes for elderly Jews living in Austria, the United States, Israel, and other countries. Rabbi Miller, the president of the Austrian claims committee described the agreement as a "major achievement."[22] Although the Austrian record on restitution is not nearly as generous as West Germany's, or as good as Jewish survivors would wish it to be, it has been infinitely better than that of the former German Democratic Republic, which until 1989 did not even respond to Israel's appeals for reparations.[23] Nor until very recently have other Eastern European governments been any more eager to admit that many of their citizens had been active collaborators in the Holocaust. Even the American government waited until 1990 to compensate the survivors of the 120,000 Japanese-Americans who lost their homes and businesses in 1942 and were "relocated" to what amounted to concentration camps; many of them remained there as late as 1945 (although almost no Japanese-Americans were killed and no citizens were forced to emigrate).[24]

Another enormous source of aggravation for Jews in Austria and abroad has been the Austrian record on de-Nazification. It should be remembered, however, that the task of prosecuting former Nazis in Austria was at first shared between the Austrian government and the four occupying powers who thought that only those "illegal" Nazis who had joined the Austrian Nazi Party before the Anschluss, or who had held important positions after 1938, ought to be punished. However, since the end of the Allied occupation in 1955 the record of the federal and state governments in Austria with regard to the punishment of Nazi crimes has been at best less than rigorous. Victims of Nazism, especially those who were forced to leave their homes and jobs and emigrate, were especially incensed by the Austrian government's restoring the property of former Austrian Nazis before the victims themselves had been compensated. Still worse was the granting of amnesty to 90 percent of the former members of the party in 1948 and nearly all the others, including the Gestapo and the SS by 1957.[25]

Many Austrians and even non-Austrians have argued that excluding 500,000 former Nazis from the franchise indefinitely might somehow threaten democracy. What is certain is that these newly enfranchised voters had substantial influence because they often held the balance of power between the two major parties, the People's Party and the Socialists. Although the government instituted proceedings against 130,000 accused war criminals, only 13,000, or 10 percent, were found guilty and only 28 were executed. Of those all but 4 had been guilty of ordinary murders unrelated to the Holocaust. Another 100,000 civil servants were dismissed, but otherwise escaped prosecution. That more former Nazi Party members did not lose their jobs was the result of Allied fears that Austria's war-torn economy could not be restored if a large part of its population was either imprisoned or barred from the labor force. The success of the IKG in Vienna in prosecuting anti-Semites has been no better than that of the government; it has lost twenty court cases of documented attacks on Austrian Jews.[26]

Critics of the Austrian de-Nazification record, especially in the United States and Great Britain, should be aware that their postwar governments considered it counterproductive to dwell on Austria's Nazi and anti-Semitic past at a time when Soviet Communism was rapidly engulfing East Central Europe. From 1946 on the American policy toward Austria was based on the half-truth, originally formulated in the Allies' "Moscow Declaration" of November 1943, that Austria was the "first victim" of Nazi aggression. Even the very real differences between the American and Austrian governments over the issue of compensation for Jewish victims were therefore kept out of the public's view because of the Cold War. This factor alone, of course, limited the amount of pressure the United States could put on Austria. Consequently, foreign pressure to make restitution to the Jews steadily declined after early 1947 whereas domestic pressures against such compensation correspondingly increased. The United States, joined by its Western allies, Britain and France, did not press the issue of reparations because it wanted a stable Austria; the Soviet Union likewise was not insistent because it wanted a neutral Austria.[27]

THE WALDHEIM AFFAIR

Whatever progress there was in combating anti-Semitism and compensating its victims seemed to be undone by the international uproar accompanying the presidential campaign of Kurt Waldheim. Any detailed discussion of whether Herr Waldheim was a war criminal or an anti-Semite lies well beyond the scope of this study; in any event it has already been thoroughly explored by Robert Herzstein. The University of South Carolina historian argues in his book, *Waldheim: The Missing Years*, that the former secretary-general of the United Nations was no war criminal according to the Nuremberg definition of the term, but a facilitator. In many respects, he could be described as clever and ambitious; however, his doctoral dissertation on the German political theorist Konstantin Frantz, written in 1944, contained no anti-Semitism even though it would have been politically advantageous for Waldheim to have resorted to it. Above all Waldheim was a careerist who had never actually lied about his wartime past but had also neglected to mention the more embarrassing aspects of it. Like many other people of his generation, he simply wanted to forget "the awkward baggage of his past."[28]

There is no clear evidence that Waldheim exploited anti-Semitism during the presidential campaign in the spring of 1986. On the other hand, he was criticized for not denouncing the phenomenon, at least not until after the first election in May and not vigorously until after the run-off election the next month when he promised to oppose discrimination against Jews and said that he would welcome a historical commission investigating his wartime activities. On the other hand, the New York Times described his apparent nonchalance about his military assignments in the Balkans as "staggering." His attempts to brush off accusations against him as having been made by "some interest groups in New York" could be interpreted as having anti-Semitic overtones.[29]

The Waldheim campaign along with the placement of the Austrian president on the infamous "Watch List" in the United States clearly led to a revival of Austrian anti-Semitism as was shown in the public opinion poll of January 1989. Sixty to seventy hate letters were sent to the Kultusgemeinde, some of them threatening violence if Waldheim lost. Other recipients of such mail were anti-Waldheim journalists; Waldheim's Socialist opponent, Kurt Steyrer, who was accused of being part of a Jewish conspiracy; Orthodox Jews, who were told to get out of the country; and even a gentile critic of anti-Semitism, the historian Gerhard Botz, who received around sixty anti-Semitic letters. Eighty-five percent of the Austrian public was especially incensed over charges leveled against Waldheim and Austria by the World Jewish Congress and its leader Edgar Bronfman. Because most of the American criticism of Waldheim originated with Jewish organizations, it appeared to many Austrians as if the whole affair was an American Jewish plot. On the other hand, Waldheim's evasive answers to allegations only deepened the mistrust of his accusers.[30]

The Austrian reaction to the Waldheim affair, however, was far from uniform and, in fact, the controversy divided the country like no other issue during the entire Second Republic. It should be recalled that the initial accusations against Waldheim were leveled by the popular Austrian magazine Profil. Austria's small Jewish population was itself divided by the whole episode, with many distinguished Jewish families steadfastly supporting the eventual winner. Even the anti-Waldheim Austrian Jews did not feel threatened enough by the rise of anti-Semitism to leave the country. Simon Wiesenthal accused the

Anti-Waldheim rally in the Stephansplatz in Vienna. The sign reads, "Our duty: to fight against fascist agitation. Away with Waldheim!" The horse symbolizes the Nazi riding club that President Waldheim belonged to in 1938. Photograph by the author, February 1988.

World Jewish Congress of stirring up anti-Semitism in Austria and denied that Waldheim was a war criminal. Paul Grosz, president of the IKG in Vienna, criticized Bronfman's attempts to block Austria's admission into the European Economic Community. Austria's intelligentsia was almost unanimously opposed to Waldheim. A petition with fifteen hundred of their signatures called for his resignation in February 1988. At the same time many intellectuals made the same demand in speeches at several large anti-Waldheim demonstrations held in front of St. Stephen's Cathedral in Vienna.[31]

RENEWED EFFORTS TO COMBAT ANTI-SEMITISM

If on balance the Waldheim campaign did reawaken anti-Semitism, it also caused Austrians to take a hard look at their Nazi and anti-Semitic past. In June 1987 Chancellor Franz Vranitzky gave a speech warning that anti-Semitism had to be stopped or Austria would face international isolation. On the fiftieth anniversary of the November Pogrom both the chancellor and President Waldheim gave speeches denouncing anti-Semitism; the chancellor even pointed out that Kristallnacht had not been an isolated incident in interwar Austria. In July the conservative People's Party also passed a resolution condemning anti-Semitism.[32]

The negative international publicity accompanying the Waldheim affair doubtless also encouraged governmental institutions in Austria to improve their relations with Austrian Jews. Memorial plaques have been placed at the sites of some synagogues. City, state, and federal governments have combined with the IKG of Vienna to restore the synagogue in St. Pölten, and a private interdenominational organization dedicated to the restoration of Austrian Jewish cultural artifacts has been founded. Austria has served as a temporary host for more than 90 percent of the Russian Jews seeking new homes in Israel and the West although the cost of their stay has been paid for by international Jewish organizations. No incidents have resulted from this program and a few thousand Soviet Jews have made Vienna their home. Public money was spent on the opening of a new Freud museum in the psychiatrist's former apartment in Vienna and the Austrian government even partly financed a new Jewish museum in the Netherlands that opened in 1987. A Jewish museum on Vienna's Seitenstettengasse in the first district, which was founded in 1895 and completely destroyed by the Nazis in 1938, was reopened in March 1990 through the financial support of the municipal and federal governments. In 1989 Vienna hosted one hundred grandchildren of Jewish emigrants as a goodwill gesture. The efforts of Vienna's mayor, Dr. Hellmut Zilk, in "helping to bring about an atmosphere of tolerance, liberalism, and solidarity with the weaker segments of society" resulted in his being awarded a gold medal by the Federal Association of Jewish Religious Communities in December 1990.[33]

The fiftieth anniversaries of the German annexation of Austria and the November Pogrom were also the occasions for an almost incredible number of international scholarly conferences in Austria. In contrast to previous anniversaries of these events, Austria was no longer portrayed almost exclusively as a mere victim of German aggression, but to a considerable extent as an active and willing participant. An exhibition of "Language and Anti-Semitism" in March 1988 showed how anti-Semitism had survived in Austria through subtle code words. For example, a campaign poster in 1970 urged voters to cast their ballots for the People's Party candidate, Josef Klaus, because he was "a real Austrian," thus implying that the Socialist candidate, Bruno Kreisky, was not *bodenständig* (indigenous) because of his Jewish origins.[34] Another exhibit on

לזכר רבבות היהודים - גברים.נשים וטף
שנפלו שדודים במחנות הריכוז של
מאטהאוזן בשנים 1945-1938 כקרבנות
חרם מפשע של משטר הרשע הנאצי.
הם נתנו את חייהם על קדוש השם.
קהילת יהודי וינה.

**VIELE ZEHNTAUSENDE JUDEN,
MÄNNER, FRAUEN UND KINDER.
MUSSTEN IM KONZENTRATIONS-
LAGER MAUTHAUSEN UND IN
SEINEN NEBENLAGERN IN DEN
JAHREN 1938-1945 ALS OPFER
NATIONALSOZIALISTISCHER
BARBAREI IHR LEBEN LASSEN.**

ISRAELITISCHE KULTUSGEMEINDE WIEN.

*Commemorative plaque erected by the Jewish Communal Organization (IKG) of
Vienna at the former Mauthausen concentration camp near Linz. The plaque
reads, "Many tens of thousands of Jewish men, women, and children lost their lives
as victims of National Socialist barbarism at the concentration camp of
Mauthausen and its satellite camps between 1938 and 1945."
Photograph by the author, 1988.*

the November Pogrom, shown at the Museum for the History of the City of Vienna in the winter of 1988–89, was unrelenting in unmasking the brutality of that event. The Federal Press Service of Austria also published a pamphlet in English in 1988 called *Resistance and Persecution in Austria, 1938–1945* in which it was openly admitted that it was Austrian Nazis who were primarily responsible for the excesses committed against Jews after the Anschluss and that too many Austrians were silent onlookers during that persecution.[35] Unfortunately, these conferences, exhibits, and publications received little attention outside Austria. On the contrary, at least one American news magazine portrayed the Austrians as still deliberately ignoring their Nazi past.[36]

Although the conferences and special exhibitions represented a promising development in enlightening the public about the history and surviving remnants of Austrian anti-Semitism, much remained to be done. The Institute of Contemporary History at the University of Vienna published a collection of documents in 1988 about Jews and anti-Semitism in Austria between 1918 and 1938.[37] In May of the same year an Institute for Austrian-Jewish History opened in the restored synagogue of St. Pölten in Lower Austria. However, Minister of Education Dr. Hilde Hawlicek stated the opinion that Austrian school texts needed to deal more explicitly with the problems of anti-Semitism, racism, violence, and inequality. In fact, Austrian schools are not mandated to deal with either Nazism or the Holocaust. Moreover, there is considerable evidence, albeit strictly anecdotal, that many Austrian teachers and principals at the secondary level actually avoid these embarrassing and controversial subjects.[38] Educating the Austrian public about anti-Semitism would not be easy because over half of all Austrians said they did not change their attitudes as a result of the commemorative activities of 1988; fully 65 percent, moreover, did not want to hear any more about the persecution of Jews. This attitude may have been the temporary result of "overexposure" in the commemorative year of 1988, however.[39]

LOOKING TO THE FUTURE

Despite the checkered record of the Austrian government toward anti-Semitism since the founding of the Second Republic and the persistence of latent and not so latent anti-Semitism in the general population, the relatively low incidence of anti-Semitism among the young and the intellectuals at the beginning of the 1990s was just one reason to hope that Austrian anti-Semitism was likely to resume its decline in the future. At any rate, it is extremely improbable that

Poster attached to a Catholic church in Vienna, which reads, "Jesus was a Jew."
Photograph by the author, 1987.

Austria will ever experience again the passionate, violent, and nearly universal anti-Semitism that existed between 1914 and 1945.

Almost none of the conditions that made anti-Semitism so virulent in the First Republic still exists today. Contemporary Austria is a far more secular country than it was six decades ago. Secular trends in art, literature, and popular entertainment that were regarded as shocking to conservatives in the First Republic and which were habitually associated with Jews are now taken for granted. The Roman Catholic church took the lead before and after the First World War in denouncing these trends and blaming them on Jews; it also continued to propagate the doctrine that Jews were collectively responsible for the "murder of God." However, in 1967 Franz Cardinal König of Vienna announced that the Austrian church was trying to implement the Ecumenical Council Vatican II by absolving the Jews of deicide by purging all references to the Jews being responsible for the crucifixion.[40] The prohibition by the Austrian church against taking an active role in politics is likely to eliminate another source of conflict that poisoned the political atmosphere of the First Republic. Furthermore, the church has played a leading role in the Second Republic in educating the faithful about the evils of anti-Semitism.

Another great molder of public opinion and a leading element in the campaign against anti-Semitism have been the intellectuals, although cynics might say it is because today such intellectuals no longer face any competition from Jews. Whatever the cause, the fact is that today academicians are relatively free of anti-Semitism, in sharp contrast with the situation in the First Republic, when they were among its staunchest proponents. On the other hand, anti-Semitism is today most prevalent among people over forty, and especially the downwardly mobile and rural people.[41]

Although anti-Semitism can survive even in places where no Jews live, there is no doubt that anti-Semitism was strong in interwar Vienna in part because of the large Jewish population, which had grown still larger during the First World War. At a time when food, fuel, and housing were in desperately short supply for everyone, and the intelligentsia competed with large numbers of Jews for a small number of professional positions, the size of the Jewish population did make a difference, even though it was never as large as rabid anti-Semites imagined.

Today, Austria's Jewish population is only about 3 or 4 percent of its former size, and any drastic change in the future is virtually impossible. The large Jewish population of interwar Vienna was solely the result of the city being the capital of a great empire with over 1.3 million Jews living in the Austrian half of the monarchy alone. Now that pool of potential immigrants has disappeared. The only sizable Jewish population in Europe is in the former Soviet Union. Even though tens of thousands of Russian Jews have passed through Austria on their way to the United States or Israel, only a few thousand have remained in Austria or are likely to remain in the future.

Therefore most of the foundations of Austrian anti-Semitism have been undermined. Secularism has largely eliminated religious and cultural anti-Semitism, and the decimation of the Jewish population has removed the cause of economic anti-Semitism. Racial anti-Semitism has been discredited by its close association with Nazi atrocities. What remains in Austria are old stereotypes, especially those concerning alleged Jewish financial power and control over the mass media. Even here, however, there is reason to hope that with time and education these views will gradually disappear, although the process is likely to be a lengthy one.

21

FINAL THOUGHTS

THE EXPLOITATION OF POLITICAL ANTI-SEMITISM

It would probably not be an exaggeration to suggest that "Jewish predominance" was the single most pervasive and persistent issue in Austrian politics in the six decades preceding the Anschluss in 1938. No other idea was denounced more frequently and by so many political parties and private organizations over so long a period of time. No political party of any significance entirely ignored the issue for long. Anti-Semitism was a political weapon that every political party adapted to its philosophy in order to embarrass its enemies and to integrate its own followers more closely to its organization.

On the other hand, anti-Semitism was rarely if ever the single most important question at any given time. Rather, it was an issue that could easily be used, especially by politicians, to obscure other much more important problems. If the real economic problem for small Viennese manufacturers and merchants in the 1880s and 1890s was their backwardness and inefficiency, politicians could blame the competition of big Jewish industrialists, bankers, and department-store owners. If the most dire need in Vienna during the First World War was the shortage of apartments, a legacy of insufficient prewar housing construction, then the Jewish refugees from Galicia were to blame. If the real cause of defeat of the Central Powers in the world war was the American intervention and the ambition of the German government to make territorial gains in both Eastern and Western Europe, anti-Semitic politicians could instead blame the catastrophe on "Jewish revolutionaries" or the "defeatism" of Jewish journalists.

The same kind of scapegoating continued into the First Austrian Republic. If the real reason for the Christian Social Party's loss of power in the Vienna municipal government was the extension of the franchise to the industrial workers, it was much easier to blame their defeat in 1919 on the Ostjuden. If the actual cause of overcrowding in Vienna's Hochschulen in the early postwar years was the sudden return of war veterans, a ready culprit could be found in the Jewish students from Eastern Europe. If the real reason for the failure of the Marxists to nationalize Austrian industries was the conservatism of the majority of the Austrian people, it was easier to lash out at Jewish bankers and capitalists. If the real reason behind the secularization of Austrian society and the decline in traditional Catholic values was the urbanization and industrialization of Western civilization, it was much easier for Christian Social politicians and Catholic clergymen to blame Jewish Socialists, journalists, book publishers, and owners of cinemas for the unwanted changes. If the real reason for the reluctance of at least two-thirds of the Austrian population to join the Third Reich was Hitler's suppression of Catholic and Socialist institutions, it was much easier for Austrian Nazis to blame it on the supposed lust for world domination of international Jewry.

The potency of anti-Semitism in fin-de-siècle and interwar Austria was such that whatever the problem, it could always be made to appear worse by associating it with Jews. If capitalism was bad, Jewish capitalism, in the eyes of Christian Social workers and Social Democrats, was worse. If modern art was objectionable, modern art produced or patronized by Jews was still worse. If socialism was bad, Jewish-led socialism was infinitely more damnable. Politicians in Austria (as well as other Central and Eastern European countries) knew that far more people would respond favorably to such associations than would object to them. In other words, anti-Semitism was a kind of political sugar-coating, not entirely unlike the role that anti-Communism has played in American politics especially during the Red Scare of the early post–World War I years and again during the McCarthy era of the early 1950s.

Not only were Jews the perfect scapegoats for Austria's many ills in the late nineteenth century and during the interwar years; they were also highly useful as an integrating device for Austria's political parties. This was less true of the Social Democratic Workers' Party and the much smaller Communist Party because there was little direct competition between industrial workers and the Jewish population of Austria. Although the SDAP never espoused or practiced religious or racial anti-Semitism, its depiction of many Jews as ultra-rich, exploiting industrialists and bankers could only reinforce already existing prejudices. In reality, there were far more impoverished and lower-middle-class Jews in Austria than wealthy ones. However, the stereotype of the fat, swarthy, hooked-nosed, cigar-chewing capitalist was utilized not just by Marxists, but also by Catholic Christian Socials and pan-German racists in the Greater German People's Party, and finally by the National Socialist German Workers' Party.

For Roman Catholics in the Christian Social Party, religious issues were still important, although by no means the only areas of conflict with Jews. To be more exact, however, it was not so much the Jewish religion that bothered Christian Socials, as it was their apparent lack of it. Relations between the Christian Social Party and Orthodox Jews and Zionists remained reasonably "correct," thus encouraging both Jewish groups to imagine that their philosophies of self-defense would save them against all anti-Semites in the future.

The indignation of Christian Socials was aimed not at those Jews who wished to withdraw at least partially from the Christian community, but at secularized Jews who wanted to play an active role in Austrian politics and culture, particularly those who had joined the Socialist Party, and most of all the Jewish leaders of the SDAP. The complete separation of church and state, including the removal of most religious influences from public schools, which was advocated by the Austrian Socialists, seemed to threaten the very foundations of Catholicism and the traditional values of the bourgeoisie.

Pan-Germans in the Greater German People's Party, the paramilitary Front Fighters' Association, part of the equally paramilitary Austrian Heimwehr, and the Nazi Party also rejected Jewish secularism. For them, however, the ultimate source of Jewish wickedness lay not in any free-will decision a Jew might make, but in their "racial characteristics." Marxists could easily accept Jews who renounced capitalism. Catholics always claimed to reject racial anti-Semitism and in theory would welcome any Jew who converted to Catholicism. But a true-believing racial anti-Semite would never accept someone who had so much as a single drop of "Jewish" blood in his veins.

The difference between pan-German nationalists and Catholics on the question of race or even religious, cultural, and economic issues should not be exaggerated, however. It is true that Catholic moderates like Ignaz Seipel and Theodor Cardinal Innitzer, or for that matter a not-so-moderate Catholic like the *Reichspost* editor, Friedrich Funder, had little difficulty accepting Jewish converts into the fold. The same could not be said, however, for hard-core anti-Semites like Leopold Kunschak or Anton Orel who would at most tolerate converted Jews only after several generations. On the other hand, moderate nationalists like Johannes Schober had cordial relations with Jews.

As a political weapon anti-Semitism had a wide variety of uses. Marxists employed it to point out the hypocrisy of Christian Socials who denounced Jews and demanded anti-Semitic legislation, but accepted baptized Jews into the party and did not enact any anti-Semitic legislation. Christian Socials and pan-Germans tried to create dissension between Socialist workers and their leadership by saying that the proletariat was being led by alien and unpatriotic

Jews. Anti-Semitism was also unsurpassed as an integrating device, not only in Austria but in Germany, Poland, and no doubt other countries as well, for all those groups that were opposed to the Enlightenment and all its modern byproducts.[1] In Austria the need for an ideological glue was particularly important for the Christian Socials and pan-Germans. For Karl Lueger, Georg von Schönerer, and Adolf Hitler, anti-Semitism gave some coherence to their otherwise contradictory anti-Socialist and anti-capitalist slogans. Members of the Christian Social Party and the NSDAP in particular came from a wide variety of social and economic backgrounds. Their dislike, envy, and even fear of Jews were among the few things they had in common. However, because these rank-and-file members had very different reasons for disliking Jews, and very different ideas about how the "Jewish problem" ought to be solved, the leadership of the CSP and even the NSDAP avoided making specific proposals that might alienate either their moderate or their more radical followers. The same was true of the Nazi leadership in Germany. The Greater German People's Party was more socially cohesive than the Christian Socials or Nazis, but it was ideologically fragmented except for its anti-Semitism and its advocacy of Anschluss with Germany.[2]

Anti-Semitism was not only an important integrating device *within* the Christian Social and pan-German parties but also *between* them; it even facilitated cooperation at the international level between right-wing elements in Germany, Austria, and Hungary. Ultraconservatives in all the bourgeois parties in Austria, including the Nazis, associated Jews with the hated ideologies of liberalism, Marxism, pacifism, and internationalism and all aspects of modern art, music, and literature. They all found it easier to equate these trends with Jews and the "Jewish spirit" than to criticize them on their own merits. They could all simply be dismissed as "Jewish" or contaminated by Jews. Right-wing anti-Semites also used the same terminology to denounce Jews. They all described the Jews as "parasitic," "cancerous," "usurous," "disintegrating," "materialistic," and "alien."

Anti-Semitism was the most important issue enabling Catholic and nationalistic students to join forces in the Deutsche Studentenschaft. The nationalistic students (and no doubt some Catholic students as well) then became a vital element in the Austrian Nazi Party. Likewise, anti-Semitism was the only thing that enabled Catholics and nationalists to cooperate in the umbrella organization known as the Antisemitenbund, not to mention innumerable anti-Semitic demonstrations. Anti-Semitism was the perfect vehicle of anti-democrats wishing to embarrass the government because there was always some "Jewish problem" that the government could not possibly solve by democratic means or whose solution would be unacceptable to the international community.[3]

Nevertheless, it would be wrong to suggest that any of Austria's political parties was utterly dependent on anti-Semitism for its very existence, at least in the interwar period. For Marxists, anti-Semitism was primarily a propaganda tool used to defend themselves against the anti-Semitic attacks of other parties, especially the CSP. There is no reason to doubt that the SDAP could have survived without such propaganda, as indeed it has in the Second Republic.

To a lesser extent anti-Semitism was also a mere propaganda tool of the CSP, which it used when pan-German anti-Semitism threatened to become too popular in the early 1920s and again a decade later. At those times the party was anxious to prove that it had been anti-Semitic long before the pan-Germans had even thought of the idea. When the competition of pan-German anti-Semitism faded in the late 1920s, so too did the anti-Semitism of the Christian Socials. And when hostility toward Jews declined as an issue for the Christian Social Party in the middle and late 1920s, there were no dire consequences for the party.

Even most Nazis did not cite anti-Semitism as a major reason for their joining the party, at least not in Germany.[4] Anti-Semitism had been part of the Austrian Nazi ideology since 1913 and a very important part since 1918; yet it was not until the Great Depression hit Austria, and the NSDAP began enjoying an astonishing series of electoral successes in Germany, that the Austrian NSDAP began its rapid ascent. In explaining the party's success in the local elections in April 1932, Walter Riehl did mention anti-Semitism; but he also said it was "above all our anti-Marxist positions" that accounted for the victory.[5] Even more important for the Austrian Nazis was their near monopoly of the Anschluss issue after 1933.

Although political anti-Semitism in Austria was primarily a weapon used to attack one's enemies and was not crucial to any party's ideology, this does not mean that it was nothing more than pure demagoguery and was not sincerely believed by its proponents. The minutes of the GDVP's committee of "experts" on the Jewish question provide us with chilling evidence to the contrary. Moreover, the demagogic character of political anti-Semitism also meant that there was never a realistic possibility of Jews eliminating anti-Semitism or escaping its consequences by changing their professions, political affiliations, religious beliefs, or their desire to integrate with Christians. To a certain extent the post–World War II phenomenon of "anti-Semitism without Jews" already existed before the war. The anti-Semites did not require real live Jews to hate; the mythical Jew sufficed, or even the "Jewish spirit."

However, it was also this highly abstract nature of anti-Semitism that enabled most Austrian Jews—especially those who lived outside the heavily Jewish district of Leopoldstadt or who did not attend a university—to lead fairly normal lives during the First Republic, often suffering few if any anti-Semitic insults or physical assaults. Anti-Semitism was almost entirely a war of words fought between the anti-Semites themselves. Each party wanted to prove that its anti-Semitism was superior to all the others. Only rarely did anti-Semitism involve direct confrontations between Jews and anti-Semites.

None of this is meant to imply that anti-Semitism had no practical consequences for Austrian Jews. On the contrary, the six decades of political and private anti-Semitism and all the propaganda that accompanied it made the anti-Semitism of both the Austrian and German Nazis seem neither novel nor particularly radical. Indeed, the sad fact is that prior to the Anschluss the Austrian Nazis had not proposed, and the Nazi government in Germany had not enacted, any legislation that had not already been demanded by the Antisemitenbund, Leopold Kunschak's "Workers' Association," the Greater German People's Party, and in some cases even the Christian Social Party and the Social Democratic Party. The Austrian Nazis simply combined all the earlier forms of religious, economic, and racial anti-Semitism. They could now also legitimately claim that their brethren in Germany had the courage actually to do what Austrian anti-Semites merely talked about. In fact, when Austrian Judeophobes commented on Nazi anti-Semitism at all, it was mostly to complain about its moderation, not its severity.

After the Anschluss the Nazis quickly enacted the anti-Semitic legislation that Austrian anti-Semites themselves had long demanded. The handful of Jews who held civil service jobs or were the managers of banks and large industries were dismissed in a matter of days. Jewish pupils were segregated into separate schools, and Jewish university students were reduced to their percentage of Austria's population (or less) and finally expelled altogether. Some Austrians were offended by the violence perpetrated against Jews, especially during the November Pogrom, but not enough to make the kinds of united and successful public protest that the Christian wives of some 6,000 Berlin Jews made in February 1943 after their husbands had been arrested and were about to be deported to death camps, or that the Catholic Church made to reinstate crucifixes in public classrooms in Bavaria in October 1944.[6] When the deportation of Austrian Jews began in 1941, it too simply fulfilled a demand that such politicians as Leopold Kunschak and Walter Riehl had made more than twenty years earlier, although neither man probably envisioned the murder of the deportees.

Even though it is impossible to prove in any empirical way, it is also highly probable that six decades of anti-Semitic propaganda had left Austrian Jews so isolated socially that few Christians were willing to help them in their hour of mortal danger. To argue otherwise is to suggest that propaganda has absolutely no influence on the public no matter how often it is repeated over no matter how long a time. This is not a thesis that the advertising industry would readily accept. The stereotype of the greedy, unscrupulous, lustful, and revolutionary Jew had already been firmly implanted in the Austrian mind long before any-one had heard of National Socialism. From an anti-Semitism of words it was only one small step to an anti-Semitism of deeds.

Should we conclude from all this that the Nazis merely followed in the foot-steps of earlier Austrian anti-Semites with no qualitative differences? No simple answers to this question are readily available. Certainly the more traditional anti-Semites must not have approved of the public humiliations of the Jews that occurred in the first days following the Anschluss. And no doubt many of them did recoil in horror at the deliberate destruction of Jewish religious houses during the November Pogrom. The anti-Semitism they advocated was "legal," nonviolent, and "respectable." The *Reichspost* had on numerous occa-sions denounced anti-Semitic violence at the University of Vienna as being harmful to the anti-Semitic cause. The Nuremberg Laws of 1935 were un-doubtedly framed to appeal to this kind of traditional anti-Semitism. And yet the imposition of a numerus clausus on professional positions held by Jews and the elimination or drastic reduction of Jewish "influence" over Austria's cultural and economic life would have resulted in massive unemployment for middle-class and upper-middle-class Jews and their forced emigration. Such an outcome would not have been altogether different from that which actually occurred in Germany after 1933, all the more so since traditional Austrian anti-Semites were unwilling to open up the civil service to Jews.

THE ETERNAL OPTIMISTS

While the war of words was raging between anti-Semites, a curiously parallel verbal battle was taking place among Austrian Jews. If anti-Semites vehemently denounced their opponents as being soft on Jews and promoted themselves as the best anti-Semites, Austrian Jews likewise accused each other of playing into the hands of anti-Semites while they themselves represented the best of Jewry. This is not to imply a kind of moral equivalency between Jews and anti-Semites. The Jewish "civil war" was to a large extent a war for survival dictated by the rise of modern political anti-Semitism. Of course, a struggle within the Jewish community in Austria and other countries would have existed in any event over the role of Jews and Judaism in the postemancipation world. However, it is reasonable to assume that it would have been fought at a much lower level of intensity had it not been for the vicious attacks of anti-Semites, which called into question whether it was even possible for Jews to survive, let alone assimilate, in a predominantly gentile as well as predominantly secularized modern world.

The Jewish war of words in interwar Austria, like the domestic politics of contemporary Israel, was so intense for the simple reason that it involved absolutely fundamental philosophical issues that might very well determine whether the Jews would survive as an identifiable group. Each Jewish faction was profoundly convinced that in the long run—and all Jews were ultimately more concerned about the distant future than the present—their philosophy would insure survival. By contrast, the philosophy of their opponents would allegedly guarantee either the end of Jewry as a separate religion or as a separate community—the argument of the Zionists—or a permanent status of legal and social inferiority, which was the position of the assimilationists organized in the Union of Austrian Jews. More crucial issues can hardly be imagined. Unfortunately, none of the philosophies of the various Jewish factions would have assured the survival of the Austrian Jews. Not only did they badly divide the Jewish community at a time when unity was desperately needed, but they also encouraged illusions about the future and weakened the urge for self-defense.

The assimilationists, clinging to their liberal belief in the goodness and rationality of mankind, were sure that the revival of anti-Semitism after 1914 had been caused merely by temporary military, political, and economic circumstances that in time would disappear. In a sense they were correct, but 65,000 Austrian Jews did not live to witness the remission of anti-Semitism after the Second World War. In the meantime, the long-held assimilationist desire to blend into the local population contradicted the need to defend themselves as Jews.

The Zionists' belief that anti-Semitism was permanent implied that any effort to combat it was essentially futile. Occasional positive comments from Catholics and even pan-Germans about Zionism encouraged them to feel that Nazis would also leave them alone if only they voluntarily withdrew from the gentile community. Orthodox Jews were convinced that anti-Semitism was being inflicted on the Jews, especially assimilationist Jews, by God as punishment for abandoning the traditional faith. The anti-Semitic threat could therefore be overcome simply by returning to Orthodoxy.

Jewish hopes for survival also rested to a very large extent on their ability to survive so many apparently similar dangers in the past. Six decades of anti-Semitic agitation accompanied by next to nothing in the way of concrete anti-Semitic legislation played a central role in giving Austrian Jews a false sense of security. Adolf Hitler recognized this fact in *Mein Kampf* when he cynically observed that "the Jew is so accustomed to this type of [Christian Social] anti-Semitism that he would have missed its disappearance more than its presence inconvenienced him."[7]

The Jews' ability to survive every historical crisis, including the one created by the Nazis, was repeatedly emphasized by all the Jewish newspapers of Vienna. Soon after the German Nazis became a mass movement in the fall of 1930, *Die Wahrheit* commented that "Judaism has already endured so much that it will also overcome Hitler and Goebbels."[8] A few days after Hitler's Machtergreifung in January 1933, the same newspaper warned that the new Nazi regime would be a serious testing time for German Jews. However, "for us Viennese Jews the developments [in Germany] are nothing new. We experienced the same thing during the rise of the Christian Social Party. Lueger's takeover of power was harmful to the livelihood of Jewish peddlers, Jewish municipal civil servants, teachers, etc., but the Jewish representatives of big capital established new business ties which were advantageous for both sides."[9] In July 1935, *Die Wahrheit* still considered the Nazi regime in Germany no more than a "passing phenomenon" that would not deflect the Union of Austrian Jews from its assimilationist philosophy.[10]

The Unionist organ was not the only newspaper to express such illusions. The *Jüdische Arbeiter* thought that the Jewish "will to live [was] stronger than the hardest blow that can hit us."[11] *Die Stimme* was a little more cautious, saying that it was wrong to say that Jews would endure the present threat because Jews had endured the persecutions of Haman (an ancient Persian prime minister) and Torquemada (the head of the Spanish Inquisition in the 1480s). Jews had survived then because they were united, true to their beliefs, and selfless. They would survive again in Hitler's day, but only if they united behind the blue and white flag of Zionism. Divided into parties the Jewish people were nothing. But united they were a mass that could determine their own fate. The Jewish people might be weak, but they were eternal. Jewry had experienced harder times than the present one. Soon there would be a reaction to Hitler.[12]

What most Austrian (and also German and French) Jews forgot was that they had survived popular outbursts of anti-Semitism so often in the past because they had enjoyed the protection of emperors, bishops, abbots, and aristocrats.[13] Under Hitler, however, legal authority changed from being the protector of Jews to their persecutor. The *Jüdische Front*, the mouthpiece of the League of Jewish Front Fighters, was virtually alone in debunking the idea that Jews would survive Hitler because they had survived so many hardships in the past. This was a dangerous error, the paper warned, that only made the Jews passive. In the past Jews had been able to escape persecution by simply emigrating to another country where there was no hostility toward Jews. This option no longer existed for the Jewish masses because all countries had (in the only slightly exaggerated words of the *Jüdische Front*) "hermetically sealed their borders."[14]

THE QUESTION OF RESPONSIBILITY

By now it should be obvious to the reader that anti-Semitism was hardly an imported item brought into Austria from Germany by Nazi Party officials in 1938. Although Austrian anti-Semitism cannot be divorced from its European context, it had been thriving on Austrian soil since the Middle Ages. For centuries it was nourished by the Catholic clergy, who taught the faithful that Jews were collectively and hereditarily responsible for the murder of Jesus. The prosperity of the last seventeen years preceding the First World War only temporarily cooled anti-Semitic passions in Austria.

This hopeful trend was suddenly and catastrophically ended in 1914. The Russian invasion of the Austrian crownlands of Galicia and Bukovina inaugurated one of the greatest mass migrations of Jews in modern European history and contributed to starvation conditions in Vienna unsurpassed anywhere else in Central or Western Europe. The breakup of the Austro-Hungarian Monarchy—which might have occurred in any case, but which was actively encouraged by the Allied Powers in 1918—was a near death blow to the Austrian economy, from which the country never fully recovered during the entire interwar period.

This combination of political and economic conditions produced the most extreme form of anti-Semitism found anywhere in Central or Western Europe during the interwar years, although it is highly unlikely that Austrian anti-Semitism was as extreme as that found in Poland, the Ukraine, Lithuania, Hungary, or Rumania.[15] Even though Austrian anti-Semitism was undoubtedly radicalized by the growing success of the German Nazis after 1930, not to mention more directly after the Anschluss, it would be utterly false to claim that this influence always flowed from north to south. As we have seen, private organizations such as academic fraternities and sporting clubs in Austria aggressively and successfully persuaded their German comrades to adopt more radical and racial forms of anti-Semitism. This influence was even more obvious after the Anschluss when Austrian Nazis were at times ahead of their German Parteigenossen in the persecution of Jews; they sometimes created organizations (and accelerated the drive for persecution) that were later adopted for the entire Third Reich.

Strong and pervasive as Austrian anti-Semitism undoubtedly was between the late 1870s and 1938, blanket generalizations must be avoided. Not all Austrians, after all, were anti-Semitic, let alone fanatically committed to the ideology. Nor were they equally responsible for advocating the prejudice. Undoubtedly the worst offenders were leading politicians, especially those having no executive powers themselves. Anti-Semitism was a kind of sport from which few politicians wished to be excluded. They competed with each other for the votes of the anti-Semitic electorate or at least (in the case of the Social Democrats) to avoid the dreaded "stigma" of being the "protective guard" of the Jews.

Only slightly less responsible for the spread of anti-Semitism were Roman Catholic clergy like Father Georg Bichlmair, and Catholic journalists like Friedrich Funder and Josef Eberle, the editor of *Schönere Zukunft*. Most Catholic spokesmen, such as Bishop Johannes Gföllner, at least warned against racism and violence. Many Catholics, however, openly called for boycotting Jewish businesses as well as publications authored by Jews. Above all their denunciations of alleged "Jewish" capitalism, materialism, secularism, liberalism, and socialism still carried enormous weight with a large segment of the Austrian public and went a long way in stereotyping the Jews as alien and corrupting.

Much less numerous and therefore less influential than the Catholic anti-Semites, but still very important, were university professors and administrators. The very people who should have been the most enlightened and tolerant of differing political, economic, and intellectual ideas instead were frequently active promoters of anti-Semitism or at least stood by and did little or nothing to combat it. The anti-Semitic violence at the University of Vienna and other Austrian universities was an almost unabating scandal, which administrators were either unwilling or unable to suppress. With few exceptions (one being the rectorship of Theodor Innitzer in 1928–29), the most they would do would be to close the affected institution for a few days—an action that hurt the innocent as much as the guilty—and perhaps scold the perpetrators for their "excessive" but nevertheless "understandable" actions. The idea of actually expelling students who broke up lectures and physically assaulted their Jewish classmates apparently never occurred to them until suggested by the American minister to Austria, Gilchrist Baker Stockton.

Compared with these other groups, the record of the imperial government of Austria and the federal government of the First Republic, though far from untarnished, was fairly good especially between 1867 and 1914. Even in the Middle Ages and early modern times Austrian Jews were generally able to look to the imperial government for protection, although there were some obvious exceptions as in 1421 and 1670, when Habsburg rulers expelled Jews from Vienna. During the reign of Joseph II in the 1780s, Austria became the European leader in emancipating Jews from medieval economic, cultural, social, and political restrictions. During most of the incredibly long reign of Franz Joseph (1848–1916), Austrian Jews made impressive progress in almost all aspects of life with the partial exception of social integration.

The record of the republican government of Austria was less admirable than that of Franz Joseph's administration. Still, at worst the government tolerated anti-Semitic demonstrations and publications, and after 1934 occasionally gave in to anti-Semitic demands for the limitation of Jewish "influence." Unlike Nazi Germany, however, the Austrian government followed rather than led public opinion and did at least protect Jews from violence. Consequently, Austrian Jews confidently continued to look to the government for protection almost literally up to the eleventh hour of the eleventh day of March 1938. This tradition of the government occasionally appeasing anti-Semitic feelings—as shown in the reluctance to grant reparations for the Jewish victims of Nazism—while protecting the physical and economic welfare of the Jewish population of Austria has at times reappeared during the Second Republic.

AMERICAN AND AUSTRIAN RACISM AND
THE PASSING OF MORAL JUDGMENTS

It is tempting for Americans, and no doubt other nationalities as well, to pass moral judgments on Austria for its history of anti-Semitism. After all, anti-Semitic violence has been almost unknown in American history. Moreover, the government of the United States played a surprisingly important role in restraining anti-Semitism in Austria during the early post–World War I years by threatening to withhold shipments of food; in 1932–33, when the American minister to Austria denounced physical assaults against American Jewish students at the University of Vienna; and finally, after the Second World War, in pressuring the Austrian government into compensating Jewish victims.

Yet these praiseworthy actions do not tell the whole story of American involvement in Austrian anti-Semitism. It is a sobering fact that Austrian anti-Semites were frequently inspired by American anti-Semitism and other forms of racism. It can hardly be argued that American racism *caused* Austrian anti-Semitism or evenly significantly influenced it. Austrian anti-Semites were, however, frequently inspired by it or at least grateful for the opportunity to justify beliefs they already held.

References to American anti-Semitism and racism can be found in Austrian newspapers at least as early as the 1880s. It should be recalled that Georg von Schönerer drafted a law to prohibit Jewish immigration to Vienna that was a verbatim copy of the American Chinese exclusion law. Austrian anti-Semites, including Adolf Hitler, were particularly impressed with the anti-Semitic publications of the American automobile magnate, Henry Ford, especially in his book, *The International Jew*.[16] The Antisemitenbund was convinced that its proposals for discriminatory legislation against Jews were moderate in comparison with the rights accorded to Negroes, Indians, and Chinese in the United States, who were not even allowed to sit next to whites on streetcars or restaurants.[17] The Nazis' *Deutsche Arbeiter-Presse* was pleased to report on the existence of the Ku Klux Klan with its 5 million members who were opposed to Jews of every description.[18] *Schönere Zukunft* pointed out that the 1.6 million Jews of New York were so thoroughly rejected socially that not even the richest among them could get into the most prestigious private clubs. Moreover, elite private universities on the East Coast strictly limited the enrollment of Jewish students during the interwar years and beyond.[19]

Most disturbing of all for Americans is the fact that even horrifying stories about the November Pogrom in the American press did not appreciably reduce anti-Semitism. In 1938, 70 to 85 percent of all Americans objected to the raising of quotas in order to help Jewish refugees. Furthermore, between 1938 and 1942 between 10 and 15 percent of the Americans polled said they were willing to support actively government-sponsored anti-Semitism, another 20 percent were sympathetic to such a policy, and only a third said they were opposed. The peak of American anti-Semitism was not even reached until 1944, eleven years after Hitler had come to power, six years after Kristallnacht, and two years after the first reports about the Holocaust reached the United States.[20]

The incarceration of 120,000 Japanese-Americans in internment camps, whose only crime was to be of Japanese descent (in some cases people who, unbeknownst to themselves, had only one Japanese great-great-grandparent),[21] produced no movement of protest remotely comparable to Irene Harand's "World Organization against Racial Hatred and Human Need." When the mayor of Tacoma, Washington, spoke out against the deportation, he was promptly defeated for reelection. Nor can the imprisonment of the Japanese-Americans be excused on the grounds that it was an unfortunate military necessity. Most of the deportees were incarcerated *after* the Battle of Midway in June 1942, which ended even the remote possibility of a Japanese invasion of the West Coast.

Americans and other critics of Austria must also remind themselves that something like 80 percent of the population of contemporary Austria was at most no more than small children during the Holocaust, let alone in any way actively involved in it. To be sure, far more Austrians (and other European nationalities) were in some sense guilty of crimes against humanity than those few people in decision-making positions. They included bureaucrats who methodically carried out orders to persecute Jews, people who gleefully confiscated Jewish businesses and homes, and numerous authors of anti-Semitic smut like Robert Körber. Nevertheless, the concept of collective guilt ignores individual responsibility and lumps together the monstrously guilty, like Adolf Hitler and Adolf Eichmann, with the ardent opponents of anti-Semitism like Irene Harand and Richard Coudenhove-Kalergi. It also bears an uncomfortable resemblance to the Nazi dogma of inherited racial characteristics and the medieval Catholic dogma that Jews were collectively and hereditarily responsible for the crucifixion of Jesus.

However inadequate the Austrian government has been in compensating Jewish survivors, and however real the remnants of anti-Semitism are in contemporary Austria, it is nevertheless beyond doubt that the Austrians have made great progress in combating anti-Semitism since the Second World War. Anti-Semitic brawls at the University of Vienna and giant anti-Semitic demonstrations in the streets of the capital city, such as those that characterized the First Republic, have been rare in the Second Republic and unknown since 1965.

Although it is both unfair and politically counterproductive for outside observers to hold the great majority of the Austrian people of today even partially responsible for the Holocaust, Austrians, for their part, should also not treat the Holocaust and their anti-Semitic past as though they were things that occurred on another continent or in another century. If collective guilt deserves to be rejected, a collective responsibility to remember ought to be embraced. Even though Austrian anti-Semitism today is vastly weaker than it was a half century ago, both Austrian and world history demonstrate the remarkable ability of the prejudice to survive long periods of dormancy. All that is required is a political, economic, or social crisis. National traditions are often enormously tenacious and do not disappear simply by being ignored. Austrian anti-Semitism certainly qualifies as such a national tradition. Moreover, recent public opinion polls show that about a third of the Austrian population is susceptible to anti-Semitism.[22] This fact is perhaps less significant for the tiny Jewish population of Austria in the 1990s, which now at least has the option of moving to Israel if necessary, than it is for Austrian democracy, which can still be corrupted by anti-Semitic demagoguery.

Another, no doubt lesser known Austrian tradition is the protection of minority rights. Anyone who doubts this need only compare the fate of national minorities in the Austro-Hungarian Monarchy with that of most of the successor states of interwar East Central Europe.[23] This other tradition is shortchanged when Austrian anti-Semites are rehabilitated and the defenders of Jews are neglected. For example, a person like Leopold Kunschak, who as late as December 1945 boasted that he was a life-long anti-Semite, is today revered as one of the great founders of the Second Republic. In 1978 he was even honored with a stamp on the twenty-fifth anniversary of his death[24] and a housing project has been named for him in the Lower Austrian town of St. Polten.

On the other hand, the incredible bravery of Irene Harand has gone largely unrecognized. She was lucky enough to be in England at the time of the Anschluss and then lived out the rest of her life in exile in New York where she continued her struggle against anti-Semitism and other forms of prejudice both during and after the Second World War before dying in almost total obscurity in 1975. In December 1969, however, Yad Vashem, the Holocaust memorial and research center in Jerusalem, did honor her with a medallion and a certificate testifying to her activities on behalf of persecuted Jews and made her one of the "Righteous Gentiles." A year later, on her seventieth birthday, the Austrian government decorated her for her opposition to National Socialism.[25] Until very recently, however, she remained almost completely forgotten in her own country. This fate may now at last be changing, however. A housing project (appropriately) on the Judengasse in Vienna's first district was named for her in a formal ceremony in early 1990 at which time her life-long achievements were lauded by Mayor Helmut Zilk and District Manager Dr. Richard Schmitz.[26] A heroine of truly international stature, she represents the very highest humanitarian and Austrian values. Her story should be told in every Austrian school.

NOTES

PREFACE

1. Fellner, "Der Novemberpogrom 1938," p. 40.
2. Johnston, *Austrian Mind*, p. 23.
3. Heer, "Judentum und österreichischer Genius," p. 295.
4. Coudenhove-Kalergi, *Anti-Semitism throughout the Ages*, p. 267.
5. Bauer, *History of the Holocaust*, p. 67.
6. Wyman, *Paper Walls*, pp. 47, 95.
7. *Washington Post*, 29 December 1987, p. A10.

CHAPTER 1

1. For a recent discussion of the definitions of fascism, see Allardyce, "What Fascism Is Not."
2. Lebzelter, *Political Anti-Semitism in England*, p. 3.
3. Quoted in Carlebach, *Karl Marx*, p. 348.
4. Grosser and Halperin, *The Causes and Effects of Anti-Semitism*, p. 315.
5. Coudenhove-Kalergi, *Anti-Semitism throughout the Ages*, p. 246.
6. Arkel, "Anti-Semitism in Austria," p. 193; Spira, *Feindbild "Jud,"* p. 83.
7. Pulzer, *Political Anti-Semitism*, p. 300; Maderegger, *Juden im Ständestaat*, p. 182.
8. Wachter, "Antisemitismus im Vereinswesen," pp. 37–38.
9. See, for example, *DAP*, 4 October 1919, p. 2; Amelung, "Die Judenfrage in christlicher Schau," p. 450; Peter, *Der Antisemitismus*, p. 6.
10. Klose et al., eds., *Katholische Soziallexikon*, p. 75.
11. *EB*, 16 April 1927, p. 1.
12. Weinzierl, "Stereotypen," p. 265.
13. The book was written by Christian Loge.
14. *JIZ*, January 1935, pp. 7–8.

15. Glockemeier, *Wiener Judenfrage*, p. 100; Pötsch, *Jüdische Rasse*, pp. 24–25, 61; Drexel, *Judenfrage*, p. 8.

16. *Juden im Staate Deutsch-Österreich*, pp. 4–9.

17. Glockemeier, *Wiener Judenfrage*, p. 95.

18. Drexel, *Judenfrage*, p. 9.

19. *DÖTZ*, 25 September 1928. Quoted in Schilling[-Schletter], *Walter Riehl*, p. 112.

20. Pötsch, *Jüdische Rasse*, p. 43.

21. Ibid.

22. Ibid., pp. 32, 34.

23. Fellner, *Antisemitismus in Salzburg*, p. 85. According to one Jewish source they were in fact convicted in thirteen of twenty-eight cases involving profiteering between 1911 and 1913 and six of twenty convictions between 1922 and 1924. See Goldhammer, *Juden Wiens*, p. 48.

24. Interviews with Ernest Rapp and Rose Hoffman.

25. Pötsch, *Jüdische Rasse*, pp. 30, 42. Pötsch cites the figures for Jewish crimes against property on p. 72 but draws no conclusions from them.

26. Pulzer, *Political Anti-Semitism*, p. 52; *EB*, 1 June 1920, p. 1.

27. Menghin, *Geist und Blut*, pp. 160–61, 168.

28. Johnson, *History of the Jews*, p. 408; Gay, *Freud, Jews and Other Germans*, p. 21; Sachar, *Modern Jewish History*, p. 398.

29. Spira, *Feindbild "Jud,"* p. 28.

30. Cohn, *Warrant for Genocide*, p. 170.

31. Glockemeier, *Wiener Judenfrage*, p. 43; *EB*, 20 March 1921, p. 4; Cohn, *Warrant for Genocide*, pp. 13, 184–85; article by Walter Riehl in the *Wiener Nachtpost* for 12 June 1933 quoted by Schilling[-Schletter] in *Walter Riehl*, p. 117.

32. Mosse, *Toward the Final Solution*, p. 119.

33. *Anti-Semitism throughout the Ages*, pp. 258–59.

34. Cohn, *Warrant for Genocide*, pp. 62–63.

35. Ibid., p. 68.

36. Ibid., p. 69.

37. Coudenhove-Kalergi, *Anti-Semitism throughout the Ages*, pp. 259, 261.

38. Johnson, *History of the Jews*, pp. 452, 455; Marcus, *Rise and Destiny of the German Jew*, p. 92.

39. See, for example, the *DVB*, 17 March 1920, p. 1; and *EB*, 20 April 1921, pp. 1, 3.

40. Cohn, *Warrant for Genocide*, p. 138; Lebzelter, *Political Anti-Semitism in England*, pp. 24–27.

CHAPTER 2

1. Grunwald, *History of Jews in Vienna*, p. 51; Kubl, "Geschichte der jüdischen Advokaten," p. 118; Wistrich, *Jews of Vienna*, p. 6.

2. Schneider, "Juden in Klagenfurt," p. 41; Salzer-Eibenstein, "Juden in Graz," p. 9; Gerhartl, "Juden in Wiener Neustadt," p. 91; Grunwald, *History of Jews in Vienna*, pp. 45–46.

3. Maccoby, "The Origins of Anti-Semitism," p. 3; Bein, *Judenfrage*, pp. 52, 55, 85, 86, 88, 100.

4. Grunwald, *History of Jews in Vienna*, p. 45; Grosser and Halperin, *Causes and Effects of Anti-Semitism*, p. 341; Cohn, *Warrant for Genocide*, p. 22.

5. Gerhartl, "Juden in Wiener Neustadt," p. 92; Altmann, "Juden in Salzburg," pp. 70–71; Schwager, "Juden in Linz," p. 53.

6. Grunwald, *History of Jews in Vienna*, p. 36; Schmidl, *Juden in der Armee*, p. 96; Weinzierl, *Zu wenig Gerechte*, p. 12; Oxaal, "Jews of Young Hitler's Vienna," pp. 16–17.

7. Spira, *Feindbild "Jud,"* p. 9; Weinzierl, *Zu wenig Gerechte*, p. 12; Grunwald, *History of Jews in Vienna*, pp. 88–90, 105; Berkley, *Vienna and Its Jews*, p. 30.

8. Wistrich, *Jews of Vienna*, p. 8; Kienzl, "Der Österreicher und seine Schande," p. 655.

9. Quoted by Wangermann, *Austrian Achievement*, p. 48.

10. Kann, A *Study in Austrian Intellectual History*, p. 78.

11. Weinzierl, *Zu wenig Gerechte*, p. 13; McCagg, *Habsburg Jews*, p. 1.

12. Berkley, *Vienna and Its Jews*, p. 30; Oxaal, "Jews of Hitler's Vienna," p. 21.

13. Grunwald, *History of Jews in Vienna*, pp. 134–36, 142–43, 222; McCagg, *Habsburg Jews*, p. 49.

14. Quoted in Grunwald, *History of Jews in Vienna*, p. 139; *Stürmer*, 30 September 1933, p. 3.

15. Grunwald, *History of Jews in Vienna*, pp. 139, 143; McCagg, *Habsburg Jews*, p. 19.

16. *Juden in Oesterreich*, p. 5; Altmann, "Juden in Salzburg," p. 73.

17. Weinzierl, *Zu wenig Gerechte*, p. 14; Schmidl, *Juden in der Armee*, p. 112; Grunwald, *History of Jews in Vienna*, p. 152; Wistrich, *Jews of Vienna*, pp. 17–20.

18. Grunwald, *History of Jews in Vienna*, pp. 147, 152–55; Spira, *Feindbild "Jud,"* p. 21; McCagg, *Habsburg Jews*, p. 29.

19. Wistrich, *Jews of Vienna*, pp. 18–19; Low, *Jews in the Eyes of the Germans*, p. 23; Bein, *Judenfrage*, p. 198.

20. Wangermann, *Austrian Achievement*, p. 97; Low, *Jews in the Eyes of the Germans*, p. 216.

21. Weinzierl, *Zu wenig Gerechte*, p. 16; Wistrich, *Jews of Vienna*, p. 20; McCagg, *Habsburg Jews*, p. 51; Grunwald, *History of Jews in Vienna*, pp. 168, 173–74, 209–10.

22. Wistrich, *Jews of Vienna*, p. 24; McCagg, *Habsburg Jews*, pp. 54, 61, 63; Grunwald, *History of Jews in Vienna*, pp. 329–30.

23. Weinzierl, *Zu wenig Gerechte*, p. 17; Black, *Ernst Kaltenbrunner*, p. 17.

24. Low, *Jews in the Eyes of the Germans*, pp. 218, 220.

25. McCagg, *Habsburg Jews*, pp. 89, 94.

26. Rath, *Viennese Revolution*, p. 103; Grunwald, *History of Jews in Vienna*, pp. 262, 286–89.

338 : NOTES TO PAGES 20–28

27. Grunwald, *History of Jews in Vienna*, p. 289.

28. Ibid., pp. 277, 292, 294; Tietze, *Juden Wiens*, pp. 200, 206; Rothschild, "Juden in Hohenems," p. 32.

29. Simon, *Österreich 1918–1938*, p. 41; Rath, *Viennese Revolution*, p. 103.

30. Volkov, "The Written Matter and the Spoken Word," p. 39; Wistrich, *Jews of Vienna*, pp. 32–33.

31. Grunwald, *History of Jews in Vienna*, pp. 267, 298–99.

32. Ibid., p. 295.

33. Ibid., pp. 308–9, 324; Weinzierl, *Zu wenig Gerechte*, p. 19; Grun, *Franz Joseph*, pp. 8–9.

34. Weinzierl, *Zu wenig Gerechte*, p. 19; Grunwald, *History of Jews in Vienna*, p. 401.

35. Grunwald, *History of Jews in Vienna*, pp. 406–7.

36. Ibid., pp. 412–13; Weinzierl, *Zu wenig Gerechte*, p. 22; Häusler, "Toleranz, Emanzipation und Antisemitismus," p. 118; *BÖW*, 24 November 1916, pp. 761–62; Grun, *Franz Joseph*, p. 22.

37. Glockemeier, *Wiener Judenfrage*, p. 9; Schechter, *Viennese Vignettes*, p. 32.

38. Rosensaft, "Jews and Antisemites," p. 59.

39. *Juden in Oesterreich*, p. 9.

40. Weinzierl, *Zu wenig Gerechte*, p. 19.

41. Wistrich, *Jews of Vienna*, pp. 42–43; Cohen, "Jews in German Liberal Politics," pp. 68–69.

42. *Juden in Oesterreich*, p. 7; Wistrich, *Jews of Vienna*, p. 41.

43. Wistrich, *Socialism and the Jews*, p. 176.

44. Rozenblit, *Jews of Vienna*, p. 21; McCagg, *Habsburg Jews*, pp. 71, 177.

45. McCagg, *Habsburg Jews*, p. 184.

46. Johnson, *History of the Jews*, pp. 363–64.

47. Lebzelter, *Political Anti-Semitism in England*, pp. 7–8; Weinberg, *A Community on Trial*, p. 3; Johnson, *History of the Jews*, p. 395.

48. Salzer-Eibenstein, "Juden in Graz," p. 14; Barkai, *Von Boykott zur Entjudung*, p. 11.

49. *Juden in Oesterreich*, pp. 14–15; McCagg, *Habsburg Jews*, p. 196.

50. McCagg, *Habsburg Jews*, p. 191.

51. Pulzer, *Political Anti-Semitism*, pp. 30, 288.

52. Ibid., pp. 138, 296; McCagg, *Habsburg Jews*, pp. 177–78; Jaszi, *Dissolution of the Habsburg Monarchy*, pp. 173, 325–26.

53. Pulzer, "Spezifische Momente," p. 126; Pulzer, *Political Anti-Semitism*, pp. 144–45.

CHAPTER 3

1. Pulzer, "Spezifische Momente," p. 122.

2. Hitler, *Mein Kampf*, Ralph Manheim trans., p. 52.

3. Ibid., p. 56.

4. Bein, *Judenfrage*, pp. 218–20.

5. Ibid., p. 232; Massing, *Rehearsal for Destruction*, pp. 101–2; Carlebach, *Karl Marx*, pp. 346–47.

6. Zimmermann, *Wilhelm Marr*, pp. 112–13, 115; Mosse, *Final Solution*; Pulzer, *Political Anti-Semitism*, pp. 49–50; Massing, *Rehearsal for Destruction*, p. 7; Niewyk, "Solving the 'Jewish Problem,'" p. 351.

7. Volkov, "Antisemitism as a Cultural Code," pp. 42–43; Zmarzlik, "Antisemitismus im Deutschen Kaiserreich," p. 255.

8. Bein, *Judenfrage*, pp. 223–25; Pulzer, *Political Anti-Semitism*, pp. 52–53.

9. Niewyk, "Solving the 'Jewish Problem,'" p. 361.

10. Ibid., pp. 343–44; Stackelberg, *Idealism Debased*, p. 6; Niewyk, *Socialist, Anti-Semite, and Jew*, p. 20.

11. Bein, *Judenfrage*, p. 239; Rosenberg, *Grosse Depression und Bismarckzeit*, p. 92.

12. Weinzierl, "Antisemitismus als Phänomen," p. 31; Kampe, *Studenten und Judenfrage*, pp. 61, 101. For a discussion of the Great Depression and its impact on liberal thought, see Good, *Economic Rise of the Habsburg Empire*, pp. 163, 168, 172, 232.

13. *Juden in Oesterreich*, p. 99.

14. Ibid., p. 102.

15. See, for example, Molisch, *Hochschulen in Österreich*, p. 134, who cites the figures for 1890–91, but ignores subsequent years.

16. See, for example, *Unverfälschte deutsche Worte*, 16 May 1885, p. 1.

17. Streibel, "Judenfrage und Antisemitismus," p, 34.

18. Kofler, "Tirol und die Juden," p. 174.

19. *Juden in Oesterreich*, p. 101.

20. Ibid., p. 102.

21. Molisch, *Hochschulen in Österreich*, pp. 136–37.

22. Ibid., p. 120; Moser, "Katastrophe der Juden in Österreich 1938–1945," p. 85; Wistrich, *Jews of Vienna*, p. 216; Haag, "Academic Antisemitism," p. 4; Weinzierl, "Stellung der Juden in Österreich," p. 90.

23. Mosse, *Final Solution*, pp. 115–16; Nicosia, "Zionism in Antisemitic Thought," p. 9.

24. Beller, *Vienna and the Jews*, p. 166; Massing, *Rehearsal for Destruction*, p. 76.

25. Tietze, *Juden Wiens*, p. 242; Hein, *Studentischer Antisemitismus*, p. 75; Scheuer, *Burschenschaften und Judenfrage*, p. 46.

26. Pulzer, *Political Anti-Semitism*, p. 253; Synnott, "Anti-Semitism and American Universities," p. 237.

27. Scheuer, *Burschenschaften und Judenfrage*, pp. 45, 67; Pulzer, *Political Anti-Semitism*, pp. 255–56; Mosse, *Crisis of German Ideology*, p. 135; Kampe, *Studenten und Judenfrage*, p. 23.

28. Schnitzler, *Jugend in Wien*, p. 156; Scheuer, *Burschenschaften und Judenfrage*, pp. 49–50, 61; Berkley, *Vienna and Its Jews*, pp. 80–81.

29. Molisch, *Hochschulen in Österreich*, p. 132; Kampe, *Studenten und Judenfrage*, p. 203.

30. Molisch, *Hochschulen in Österreich*, p. 132; Kampe, *Studenten und Judenfrage*, p. 204; Kuppe, *Karl Lueger*, p. 62.

31. Molisch, *Hochschulen in Österreich*, pp. 126–28, 132.

32. Stadler, *Austria*, pp. 138–39.

33. Zweig, *World of Yesterday*, p. 25.

34. Whiteside, *Socialism of Fools*, pp. 89, 105.

35. Morton, *A Nervous Splendor*, p. 73.

36. Wache, "Land und Volk," p. 33; Hantsch, *Geschichte Österreichs*, 2:445; Fuchs, *Geistige Strömungen*, p. 182.

37. Quoted in Pulzer, *Political Anti-Semitism*, p. 153.

38. Wistrich, *Socialism and the Jews*, p. 225; Boyer, *Political Radicalism*, p. 64; Katz, *From Prejudice to Destruction*, p. 284. The franchise statistics are from Pulzer, *Political Anti-Semitism*, pp. 174–75.

39. Pulzer, *Political Anti-Semitism*, p. 295.

40. Boyer, *Political Radicalism*, pp. 92–93; McCagg, *Habsburg Jews*, p. 164; Moser, "Emanzipation zur antisemitischen Bewegung," pp. 61, 65. The quotation is from Karbach, "Grundlagen des Antisemitismus," p. 4.

41. Kuppe, *Karl Lueger*, p. 56; Moser, "Emanzipation zur antisemitischen Bewegung," p. 49; McCagg, *Habsburg Jews*, p. 164; Carsten, *Rise of Fascism*, p. 34.

42. Boyer, *Political Radicalism*, p. 98; Moser, "Emanzipation zur antisemitischen Bewegung," pp. 63–64; Berkley, *Vienna and Its Jews*, p. 94.

43. Kuppe, *Karl Leuger*, p. 61; Molisch, *Hochschulen in Österreich*, p. 125; Moser, "Emanzipation zur antisemitischen Bewegung," pp. 50, 53.

44. Moser, "Emanzipation zur antisemitischen Bewegung," p. 66; Whiteside, *Socialism of Fools*, p. 113; Kuppe, *Karl Lueger*, p. 195; Wistrich, *Socialism and the Jews*, pp. 195, 201.

45. Fuchs, *Geistige Strömungen*, p. 296, n. 10; Pulzer, *Political Anti-Semitism*, pp. 159–60.

46. Whiteside, *Socialism of Fools*, pp. 217, 282, 316.

47. May, *Hapsburg Monarchy*, p. 47; Boyer, *Political Radicalism*, p. 418.

48. May, *Hapsburg Monarchy*, p. 48.

49. Katz, *Prejudice to Destruction*, p. 227; Streibel, "Judenfrage und Antisemitismus," p. 18; Macartney, *Habsburg Monarchy*, pp. 458, 574.

50. Heer, *Gottes erste Liebe*, pp. 354, 357.

51. Pulzer, *Political Anti-Semitism*, pp. 132–34; Tietze, *Juden Wiens*, p. 239; Spira, *Feindbild "Jud,"* pp. 22–23; Mosse, *Final Solution*, p. 138.

52. Pulzer, *Political Anti-Semitism*, pp. 167, 207; Rosensaft, "Jews and Antisemites," pp. 75, 81–82; Wistrich, *Jews of Vienna*, p. 229; Schorske, *Fin-de-Siècle Vienna*, pp. 133, 140, 145–46.

53. Botz, "*Anschluss* to Holocaust," p. 186; Wistrich, *Socialism and the Jews*, p. 199; Boyer, *Political Radicalism*, p. 78.

54. Holzmann, "Antisemitismus in österr. Innenpolitik," p. 16; Pulzer, *Political Anti-Semitism*, p. 272; Charmatz, *Deutsch-österreichische Politik*, p. 94; Braunthal,

Tragedy of Austria, p. 61; Boyer, *Political Radicalism*, pp. 43, 46–47. The quotation is from Boyer, *Political Radicalism*, p. 70.

55. Charmatz, *Deutsch-österreichische Politik*, p. 94.

56. Katz, *Prejudice to Destruction*, p. 285. The quotation is from Charmatz, *Deutsch-österreichische Politik*, pp. 96–97.

57. Wistrich, *Socialism and the Jews*, p. 192; Pulzer, *Political Anti-Semitism*, p. 174; Kuppe, *Karl Lueger*, p. 196. The quotation is from Holzmann, "Antisemitismus in österr. Innenpolitik," p. 174.

58. Charmatz, *Deutsch-österreichische Politik*, pp. 95–96; Karbach, "Grundlagen des Antisemitismus," p. 111. The quotation is from Boyer, *Political Radicalism*, p. xiii.

59. May, *Hapsburg Monarchy*, pp. 309–11; Wistrich, *Jews of Vienna*, p. 205.

60. Tietze, *Juden Wiens*, p. 252.

61. Boyer, *Political Radicalism*, p. 418.

62. Pulzer, "Austrian Liberals," p. 142.

63. *Political Anti-Semitism*, p. 135.

CHAPTER 4

1. Beller, "Class, Culture and the Jews of Vienna," p. 52.

2. Wassermann, *My Life as a German and a Jew*, pp. 186–87.

3. *MU*, May–June 1914, p. 18.

4. Berkley, *Vienna and Its Jews*, p. 105; Geehr, *Karl Lueger*, p. 312.

5. Quoted in Kann, *A Study in Austrian Intellectual History*, p. 112n.

6. Berkley, *Vienna and Its Jews*, p. 106; Gold, *Geschichte der Juden in Wien*, p. 40; Good, *Economic Rise of the Habsburg Monarchy*, pp. 165, 240–41.

7. Wistrich, *Jews of Vienna*, pp. 236–37; Geehr, *Karl Lueger*, pp. 292–93, 360; Boyer, "Karl Lueger and the Viennese Jews," p. 128.

8. Weinzierl, "Die Stellung der Juden in Österreich," p. 89.

9. Schwager, "Juden in Linz," p. 57; Altmann, "Juden in Salzburg," p. 78.

10. Pulzer, *Political Anti-Semitism*, p. 202.

11. Wistrich, *Socialism and the Jews*, p. 298.

12. *Political Anti-Semitism*, p. 290. The quotation is from p. 219.

13. Carsten, *Fascist Movements in Austria*, p. 15.

14. *Wahrheit*, 8 March 1918, p. 3.

15. Petting [pseudonym for Petwaidi-Petting], *Wiens antisemitische Presse*, p. 12.

16. Ibid., p. 8; Jenks, *Vienna and the Young Hitler*, p. 133.

17. Hitler, *Mein Kampf*, p. 55.

18. Petting, *Wiens antisemitische Presse*, pp. 14–18; ODR, 8 August 1919, p. 1.

19. Hanisch, "Nationalsozialismus in Salzburg," p. 373.

20. Oxaal, "Jews of Young Hitler's Vienna," p. 64.

21. Hitler, *Mein Kampf*, p. 52.

22. Pollak, "Cultural Innovation," p. 64; Petting, *Wiens antisemitische Presse*, p. 22; Grunwald, *History of Jews in Vienna*, p. 324; Tietze, *Juden Wiens*, p. 258.

23. Grunwald, *History of Jews in Vienna*, p. 442; Heer, *Gottes erste Liebe*, p. 301.

24. Grunwald, *History of Jews in Vienna*, pp. 367, 370; Weinzierl, *Zu wenig Gerechte*, p. 22.

25. Weinzierl, "Stereotypen," pp. 261–62; Mosse, *Final Solution*, p. 140; Mosse, *Crisis of German Ideology*, pp. 129–30; Grunwald, *History of Jews in Vienna*, pp. 430, 433; Berkley, *Vienna and Its Jews*, pp. 77–78.

26. Berkley, *Vienna and Its Jews*, p. 78.

27. Quoted by Weinzierl in "Stereotypen," pp. 262–63.

28. Ibid., p. 263.

29. Ibid.; Grunwald, *History of Jews in Vienna*, pp. 437, 447.

30. Wistrich, *Jews of Vienna*, p. 297.

31. *BÖW*, 2 January 1914; Weitzmann, "Politics of the Viennese Jewish Community," p. 128; Grunwald, *History of Jews in Vienna*, p. 444; Wistrich, *Jews of Vienna*, pp. 287, 298.

32. Bloch, *Erinnerungen*, 3:267; Grunwald, *History of Jews in Vienna*, pp. 439, 441–42; *BÖW*, 2 January 1914, p. 2; Weitzmann, "Politics of the Viennese Jewish Community," p. 127.

33. Wistrich, *Jews of Vienna*, pp. 289, 291; Bloch, *Erinnerungen*, 1:201; Rozenblit, *Jews of Vienna*, p. 155.

34. Bloch, *Erinnerungen*, 1:202; Weitzmann, "Politics of the Viennese Jewish Community," p. 129; Wistrich, *Jews of Vienna*, p. 193.

35. Toury, "Defense Activities," pp. 168–69, 187, 189.

36. Wistrich, *Jews of Vienna*, pp. 199–200, 291.

37. Rosensaft, "Jews and Antisemites in Austria," p. 71; Wistrich, *Jews of Vienna*, pp. 186–87, 190; Levy, *Anti-Semitic Political Parties in Imperial Germany*, p. 146; Schorsch, *Jewish Reactions to German Anti-Semitism*, p. 83; Weinzierl, "Antisemitismus als Phänomen," p. 32.

38. Daviau, "Hermann Bahr," pp. 25–27.

39. Ibid., pp. 22–25.

40. Wistrich, *Socialism and the Jews*, p. 310; Sacher, *Modern Jewish History*, p. 261.

41. Wistrich, *Jews of Vienna*, pp. 348, 362, 366; Rozenblit, "The Assertion of Identity," pp. 177–78, 182; Schoeps, "Modern Heirs of the Maccabees," pp. 155, 164, 168.

42. Bihl, "Jews of Austria-Hungary," p. 9; McCagg, *Habsburg Jews*, p. 199.

43. Wistrich, *Jews of Vienna*, p. 407; Berkley, *Vienna and Its Jews*, p. 114. The quotation is from Johnson, *History of the Jews*, p. 391. Some highly assimilated Jews went so far as to give their small children Christmas presents and Easter eggs. See Clare, *Last Waltz in Vienna*, p. 272.

44. Grunwald, *History of Jews in Vienna*, p. 451; Schorske, *Fin-de-Siècle Vienna*, p. 162; Wistrich, *Jews of Vienna*, pp. 443–44.

45. Sachar, *Modern Jewish History*, p. 270; Poppel, *Zionism in Germany*, p. 41; Schorske, *Fin-de-Siècle Vienna*, p. 172; Wistrich, *Jews of Vienna*, pp. 452–53.

46. Tietze, *Juden Wiens*, p. 265; Laqueur, *History of Zionism*, pp. 96, 98, 398–401,

404–7; Johnston, *Austrian Mind*, p. 359; Grayzel, *History of the Jews*, pp. 578–79; Grunwald, *History of Jews in Vienna*, pp. 452–53. The quotation is from Wistrich, *Socialism and the Jews*, p. 213.

47. Berkley, *Vienna and Its Jews*, pp. 117, 122; Oxaal and Weitzmann, "The Jews in Pre-1914 Vienna," p. 418; Weitzmann, "Politics of the Viennese Jewish Community," pp. 146–47; Wistrich, *Jews of Vienna*, p. 192; Freidenreich, *Jewish Politics in Vienna*, p. 72; Laqueur, *History of Zionism*, p. 398.

48. Weitzmann, "Politics of the Viennese Jewish Community," pp. 122–23; Laqueur, *History of Zionism*, p. 389; McCagg, *Habsburg Jews*, p. 4; Janik, "Viennese Culture and Jewish Self-hatred," p. 84.

49. Rozenblit, *Jews of Vienna*, p. 127. The desire to avoid paying taxes to the Jewish Gemeinde was significant in Graz, and we can safely assume in Vienna as well. See Salzer-Eibenstein, "Juden in Graz," p. 15.

50. Tietze, *Juden Wiens*, p. 205; Bihl, "Jews of Austria-Hungary," p. 4; Rozenblit, *Jews of Vienna*, p. 32; Oxaal, "Jews of Young Hitler's Vienna," p. 32.

51. Goldhammer, *Juden Wiens*, p. 32; Goldfarb interview; Schmidl, *Juden in der Armee*, p. 134; Beller, *Vienna and the Jews*, p. 35; *Juden in Oesterreich*, pp. 69–72, 75.

52. Cohen, "Jews in German Society," p. 39; Oxaal and Weitzmann, "The Jews in Pre-1914 Vienna," p. 405; Wistrich, *Jews of Vienna*, p. 48.

53. Honigmann, "Austritte aus dem Judentum in Wien," pp. 452, 459–62, 464.

54. Thalberg, *Kunst, Österreicher zu sein*, p. 48.

55. McCagg, *Habsburg Jews*, p. 6.

56. Oxaal and Weitzmann, "Jews in Pre-1914 Vienna," p. 416.

57. Rozenblit, *Jews of Vienna*, pp. 8, 128–29; Beckermann, *Mazzesinsel*, p. 12; Salzer-Eibenstein, "Juden in Graz," p. 15.

58. Haag, "Students at the University of Vienna," pp. 301–2.

59. Laqueur, *History of Zionism*, p. 392.

60. McCagg, *Habsburg Jews*, p. 225.

CHAPTER 5

1. Laqueur, *History of Zionism*, p. 172; Maurer, *Ostjuden in Deutschland*, p. 42. The quotation is from *BÖW*, 4 September 1914, first page.

2. *Wahrheit*, 28 August 1914, p. 1.

3. *MU*, July–August 1914, p. 2. For a similar view, see *BÖW*, 4 September 1914, front page.

4. *BÖW*, 3 July 1914, pp. 461–62; *Wahrheit*, 7 August 1914, pp. 1, 5; 28 August 1914, p. 6.

5. *BÖW*, 4 September 1914, p. 643.

6. *MU*, June–August 1916, p. 2; *JZ*, 24 November 1916, p. 1.

7. *BÖW*, 5 January 1917, front page.

8. *BÖW*, 20 April 1917, pp. 229–30.

9. Deak, "Pacesetters of Integration," pp. 23–25, 29.

10. Schmidl, *Juden in der Armee*, p. 144.

11. Deak, "Pacesetters of Integration," p. 46; *JF*, 7 January 1938, p. 1; Andics, *Juden in Wien*, p. 215.

12. Greive, *Antisemitismus in Deutschland*, pp. 100–103.

13. Karbach, "Grundlagen des Antisemitismus," p. 170; Kreppel, *Juden von heute*, p. 143.

14. *Wahrheit*, 16 October 1914, p. 4.

15. [Ornstein], *Festschrift*, p. 9.

16. Harand, *Sein Kampf*, pp. 179–83; *JF*, 29 December 1934, p. 3; 15 November 1934, p. 2; *BÖW*, 17 November 1917, p. 390.

17. *MU*, January–February 1915, p. 1.

18. Kreppel, *Juden von heute*, p. 147; Daniek, *Judentum im Kriege*, pp. 7–8.

19. Holter, "Kriegsflüchtlinge in Wien," pp. 20, 54; *MU*, October–December 1917, pp. 6–7; *JF*, 7 January 1938, p. 1; Daniek, *Judentum im Kriege*, foreword, pp. 1, 4–6; Körber, *Rassesieg in Wien*, p. 280; *WMZ*, 20 July 1924, p. 1; Kreppel, *Juden von heute*, p. 138.

20. *BÖW*, 7 February 1919, front page.

21. *BÖW*, 8 November 1918, p. 691; Rozenblit, *Jews of Vienna*, p. 37; Wistrich, *Socialism and the Jews*, p. 185; McCagg, *Habsburg Jews*, p. 183; Rosenfeld, "Autonomie der Juden," p. 292; Holter, "Kriegsflüchtlinge in Wien," p. 5.

22. Ettinger, "Jews and Non-Jews in Eastern and Central Europe," p. 3; Pollack, "Cultural Innovation," p. 60; Goldfarb interview; Birnbaum, *Den Ostjuden ihr Recht!*, p. 16; Hilsenrad, *Brown Was the Danube*, p. 86.

23. Rozenblit, *Jews of Vienna*, p. 43; Wistrich, *Socialism and the Jews*, p. 205; Holter, "Kriegsflüchtlinge in Wien," p. 9; Wertheimer, *Unwelcome Strangers*, p. 161; Wistrich, *Jews of Vienna*, p. 51; Coudenhove-Kalergi, *Anti-Semitism throughout the Ages*, pp. 226, 270.

24. Holter, "Kriegsflüchtlinge in Wien," p. 14. Tartakower holds a minority view that there were only 77,000 Jewish refugees in Vienna during the war out of a total of 137,000 refugees. See his chapter, "Jewish Migratory Movements," p. 290.

25. Bloch, *Erinnerungen*, 3:253.

26. Holter, "Kriegsflüchtlinge in Wien," pp. 11–12; *MU*, November–December 1914, p. 3.

27. Holter, "Kriegsflüchtlinge in Wien," p. 13; Bauer, *History of the Holocaust*, p. 53; Spira, *Feindbild "Jud,"* p. 72.

28. Holter, "Kriegsflüchtlinge in Wien," pp. 48–49.

29. *MU*, November–December 1914, pp. 3–5.

30. *BÖW*, 5 March 1915, p. 174. See also Holter, "Kriegsflüchtlinge in Wien," p. 22.

31. Holter, "Kriegsflüchtlinge in Wien," pp. 27–28.

32. Sachar, *Modern Jewish History*, p. 425; Niewyk, "Jews in Revolution," p. 48.

33. Kreppel, *Juden von heute*, p. 154; Häusler, "Toleranz, Emanzipation und Antisemitismus," pp. 132–33.

34. Kreppel, *Juden von heute*, pp. 149–50; Holter, "Kriegsflüchtlinge in Wien," pp. 16–19, 56; Bunzl, "Arbeiterbewegung, 'Judenfrage,'" p. 746.

35. Holter, "Kriegsflüchtlinge in Wien," p. 63.

36. Janik and Toulmin, *Wittgenstein's Vienna*, p. 50; Kreppel, *Juden von heute*, p. 153; Holter, "Kriegsflüchtlinge in Wien," pp. 57, 63, 64, 70; Daniek, *Juden im Kriege*, pp. 10–11; Paumgarten, *Judentum und Sozialdemokratie*, p. 62; *BÖW*, 27 September 1918, front page.

37. Fellner, *Antisemitismus in Salzburg*, p. 85; Streibel, "Judenfrage und Antisemitismus," p. 89.

38. Grunwald, *History of Jews in Vienna*, p. 463.

39. Holzmann, "Antisemitismus in österr. Innenpolitik," p. 37; Daniek, *Juden im Kiege*, pp. 13, 14, 18, 20–22.

40. Coudenhove-Kalergi, *Anti-Semitism throughout the Ages*, p. 236; Moser, "Katastrophe der Juden," p. 70.

41. *MU*, October–December 1917, pp. 3–4; *BÖW*, 26 November 1915, front page; *Wahrheit*, 8 March 1918, p. 3.

42. *MU*, June–September 1917, p. 1; *BÖW*, 20 July 1917, p. 454.

43. *ODR*, 18 June 1918, p. 1; *BÖW*, 21 June 1918, front page; *Selbstwehr*, 9 August 1918, pp. 1–2.

44. *Selbstwehr*, 9 August 1918, p. 1; [Ornstein], *Festschrift*, p. 13; open letter of Sigmund Schonau to Dr. Alfred Stern, president of the Vienna IKG, Vienna, 8 November 1917, pp. 1–2, CAHJP, A/W 325.

45. *Wahrheit*, 23 August 1918, p. 4; Gordon, *Hitler and the "Jewish Question,"* p. 3.

CHAPTER 6

1. *Wahrheit*, 1 November 1918, p. 1. See also Schwarz, "Lost World of Joseph Roth."

2. *BÖW*, 25 October 1918, pp. 673, 675; 15 November 1918, front page.

3. Tartakower, "Jewish Migratory Movements," p. 292.

4. Kreppel, *Juden von heute*, p. 159.

5. Holter, "Kriegsflüctlinge in Wien," p. 45.

6. McCagg, *Habsburg Jews*, pp. 213–14; Bunzl, "Arbeiterbewegung, 'Judenfrage,'" pp. 751–53.

7. Bunzl, "Arbeiterbewegung, 'Judenfrage,'" pp. 751–52; Bunzl, *Klassenkampf in der Diaspora*, pp. 127–28.

8. Gold, *Geschichte der Juden in Wien*, pp. 80, 91; Timms, *Karl Kraus*, p. 361.

9. Bunzl, "Arbeiterbewegung, 'Judenfrage,'" p. 754.

10. Valentin, *Antisemitismus*, p. 70.

11. *WS*, 3 December 1919, p. 1.

12. Bunzl, "Arbeiterbewegung und Antisemitismus," p. 167; Freidenreich, *Jewish Politics in Vienna*, p. 87.

13. Buttinger, *Am Beispiel Österreichs*, p. 95.

14. Pulzer, *Political Anti-Semitism*, pp. 259–60; Bunzl, "Arbeiterbewegung und Antisemitismus," p. 167; Maderegger, *Juden im Ständestaat*, p. 73.

15. Ettinger, "Jews and Non-Jews in Eastern and Central Europe," p. 8; Gold, *Geschichte der Juden in Wien*, p. 44.

16. *WMZ*, 13 April 1919, p. 1.

17. Statements of these kinds were legion in the First Republic. See, for example, *Wahrheit*, 1 January 1927, p. 2. See also Zernatto, *Wahrheit über Österreich*, p. 67.

18. Bunzl, "Arbeiterbewegung, 'Judenfrage,'" p. 167; Knütter, *Juden in der Weimarer Republik*, p. 73.

19. *WMZ*, 21 September 1921, p. 1.

20. On St. Germain and the question of Austria's viability, see Pauley, "Austria's *Lebensunfähigkeit*," pp. 21–37.

21. *DAP*, 28 June 1919, p. 1; Whiteside, "Austria," p. 329; Gerlach, *Einfluss der Juden*, pp. 168–69, 175; Kerekes, *Von St. Germain bis Genf*, p. 47.

22. Berkley, *Vienna and Its Jews*, p. 150. For comparable allegations in Germany, see Marcus, *Destiny of the German Jew*, p. 135.

23. *WMZ*, 21 September 1921, p. 1.

24. Streibel, "Judenfrage und Antisemitismus," p. 58.

25. Holter, "Kriegsflüchtlinge in Wien," p. 60.

26. Streibel, "Judenfrage und Antisemitismus," p. 66.

27. Tartakower, "Jewish Migratory Movements," p. 293.

28. *BÖW*, 18 October 1918, p. 659; Schuschnigg, *Brutal Takeover*, pp. 61–62. Oswald Dutch [pseud. for Deutsch] estimates that there were about 200,000 Jews and 100,000 "half Jews" and their dependents in Austria by the 1930s. Of these, 180,000 Jews and 80,000 half Jews lived in Vienna. See "Seeds of a Noble Inheritance," p. 178. For the impact of the Nuremberg Laws on Austro-Jewish census figures, see DÖW, *Widerstand und Verfolgung*, 3:202.

29. *WMZ*, 26 September 1919, p. 1; *DAP*, 11 October 1919, p. 2; *ODR*, 10 October 1919, pp. 1–2.

30. *WMZ*, 12 June 1920, p. 4.

31. *DAP*, 4 September 1920, p. 1; excerpt from the *NFP*, 1 September 1920, AVA.

32. *EB*, 20 March 1921, p. 1.

33. Ibid., pp. 1, 2, 5–6; *DÖTZ*, 14 March 1921, p. 1; *RP*, 13 March 1921, p. 2; *NFP*, 14 March 1921, p. 4.

34. Auer, "Antisemitische Strömungen," p. 26; Zoitl, "Kampf um Gleichberechtigung" p. 385; *WMZ*, 23 January 1923, p. 2; *NFP*, 22 January 1923, p. 5.

35. *WMZ*, 5 February 1923, p. 1; 6 February 1923, p. 1.

36. *WMZ*, 28 February 1923, p. 1; 4 March 1923, p. 1; *RP*, 4 March 1923, p. 2; Zoitl, "Kampf um Gleichberechtigung," p. 389.

37. *WMZ*, 12 July 1919, p. 4; Hinteregger, *Judenschwindel*, p. 71; Spira, *Feindbild "Jud*," p. 80; Holter, "Kriegsflüchtlinge in Wien," pp. 23, 68, 84.

38. McCagg, *Habsburg Jews*, pp. 204, 212; *DAP*, 11 October 1919, p. 1; 4 August 1923, p. 1; Johnson, *History of the Jews*, p. 459.

39. Knütter, *Juden in der Weimarer Republik*, pp. 86–87; Maurer, *Ostjuden in Deutschland*, pp. 185, 418, 422, 427, 763.

40. Holzmann, "Antisemitismus in österr. Innenpolitik," pp. 104–6; Spira, *Feindbild "Jud,"* p. 76.

41. Holzmann, "Antisemitismus in österr. Innenpolitik," p. 106; Spira, *Feindbild "Jud,"* p. 79; Staudinger, "Christlichsoziale Judenpolitik," p. 28; *DAP*, 4 October 1919, p. 1.

42. *NYT*, 28 September 1919, 2:1; Streibel, "Judenfrage und Antisemitismus," p. 73.

43. Pelinka, *Stand oder Klasse?*, p. 216; Holter, "Kriegsflüchtlinge in Wien," pp. 68, 83; *Stenographische Protokolle der Nationalversammlung der Republik Österreich*, 78. Sitzung am 29 April 1920, p. 2379; *WMZ*, 15 January 1921, p. 2.

44. *DÖTZ*, 5 February 1921, p. 7.

45. Pötsch, *Jüdische Rasse*, p. 66.

46. *WMZ*, 9 January 1921, p. 1; *DÖTZ*, 7 January 1921, p. 1.

47. *DÖTZ*, 7 January 1921, p. 1; *Wahrheit*, 12 October 1923, p. 9.

48. *DÖTZ*, 6 March 1921, p. 1.

49. *Wahrheit*, 12 October 1923, p. 9.

50. Ibid.

51. Holter, "Kriegsflüchtlinge in Wien," pp. 72–73, 91; Knütter, *Juden in der Weimarer Republik*, p. 87.

CHAPTER 7

1. Excerpt from the *RP*, 17 October 1919, AVA, NS-P, K. 64.

2. Goldhammer, *Juden Wiens*, p. 39.

3. Pulzer, *Political Anti-Semitism*, pp. 248, 308; Niewyk, *Jews in Weimar Germany*, p. 62; Stadler, *Austria*, p. 139.

4. Thieberger, "Assimilated Jewish Youth," pp. 176, 180, 182; Boyer, *Political Radicalism*, p. 89.

5. Goldhammer, *Juden Wiens*, p. 39; *Juden im Staate Deutsch-Österreich*, p. 30; Streibel, "Judenfrage und Antisemitismus," p. 33.

6. *MU*, January–February 1915, p. 11; Kreppel, *Juden von heute*, p. 148; Haag, "Students at the University of Vienna," pp. 305–6; Haag, "Academic Antisemitism," p. 8.

7. Zoitl, "Kampf um Gleichberechtigung," p. 190.

8. Ibid., pp. 371, 379; Mendelsohn, "Relations between Jews and Non-Jews in Eastern Europe," p. 80.

9. Haag, "Blood on the Ringstrasse," p. 32.

10. Ibid.; Macartney and Palmer, *Independent Eastern Europe*, p. 201.

11. *AZ*, 4 March 1919, p. 5.

12. Zoitl, "Kampf um Gleichberechtigung," p. 192; *AZ*, 16 March 1921, p. 2; *WMZ*, 8 January 1921, p. 1; Goldhammer, *Juden Wiens*, p. 39.

13. Wistrich, *Jews of Vienna*, p. 59. At the University of Vienna Jewish coeds were particularly overrepresented in the fields of literature, history, law, and medicine, a trend that *Dr. Bloch's Wochenschrift* said was not welcome because it threatened Jewish reproduction (15 March 1918, p. 162. See also Schaukal, "Studentenrecht und Judenfrage," p. 304). For comparisons with the attitude of middle-class German Jewish families toward higher education, see Niewyk, *Jews in Weimar Germany*, p. 62.

14. *Juden in Oesterreich*, p. 91.

15. Boyer, *Political Radicalism*, p. 83; Streibel, "Judenfrage und Antisemitismus," pp. 30, 73; Goldhammer, *Juden Wiens*, pp. 15–16, 37.

16. Pötsch, *Jüdische Rasse*, p. 63.

17. *Last Waltz in Vienna*, p. 93. See also Thieberger, "Assimilated Jewish Youth," p. 176, and my interviews with Goldfarb, Flick, Hoffmann, and Pollock.

18. Haag, "Academic Antisemitism," p. 9; Scheuer, *Burschenschaften und Judenfrage*, p. 60; Hein, *Studentischer Antisemitismus*, p. 72.

19. Scheuer, *Burschenschaften und Judenfrage*, p. 60.

20. Führer, "Antisemitismus in neuen Österreich," p. 198; Zoitl, "Kampf um Gleichberechtigung," p. 374.

21. Zoitl, "Kampf um Gleichberechtigung," pp. 390, 400–403, 405.

22. Ibid., p. 378; *WMZ*, 27 September 1920, p. 1; Synnott, "Anti-Semitism and American Universities," pp. 233–35, 239.

23. Zoitl, "Kampf um Gleichberechtigung," pp. 185, 190.

24. Memorandum on the background to incident at the Social Welfare Office [Wirtschaftstelle] of the College of International Trade, 22 December 1922, CZA, Z4/2094 I.

25. Holter, "Kriegsflüchtlinge in Wien," p. 75; *NYT*, 13 December 1922, p. 14; Zoitl, "Kampf um Gleichberechtigung," pp. 376–78, 380–81. The quotation is from p. 382.

26. Zoitl, "Kampf um Gleichberechtigung," p. 383.

27. Ibid., p. 386.

28. Goldhammer, *Juden Wiens*, p. 42; *WMZ*, 6 March 1923, p. 1; 7 March 1923, p. 1; *Wahrheit*, 13 April 1923, p. 9.

29. Goldhammer, *Juden Wiens*, p. 41. The quotation is cited in Zoitl, "Kampf um Gleichberechtigung," p. 534.

30. Schechter, *Viennese Vignettes*, pp. 28, 48; Schoeps, "Modern Heirs of the Maccabees," p. 167; Pulzer, "Antisemitism in Austria," p. 440.

31. Haag, "Academic Antisemitism," pp. 5–6, 13; Sablik, *Julius Tandler*, p. 298; *WMZ*, 29 April 1920, p. 3.

32. *WMZ*, 30 April 1920, p. 1.

33. *Stenographische Protokolle der 78. Sitzung der Konstituierenden Nationalversammlung der Republik Österreich am 29 April*, pp. 2361, 2378, 2381; *NT*, 30 April 1920, p. 1.

34. *WMZ*, 6 March 1923, p. 2.

35. *AZ*, 20 November 1923, p. 6; *Abend*, 20 November 1923, p. 1; *RP*, 20 November 1923, p. 6; *NYT*, 20 November 1923, p. 2.

36. *RP*, 20 November 1923, p. 5.

37. *AZ*, 20 November 1923, p. 6.

38. *RP*, 24 November 1923, pp. 1–2.

39. *AZ*, 20 November 1923, p. 1.

40. *Wahrheit*, 2 December 1923, pp. 9–10.

41. Oberkofler, "Deutschnationalismus und Antisemitismus," pp. 65–71; Field, *The Last Days of Mankind*, pp. 142–43.

42. Scheuer, *Burschenschaften und Judenfrage*, pp. 45, 67; Niewyk, *Jews in Weimar Germany*, p. 65.

43. Quoted in Hein, *Studentischer Antisemitismus*, p. 74.

44. Ibid.

45. Ibid.

46. Quoted in Pulzer, *Political Anti-Semitism*, pp. 307–8.

47. Goldhammer, *Juden Wiens*, pp. 39, 42.

48. Letter from two officers of the Zionist State Committee for Austria (signatures illegible) to the Zionist Executive in London. Vienna, 22 December 1922, CZA, Z4/ 2094 I. 4 pp.

49. *EB*, 31 December 1926, p. 1.

CHAPTER 8

1. Hall, *Erotik*, p. 9; Lea, "*Die Stadt ohne Juden*," pp. 1–2.

2. Hall, *Erotik*, p. 24; Lea, "*Die Stadt ohne Juden*," pp. 3–6; Sachar, *Modern Jewish History*, p. 394.

3. Botz, *Gewalt in der Politik*, p. 132; Lea, "*Die Stadt ohne Juden*," pp. 4, 7, 10; Hall, *Erotik*, pp. 20–21, 24, 27.

4. Hall, *Erotik*, pp. 7, 54, 56–57, 59, 99; Lea, "*Die Stadt ohne Juden*," p. 11; *EB*, 20 March 1925, p. 1; *NFP*, 11 March 1925, p. 1.

5. Hall, *Erotik*, pp. 72–73, 124.

6. Quoted in Botz, *Gewalt in der Politik*, pp. 132–33.

7. Ibid., p. 134; *WS*, 11 March 1925, p. 1; Hall, *Erotik*, pp. 100–101.

8. Hall, *Erotik*, pp. 88, 98; Botz, *Gewalt in der Politik*, p. 136.

9. Hall, *Erotik*, p. 99; Holzmann, "Antisemitismus in österr. Innenpolitik," p. 41.

10. Botz, *Gewalt in der Politik*, p. 135; Hall, *Erotik*, pp. 86, 89; *EB*, 9 October 1925, pp. 1–2. The quotation is cited in Holzmann, "Antisemitismus in österr. Innenpolitik," p. 41.

11. *EB*, 9 October 1925, p. 2; Hall, *Erotik*, pp. 125, 132, 182; Botz, *Gewalt in der Politik*, p. 137.

12. *NFP*, 3 August 1925, pp. 1–2; Botz, *Gewalt in der Politik*, pp. 106–7; *EB*, 3 December 1925, p. 1; *AZ*, 2 August 1925, p. 8.

13. Johnson, *History of the Jews*, p. 400; *WS*, 27 December 1919, AVA, K. 64; Streibel, "Judenfrage und Antisemitismus," pp. 29, 105; 15 August 1925, pp. 1–2; *SZ*, 18 October 1925, p. 69. The quotation is from the *RP*, 9 November 1918, p. 2.

14. Fellner, *Antisemitismus in Salzburg*, p. 138; Gstrein, *Jüdisches Wien*, p. 50.

15. *AZ*, 16 August 1920, AK, folder "Judentum, Antisemitismus, Zionismus"; *WMZ*, 5 August 1925, p. 1.

16. Niewyk, "Solving the Jewish Problem," pp. 364–67; Nicosia, "Zionism in Anti-semitic Thought," pp. 14–15.

17. *ODR*, 7 February 1918, p. 5; *EB*, 10 January 1924, p. 1; *DAP*, 18 July 1925, p. 1; 1 August 1925, pp. 1–2; 22 August 1925, p. 3.

18. *DAP*, 6 June 1925, p. 1; 11 July 1925, p. 1; 25 July 1925, p. 2; *DÖTZ*, 8 August 1925, p. 1; *AZ*, 19 August 1925, p. 9; *EB*, 7 August 1925, p. 2; 28 August 1925, p. 1. The Zionist *Wiener Morgenzeitung* also estimated that 10,000 delegates had attended the Congress and thought the figure might have been three times higher without the anti-Semitic violence that accompanied the meeting (16 September 1925, p. 3).

19. Bundesrat, 93 Sitzung vom 30. Juli 1925, Anfrage, AVA, BKA Inneres, K. 32, 108872.

20. *NYT*, 1 August 1925, p. 5.

21. *DAP*, 27 June 1925, p. 2. The quotation is from a letter with an illegible signature to the Zionist Executive in London, 10 June 1925, CZA, Z4/214/4, 3 pp.

22. *NYT*, 18 August 1925, 2:1.

23. Ibid.; letter of Schober to the BKA, Abteilung 14, 15 July 1925, AVA, BKA Inneres, 1925, K. 32, 103.533, 2 pp.

24. *WMZ*, 8 August 1925, p. 1; 9 August 1925, p. 1.

25. *Wahrheit*, 28 August 1925, p. 1; *RP*, 19 August 1925, p. 1; *DAP*, 20 August 1925, p. 1; 22 August 1925, p. 1; *EB*, 25 September 1925, p. 1.

26. *DAP*, 15 August 1925, p. 5; *AZ*, 17 August 1925, p. 4; *NFP*, 17 August 1925, p. 2; *RP*, 17 August 1925, p. 1; *NWT*, 17 August 1925, p. 1.

27. *NWJ*, 18 August 1925, p. 3; *RP*, 18 August 1925, pp. 2, 4.

28. *DÖTZ*, 23 August 1925, p. 1; *NWJ*, 18 August 1925, p. 3; *NYT*, 18 August 1925, p. 1; 19 August 1925, p. 1; *WMZ*, 18 August 1925, p. 2; 29 August 1925, p. 4; *NFP*, 18 August 1925, p. 1; *AZ*, 18 August 1925, p. 6; *NWA*, 18 August 1925, p. 1; *WZ*, 22 August 1925, p. 1.

29. *NFP*, 19 August 1925, p. 7; *WMZ*, 19 August 1925, p. 8; 20 August 1925, p. 7; *WZ*, 22 August 1925, p. 1.

30. *RP*, 20 August 1925, p. 1; 21 August 1925, p. 3; *NFP*, 18 August 1925, p. 3; Carsten, *First Austrian Republic*, p. 109.

31. *NWJ*, 23 August 1925, AVA, K. 64; *RP*, 23 August 1925, pp. 5–6; *DÖTZ*, 23 August 1925, p. 1.

32. *RP*, 20 August 1925, p. 1.

33. *WS*, 18 August 1925, pp. 1–2.

34. *RP*, 18 August 1925, p. 1; 23 August 1925, p. 1.

35. *NFP*, 18 August 1925, p. 1.

36. *AZ*, 18 August 1925, p. 1. The editorial was printed on 19 August 1925, p. 6.

37. *NYT*, 13 October 1925, p. 8.

38. *WMZ*, 21 August 1925, p. 6; *NYT*, 19 August 1925, p. 1. The quotation is from the *NYT*, 20 August 1925, p. 7.

39. *NYT*, 23 August 1925, p. 24.

CHAPTER 9

1. *EB*, 20 May 1921, p. 3.

2. *WMZ*, 29 October 1921, AVA, K. 64, p. 1; 22 July 1924, p. 4; Wachter, "Antisemitismus im Vereinswesen," p. 94.

3. *RP*, 11 April 1921, p. 4.

4. Krammer, "Die Turn- und Sportbewegung," pp. 734–35; Wachter, "Antisemitismus im Vereinswesen," pp. 157, 160; Ardelt, *Zwischen Demokratie und Faschismus*, pp. 100–101.

5. Wachter, "Antisemitismus im Vereinswesen," pp. 181, 183–84, 191, 198, 206, 208.

6. Ibid., pp. 136–37, 147, 152.

7. Schilling[-Schletter], *Walter Riehl*, p. 13; *Mitteilungen der Vereinigung christlich-deutscher Ärtze Österreichs*, September 1935, p. 4.

8. [Eberle], "Judentum und Rechtsanwaltsberuf in Wien," p. 2667; "Beilage zu den *Mitteilungen des Verbandes deutsch-arischer Rechtsanwalte Österreich*" (n.d.).

9. Maderegger, *Juden im Ständestaat*, p. 211.

10. *Wahrheit*, 14 October 1927, p. 12; Bentwich, "Destruction of the Jewish Community in Austria," p. 467; Maderegger, *Juden im Ständestaat*, p. 153.

11. Thieberger, "Assimilated Jewish Youth," p. 182; *WMZ*, 27 July 1934, p. 2; Boerner, *Antisemitismus, Rassenfrage, Menschlichkeit*, p. 12.

12. *NFP*, 12 March 1925, p. 1; *Wahrheit*, 23 October 1925, p. 3.

13. Sablik, *Julius Tandler*, p. 299.

14. Letter from the Vorstand of the IKG to Dr. Rudolf Ramek, 26 May 1925, CAHJP, A/W 328, 3 pp.; *AZ*, 29 May 1925, p. 6; 30 May 1925, p. 6.

15. *AZ*, 6 March 1927, p. 3.

16. Letter of Leopold Tlimef (Vienna) to Gauleiter Alfred E. Frauenfeld, 23 April 1930, AVA, NS-P, K. 5, 5 pp.; Carsten, *Fascist Movements*, pp. 154–55.

17. Letter of Leopold Tlimef (Vienna) to Gauleiter Alfred E. Frauenfeld, 23 April 1930, AVA, NS-P, K. 5, 5 pp. See also *Wahrheit*, 15 November 1929, p. 4.

18. *NYT*, 30 October 1929, p. 13; 6 November 1929, p. 15; 8 November 1929, p. 3; 11 November 1930, p. 8; 7 December 1930, 3:2.

19. *NFP*, 3 February 1931, p. 4; 4 February 1931, p. 2; *AZ*, 3 February 1931, p. 3; *NYT*, 3 February 1931, p. 13. The quotation is from the *NYT* for 4 February 1931, p. 9.

20. Körber, *Rassesieg in Wien*, p. 236; Fenz, "Zur Ideologie der 'Volksbürgerschaft,'" p. 132; Thieberger, "Assimilated Jewish Youth," pp. 180–81; *JVZ*, 9 February 1932, p. 2.

21. Rill, "Auseinandersetzung des Cartellverbandes," p. 55; Fenz, "Ideologie der 'Volksbürgerschaft,'" pp. 125–26; Haag, "Academic Antisemitism," p. 11; Führer, "Antisemitismus im neuen Österreich," p. 200; Schaukal, "Studentenrecht und Judenfrage," p. 303.

22. Fenz, "Ideologie der 'Volksbürgerschaft,'" pp. 132, 138; *Wahrheit*, 18 April 1930, p. 2; *NFP*, 23 June 1931, p. 4.

23. AZ, 24 June 1931, p. 5; 25 June 1931, p. 4; Weinzierl, *Universität und Politik,* p. 18; NYT, 24 June 1931, p. 48; NFP, 26 June 1931, p. 6.

24. Weinzierl, *Universität und Politik,* p. 18; NFP, 26 June 1931, p. 6; *Stimme,* 19 November 1931, p. 1.

25. RP, 24 June 1931, p. 7.

26. Fenz, "Ideologie der 'Volksbürgerschaft,'" p. 142; Rill, "Auseinanderandersetzung des Cartellverbandes," p. 54.

27. *Wahrheit,* 15 November 1929, *Volksstimme,* 18 October 1930, p. 2.

28. *Bericht der IKG,* 1929–1932, pp. 11–12; *Stimme,* 3 July 1931, p. 7; JA, 4 December 1931, p. 1.

29. *Stimme,* 3 July 1931, p. 7; NYT, 1 July 1931, p. 52; *The Minister in Austria to the Secretary of State,* 2 March 1932, in FRUS 1932, 2:122.

30. NYT, 21 May 1933, p. 25; Spaulding, *Quiet Invaders,* p. 271; Synnott, "Anti-Semitism and American Universities," p. 251.

31. NYT, 18 October 1932, p. 7; 27 October 1932, p. 8.

32. *The Minister in Austria to the Secretary of State,* 22 October 1932, 27 October 1932, 29 October 1932, in FRUS 1932, 2:124–29, 132–33. The quotations are on pp. 125 and 128.

33. *Wahrheit,* 4 November 1932, p. 1; NYT, 27 October 1932, p. 8; *The Minister in Austria to the Secretary of State,* 29 October 1932, in FRUS 1932, 2:124–29, 132–33.

34. DÖTZ, 20 October 1932, p. 3.

35. *Bericht der IKG,* 1929–32, p. 13.

CHAPTER 10

1. Johnson, *History of the Jews,* p. 347.

2. See, for example, ibid., p. 352.

3. Marx, "On the Jewish Question," pp. 58–60.

4. Ibid., p. 60.

5. Carlebach, *Karl Marx,* pp. 266, 356–57; Massing, *Rehearsal for Destruction,* p. 159; Simon, *Österreich 1918–1938,* p. 43; Niewyk, *Socialist, Anti-Semite, and Jew,* pp. 5, 15.

6. Carlebach, *Karl Marx,* p. 261; Hanisch, "Friedrich Engels," pp. 118–19; Moser, "Katastrophe der Juden," p. 95.

7. Hanisch, "Friedrich Engels," pp. 118–19; Moser, "Katastrophe der Juden," p. 95.

8. Katz, *From Prejudice to Destruction,* p. 6; Bunzl, "Arbeiterbewegung und Anti-semitismus," pp. 164–65; Wistrich, "Social Democracy," p. 118; Stuhlpfarrer, "Anti-semitismus, Rassenpolitik," p. 149; Wistrich, *Socialism and the Jews,* p. 340; letter from the Zionist State Committee [Landeskomitee] for Austria in Vienna to the Zionist Executive in London, 3 February 1926, CZA, Z4/2422, pp. 12–13.

9. Gold, *Geschichte der Juden in Wien,* p. 49; Frei, *Jüdisches Elend in Wien,* p. 12; Spira, *Feindbild "Jud,"* p. 45; Silberner, "Austrian Social Democracy," pp. 126–27; Simon, "Jewish Vote in Austria," p. 110.

10. Wistrich, *Socialism and the Jews*, pp. 280–81, 313; Spira, *Feindbild "Jud,"* p. 46.

11. Wistrich, *Socialism and the Jews*, pp. 233, 282, 352; Wistrich, "Social Democracy," p. 120. The quotation is cited in Silberner, "Austrian Social Democracy," p. 128.

12. All of the Austrian Jewish refugees interviewed by the present author cited these reasons to explain why their families voted for the Socialist Party.

13. Simon, "Jewish Vote in Austria," p. 108; *JVZ*, 18 April 1932, p. 3; *Stimme*, 21 April 1932, p. 1.

14. Simon, "Jewish Vote in Austria," pp. 120–21.

15. Beller, "Class, Culture and the Jews of Vienna," pp. 42–43; Black, *Ernst Kaltenbrunner*, p. 36; Schwarz, "Antisemitism and Socialism," p. 446; Spira, *Feindbild "Jud,"* p. 33.

16. Spira, *Feindbild "Jud,"* pp. 55, 61; Wistrich, *Socialism and the Jews*, p. 338; letter of Josiah C. Wedgwood to Dr. Gelber, Vienna, 6 February 1927, CZA, Z4/3563/I; *HZ*, 23 July 1932, p. 2; Wistrich, *Jews of Vienna*, p. 225; Bunzl, "Arbeiterbewegung, 'Judenfrage,'" p. 761.

17. Bunzl, "Arbeiterbewegung und Antisemitismus," p. 168; Pulzer, *Political Antisemitism*, p. 263.

18. Holzmann, "Antisemitismus in österr. Innenpolitik," pp. 87, 92.

19. AZ, 8 August 1923, AVA, SD Parteistellen, K. 52; Fellner, *Antisemitismus in Salzburg*, p. 187.

20. Holzmann, "Antisemitismus in österr. Innenpolitik," pp. 93–94.

21. Fellner, *Antisemitismus in Salzburg*, pp. 124–25; Binder, "Der 'reiche' Jude," p. 48; Greive, *Antisemitismus in Deutschland*, p. 97; marginal note by Robert Schwarz.

22. Holzmann, "Antisemitismus in österr. Innenpolitik," pp. 87, 92.

23. Hinteregger, *Judenschwindel*; see esp. pp. 28, 64, 77–78, 82–83. See also, Jacobs, "Austrian Social Democracy," p. 158.

24. Hinteregger, *Judenschwindel*, pp. 16–18, 86.

25. AZ, 14 November 1918, AK, folder 516.

26. WMZ, 6 December 1919, p. 1.

27. Fellner, *Antisemitismus in Salzburg*, p. 123; WMZ, 13 August 1919, p. 5; 24 July 1919, p. 5.

28. NYT, 31 August 1924, 2:5; Bunzl, "Arbeiterbewegung und Antisemitismus," p. 170.

29. Niewyk, *Socialist, Anti-Semite, and Jew*, pp. 118, 122; Massing, *Rehearsal for Destruction*, pp. 160, 206; Laqueur, *History of Zionism*, p. 421; Greive, *Antisemitismus in Deutschland*, p. 115.

30. Niewyk, *Socialist, Anti-Semite, and Jew*, pp. 24, 52–54, 94; Massing, *Rehearsal for Destruction*, p. 164.

31. Solow, "Letters from Abroad," p. 139; Niewyk, *Socialist, Anti-Semite, and Jew*, p. 216; Simon, "Jewish Vote in Austria," p. 110.

32. Paumgarten, *Judentum und Sozialdemokratie*; see esp. pp. 4, 8, 12–14, 18, 24–25, 31.

33. Ibid., pp. 34–35.

34. *Juden im Staate Deutsch-Österreich*, pp. 16–18; Daniek, *Judentum im Kriege*,

p. 30; Gerlach, *Juden in Sozialdemokratie*, pp. 182–83; Pötsch, *Jüdische Rasse*, p. 51.

35. Schwarz, "Antisemitism and Socialism," p. 447.

36. Ibid., p. 448.

37. Ibid., p. 450; Austria, Political Situation (no name), 2 June 1934, NA, T-120, R. 900, frame 5652945; Braunthal, *Tragedy of Austria*, p. 121.

38. Bunzl, "Arbeiterbewegung 'Judenfrage,'" p. 761.

39. Poppel, *Zionism in Germany*, p. 113.

40. AZ, 5 October 1919, p. 1.

CHAPTER 11

1. Coudenhove-Kalergi, *Anti-Semitism throughout the Ages*, p. 244; Heller, *Edge of Destruction*, p. 113.

2. Bein, *Judenfrage*, p. 241; Simon, *Österreich 1918–1938*, p. 42.

3. Busshoff, *Dollfuss-Regime*, p. 261.

4. Weinzierl, "Wurzeln des Antisemitismus," p. 64.

5. Eppel, *Zwischen Kreuz und Hakenkreuz*, pp. 146–47.

6. Heer, *Gottes erste Liebe*, p. 360; Weinzierl, "Antisemitismus in Österreich," p. 312; [Eberle], "Jüdische Vorherrschaft," p. 362.

7. Eberle, "Katholiken und Judenfrage," pp. 699, 701; Balas, "Zur Judenfrage," p. 11; Eberle, "Umschau," p. 142; Senn, "Christen—kauft bei Christen!" pp. 197–98.

8. Mager, "Die religiöse Seite der Judenfrage," p. 563.

9. Balas, "Zur Judenfrage," p. 11.

10. *Juden im Staate Deutsch-Österreich*; see esp. pp. 22, 24–25, 32–43.

11. *RP*, 20 August 1925, p. 6.

12. Waldinger, "Vor Sonnenuntergang," p. 64.

13. Salzer-Eibenstein, "Juden in Graz," p. 15; *BÖW*, 1 March 1918, p. 1; *NW*, 28 July 1933, pp. 1–2; *Wahrheit*, 26 December 1930, p. 1; *Klerus-Zeitschrift für soziale Arbeit*, 1919, p. 110; reprinted in Hodik, Malina, and Spann, *Juden in Österreich*, p. 64.

14. Csoklich, "Presse und Rundfunk," pp. 719–20; Pfarrhofer, *Friedrich Funder*, p. 296.

15. Pfarrhofer, *Friedrich Funder*, pp. 295, 300; Streibel, "Judenfrage und Antisemitismus," p. 16.

16. Streibel, "Judenfrage und Antisemitismus," pp. 15, 92; *BÖW*, 29 November 1918, p. 754; *RP*, 16 November 1918, p. 2; Staudinger, "Christlichsoziale Judenpolitik," p. 30; Zoitl, "Kampf um Gleichberechtigung," p. 546.

17. Streibel, "Judenfrage und Antisemitismus," pp. 94–95, 99.

18. See Chapter 8.

19. Streibel, "Judenfrage und Antisemitismus," pp. 104, 107, 112.

20. Ibid., p. 16; Pfarrhofer, *Friedrich Funder*, pp. 297–99; *Wahrheit*, 26 December 1930, p. 1.

21. Tietze, *Juden Wiens*, p. 255; *RP*, 22 January 1919, pp. 1–2; *WMZ*, 25 January 1919, p. 1; Kobler, "The Contribution of Austrian Jews to Jurisprudence," p. 34; Streibel, "Judenfrage und Antisemitismus," pp. 19, 23–24, 28.

22. Vago, "Attitude toward the Jews," p. 44; Karbach, "Grundlagen des Antisemitismus," p. 108.

23. Spira, *Feindbild "Jud,"* pp. 80–81.

24. Berchtold, *Österreichische Parteiprogramme*, pp. 357, 364–65.

25. Holzmann, "Antisemitismus in österr. Innenpolitik," p. 110; Staudinger, "Christlichsoziale Judenpolitik," p. 32.

26. Ibid., pp. 48–49; Bihl, "The Austrian Jews from 1918 to 1938," p. 6.

27. Moser, "Katastrophe der Juden," p. 100; *NWT*, 16 January 1927, p. 1; *Wahrheit*, 21 May 1926, p. 1.

28. Pelinka, *Stand oder Klasse*, p. 211; Geehr, *Karl Lueger*, p. 157; Stubenvoll, "Christliche Arbeiterbewegung," p. 603.

29. Pelinka, *Stand oder Klasse*, p. 222.

30. Hilberg, *Destruction of the European Jews*, p. 2; Geehr, *Karl Lueger*, p. 226.

31. Pelinka, *Stand oder Klasse*, pp. 213–14, 217–18, 220, 224, 232; Stubenvoll, "Christliche Arbeiterbewegung," pp. 604, 607–8.

32. Stubenvoll, "Christliche Arbeiterbewegung," pp. 606, 610; Holzmann, "Antisemitismus in österr. Innenpolitik," pp. 51, 109; letter of Siegmund Schonau (Baden [bei Wien]), to Dr. Wilhelm Pappenheim (Vienna), 15 July 1918, CAHJP, A/W, 326. See also Chapter 6.

33. The complete text of Kunschak's proposed law together with the comments of Ignaz Seipel on each point has been reprinted by Pelinka in *Stand oder Klasse*, pp. 297–300. See also Staudinger, "Christlichsoziale Judenpolitik," pp. 36–37.

34. Pelinka in *Stand oder Klasse*, p. 300; Botz, *Gewalt in der Politik*, p. 131; Staudinger, "Katholischer Antisemitismus," p. 260; Holzmann, "Antisemitismus in österr. Innenpolitik," p. 110.

35. The quotation is cited in Pelinka, *Stand oder Klasse*, pp. 213–14.

36. Ibid., p. 216; Seliger and Ucaker, *Wiens politische Geschichte*, p. 1186; *NW*, 5 February 1932, p. 1. The quotation is from *DVB*, 21 March 1936, p. 1.

37. Rosenkranz, "Bemerkungen," p. 92; Heer, *Gottes erste Liebe*, p. 363; *RP*, 19 March 1936, AK, folder Juden-Katholizismus; *JW*, 25 March 1936, p. 1; *SZ*, 2 August 1936, p. 1172.

38. *NWJ*, 3 December 1922, AVA, K. 64; [Ornstein], *Festschrift*, p. 34; Rennhofer, *Ignaz Seipel*, pp. 222, 495; Klemperer, *Ignaz Seipel*, p. 256; Moser, "Katastrophe der Juden," p. 100; *DVB*, 28 December 1919, AVA. NS-P, K. 64c; *EB*, 29 January 1927, p. 1.

39. Staudinger, "Christlichsoziale Judenpolitik," pp. 17–18; Moser, "Katastrophe der Juden," pp. 84–85; Spira, *Feindbild "Jud,"* p. 24.

40. Berkley, *Vienna and Its Jews*, p. 204; *WMZ*, 3 June 1924, p. 1; *Wahrheit*, 5 August 1932, p. 2; Klemperer, *Ignaz Seipel*, pp. 431–32.

41. *Wahrheit*, 1 November 1935, p. 2.

42. Czermak and Karbach, *Ordnung in der Judenfrage*, pp. 8–9. The quotation is from p. 8.

43. Ibid., pp. 24–27.

44. Ibid., pp. 30, 41, 43, 46.

45. Ibid., pp. 53–55, 61, 67.

46. Ibid., pp. 90–91, 106, 113.

47. *Wahrheit*, 27 October 1933, p. 1; 8 November 1933, p. 1; 15 November 1933, p. 2.

48. *Stimme*, 21 December 1933, p. 3; *JF*, 15 November 1933, pp. 1, 4; *JA*, 19 January 1934, p. 1.

49. *Gerechtigkeit*, 3 November 1933, p. 1.

50. *SZ*, 10 December 1933, p. 266; *Stürmer*, 11 November 1933, p. 1.

51. On the Austrian Nazi renaissance between 1931 and the spring of 1933, see Pauley, *Hitler and the Forgotten Nazis*, pp. 69–86.

52. Eberle, "Katholiken und Judentum," p. 700.

53. Eppel, *Zwischen Kreuz und Hakenkreuz*, pp. 179–80, 184.

54. Busshoff, *Dollfuss-Regime*, p. 280; Spira, *Feindbild "Jud,"* p. 92; Pfarrhofer, *Friedrich Funder*, p. 300; Maderegger, *Juden im Ständestaat*, p. 203; *Wahrheit*, 1 May 1936, p. 1.

55. Eibl, "Aufstieg des Nationalsozialismus, II," pp. 790–91; Heer, *Gottes erste Liebe*, p. 364. The quotation is cited in Maderegger, *Juden im Ständestaat*, p. 135.

56. [Eberle], "Judenfrage in Österreich," p. 206.

57. Stubenvoll, "Christliche Arbeiterbewegung," p. 612.

58. Ibid., p. 614; Pelinka, *Stand oder Klasse*, pp. 141, 218, 227–28.

59. *RP*, 24 January 1933, pp. 1–2.

60. Ibid., p. 4.

61. Stubenvoll, "Christliche Arbeiterbewegung," p. 613; *Stimme*, 2 February 1933, p. 7; Glockemeier, *Wiener Judenfrage*, p. 106; *Volksstimme*, 4 February 1933, p. 7; Heer, *Gottes erste Liebe*, pp. 363–64.

62. Stehle, "Bischof Hudal und SS-Führer Meyer," p. 300.

63. Maderegger, *Juden im Ständestaat*, p. 138; Adler, *Die historischen Fakten*, p. 10; Spira, *Feindbild "Jud,"* pp. 88–89; Ebneth, "Der christliche Ständestaat," p. 186; Staudinger, "Katholischer Antisemitismus," p. 268.

64. Lewy, *The Catholic Church and Nazi Germany*, p. 274.

CHAPTER 12

1. For elections results during the First Republic, see Stadler, *Austria*, p. 116.

2. Berchtold, *Österreichische Parteiprogramme*, pp. 482–83.

3. *Vormarsch*, 9 April 1932, p. 6; Cohn, *Warrant for Genocide*, p. 172; *Bauernsturm*, 19 March 1932, p. 3.

4. For a general history of the Heimwehr, see Edmondson, *The Heimwehr and Austrian Politics*. On the Heimwehr's racist and pan-German wing in Styria, see Pauley,

Hahnenschwanz und Hakenkreuz. On the fascist proclivities of the Heimwehr and the Styrian Heimatschutz, see Pauley, "Fascism and the *Führerprinzip.*"

5. Macartney, "The Armed Formations of Austria," p. 630; Bunzl and Marin, *Antisemitismus in Österreich,* p. 46; Bullock, *Austria 1918–1938,* pp. 185–86; NYT, 17 March 1929, 3:6.

6. *Wahrheit,* 4 October 1929, p. 24; Carsten, *First Austrian Republic,* p. 202; Wiltschegg, *Die Heimwehr,* p. 265.

7. AZ, 5 October 1930, AK, folder "HW, Antisemitismus"; Spira, *Feindbild "Jud,"* p. 32. The quotation is from the AZ, 26 October 1930, AK, folder "HW-Antisemitismus"; Solow, "Letters from Abroad," p. 145; Carsten, *First Austrian Republic,* p. 241.

8. Spira, *Feindbild "Jud,"* p. 31.

9. Quoted in Winkler, *Diktatur in Österreich,* p. 40.

10. *OHZ,* 25 February 1933, p. 1.

11. *Wahrheit,* 2 March 1934, p. 2; *Stimme,* 27 March 1934, p. 2; NW, 27 March 1934, p. 1.

12. AZ, 20 April 1929, AK, folder "HW-Antisemitismus"; Statutes of the Heimatschutzverbandes Steiermark, AVA, NS-P, K. 12; *Panther,* 22 April 1932, p. 3.

13. Pauley, *Hahnenschwanz und Hakenkreuz,* pp. 175–84, 204–5.

14. Kondert, "Early History of the Austrian 'Heimwehr' Movement," p. 29.

15. Messerer, "Frontkämpfervereinigung," pp. 134–35. For the participation of the FKV in anti-Semitic rallies, see Chapter 6.

16. Messerer, "Frontkämpfervereinigung," pp. 41, 49.

17. Johnson, *History of the Jews,* p. 392.

18. Ardelt, *Zwischen Demokratie und Faschismus,* pp. 75–77.

19. Ibid., pp. 78–79, 87.

20. Ackerl, "Grossdeutsche Volkspartei," pp. 46–47, 71, 312, 314–15.

21. Ibid., p. 313; Stuhlpfarrer, "Antisemitismus, und Judenverfolgungen," p. 147.

22. Berchtold, *Österreichische Parteiprogramme,* pp. 478–83.

23. Ibid., p. 483.

24. *DÖTZ,* 10 July 1921, AVA, NS-P, K. 64/P.

25. Ibid.; Polleross, *Antisemitismus im Waldviertel,* p. 53; minutes of the Expert Committee for the Jewish Question, 21 April 1921, pp. 2, 5; 19 May 1921, p. 2; 6 December 1921, pp. 1–2, AVA, BKA, GVDP, VI-36 (Judenausschuss).

26. Ibid., 18 January 1924, pp. 1–2; 7 February 1924, pp. 1–3; 22 February 1924, p. 1.

27. NWT, 13 February 1923,. pp. 1–2; *Wahrheit,* 1 February 1923, p. 10; WMZ, 27 February 1923, p. 1; Moser, "Katastrophe der Juden," p. 88.

28. Ackerl, "Grossdeutsche Volkspartei," pp. 70, 317.

29. Fellner, *Antisemitismus in Salzburg,* pp. 130–31; Pelinka, *Stand oder Klasse,* p. 230; Staudinger, "Christlichsoziale Judenpolitik," p. 34; unsigned letter from an official of the AB in Vienna to the security director for Lower Austria, 27 April 1935, AVA, BKA, GD (Antisemitenbund), doc. 33000 4 GD 2/1935, 2 pp.; Holter, "Kriegsflüchtlinge in Wien," p. 69.

30. Ibid., p. 131. See also Chapter 6.

31. Fellner, *Antisemitismus in Salzburg*, pp. 128–30; *ATA*, 24 December 1919, AVA, NS-P, K. 64/c.

32. Fellner, *Antisemitismus in Salzburg*, p. 137.

33. Ibid., pp. 106–7, 128–30; *EB*, 20 May 1921, p. 1; *NYT*, 16 May 1921, p. 20; *RP*, 11 May 1921, AVA, NS-P, K. 64.

34. *EB*, 22 November 1921, p. 1; 18 December 1923, p. 3; 1 October 1931, p. 1; 12 March 1932, p. 1; Hanisch, "Nationalsozialismus in Salzburg," pp. 374–75; Fellner, *Antisemitismus in Salzburg*, p. 133; [Ornstein], *Festschrift*, p. 22.

35. Unsigned letter from the Antisemitenbund to the security director of Lower Austria, 27 April 1935, AVA, BKA, GD (Antisemitenbund), doc. 330000 4 GD 2/35; letter of Michael Skubl [chief of the police in Vienna] to the BKA, Generaldirektion für die öffentliche Sicherheit, 31 October 1934, ibid., doc. 191611-34, p. 7; report dated 13 January 1937 on a meeting of the Antisemitenbund, DÖW, folder 6895, no. 4, 2 pp.; Jedlicka, "Tagebuch Emmerich Czermak," p. 359; Denkschrift des Deutschösterreichische Schutzvereines Antisemitenbund, 4 October 1935, AVA, BKA (Antisemitenbund), GD, doc. 365940.

36. *DVB*, 3 April 1937, p. 3; *Wahrheit*, 17 December 1937, p. 3; VF report dated 11 November 1937 on a meeting of the Antisemitenbund, DÖW, folder 6895, no. 10, 2 pp.; letter from the security director to the BKA, Generaldirektion für die öffentliche Sicherheit, 15 February 1937, AVA, BKA, Akten, doc. 312025/3f, 3 pp.; report of the Bundespolizeidirektion of Vienna, 5 February 1938, p. 1, DÖW, folder 6895, no. 14; unsigned report in the files of the BKA, Akten, doc. 67.453-DGr, 1 January 1937, 1 p.

37. *DVB*, 7 July 1936, p. 3.

38. DÖW, folder 6895, Antisemitenbund, no. 14, Bundespolizeidirektion in Wien, 5 February 1938, p. 10; Peter, *Der Antisemitismus*, Foreword, pp. 2, 12, 14–15. *Der Antisemitismus* consisted of articles first printed in the *Deutsches Volksblatt*.

39. *EB*, 7 November 1930, p. 1; the quotation is from 30 April 1932, p. 1.

40. Letter of police director Ferraris to the Bundespolizeidirektion, Staatspolizeiliches Büro Graz, 26 May 1937, AVA, GD (Antisemitenbund), doc. 335043, 2 pp.; confidential [vertraulich] police report dated 26 January 1938, DÖW, folder 6895, no. 12.

CHAPTER 13

1. Pulzer, *Political Anti-Semitism*, p. xvi; Stackelberg, *Idealism Debased*, p. 156.

2. Draft for a poster entitled "Ihre Existenz ist in Gefahr!" AVA, NS-P, K. 14; Führer, "Antisemitismus im neuen Österreich," pp. 188–90; *Stürmer*, 3 March 1934, p. 1.

3. Reichmann, *Hostages of Civilization*, p. 198; Barkai, *Von Boykott zur Entjudung*, p. 19.

4. Fodor, *Plot and Counterplot in Central Europe*, p. 163.

5. Brandstötter, "Riehl und die NS Bewegung," pp. 137–38; *DAP*, 16 October 1920,

p. 1. The quotation is from Carsten, *Fascist Movements*, p. 35.

6. Whiteside, *Austrian National Socialism before 1918*, p. 104; Frischauer, *The Rise and Fall of Hermann Goering*, p. 43; Schilling[-Schletter], *Walter Riehl*, p. 96.

7. Brandstötter, "Riehl und die NS Bewegung," p. 19.

8. *Wahrheit*, 8 April 1927, p. 1.

9. Botz, "Changing Patterns," p. 204; Abel, *Why Hitler Came to Power*, p. 156; Zoitl, "Kampf um Gleichberechtigung," p. 405.

10. Letter of Schober to the BKA, Abteilung 14, 1 September 1923, AVA, BKA Inneres 1923, doc. 52.921, 4 pp.

11. Hall, *Erotik*, p. 95.

12. NYT, 17 July 1925, p. 4.

13. Letter of Schober to the BKA, Abteilung 14, 15 July, AVA, BKA Inneres 1925, K. 32, doc. 103.533, 2 pp.; Brandstötter, "Riehl und die NS Bewegung," p. 227. See also Chapter 8.

14. *DAP*, 6 March 1926, p. 1.

15. *WMZ*, 24 April 1924, p. 5; *Wahrheit*, 15 November 1929, p. 4.

16. *Wahrheit*, 4 October 1929, p. 24.

17. Furth letter, p. 5.

18. Führer, "Antisemitismus im neuen Österreich," p. 190.

19. Carsten, *First Austrian Republic*, p. 163; NYT, 2 July 1932, p. 8.

20. *Stimme*, 6 October 1932, p. 1; 9 February 1932, p. 4; letter of Braudi (Vienna) to the BKA, Generaldirektion für die öffentliche Sicherheit, 4 November 1932, AVA, BKA Inneres 1932, K. 32, doc. 231208, 2 pp.; Weinzierl, "Antisemitismus in Öster-reich," p. 316; NYT, 29 March 1933, p. 1; 5 May 1933, p. 9; 22 May 1933, p. 9; 13 June 1933, p. 6; AZ, 13 June 1933, p. 1.

21. *Wahrheit*, 5 February 1926, p. 1.

22. Information for speakers, speakers' letters, the press and posters, Office for the Handling of the Jewish Question, 16 January 1933, AVA, NS-P, K. 5; Office for the Handling of the Jewish Question, AVA, NS-P, K. 18, p. 2.

23. *Stürmer*, 19 August 1933, pp. 1, 3; 16 September 1933, p. 3.

24. *Wahrheit*, 5 February 1926, p. 1.

25. *Wahrheit*, 21 November 1929, p. 9.

26. Educational materials for the meeting of block wardens, nr. 7: "Jewry in the German cultural community," 24 January 1933, AVA, NS-P 18, p. 6.

27. Ibid., p. 7.

28. Niewyk, *Jews in Weimar Germany*, p. 4; Glockemeier, *Wiener Judenfrage*, p. 109.

29. DÖTZ, 5 January 1931, p. 1; 10 January 1931, p. 1; *Stimme*, 8 January 1931, p. 1.

30. Press brochure of Gau Vienna, AVA, NS-P, K. 16; *Wahrheit*, 15 July 1923, p. 11. The quotation is from Führer, "Antisemitismus im neuen Österreich," p. 192.

31. *Kampfruf*, 2 May 1931, p. 1; AZ, 28 January 1926, p. 1; Jung, "Die völkische Presse in Österreich," pp. 345–46.

32. Layton, "*Völkischer Beobachter*," p. 377.

33. *Kampf*, 8, 15 August, 26 September 1931.

34. Landespressechef Haintz (Linz) to J. Müller (Vienna), 16 January 1933 and several attached letters, AVA, NS-P, K. 8; Carsten, *Fascist Movements*, pp. 285–86.

35. *DÖTZ*, 24 September 1932, p. 5. The quotation is from 7 October 1932, p. 8.

36. Holzmann, "Antisemitismus in österr. Innenpolitik," pp. 81–82; *DAP*, 25 July 1925, p. 3; *Kampf*, 13 August 1932, SD-Parteistellen, K. 58; *Stürmer*, 14 October 1933, p. 5.

37. Letter of Alfred Proksch to the Landes USCHLA in Linz, 15 April 1931, AVA, K. 14; letter of Alfred Frauenfeld to Gregor Strasser, 27 January 1932, Slg. Sch., 305 folder 2; letter of Frauenfeld (Vienna), to Dr. Georg Ettingshausen, 19 January 1933, NS-P, 5.

38. Jedlicka, "Gauleiter Josef Leopold," p. 150; Persche, "Hauptmann Leopold," p. 90.

39. Levine, "The Jewish Leadership in Germany," p. 205.

40. *DAP*, 6 June 1925, p. 1.

41. Rosenkranz, "Tragedy of Austrian Jewry," p. 480.

42. *Kampfruf*, Sonderdruck, June 1932 (unnumbered page).

43. *Stürmer*, 14 October 1933, p. 1.

44. Führer, "Antisemitismus im neuen Österreich," p. 204.

45. *Stürmer*, 14 October 1933, p. 1; 2 June 1934, p. 2; Maderegger, *Juden im Ständestaat*, p. 197; Führer, "Antisemitismus im neuen Österreich," p. 202. For other Nazi attitudes toward Zionism, see Chapter 8.

46. *JW*, 28 December 1932, p. 1; [Ornstein], *Festschrift*, p. 14.

47. *Wahrheit*, 26 December 1930, p. 1.

48. Hanisch, "Nationalsozialismus in Salzburg," p. 376; "Ihre Existenz ist in Gefahr," AVA, NS-P, K. 14, 4 September 1931; Carsten, *Fascist Movements*, pp. 284–85; *Stimme*, 22 December 1932, p. 1.

49. *DVB*, 22 June 1935, p. 12.

50. *JW*, 28 December 1932, p. 1.

51. Letter from Josef Fodinger (Vienna) to *Kampfruf*, 30 October 1932, AVA, NS-P, K. 12, 1 p.

52. Maderegger, *Juden im Ständestaat*, p. 244; *JW*, 28 December 1932, p. 1.

53. Letter of Riehl (Vienna), to Alfred Proksch (Linz), 26 April 1932, Slg. Sch. 305, 2:1.

54. Botz, "Changing Patterns," p. 212.

55. Wandruszka, " Österreichs politische Struktur," p. 405.

56. Fellner, *Antisemitismus in Salzburg*, p. 188; Bunzl and Marin, *Antisemitismus in Österreich*, p. 53; Valentin, *Antisemitism: Historically and Critically Examined*, p. 120; Heller, *Edge of Destruction*, p. 77.

57. For comparisons with Germany, see Kershaw, "Ideology, Propaganda," p. 168, and Niewyk, *Jews in Weimar Germany*, p. 80.

58. Botz, "*Anschluss* to the Holocaust," p. 202.

CHAPTER 14

1. Friedrich and Brzezinski, *Totalitarian Dictatorship*, p. 131.
2. See Chapter 6.
3. GVP Judenausschuss, meeting of 7 May 1921, AVA, VI-36.
4. *DAP*, 18 July 1925, p. 2.
5. *DÖTZ*, 14 June 1932, p. 9.
6. Pötsch, *Jüdische Rasse*, pp. 52–55, 60.
7. "Deutsche Kultur," Beiblatt des *Kampfrufs*, 4 July 1931, p. 7; draft of a speech by Heinz Cohrs, enclosed in a letter by Robert Körber dated 4 April 1933, AVA, NS-P. K. 16; *Stürmer*, 21 October 1933, p. 4. A scholarly study conducted by both Jewish and non-Jewish statisticians in 1936 revealed that there were only 16,291,000 Jews in the entire world. See *Wahrheit*, 7 August 1936, p. 4.
8. Educational material for Blockwartsitzung number 5, "The Jewish Question," Vienna, 10 January 1933, AVA, NS-P. K. 18, p. 4.
9. Goldhammer, *Juden Wiens*, p. 6; Haubenberger, "Judentum in Österreich," p. 618.
10. Rosenkranz, "Tragedy of Austrian Jewry," pp. 486–87; *B'nai-Brith—Mitteilungen für Oesterreich*, January–February 1937, p. 58; Rosenkranz, *Verfolgung und Selbstbehauptung*, p. 13.
11. *Bericht der IKG*, 1933–1936, p. 119; *Gerechtigkeit*, 10 March 1938, p. 2; *Wahrheit*, 6 February 1931, p. 4; Glockemeier, *Wiener Judenfrage*, pp. 114–15.
12. Okladek, "Returnee Movement," p. 29.
13. *Bericht der IKG*, 1933–1936, pp. 109–10; Berkley, *Vienna and Its Jews*, p. 189; Freidenreich, *Jewish Politics in Vienna*, p. 17; Goldhammer, *Juden Wiens*, p. 12.
14. *Wahrheit*, 6 February 1931, p. 4.
15. Bangha, Trebitsch, and Kris, *Klärung in der Judenfrage*, p. 160; Goldhammer, *Juden Wiens*, pp. 11, 15.
16. *Stimme*, 24 May 1928, p. 6.
17. *Wahrheit*, 30 January 1931, p. 3; Rosenkranz, *Verfolgung und Selbstbehauptung*, p. 13.
18. Kreppel, *Juden von heute*, p. 710.
19. Goldhammer, *Juden Wiens*, p. 63; Rozenblit, *Jews of Vienna*, p. 3; Heller, *Edge of Destruction*, p. 59; Weinberg, *Community on Trial*, p. 6.
20. M. Freud, "Who Was Freud?" p. 204.
21. Rozenblit, *Jews of Vienna*, p. 71. See also Weitzmann, "Politics of the Viennese Jewish Community," p. 135. There were some exceptions to this pattern of Jewish social isolation, however. Both Hedi Goldfarb (interview) and J. Herbert Furth (letter) have asserted that they had a wide circle of gentile friends.
22. *Wahrheit*, 20 February 1931, p. 6.
23. Niewyk, *Jews in Weimar Germany*, p. 16; Frei, *Jüdisches Elend in Wien*, pp. 22, 27, 38, Goldhammer, *Juden Wiens*, pp. 60, 66.
24. Goldhammer, *Juden Wiens*, pp. 60, 66, 68; *Wahrheit*, 13 February 1931, p. 4; Gold, *Geschichte der Juden in Wien*, p. 65; Maderegger, *Juden im Ständestaat*, p. 54.

25. Wistrich, *Jews of Vienna*, p. 165; Furth letter, p. 1.

26. Beller, "Class, Culture and the Jews of Vienna," p. 49; Boyer, *Political Radicalism*, p. 80.

27. *Wahrheit*, 20 February 1931, p. 6; Sachar, *Modern Jewish History*, p. 395; Grunwald, *History of Jews in Vienna*, p. 253.

28. *DÖTZ*, 6 September 1925, p. 1; Glockemeier, *Wiener Judenfrage*, pp. 72, 77; Pötsch, *Jüdische Rasse*, p. 64; Bangha, Trebitsch, and Kris, *Klärung in der Judenfrage*, p. 176.

29. Maderegger, *Juden im Ständestaat*, p. 220; Andics, *Der ewige Jude*, p. 241.

30. Ludwig and Rosenberg, *Zur jüdischen Frage*, p. 9; *Wahrheit*, 8 March 1935, p. 1; *Stimme*, 5 March 1935, p. 2; *JF*, 1 January 1935, p. 1.

31. Thalberg, *Kunst, Österreicher zu sein*, p. 79.

32. Botz, "'Ausmerzung,'" p. 19; Goldhammer, *Juden Wiens*, p. 56; Oxaal and Weitzmann, "Jews in Pre-1914 Vienna," p. 432.

33. Rosenkranz, "Tragedy of Austrian Jewry," p. 480; Maderegger, *Juden im Ständestaat*, p. 220; Glockemeier, *Wiener Judenfrage*, pp. 76–77.

34. Grunwald, *History of Jews in Vienna*, p. 425; Boyer, *Political Radicalism*, pp. 80–81; Polleross, *Antisemitismus im Waldviertel*, p. 64; Sylvia Rapp interview.

35. Sozius [pseudonym for Eli Rubin], *Juden in Oesterreich*, pp. 9, 14, 17, 21; Polleross, *Antisemitismus im Waldviertel*, p. 65; Rosenkranz, "Tragedy of Austrian Jewry," p. 480; Körber, *Rassesieg in Wien*, p. 259.

36. Roth, *Juden auf Wanderschaft*, pp. 57, 59, 61, 62; Rozenblit, *Jews of Vienna*, p. 49.

37. Roth, *Juden auf Wanderschaft*, p. 62; McCagg, *Habsburg Jews*, p. 208.

38. Reichmann, *Hostages of Civilization*, pp. 46–47.

39. Ibid., pp. 44, 143.

40. Boyer, *Political Radicalism*, p. 84; *Gerechtigkeit*, 31 October 1935, p. 1; *Stimme*, 2 March 1934, p. 1; Bangha, Trebitsch, and Kris, *Klärung in der Judenfrage*, p. 178.

41. *Juden im Staate Deutsch-Österreich*, pp. 20–22, 26–29; Daniek, *Judentum im Kriege*, p. 28; Glockemeier, *Wiener Judenfrage*, pp. 60, 98; Ardelt, *Zwischen Demokratie und Faschismus*, p. 82; *Volksstimme*, 6 February 1932, p. 3. The quotation from *Mein Kampf* is on p. 63 of the German edition of 1937.

42. Jenks, "Jews in the Habsburg Empire," p. 155; Whiteside, "Comments on the Papers of Jenks and Niewyk," pp. 176–77; Johnson, *History of the Jews*, p. 476; Janik and Toulmin, *Wittgenstein's Vienna*, p. 70.

43. Csoklich, "Presse und Rundfunk," pp. 718, 724; Grunberger, "Jews in Austrian Journalism," pp. 93, 95; Tietze, *Juden Wiens*, pp. 211–12.

44. Tietze, *Juden Wiens*, p. 210; Johnson, *History of the Jews*, p. 481; Steed, *Hapsburg Monarchy*, p. 184.

45. Moser, "Katastrophe der Juden," p. 79; Ardelt, *Zwischen Demokratie und Faschismus*, pp. 84–85; Coudenhove-Kalergi, *Antisemitism throughout the Ages*, pp. 185, 187.

46. *Wahrheit*, 6 December 1929, p. 1; Stricker, *Der jüdische Nationalismus*, pp. 42–44, 46; Maderegger, *Juden im Ständestaat*, p. 188.

CHAPTER 15

1. *WJFB*, November 1933, p. 1.

2. Weitzmann, "Politics of the Viennese Jewish Community," pp. 136, 142–43, 148; Johnston, *Austrian Mind*, p. 360; *Wahrheit*, 7 July 1920, p. 3; Wistrich, *Jews of Vienna*, p. 662; Poppel, *Zionism in Germany*, p. 94. The quotation is from Zweig, *World of Yesterday*, p. 107.

3. *Wahrheit*, 1 January 1922, p. 3; 5 October 1934, p. 1; Gold, *Geschichte der Juden in Wien*, p. 48.

4. Wistrich, *Jews of Vienna*, p. 189; Pollak, "Cultural Innovation and Social Identity," p. 68.

5. *Stimme*, 2 March 1934, p. 1; Stricker, *Jüdische Politik*, p. 20; *Wahrheit*, 2 December 1932, p. 2; Maderegger, *Juden im Ständestaat*, p. 9. For similar Zionist attitudes in Germany, see Niewyk, *Jews in Weimar Germany*, pp. 107, 164; Grunwald, *History of Jews in Vienna*, pp. 454–55.

6. Rozenblit, *Jews of Vienna*, p. 165; Stricker, *Der jüdische Nationalismus*, pp. 22–23; marginal comment by Carl Flick; Niewyk, *Jews in Weimar Germany*, pp. 126, 128; Poppel, *Zionism in Germany*, p. 30.

7. Stricker, *Jüdische Nationalismus*, pp. 32–33; *Stimme*, 21 December 1933, p. 3; Berkley, *Vienna and Its Jews*, p. 191.

8. *Wahrheit*, 2 December 1932, p. 2; 1 September 1933, p. 1; 4 September 1936, p. 1; Clare, *Last Waltz in Vienna*, pp. 90–91; Levine, "Jewish Leadership in Germany," p. 197.

9. *Wahrheit*, 17 August 1925, p. 2; 21 March 1936, p. 4; 1 May 1936, p. 5; 16 October 1936, p. 3; 23 October 1936, p. 1; Häusler, "Toleranz, Emanzipation und Antisemitismus," pp. 128–29.

10. *Stimme*, 5 January 1928, p. 1; 5 October 1933, p. 1.

11. Maderegger, *Juden im Ständestaat*, p. 20.

12. Freidenreich, *Jewish Politics in Vienna*, p. 57; Niessner, "Entwicklungen im Judentum," p. 68; *JA*, 4 January 1933, p. 1; Bunzl, *Klassenkampf in der Diaspora*, p. 130; letter of Dr. Oscar Gruenbaum (Vienna) to the Zionist Executive in London, 25 February 1934, CZA, file 3563; NW, 16 September 1932, p. 1; 28 February 1934, p. 1; Schechter, *Viennese Vignettes*, p. 72.

13. Freidenreich, *Jewish Politics in Vienna*, p. 115; Kreppel, *Juden von heute*, pp. 711–12; Wistrich, *Jews of Vienna*, p. 27; Maderegger, *Juden im Ständestaat*, p. 12; Laqueur, *History of Zionism*, p. 408.

14. Freidenreich, *Jewish Politics in Vienna*, p. 27; *Wahrheit*, 23 October 1936, p. 1.

15. McCagg, *Habsburg Jews*, pp. 154–55; Baker, *Days of Sorrow and Pain*, p. 93; Berkley, *Vienna and Its Jews*, p. 238.

16. Weitzmann, "Politics of the Viennese Jewish Community," pp. 122, 124; Gold, *Geschichte der Juden in Wien*, p. 42; *Wahrheit*, 30 October 1936, p. 4; Wistrich, *Jews of Vienna*, p. 92.

17. Holter, "Kriegsflüchtlinge in Wien," p. 44.

18. Niewyk, "German Jews in Revolution and Revolt," p. 50.

19. Freidenreich, *Jewish Politics in Vienna*, p. 52; Streibel, "Judenfrage und Anti-semitismus," p. 106; *RP*, 5 November 1918, p. 3; Moser, "Katastrophe der Juden," p. 75; *ODR*, 17 October 1918, AK, folder "Zionismus"; *Wahrheit*, 6 January 1921, p. 3.

20. *BÖW*, 8 November 1918, first page; Weltsch, " Österreichische Revolutions-chronik," p. 357.

21. Hawlik, "Die politische Parteien Deutschösterreichs bei der wahlen zur kon-stuierenden Nationalversammlung," p. 684; *Stimme*, 8 July 1932, p. 2; Rosenkranz, *Verfolgung und Selbstbehauptung*, pp. 13–14; letter from the Union of Austrian Jews to Mayor Richard Schmitz, 5 February 1936, AVA, BKA Inneres 1936, K. 32, doc. 312.977, p. 10; Freidenreich, *Jewish Politics in Vienna*, p. 41; Palmon, "Jewish Community of Vienna," pp. XI, XIV.

22. *Wahrheit*, 7 July 1920, p. 3; *JZ*, 9 July 1920, p. 1; *Bericht der IKG*, 1929–1932, p. 3.

23. *Stimme*, 8 December 1932, p. 1; *Wahrheit*, 9 December 1932, p. 1.

24. *Stimme*, 6 December 1928, p. 1; *NW*, 10 November 1936, p. 1.

25. Palmon, "Jewish Community of Vienna," p. XX; *Wahrheit*, 7 July 1920, pp. 3–4; 13 November 1936, pp. 1–2; 20 November 1936, p. 1; Freidenreich, *Jewish Politics in Vienna*, p. 175.

26. *NW*, 10 November 1936, p. 2; *Stimme*, 8 December 1932, p. 2.

27. Letter of Dr. Koepf, Wiener Magistrat, to the Union of Austrian Jews, 30 June 1936, AVA, BKA Inneres 1936, K. 32. doc. 309507; Gold, *Geschichte der Juden in Wien*, p. 65.

28. Bihl, "Austrian Jews from 1918 to 1938," p. 4; Freidenreich, *Jewish Politics in Vienna*, pp. 65–68.

CHAPTER 16

1. Palmon letter, pp. 1–2.
2. *Wahrheit*, 12 July 1935, p. 1.
3. Niewyk, *Jews in Weimar Germany*, pp. 54, 85.
4. *Wahrheit*, 4 October 1929, p. 24. The quotation is from 18 December 1925, p. 1.
5. *Wahrheit*, 25 July 1930, p. 1.
6. *Wahrheit*, 22 August 1930, p. 2.
7. *Wahrheit*, 22 September 1930, p. 7.
8. *NW*, 19 September 1930, p. 1.
9. *Wahrheit*, 25 September 1931, p. 1.
10. *Wahrheit*, 6 May 1932, p. 2; *NW*, 29 April 1932, p. 1.
11. *Wahrheit*, 17 June 1932, p. 1.
12. *Wahrheit*, 5 August 1932, p. 1.
13. *Wahrheit*, 23 September 1932, p. 1.
14. *Wahrheit*, 11 November 1932, p. 1.
15. *NW*, 11 November 1932, p. 2.

16. *Stimme*, 2 June 1932, p. 2.

17. *Stimme*, 22 December 1932, p. 1.

18. *Wahrheit*, 10 February 1933, p. 1.

19. *Wahrheit*, 10 March 1933, pp. 3–4; 24 March 1933, p. 1.

20. *Wahrheit*, 10 March 1933, p. 4.

21. *Mein Kampf*, p. 52; *Wahrheit*, 31 March 1933, p. 1; Marcus, *Destiny of the German Jew*, p. 261.

22. *Wahrheit*, 10 April 1933, p. 3. On the dismissal of Jews, see Marcus, *Destiny of the German Jew*, pp. 8–13.

23. *Wahrheit*, 17 November 1933, p. 1.

24. *Stimme*, 2 February 1933, p. 1.

25. *Stimme*, 18 May 1933, pp. 1–2.

26. *JA*, 3 February 1933, p. 1; 10 March 1933, p. 1.

27. *NW*, 3 February 1933, p. 1; 31 March 1933, p. 1; 10 March 1933, p. 1. The quotation is from 4 August 1933, p. 1.

28. *JP*, 3 February 1933, p. 1.

29. Boas, "German-Jewish Internal Politics under Hitler," pp. 3–4.

30. *Wahrheit*, 6 July 1934, pp. 1–2.

31. Marcus, *Destiny of the German Jew*, p. 252.

32. Schleunes, *Twisted Road to Auschwitz*, pp. 125–26, 128; Gordon, *Hitler and the "Jewish Question,"* p. 122; Johnson, *History of the Jews*, p. 484.

33. *Wahrheit*, 20 September 1935, p. 1.

34. *Wahrheit*, 22 November 1935, p. 1; *Jude*, October 1935, p. 1.

35. *Wahrheit*, 6 April 1936, p. 5; 20 November 1936, p. 2.

36. *NW*, 11 May 1937, p. 1.

37. Barkai, *Von Boykott zur Entjudung*, p. 88.

CHAPTER 17

1. *Wahrheit*, 1 January 1927, p. 3; 25 March 1927, p. 1; Harand, *So oder So?*, p. 20.

2. Simon, *Österreich 1918–1938*, pp. 46–47.

3. Stricker, *Der jüdische Nationalismus*, p. 9.

4. *JP*, 9 December 1932, p. 1.

5. *JP*, 24 March 1933. See also *JP*, 21 April 1933, p. 1, and 6 May 1932, p. 1.

6. *Wahrheit*, 13 May 1932, p. 1; *WMZ*, 15 March 1923, p. 1; *EB*, 23 January 1932, p. 1; *Stürmer*, 2 September 1933, p. 1; *NYT*, 28 September 1934, p. 9; Hodik, "Israelitische Kultusgemeinde," pp. 27, 30; *Bericht der IKG*, 1929–1932, p. 14.

7. *EB*, 18 June 1927, p. 3; *DVB*, 22 June 1935, p. 11; Polleross, *Antisemitismus im Waldviertel*, pp. 44–45; Schilling [-Schletter], *Walter Riehl*, pp. 132–33.

8. *EB*, 15 May 1920, p. 1; 13 June 1927, p. 3; *Wahrheit*, 10 September 1923, p. 25; 6 May 1932, p. 1; *WMZ*, 26 July 1921, p. 3; *Stimme*, 7 June 1928, p. 1.

9. Letter dated 21 June 1929 from the Union of German Austrian Jews to Department 9 of the BKA, AVA, BKA Inneres 1929, K. 32, doc. 132964-6, 2 pp.; *NFP*,

21 June 1929, p. 1; 6 July 1929, p. 1; 19 July 1929, p. 4; *EB*, 19 July 1929, p. 4. The only two people interviewed for this book who took numerous summer vacations in Austria during the interwar period, Hedi Goldfarb and Lillian Axel, reported no anti-Semitic incidents. On the other hand, Mrs. Axel was denied admittance to a hotel in the Adirondack Mountains of New York in 1944 when she was eight months pregnant (Axel letter, pp. 4, 17).

10. [Ornstein], *Festschrift*, pp. 25, 100–103; letter from the president of the Union of Austrian Jews to the Police Directorate, 10 March 1937, 2 pp., DÖW, doc. 6895/7.

11. Toury, "Defense Activities," pp. 173–78; *Wahrheit*, 8 April 1925, p. 1; *NFP*, 31 October 1929, AK, folder "Union österr. Juden."

12. *Wahrheit*, 16 October 1936, p. 4; 1 February 1923, p. 10; 15 October 1926, p. 2; 6 February 1931, p. 3. The quotation is from 30 January 1931, p. 3.

13. For Zionist attitudes toward anti-Semitism in Germany, see Reinharz, "Zionist Response to Antisemitism," pp. 266–93; Niewyk, *Jews in Weimar Germany*, p. 95; and Edelheim-Mühsam, "Reactions of the Jewish Press to the Nazi Challenge," p. 312.

14. *Stimme*, 20 February 1934, p. 2; NW, 1 March 1938, p. 1; Sachar, *Modern Jewish History*, pp. 354–55; *BÖW*, 2 January 1920, p. 4; *Wahrheit*, 2 December 1932, p. 2; letter from the Zionist Landeskomitee für Österreich (Vienna) to the Zionist Executive in London, 22 December 1922, CZA, Z4/2094 I.

15. *B'nai-Brith—Mitteilungen Oesterreich*, January 1934, p. 2; Frei, *Jüdisches Elend in Wien*, p. 25.

16. Lebzelter, *Political Anti-Semitism in England*, p. 139; Weinberg, *Community on Trial*, pp. xi, 19; Mendelsohn, *Jews of East Central Europe*, p. 81; Baker, *Days of Sorrow and Pain*, p. 14.

17. *Wahrheit*, 1 February 1923, p. 11; 1 April 1923, p. 10; 5 October 1923, p. 12; Simon, "Jewish Vote in Austria," p. 114.

18. Gold, *Geschichte der Juden in Wien*, p. 47.

19. Letter of O. Braudi (Vienna) to the BKA, Generaldirektion für die öffentliche Sicherheit, 4 November 1932, BKA Inneres 1932, K. 32, doc. 231208, pp. 1, 4.

20. Ibid., p. 3.

21. On the Reichsbund, see Duncker, *Der Reichsbund jüdischer Frontsoldaten*, and Boas, "Jewish Internal Politics under Hitler," pp. 10–11.

22. *JF*, 1 May 1935, p. 1; 17 April 1936, p. 3; Maderegger, *Juden im Ständestaat*, p. 56. An unidentified document in the CZA claims that 70 to 80 percent of the members of the BJF were Zionists. See "Note in regard to the position of the 'Bund jüdischer Frontsoldaten Österreichs,'" n.d., file S5 2228, p. 1. This view is confirmed by the Israeli scholar, Avraham Palmon, who, in a letter to the author says that "it can be assumed with the utmost certainty that the majority of the Bund's members were Zionists. The more so since the leader of the Bund, Sigmund Edler von Friedmann, was a Zionist" (p. 2).

23. *JF*, 1 June 1935, p. 3.

24. For the best overall description of the BJF, see *Drei Jahre BJF-Bund Jüdischer Frontsoldaten Österreichs*. See also Schmidl, *Juden in der Armee*, pp. 148–49, and Körber, *Rassesieg in Wien*, p. 251.

25. Palmon letter, p. 1; *Stimme*, 6 October 1932, p. 2; NW, 5 August 1932, p. 2; *JF*, 1 May 1937, p. 3; 15 May 1937, p. 1.

26. See, for example, *JF*, 29 December 1932, p. 3; 15 November 1934, p. 3.

27. *JF*, 20 July 1936, p. 11.

28. *JF*, 15 October 1935, p. 1; 15 January 1936, p. 1; 1 April 1936, p. 3.

29. *JF*, 12 April 1934, p. 1.

30. Letter from the secretary of the IKG in Graz to the IKG in Vienna, 4 November 1934, 5 pp., CAHJP, A/W 2819; letter of the Vienna magistrate, Dept. 2 to the Executive Committee of the IKG of Vienna, 23 January 1936, 2 pp., ibid.; minutes of the meeting of the "Arbeitsgemeinschaft" of the IKG of Austria, 14 November 1937, 15 pp. ibid.

31. BÖW, 9 January 1920, first page; *Wahrheit*, 30 April 1937, p. 1. The quotation is from 4 December 1931, p. 1.

32. *WJFB*, February 1934, p. 2; *Gerechtigkeit*, 21 March 1935, p. 1; *JIZ*, January 1935, pp. 5–6; Eppel, *Zwischen Kreuz und Hakenkreuz*, pp. 175–76, 191.

33. Ebneth, "*Der christliche Ständestaat,*" p. 184.

34. Johnston, *Austrian Mind*, pp. 320–21; *Wahrheit*, 8 October 1926, p. 1.

35. Coudenhove-Kalergi, *Anti-Semitism throughout the Ages*, p. 198.

36. Daviau, "Hermann Bahr," p. 30.

37. Boerner, *Antisemitismus*, pp. 18, 22.

38. Ibid., pp. 16–17, 20–21, 23.

39. Haag, "A Woman's Struggle against Nazism," p. 66.

40. Leonard, "Anti-Semitism Disgraces Christianity," DÖW, doc. 11059, 4; Harand, *So oder So*, pp. 16–17.

41. *The Anti-Nazi Economic Bulletin*, December 1936, p. 8, DÖW, doc. 11059, 3a; *Stimme*, 3 November 1933, p. 3; *Gerechtigkeit*, 3 September 1936, p. 1; 12 August 1937, p. 1.

42. *The Anti-Nazi Economic Bulletin*, DÖW, doc. 11059, folder 3a; Leonard, "Anti-Semitism Disgraces Christianity," DÖW, doc. 11059, 4; *Gerechtigkeit*, 14 March 1935, p. 1.

43. *JIZ*, January 1935, p. 9; Harand, *So oder So?*, p. 2; Harand, *Sein Kampf*, p. 275. The quotation is from *Sein Kampf*, p. 278.

44. *Gerechtigkeit*, 4 January 1934, p. 1; 23 April 1936, pp. 3–4; 19 August 1937, p. 1.

45. See Harand, *So oder So?*, esp. pp. 6, 8, 24.

46. *Gerechtigkeit*, 23 April 1936, p. 2.

47. "The Harand Movement—How propaganda labels were used to fight Hitler's anti-Semitism," DÖW, doc. 11059, pp. 2–3.

48. *Gerechtigkeit*, 2 August 1934, p. 1; 4 January 1935, p. 1; 23 February 1935, p. 1; 13 August 1935, p. 1; 16 July 1936, p. 1; 17 February 1938, p. 1.

49. *Gerechtigkeit*, 26 April 1934, p. 1; 13 August 1935, p. 1; 9 July 1936, p. 1; Weinzierl, "Antisemitismus in Österreich," p. 314.

50. *Wahrheit*, 11 October 1933, p. 3; *Stimme*, 3 November 1933, p. 1; Leonard, "Anti-Semitism Disgraces Christianity," DÖW, doc. 11059, 4; "Die Wahrheit über die

Harand Bewegung," DÖW, doc. 11059, 3b; Körber, *Rassesieg in Wien*, p. 265; *Gerechtigkeit*, 14 March 1935, p. 1; 23 April 1935, p. 1; 2 May 1935, p. 1; 19 August 1937, p. 1.

51. Levy, *The Downfall of the Anti-Semitic Political Parties*, p. 153.

52. Massing, *Rehearsal for Destruction*, p. 168.

53. Mendelsohn, "Jewish Reactions to Antisemitism," p. 310; Levine, "The Jewish Leadership in Germany," p. 187; Knütter, *Die Juden und die deutsche Linke*, pp. 92–93; Lebzelter, *Political Anti-Semitism in England*, p. 145.

54. *BÖW*, 2 January 1920, pp. 1–2.

CHAPTER 18

1. Maderegger, *Juden im Ständestaat*, pp. 67, 266.

2. Ibid., p. 115; *Stürmer*, 28 October 1933, p. 1. The quotation is from Bunzl and Marin, *Antisemitismus in Österreich*, p. 48.

3. For details of political events in the late winter and spring of 1933, see Pauley, *Hitler and the Forgotten Nazis*, pp. 104–9.

4. *Wahrheit*, 24 March 1931, p. 1; Clare, *Last Waltz in Vienna*, p. 128.

5. Karbach, "Grundlagen des Antisemitismus," p. 176; Boas, "German-Jewish Internal Politics under Hitler," pp. 5–6.

6. *Stimme*, 30 March 1933, p. 6; letter from Grunbaum (Vienna) to Paul Goodman (London), 24 March 1933, CZA, Z4/3563.

7. *Wahrheit*, 28 April 1933, p. 1.

8. *RP*, 31 August 1933, p. 1. The quotation is from *Wahrheit*, 2 June 1933, p. 1.

9. *Wahrheit*, 23 June 1933, p. 1. The quotation is from 9 June 1933, p. 1.

10. *Protokolle des Ministerrates*, 3:578.

11. *Wahrheit*, 4 May 1934, p. 1; *JP*, 23 February 1934, p. 1.

12. Gold, *Geschichte der Juden in Wien*, p. 70; *Wahrheit*, 9 March 1934, p. 1; Wachter, "Antisemitismus im Vereinswesen," pp. 158, 202; Berkley, *Vienna and Its Jews*, p. 223.

13. *Stimme*, 5 October 1933, p. 1.

14. *Wahrheit*, 27 July 1934, p. 1.

15. *Stimme*, 27 July 1934, p. 1.

16. *The Minister in Austria (Stockton) to the Secretary of State*, Vienna, 29 October 1932, in *FRUS*, 1932, 2:125.

17. Zeller, "Lösung der Judenfrage," p. 558.

18. See Chapter 6.

19. See Chapter 9.

20. Sablik, *Julius Tandler*, p. 300; *NYT*, 11 May 1933, p. 10; 21 May 1933, p. 25.

21. *NYT*, 15 November 1933, p. 4; 18 November 1933, p. 34; *Wahrheit*, 23 February 1934, p. 1.

22. *SZ*, 14 January 1934, p. 396.

23. *DVB*, 28 August 1937, p. 3.

24. *Wahrheit*, 4 October 1929, p. 25. The quotation is from 1 January 1927, p. 1.

25. *Wahrheit*, 17 February 1934, p. 1.

26. *Stimme*, 27 February 1934, p. 1; 9 March 1934, p. 1.

27. *Wahrheit*, 23 February 1934, p. 1; *JP*, 23 February 1934, p. 1. The quotation is from *Stimme*, 16 February 1934, p. 1.

28. *Stimme*, 21 September 1934, p. 1; 26 October 1934, p. 1; 5 March 1935, p. 2; *Wahrheit*, 22 October 1937, p. 1; *NW*, 26 October 1937, p. 1.

29. Fellner, *Antisemitismus in Salzburg*, pp. 200–201.

30. *JP*, 27 March 1936, p. 1; *NW*, 30 November 1937, p. 1; Freidenreich, *Jewish Politics in Vienna*, pp. 190, 192.

31. *JA*, 10 March 1933, p. 2; *Wahrheit*, 28 July 1933, p. 1; *NW*, 23 September 1933. The quotation is from *JIZ*, January 1935, p. 11.

32. Letter of Kurt Rieth (Vienna) to the AA, 9 September 1933, NA, T-120, R. 5415/K287235; Rieth to the AA, 12 December 1933, ibid./K287243; letter of Franz von Papen (Vienna) to the AA, 8 May 1935, ibid./K287372; letter of Bade to the German Legation in Vienna, 24 June 1936, ibid./K287497; *NYT*, 14 December 1934, p. 10.

33. *Gerechtigkeit*, 10 May 1934, p. 1; 31 May 1934, p. 2; *Stürmer*, 20 January 1934, p. 1.

34. *JIZ*, January 1935, pp. 3–4.

35. *NW*, 5 March 1935, pp. 1–2; Maderegger, *Juden im Ständestaat*, p. 116.

36. Maderegger, *Juden im Ständestaat*, pp. 225, 230, 241; *Wahrheit*, 30 March 1934, p. 4; Fuchs, *Showdown in Vienna*, pp. 71–72; *JIZ*, January 1935, p. 12.

37. *NW*, 30 October 1934, p. 1; 3 November 1935, p. 1; Gstrein, *Jüdisches Wien*, p. 52; *Jude*, 10 December 1937, p. 1.

38. Lefwich, "Thinking of Vienna," p. 236; Kubl, "Geschichte der jüdischen Advokaten," pp. 122–23; *JP*, 8 March 1935, p. 1; *American Ambassador in Germany (Wilson) to the Secretary of State*, Berlin, 30 March 1938, in *FRUS*, 1938, 1:471.

39. Fuchs, *Showdown in Vienna*, p. 221; *NW*, 6 December 1934, p. 1.

40. Bärnthaler, *Vaterländische Front*, p. 176; Busshoff, *Dollfuss-Regime*, p. 251; Maderegger, *Juden im Ständestaat*, p. 125.

41. Freidenreich, *Jewish Politics in Vienna*, p. 196; Staudinger, "Katholischer Antisemitismus," p. 269; *NYT*, 13 December 1934, p. 10; 30 March 1936, p. 3; Schwarz, "Antisemitism and Socialism," p. 448; *Gerechtigkeit*, 18 April 1935, p. 1; letter of von Papen (Vienna) to the Führer and Reichskanzler Hitler, 20 March 1936, in *Akten zur deutschen auswärtigen Politik 1918–1945*, Series C: 1933–36, vol. 5, pp. 209–10, reprinted in Hodik, Malina, and Spann, *Juden in Österreich*, pp. 95–96; *JP*, 14 January 1938, p. 1; *NW*, 14 January 1938, p. 1.

42. Botz, "*Anschluss* to Holocaust," p. 190.

43. *JP*, 5 October 1934, p. 1; 24 May 1935, p. 1; *Wahrheit*, 28 September 1934, p. 1; 8 March 1935, p. 2; *Stimme*, 21 September 1934, p. 1; Pulzer, *Political Anti-Semitism*, p. 321; *NYT*, 9 September 1934, p. 9; 23 September 1934, p. 3; 28 September 1934, p. 9; Freidenreich, *Jewish Politics in Vienna*, p. 199.

44. *NYT*, 1 January 1937, p. 3; 10 March 1937, p. 26; 7 April 1937, p. 15.

45. Clare, *Last Waltz in Vienna*, pp. 42, 126.

46. *NYT*, 30 March 1936, p. 3.

CHAPTER 19

1. Zweig, *World of Yesterday*, pp. 402–3; Thalberg, *Kunst, Österreicher zu sein*, p. 60; Baron letter, p. 2. See also Hilsenrad, *Brown Was the Danube*, p. 206.

2. Clare, *Last Waltz in Vienna*, pp. 160–61.

3. *JP*, 11 February 1938, p. 1; 18 February 1938, p. 1; 25 February 1925, p. 1; *Wahrheit*, 4 March 1938, p. 1.

4. *NYT*, 20 February 1938, p. 1.

5. *NW*, 22 February 1938, p. 1; Clare, *Last Waltz in Vienna*, p. 173.

6. Gold, *Geschichte der Juden in Wien*, p. 74; Dr. Leo Landau, "Zu Wien von 1909 bis 1939," YV, doc. 0-1/244, p. 9; Moser, "Katastrophe der Juden," p. 107. The "Rosenkranz" religious celebration of 7 October 1938 did take on an at least partly political character when 6,000 to 8,000 young celebrants demonstrated outside the bishop's palace on St. Stephen's Square in Vienna amid chants of "Austria, Austria" and "Christ is our leader." The demonstration was not purely political, however, and far from producing positive results, only led to retaliation the next day by the Hitler Youth. See Botz, *Wien vom "Anschluss" zum Krieg*, pp. 383–84.

7. Clare, *Last Waltz in Vienna*, p. 178; Thalberg, *Kunst, Österreicher zu sein*, p. 62; Hilsenrad, *Brown Was the Danube*, p. 292.

8. Interviews with Goldfarb, Pollack, and Sylvia and Ernest Rapp; Axel letter, p. 6.

9. Gedye, *Fallen Bastions*, pp. 303, 308, 310–11.

10. Shirer, *Berlin Diary*, pp. 110–11; *SK*, 16 June 1938, p. 45.

11. Gedye, *Fallen Bastions*, pp. 303–4; Hilsenrad, *Brown Was the Danube*, pp. 245, 281.

12. Gedye, *Fallen Bastions*, p. 301; Clare, *Last Waltz in Vienna*, pp. 208–9.

13. Botz, *Wien vom "Anschluss" zum Krieg*, pp. 93–94.

14. Weinzierl, *Zu wenig Gerechte*, p. 29; Bentwich, "Destruction of the Jewish Community in Austria," p. 470; *SK*, 16 June 1938, p. 45; Gold, *Geschichte der Juden in Wien*, p. 84.

15. Moser, "Das Schicksal der Wiener Juden," p. 172; *SK*, 16 June 1938, p. 44.

16. Ibid., pp. 44–45; Moser, "Österreichs Juden unter der NS-Herrschaft," p. 191; Flick interview.

17. Botz, *Wien vom "Anschluss" zum Krieg*, pp. 103–4; Berkley, *Vienna and Its Jews*, p. 265.

18. Botz, *Wohnungspolitik*, p. 64; Botz, *Wien vom "Anschluss" zum Krieg*, pp. 98, 335, 337, 502; Gedye, *Fallen Bastions*, p. 360; Witek, "'Arisierungen' in Wien," pp. 210–13.

19. Botz, "Anschluss to Holocaust," p. 192.

20. Weinzierl, *Zu wenig Gerechte*, p. 57.

21. Botz, *Wien vom "Anschluss" zum Krieg*, p. 333.

22. Botz, "Anschluss to Holocaust," p. 190; Safrian and Witek, Keiner war Dabei, p. 98; Botz, Wohnungspolitik, p. 122.

23. Berkley, Vienna and Its Jews, p. 306; Botz, Wien vom "Anschluss" zum Krieg, pp. 330–31; Safrian and Witek, Keiner war Dabei, p. 40.

24. Schleunes, Twisted Road to Auschwitz, pp. 214–21, 258; Barkei, Von Boykott zur Entjudung, pp. 68, 71, 73, 87, 123, 139; Carr, "Nazi Policy against the Jews," pp. 72–73.

25. Botz, Wien vom "Anschluss" zum Krieg, p. 397.

26. Ibid., pp. 398, 400; Rosenkranz, "Tragedy of Austrian Jewry," p. 496; Gold, Geschichte der Juden in Wien, p. 89. For a complete description of the assassination in Paris and subsequent preparations for a trial of the perpetrator, see Gerald Schwab, The Day the Holocaust Began.

27. Rosenkranz, "Tragedy of Austrian Jewry," pp. 496–97; Gold, Geschichte der Juden in Wien, p. 78; Botz, Wien vom "Anschluss" zum Krieg, p. 402; Weinzierl (Zu wenig Gerechte, p. 63) estimates that 4,600 Austrian Jews were sent to Dachau.

28. Rosenkranz, "Tragedy of Austrian Jewry," pp. 496–97; Berkley, Vienna and Its Jews, pp. 278–79, 311.

29. Weinzierl, Zu wenig Gerechte, pp. 60, 62; Binder, "Das Schicksal der Grazer Juden 1938," pp. 222–23; Rosenkranz, "Tragedy of Austrian Jewry," pp. 488, 498.

30. For a recent comparison of Kristallnacht in Vienna and other parts of the German Reich, see Fellner, "Der Novemberpogrom 1938," esp. pp. 37, 44. See also Botz, "'Ausmerzung,'" pp. 25, 29; Weinzierl, Zu wenig Gerechte, p. 69; Gordon, Hitler and the "Jewish Question," p. 175; and Berkley, Vienna and Its Jews, pp. 310–11.

31. Safrian and Witek, Keiner war Dabei, p. 15; Botz, Wohnungspolitik, pp. 120–21; Botz, "'Ausmerzung,'" p. 33.

32. Botz, Wien vom "Anschluss" zum Krieg, p. 96; Botz, Wohnungspolitik, pp. 58, 60; Ronzoni, "Lebensverhältnisse der jüdischen Bevölkerung in Österreich zwischen Herbst 1938 und Frühjahr 1939," p. 12.

33. Botz, Wohnungspolitik, pp. 57, 89; Botz, Wien vom "Anschluss" zum Krieg, p. 459; Rosenkranz, "Tragedy of Austrian Jewry," p. 509.

34. Botz, Wohnungspolitik, p. 76; Botz, "Anschluss to Holocaust," pp. 198–99.

35. Weinzierl, Zu wenig Gerechte, p. 36.

36. Ibid., p. 32; SK, 16 June 1938, p. 46; Botz, "Anschluss to Holocaust," p. 190; Flick interview.

37. Berkley, Vienna and Its Jews, p. 324; Weinzierl, Zu wenig Gerechte, p. 35; Kubl, "Geschichte der jüdischen Advokaten," p. 123; Safrian and Witek, Keiner war Dabei, p. 160; Botz, Wien vom "Anschluss" zum Krieg, p. 244.

38. Rosenkranz, "Tragedy of Austrian Jewry," pp. 502, 506, 519; Weinzierl, Zu wenig Gerechte, pp. 37–38, 41–43.

39. See Körber, Rassesieg in Wien, esp. pp. 201, 202, 206, 211, 221, 254, 257, 261.

40. Ibid., pp. 292–93, 298–99, 301, 302.

41. Bentwich, "Destruction of the Jewish Community," p. 468; Weinzierl, "Schuld durch Gleichgültigkeit," p. 183; minutes of the meeting of the Kultusgemeinden of Austria, 7 August 1938, CAHJP, A/W 2819, p. 2.

42. Hodik, "Israelitische Kultusgemeinde," p. 33; Weinzierl, *Zu wenig Gerechte*, p. 51; Botz, *Wohnungspolitik*, p. 71; Goldfarb interview.

43. *German Ambassador in the United States (Dieckhoff) to the German Foreign Ministry*, Washington, D.C., 18 April 1938, in *DGFP*, D, I, no. 401, p. 619.

44. Botz, *Wien vom "Anschluss" zum Krieg*, p. 254; Botz, *Wohnungspolitik*, p. 101; Rosenkranz, "Tragedy of Austrian Jewry," pp. 469, 490.

45. Botz, *Wien vom "Anschluss" zum Krieg*, pp. 250-51; Ganglmair, *Resistance and Persecution*, p. 43; Clare, *Last Waltz in Vienna*, p. 200.

46. Botz, "Anschluss to Holocaust," p. 195; Dutch [pseud. Otto Deutsch], "Seeds of a Noble Inheritance," p. 179; Botz, *Wohnungspolitik*, p. 68; Weinzierl, *Zu wenig Gerechte*, p. 52; *NYT*, 23 May 1958, p. 22; Rosenkranz, "Tragedy of Austrian Jewry," pp. 510, 514.

47. *SK*, 13 January 1940, pp. 3-5.

48. Ibid. See also Botz, *Wohnungspolitik*, pp. 106-7.

49. Fellner, "Der Novemberpogrom 1938," pp. 46-47; Gordon, *Hitler and the "Jewish Question*," p. 312.

50. Rosenkranz, "Tragedy of Austrian Jewry," p. 486; Botz, *Wien vom "Anschluss" zum Krieg*, pp. 251-52.

51. Schleunes, *Twisted Road to Auschwitz*, pp. 212, 229-30; Riedl, "Geht doch in die Donau," p. 166.

52. Berkley, *Vienna and Its Jews*, p. 312; Rosenkranz, "Tragedy of Austrian Jewry," pp. 500, 517.

53. Berkley, *Vienna and Its Jews*, pp. 315, 317; Botz, "Anschluss to Holocaust," p. 202.

54. Rosenkranz, "Tragedy of Austrian Jewry," pp. 517, 519; Gold, *Geschichte der Juden in Wien*, p. 102.

55. Rosenkranz, "Tragedy of Austrian Jewry," pp. 513, 522; Botz, *Wohnungspolitik*, p. 114; Weinzierl, *Zu wenig Gerechte*, p. 88; Binder, "Schicksal der Grazer Juden," p. 227; Bukey, *Hitler's Home Town*, p. 189.

56. Weinzierl, "Die Stellung der Juden in Österreich," p. 94; Berkley, *Vienna and Its Jews*, p. 320; Weinzierl, *Zu wenig Gerechte*, p. 88; Rosenkranz, "Tragedy of Austrian Jewry," p. 526.

57. Rosenkranz, "Bemerkungen," pp. 90-91; *Morgen*, 5 November 1934, p. 2.

58. Rosenkranz, "Bemerkungen," pp. 92-94, 96; Weinzierl, " Österreichische Katholiken," pp. 362-65; Gordon, *Hitler and the "Jewish Question*," pp. 248-49; Berkley, *Vienna and Its Jews*, pp. 326-27. German bishops meeting in Fulda in 1943 also protested the possibility of dissolving mixed marriages and the Vatican intervened with the Berlin government. In the end, the Nazis never went through with their plans, one of several interesting examples of how unified protests against Nazi actions could bring positive results. See Weinzierl, " Österreichische Katholiken," pp. 364-65; Reimann, *Innitzer*, pp. 249, 256-57, 263-64; Luža, *The Resistance in Austria*, pp. 41-42.

59. Rosenkranz, "Tragedy of Austrian Jewry," pp. 486-87.

60. *SK*, 16 June 1938, p. 45.

61. Lipstadt, *Beyond Belief.*

62. Kolin interview.

CHAPTER 20

1. *NYT*, 3 May 1981, 6:127; Botz letter; Wodak and de Cillia, "Judenfeindlichkeit im öffentlichen Diskurs," p. 5; Beckermann, *Unzugehörig*, pp. 99–100; Kraus, "Austria's Future Jewish Problem," 24, 31 January 1947, in Wagnleitner, *Understanding Austria*, p. 118; Binder, "Schicksal der Grazer Juden," p. 228.

2. Weiss, *Antisemitische Vorurteile?*, p. 127.

3. Rathkolb, "Vorurteile in Österreich 1945/1950," p. 176. On the attitude of Socialists toward their former Jewish leaders, see Schwarz, "Antisemitism and Socialism," pp. 453–55.

4. Albrich, *Exodus durch Österreich*, pp. 8, 180, 184–85, 188; the American Minister (Erhardt) to the Secretary of State, Vienna, 4 March 1947, in Wagnleitner, *Understanding Austria*, p. 113.

5. Albrich, *Exodus durch Österreich*, pp. 182, 187; the American Minister (Erhardt) to the Secretary of State, Vienna, 4 March 1947, in Wagnleitner, *Understanding Austria*, p. 113.

6. Rathkolb, "Vorurteile in Österreich 1945/50," p. 168.

7. Ibid., p. 172; reprint of an article by Mayor Körner dated 9 February 1947 in Wagnleitner, *Understanding Austria*, pp. 114–15; Pfarrhofer, *Friedrich Funder*, pp. 301–2.

8. *NYT*, 3 May 1981, 6:142.

9. Gärtner, "Right-Wing Student Politics," pp. 280, 282–83, 285, 291; *NYT*, 28 March 1965, p. 18; 4 April 1965, p. 16.

10. *NYT*, 27 February 1966, p. 17.

11. Marin, "Antisemitism before and after the Holocaust," pp. 218–19, 226; Weiss, *Antisemitische Vorurteile?*, p. 126. See also, Marin, "A Post-Holocaust 'Anti-Semitism without Anti-Semites'?," esp. p. 59.

12. Bunzl, "'Austrian Identity' and Antisemitism," p. 6.

13. Marin, "Antisemitism before and after the Holocaust," p. 221.

14. Weinzierl, "Religious Antisemitism," p. 348.

15. Weiss, *Antisemitische Vorurteile?*, pp. 128–29; Hitler, *Mein Kampf*, p. 57.

16. Peres, "Antisemitismus in Österreich," p. 84; Lukawetz, "Antisemitismus," p. 80; Gordon, *Hitler and the "Jewish Question,"* p. 260; Wodak and de Cillia, "Judenfeindlichkeit," p. 6.

17. Haerpfer, *Anti-Semitic Attitudes in Austrian Society*, pp. 1, 4, 6–7, 11, 13–15.

18. Ibid., pp. 7–8; Pelinka, "SPÖ, ÖVP, and the 'Ehemaligen,'" p. 267.

19. Jellinek, "Wiedergutmachung," p. 399; OÖT, reprinted in ÖB, no. 33/189, 8 August 1987, Kulturbeilage.

374 : NOTES TO PAGES 308-15

20. Jellinek, "Wiedergutmachung," p. 426; *Presse*, reprinted in *ÖB*, no. 275, 23 November 1988, p. 2; Beckermann, *Unzugehörig*, p. 63; Walch, *Wiedergutmachung*, p. 14.

21. Knight, *Ich bin dafür*, pp. 42, 52, 59; Beckermann, *Unzugehörig*, pp. 89–90; Berkley, *Vienna and Its Jews*, p. 351; *Time*, 26 March 1990, p. 34; Walch, *Wiedergutmachung*, pp. 1, 5, 9–10, 229–30; *NYT*, 22 December 1953, p. 16; 3 April 1988, 4:16.

22. Petritsch letter with an enclosed article from the *NYT* dated 14 February 1990.

23. *Presse*, reprinted in *ÖB*, no. 275, 23 November 1988, p. 2; Jellinek, "Wiedergutmachung," p. 397.

24. On the long and tortuous efforts of the Japanese-Americans to receive compensation for their wartime incarceration, see Hosokawa, *JACL*.

25. Herzstein, *Waldheim*, p. 174; Meissl, Mulley, and Rathkolb, *Verdrängte Schuld, verfehlte Sühne*, p. 29; *NYT*, 19 December 1953, p. 2; Walch, *Wiedergutmachung*, p. 148; Stiefel, "Nazifizierung plus Entnazifizierung," p. 34.

26. Stiefel, "Nazifizierung plus Entnazifizierung," p. 34; Rubenstein, "After the Holocaust," p. 5; Köfler, "Tirol und die Juden," p. 179; *AZ*, in *ÖB*, no. 182, 8 August 1987, p. 2; Herzstein, *Waldheim*, p. 174; Safrian and Witek, *Und Keiner war Dabei*, p. 197.

27. Knight, *Ich bin dafür*, pp. 34, 50, 55; Knight, "Kalter Krieg, Entnazifierung und Österreich," p. 46.

28. Herzstein, *Waldheim*, pp. 117, 215, 254. The quotation is from p. 23.

29. Basset, *Waldheim and Austria*, p. 157; *NYT*, 29 March 1986, p. 20; 27 April 1986, 4:2; 5 May 1986, p. 4; 12 June 1986, p. 3.

30. Basset, *Waldheim and Austria*, pp. 98, 122; *NYT*, 11 April 1986, p. 12; 2 June 1986, 6:16; Herzstein, *Waldheim*, p. 252.

31. Langbein, "Darf man vergessen?" p. 13; Grunberger, "Waldheim in the Press," p. 12; Basset, *Waldheim and Austria*, pp. 138, 163; *NYT*, 11 April 1986, p. 12; 4 May 1986, p. 23; 17 May 1986, p. 4; 15 February 1988, p. 1; 16 February 1988, p. 6; Botz interview; Wodak and de Cillia, "Judenfeindlichkeit," p. 8, *AZ*, reprinted in *ÖB*, no. 58, 10 March 1988, p. 1.

32. *Presse*, reprinted in *ÖB*, no. 278, 27 November 1987, p. 2; *AZ*, reprinted in *ÖB*, no. 147, 29 June 1987, p. 1; *WZ*, reprinted in *ÖB*, no. 157, 10 July 1987, p. 1; *WZ*, reprinted in *ÖB*, no. 260, 9 November 1988, p. 1.

33. *OÖT*, reprinted in *ÖB*, no. 33/189, 8 August 1987, Kulturbeilage; *NYT*, 3 May 1981, 6:140, 144; *Kurier*, reprinted in *ÖB*, no. 98, 22 April 1989, p. 2; Sully, "Waldheim Connection," p. 307; *AZ*, reprinted in *ÖB*, no. 56, 8 March 1990, p. 2; "Vienna Welcomes Grandchildren of Survivors," p. 6; *Austrian Information*, p. 2.

34. Wodak and de Cillia, "Judenfeindlichkeit," pp. 12–13.

35. Ganglmair, *Resistance and Persecution*, pp. 23, 37.

36. See for example, *Presse*, reprinted in *ÖB*, no. 217, 17 September 1988, p. 2; *Furche*, reprinted in *ÖB*, no. 238, 30 September 1988, p. 2; Joffe, "Where Hitler Fell Down the Memory Hole," p. 32. See also the catalog of the November Pogrom exhibit called *Der Novemberpogrom*.

37. Hodik, Malina, and Spann, *Juden in Österreich.*

38. *Austrian Studies Newsletter,* p. 10; WZ, reprinted in ÖB, no. 5, 8 January 1988, p. 1; *Presse,* reprinted in ÖB, no. 300, 22 December 1988, p. 2; "SWS-Meinungsprofile," p. 91. See also Kienzl, "Der Österreicher und seine Schande," p. 657.

39. Koppel, "Holocaust in Austrian Schools," esp. pp. 3, 10.

40. NYT, 29 August 1967, p. 3.

41. Marin, "Antisemitism before and after the Holocaust," p. 223; Lukawetz, "Antisemitismus," p. 79.

CHAPTER 21

1. Valentin, *Antisemitism,* p. 120; Heller, *Edge of Destruction,* p. 77; Zmarzlik, "Antisemitismus im Deutschen Kaiserreich," p. 258.

2. Bukey, *Hitler's Home Town,* pp. 54–55; Fellner, *Antisemitismus in Salzburg,* p. 166.

3. Karbach, "Grundlagen des Antisemitismus," p. 8.

4. Gordon, *Hitler and the "Jewish Question,"* pp. 53–55; Niewyk, *Jews of Weimar Germany,* p. 80.

5. Letter of Walter Riehl (Vienna) to Alfred Proksch (Linz), 26 April 1932, Slg. Sch., 305 folder 2, p. 1.

6. Kershaw, *Popular Opinion and Political Dissent in the Third Reich,* p. 347; Lewy, *The Catholic Church and Nazi Germany,* p. 289.

7. *Mein Kampf,* p. 121.

8. *Wahrheit,* 24 April 1931, p. 4.

9. *Wahrheit,* 10 February 1933, p. 1.

10. *Wahrheit,* 12 July 1935, p. 1.

11. JA, 2 February 1934, p. 1.

12. *Stimme,* 2 June 1932, p. 2; 22 December 1932, p. 1; 31 July 1934, p. 1.

13. Heer, "Judentum und österreichischer Genius," p. 297. On the illusions of German and French Jews about Hitler, see Niewyk, *Jews in Weimar Germany,* p. 143; Baker, *Days of Sorrow and Pain,* p. 180; and Weinberg, *Community on Trial,* p. 196.

14. JF, 15 April 1937, p. 1.

15. See Mendelsohn, *Jews of East Central Europe,* and Valentin, *Der Antisemitismus,* p. 102.

16. DÖTZ, 13 January 1921, p. 5; EB, 16 October 1924, p. 2; Cohn, *Warrant for Genocide,* p. 162.

17. ATA, 24 December 1919, AVA, NS-P, K. 64; Peter, *Der Antisemitismus,* p. 11.

18. DAP, 21 February 1925, p. 5.

19. [Eberle], "Die gesellschaftliche Stellung der Juden in Nordamerika," p. 575.

20. Bauer, *History of the Holocaust,* pp. 67, 470.

21. Hosokawa, *JACL,* p. 183.

22. Haerpfer, *Anti-Semitic Attitudes in Austrian Society,* p. 16.

23. For such comparisons, see Pauley, *Habsburg Legacy*. An exception is Czecho-slovakia, which undoubtedly treated its Jewish population better than Austria or the other successor states did.

24. Cummings, *Scott 1990 Standard Postage Stamp Catalogue*, 2:166.

25. Haag, "A Woman's Struggle against Nazism," p. 71.

26. Marboe letter.

BIBLIOGRAPHY

DOCUMENTS AND MANUSCRIPTS

Allgemeines Verwaltungsarchiv (AVA) (General Administrative Archive), Vienna.
  Bundeskanzleramt (BKA) Inneres
    Akten (documents), Karton (carton, K.), 32, Generaldirektion für die öffentliche
      Sicherheit: 1923, 1925, 1928, 1932, 1936.
  NS-Parteistellen (NS-P)
    Karton 5, Gauleiter A. E. Frauenfeld, Korrespondenz, 1930–33.
    Karton 8, *Der Kampfruf*, Redaktion.
    Karton 12, Information über Gegner—Heimatschutz.
    Karton 14, Organisation, Prozesse.
    Karton 16, Propagandamanuskripte.
    Karton 18, Rassenhygiene; Schulung des Amtes für Bearbeitung der Judenfrage.
    Karton 32, Zeitungsausschnitte: Rasse.
    Karton 64, Zeitungsausschnitte: Juden.
  Grossdeutsche Volkspartei
    Antisemitenbund.
    VI-36, Judenausschuss.
  SD-Parteistellen
    Karton 52, Zeitungsausschnitte.
    Karton 58, Zeitungsausschnitte.
Bundesarchiv (Federal Archives), Koblenz, Germany.
  Sammlung Schumacher (Slg. Sch.).
    305 Folder 2. Korrespondenz der Landesleitung der NSDAP in Österreich mit
      den einzelnen Ortsgruppen sowie der Reichsleitung in München.
Central Archive for the History of the Jewish People (CAHJP), Jerusalem.
  Archives of the Kultusgemeinde in Vienna.
    A/W 326, 328, 2819.
Central Zionist Archives, Jerusalem (CZA).
  Correspondence between the Zionist Organization, Central Office in London and
    Zionist officials in Vienna

Z4, 414/4; 2094 I; 2422 I; S 5 2228; 3563, I, III

Dokumentationsarchiv des österreichischen Widerstandes (DÖW), Vienna.

Folders: 6895: 4, 7, 10, 12, 14; 11059: 1, 3a, 3b, 4.

A folder not fully cited in the notes is 1460, Alfred Persche, "Hauptmann
Leopold: Der Abschnitt 1936–1938 der Geschichte der nationalsozialistischen
Machtergreifung in Österreich." Unpublished manuscript (n.d.).

Kammer für Arbeiter und Angestellte in Wien (AK), Abteilung:
Dokumentation, Vienna
Newspaper clippings. Folders:
HW-Antisemitismus.
Juden-Katholizismus.
Judentum, Antisemitismus, Zionismus.
Union österr. Juden.
Zionismus.

National Archives (NA), Washington, D.C.
World War II Collection of Seized Enemy Records
Records filmed at Whaddon Hall, Bucks, England
Microcopy T-120, 1920–36, reels 900, 5415.

Protokolle des Ministerrates der Ersten Republik: Kabinett Dr. Engelbert Dollfuss,
Abteilung VIII, 20 Mai 1932 bis 25 Juli 1934, edited by Isabella Ackerl and Rudolf
Neck, vol. 3. Vienna: Verlag der österreichischen Staatsdruckerei, 1983.

Stenographische Protokolle der Konstituierenden Nationalversammlung der Republik
Österreich, 1920, vol. 78. Sitzung am 29 April 1920.

United States Department of State. *Documents on German Foreign Policy, 1918–1945*
(DGFP). Series D, *From Neurath to Ribbentrop,* vol. 1. Washington, D.C.: U.S.
Government Printing Office, 1949.

⸻. *Papers Relating to the Foreign Relations of the United States* (FRUS),
1932, vol. 2; 1938, vol. 1. Washington, D.C.: U.S. Government Printing Office,
1947, 1955

Yad Vashem (YV), Jerusalem.
Doc. 0-1/244

NEWSPAPERS AND PERIODICALS

Allgemeine Tiroler Anzeiger (ATA, Innsbruck), 24 December 1919.

Anti-Nazi Economic Bulletin, December 1936.

Arbeiter-Zeitung: Zentralorgan der Sozialdemokratie Deutschösterreichs (AZ, Vienna),
14 November 1918–12 August 1991.

Austrian Information 44, no. 1 (1991).

Austrian Studies Newsletter 2, no. 3 (Winter 1990).

Bauernsturm. Beilage der *Volksstimme* (Linz), 18 March 1932.

Dr. Blochs Oesterreichische Wochenschrift: Zentralorgan für die gesamten Interessen des

Judentums (*BÖW*, Vienna. Called *Dr. Blochs Wochenschrift* after 1919.), 2 January 1914–20 January 1920.

B'nai-Brith—Mitteilungen für Oesterreich (Vienna), January–February 1934—January–February 1937.

Deutsche Arbeiter-Presse: Nationalsozialistisches Kampfblatt für Deutschösterreich (DAP, Vienna), 28 June 1919–6 November 1926.

Deutsches Volksblatt (DVB, Vienna), 17 March 1920; 21 March 1936–3 April 1937.

Deutschösterreichische Tages-Zeitung: Unabhängiges Blatt für völkische Politik (DÖTZ, Vienna), 7 January 1921–10 January 1931.

Der eiserne Besen: Ein Blatt der Notwehr (EB, Salzburg), 15 May 1920–12 March 1932.

Die Furche (Vienna), 30 September 1988.

Gerechtigkeit: Gegen Rassenhass und Menschennot (Vienna), 4 January 1934–10 March 1938.

Der Jude: Ein Monatschrift (Berlin, Vienna), 1916–19.

Der Jude: Organ für der arbeitende Palästina (Vienna), October 1935.

Jüdische Front: Offizielle Organ des Bundes jüdischer Frontsoldaten Österreichs (JF, Vienna) 12 April 1934–7 January 1938.

Jüdische Information Zentrale (JIZ), January 1935.

Jüdische Presse: Organ für die Interessen des Orthodoxen Judentums (JP, Vienna), 6 May 1932–25 February 1938.

Der jüdischer Arbeiter: Organ der Vereinigten Zionistisch-sozialistischen Arbeiter-organisation Poale Zion-Hitachduth in Österreich (JA, Vienna), 4 January 1933–19 January 1934.

Jüdischer Volkszeitung (JVZ, Vienna), 9 February 1932–18 April 1932.

Jüdische Weg (JW, Vienna), 28 December 1932–25 March 1936.

Jüdische Zeitung (JZ, Vienna), 9 July 1920.

Der Kampf (Graz), 8 August 1931–16 September 1931.

Der Kampfruf (Vienna), 2 May 1931–June 1932.

Kurier (Vienna), 22 April 1989.

Mitteilungen der Vereinigung christlich deutscher Ärzte Österreichs (Vienna), September 1935.

Monatschrift der Österreichisch-israelitischen Union (MU, Vienna), July–August 1914—October–December 1917.

Der Morgen: Wiener Montagblatt (Vienna), 5 May 1934.

Neue Freie Presse (NFP, Vienna), 1 January 1920–29 January 1932.

Der Neue Tag (NT, Vienna), 30 April 1920.

Die Neue Welt (NW, Vienna), 5 February 1932–1 March 1938.

Neues Wiener Abendblatt (NWA, Vienna), 18 August 1925.

Neues Wiener Journal (NWJ, Vienna), 3 December 1922–18 August 1925.

Neues Wiener Tagblatt: Demokratisches Organ (NWT, Vienna), 13 February 1923–16 January 1927.

The New York Times (NYT), 28 September 1919–20 February 1938; 19 December

1953; 28 March 1965–29 August 1967; 3 May 1981–14 February 1990.

Oberösterreichisches Tagblatt (OÖT, Linz), 8 August 1987.

Ostdeutsche Rundschau: Wiener Wochenschrift für Politik, Volkswirtschaft, Kunst und Literatur (ODR, Vienna), 7 February 1918–10 October 1919.

Der Österreich-Bericht: Presseübersicht Zusammengestellt vom Bundespressedienst des Bundeskanzleramtes (ÖB, Vienna), 29 June 1987–8 March 1990.

Österreichische Heimatschutz-Zeitung (ÖHZ, Vienna), 25 February 1933.

Der Panther (Judenburg), 12 April 1932.

Die Presse (Vienna), 17 September 1988–22 December 1988.

Reichspost: Unabhängiges Tagblatt für das christliche Volk (RP, Vienna), 9 November 1918–31 August 1937.

Schönere Zukunft (SZ, Vienna), 18 October 1925–28 February 1937.

Selbstwehr: Unabhängiger jüdische Wochenschrift (Prague), 9 August 1918.

Der Sozialistische Kampf (SK, Paris), 16 June 1938–13 January 1940.

Die Stimme: Jüdische Zeitung (Vienna), 5 January 1928–5 March 1935.

Der Stürmer: Unabhängiges Wochenblatt für alle Schaffenden (Vienna), 21 October 1933–3 March 1934.

Time, 26 March 1990.

Unverfälschte deutsche Worte (Vienna), 16 May 1885.

Die Volksstimme (Linz), 4 February 1933.

Der Vormarsch: NS Nachrichtenblatt (Klagenfurt), 9 April 1932.

Die Wahrheit: Unabhängige Zeitschrift für jüdische Interessen (Vienna), 7 August 1914–4 March 1938.

The Washington Post, 29 December 1987.

Wiener jüdisches Familienblatt (WJFB, Vienna), November 1933–February 1934.

Wiener Morgenzeitung (WMZ, Vienna), 25 January 1919–29 August 1925.

Wiener Stimmen (WS, Vienna), 3 December 1919.

Wiener Zeitung (WZ, Vienna), 23 August 1925; 10 July 1987; 9 November 1988.

INTERVIEWS AND PERSONAL CORRESPONDENCE

Axel, Lillian (New Rochelle, New York). Letter to the author, 14 March 1989, 25 pp.

Baron, Fred E. (Golden Valley, Minneapolis). Letter to the author, 5 March 1989, 2 pp.

Botz, Gerhard. Interview in Oviedo, Florida, 12 October 1988.

——— (Salzburg). Letter to the author, 1 February 1991.

Flick, Carl. Interview in Orlando, Florida, 5 December 1988.

Furth, J. Herbert. Letter to Professor Gottfried Haberler, 24 June 1979, forwarded to the author, 6 pp.

Goldfarb, Hedi. Interview in Longwood, Florida, 2 December 1988.

Hoffmann, Rose. Interview in Casselberry, Florida, 1 December 1988.

Kolin, Jean. Interview in Winter Park, Florida, 6 December 1988.

Marboe, Peter (Vienna). Letter (with an enclosure) to Irene Freudenschuss-Reichl (New York), 18 May 1990, forwarded to the author.

Palmon, Avraham (Jerusalem). Letter to the author, 20 August 1990, 2 pp.

Petritsch, Wolfgang (New York). Letter to the author, 27 June 1990, 2 pp.

Pollack, Felix. Interview in Longwood, Florida, 6 December 1988.

Rapp, Ernest and Sylvia. Interview in Longwood, Florida, 7 December 1988.

GENERAL

(Books, Articles in Journals and Books, Theses and Dissertations)

Abel, Theodore. *Why Hitler Came to Power*. 1938. Reprint. Cambridge: Harvard University Press, 1986.

Ackerl, Isabella. "Die Grossdeutsche Volkspartei." Ph.D. dissertation, University of Vienna, 1967.

Adler, Alois. *Die historischen Fakten des Nationalsozialismus in Österreich*. Leibnitz: Retzhof, 1968.

Albrich, Thomas. *Exodus durch Österreich: Die jüdischen Flüchtlinge 1945–1948*. Innsbruck: Haymon-Verlag, 1987.

Allardyce, Gilbert. "What Fascism Is Not: Thoughts on the Deflation of a Concept." *American Historical Review* 84 (April 1979): 367–98.

Altmann, Adolf. "Geschichte der Juden in Salzburg." In *Geschichte der Juden in Österreich*, edited by Hugo Gold, pp. 67–80. Tel Aviv: Olamenu, 1971.

Amelung, Eugen. "Die Judenfrage in christlicher Schau." *Schönere Zukunft* (14 February 1932): 450–51.

Andics, Hellmut. *Der ewige Jude: Ursachen und Geschichte des Antisemitismus*. Vienna: Fritz Molden Verlag, 1969.

————. *Die Juden in Wien*. Vienna: Verlag Kremayr & Scheriau, 1988.

Ardelt, Rudolf. *Zwischen Demokratie und Faschismus: Deutschnationales Gedanken-gut in Österreich 1919–1930*. Vienna: Geyer, 1972.

Arkel, Dirk van. "Anti-Semitism in Austria." Ph.D. dissertation, University of Leiden, 1966.

Auer, Johann. "Antisemitische Strömungen in Wien, 1921–1923." *Österreich in Geschichte und Literatur* 10 (1966): 23–27.

Baker, Leonard. *Days of Sorrow and Pain: Leo Baeck and the Berlin Jews*. New York: Oxford University Press, 1978.

Balas, Karl von. "Zur Judenfrage." *Schönere Zukunft* (2 October 1927): 11–12.

Bangha, Bela, Oskar Trebitcsh, and Paul Kris. *Klärung in der Judenfrage*. Vienna: Reinhold Verlag, 1934.

Barkai, Avraham. *Von Boykott zur Entjudung: Der wirtschaftliche Existenzkampf der Juden im Dritten Reich 1933–1943*. Frankfurt am Main: Fischer Verlag, 1988.

Bärnthaler, Imgard. *Die Vaterländische Front: Geschichte und Organisation*. Vienna: Europa Verlag, 1971.

Bassett, Richard. *Waldheim and Austria*. New York: Viking Press, 1989.

Baudisch, Ursula. "Der Antisemitismus der Christlichsozialen im Spiegel der parteinahen Presse, 1890 bis April 1897." Ph.D. dissertation, University of Vienna, 1967.

Bauer, Yehuda. *A History of the Holocaust*. New York: Franklin Watts, 1982.

Beckermann, Ruth. *Die Mazzesinsel: Juden in der Wiener Leopoldstadt 1918–1939*. Vienna: Löcker Verlag, 1984.

——— . *Unzugehörig: Oesterreicher und Juden nach 1945*. Vienna: Löcker Verlag, 1989.

Bein, Alex. *Die Judenfrage: Biographie eines Weltproblems*. 2 vols. Stuttgart: Deutsche Verlags-Anstalt, 1980.

Beller, Steven. "Class, Culture and the Jews of Vienna, 1900." In *Jews, Antisemitism and Culture in Vienna*, edited by Ivar Oxaal, Michael Pollack, and Gerhard Botz, pp. 39–58. London: Routledge and Kegan Paul, 1987.

——— . *Vienna and the Jews, 1867–1938: A Cultural History*. Cambridge: Cambridge University Press, 1989.

Benedikt, Heinrich, ed. *Geschichte der Republik Österreich*. Vienna: Verlag für Geschichte und Politik, 1954.

Bentwich, Norman. "The Destruction of the Jewish Community in Austria 1938–1942." In *The Jews of Austria: Essays on Their Life, History and Destruction*, edited by Josef Fraenkel, pp. 467–78. London: Vallentine, Mitchell, 1967.

Berchtold, Klaus, ed. *Österreichische Parteiprogramme 1868–1966*. Vienna: Verlag für Geschichte und Politik, 1967.

Bericht der Israelitischen Kultusgemeinde Wien über die Tätigkeit in der Periode 1929–1932, 1933–1936. 2 vols. Vienna: Verlag der Israelitischen Kultusgemeinde Wien, 1932, 1936.

Berkley, George E. *Vienna and Its Jews: The Tragedy of Success, 1880–1980s*. Foreword by Harry Zohn. Landham, Md.: Madison Books, 1988.

Bessel, Richard, ed. *Life in the Third Reich*. Oxford: Oxford University Press, 1987.

Bihl, Wolfdieter. "The Austrian Jews from 1918–1938." Unpublished paper presented to the International Symposium on "The Jews of Austria." Center for Austrian Studies, University of Minnesota, May 1986.

——— . "The Jews of Austria-Hungary (Austria) 1848–1918." Unpublished paper presented to the International Symposium on "The Jews of Austria." Center for Austrian Studies, University of Minnesota, May 1986.

Binder, Dieter. "Der 'reiche' Jude: Zur sozialdemokratischen Kapitalismus-Kritik und zu deren antisemitischen Feindbildern in der Ersten Republik." *Geschichte und Gegenwart* 1, no. 1 (March 1985): 43–53.

——— . "Das Schicksal der Grazer Juden 1938." In *Historisches Jahrbuch der Stadt Graz*, pp. 203–28. Graz: Stadt Graz, 1988.

Birnbaum, Nathan. *Den ostjuden ihr Recht!* Vienna: R. Löwit, 1915.

Black, Peter R. *Ernst Kaltenbrunner: Ideological Soldier of the Third Reich*. Princeton: Princeton University Press, 1984.

Bloch, Josef. *Erinnerungen aus meinem Leben*. Vols. 1, 3. Vienna: R. Löwit, 1922.

Boas, Jacob. "German-Jewish Internal Politics under Hitler, 1933–1938." *Leo Baeck Institute Yearbook* 29 (1984): 3–25.

Boerner, Wilhelm. *Antisemitismus, Rassenfrage, Menschlichkeit.* Vienna: Flugschrift der Ethischen Gemeinde, 1936.

Botz, Gerhard. " 'Ausmerzung': Von der Ächtung zur Vernichtung: Steigerungsstufen der Judenverfolgung in Österreich nach dem 'Anschluss' (1938–1942)." *Journal für Sozialforschung* 28, no. 1 (1988): 5–50.

————. "The Changing Patterns of Social Support for Austrian National Socialism." In *Who Were the Fascists: Social Roots of European Fascism*, edited by Stein U. Larsen, Bernt Havet, and Jan P. Myklebust, pp. 202–23. Bergen: Universitetsforlaget, 1980.

————. *Gewalt in der Politik: Attentate, Zusammenstösse, Putschversuche, Unruhen in Österreich 1918–1938.* 2d ed. Munich: Wilhelm Fink Verlag, 1983.

————. "The Jews of Vienna from the *Anschluss* to the Holocaust." In *Jews, Antisemitism and Culture in Vienna*, edited by Ivar Oxaal, Michael Pollack, and Gerhard Botz, pp. 185–204. London: Routledge and Kegan Paul, 1987.

————. *Wien vom "Anschluss" zum Krieg: Nationalsozialistische Machtübernahme und politisch-soziale Umgestaltung am Beispiel der Stadt Wien 1938/39.* Vienna: Verlag für Jugend und Volk, 1978.

————. *Wohnungspolitik und Judendeportation in Wien 1938 bis 1945.* Vienna: Geyer-Edition, 1975.

Botz, Gerhard, Hans Hautmann, and Helmut Konrad, eds. *Geschichte und Gesellschaft: Festschrift für Karl R. Stadler.* Vienna: Europa Verlag, 1974.

Botz, Gerhard, Ivar Oxaal, and Michael Pollak, eds. *Eine zerstörte Kultur: Jüdisches Leben und Antisemitismus in Wien seit dem 19. Jahrhundert.* Vienna: Druck und Verlag Obermayer, 1990.

Boyer, John W. "Karl Lueger and the Viennese Jews." *Leo Baeck Institute Yearbook* 21 (1981): 125–41.

————. *Political Radicalism in Late Imperial Vienna: Origins of the Christian Social Movement, 1848–1897.* Chicago: University of Chicago Press, 1981.

Braham, Randolph L., ed. *The Origins of the Holocaust: Christian Anti-Semitism.* Boulder, Colo.: Social Science Monographs and Institute for Holocaust Studies of New York, 1986. Distributed by Columbia University Press, New York.

Brandstötter, Rudolf. "Dr. Walter Riehl und die nationalsozialistische Bewegung in Österreich." Ph.D. dissertation, University of Vienna, 1970.

Braunthal, Julius. *The Tragedy of Austria.* London: Victor Gollancz, 1938.

Bukey, Evan B. *Hitler's Hometown: Linz, Austria, 1908–1945.* Bloomington: Indiana University Press, 1986.

Bullock, Malcolm. *Austria 1918–1938: A History of Failure.* London: Macmillan, 1939.

Bunzl, John. "Arbeiterbewegung, 'Judenfrage' und Antisemitismus. Am Beispiel des Wiener Bezirks Leopoldstadt." In *Bewegung und Klasse*, edited by Gerhard Botz, Hans Hautmann, Konrad Helmut, and Josef Weidenholzer, pp. 743–63. Vienna: Europa Verlag, 1978.

————. "Arbeiterbewegung und Antisemitismus in Österreich vor und nach dem Ersten Weltkrieg." *Zeitgeschichte* 4 (1976–77): 161–71.

————. "'Austrian Identity' and Antisemitism." *Patterns of Prejudice* 21, no. 1 (1987): 3–8.

————. *Klassenkampf in der Diaspora: Zur Geschichte der jüdischen Arbeiterbewegung.* Foreword by Karl R. Stadler. Vienna: Europa Verlag, 1975.

Bunzl, John, and Bernd Marin. *Antisemitismus in Österreich: Sozialhistorische Studien.* Foreword by Anton Pelinka. Innsbruck: Inn-Verlag, 1983.

Busshoff, Heinrich. *Das Dollfuss-Regime in Österreich in geistesgeschichtlicher Perspektive unter besonderer Berücktsichtigung der "Schöneren Zukunft" und "Reichspost."* Berlin: Duncker und Humblot, 1968.

Buttinger, Joseph. *Am Beispiel Österreichs: Ein geschichtlicher Beitrag zur Krise der sozialistischen Bewegung.* Cologne: Kiepenheuer und Witsch, 1953.

Carlebach, Julius. *Karl Marx and the Radical Critique of Judaism.* London: Henley and Boston, 1978.

Carr, William. "Nazi Policy against the Jews." In *Life in the Third Reich*, edited by Richard Bessel, pp. 69–82. Oxford: Oxford University Press, 1987.

Carsten, F. L. *Fascist Movements in Austria: From Schönerer to Hitler.* London: Sage Publications, 1977.

————. *The First Austrian Republic, 1918–1939: A Study Based on British and Austrian Documents.* Hants, England: Gower/Maurice Temple Smith, 1986.

————. *The Rise of Fascism.* Berkeley: University of California Press, 1976.

Charmatz, Richard. *Deutsch-österreichische Politik: Studien über den Liberalismus und die auswärtige Politik Österreichs.* Leipzig: Verlag von Duncker und Humblot, 1907.

Clare, George. *Last Waltz in Vienna: The Rise and Destruction of a Family.* New York: Holt, Rinehart and Winston, 1980.

Cohen, Gary B. "Jews in German Liberal Politics: Prague, 1880–1914." *Jewish History* 1, no. 1 (Spring 1986): 55–74.

————. "Jews in German Society: Prague, 1860–1914." *Central European History* 10, no. 1 (March 1977): 28–54.

Cohn, Norman. *Warrant for Genocide: The Myth of the Jewish World Conspiracy and the Protocols of the Elders of Zion.* Chico, Calif.: Scholars Press, 1969. Reprint. 1981.

Coudenhove-Kalergi, Count Heinrich. *Anti-Semitism throughout the Ages.* Edited and brought up to date by Count Richard Coudenhove-Kalergi. Authorized English translation from the German by Angelo S. Rappaport. London: Hutchinson, 1935.

Csoklich, Fritz. "Presse und Rundfunk." In *Österreich 1918–1938*, edited by Erika Weinzierl and Kurt Skalnik, pp. 715–30. Graz: Styria Verlag, 1983.

Cummings, William W., ed. *Scott 1990 Standard Postage Stamp Catalogue.* 146th ed. Vol. 2: *European Countries and Colonies. Independent Nations of Africa, Asia, Latin America, A–F.* Sidney, Ohio: Scott Publishing Co., 1989.

Czermak, E[mmerich], and O[skar] Karbach. *Ordnung in der Judenfrage: Verständigung mit dem Judentum?* Vienna: Reinhold Verlag, 1933.

Daniek, Edmund. *Das Judentum im Kriege.* Vienna: Verlag der Deutschnationalen Vereinigung, 1919.

Daviau, Donald. "Hermann Bahr und Antisemitismus, Zionismus und die Judenfrage." *Literatur und Kritik* 221–22 (1988): 21–41.

Deak, Istvan. "Pacesetters of Integration: Jewish Officers in the Habsburg Monarchy." *Eastern European Politics and Societies* 3 (Winter 1989): 22–50.

Dokumentationsarchiv des österreichischen Widerstandes. *Widerstand und Verfolgung in Wien 1934–1945: Eine Dokumentation.* Vol. 3: 1938–1945. Vienna: Österreichischer Bundesverlag für Unterricht, Wissenschaft und Kunst. Vienna: Jugend und Volk Verlagsges., 1975.

Drabek, Anne, et al. *Das österreichische Judentum: Voraussetzungen und Geschichte.* Vienna: Jugend und Volk, 1974.

Drei Jahre BJF-Bund jüdischer Frontsoldaten Österreichs. Vienna: BJF, 1935.

Drexel, Albert. *Die Judenfrage in wissenschaftlicher Beleuchtung.* Innsbruck: Wagner Verlag, 1936.

Duncker, Ulrich. *Der Reichsbund jüdischer Frontsoldaten 1919–1938.* Düsseldorf: Droste Verlag, 1977.

Dutch, Oswald O. [Otto Deutsch]. "Seeds of a Noble Inheritance: The Influence of Austrian Jewish Emigration upon the Anglo-American World." In *The Jews of Austria*, edited by Josef Fraenkel, pp. 177–93. London: Vallentine, Mitchell, 1967.

Eberle, Josef. "Eine bemerkenswerte Stimme zur Judenfrage in Österreich." *Schönere Zukunft* (19 November 1933): 200.

[———]. "Die gesellschaftliche Stellung der Juden in Nordamerika." *Schönere Zukunft* (28 February 1937): 575.

———. Introduction to "*Ordnung in der Judenfrage* von Emmerich Czermak." *Schönere Zukunft* (10 December 1933): 266.

[———]. "Judentum und Rechtsanwaltsberuf in Wien." *Schönere Zukunft* (2 December 1934): 267.

———. "Umschau." *Schönere Zukunft* (13 November 1927): 141–43.

———. "Umschau: Katholiken und Judenfrage." *Schönere Zukunft* (18 April 1926): 698–701.

[———]. "Zum Thema: Jüdische Vorherrschaft in Presse und Geschäftswelt." *Schönere Zukunft* (17 January 1929): 362.

Ebneth, Rudolf. *Die österreichische Wochenschrift "Der christliche Ständestaat." Deutsche Emigration in Österreich 1933–1938.* Mainz: Matthias-Grunewald, 1976.

Edelheim-Mühsam, Margaret. "Reactions of the Jewish Press to the Nazi Challenge." *Leo Baeck Institute Yearbook* 5 (1960): 308–29.

Edmondson, C. Earl. *The Heimwehr and Austrian Politics, 1918–1936.* Athens: University of Georgia Press, 1978.

Eibl, Hans. "Lehren aus dem Aufstieg des Nationalsozialismus, II." *Schönere Zukunft* (22 May 1933): 790–91.

Eppel, Peter. *Zwischen Kreuz und Hakenkreuz: Die Haltung der Zeitschrift "Schönere Zukunft" zum Nationalsozialismus in Deutschland 1934–1938*. Vienna: Hermann Böhlaus Nachf., 1980.

Ettinger, S. "Jews and Non-Jews in Eastern and Central Europe between the Wars: An Outline." In *Jews and Non-Jews in Eastern Europe, 1918–1945*, edited by Bela Vago and George L. Mosse, pp. 1–19. Jerusalem: Israel Universities Press, 1974.

Fellner, Günter. *Antisemitismus in Salzburg 1918–1938*. Vienna: Veröffentlichungen der Historische Institut der Universität Salzburg, 1979.

————. "Der Novemberpogrom 1938: Bemerkungen zur Forschung." *Zeitgeschichte* 15, no. 2 (November 1988): 35–58.

Fenz, Brigitte. "Zur Ideologie der 'Volksbürgerschaft': Die Studentenordnung der Universität Wien von 8 April 1930 vor dem Verfassungsgerichtshof." *Zeitgeschichte* 5, no. 4 (January 1978): 125–44.

Field, Frank. *The Last Days of Mankind: Karl Kraus and His Vienna*. New York: St. Martin's Press, 1967.

Fink, Carole, Isabel V. Hull, and MacGregor Knox, eds. *German Nationalism and the European Response, 1890–1945*. Norman: University of Oklahoma Press, 1985.

Fodor, M. W. *Plot and Counterplot in Central Europe*. London: Harper and Brothers, 1939.

Fraenkel, Josef, ed. *The Jews of Austria: Essays on Their Life, History and Destruction*. London: Vallentine, Mitchell, 1967.

Frei, Bruno. *Jüdisches Elend in Wien: Bilder und Daten*. Vienna: R. Löwit, 1920.

Freidenreich, Harriet Pass. *Jewish Politics in Vienna, 1918–1938*. Bloomington: Indiana University Press, 1991.

Freud, Martin. "Who Was Freud?" In *The Jews of Austria*, edited by Josef Fraenkel, pp. 197–211. London: Vallentine, Mitchell, 1967.

Friedrich, Carl J., and Zbigniew K. Brzezinski. *Totalitarian Dictatorship and Autocracy*. 2d edition. New York: Praeger, 1966.

Frischauer, Willi. *The Rise and Fall of Hermann Goering*. New York: Ballantine, 1951.

Fuchs, Albert. *Geistige Strömungen in Österreich 1867–1918*. Vienna: Globus Verlag, 1949.

Fuchs, Martin. *Showdown in Vienna*. New York: G. P. Putnam's Sons, 1939.

Führer, Erich. "Antisemitismus im neuen Österreich." In *Antisemitismus in Wort und Bild*, edited by Robert Körber and Theodor Pügel, pp. 183–204. Dresden: M. O. Groh, 1935.

Furret, Francois. *Unanswered Questions: Nazi Germany and the Genocide of the Jews*. New York: Schocken Books, 1989.

Ganglmair, Siegwald. *Resistance and Persecution in Austria, 1938–1945*. Vienna: Federal Press Service, 1988.

Gärtner, Reinhold. "Right-Wing Student Politics in Austria after 1945." In *Conquering the Past: Austrian Nazism Yesterday and Today*, edited by Fred Parkinson, pp. 279–93. Detroit: Wayne State University Press, 1989.

Gay, Peter. *Freud, Jews and Other Germans: Masters and Victims in Modernist Culture.* Oxford: Oxford University Press, 1978.

Gedye, G. E. R. *Fallen Bastions: The Central European Tragedy.* London: Victor Gollancz, 1939.

Geehr, Richard S. *Karl Lueger: Mayor of Fin de Siècle Vienna.* Detroit: Wayne State University Press, 1989.

Der gelbe Stern in Österreich: Katalog und Einführung zu einer Dokumentation. Vol. 5 of *Studia Judaica Austriaca.* Eisenstadt: in Kommission bei Edition Roetzer, 1977.

Gerber, David A., ed. *Anti-Semitism in American History.* Urbana: University of Illinois Press, 1986.

Gerhartl, Gertrud. "Geschichte der Juden in Wiener Neustadt." In *Geschichte der Juden in Österreich: Ein Gedenkbuch,* edited by Hugo Gold, pp. 91–102. Tel Aviv: Olamenu, 1971.

Gerlach, Aurelia. *Der Einfluss der Juden in der österreichischen Sozialdemokratie.* Vienna: Wilhelm Braumüller, 1939.

Glockemeier, Georg. *Zur Wiener Judenfrage.* Vienna: Günther, 1936.

Gold, Hugo, ed. *Geschichte der Juden in Österreich: Ein Gedenkbuch.* Tel Aviv: Olamenu, 1971.

———. *Geschichte der Juden in Wien: Ein Gedenkbuch.* Tel Aviv: Olamenu, 1966.

Goldhammer, Leo. *Die Juden Wiens: Eine statistische Studie.* Vienna: R. Löwit, 1927.

Good, David F. *The Economic Rise of the Habsburg Empire, 1750–1914.* Berkeley: University of California Press, 1984.

Gordon, Sarah. *Hitler, Germans, and the "Jewish Question."* Princeton: Princeton University Press, 1984.

Grayzel, Solomon. *A History of the Jews: From the Destruction of Judah in 586 B.C. to the Present Arab-Israeli Conflict.* New York: New English Library, 1947.

Greive, Hermann. *Geschichte der modernen Antisemitismus in Deutschland.* Darmstadt: Wissenschaftliche Buchgesellschaft, 1983.

Grosser, Paul E., and Edwin G. Halperin. *The Causes and Effects of Anti-Semitism: The Dimensions of a Prejudice. An Analysis and Chronology of 1900 Years of Anti-Semitic Attitudes and Practices.* New York: Philosophy Library, 1978.

Grun, Oskar. *Franz Joseph der Erste in seinem Verhältnis zu den Juden.* Zurich: Buchdruckerei G. v. Ostheim, 1916.

Grunberger, Richard. "Jews in Austrian Journalism." In *The Jews of Austria,* edited by Josef Fraenkel, pp. 83–95. London: Vallentine, Mitchell, 1967.

———. "Waldheim in the Press: A Selected Survey." *Patterns of Prejudice* 21, no. 1 (1987): 9–13.

Grunwald, Max. *History of the Jews in Vienna.* Philadelphia: Jewish Publication Society of America, 1936.

Gstrein, Heinz. *Jüdisches Wien.* Vienna: Herold, 1984.

Haag, John. "Academic Antisemitism in Austria—1878–1938." Unpublished paper presented to the German Studies Association, Milwaukee, Wisconsin, October 1989.

——. "Blood on the Ringstrasse: Vienna's Students, 1918–33." *Wiener Library Bulletin* 29 (1976), new ser., nos. 39–40: 29–34.

——. "Students at the University of Vienna in the First World War." *Central European History* 17, no. 4 (December 1984): 299–309.

——. "A Woman's Struggle against Nazism: Irene Harand and *Gerechtigkeit.*" *Wiener Library Bulletin* 34 (1981), new ser., nos. 53–54: 64–72.

Haerpfer, Christian. *Anti-Semitic Attitudes in Austrian Society, 1973–1989: A Study for the Liga der Freunde des Judentums, Vienna.* Vienna: Institute for Conflict Research, July 1989.

Hall, Murray G. *Erotik und Hakenkreuz auf der Anklagebank: Der Fall Bettauer.* Vienna: Löcker Verlag, 1978.

Hanisch, Ernst. "Friedrich Engels und der Antisemitismus in Wien." *Archiv: Mitteilungsblatt des Vereins für Geschichte der Arbeiterbewegung* 15 (1975): 116–21.

——. "Zur Frühgeschichte des Nationalsozialismus in Salzburg (1913–1925)." *Mitteilungen der Gesellschaft für Salzburger Landeskunde* 117 (1977): 371–410.

Hantsch, Hugo. *Die Geschichte Österreichs.* Vol. 2: *1648–1918.* Graz: Verlag Styria, 1953.

Harand, Irene. *Sein Kampf: Antwort an Hitler.* Vienna: privately printed, 1937. English edition: *His Struggle: An Answer to Hitler.* Chicago: Art Craft Press, 1937.

——. *So oder So? Die Wahrheit über den Antisemitismus.* Vienna: privately printed, 1933.

Haubenberger, Leo. "Das Judentum in Österreich." *Deutschlands Erneuerung: Monatschrift für das deutsche Volk* 4, no. 10 (October 1920): 618–22.

Häusler, Wolfgang. "Toleranz, Emanzipation und Antisemitismus: Das österreichische Judentum des bürgerlichen Zeitalters (1782–1918)." In Anna Drabek et al. *Das österreichische Judentum: Voraussetzungen und Geschichte,* pp. 83–140. Vienna: Jugend und Volk, 1974.

Hawlik, Johannes. "Die politische Parteien Deutschösterreichs bei der Wahlen zur konstituierenden Nationalversammlung 1919." Ph.D. dissertation, University of Vienna, 1971.

Heer, Friedrich. *Gottes erste Liebe: 2000 Jahre Judentum und Christentum: Genesis des österreichischen Katholiken Adolf Hitler.* Munich: Bechtle, 1967.

——. "Judentum und österreichischer Genius." In *Land im Strom der Zeit: Österreich gestern, heute, morgen,* edited by Friedrich Heer, pp. 293–314. Vienna: Verlag Herold, 1958.

Heer, Friedrich, ed. *Land im Strom der Zeit: Österreich gestern, heute, morgen.* Vienna: Verlag Herold, 1958.

Hein, Robert. *Studentischer Antisemitismus in Österreich.* Vienna: Österreichischer Verein für Studentengeschichte, 1984.

Heller, Celia S. *On the Edge of Destruction: Jews of Poland between the Two World Wars.* New York: Schocken Books, 1977.

Herzstein, Robert E. *Waldheim: The Missing Years.* New York: Arbor House/William Morrow, 1988.

Hilberg, Raul. *The Destruction of the European Jews.* New York: Harper Colophon Books, 1979.

Hilsenrad, Helen. *Brown Was the Danube.* New York: Thomas Yoseloff, 1966.

Hinteregger, C[hristian]. *Der Judenschwindel.* Vienna: Verlag der Wiener Volksbuch-handlung, 1923.

Hitler, Adolf. *Mein Kampf.* Translated from the German by Ralph Manheim. Boston: Houghton Mifflin Company, 1943. Originally published in 1927. German edition: Munich: Zentralverlag der NSDAP. Fritz Eher Nachf., 1937.

Hodik, Avshalom. "Die Israelitische Kultusgemeinde 1918–1938." In *Juden in Öster-reich 1918–1938*, edited by Avshalom Hodik, Peter Malina, and Gustav Spann, pp. 10–34. Vienna: Institut für Zeitgeschichte, 1982.

Hodik, Avshalom, Peter Malina, and Gustav Spann, eds. *Juden in Österreich 1918–1938.* Vienna: Institut für Zeitgeschichte, 1982.

Holter, Beatrix. "Die ostjüdischen Kriegsflüchtlinge in Wien (1914–1923)." Hausar-beit aus Geschichte. University of Salzburg, 1978.

Holzmann, Hermann. "Antisemitismus in der österreichischen Innenpolitik 1918–1933: Der Umgang der drei politischen Lager mit diesem Phänomen." Diplomarbeit, University of Vienna, 1986.

Honigmann, Peter. "Die Austritte aus dem Judentum in Wien 1868–1914." *Zeitgeschichte* 16, nos. 1–2 (August–September 1988): 452–66.

Hosokawa, Bill. *JACL in Quest of Justice.* New York: William Morrow, 1982.

Jacobs, Jack. "Austrian Social Democracy and the Jewish Question." In *The Aus-trian Socialist Experiment, 1918–1934*, edited by Anson Rabinbach, pp. 157–68. Boulder, Colo.: Westview Press, 1985.

Janik, Allan. "Viennese Culture and Jewish Self-hatred." In *Jews, Antisemitism and Culture in Vienna*, edited by Ivar Oxaal, Michael Pollak, and Gerhard Botz, pp. 75–88. London: Routledge and Kegan Paul, 1987.

Janik, Allan, and Stephen Toulmin. *Wittgenstein's Vienna.* New York: Simon and Schuster, 1973.

Jaszi, Oscar. *The Dissolution of the Habsburg Monarchy.* 1929. Reprint. Chicago: University of Chicago Press, 1961.

Jedlicka, Ludwig. "Aus dem politischen Tagebuch des Unterrichtsministers a.D. Dr. Emmerich Czermak, 1937 bis 1938." *Österreich in Geschichte und Literatur* 8 (1964): no. 6, 268–73; no. 7, 323–33; no. 8, 358–68.

———. "Gauleiter Josef Leopold (1889–1941)." In *Geschichte und Gesellschaft: Festschrift für Karl R. Stadler*, edited by Gerhard Botz, Hans Hautmann, and Helmut Konrad, pp. 143–61. Vienna: Europa Verlag, 1974.

Jellinek, Gustav. "Die Geschichte der österreichischen Wiedergutmachung." In *The Jews of Austria*, edited by Josef Fraenkel, pp. 395–426. London: Vallentine, Mitchell, 1967.

Jenks, William A. "The Jews in the Habsburg Empire, 1879–1918." *Leo Baeck Institute Yearbook* 16 (1971): 155–62.

————. *Vienna and the Young Hitler*. New York: Columbia University Press, 1960.

Joffe, Josef. "Where Hitler Fell Down the Memory Hole." *U.S. News and World Report* (14 March 1988): 32.

Johnson, Paul. *A History of the Jews*. New York: Harper and Row, 1987.

Johnston, William M. *The Austrian Mind: An Intellectual and Social History*. Berkeley: University of California Press, 1972.

Die Juden in Oesterreich: Veröffentlichungen des Bureaus für Statistik der Juden. Berlin-Halensee: L. Lamm, 1908.

Die Juden im Staate Deutsch-Österreich. Innsbruck: Pius-Verein, 1920.

Jung, Karl. "Die völkische Presse in Österreich." In *Deutscher Geist in Österreich*, edited by Karl Wache, pp. 345–52. Dornbirn: C. Bruton-Verlag, 1933.

Kampe, Norbert. *Studenten und Judenfrage in der Kaiserreich: Die Entstehung einer akademischen Trägerschicht des Antisemitismus*. Göttingen: Vandenhoeck und Ruprecht, 1988.

Kann, Robert A. *A Study in Austrian Intellectual History: From the Late Baroque to Romanticism*. New York: Praeger, 1960.

Karbach, Oskar. "Die politischen Grundlagen des deutsch-österreichischen Antisemitismus." *Zeitschrift für die Geschichte der Juden* 1, nos. 1, 2, 4 (1964): 1–8, 103–16, 169–78.

Katz, Jacob. *From Prejudice to Destruction: Anti-Semitism, 1700–1933*. Cambridge: Harvard University Press, 1980.

Kerekes, Lajos. *Von St. Germain bis Genf: Österreich und seine Nachbarn 1918–1922*. Vienna: Hermann Böhlaus Nachf., 1979.

Kershaw, Ian. "Ideology, Propaganda, and the Nazi Party." In *The Nazi Machtergreifung*, edited by Peter D. Stachura, pp. 162–81. Boston: George Allen and Unwin, 1983.

————. *Popular Opinion and Political Dissent in the Third Reich: Bavaria, 1933–1945*. Oxford: Clarendon Press, 1983.

Kienzl, Heinz. "Der Österreicher und seine Schande: Erster Versuch einer empirischen Studie über Antisemitismus." *Forum* 13, no. 154 (1966): 655–57.

Klemperer, Klemens von. *Ignaz Seipel: Christian Statesman in a Time of Crisis*. Princeton: Princeton University Press, 1972.

Klose, Alfred, et al., eds. *Katholische Soziallexikon*. 2d ed. Graz: Verlag Styria, 1980.

Knight, Robert. *Ich bin dafür, die Sache in die Länge zu ziehen: Wortprotokolle der österreichischen Bundesregierung von 1945–52 über die Entschädigung der Juden*. Frankfurt am Main: Athenäum Verlag, 1988.

————. "Kalter Krieg, Entnazifierung und Österreich." In *Verdrängte Schuld, verfehlte Sühne*, edited by Sebastian Meissl, Klaus-Dieter Mulley, and Oliver Rathkolb, pp. 37–57. Munich: R. Oldenbourg Verlag, 1986.

Knütter, Hans-Helmuth. *Die Juden und die deutsche Linke in der Weimarer Republik 1918–1933*. Düsseldorf: Bonner Schriften zur Politik und Zeitgeschichte, 1971.

Kobler, Franz. "The Contribution of Austrian Jews to Jurisprudence." In *The Jews of Austria*, edited by Josef Fraenkel, pp. 25–40. London: Vallentine, Mitchell, 1967.

Köfler, Gretl. "Tirol und die Juden." In *Tirol und der Anschluss: Voraussetzungen, Entwicklungen, Rahmenbedingungen 1918–1938*, edited by Thomas Albrich, Klaus Eisterer, and Rolf Steininger, pp. 169–82. Innsbruck: Haymon-Verlag, 1988.

Kondert, Reinhart. "The Rise and Early History of the Austrian 'Heimwehr' Movement." Ph.D. dissertation, Rice University, 1971.

Koppel, Reynold S. "Heikle Sache: The Holocaust in Austrian Schools." Unpublished paper presented to the German Studies Association, Buffalo, New York, October 1990.

Körber, Robert. *Rassesieg in Wien: Der Grenzfeste des Reiches*. Vienna: Wilhelm Braumüller, 1939.

Körber, Robert, and Theodor Pugel. *Antisemitismus der Welt in Wort und Bild*. Dresden: M. O. Groh, 1935.

Krammer, Reinhard. "Die Turn- und Sportbewegung." In *Österreich 1918–1938*, edited by Erika Weinzierl and Kurt Skalnik, pp. 731–41. Graz: Styria Verlag, 1983.

Kreissler, Felix, ed. *Austriaca: Cahiers universitaires d'information sur l'Autriche. Colloque special. Deux fois l'Autriche. Après 1918 et après 1945*. Rouen: Imprimerie Lecerf, 1978.

Kreppel, J[onas]. *Juden und Judentum von heute*. Vienna: Amalthea-Verlag, 1925.

Kubl, Friedrich. "Geschichte der jüdischen Advokaten und Rechtsgelehrten in Österreich." In *Geschichte der Juden in Österreich*, edited by Hugo Gold, pp. 117–26. Tel Aviv: Olamenu, 1971.

Kuppe, Rudolf. *Karl Lueger und seine Zeit*. Vienna: Österreichische Volksschriften, 1933.

Langbein, Hermann. "Darf man vergessen?" In *Das grosse Tabu*, edited by Anton Pelinka and Erika Weinzierl, pp. 8–16. Vienna: Verlag der österreichische Staatsdruckerei, 1987.

Laqueur, Walter. *A History of Zionism*. New York: Schocken Books, 1976.

Larsen, Stein, Bernt Hagvet, and Jan P. Myklebust, eds. *Who Were the Fascists: Social Roots of European Fascism*. Bergen: Universitetsforlaget, 1980.

Layton, Roland V. "The *Völkischer Beobachter*, 1920–1933: The Nazi Party Newspaper in the Weimar Era." *Central European History* 3 (December 1970): 353–82.

Lea, Henry A. "Hugo Bettauer's *Die Stadt ohne Juden*: A Prophetic Novel of Austria's Interwar Years." Unpublished paper presented to the German Studies Association, St. Louis, 1987.

Lebzelter, Gisela C. *Political Anti-Semitism in England, 1918–1939*. New York: Holmes and Meier Publishers, 1978.

Lefwich, Joseph. "Thinking of Vienna." In *The Jews of Austria*, edited by Josef Fraenkel, pp. 231–39. London: Vallentine, Mitchell, 1967.

Levine, Herbert S. "The Jewish Leadership in Germany and the Nazi Threat in 1933." In *German Nationalism and the European Response, 1890–1945*, edited by Carole Fink, Isabel V. Hull, and MacGregor Knox, pp. 181–206. Norman: University of Oklahoma Press, 1985.

Levy, Richard S. *The Downfall of the Anti-Semitic Political Parties in Imperial Germany*. New Haven: Yale University Press, 1975.

Lewy, Guenter. *The Catholic Church and Nazi Germany*. New York: McGraw-Hill Book Company, 1964.

Lipstadt, Deborah. *Beyond Belief: The American Press and the Coming of the Holocaust, 1933–1945*. New York: Free Press, 1980.

Loge, Christian [pseud.]. *Gibt es jüdische Ritualmorde? Eine Sichtung und psychologische Klärung des geschichtlichen Materials*. Graz: Moser, 1934.

Lohrmann, Klaus, ed. *1000 Jahre österreichisches Judentum*. Eisenstadt: Edition Roetzer, 1982.

Low, Alfred D. *Jews in the Eyes of the Germans: From the Enlightenment to Imperial Germany*. Philadelphia: Institute for the Study of Human Issues, 1979.

Ludwig, Eduard, and Arthur Rosenberg. *Zur jüdischen Frage: 2 Reden an das österreichische Volk*. Vienna: E. Muller, 1946.

Lukawetz, Gerd. "Antisemitismus — Versuch einer Klärung: Theorieorientierte Analyse der grossen Antisemitismusumfrage 1986." *SWS Rundschau* 27, no. 1 (1987): 75–81.

Luža, Radomir V. *The Resistance in Austria, 1938–1945*. Minneapolis: University of Minnesota Press, 1984.

Macartney, C. A. "The Armed Formations in Austria." *Journal of the Royal Institute of International Affairs* 8 (November 1929): 617–32.

———. *The Habsburg Monarchy, 1790–1918*. New York: Macmillan, 1969.

Macartney, C. A., and A. W. Palmer. *Independent Eastern Europe: A History*. New York: St. Martin's Press, 1966.

Maccoby, Hyam. "The Origins of Anti-Semitism." In *The Origins of the Holocaust: Christian Anti-Semitism*, edited by Randolf L. Braham, pp. 1–16. New York: Columbia University Press, 1986.

Maderegger, Sylvia. *Die Juden im österreichischen Ständestaat 1934–1938*. Vienna: Verlag Geyer, 1973.

Mager, Alois. "Die religiöse Seite der Judenfrage." *Schönere Zukunft* (25 March 1928): 563.

Marcus, Jacob R. *The Rise and Destiny of the German Jew*. Cincinnati: Department of Synagogue and School Extension of the Union of American Hebrew Congregations, 1934.

Marin, Bernd. "Antisemitism before and after the Holocaust: The Austrian Case." In *Jews, Antisemitism and Culture in Vienna*, edited by Ivar Oxaal, Gerhard Botz, and Michael Pollak, pp. 216–33. London: Routledge and Kegan Paul, 1987.

———. "A Post-Holocaust 'Anti-Semitism without Anti-Semites'? Austria as a Case in Point." *Political Psychology* 2, no. 1 (Spring 1980): 57–74.

Marin, Bernd, and Ernst Schulin, eds. *Die Juden als Minderheit in der Geschichte*. Munich: Deutscher Taschenbuch Verlag, 1981.

Marx, Karl. "On the Jewish Question." In *Karl Marx: Selected Writings*, edited by David McLellen, pp. 38–62. Oxford: Oxford University Press, 1977.

Massing, Paul W. *Rehearsal for Destruction: A Study of Political Anti-Semitism in Imperial Germany.* 1949. Reprint. New York: Howard Fertig, 1967.

Maurer, Trude. *Ostjuden in Deutschland 1918–1933.* Hamburg: Hans Christians, 1986.

May, Arthur J. *The Hapsburg Monarchy, 1867–1914.* Cambridge: Harvard University Press, 1951. Reprint. 1961.

McCagg, William O., Jr. *A History of Habsburg Jews, 1670–1918.* Bloomington: Indiana University Press, 1989.

McLellan, David, ed. *Karl Marx: Selected Writings.* Oxford: Oxford University Press, 1977.

Meissl, Sebastian, Klaus-Dieter Mulley, and Oliver Rathkolb, eds. *Verdrängte Schuld, verfehlte Sühne: Entnazifizierung in Österreich 1945–1955.* Munich: R. Oldenbourg Verlag, 1986.

Mendelsohn, Ezra. "Jewish Reactions to Antisemitism in Interwar East Central Europe." In *Living with Antisemitism,* edited by Jehuda Reinharz, pp. 296–310. Hanover, N.H.: University Press of New England (for the Brandeis University Press), 1987.

———. *The Jews of East Central Europe between the World Wars.* Bloomington: Indiana University Press, 1983.

———. "Relations between Jews and Non-Jews in Eastern Europe between the Two World Wars." In *Unanswered Questions: Nazi Germany and the Genocide of the Jews,* edited by François Furet, pp. 71–83. New York: Schocken Books, 1989.

Menghin, Oswald. *Geist und Blut: Grundsätzliches um Rasse, Sprache, Kultur und Volkstum.* Vienna: Schnoll, 1934.

Messerer, Ingeborg. "Die Frontkämpfervereinigung Deutsch-Österreichs: Ein Beitrag zur Geschichte der Wehrverbände in der Republik Österreich." Ph.D. dissertation, University of Vienna, 1964.

Molisch, Paul. *Politische Geschichte der deutschen Hochschulen in Österreich von 1848 bis 1918.* Vienna: Wilhelm Braumüller, 1939.

Morton, Frederic. *A Nervous Splendor: Vienna 1888/1889.* New York: Penguin Books, 1979.

Moser, Jonny. "Die Katastrophe der Juden in Österreich, 1938–1945—ihre Voraussetzungen und ihre Überwindung." In *Studia Judaica Austriaca.* Vol. 5: *Der gelbe Stern in Österreich,* pp. 67–134. Eisenstadt: im Kommission bei Edition Roetzer, 1977.

———. " Österreichs Juden unter der NS-Herrschaft." In *NS-Herrschaft in Österreich 1938–1945,* edited by Emmerich Talos, Ernst Hanisch, and Wolfgang Neugebauer, pp. 185–98. Vienna: Verlag für Gesellschaftskritik, 1988.

———. "Das Schicksal der Wiener Juden in den März- und Apriltagen 1938." *Forschungen und Beiträge zur Wiener Stadtgeschichte* 5, no. 2 (1978): 172–82.

———. "Von der antisemitischen Bewegung zum Holocaust." In *1000 Jahre österreichische Judentum,* edited by Klaus Lohrmann, pp. 250–70. Eisenstadt: Edition Roetzer, 1982.

————. "Von der Emanzipation zur antisemitischen Bewegung: Die Stellung Georg Ritter von Schönerers und Heinrich Friedjungs in der Entwicklungsgeschichte des Antisemitismus in Österreich (1848–1896)." Ph.D. dissertation, University of Vienna, 1962.

Mosse, George L. *The Crisis of German Ideology: Intellectual Origins of the Third Reich.* New York: Universal Library, Grosset and Dunlap, 1964.

————. *Toward the Final Solution: A History of European Racism.* New York: Harper Colophon Books, 1978.

Nicosia, Francis R. "Zionism in Antisemitic Thought in Imperial Germany." Unpublished paper presented to the German Studies Association, Buffalo, New York, October 1990.

Niessner, Ernst. "Entwicklungen im Judentum." *Schönere Zukunft* (18 October 1925): 68–69.

Niewyk, Donald L. "The German Jews in Revolution and Revolt, 1918–19." In *Studies in Contemporary Jewry an Annual,* vol. 4: *The Jews and the European Crisis, 1914–21,* edited by Jonathan Frankel, pp. 41–66. New York: Oxford University Press, 1988.

————. *The Jews in Weimar Germany.* Baton Rouge: Louisiana State University Press, 1980.

————. *Socialist, Anti-Semite, and Jew: German Social Democracy Confronts the Problem of Anti-Semitism, 1918–1933.* Baton Rouge: Louisiana State University Press, 1971.

————. "Solving the 'Jewish Problem': Continuity and Change in German Antisemitism." *Leo Baeck Institute Yearbook* 35 (1990): 335–70.

Der Novemberpogrom: Die "Kristallnacht" in Wien. Vienna: Einverlag der Museen der Stadt Wien, 1988.

Oberkofler, Gerhard. "Deutschnationalismus und Antisemitismus in der Innsbrucker Studentenschaft um 1920." *Tiroler Heimatblätter* 56, no. 2 (1981): 65–71.

Okladek, F[riedrich]. *The Returnee Movement of Jews to Austria.* London, 1965.

[Ornstein, Jakob]. *Festschrift zur Feier des 50 jährigen Bestandes der Union Österreichischer Juden.* Vienna: Union Österreichischer Juden, 1937.

Oxaal, Ivar. "The Jews of Hitler's Vienna: Historical Sociological Aspects." In *Jews, Antisemitism and Culture in Vienna,* edited by Ivar Oxaal, Michael Pollak, and Gerhard Botz, pp. 11–38. London: Routledge and Kegan Paul, 1987.

Oxaal, Ivar, Michael Pollak, and Gerhard Botz, eds. *Jews, Antisemitism and Culture in Vienna.* London: Routledge and Kegan Paul, 1987.

Oxaal, Ivar and Walter R. Weitzmann. "The Jews in Pre-1914 Vienna: An Explanation of Basic Sociological Dimensions." *Leo Baeck Institute Yearbook* 30 (1985): 395–432.

Palmon, Avraham. "The Jewish Community of Vienna between the Two World Wars, 1918–1938." Ph.D. dissertation, Hebrew University, 1985. In Hebrew except for a 27-page abstract in English.

Parkinson, Fred, ed. *Conquering the Past: Austrian Nazism Yesterday and Today.* Detroit: Wayne State University Press, 1989.

Pauley, Bruce F. "Fascism and the *Führerprinzip*: The Austrian Example." *Central European History* 12 (September 1979): 272–96.

―――. *The Habsburg Legacy, 1867–1939*. 1972. Reprint. Malabar, Fla.: Robert E. Krieger, 1981.

―――. *Hahnenschwanz und Hakenkreuz: Steirischer Heimatschutz und österreichischer Nationalsozialismus 1918–1934*. Vienna: Europa Verlag, 1972.

―――. *Hitler and the Forgotten Nazis: A History of Austrian National Socialism*. Chapel Hill: University of North Carolina Press, 1981.

―――. "The Social and Economic Background of Austria's *Lebensunfähigkeit*." In *The Austrian Socialist Experiment, 1918–1934*, edited by Anson Rabinbach, pp. 21–37. Boulder, Colo.: Westview Press, 1985.

Paumgarten, Karl. *Judentum und Sozialdemokratie*. Graz: Heimatverlag, 1921.

Pelinka, Anton. "SPÖ, ÖVP, and the 'Ehemaligen': Isolation or Integration?" In *Conquering the Past: Austrian Nazism Yesterday and Today*, edited by Fred Parkinson, pp. 245–56. Detroit: Wayne State University Press, 1989.

―――. *Stand oder Klasse: Die christliche Arbeiterbewegung Österreichs 1933–1938*. Vienna: Europaverlag, 1972.

Pelinka, Anton, and Erika Weinzierl, eds. *Das grosse Tabu: Österreichs Umgang mit seiner Vergangenheit*. Vienna: Verlag der österreichischer Staatsdruckerei, 1987.

Peres, Yochanan. "Antisemitismus in Österreich: Bemerkungen und Eindrücke." *SWS Rundschau* 17, no. 1 (1987): 83–86.

Peter, Karl. *Der Antisemitismus*. Vienna: privately printed, 1936.

Petting, Otto [Otto Petwaidic-Petting]. *Wiens antisemitische Presse*. Vienna: privately printed, 1896.

Pfarrhofer, Hedwig. *Friedrich Funder: Ein Mann zwischen Gestern und Morgen*. Graz: Verlag Styria, 1978.

Pollak, Michael. "Cultural Innovation and Social Identity in Fin-de-Siècle Vienna." In *Jews, Antisemitism and Culture in Austria*, edited by Ivar Oxaal, Michael Pollak, and Gerhard Botz, pp. 59–74. London: Routledge and Kegan Paul, 1987.

Polleross, Fredrich B. *100 Jahre Antisemitismus im Waldviertel*. Krems an der Donau: Waldviertel Heimatbund, Faber Verlag, 1983.

Poppel, Stephen M. *Zionism in Germany, 1897–1933: The Shaping of a Jewish Identity*. Philadelphia: Jewish Publication Society of America, 1977.

Pötsch, Walter. *Die jüdische Rasse im Lichte der Straffälligkeit: Zuchtstatten der Minderrassigkeit*. Vienna: Sudostdeutscher Kulturverlag, 1932.

Pulzer, P. G. J. "Austrian Liberals and the Jewish Question, 1867–1914." *Journal of Central European Affairs* 33 (1963): 131–42.

―――. "The Development of Political Antisemitism in Austria." In *The Jews of Austria*, edited by Josef Fraenkel, pp. 429–43. London: Vallentine, Mitchell, 1967.

―――. *The Rise of Political Anti-Semitism in Germany and Austria*. 1964. Revised edition. Cambridge: Harvard University Press, 1988.

―――. "Spezifische Momente und Spielarten des österreichischen und des Wiener Antisemitismus." In *Eine zerstörte Kultur: Jüdisches Leben und Antisemitismus in*

Wien seit den 19. Jahrhundert, edited by Gerhard Botz, Ivar Oxaal, and Richard Pollack, pp. 121–40, 373–74. Buchloe: Druck und Verlag Obermayer, 1990.

Rabinbach, Anson, ed. *The Austrian Socialist Experiment, 1918–1934*. Boulder, Colo.: Westview Press, 1985.

Rath, R. John. *The Viennese Revolution of 1848*. Austin: University of Texas Press, 1957.

Rathkolb, Oliver. "Zur Kontinuität antisemitischer und rassistischer Vorurteile in Österreich 1945/1950." *Zeitgeschichte* 16, no. 5 (February 1989): 167–79.

Reichmann, Eva G. *Hostages of Civilization: The Social Sources of National Socialist Anti-Semitism*. Boston: Beacon Press, 1951.

Reimann, Viktor. *Innitzer, Kardinal zwischen Hitler und Rom*. Vienna: Verlag Fritz Molden, 1967.

Reinharz, Jehuda, ed. *Living with Antisemitism: Modern Jewish Responses*. Hanover, N.H.: University Press of New England (for the Brandeis University Press), 1987.

———. "The Zionist Response to Antisemitism in the Weimar Republic." In *The Jewish Response to German Culture: From the Enlightenment to the Second World War*, edited by Jehuda Reinharz and Walter Schatzberg, pp. 266–93. Hanover, N.H.: University Press of New England, 1985.

Reinharz, Jehuda, and Walter Schatzberg, eds. *The Jewish Response to German Culture: From the Enlightenment to the Second World War*. Hanover, N.H.: University Press of New England, 1985.

Rennhofer, Friedrich. *Ignaz Seipel: Mensch und Staatsmann: Eine biographische Dokumentation*. Vienna: Hermann Böhlaus Nachf, 1978.

Riedl, Joachim. "Geht doch in die Donau: Über den österreichischen Anteil am Holocaust." In *Versunkene Welt*, edited by Joachim Riedl, pp. 165–70. Vienna: Jewish Welcome Service, 1984.

Riedl, Joachim, ed. *Versunkene Welt*. Vienna: Jewish Welcome Service, 1984.

Rill, Robert. "Die Auseinandersetzung des Cartellverbandes in Österreich mit dem Nationalsozialismus." Ph.D. dissertation, University of Vienna, 1986.

Rogger, Hans, and Eugen Weber, eds. *The European Right: A Historical Profile*. Berkeley: University of California Press, 1966.

Ronzoni, Michaela. "Lebensverhältnisse der jüdischen Bevölkerung in Österreich zwischen Herbst 1938 und Frühjahr 1939." Diplomarbeit, University of Vienna, 1985.

Rosenberg, Hans. *Grosse Depression und Bismarckzeit*. Berlin: Gruyter, 1967.

Rosenfeld, Max. "Für eine nationale Autonomie der Juden in Österreich." *Der Jude* 1 (1916–17): 290–97.

Rosenkranz, Herbert. "The Anschluss and the Tragedy of Austrian Jewry." In *The Jews of Austria*, edited by Josef Fraenkel, pp. 479–545. London: Vallentine, Mitchell, 1967.

———. "Bemerkungen zu neueren Arbeiten über das Problem der Judenverfolgung und des Antisemitismus in Österreich." *Österreich in Geschichte und Literatur* 22, no. 2 (March–April 1978): 90–100.

————. *Verfolgung und Selbstbehauptung: Die Juden in Österreich*. Vienna: Verlag Herold, 1978.

Rosensaft, Menachem Z. "Jews and Antisemites in Austria at the End of Nineteenth Century." *Leo Baeck Institute Yearbook* 21 (1976): 57–86.

Roth, Joseph. *Juden auf Wanderschaft: Berichte aus der Wirklichkeit*. Berlin: Die Schmiede, 1927.

Rothschild, Lothar. "Geschichte der Juden in Hohenems." In *Geschichte der Juden in Österreich*, edited by Hugo Gold, pp. 27–32. Tel Aviv: Olamenu, 1971.

Rozenblit, Marsha. "The Assertion of Identity: Jewish Student Nationalism at the University of Vienna before the First World War." *Leo Baeck Institute Yearbook* 27 (1982): 171–86.

————. *The Jews of Vienna, 1867–1914: Assimilation and Identity*. Albany: State University of New York, 1983.

Rubenstein, Richard L. "After the Holocaust: Waldheim, the Pope and the Holocaust." *Holocaust and Genocide Studies* 4, no. 1 (1989): 1–13.

Sablik, Karl. *Julius Tandler: Mediziner und Sozialreformer*. Vienna: Verlag A. Schendl, 1983.

Sachar, Howard M. *The Course of Modern Jewish History*. London: Weidenfeld and Nicolson, 1958.

Safrian, Hans, and Hans Witek, eds. *Und Keiner War Dabei: Dokumente des Alltäglichen Antisemitismus in Wien 1938*. Foreword by Erika Weinzierl. Vienna: Pius Verlag, 1988.

Salzer-Eibenstein, Gerd W. "Geschichte der Juden in Graz." In *Geschichte der Juden in Österreich*, edited by Hugo Gold, pp. 9–21. Tel Aviv: Olamenu, 1971.

Schaukal, Richard von. "Studentenrecht und Judenfrage." *Schönere Zukunft* (27 December 1931): 303–4.

Schechter, Edmund. *Viennese Vignettes: Personal Recollections*. New York: Vantage Press, 1983.

Scheuer, O[skar] F[ranz]. *Burschenschaften und Judenfrage: Die Rassenfrage in der deutschen Studentenschaft*. Berlin: Verlag Berlin-Wien, 1927.

Schilling [-Schletter], Alexander. *Dr. Walter Riehl und die Geschichte des Nationalsozialismus*, mit einem Anhang: *Hitler in Österreich*. Leipzig: Forum Verlag, 1933.

Schleunes, Karl A. *The Twisted Road to Auschwitz: Nazi Policy toward German Jews, 1933–1939*. Urbana: University of Illinois Press, 1970.

Schmidl, Erwin A. *Juden in der k. (u.) k. Armee, 1788–1918. Jews in the Habsburg Armed Forces*. Eisenstadt: Österreichisches jüdisches Museum, 1989.

Schneider, Hermann. "Geschichte der Juden in Klagenfurt." In *Geschichte der Juden in Österreich*, edited by Hugo Gold, pp. 41–44. Tel Aviv: Olamenu, 1971.

Schnitzler, Arthur. *Jugend in Wien: Eine Autobiographie*. Vienna: Verlag Fritz Molden, 1968.

Schoeps, Julius H. "Modern Heirs of the Maccabees: The Beginning of the Vienna Kadimah, 1882–1897." *Leo Baeck Institute Yearbook* 27 (1982): 155–70.

Schorsch, Ismar. *Jewish Reactions to German Anti-Semitism, 1870–1914*. New

York: Columbia University Press; Philadelphia: Jewish Publication Society of America, 1972.

Schorske, Carl E. *Fin-de-Siècle Vienna: Politics and Culture*. New York: Alfred A. Knopf, 1980.

Schuschnigg, Kurt von. *The Brutal Takeover*. London: Weidenfeld and Nicolson, 1969.

Schwab, Gerald. *The Day the Holocaust Began: The Odyssey of Herschel Grynszpan*. New York: Praeger, 1990.

Schwager, Karl. "Geschichte der Juden in Linz." In *Geschichte der Juden in Österreich*, edited by Hugo Gold, pp. 53–62. Tel Aviv: Olamenu, 1971.

Schwarz, Robert. "Antisemitism and Socialism in Austria, 1918–1962." In *The Jews of Austria*, edited by Josef Fraenkel, pp. 445–66. London: Vallentine, Mitchell, 1967.

————. "The Lost World of Joseph Roth." *Zeitschrift für die Geschichte der Juden* 3, no. 1 (1966): 37–41.

Seliger, Maren, and Karl Ucakar. *Wiens politische Geschichte 1740–1934: Entwicklung und Bestimmungskräfte grossstädtischer Politik*. Vol. 2. Vienna: Verlag Jugend und Volk, 1985.

Senn, Pfarrer Wilhelm. "Christen—kauft bei Christen!" *Schönere Zukunft* (2 December 1928): 197–98.

Shirer, William L. *Berlin Diary: The Journal of a Foreign Correspondent, 1934–1941*. 1941. Reprint. New York: Penguin Books, 1979.

Silberner, Edmund. "Austrian Social Democracy and the Jewish Problem." *Historia Judaica* 13 (1951): 121–40.

Simon, Walter. "The Jewish Vote in Austria." *Leo Baeck Institute Yearbook* 16 (1971): 97–121.

————. *Österreich 1918–1938: Ideologien und Politik*. Vienna: Hermann Böhlaus Nachf., 1984.

Solow, Herbert. "Letters from Abroad: Unrest in Austria." *Menorah Journal* 18, no. 2 (February 1930): 137–47.

Sozius [Eli Rubin]. *Die Juden in Oesterreich: Schädlinge oder wertvolle Staatsbürger?* Vienna: privately printed, 1923.

Spaulding, E. Wilder. *The Quiet Invaders: The Story of the Austrian Impact upon America*. Foreword by Josef Stumm Voll. Vienna: Österreichischer Bundesverlag für Unterricht, Wissenschaft und Kunst, 1968.

Spira, Leopold. *Feindbild "Jud": 100 Jahre politischer Antisemitismus in Österreich*. Foreword by Heinz Brandt. Vienna: Löcker Verlag, 1981.

Stachura, Peter D., ed. *The Nazi Machtergreifung*. London: George Allen and Unwin, 1983.

Stackelberg, Roderick. *Idealism Debased: From Völkisch Ideology to National Socialism*. Kent, Ohio: Kent State University Press, 1981.

Stadler, Karl R. *Austria*. New York: Praeger, 1971.

Staudinger, Anton. "Christlichsoziale Judenpolitik in der Grundungsphase der österreichischen Republik." In *Jahrbuch für Zeitgeschichte 1978*, edited by Karl Stuhlpfarrer, pp. 11–48. Vienna: Löcker Verlag, 1979.

————. "Katholischer Antisemitismus in der Ersten Republik." In *Eine zerstörte Kultur: Jüdisches Leben und Antisemitismus in Wien seit dem 19. Jahrhundert*, edited by Gerhard Botz, Ivar Oxaal, and Michael Pollak, pp. 247–70, 393–97. Buchloe: Druck und Verlag Obermayer, 1990.

Steed, Henry W. *The Hapsburg Monarchy*. New York: Charles Scribner's Sons, 1913.

Stehle, Hansjakob. "Bischof Hudal und SS-Führer Meyer: Ein Kirchenpolitischer Friedensversuch 1942/43." *Vierteljahrshefte für Zeitgeschichte* 37, no. 2 (April 1989): 299–322.

Stiefel, Dieter. "Nazifizierung plus Entnazifizierung in Österreich." In *Verdrängte Schuld, verfehlte Sühne: Entnazifizierung in Österreich 1945–1955*, edited by Sebastian Meissl, Klaus-Dieter Mulley, and Oliver Rathkolb, pp. 28–36. Munich: R. Oldenbourg Verlag, 1986.

Streibel, Elisabeth. "Judenfrage und Antisemitismus im Spiegel der 'Reichspost' in den Jahren 1918 bis 1923." Hausarbeit am Institut für Geschichte, University of Vienna, 1981.

Stricker, Robert. *Der jüdische Nationalismus: Die wirksame Abwehr des Antisemitismus*. Vienna: R. Löwit, 1929.

————. *Jüdische Politik in Österreich: Tätigkeitsbericht und Auszuge aus den im österreichischen Parlamente 1919 und 1920 gehaltenen Reden*. Vienna: Verlag der *Wiener Morgenzeitung*, 1920.

Stubenvoll, Karl. "Die christliche Arbeiterbewegung Österreichs 1918 bis 1933: Organisation, Politik, Ideologie." Ph.D. dissertation, University of Vienna, 1982.

Stuhlpfarrer, Karl. "Antisemitismus, Rassenpolitik und Judenverfolgungen in Österreich nach dem Ersten Weltkrieg." In *Das österreichische Judentum*, by Anna Drabek et al., pp. 141–64. Vienna: Jugend und Volk, 1974.

Sully, Melanie. "The Waldheim Connection." In *Conquering the Past: Austrian Nazism Yesterday and Today*, edited by Fred Parkinson, pp. 294–312. Detroit: Wayne State University Press, 1989.

"SWS-Meinungsprofile: Antisemitismus in Österreich." *SWS-Rundschau* 27, no. 1 (1987): 89–96.

Synnott, Marcia Graham. "Anti-Semitism and American Universities: Did Quotas Follow the Jews?" In *Anti-Semitism in American History*, edited by David A. Gerber, pp. 233–71. Urbana: University of Illinois Press, 1986.

Talos, Emmerich, Ernst Hanisch, and Wolfgang Neugebauer, eds. *NS-Herrschaft in Österreich 1938–1945*. Vienna: Verlag für Gesellschaftskritik, 1988.

Tartakower, Arieh. "Jewish Migratory Movements in Austria in Recent Generations." In *The Jews of Austria*, edited by Josef Fraenkel, pp. 285–310. London: Vallentine, Mitchell, 1967.

Thalberg, Hans J. J. *Von der Kunst, Österreicher zu sein: Erinnerungen und Tagebuchnotizen*. Vienna: Hermann Böhlau Verlag, 1984.

Thieberger, Richard. "Assimilated Jewish Youth and Viennese Cultural Life around

1930." In *Jews, Antisemitism and Culture in Vienna*, edited by Ivar Oxaal, Michael Pollack, and Gerhard Botz, pp. 174–84. London: Routledge and Kegan Paul, 1987.

Tietze, Hans. *Die Juden Wiens: Geschichte, Wirtschaft, Kultur*. Leipzig and Vienna: E. P. Tal, 1933.

Timms, Edward. *Karl Kraus, Apocalyptic Satirist: Culture and Catastrophe in Habsburg Vienna*. New Haven: Yale University Press, 1986.

Toury, Jacob. "Defense Activities of the Österreichisch-Israelitische Union." In *Living with Antisemitism*, edited by Jehuda Reinharz, pp. 167–92. Hanover, N.H.: University Press of New England, 1987.

Vago, Bela. "The Attitude toward the Jews as a Criterion of the Left-Right Concept." In *Jews and Non-Jews in Eastern Europe, 1918–1945*, edited by Bela Vago and George L. Mosse, pp. 21–49. Jerusalem: Israel Universities Press, 1974.

Vago, Bela, and George L. Mosse. *Jews and Non-Jews in Eastern Europe, 1918–1945*. Jerusalem: Israel Universities Press, 1974.

Valentin, Hugo. *Antisemitism: Historically and Critically Examined*. Translated from the Swedish by A. G. Chater. New York: Viking Press, 1936. *Der Antisemitismus: Geschichte, Kritik, Soziologie*. Translated from the Swedish by Hans Hellwig. Vienna: Glanz, 1937.

"Vienna Welcomes Grandchildren of Survivors." *Martyrdom and Resistance* 16, no. 1 (September–October 1980): 6.

Volkov, Shulamit. "Antisemitism as a Cultural Code: Reflections on the History and Historiography of Antisemitism in Imperial Germany." *Leo Baeck Institute Yearbook* 23 (1978): 24–46.

———. "The Written Matter and the Spoken Word: On the Gap Between Pre-1914 and Nazi Anti-Semitism." In *Nazi Germany and the Genocide of the Jews*, edited by François Furet, pp. 33–55. New York: Schocken Books, 1989.

Wache, Karl. "Land und Volk: Ursprung und Werdegang." In *Deutscher Geist in Österreich*, edited by Karl Wache, pp. 9–69. Dornbirn: C. Bruton-Verlag, 1933.

Wache, Karl, ed. *Deutscher Geist in Österreich: Ein Handbuch des völkischen Lebens*. Dornbirn: C. Bruton-Verlag, 1933.

Wachter, Andrea. "Antisemitismus im österreichischen Vereinswesen für Leibesübungen 1918–1938 am Beispiel ausgewählter Vereine." Ph.D. dissertation, University of Vienna, 1983.

Wagnleiter, Reinhold, ed. *Understanding Austria: The Political Reports and Analyses of Martin F. Herz, Political Officer of the U.S. Legation in Vienna 1945–1948*. Salzburg: Wolfgang Neugebauer Verlag, 1984.

Walch, Dietmar. *Der jüdischen Bemühungen um die materielle Wiedergutmachung durch die Republik Österreich*. Vienna: Geyer, 1971.

Waldinger, Ernst. "Vor Sonnenuntergang: Über eine jüdische Kindheit in der Wiener Vorstadt." In *Versunkene Welt*, edited by Joachim Riedl, pp. 61–67. Vienna: Jewish Welcome Service, 1984.

Wandruszka, Adam. " Österreichs politische Struktur: Die Entwicklung der Parteien und politischen Bewegungen." In *Geschichte der Republik Österreich*, edited by Heinrich Benedikt, pp. 289–485. Vienna: Verlag für Geschichte und Politik, 1954.

Wangermann, Ernst. *The Austrian Achievement, 1700–1800*. London: Harcourt Brace Jovanovich, 1973.

Wassermann, Jakob. *My Life as a German and a Jew*. Translated from the German by S. N. Brainin. London: George Allen and Unwin, Ltd., 1933.

Weinberg, David H. *A Community on Trial: The Jews of Paris in the 1930s*. Chicago: University of Chicago Press, 1977.

Weinzierl, Erika. "Antisemitismus als österreichischen Phänomen." *Die Republik* 3 (1970): 28–35.

———. "Antisemitismus in der österreichischen Literatur 1900–1938." *Mitteilungen des österreichischen Staatsarchiv* 20 (1967): 356–71.

———. "Antisemitismus in Österreich." In *Austriaca: Cahiers universitaires d'information sur l'Autriche*. *Colloque special*. *Deux fois l'Autriche*. *Apres 1918 et après 1945*, edited by Felix Kreissler, pp. 309–27. Rouen: Imprimerie Lecerf, 1978.

———. "Österreichische Katholiken und die Juden." In *Ecclesia semper reformanda*, edited by Erika Weinzierl, pp. 339–71. Vienna: Geyer, 1985.

———. "Religious Antisemitism." In *Ecclesia semper reformanda*, edited by Erika Weinzierl, pp. 343–50. Vienna: Geyer, 1985.

———. "Schuld durch Gleichgültigkeit." In *Das grosse Tabu*, edited by Anton Pelinka and Erika Weinzierl, pp. 174–95. Vienna: Verlag der österreichischen Staatsdruckerei, 1987.

———. "Die Stellung der Juden in Österreich seit dem Staatsgrundgesetz von 1867." *Zeitschrift für die Geschichte der Juden* 5 (1968): 89–96.

———. "Stereotypen christliche Judenfeindschaft." In *Ecclesia semper reformanda*, edited by Erika Weinzierl, pp. 257–69. Vienna: Geyer, 1985.

———. *Universität und Politik*. Salzburg: Pustet, 1969.

———. "Wurzeln des Antisemitismus." *Die österreichische Nation* 27, nos. 5–6 (1974): 64–66.

———. *Zu wenig Gerechte: Österreicher und Judenverfolgung 1938–1945*. Graz: Verlag Styria, 1969. 2d revised edition, 1985.

Weinzierl, Erika, ed. *Ecclesia semper reformanda: Beiträge zur österreichischen Kirchengeschichte im 19. und 20. Jahrhundert. Festgabe für Erika Weinzierl*. Vienna: Geyer, 1985.

Weinzierl, Erika, and Kurt Skalnik, eds. *Österreich 1918–1938: Geschichte der Ersten Republik*. 2 vols. Graz: Verlag Styria, 1983.

Weiss, Hilde. *Antisemitische Vorurteile in Österreich? Theoretische und empirische Analysen*. Vienna: Wilhelm Braumüller, 1984.

Weitzmann, Walter R. "The Politics of the Viennese Jewish Community, 1890–1914." In *Jews, Antisemitism and Culture in Vienna*, edited by Ivar Oxaal, Michael Pollak, and Gerhard Botz, pp. 121–51. London: Routledge and Kegan Paul, 1987.

Weltsch, Robert. "Österreichische Revolutionschronik." *Der Jude* 3 (1918–19): 350–58.

Wertheimer, Jack. *Unwelcome Strangers: East European Jews in Imperial Germany*. Oxford: Oxford University Press, 1987.

Whiteside, Andrew G. "Austria." In *The European Right*, edited by Hans Rogger and

Eugen Weber, pp. 308–63. Berkeley: University of California Press, 1966.
———. *Austrian National Socialism before 1918.* The Hague: Martinus Nujhoff, 1962.
———. "Comments on the Papers of William A. Jenks and Donald L. Niewyk." *Leo Baeck Institute Yearbook* 16 (1971): 174–77.
———. *The Socialism of Fools: Georg von Schönerer and Austrian Pan-Germanism.* Berkeley: University of California Press, 1975.
Wiltschegg, Walter. *Die Heimwehr: Eine unwiderstehliche Volksbewegung?* Munich: R. Oldenbourg Verlag, 1985.
Winkler, Franz. *Die Diktatur in Österreich.* Zurich: Orell Fussli, 1935.
Wistrich, Robert S. *The Jews of Vienna in the Age of Franz Joseph.* Oxford: Oxford University Press (published for The Littman Library), 1989.
———. "Social Democracy, Antisemitism and the Jews of Vienna." In *Jews, Antisemitism and Culture in Vienna*, edited by Ivar Oxaal, Michael Pollak, and Gerhard Botz, pp. 111–51. London: Routledge and Kegan Paul, 1987.
———. *Socialism and the Jews: The Dilemmas of Assimilation in Germany and Austria-Hungary.* London: Associated University Presses, 1982.
Witek, Hans. "'Arisierungen' in Wien: Aspekte nationalsozialistischer Enteignungspolitik 1938–1942." In *NS-Herrschaft in Österreich*, edited by Emmerich Talos, Ernst Hanisch, and Wolfgang Neugebauer, pp. 199–216. Vienna: Verlag für Gesellschaftskritik, 1988.
Wodak, Ruth, and Rudolf de Cillia. "Judenfeindlichkeit im öffentlichen Diskurs in Österreich." *Sprache und Antisemitismus: Ausstellungskatalog* 43, no. 3 (March 1988).
Wyman, David S. *Paper Walls: America and the Refugee Crisis, 1938–1941.* New York: Pantheon Books, 1985.
Zeller, Stephan. "Wie sich Dr. Seipel die Lösung der Judenfrage in Österreich dachte." *Schönere Zukunft* (1 March 1936): 558–59.
Zernatto, Guido. *Die Wahrheit über Österreich.* New York: Longmans Green and Co., 1939.
Zimmermann, Moshe. *Wilhelm Marr: The Patriarch of Anti-Semitism.* Oxford: Oxford University Press, 1986.
Zmarzlik, Hans-Günter. "Antisemitismus im Deutschen Kaiserreich 1871–1914." In *Die Juden als Minderheit in der Geschichte*, edited by Bernd Marin and Ernst Schulin, pp. 249–70. Munich: Deutscher Taschenbuch Verlag, 1981.
Zoitl, Helge. "Kampf um Gleichberechtigung: Die Sozialdemokratische Studentenbewegung in Wien 1914–1925." Ph.D. dissertation, University of Salzburg, 1976.
Zweig, Stefan. *The World of Yesterday.* New York: Viking Press, 1943.

INDEX

Abel, Othenio, 98, 129
Abend, Der, 195, 218
Abraham a Sancta Clara, 16
Abwehr-Verein, 258
Adenauer, Konrad, 308
Adler, Friedrich, 61
Adler, Viktor, 35, 53, 61, 136
Agricultural College, 95, 127
Agudas Jisroel (Association of Israel),
  141–42
Akademischer Verein Kadimah, 54,
  96, 298
Albrecht (duke of Austria), 14
Albrecht V (archduke of Austria), 15
Allexin, R. E., 64
Allgemeiner österreichischer Schiver-
  vand (General Austrian Skiing Asso-
  ciation, 119
Alliance Israelite Universelle, 8, 87
All Quiet on the Western Front, 198
American Jewish Congress, 115
American Jewish Joint Distribution
  Committee, 96, 294, 302
American League for the Protection of
  Foreign Students, 128
American Medical Association, 128
American Relief Administration, 101
Amsterdam, 84
Anatomy Institute, 96, 97, 122, 124,
  129, 265
Anschluss, xvii, 76, 208; discriminatory

legislation, xix, 290, 323; Treaty of
St. Germain and, 79–80; Austrian
Nazi Party and, 132, 179, 189, 296,
322, 328; Jews in favor of, 139; Austrian political parties and, 176, 180,
202, 203, 321; *Mein Kampf* and, 231,
277; Dollfuss and, 261; violence and
persecution following, 275, 280–84,
289, 299, 324, 327; German invasion,
279–80; Catholics and, 298; fiftieth
anniversary of, 308–9, 313
Anticapitalism, 36, 42, 78, 131–32, 133,
136, 159, 190
Anti-Catholicism, 37
Anticlericalism, 38, 74, 151, 153, 266
Anti-Communism, 319
Anti-Marxism, 48, 74; Jews and, 78–
79, 176; and anti-Semitism, 124, 252;
Nazi, 169, 202, 203, 322
Antimodernism, 150, 159
Antisemitenbund (League of Anti-
Semites), 183–85, 191, 197, 321;
rallies, 81, 82, 85, 185, 194, 245;
legislative demands, 182–83, 185–
86, 190, 323, 330; and Nazi Party,
186–88, 189; Dollfuss and, 263–64;
government toleration of, 273
Anti-Semitic League, 25
Anti-Semitic newspapers, 47–49, 67, 70,
101, 186, 218, 244, 269; and World
Zionist Congress, 108, 110

: 403 :

AM7087-MN
92